WITHDRAWN
PILGRIM LIBRARY

D0140525

READINGS
ON
SOCIAL
PROBLEMS

READINGS ON SOCIAL PROBLEMS

Probing the Extent, Causes, and Remedies of America's Social Problems

PROPERTY OF THE PILGRIM LIBRARY THE DEFIANCE COLLEGE DEFIANCE, OHIO

WITHDRAWN PILGRIM LIBRARY

Edited by

William Feigelman
Nassau Community College

HOLT, RINEHART AND WINSTON, INC.

Fort Worth	Chicago	San Francisco
Philadelphia	Montreal	Toronto
London	Sydney	Tokyo

Publisher	Ted Buchholz
Acquisitions Editor	Christopher P. Klein
Senior Project Editor	Charlie Dierker
Manager of Production	Tad Gaither
Manager of Art & Design	Guy Jacobs
Text Design	Tom Dawson
Cover	Faith Nichols and Gregg Weitzel

Library of Congress Cataloging-in-Publication Data

Readings on social problems : probing the extent, causes,
   and remedies of America's problems / edited by
   William Feigelman.
      p.   cm.
    Includes index.
    1. United States—Social conditions—1980-
  2. Social problems. I. Feigelman, William.
  HN59.2.R43 1990
  361.1'0973—dc20   89-30467
                                        CIP
                                        AC

ISBN: 0-03-028913-0

Copyright © 1990 by Holt, Rinehart and Winston, Inc.

All rights reserved. No part of this publication may be
reproduced or transmitted in any form or by any means,
electronic or mechanical, including photocopy,
recording or any information storage and retrieval
system, without permission in writing from the
publisher.

Requests for permission to make copies of any part of
the work should be mailed to: Copyrights and
Permissions Department, Holt, Rinehart and Winston,
Inc., Orlando, FL 32887

Address Editorial Correspondence To:
        301 Commerce Street, Suite 3700,
        Fort Worth, TX 76102

Address Orders To:
        6277 Sea Harbor Drive,
        Orlando, FL 32887
        1-800-782-4479, or
        1-800-433-0001 (in Florida)

Printed in the United States of America

0 1 2 3   039   9 8 7 6 5 4 3 2 1

Holt, Rinehart and Winston, Inc.
The Dryden Press
Saunders College Publishing

HV
59.2
.R3
1986

JUL 28 1997

VCYW9

For Jesse and Ana

This work is conceived primarily to complement one of the many textbooks used in the very popular undergraduate course Social Problems. Some students, encountering this book *and* their text for the first time, may feel overwhelmed by a seemingly enormous amount of reading. Some might wonder why isn't the textbook enough? Why do we need to read these additional selections? Can't the important aspects of the readings be summarized by the text?

Instructors acquainted with the benefits of anthologies will of course not need to be persuaded about their value. But those unfamiliar with these teaching tools may need some explanation of their advantages. Too often, students exposed only to a textbook end up obtaining an erroneous and unrealistic conception of their subject of study. As one attempts to acquire knowledge in almost any discipline, one learns that it ordinarily does not come out of one central headquarters; erudition usually emerges from many sources of inspiration and from a careful review by students themselves of all the available materials. Many students who have no more to guide them than their text become lulled into thinking that wisdom is embodied in the authoritative pronouncements of their textbook author. They may become overinclined to apply rote memory—memorizing the five factors that cause the "Y" problem—rather than to invoke their critical-thinking capabilities.

An anthology serves important functions for beginning students in any discipline. In sociology, it enables them to observe directly what sociologists actually do. It affords for the student firsthand experience in confronting the sociological literature and in evaluating the actual products of sociologists. Students are also encouraged from such exposure to learn that problems are not always conceptualized in the same way by all scientific practitioners and are thereby encouraged to sift all the available evidence, to come to their own scientific conclusions.

Anthologies also permit students to acquire an in-depth understanding of some selected issues. Instead of the encyclopedic overview of a text, an anthology provides some detailed focus. Accordingly, with text and reader together, students are encouraged to derive a more balanced and complete viewpoint.

In this collection, I have tried to offer selections paralleling the topics usually investigated in Social Problems courses: problems of poverty, drug and alcohol abuse, crime, racism, family disorganization problems, and the like. These selections are derived from recent social science contributions. Many have come from highly acclaimed and prize-winning studies. Some of the selections have appeared in such professional social science journals as *Social Problems, Psychiatry,* and *Social Forces;* others have come from books and monographs; and still others originally appeared in popular magazines like the *New York Times Magazine, The Public Interest,* and *Reader's Digest.* They span the broad range of social-problems thinking that has been developed not only from sociologists and other behavioral scientists but also by journalists, politicians, and educated laypeople. Those aiming for the most complete understanding of the nature of social problems must inevitably assume a broad-based and open-ended attitude; indeed, it would be arrogant and foolhardy to assume that such knowledge would be confined only to social science practitioners.

Yet, sociologists like myself are inclined to put a sociological framework at the centerpiece of efforts to interpret social problems. The organization of selections presented here is meant to conform to a sociological approach to studying social problems. And what does that consist of? First, we must identify the definition and incidence of social problems: what the problem is and how pervasive it is in the community. We might call this the **epidemiology** of a social problem. (Does the problem represent an epidemic, or how much of an epidemic is it?) Second, we are concerned with the **etiology** of social problems. What causes the problem; what are its social bases or group correlates; and how does the problem interpenetrate with other social problems? Last, but by no means least, we are concerned with the problem's **remediation**. Through what kinds of actions or social policies can we reduce or eliminate this problem? Today's sociological social-problems analysts are concerned with each of these three important dimensions of social problems. They are committed to using the scientific method of systematically collecting and comparing empirical data to address each of these major aspects to social problems. In assembling these readings I have attempted to represent each of these three major attributes of interpreting social problems throughout.

Those studying sociology for the first time are often advised about the three dominant theoretical perspectives shared by most sociologists: functionalism, conflict theory, and symbolic interactionism. These viewpoints are very relevant in the sociology of social problems. Most social-problems analysts would be inclined to emphasize one or another of these three fundamental overviews in attempting to understand and deal with the various social problems plaguing us in urban–industrial societies.

FUNCTIONALISM: SOCIAL PROBLEMS OFTEN RESULT FROM SOCIAL DISORGANIZATION

The theory of functionalism holds that society consists of a system of interrelated parts. Under optimal conditions, the institutions of society are integrated with one another, satisfying individual needs and binding the members of society together. As an example, let us consider the development of work values, imparted by parents and reinforced by extended kin. The individual learns various things about work: work is inherently gratifying; a task well done is a source of self-pride; work is the primary vehicle for attaining financial and adult autonomy; promptness, ambition, and assuming responsibility are desirable personal traits. As these values are imparted within the context of the family, they are also supported by the institutions of the church and the schools. This, in turn, eventually inspires young people to seek employment, which not only relieves family members of the burden of their continuing dependency but also fulfills the needs of the industrial economy. Such would represent a state of institutional integration, the antithesis of social disorganization.

Functionalists see social problems as emerging from social disorganization. Social disorganization arises when the institutions of society are malintegrated with one another. Returning again to our example, social disorganization might arise when the industrial community is unable to generate a sufficient number of jobs for all those desiring work. Among those unable to find work, some of the possible social-problem by-products could be poverty, an overpowering sense of guilt that is temporarily allayed by drug abuse, or resentment to conventional social institutions expressed in criminal or violent actions, among other possible problems.

In any complex society, institutions exert compound consequences upon each other. These multifold relationships may be functional in some respects and disorganizing in others. For example, the industrial system may generate sufficient employment opportunities but it may also pollute the environment. As it may require its employees to relocate often or to subordinate their family lives for the company, it may contribute to marital instability.

Often, social disorganization results from rapid and uneven rates of social change. Change may take place in one institutional realm but adaptive responses may lag behind in other areas. Thus social disorganization becomes the inevitable result. Developments in medical science, greatly extending life expectancy through inoculations and insect control, have produced alarming rises in world population. Many third-world countries absorbed new technological measures but have not modified their religious prohibitions against modern birth-control techniques and traditional values venerating large families.

CONFLICT THEORY: SOCIAL PROBLEMS RESULT FROM GROUP AND VALUE CONFLICT

In sharp relief to the scheme above is another theoretical perspective: conflict theory. Conflict theory presupposes that social problems result from the hegemony of the socially dominant forces of society. The powerful and economically dominant strive to promote values that are consistent with their needs and interests, which necessarily involves subordination for the rest of society. The dominating elite foists its commitments to corporate capitalism upon a citizenry whose interests would probably be better served by more socialistic economic practices; thus social problems become the inevitable result. In the conflict perspective social problems exist because the interests of the most powerful members of society often prevail at the expense of the many.

For example, the problem of poverty in society could be dramatically reduced if wealthier members were willing to give up some of their many tax loopholes and tax themselves at the same rates paid by lower-income wage earners. But elite members use their dominance in the political process to blunt more far-reaching tax-reform proposals. The rich are also highly critical of proposals to expand welfare state practices, arguing that such aid will only weaken incentives to work and produce other demoralizing consequences among their recipients. The rich also gain by the presence of poverty: it means that people will be willing to work for low wages, pay high amounts for borrowing privileges, perform unpleasant tasks, buy inferior and secondhand merchandise, and do other things that help sustain the power and wealth of the rich. Many conflict theorists claim that substantial change or the amelioration of social problems can only be accomplished if power is seized from the ruling class.

Akin to the notion of conflict theory is the value-conflict approach. While most conflict theorists see fundamental structural change as essential for combating social problems, many value-conflict theorists do not necessarily link drastic restructuring of society to the remediation of particular social problems. Many posit that value conflicts can also be resolved by compromise, bargaining, and accommodation among the various contending interests.

This analytical scheme provides additional insight into the causation and persistence of social problems. Its principal assumption is that society is composed of a variety of groups who pursue diverging and competing interests and values. As groups attempt to promote their concerns, conflict inevitably results—and with it social problems. Conflicts vary in intensity from mild differences of opinion to violent opposition. Although certain conflicts may engender changes that avoid stagnation and enhance adaptation, others may tear a society apart, resulting in massive destruction of human material resources. A great many contemporary social problems are either caused, exacerbated, or sustained by value conflicts.

For example, problems associated with the unequal availability of health care largely reflect the successful efforts of the health care industry—physicians, drug and medical equipment manufacturers, health insurance companies, hospital management, and the like—to maintain the existing fee-for-service, profit-oriented system against more socialized medical systems favored by their detractors—the poor, consumer advocate interests, leftists, among others. Despite the proven dangers associated with cigarette smoking, the tobacco industry has strenuously opposed most all anti-tobacco legislation, launching extensive efforts in its own behalf to obtain favored treatment and governmental supports. Thus the poor health of many Americans attributable to smoking owes its existence in part to the successful value and interest advocacy of tobacco industrialists.

SYMBOLIC INTERACTIONISM: SOCIAL PROBLEMS OFTEN RESULT FROM ASSIGNING MEANING TO ACTION AND LABELING BEHAVIOR AS DEVIANT

Another dominant sociological viewpoint is the theory of symbolic interactionism. Symbolic interactionists maintain that as people interact socially they assign meaning to their actions. As

W. I. Thomas once said, "if men define situations as real, they are real in their consequences." In this perspective, it is the assignment of meanings or social labeling that creates social problems. This viewpoint holds that many social problems result from labeling behavior as deviant. Here it is emphasized that the members of society make and enforce social rules and apply them to different groups and individuals. As the behavior of particular people departs from normative expectations, labels are assigned to them; they may be designated criminal, mentally ill, homosexual, old, alcoholic, and the like. As such labels are applied to particular persons, so-called deviants are also likely to be subject to exclusionary and inferior treatment. As a consequence, labeling may serve to elicit further disapproved behavior. Thus the occasional drinker may be encouraged to drink more heavily if those within his social circle expect him to do so. Moreover, if close associates link drinking with irresponsibility, "drinkers" may be inclined to doubt their abilities to take initiatives and they may act unreliably. Such associated additional deviant patterns are termed secondary deviance.

When labeling takes place on an institutional level as well as informally, its effects are likely to be even more personally damaging. Thus persons who may be denied employment because of their drinking problems may be inclined to drink more heavily to allay their anxiety and guilt for failing to comply with work values. Or in other cases of deviance, the same would be true for officially convicted criminals or for persons subjected to mandatory retirement, despite their desires to continue with their careers. Labeling at the institutional level drastically circumscribes the conventional opportunities available to the deviant.

People who are similarly stigmatized may be inclined to gravitate toward each other and form groups—deviant subcultures. Such memberships may have multifold consequences: they may insulate deviants from the critical and condemnatory responses of conventional society and they may contribute to further deviance. For example, former criminals who evoke much suspicion and encounter considerable employment discrimination may find their only acceptance within the criminal subculture, which may enlist them to do more crime. Thus deviant labels, when applied to people, tend to generate self-confirming and self-perpetuating response patterns.

Reading through many of the selections offered in this text, students will note that many of the analyses converge with these three dominant theoretical interpretations. It may even comprise a worthy academic enterprise to identify some of the theoretical underpinnings of the selections offered here. Yet it would be a gross oversimplification to assume that all or most of the analyses can be neatly pigeonholed into one or another of these predominating theoretical schemes.

In arranging the collection, I made certain arbitrary decisions about the ordering of all these selections. The interpenetrating nature of many social problems is often so deep that some instructors may feel more comfortable assigning an essay under another problem topic than the one under which it was placed here.

My main objective in making these selections was to offer students a sense of the rich and varied array of sociological work on social problems. If this collection succeeds in conveying a sense of the value of the sociological approach to illuminate the causes of and remedies to our social problems, it will have more than fulfilled its ambitions.

ACKNOWLEDGMENTS

Finally, I would like to thank the following reviewers for their kind and constructive comments about this project: Gregg Carter, Bryant College; Lois M. Easterday, Onandago Community College; James Floyd, Macon College; Marietta Morrissey, Texas Tech University; Kathryn Mueller, Baylor University; Charles Norman, Indiana State University; Margaret Ortigo, Louisiana State University at Alexandria; Ed Ponczek, William Rainey Harper College; and William A. Roberts, Clinton Community College.

Contents

Introduction————————— vii

PART ONE
Overview on Social Problems

1 THE SOCIOLOGY OF SOCIAL PROBLEMS

Jerome G. Manis: *Assessing the
Seriousness of Social Problems*———— 3

Joel Best: *Missing Children,
Misleading Statistics*——————— 11

PART TWO
The American Scene

2 PROBLEMS OF PHYSICAL HEALTH

Geraldine Dallek: *Hospital Care
for Profit*————————————— 19

Peter Conrad: *The Social Meaning
of AIDS*————————————— 27

3 PROBLEMS OF MENTAL HEALTH

James S. House, Karl R. Landis, and
Debra Umberson: *Social Relationships
and Health*——————————— 36

Stuart A. Kirk and Mark E. Therrien:
*Community Mental Health Myths
and the Fate of Former
Hospitalized Patients*——————— 45

4 THE CRIME PROBLEM

William Kornblum and Vernon Boggs:
New Alternatives for Fighting Crime—— 55

Eugene H. Methvin: *The Proven Key
to Crime Control*————————— 62

James D. Wright: *Second Thoughts
About Gun Control*———————— 65

James Traub: *Into the Mouths of
Babes*————————————— 75

5 ALCOHOL AND DRUG ABUSE

Gerald E. Markle and Ronald J. Troyer:
*Smoke Gets in Your Eyes: Cigarette
Smoking as Deviant Behavior*———— 82

Herbert Fingarette: *Alcoholism: The
Mythical Disease*————————— 95

Patricia A. Adler and Peter Adler:
*Shifts and Oscillations in Deviant
Careers: The Case of Upper-Level Drug
Dealers and Smugglers*——————— 107

6 PROBLEMS OF THE ECONOMY

James D. Wright: *The Worthy and
Unworthy Homeless*———————— 121

William J. Wilson with Robert Aponte
and Kathryn Neckerman: *Joblessness
versus Welfare Effects: A Further
Reexamination*—————————— 129

Robert Blauner: *Work Satisfaction and
Industrial Trends in Modern Society*—— 139

Michael Lipsky: *The Welfare State As
Workplace*———————————— 157

7 PROBLEMS OF FAMILY LIFE

Steven Mintz and Susan Kellogg:
*Coming Apart: Radical Departures
Since 1960*———————————— 164

Lenore J. Weitzman: *The Economic
Consequences of Divorce*—————— 179

8 SEX DEVIANCE

David F. Luckenbill: *Entering Male
Prostitution*——————————— 202

Susan H. Gray: *Exposure to Pornography
and Aggression Toward Women: The
Case of the Angry Male*——————— 213

Contents

9 PROBLEMS OF THE CITIES

John D. Kasarda: *Caught in the Web of Change* _____ 223

J. Allen Whitt and Glenn Yago: *Corporate Strategies and the Decline of Transit in U.S. Cities* _____ 232

10 PROBLEMS IN THE EDUCATIONAL SYSTEM

Jonathan Kozol: *A Third of the Nation Cannot Read These Words* _____ 249

Robert Rosenthal and Lenore F. Jacobson: *Teacher Expectations for the Disadvantaged* _____ 255

11 AGEISM

Arnold Arluke and Jack Levin: *"Second Childhood": Old Age in Popular Culture* _____ 261

Arlie Russell Hochschild: *Communal Life-Styles for the Old* _____ 266

12 SEXISM

Kathryn Strother Ratcliff and Janet Bogdan: *Unemployed Women: When "Social Support" Is Not Supportive* _____ 276

Judith Lewis Herman and Lisa Hirschman: *Incestuous Fathers and Their Families* _____ 284

13 RACISM

William Julius Wilson: *Inner-City Dislocations* _____ 301

Douglas S. Massey, Gretchen A. Condran, and Nancy A. Denton: *The Effect of Residential Segregation on Black Social and Economic Well-Being* _____ 310

PART THREE

The World at Large

14 OVERPOPULATION

Jodi L. Jacobson: *Family Planning and World Health* _____ 329

Elise F. Jones, Jacqueline Darroch Forrest, Noreen Goldman, Stanley K. Henshaw, Richard Lincoln, Jeannie I. Rosoff, Charles F. Westoff, and Deirdre Wulf: *Teenage Pregnancy in Developed Countries: Determinants and Policy Implications* _____ 338

15 THE ECOLOGICAL CRISIS

Joseph Collins and Frances Moore Lappé: *Still Hungry after All These Years* _____ 353

Anastasia Toufexis: *The Dirty Seas* _____ 360

16 PROBLEMS IN INTERNATIONAL RELATIONS

Malcolm W. Browne: *Will the Stealth Bomber Work?* _____ 368

Carl Sagan: *Nuclear War and Climatic Catastrophe: Some Policy Implications* _____ 374

Name Index _____ 389

Subject Index _____ 395

READINGS ON SOCIAL PROBLEMS

Part

ONE

Overview on
Social Problems

The Sociology of Social Problems

Assessing the Seriousness of Social Problems

JEROME G. MANIS
Western Michigan University

The definition of a concept inevitably influences the nature of the related hypotheses or theory. A well-conceived concept is heuristic and realistic—that is, it generates hypotheses that improve our understanding of phenomena. Such a concept will direct researchers toward significant data. As Max Planck (1962:841) has contended, however, there are many "phantom problems—in my opinion, far more than one would ordinarily suspect—even in the realm of science." It is the recognition of anomalies in "normal science" that results in the collapse of accepted paradigms (Kuhn, 1962).

. . . . To most sociologists, social problems are defined by popular beliefs and interest groups.

Exponents of leading sociological perspectives—symbolic interactionism and functionalism—have essentially similar conceptions of social problems. To Blumer (1971:298, 301–302), "social problems are fundamentally products of collective definition. . . . A social problem does not exist for a society unless it is recognized by that society to exist." Merton (1971:799) is somewhat more inclusive: "The first and basic ingredient of a social problem consists of a substantial discrepancy between widely shared standards and actual conditions of social life." Although he distinguishes between manifest or recognized and latent or unrecognized discrepancies, his definition centers upon "widely shared standards," i.e., society's norms and values. . . .

One of the shortcomings of the public definition of social problems is the inclusion of possibly spurious or "phantom" conditions. . . .

Indeed, the "subjective" definition must include witchhunting, long hair, and possession of marihuana as social problems as long as the public is in opposition to them. So defined, the concern of the sociology of social problems is with social issues or controversies rather than the objective conditions detrimental to human or societal well-being.

A related deficiency of the "public opinion" approach to social problems is its inability to assess the seriousness of social problems. Some advocates of this viewpoint are aware of the limitation.

> . . . it is the values held by people occupying different social positions that provide the rough basis for the relative importance assigned to social problems . . . this sometimes leads to badly distorted impressions of various problems, even when these are judged in the light of reigning values (Merton, 1971:801).

Nor are public definitions sound guides to the magnitude of social problems. . . . Influential publics, moreover, have little if any basis on which to *compare* the relative seriousness—extent and effects—of problems . . . . This definition of social problems explores certain absurdities. Public recognition is in nearly all respects a bad basis for collective judgment . . . . In spite of these difficulties, the definition stands: A social problem is a condition that has been defined by significant groups as a deviation from some social standard, or breakdown of social organization (Dentler, 1971: 14–15).

Despite these admissions of "distortions" and "absurdities," sociologists have continued

I would like to thank James J. Bosco, Paul A. Dorsey, Charles B. Keely, Bernard N. Meltzer, and Stanley S. Robin for their helpful criticisms and suggestions.

From the article originally published in *Social Problems,* Vol. 22, No. 1 (1974): 1–15. © 1974 by the Society for the Study of Social Problems. Used with permission.

to use popular values as the only criteria of social problems. Considerations of the severity or magnitude of social problems are restricted to the numbers of concerned citizens or to the intensity of their feelings (Tallman and McGee, 1971:42). . . .

THE IDENTIFICATION OF SOCIAL PROBLEMS

For present purposes, social problems are defined as "those social conditions, identified by scientific inquiry and values as detrimental to the well-being of human societies" (Manis, 1974). Four perspectives or viewpoints appear useful in determining and specifying such conditions. These are: (1) public conceptions; (2) the views of appropriate professionals; (3) sociological knowledge; (4) the norms and values of science. The order in which the categories are presented is based upon their increasing importance as criteria for identifying social problems. Consistent application of these criteria can help to reduce or eliminate the anomalies arising from current definitions of social problems.

Public conceptions. A basic source of information concerning social problems is the opinions and attitudes of the members of a group or society. This information is necessary for understanding social behavior. As Blumer (1971:301) points out, "the process of collective definition determines the career and fate of social problems, from the initial point of their appearance to whatever may be the terminal point in their course." Though most textbooks accept "collective definition" as the essence of social problems, they do not disclose any evidence for the choice of their topics.

The content of the sociological literature— crime, divorce, alcoholism, etc.—*appears* to be congruent with the views of the populace. However, the justification for their inclusion or for the assessment of their assumed seriousness is not revealed to the reader. The absence of such data is a major deficiency in our knowledge. . . .

Public conceptions of deviance, and of social problems generally, are necessary but insufficient knowledge. Certainly, we need to know what a society abhors and why it does so. We also need to know the consequences of these conceptions. Accepting social values as criteria of "harmful people" or "undesirable conditions" lends an aura of scientific respectability to beliefs which may be based on ignorance or prejudice. Accepting these values as the ultimate criteria of social problems is a specious justification for claims of value-neutrality.

Professional expertise. At times, public opinion differs substantially from the views of experts. A current example is the widespread antagonism to users of marihuana. The public position seems to be based upon many erroneous beliefs: that it is addictive; that it is debilitating; that it invariably leads to other addictions; that users are sexually depraved. The differing views of physicians, psychiatrists, and sociologists apparently have not greatly altered its popular image.

According to current definitions, marihuana is a social problem since it is contrary to social values. Presumably it is a serious problem if many people are strongly opposed to its usage. The views of trained experts are considered relevant because of their disagreement with the public, not for their technical knowledge. Sociologists may agree with the professional definition—but the public definition is the usual standard for identifying social problems.

There are, of course, many experts; and they are not always in agreement. But in agreement or not, their professional training and intimate contact with conditions viewed by the public as undesirable can provide needed correctives. Sociologists do question the medical perspective of psychiatry. Should they not also raise questions about the category of "crazy people"? The latter conception helps to explain the responses of society to those so identified and the effects of these labels. It is less helpful in the search for social causation and consequences.

Sociologists draw upon the data of other experts and disciplines in their analyses of mental disorder, drop-outs, divorce, and riots. This expertise receives special weight in the analyses but not in the definition of social problems. To be consistent with current definitions, the seriousness of social problems should be based not on the weight of technical data but the extent of popular concern.

To propose that the expert's interpretation be included in defining and assessing social problems is not a claim for their absolute correctness. It is only a means for incorporating more technical knowledge into our inquiries. Such knowledge can help to recognize trivial or spurious social problems as well as to identify serious ones.

Sociological knowledge. Although social problems are defined in terms of public conceptions, values, and controversies, sociologists do not ignore the causes and the consequences of the "undesirable conditions." Indeed, Blumer (1971:300) has contended that sociologists have concentrated on the latter and have "conspicuously failed . . . to study the process by which a society comes to recognize its social problems." What sociologists actually do is different from what they say about social problems.

The discrepancy stems, I believe, from the unwillingness of researchers to accept the implications of the accepted definition. If the public views busing, atheism, subversives, women's liberation, and radical professors as major social problems, will the textbook writers allocate substantial sections to these topics? If not, why not? A reasonable conjecture is that their knowledge and values are the implicit criteria.

To understand social behavior, we must explore public beliefs and values. Collective behavior is guided by social perceptions. To adopt these perceptions of social realities, however, is to equate common sense with analytic sociology (Schutz, 1963; Manis, 1972). Understanding of everyday knowledge is needed by sociology; understanding does not require its endorsement. . . .

The values of science. A major justification for the accepted definitions of social problems is the presumed value-neutrality of science. A scientific sociology must avoid any appearance of bias derived from personal values. The aim is laudable. The accepted solution—adopting popular values as the standards for identifying social problems—is a substitution of values, not their elimination. The outcome is an illusory value-neutrality.

Values are an integral aspect of the sociological enterprise. . . .

That science is a social institution with distinctive norms and values can hardly be questioned. Among the accepted values are: the search for knowledge, the empirical testing of belief, the provisional standing of accepted viewpoints, the freedom of critics to dissent and propose new interpretations, and the dissemination of knowledge (Merton, 1967; Kaplan, 1964). The socialization of would-be scientists includes the inculcation of these values.

Scientists seldom discuss, since they take for granted, certain underlying values. In totalitarian states, protection of life, safety, subsistence, and freedom of inquiry for the scientist may be uncertain. The institution of science depends upon societal tolerance and support. Obviously, science cannot exist without society and functioning scientists. Is it less obvious to contend that science must value an open, supportive society?

A current value-controversy among scientists concerns the social responsibility of science. To take an extreme illustration, does the nuclear scientist have the obligation to test a fission hypothesis which will set off a continuous, endless, chain reaction (Z-bomb?)? Traditionally, scientists have contended that science can only describe "what is, not should be." Contemporary science is *not* limited to this role of passive observation. The rapid tempo of discovery and, particularly, the creation of new phenomena—synthetic atoms, plastics, nylon, etc.—reflect the intentional innovations which have helped to transform the world around us. These creations have blurred the lines between basic and applied science as well as between science and technology.

The thesis here is that the knowledge and the values of science can provide sociology with needed guidelines for appraising social phenomena. Certainly, scientists neither possess all of the needed knowledge nor agree upon scientific values. Nevertheless, existing knowledge and values are more uniform, more rational, and more fruitful criteria than the divergent beliefs and values of any given society. . . .

To say that science is guided by values is not to deny its efforts at objectivity. All knowledge is subjective, a product of mental activity. Scientific knowledge, however, is guided by norms of conceptual clarification, descriptive accuracy, and theoretical understanding. In current definitions of social problems, "subjective" knowledge refers to personal and group beliefs whatever their source may be. Studying these beliefs is needed to help account for individual and collective behavior; it is insufficient for explaining the nature, the causes, and the consequences of specific social problems.

Proposing the use of scientific criteria to assess the existence or the severity of social problems need not imply absolutism. Specifying their criteria does not require the crowning of scientists. The concepts, hypotheses, theories, and values of science are open to continuing criticism, revision, or rejection on the basis of rational judgments and knowledge. No implication that science be empowered to coerce society to accept its conclusions is intended. All that is suggested here is to permit the knowledge and values of science to identify and to assess conditions deemed harmful to science and to society.

To summarize, scientific knowledge and values are proposed as criteria for identifying socially harmful conditions. These criteria can help to distinguish spurious from genuine social problems. We also need to consider ways of differentiating minor or trivial social problems from major or serious ones. By seriousness is meant the primacy, the magnitude, and the severity of social problems.

THE PRIMACY OF SOCIAL PROBLEMS

An examination of the interrelationships among social problems provides one way of assessing their importance. To illustrate, let us consider the hypothesis that poverty is associated with higher rates of malnutrition, mortality, desertion, delinquency, drop-outs, addiction, and mental disorder. Although sociologists are cautious about attributing causality in statistical relationships, the temporal priority of poverty to many of the other variables suggests its consideration as an independent variable. Viewing poverty as an antecedent to many other social problems is a basis for appraising its importance of primacy.

Social problems which produce or exacerbate other social problems are more serious or critical to society than those which have less

effects. On such grounds, Perrucci and Pilisuk (1971:xix) refer to "central" or "underlying" social problems as distinguished from the "peripheral" ones produced by the former. Despite the brevity of their discussion, it is evident that they consider cause-effect relationships as their basic criterion.

For my purposes, the term "primary social problems" will be used to refer to these influential conditions. The search for independent or causal social problems may imply an endless, circuitous task, since society is a complex system. This difficulty, however, applies to any investigation of causality. Still, there are established ways for reducing the possibility of error and the level of difficulty. Temporal priority, statistical association, and control of related variables are commonly accepted standards for causal analysis.

By influence, we refer not only to the degree of relationship between two variables but also to the relationships between a variable and a number of others. A social problem that directly or indirectly causes or increases many other social problems can be considered more influential than its consequences. Designating the former as a primary social problem differentiates it from secondary or tertiary ones. Although finer gradations may appear desirable, limiting the categories facilitates their clarification.

A more specific definition can be proposed at this point. *Primary social problems are influential social conditions which have multiple detrimental consequences for society.* For example, we may predict that a conventional war will result in higher death rates, waste of human and other resources, increases in family disorganization, disruption of careers, and neglected solutions to other undesirable conditions. Racism seems conducive to separatism, conflict, individual alienation, etc. On the basis of their multiplicative influences, war and racism can be viewed as primary social problems; their socially harmful effects may be defined as secondary or tertiary problems. . . .

In the absence of detailed, accurate, and precise knowledge, the proposed distinctions between specific primary and secondary or tertiary social problems remain as hypotheses rather than established conclusions. Even so, they are preferable to such criteria as numbers of concerned citizens or level of their emotional outrage. Not only is the distinction more objective, but it requires empirical data concerning the relationships between problem variables. The formulation of more and improved social indicators would facilitate study of such relationships.

Secondary social problems are less critical for a society than primary ones in that the former are products of the latter. Likewise, tertiary social problems are least important in that they are the products of primary and secondary problems. Secondary social problems may be viewed as intervening variables or as the immediate influences upon tertiary social problems.

To be explicit, *secondary social problems are those harmful conditions resulting mainly from more influential social problems and, in turn, generating additional problems. Tertiary social problems are harmful conditions which are, directly or indirectly, the results of more dominant problems.* Figure 1 contains an illustrative diagram of hypothetical relationships between these categories of social problems. . . .

THE MAGNITUDE OF SOCIAL PROBLEMS

. . . . Whatever the terminology—amount, prevalence, rates, extent, or magnitude—sociologists seek to achieve the most accurate and precise measures as indicators of seriousness. Studies of the frequency of occurrence of social problems have raised questions about the data available from the most knowledgeable and expert sources. Hospitalization rates of mental disorders are considered inadequate measures of true incidence (Davis, 1970:179; Julian, 1973:39). Similar criticism has been leveled at the official statistics concerning the amount of crime (Horton and Leslie, 1970:119; Birenbaum and Sagarin, 1972:420). Their definitions notwithstanding, sociologists report the extent or rate of the "harmful conditions" as a central basis for determining their importance rather than the extent of public concern or the public's beliefs about magnitude.

The discrepancy between "subjective" definitions and "objective" data is a major anomaly of social problems analysis. A solution requires

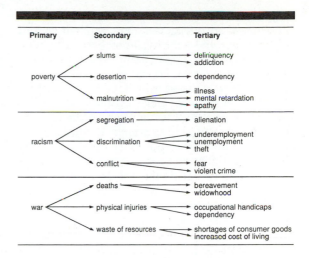

FIGURE 1. A paradigm for classifying social problems on the basis of hypothesized influences.

revision of the definition, changes in the types of data, or both. The latter appears most desirable. Viewing public conceptions as *perceived* social problems would encourage researchers concerning the magnitude of public concern. Comparing the extent of public concern with public beliefs about the extent of the condition can help account for societal reactions. Comparing such data with factual prevalence or rates is needed to understand the impact of these conditions.

Determining the magnitude of social problems also requires careful attention to the units of analysis. The basic question is, who defines these units? If social norms are used to identify problems, should sociologists rely on popular opinion for specifying the criteria of the units? Apparently official data (legal, psychiatric, economic, etc.) are preferred over the views of the public. However, the recognized shortcomings of official definitions of crime, as well as those based on the public fear of crime, are evidence of sociological awareness of the need for more objective data as well as for subjective interpretations.

However the units are defined, their prevalence and incidence are accepted indicators of the seriousness of social problems. Difficulties arise when attempts are made to compare the magnitude of different phenomena. Some of the suggested difficulties may be exaggerated, particularly when the differences in the units are emphasized. For example, Merton (1971: 801) asks, "Shall we conclude that the approximately 9000 murders in 1969 represent about one-fifth as great a social problem as the approximately 56,700 deaths from vehicular accidents in that year?" Although his response is negative, one may respond, why not? Certainly, the causes differ and the public concern about homicide differs from the public apathy toward traffic fatalities. The consequences *are* similar, as they are also for suicide and for war-related deaths. Vital statistics provide useful sources for appraising the magnitude of social problems.

Another useful comparison can be made of the prevalence of forms of addiction. While the public is more greatly aroused by heroin addiction than by addiction to alcohol or barbiturates, it is the resulting legal penalties for the former which compound its seriousness. That there are about ten million alcoholics as compared to several hundred thousand heroin addicts is considered by medical professionals to be the more serious health problem. Should not sociologists adopt similar criteria?

Comparing more divergent conditions, of course, is much more difficult. Assessing the magnitude of poverty requires different standards from those used in appraising the rates of juvenile delinquency. Are equal numbers of the poor and of juvenile delinquents equivalent in seriousness as social problems? Though their differences appear to defy attempts to compare their magnitude, the effort to do so is important. One method of comparing their seriousness would be a consideration of their effects—as noted in the previous section. If poverty is indeed a major source of other problems, we can give its prevalence a greater emphasis or weighting in our deliberations. Furthermore, we can appraise the differential severity of its consequences.

THE SEVERITY OF SOCIAL PROBLEMS

By severity is meant the varying impact, the degree of damage, harshness, or impairment, of social conditions upon the well-being of individuals and society. The harmfulness of some social problems can be assessed more readily than others. Loss of life is clearly a more critical outcome of war than minor injuries. A ten-year prison term is a harsher penalty than a one-year term; these differences of sentence are imposed on the basis of some judgment of differential social injury. In these comments, no implication is intended that assessing severity is a simple or easy task. Here, as elsewhere in this analysis, the aim is to further discussion of the topic.

In the absence of clearcut criteria for defining social problems, evaluation of their severity may be begun with conditions harmful to the physical well-being of individuals. Severity can be ranked from the finality of death, through total, major, and minor incapacity. These are crude but useful categories for assessing impairment. The distinctions are no more arbitrary than those used to distinguish social classes, small groups, or subcultures.

Similar procedures have been applied to the severity of mental disorders. The American Psychiatric Association (1952) has considered "psychiatric impairment" in terms of mild to severe categories. Their ratings are based on judgments of the individual's ability to function socially and occupationally. Such evaluations are appropriate ways of assessing social problems.

Also similar are the methods used in comparing the severity of crimes. Homicide and aggravated assault are characterized as major crimes while disorderly conduct is not. The alleged criterion is differential harmfulness. On this basis, some sociologists have favored the decriminalization of gambling, homosexual behavior, and other acts which are not clearly detrimental to individuals or to the society. The concept of "crimes without victims" helps to identify trivial or spurious problems.

Closely related to the degree of severity of a social problem is its duration or recurrence. Ignoring their other effects, addictive drugs are considered to be more harmful than non-addictive drugs. Other parallels to this temporal aspect of severity are the medical concern with "chronic" conditions and the penologist's concern with recidivism. Transitory conditions may be considered less severe than continuing or permanent ones. . . .

CONCLUSION

An aim of this discussion has been to emphasize the importance of demonstrable knowledge and reasoned evaluation in identifying and appraising social problems. The knowledge and values of science are less ethnocentric, less erratic, and less influenced by vested interests than those of a majority or significant numbers of a society. Using the views of the latter as the criterion of social problems is a more knowledge-free than value-free definition of social problems.

Adopting scientific knowledge and values as criteria does not imply disregard for public perceptions. Certainly, research is needed to clarify the ways by which individuals come to believe that certain social conditions are undesirable. We need to know more of the processes of collective action, of the influences of mass media and pressure groups, and of the consequences of group reactions. Knowledge of public concerns can reduce the risk of an ivory-towered isolation of sociology.

The effort to determine the seriousness of social problems requires procedures for distinguishing between trivial or spurious and important or genuine ones. That public judgments are made, at times, on the basis of erroneous information or emotionality can hardly be doubted. Such judgments need not be given equality in assessing social problems with those based on facts and reasoned judgments.

The proposed procedures for studying the seriousness of social problems—their primacy, magnitude, and severity—are not unfamiliar to sociologists. Despite the widespread "subjective" definition of social problems, most sociologists stress "objective" data in their analyses of specific social problems. The confusion stems from the disjunctions between the various goals of social problems analysis. Phenomenological study is necessary to understand how members of a group conceive of "undesirable" conditions in order to explain such behavior as labelling, imprisonment, or social movements. Determining the causes, effects, and seriousness of these conditions requires more objective criteria and data.

To espouse scientific knowledge and values for the appraisal of social phenomena implies no claims of omniscience and certainly not of omnipotence. Similar limitations are applicable to public opinion. The latter is influenced by advertising, political ideologies, religious beliefs, etc. Accepting public opinion as the standard for defining and assessing social problems is incongruent with the rational basis of scientific inquiry.

The place of values remains the central dilemma of the sociological enterprise. Values are involved in the choice of concepts, research topics, and methods of inquiry. They are clearly relevant to the definition of social problems and to assessments of their seriousness. The knowledge values of science provide a more appropriate perspective for sociology than those of "significant numbers" of a given society.

REFERENCES

American Psychiatric Association. Diagnostic and Statistical Manual, Mental Disorders, Washington, D.C. (1952).

Becker, Howard S. Outsiders: Studies in the Sociology of Deviance. Glencoe: Free Press. (1963).

———. "Whose side are we on?" Social Problems 14 (Winter): 239–247. (1967).

Birenbaum, Arnold and Edward Sagarin (eds.) Social Problems: Private Troubles and Public Issues. New York: Scribners. (1972).

Blumer, Herbert "Social problems as collective behavior." Social Problems 18 (Winter): 298–306. (1971).

Davis, F. James Social Problems: Enduring Major Issues and Social Change. New York: Free Press. (1970).

Dentler, Robert A. Basic Social Problems. Chicago: Rand McNally. (1971).

Dewey, John Logic: The Theory of Inquiry. New York: Holt. (1938).

Gans, Herbert J. "The positive functions of poverty." American Journal of Sociology 78 (September): 275–289. (1972).

Hewitt, John P. and Peter M. Hall "Social Problems, Problematic Situations, and Quasi-Theories." American Sociological Review 38 (June): 367–374. (1973).

Horton, Paul B. and Gerald R. Leslie The Sociology of Social Problems. New York: Appleton-Century-Crofts. (1970).

Johnson, Elmer H. Social Problems of Urban Man. Homewood, Illinois: Dorsey. (1973).

Julian, Joseph Social Problems. New York: Appleton-Century-Crofts. (1973).

Kitsuse, John I. and Malcolm Spector "Toward a sociology of social problems: Social conditions, value-judgments, and social problems." Social Problems 20 (Spring): 407–419. (1973).

Kuhn, Thomas S. The Structure of Scientific Revolutions Chicago: University of Chicago Press. (1970).

Lemert, Edward M. Social Pathology. New York: McGraw-Hill. (1951).

Manis, Jerome G. "Common sense sociology and analytic sociology." Sociological Focus 5 (Spring): 1–15. (1972).

———. "The concept of social problems: Vox populi and sociological analysis." Social Problems 21:305–315. (1974).

Merton, Robert K. On Theoretical Sociology. New York: Free Press. (1967).

———. "Social problems and sociological theory," pp. 793–845 in Robert K. Merton and Robert Nisbet (eds.), Contemporary Social Problems. New York: Harcourt Brace Jovanovich. (1971).

Perrucci, Robert and Marc Pilisuk (eds.) The Triple Revolution Emerging: Social Problems in Depth. Boston: Little, Brown. (1971).

Planck, Max "Phantom problems in science," pp. 840–852 in Dagobert D. Runes (ed.), Treasury of World Science. New York: Philosophical Library. (1962).

Schutz, Alfred "Common-sense and scientific interpretations of human action," pp. 302–346 in Maurice Natanson (ed.), Philosophy of the Social Sciences: A Reader. New York: Random House. (1963).

Simmons, J. L. "Public sterotypes of deviants." Social Problems 13 (Fall): 223–232. (1965).

Tallman, Irving and Reece McGee "Definition of a social problem," pp. 19–58 in Erwin O. Smigel (ed.), Handbook on the Study of Social Problems. Chicago: Rand McNally. (1971).

Theodorson, George A. and Achilles G. Theodorson A Modern Dictionary of Sociology. New York: Crowell. (1969).

Tumin, Melvin "The functionalist approach to social problems." Social Problems 12 (Spring): 379–388. (1965).

Westhus, Kenneth "Social problems as systemic costs." Social Problems 12 (Spring): 379–388. (1973).

Missing Children, Misleading Statistics

JOEL BEST

During the 1980s, a small but nasty debate emerged over the number of children abducted by strangers. Competing estimates appeared in speeches, press reports, and testimony before congressional committees. This fall, the federal Office of Juvenile Justice and Delinquency Prevention (OJJDP) will try to resolve the issue by releasing the results of the National Studies of the Incidence of Missing Children. Reporters covering the debate over the stranger-abduction problem seem to assume that these studies' findings will be authoritative.

This debate's history reveals the importance of statistics in bringing social problems to public notice. Proponents of different causes must compete for the attention of policymakers and the public. If missing children capture their attention, then other issues, such as homelessness, are more likely to be neglected. Promoting new social problems becomes a matter of persuasion, and statistics play a key role in this process.

The fear of kidnappings by strangers propelled the missing-children movement into prominence. The movement emerged in 1981, following intense media coverage of the disappearance of Etan Patz, the brutal slaying of Adam Walsh, and the murders of twenty-eight Atlanta schoolchildren. John Walsh, Adam's father, quickly became the most visible missing-children crusader—and a reminder of the reality of stranger abductions. Although the term "missing children" encompassed runaways and child snatchings (children taken by noncustodial parents), stranger abductions received the lion's share of the attention. Widely publicized recommendations that all parents assemble identification files with their children's photographs, dental records, and fingerprints suggested that every child was in danger.

ESTIMATING THE PROBLEM'S MAGNITUDE

The crusaders described a stranger-abduction problem of astonishing dimensions. Then U.S. Representative Paul Simon offered "the most conservative estimate you will get anywhere"—50,000 children abducted by strangers annually. Child Find, a leading child-search organization, estimated that parents recovered only 10 percent of these children, that another 10 percent were found dead, and that the remainder—40,000 cases per year—remained missing. In short, the crusaders described a large number of stranger abductions with very serious consequences.

To be sure, everyone agreed that stranger abductions accounted for only a small minority of missing children; estimates for child-snatchings and runaways were far larger. But stranger abductions served to typify the problem: the television movie "Adam" brought widespread attention to missing children, and Adam Walsh came to represent the larger phenomenon. Sociologist Michael Agopian testified that "there are tens of thousands of additional Adams that are not so prominently reported by the media."

The public certainly came to perceive child abduction as a serious problem. Surveys revealed widespread concern. Eighty-nine percent

Reprinted with permission of the author from *The Public Interest,* No. 92 (Summer 1988), pp. 84–92. © 1988 by National Affairs, Inc.

of Illinois parents viewed stranger abductions as a "very" or "quite" serious national problem. Thirty-seven percent of California adults believed that "there is a great deal of danger today of children being abducted by a stranger"—and another 47 percent said that there was "some" danger. A national survey of youth (ages 8–17) found that 76 percent reported being very concerned about the kidnapping of children and teenagers. (In comparison, 65 percent were very concerned about the possibility of nuclear war.)

By 1985, the movement was well established. There was a federally funded National Center for Missing and Exploited Children (NCMEC), and pictures of missing children graced billions of milk cartons and utility bills. The NCMEC was now offering a lower estimate of 4,000–20,000 stranger abductions per year, but the early estimates had a life of their own. The 50,000 figure continues to be quoted—and even higher estimates have appeared. One 1987 child-safety guide put the annual number of stranger abductions at 400,000.

These estimates reflect the typical manner in which neglected social problems gain recognition: activists call our attention to them. One feature of past neglect is the absence of official statistics—no one has been charged with keeping track of the phenomenon. Activists inevitably present themselves as knowledgeable enough about some social condition to bring it to our attention. With no official statistics available, this putative knowledge seems to give the crusaders' estimates the weight of authority. The activists seek to emphasize the problem's magnitude and importance; they have nothing to lose by providing big numbers.

In the early stages of social-problem construction, these estimates may be the best— even the only—numbers available. And the media repeat these figures, although they tend to treat them carefully. Thus, the first ABC news story on missing children contained the following statement: "By conservative estimate, 50,000 children are abducted each year, not counting parental kidnappings and custody fights. Most are never found. Four to eight thousand a year are murdered." Press reports routinely attribute statistics to "authorities,"

"experts," and "estimates." As long as some source actually gave these figures, the press report is accurate: it is true that authorities gave statistic X, even if X is wildly wrong.

THE AUTHORITY OF OFFICIAL STATISTICS

Given the ease with which activists' statistics find their way into policy discussions, it is remarkable that the missing-children crusaders' claims came under closer, more critical attention in 1985. Led by the *Denver Post* (which received a Pulitzer Prize for its coverage of the issue), the press began suggesting that the risk of child abduction had been blown out of proportion. The *Post* spoke of a "numbers gap," contrasting the well-publicized 50,000 figure with the sixty-seven FBI investigations of children abducted by strangers in 1984. A *Post* editorial suggested that the actual number of stranger abductions was "fewer than the number of preschoolers who choke to death on food each year." Other journalists and social scientists joined this attack, using the contrast between FBI statistics and the crusaders' estimates as proof that stranger abductions were uncommon. These critics betrayed a touching faith in official statistics.

The press seemed to share the widespread assumption that the FBI has jurisdiction in all kidnapping cases. This is not true. Before beginning an investigation, the Bureau demands evidence that the offense somehow violates a federal statute—for example, using the mail to deliver a ransom note, or transporting a hostage across a state line. Only a fraction of the kidnappings "opened"—that is, brought to the Bureau's attention—are found to involve violations of the Federal Kidnapping Statute. In 1984, the FBI decided to investigate 169 of 1035 opened cases. Most investigations involved adult hostages; the FBI investigated only sixty-nine cases of abducted children in 1984. (The slightly smaller figure that was quoted in the press came from a preliminary compilation.)

These FBI figures were not authoritative measures of stranger abductions. In fact, missing-children crusaders regularly criticized the FBI's reluctance to enter these cases. Several congressional hearings featured testimony from parents of children abducted by strangers—most notably John Walsh—who had found the FBI unwilling to investigate; the Senate Subcommittee on Juvenile Justice devoted one 1983 hearing to this problem. If the crusaders' 50,000 estimate now seemed too high, the FBI figure of sixty-seven repeated by the movement's critics was certainly too low.

In 1985, the media adopted the FBI statistics with the same uncritical enthusiasm with which they had accepted the activists' estimates four years earlier. Of course, the official statistics had an advantage. The press seeks authoritative sources, and the FBI, which has served as the principal source of crime statistics for decades, has great authority. In promoting new social problems, official statistics count more than unofficial statistics. Embarrassed by criticism that their estimates were unfounded, the missing-children crusaders turned to making their own figures official.

REDEFINING CHILD ABDUCTION

The contradictory official statistics made the missing-children cause controversial. In a 1986 congressional hearing, Representative Thomas Tauke of Iowa questioned the accuracy of NCMEC statistics. NCMEC President Ellis E. Meredith responded:

I don't think anything has surprised me more than this preoccupation with numbers, and the "only 67 or only 68 or only 69." . . . These are little helpless citizens of this country being held hostage, scared to death, totally unable to take care of themselves, being held hostage by terrorists. What is it with the "only," sir?

The missing-children movement gave great weight to its own estimates—until these became the subject of dispute. Once the controversy emerged, Meredith and other crusaders argued that numbers were irrelevant; they frequently asserted that "one missing child is too many."

At the same time, NCMEC officials began trying to redefine the missing-children problem: they advocated expanding the domain of stranger abduction, including offenses quite different from those described during the early stages of the missing-children movement. This more inclusive definition will inevitably produce larger numbers, justifying continued concern.

In 1986, the NCMEC responded to its critics by releasing a study of 1299 recent cases of stranger abduction. Most of these data were collected haphazardly, making it impossible to generalize from the findings. However, the study did include an analysis of police records of every reported crime involving a kidnapping or attempted kidnapping of a child by a non-relative in Jacksonville, Florida, and Houston, Texas, during 1984. There were 269 such cases. Since these two cities held 0.9 percent of the U.S. population, extrapolation suggests that there were roughly 29,889 stranger abductions nationwide during 1984—a figure that many might consider to be in the same ballpark as 50,000. This extrapolation is easy to challenge, however, because both cities have unusually high rates of serious violent crimes. In 1984, the national rate for murder and non-negligent manslaughter was 7.9 per 100,000; but Jacksonville's murder rate was 17.7 and Houston's 26.2. Similarly, the rates for forcible rape were 35.7 nationwide, 100.8 in Jacksonville, and 70.3 in Houston. Since the two cities had two to three times the national incidence of serious violent crimes, we can probably halve the extrapolated number of kidnappings, to something like 15,000.

It is important to understand, moreover, what sorts of offenses fell within this study's definition of stranger abduction. The NCMEC researchers included both attempted and completed kidnappings. (Over a fifth of the cases involved an unsuccessful attempt.) And the Jacksonville and Houston cases reveal another pattern: 88 percent of the victims were female, 97 percent were missing for less than twenty-four hours, and the police recorded 61 percent of the cases as sex offenses. In short, most were cases of molestation, albeit technically involving kidnapping (that is, moving the victim to a different place). Nor did the authorities list these offenses as kidnappings: "Only 15% of the reports had classifications that included the words *kidnapping, attempted kidnapping,* or *abduction*" (emphasis in the original). In some cases, the victim might have been missing for no more than a few minutes. Without discounting the seriousness of these experiences for the victims, these crimes do not fit the image of child abduction promoted by the early missing-children crusaders.

The Jacksonville/Houston data did include some very serious cases: six children were murdered, and at least four were gone for more than twenty-four hours. Unfortunately, the NCMEC's report doesn't reveal whether these categories overlapped. Assuming that the two cities had ten very serious incidents, extrapolation yields a nationwide figure of 1111 stranger abductions involving either murder or a child's being missing for more than one day. And considering the two cities' high rate of violent crime, we might reasonably cut the estimate in half, to roughly 550 very serious cases.

THE IMPORTANCE OF DEFINITIONS

Definitions make a difference. Defining stranger abduction broadly, so as to include attempted offenses and short-term abductions (typically for the purpose of sexual molestation), will produce a statistic of perhaps 15,000 cases annually. A narrower definition—which takes into account, for example, only children who are killed or missing overnight—will lead to a much smaller number, perhaps 550 cases a year.

There are signs that the broader definition is gaining acceptance. Other official agencies have begun to adopt the NCMEC's definition. Thus, a review of missing-children reports in New York State found that 85 percent of all cases involved teenagers, half of all cases were canceled—i.e., the child was reported found—within four days, and 99 percent of the cases reported in 1985 had been canceled by May 1986. While the New York records do not classify types of missing children, these findings might seem consistent with a high proportion of runaways. However, citing the NCMEC's

claim that many stranger abductions are short-term crimes, the report warns that "there is no evidence that would justify defining New York State's missing children as essentially a 'runaway' problem."

Missing-children activists also support the more inclusive definition. The Kevin Collins Foundation for Missing Children (an organization specializing in the problem of stranger abduction) has criticized criminal-justice record-keeping practices for misclassifying stranger abductions:

> Current police statistics (including the FBI statistics) fail to show that stranger abduction of children is a significant problem requiring national attention to correct it. . . . There is a reason why the current crime statistics fail to reflect a true picture of the numbers of stranger abductions. That reason is that whenever a previous or subsequent crime occurs in conjunction with stranger abduction . . . the crime of abduction (kidnapping) most often ceases to be shown. . . . [Stranger abduction] would be a recognized problem if statistics were kept. . . . When statistics make the problem graphic police/public attention will be directed to the problem and it will be diminished.

John Walsh put the case for a broad definition in more dramatic terms: "If it was your daughter . . . and you were waiting for her and she didn't come home for four hours and after that time she came home with bloody underpants and she had been raped, was she a missing child? Damn well she was."

THE USE AND ABUSE OF STATISTICS

The debate over stranger abduction reveals the importance of statistics in the discussion of social problems. Three principles seem clear: big numbers are better than little numbers; official numbers are better than unofficial numbers; and big official numbers are best of all.

For several years journalists, politicians, and missing-children crusaders have suggested that research will provide an authoritative measure of the number of missing children. Obviously, how many stranger abductions are counted will depend upon what counts. There are indications that the National Studies of the Incidence of Missing Children will adopt a broad definition. One of the pilot surveys sponsored by OJJDP used a broad definition in phrasing a key question: "Since the first of this year, was there any time when [name] was missing from your household and you were worried about where (he) (she) was . . . even if it was only for a few hours?" In addition to surveys, the proposed research design includes "a separate study of law enforcement records," in which researchers will select a representative sample of law-enforcement agencies, from which "records concerning all nonfamily abduction situations will be identified." While this says nothing about the definition of stranger abduction, the methodology is similar to that of the NCMEC study.

The problem, of course, is that this research will have policy consequences. However sophisticated the research design, the results are likely to be presented in a manner that will maximize their rhetorical effect. A research report—perhaps several hundred pages long—will be condensed into a brief press release, and that press release is likely to give a single, official number for stranger abductions. If that number is large, it will establish that stranger abduction is indeed widespread.

In advocating the broad definition of stranger abduction, moreover, those who make claims continue to use frightening language and horrifying examples. Thus, NCMEC President Meredith speaks of little children "held hostage by terrorists," and Jay Howell, the NCMEC's Executive Director, has provided the following testimony:

> Unfortunately, a lot of the children, whether it is Adam Walsh, Vicki Lynn, a lot of the kids that are well known in this country were killed in a very short period of time, so you typically have a scenario where one person kidnaps a child, takes them to a second location, usually somewhere in that geographic area, sexually assaults them and releases them hours later, and sometimes they are murdered.

There is a rule of thumb that the more serious the crime, the less common it is. But activists are aware of the advantages of typifying a problem by drawing their examples from the most serious cases.

A broad definition of stranger abduction will generate high incidence rates. And high incidence rates—especially when they are illustrated with atrocity tales about raped or murdered children—will lead to perceptions that the problem is serious, that new policies are needed. Most missing-children crusaders advocate two sorts of policies: education/prevention and expansion of the social-control apparatus. Currently, parents can choose among dozens of antikidnapping books, games, videotapes, ID kits, and other commercial products designed to educate children about the dangers of abduction. Most are reasonably priced, but it is more difficult to calculate the social costs of encouraging both children and adults to believe that terrifying crimes are commonplace. The missing-children movement also emphasizes the need for greater social control: schools should require detailed identification records for every student; police should have the power to hold runaways; federal police powers should be expanded; courts should accept testimony from very young children; and so on. The unspeakable threat posed by the stranger-abduction epidemic justifies these changes; the new policies' potential costs and dangers receive little attention.

Former U.S. Senator Paula Hawkins of Florida, a leader of the missing-children movement, asks: "When you think about it, does it really matter whether the number [of stranger abductions] is 4000, 20,000, or 50,000? . . . No abstract statistics should distract us from the plight of even one innocent child who is in danger of any kind of exploitation." In fact, those abstract statistics shape our sense of a problem's urgency, which in turn affects policy.

There is nothing unique about the rhetoric of the missing-children movement. Activists routinely offer large estimates. This is particularly true in making claims about crime. Because crime is secretive, because it inevitably involves a "dark figure," there are few constraints on the crusaders' imaginations. One million is a nice round number that routinely turns up; we frequently hear that there are a million abused children, and equal numbers of boy prostitutes, runaways, and victims of elder abuse. In each case the problem, because of its magnitude, demands action.

Activists use statistics to persuade; but these numbers must be understood for what they are—part of the rhetoric of social-problems promotion. Statistics are products of social processes, and they can have social consequences. When trying to understand social problems, we need figures we can count on, but we especially need to know what it is we're counting.

The American Scene

CHAPTER

2

Problems of Physical Health

Hospital Care for Profit

GERALDINE DALLEK

In 1961, four men set out for a game of golf. Two were real estate agents, two, young lawyers from a prestigious Louisville, Kentucky, law firm. That golf game was the beginning of what was to become an international corporation with $2.6 billion in annual revenue—Humana, Incorporated. Only a few years later, in 1968, two Nashville doctors met with Jack Massey, a founder of Kentucky Fried Chicken, and Hospital Corporation of America (HCA), the nation's largest for-profit hospital chain, was born. By 1984, HCA owned or managed 260 hospitals in 41 states and grossed more than $3.9 billion from its hospitals and nursing homes. By the mid-1980s, proprietary hospitals controlled 12 percent of the acute care hospital market in the United States, 21 percent in the South.

It is possible to understand the rapid growth and impact of these proprietary chains only by examining the environment that nurtured them. In many ways, the medical care industry is like the defense industry. First, the goals of each—protecting our nation and protecting our health—are intrinsically valued by our society. Second, medical care and national defense are extremely costly. We spend $300 billion on defense each year, three-fourths as much as the $400 billion spent on health care. Third, both industries, in what is clearly aberrant free-market behavior, have been permitted to set the price of the goods and services they produce. In defense, it is the weapons contractors who have been virtually given a blank check; in the medical industry, hospitals, nursing homes, drug manufacturers, and physicians have, until very recently, also had carte blanche to determine how much their product is worth.

Given these factors, is it any wonder that both industries are highly profitable?

The ability to make money from the delivery of medical care is not new. In the late nineteenth century, as hospitals became safe and attractive places in which to care for the ill, small for-profit hospitals sprang up in the United States and Western Europe. In Europe, individual for-profit hospitals faded from the scene as government assumed more responsibility for ensuring the provision of health care. By contrast, the for-profit hospital industry in the United States flourished.

In the early 1980s, for-profit chains were the darling of Wall Street with a 20 percent growth rate. During 1982, a recession year for most businesses, stocks of the top four hospital chains rose 30 percent. Profits of the twenty largest chains went up 38 percent in 1983 and 28.5 percent the following year. In 1984, HCA's chief executive officer was the second-highest-paid executive in the nation, and the head of National Medical Enterprises (NME) beat out the movie moguls as the highest-paid executive in Southern California.

What accounts for the rapid expansion and huge profits of these new hospital organizations? Traditional reimbursement policies go far to explain the attractiveness of the hospital industry to entrepreneurs. Hospitals, until adoption of the new Medicare diagnosis-related group (DRG) payment system in 1983, were generally paid by a retrospective cost-based reimbursement system. This open-ended system for paying hospitals, begun by Blue Cross plans (acting almost as agents for the hospitals) after World War II, was adopted by the federal government as the

Geraldine Dallek is a health policy analyst at the National Health Law Program, which is a legal services support center specializing in health law issues affecting the poor. She has written extensively on problems of access to health care by the uninsured and Medicaid populations.

From *Society*, July/August 1986. Published by permission of Transaction Publishers, from *Society*, Vol. 23, No. 5. Copyright © 1986 by Transaction Publishers.

quid pro quo for the hospital industry's support of Medicare and Medicaid legislation in 1965. The potential for profits in this reimbursement system cannot be overstated. "It was hard not to be successful," commented the chief executive officer of National Medical Enterprises in a 1985 *Wall Street Journal* article. Profits could be made by simply buying existing hospitals and making sure that bills to both private and public insurers contained an add-on profit.

Hospitals could be bought easily in the seventies and early eighties. For-profit chains' access to capital through the sale of stock gave them an advantage over their nonprofit brethren for purposes of both building and buying hospitals. Because of their large revenue, assets, and equity base, they were viewed as sound financial risks.

The major growth of for-profit chains came from the purchase of financially troubled hospitals. Between 1980 and 1982, 43 percent of the growth of the six largest for-profit chains came from the purchase of other for-profit hospitals, mostly independent facilities. A third of the growth came from the construction of new hospitals and a fourth from the purchase of public and voluntary nonprofit hospitals. Following a for-profit purchase, ailing hospitals were brought back to health by building new facilities to attract physicians, substantially increasing charges, and reducing services to those who could not pay. Public hospitals owned and run by local governments were often receptive to being bailed out by for-profit chains. Faced with aging facilities, unable to attract privately insured patients, and confronted with increased numbers of the poor seeking care, public hospitals awash with red ink were all too happy to sell to for-profit chains.

In assessing the impact of the for-profit hospital industry, we must go well beyond the counting of beds. The industry has had a far-reaching impact on the cost of hospital care, the delivery of services to the poor, and the behavior of other health care providers.

COSTLY CARE

For-profit chains have often been viewed favorably because of their promise to bring man-agerial efficiency to the "wasteful" nonprofit sector. It does not appear that they possess superior managerial talents. After reviewing a number of studies on multihospital systems, Ermann and Gabel concluded in a May 1985 article in *Medical Care* that "There is little empirical evidence that [multihospital] systems have realized economies of scale of mass purchasing or use capital facilities more efficiently." Nor have chains served as a competitive catalyst to an industry grown fat by its insulation from free-market forces. Theoretically, competition and efficiency would lead to reduced costs. Judged by this standard, for-profit hospital chains also failed, as they increased, not lowered, the cost of hospital care.

For-profit chain costs have been higher than nonprofit hospital costs for three reasons: they mark up charges well above expenses; they use more expensive ancillary services than nonprofit facilities; and charges must cover their higher capital costs. According to several studies, the difference in costs between for-profit and not-for-profit hospitals is substantial. A comparison of charges at 280 California for-profit and nonprofit hospitals showed that for-profit hospital charges per admission were 24 percent higher than those of the voluntary hospitals and 47 percent higher than public hospital charges. According to this study—by Robert Pattison and Hallie Katz, reported in the August 1983 *New England Journal of Medicine*—huge profits were made in ancillary services such as pharmacy and laboratory services. The study also showed that despite the claims of administrative savings, costs for "fiscal services" and "administrative services" (which include costs to maintain corporate headquarters elsewhere) were 32 percent higher in for-profit chain hospitals than in voluntary hospitals. The authors concluded that the data "do not support the claim that investor-owned chains enjoy overall operating efficiencies or economies of scale in administrative fiscal services."

Results of a more recent study, by Lewin and Associates and health-policy analysts at Johns Hopkins University, of eighty matched pairs of investor-owned chain and not-for-profit hospitals in eight states were remarkably similar to the Pattison and Katz study: prices charged by for-profit chain hospitals were 22 percent more per admission than those charged by matched not-for-profit hospitals.

For-profit hospitals also charge more for several procedures, according to a 1983 Blue Cross/ Blue Shield of North Carolina study. Comparing charges for three commonly performed hospital procedures—gall bladder removals, hysterectomies, and normal deliveries of babies—at six for-profit hospitals and six matched nonprofit hospitals, the study found that in all but one case the average total charge was from 6 percent to 58 percent higher in the for-profit hospitals.

Patients have generally been insulated from higher for-profit charges by their third-party coverage. Nevertheless, at least one Las Vegas man found the cost of care at his local for-profit hospital upsetting. In a June 1985 letter to the *Las Vegas Review Journal,* the gentleman recounted how he had

> recently had the misfortune of requiring emergency room treatment at Humana Sunrise Hospital for kidney stone problems. This was my second encounter with this problem. The first encounter occurred last July, and I was treated at Southern Nevada Memorial Hospital.
>
> As the treatment was almost identical, I have had the opportunity to compare the costs of the two facilities. I was not surprised to find that Humana hospitals were more expensive; however, I was shocked to discover that the cost was fully 50% above that of Southern Nevada.
>
> As I was curtly informed by administrative personnel at Humana, the costs were higher because Humana is a "private" hospital, and Southern Nevada is a county hospital. Now this is a point well taken and probably could account for a 15 or 20% difference, but 50%—Come on, who does Humana think they are fooling?

For-profit hospitals have also increased health-care costs indirectly by building unneeded hospitals. For example, primarily because of the growth of for-profit hospitals, twelve Florida counties, underbedded in 1972, had 6600 excess beds three years later. The for-profit chains that had controlled 16.7 percent of beds in 1972 had built 60 percent of the new beds.

If efficiency is measured by maximum use

of the physical plant, for-profit chains are once again found wanting. In 1985, average hospital occupancy rates for the four largest proprietary chains ranged from 46 percent to 56 percent. Empty beds were not as important under the old cost-based reimbursement system, as charges to insurers for patients in the occupied beds could be increased to cover the cost of unoccupied beds. This changed with Medicare's new reimbursement system which pays a flat rate based on a patient's diagnosis and vigorous cost containment programs begun by Medicaid and private health insurers in 1983 and 1984.

The old cost-based reimbursement systems not only rewarded hospitals for providing extra services and hiking up prices but failed to penalize them for empty beds. Medicare's new flat-rate reimbursement scheme provides opposite incentives: it rewards hospitals for reducing services (the fewer services provided, the more money made) and penalizes them for their empty beds. This dramatic change in the way hospitals are paid would, it could be supposed, hurt most those hospitals that had taken greatest advantage of the old system. This seems to have happened. In October of 1985, announcements by the leading chains of flat or reduced earnings stunned Wall Street and resulted in a steep decline in their stocks.

In response to changes in hospital reimbursement and declining hospital revenues, chains began to diversify—investing in more lucrative areas of medial care, including nursing homes, insurance companies, health maintenance organizations (HMOs), neighborhood emergicenters (often called doc-in-the-box), and home health agencies. Their proven ability to maximize profits from the provision of medical services will thus be tested in new arenas. Called a "managed system" approach, this vertical integration of the health industry gives proprietary chains added power to shape the future of health care delivery in this country.

Analysts may argue over the exact impact of the growth of the proprietary chains, but most agree that in subtle and not-so-subtle ways chains have irrevocably changed the milieu in which hospitals operate. Nowhere has the change been more profound than in the provision of hospital care to the poor.

TURNING AWAY THE POOR

Chains make no secret of their view that health care is nothing more than an economic commodity to be sold in the marketplace for a profit. One Humana senior vice president put it this way: "Health care is a necessity, but so is food. Do you know of any neighborhood grocery store where you can walk out with $3000 worth of food that you haven't paid for?" Chain spokesmen are also commonly heard to claim that their hospitals' commitment to the poor is taken care of by the payment of taxes. Given this view, it is not surprising that several state studies have found large disparities in the amount of care for the indigent provided by for-profit hospitals and voluntary and public hospitals. Typically, public hospitals provide the lion's share of uncompensated care; voluntary hospitals come in a poor second, with for-profit facilities running a dismal third.

Although for-profit hospitals constituted 32 percent of Florida's hospitals in 1983, they provided only 4 percent of the net charity care provided within the state. Florida's Hospital Cost Containment Board openly criticized for-profit hospitals in its 1983–84 annual report for their failure to share the burden of serving the uninsured poor. According to a report by the Texas Task Force on Indigent Health Care, for-profit hospitals made up 19.1 percent of the hospitals in that state in 1983, but provided less than 1 percent of the charity care and only 2.7 percent of the bad debt. Nonprofit hospitals, while making up 36.1 percent of the hospital facilities in Texas, provided 13.1 percent of charity care and 42.8 percent of the bad debt. Texas's public facilities provided most of the care of the poor: public hospitals, constituting 44.7 percent of the hospitals in the state, provide 86.9 percent of the charity care and 54.6 percent of the bad debt.

Some national data on provision of care for the indigent are available from the January 1981 Office of Civil Rights (OCR) survey of all general, short-term hospitals in the United States. An analysis of OCR data on inpatient admitting practices showed that 9.5 percent of all hospital patients were uninsured in 1981; yet only 6 percent of patients treated at for-profit hospitals

were uninsured while 16.8 percent of those treated at hospitals owned by state and local governments were uninsured. Alan Sager also used OCR data in his study of hospital closures and relocation in 52 cities. He found that of the 4038 patients categorized on admission as charity care patients (not to be charged) during the OCR survey, only one received care at a for-profit facility.

To some extent, the amount of charity care provided by for-profit hospitals is limited by their locations—in suburban white communities where few of the poor reside. When those hospitals are matched with similarly located nonprofit facilities, the amount of care to the poor differs little by ownership. However, geography does not explain why chain hospitals located in areas with significant numbers of uninsured populations provide so little in the way of charity.

The plight of one fifty-six-year-old uninsured laborer described in a recent *Washington Post* article is a case in point. Mr. G. R. Lafon sought care for third-degree grease burns on his side and back at the hospital nearest his home, a for-profit facility. The hospital and two other for-profit hospitals refused him emergency care because he did not have a deposit ranging from $500 to $1500. One of the hospitals did take the precaution of inserting an intravenous tube and a catheter to stabilize his liquids before sending him on his way. After seven hours and a seventy-mile trek, Lafon arrived at Parkland Memorial Hospital in Dallas, the city's public hospital, where he was immediately admitted. Lafon required nineteen days of hospitalization and a skin graft for a cost of $22,000. Soon after discharge, he began receiving notices for an overdue hospital bill—not for the $22,000 owed to Parkland (that will be written off because Lafon is poor and uninsured) but for $373.75 from the for-profit facility to cover the cost of the catheter and intravenous tube.

Similar horror stories can be heard all over the South. In Memphis, for example, the city's largest HCA hospital threatened early in 1985 that it would stop chemotherapy treatments for a farmer with lung cancer when his family ran out of cash to continue the treatments. It was not until the day a suit was to be filed against the hospital claiming abandonment, denial of emergency medical care, intentional infliction of mental distress, and extortion that the HCA relented and agreed to continue treatment.

Voluntary hospitals and even some public hospitals also turn away the poor. What distinguishes the actions of for-profit chain hospitals from those of individual voluntary or public facilities is that the for-profit hospitals' policy of denying access is established at corporate headquarters and affects all their facilities throughout the nation. Although many voluntary hospitals are reducing their uncompensated care load in order to survive, others continue to view care for the poor as part of their mission.

The impact of care to the uninsured goes beyond the number of poor that proprietary chains do and do not serve. In the past five years, 180 public hospitals have been bought or managed by for-profit companies. This has resulted in an inexorable diminution of care to the poor: public officials do not sell hospitals in order to continuing providing indigent care; they do so in order to relieve themselves from what they perceive as an onerous burden. These sales, in turn, add to the financial troubles of the public and voluntary hospitals which continue to serve the indigent population. Chains also have had one other far-reaching effect on the provision of care to the poor: they have caused what Louanne Kennedy of the City University of New York describes as "the proprietarization of voluntary hospitals."

BEAT 'EM OR JOIN 'EM

Nonprofit hospitals have long had a split personality, torn by the need to make money (their business side) and the need to succor the poor and sick (their humanitarian or social side). The rapid growth of for-profit chains forced nonprofit facilities to come to terms with this dichotomy. In the process, hospitals became more businesslike and less concerned with humanitarian goals.

Interestingly, for-profit chains did promote competition in the delivery of hospital services but not, as the supply/demand curve predicts, on the basis of price. In the middle and late seventies, as the number of empty beds increased, hospital survival became in-

creasingly predicated on attracting physicians who would admit their privately insured patients. In the competition for doctors, a hospital belonging to a large chain with easy access to capital had distinct advantages over the local voluntary and especially the public facility. A choice between a thirty-year-old public hospital with its leaky roof, overcrowded emergency room (filled with poor people), and frequent equipment breakdowns and the spanking-new Humana or HCA hospital with the latest in diagnostic equipment and nary a poor person in sight, was no choice at all.

Chains also had the money to recruit doctors to their hospitals. For example, an April 5, 1982, Humana recruiting letter to pediatricians offered the following inducements to join a five-physician multispecialty group in Springhill, Louisiana:

> guaranteed income—$5,500 per month for the first six months; the lowest projected first-year income is $150,000;

> rent-free office—absolutely no business or other overhead expenses the first year; this includes a paid nurse, secretarial and office equipment and furniture, free utilities, and more;

> paid health/dental/life/malpractice insurance;

> company car; paid moving expenses; paid country club membership; paid on-site visit.

The most famous for-profit hospital recruit, Dr. William DeVries, was brought to the Humana Heart Institute in Louisville, Kentucky, with the promise of 100 artificial heart transplants.

In the competition over physicians, chains did not ignore the patient. Although price was not a consideration, well-heeled patients were lured to specialized chain facilities which touted the latest in sports medicine, treatment of diet disorders, wine and candlelight dinners for new parents, and a free hairstyle with a "tummy tuck." If patients were to be appealed to directly, then chain products had to be merchandized, and so advertising budgets became part and parcel of the cost of providing medical care.

At the same time as voluntary hospitals were losing private, paying patients to the new hospital on the block, they were also getting less money for the private, paying patients still filling their beds. Generally, under the blank-check reimbursement system, hospitals simply passed on the costs of their nonpaying patients to their privately insured patients whose care was paid for through employer-subsidized insurance. Thus, employers were subsidizing care for the poor through higher insurance premiums. While hospital access for the poor has been far from universal, a great deal of service was paid for by this cost shift. The health-insurance industry estimated that it was charged an extra $8 billion in 1983 to subsidize the provision of care to those who could not pay and were uninsured.

As hospital costs kept spiraling (in some years by 20 percent) and as the number of uninsured poor increased, commercial insurers and business interests became less willing to pay this cost shift or what they called a "sick tax." Arguing that they should only have to pay premium costs to cover care for their work force, not the nation's poor, employers demanded and got reductions in their premium costs and the beginnings of competition based on price.

Voluntary and public hospitals subsidizing the poor are at a distinct disadvantage in any game based on price competition because they are, according to policy analysts, playing on an "uneven playing field." To even stay in the game, they are forced to act like their opponents, which means toughening up their billing and collection practices and managing their indigent patient load. Unfortunately, "managing" is often synonymous with "excluding." An American Hospital Association study found that in 1981 and 1982 about 15 percent of nonprofit hospitals adopted limits on the amount of charity care they provided, and 84 percent increased billing and collection efforts.

There is no question that many tax-exempt charitable institutions provided little or no care to the poor well before the proprietary chains came on the scene. For these hospitals, for-profit chains made barring the poor an acceptable way of doing business. For nonprofit hospitals that took their charitable status seriously, the chains made it difficult and in some instances impossible for them to continue fulfilling their mission. The traditional behavior of tax-exempt hospitals that provide little or no charity care is being challenged in state courts.

A June 1985 decision by the Utah Supreme Court denied tax-exempt status to two nonprofit hospitals owned by Intermountain Health Care, a nonprofit hospital chain, because the hospitals did not meet their obligation to provide charity care.

"If you can't beat 'em, join 'em" was a slogan adopted by a large number of voluntary and public hospitals in the early eighties. In addition to conscious efforts to reduce services to the poor, nonprofit hospitals embarked on a mad scramble to buy nursing homes, establish home health agencies, "unbundle" hospital services (remove services such as pharmacy, laboratory, and X-ray from the hospital to get the higher reimbursement rates), specialize in highly profitable ventures such as sports medicine and wellness centers, structure patient care to achieve optimal reimbursement, consider terminating unprofitable services, and advertise.

While most hospitals argue these changes are necessary for survival, others maintain their efforts are directed toward continuing to subsidize charity care. This latter justification is commonly used by public hospitals which began in 1984 and 1985 to undertake corporate restructuring as an alternative to outright sale or transfer of management to a for-profit firm. While the exact configurations vary, the basic idea is to create several new nonprofit and for-profit subsidies. One of the nonprofits will lease the existing hospital for a nominal amount and operate it for the actual public owners, blurring what had once been a clear-cut distinction between for-profit and public hospitals.

Nonprofit hospitals copied the for-profit giants in one other way. Finding strength in numbers, voluntary hospitals began to form their own nonprofit chains. Although some chains of voluntary facilities (such as religious hospitals) predated the rise of for-profit chains, the impetus for increased horizontal integration among nonprofit hospitals in the early 1980s was competition from the proprietary chains.

GOOD BUSINESS OR BASIC CARE?

In 1979 one health analyst commented that "We could wake up in a few years with a few Exxons controlling half the hospitals." It did not take long for this prediction to come true. By 1990 it is likely that ten or so for-profit and non-profit-managed systems will compete with one another to serve the paying customer, while the few public hospitals left (primarily large inner-city facilities which cannot be closed for fear of adverse political repercussions) will continue their struggle to serve the impoverished of the nation. Is this the legacy of the proprietarization of American hospitals? The answer is no. The growth of for-profit chains was simply the natural development of a society that never viewed health care as a right, guaranteed to every citizen, and a government adverse to bucking the prevailing notion that medical providers should be left to their own devices to shape the nation's health care delivery system. If, in the shaping, no space was available for millions of Americans, so be it.

Uwe Reinhardt, a Princeton economist, argues that America's political ideology—its fear of big government—helped to create a medical system that tolerates "visible social pathos in our streets." This system accepts the existence of 35 million uninsured, most of whom are poor and near-poor; denial of prenatal and some-times delivery care to poor women; the trans-ferring or "dumping" of 500 patients a month from private Chicago hospitals to Cook County General, a public facility; excessive markups on drugs needed to control hypertension and other chronic illnesses; inhuman conditions in many of our nursing homes; and, lately, the premature discharge of elderly patients from hospitals when Medicare payments prove inad-equate to cover the costs of care.

Our response to this social pathos depends in large degree on how we view the delivery of medical care. If, as for-profit hospitals maintain, health care is a business, if HCA and Humana are no different than a McDonald's or a Macy's, then our response is obvious: protect against the grossest anticompetitive behavior, but gen-erally adopt a laissez-faire attitude and let mar-ket forces dictate the supply and price of goods. If, however, we believe that health care is more than a business, but a societal good, then our response is different indeed. Laws will be needed to assure that prices are controlled, profits limited, and people guaranteed the pro-vision of basic health care.

Which is it? To date, we have either ignored the question or, when forced to confront it, tried to have it both ways. This has led to am-biguous policies at best and huge holes in the nation's health-care safety net. The "let's have it both ways" mentality is evident in the govern-ment's Medicare policies. Although the provi-sion of medical care to the elderly and disabled is clearly seen as a societal good, the federal government's Medicare reimbursement policy with its substantial return on investment and unlimited passing through of the capital costs resulted in huge profits for investor-owned hos-pital chains and more money going for fewer services. It is only recently, with the advent of DRGs and 1986 legislation to eliminate return on equity (over three years) and proposals to cap federal reimbursements for capital costs, that we have begun to realize that unlimited profits may be at odds with the nation's commitment to providing health care for the elderly.

States have not been any more certain of now to reconcile the needs of the ill and the needs of the medical-care marketplace. A few Northeastern states have controlled the growth of for-profit hospitals through hospital rate reg-ulation; by limiting rates hospitals can charge, states limit the profits hospitals can make. These states also include payment for care of the indigent in their controlled rates. Other states have sought to require good citizenship of all their hospitals, for-profit and voluntary alike. Florida, South Carolina, and Virginia tax hospitals in order to pay for increased care of the indigent. Tougher emergency-room laws in a few states, most notably Texas, have made it more difficult for hospitals to refuse emergency care to the poor or inappropriately transfer them to the nearest public hospital. Efforts have also been made, primarily through the health planning program, to require hospitals wanting to build or modernize to provide a small amount of charity care. North Carolina now requires for-profit hospitals that buy public hospitals to continue to provide care to the poor of the community.

Unfortunately, these efforts are too little too late; the poor and, increasingly, the middle class with inadequate insurance are not guaran-teed access to even basic hospital care when ill.

Neither the federal government nor the states have been willing to limit profits made from providing hospital care, to require all hospitals to serve a minimum of uninsured and Medicaid recipients, or to provide health-care coverage for all in need.

Unlike other Western industrialized nations, we treat medical care as a commodity to be bought and sold in the marketplace. This marketplace mentality is allowing corporate medicine to distort our medical-care system into one that costs us a great deal even while it serves a diminishing share of our people.

READINGS SUGGESTED BY THE AUTHOR

Dallek, G. and Lowe, L. "The For-Profit Hospital Juggernaut." *Southern Exposure* 13 (1985).

Ermann, D. and Gabel, J. "Multihospital Systems: Issues and Empirical Findings." *Health Affairs* 3 (1984).

Kennedy, L. *The Losses in Profits: How Proprietaries Affect Public and Voluntary Hospitals.* Washington D.C.: Health/PAC.

Pattison, R. and Katz, H. "Investor-Owned and Not-for-Profit Hospitals: A Comparison Based on California Data." *The New England Journal of Medicine* 309 (1983).

Watt, J. et al. "The Comparative Economic Performance of Investor-Owned Chains and Not-for-Profit Hospitals." *The New England Journal of Medicine* 314 (1986).

The Social Meaning of AIDS

PETER CONRAD

Disease and illness can be examined on different levels. Disease is understood best as a bio-physiological phenomenon, a process or state that affects the body. Illness, by contrast, has more to do with the social and psychological phenomena that surround the disease. The world of illness is the subjective world of meaning and interpretation; how a culture defines an illness and how individuals experience their disorder.

In this article I am going to examine the social and cultural meanings of Acquired Immunodeficiency Syndrome or AIDS as it is manifested in late-20th-century America and relate these meanings to the social reaction that it has engendered. When I talk about the social meaning of AIDS, I am including what Susan Sontag has termed the metaphorical aspects of illness: those meanings of diseases that are used to reflect back on some morally suspect element of society.[1] As Sontag suggests, metaphorical aspects of illness are especially prevalent with dread diseases that have great unknowns about them. We need to look at AIDS not only as a biomedical entity, but as an illness that has a socially constructed image and engages particular attitudes. The social meanings of AIDS are simultaneously alarmingly simple and bafflingly complex, but are key to understanding the social reaction to AIDS.

THE SOCIAL REACTION TO AIDS

Five years ago virtually no one had heard of AIDS. In the past five years, however, AIDS has become a household term and a feared intruder in the society.

The medical reality of AIDS, as we know it, remains puzzling but is becoming clearer. AIDS is a disease caused by a virus that breaks down the immune system and leaves the body unprotected against "opportunistic infections" that nearly invariably lead to death. The number of AIDS cases is growing dramatically and AIDS is considered an epidemic in the society. Over 19,000 cases have been diagnosed, with four or five times that many people having a chronic disorder called AIDS-Related Complex (ARC) and perhaps over a million individuals having an antibody-positive response to HTLV-III, the virus believed to cause AIDS. It is estimated that 5 to 20 percent of this exposed group will contract AIDS, but no one knows who they will be.

Over 90 percent of AIDS victims come from two risk groups: homosexual or bisexual men and intravenous drug users. (Hemophiliacs and others requiring frequent blood transfusions and infants born to mothers with AIDS are also considered risk groups.) The evidence is clear that the AIDS virus is transmitted through the direct exchange of bodily fluids, semen and blood; the most common mode of transmission is anal intercourse among male homosexuals and unsterile needle-sharing among intravenous drug users. There is virtually *no* evidence that the virus can be transmitted by everyday "casual contact," including kissing or shaking hands, or exposure to food, air, water, or whatever.[2] With the exception of very specific modes of semen- or blood-related transmission, it does not appear that the AIDS virus is very easy to "catch."

Peter Conrad is associate professor of sociology at Brandeis University.

From *Social Policy* 17 (1), Summer 1986: 51–56. Published by Social Policy Corporation, New York. Copyright 1986 by Social Policy Corporation.

27

Yet the public reaction to AIDS has bordered on hysteria. Below are a few examples of the reactions to AIDS or AIDS victims.

- 11,000 children were kept out of school in Queens, New York, as parents protested the decision to allow a 7-year-old girl with AIDS to attend second grade (despite no evidence of transmission by school children).
- Hospital workers in San Francisco refused to enter the room of an AIDS patient. When ordered to attend the patient, they appeared wearing masks, gowns, and goggles.
- A Baltimore policeman refused to enter the office of a patient with AIDS to investigate a death threat and donned rubber gloves to handle the evidence.
- A local school district in New Jersey tried to exclude a healthy 9-year-old boy whose sister has ARC (despite no sign of sibling transmission).
- An Amarillo, Texas, hospital fired a cafeteria worker who participated in a blood drive. This worker showed no signs of being ill or unable to perform his duties, but his blood had registered seropositive.
- In early 1985, Delta Airlines proposed a rule (later dropped) forbidding the carrying of AIDS patients.
- In New York, undertakers refused to embalm AIDS victims, householders fired their Haitian help, and subway riders wore gloves, all from fear of contracting AIDS.
- One child, hospitalized with AIDS, had a "do not touch" sign on her bed and was isolated from all physical contact with her parents.
- *The New York Times* reported cases of dentists who refused to treat gay patients (not just confirmed AIDS cases).
- In Dallas, a small group of doctors and dentists formed Dallas Doctors Against AIDS and began a campaign to reinstate Texas' sodomy laws.
- In a Boston corporation, employees threatened to quit en masse if the company forced them to work with an AIDS patient.
- Dade County, Florida, voted to require the county's 80,000 food workers to carry cards certifying they are free of communicable diseases, including AIDS, despite no known cases of AIDS transmitted through food and even though public health officials opposed this policy.
- The U.S. military is beginning to screen all new recruits for AIDS antibodies, with the likely result of declaring those who test seropositive ineligible for service.
- Several major life insurance companies are requiring certain applicants (young, single, male, living in certain areas) to undergo an HTLV-III antibody test.
- Public health officials in Texas passed a measure allowing quarantine of certain AIDS patients. A candidate with a platform calling for the quarantining of all people with AIDS won the Democratic party's nomination for lieutenant governor in Illinois.

The list could go on. There is clearly a great fear engendered by the specter of AIDS, a fear that has led to an overreaction to the actual problem. This is in no way to say that AIDS is not a terrible and devastating disease—it is—or to infer that it is not a serious public health concern. What we are seeing is an overblown, often irrational, and pointless reaction to AIDS that makes the disease more difficult for those who have it and diverts attention from the real public health concerns.

THE SOCIAL AND CULTURAL MEANINGS OF AIDS

To better understand the reaction to AIDS, it is necessary to examine particular social features of the disease: (1) the effect of marginal and stigmatized "risk groups"; (2) sexually related transmission; (3) the role of contagion; and (4) the deadly nature of the disease.

The effect of marginal and stigmatized "risk groups." There are some illnesses that carry with them a certain moral devaluation, a stigma. Leprosy, epilepsy, mental disorder, venereal disease, and by some accounts, cancer, all reflect moral shame on the individuals who had the ill luck to contract them. Stigmatized illnesses are usually diseases that in some fashion are connected to deviant behavior: either they are deemed to produce it as with epilepsy or are produced by it, as in the case of VD.

The effect of the early connection of AIDS to homosexual conduct cannot be underestimated in examining its stigmatized image. The early designation of the disorder was Gay Related Immune Deficiency Syndrome (GRID) and was publicly proclaimed as a "gay plague." It was first thought to be caused by the use of "poppers" (amylnitrate) and later by promiscuity.[3] Something those fast-track gays were doing was breaking down their immune system. However, AIDS is not and never was specifically related to homosexual conditions; viruses don't know homosexuals from heterosexuals.

Within a short time, other "risk" groups were identified for what was now called AIDS—intravenous drug users, Haitians, and hemophiliacs. With the exception of hemophiliacs (who made up less than 2 percent of the cases), AIDS' image in the public eye was intimately connected with marginal populations. It was a disease of "those deviants," considered by some a deserved punishment for their activities. In 1983 Patrick J. Buchanan, who later became a White House staffer, wrote: "Those poor homosexuals. They have declared war on nature, and nature is exacting an awful retribution."[4] It is certain that fear of AIDS was amplified by the widespread and deeply rooted "homophobia" in American society.

Sexually related transmission. The dominant vector of transmission of AIDS is through sexual activity, particularly anal intercourse of male homosexuals. Although scientifically AIDS is better seen as a "blood disease" (since contact with blood is necessary for transmission), this common form of transmission has contributed to its image as a sexually transmitted disease.

Venereal diseases are by nature also stigmatized. They are deemed to be the fault of the victims and would not occur had people behaved better. As Allen Brandt points out, venereal diseases have become a symbol of pollution and contamination: "Venereal disease, the palpable evidence of unrestrained sexuality, became a symbol for social disorder and moral decay—a metaphor of evil."[5]

AIDS, with its connection to multiple sex encounters and once-forbidden "sodomy,"

touches deep Puritanical concerns and revives alarms of promiscuity and "sexual permissiveness" that have become more muted in recent decades. The connection of AIDS to "sexual irresponsibility" has been made repeatedly.

Now that it appears AIDS can be transmitted through heterosexual intercourse as well, although apparently not as efficiently and rapidly, there is increasing concern among sexually active people that they may be betrayed in their most intimate moments. This connection with intimacy and sexuality amplifies our anxieties and creates fears that one sexual act may bring a lifetime of pollution and ultimately death.

The role of contagion. We have almost come to believe that large-scale deadly epidemics were a thing of the past. The polio panics of the early 1950s have receded far into our collective memory, and the wrath of tuberculosis, cholera, or diphtheria have become, in American society at least, artifacts of the past. Everyday models for contagion are more limited to the likes of herpes, chicken pox, and hepatitis. When we encounter AIDS, which is contagious but apparently in a very specific way, our fear of contagion erupts almost without limits. When little is known about a disease's transmission, one could expect widespread apprehensions about contagion. But a great deal is known about AIDS' transmission—it appears only to be transmitted through the exchange of bodily fluids and in *no* cases through any type of casual contact. In fact, compared to other contagious diseases it has a relatively low infectivity. Yet the fear of contagion fuels the reaction to AIDS.

Given our extant medical knowledge, what are the sources of fear? We live in a society where medicine is expected to protect us from deadly contagious diseases, if not by vaccine, then by public health intervention. And when medicine does not do this, we feel we must rely on our own devices to protect ourselves and our loved ones. Contagion, even of minor disorders, can engender irrational responses. Several months ago my 5-year-old daughter was exposed to a playmate who came down with chicken pox. A good friend of mine, who happens to be a pediatrician, did not want his 4-year-old to ride in the car with my daughter to gymnastics class, even though he knew medically that she could not yet be infectious. He just did not want to take any chances. And so it is with us, our reactions to contagion are not always rational.

With AIDS, of course, the situation is much worse. When we read in the newspapers that the AIDS virus has been found in saliva or tears, though only occasionally, we imagine in our commonsense germ-theory models of contagion that we could "catch AIDS" in this manner. Reports that no transmission has ever occurred in this fashion become secondary. The public attitudes seem to be that exposure to the AIDS virus condemns one to the disease.

While AIDS is contagious, so is the fear and stigma. The fear of AIDS has outstripped the actual social impact of the disease. But, more importantly for families of people who suffer from AIDS, the stigma of AIDS becomes contagious. They develop what Erving Goffman has called a courtesy stigma, a taint that has spread from the stigmatized to his or her close connections.[6] Family members of people with AIDS are shunned and isolated by former friends and colleagues, for fear that they too might bring contagion.

A deadly disease. AIDS is a devastating and deadly disease. It is virtually 100 percent lethal: 75 percent of people with AIDS die within two years. There are few other diseases that, like AIDS, attack and kill people who are just reaching the prime of their lives. Currently, AIDS is incurable; since there are no treatments for it, to contract AIDS in the 1980s is to be served with a death warrant. Many sufferers waste away from Kaposi's sarcoma or some rare form of chronic pneumonia.

As various researchers have shown, caretakers and family alike tend to distance themselves from sufferers who are terminally ill with diseases that waste away their bodies.[7] The pain of suffering and the pollution of dying are difficult for many people to encounter directly in a society that has largely removed and isolated death from everyday life.

Taken together, these features form a cultural image of AIDS that is socially as well as medically devastating. It might even be said that AIDS is an illness with a triple stigma: it is connected to stigmatized groups (homosexuals and drug users); it is sexually transmitted; and, like cancer, it is a terminal, wasting disease. It would be difficult to imagine a scenario for a more stigmatizing disease, short of one that also makes those infected obviously visible.

THE EFFECTS OF AIDS

The social meaning affects the consequences of AIDS, especially for AIDS sufferers and their families and the gay community but also for medicine and the public as well.

The greatest consequences of AIDS are of course for AIDS sufferers. They must contend with a ravaging disease and the stigmatized social response that can only make coping with it more difficult. In a time when social support is most needed, it may become least available. And in the context of the paucity of available medical treatments, those with AIDS must face the prospect of early death with little hope of survival.

People with ARC or those who test antibody-positive must live with the uncertainty of not knowing what the progression of their disorder will be. And living with this uncertainty, they must also live with the fear and stigma produced by the social meanings of AIDS. This may mean subtle disenfranchisement, overt discrimination, outright exclusion, or even total shunning. The talk of quarantine raises the anxiety of "why me?" Those symptomless seropositive individuals, who experts suggest have a 5 to 20 percent chance of developing full-blown AIDS, must live with the inner conflict of who to tell or not to tell, of how to manage their sexual and work lives, and the question of whether and how they might infect others. The social meanings of AIDS make this burden more difficult.

Families and lovers of people with AIDS, ARC, or an antibody-positive test are placed in an uncomfortable limbo status. Many live in constant fear that they might contract the AIDS virus, and thus limit their contact with the infected individual. Others wonder whether they too might be or become infectious. As mentioned earlier, families often share the AIDS stigma, as others see them as tainted, cease visiting their home, or even sever all contact with them. In one recent study of screening for AIDS among blood donors, the researchers noted they "have interviewed people in the pilot phase of [their] notification program who have been left by their spouses or significant others after telling them about their blood test results."[8]

The gay community has been profoundly affected by AIDS. The late 1960s and 1970s were an exciting and positive period of the American gay community. Thousands of gay men and women came "out of the closet" and proclaimed in a variety of ways that "gay is good." Many laws forbidding gay sexual activity were removed from the books. Gay people developed their own community institutions and more openly experimented and practiced alternative lifestyles. Although the celebration of anonymous sex among some gay males resulted in high rates of sexually transmitted diseases and hepatitis B, the social atmosphere in the gay community remained overwhelmingly positive. While the attitudes toward homosexuality never became totally accepting, public moral opprobrium toward gays was perceptibly reduced.[9]

And along came AIDS. With its image as a "gay disease" related to a fast-track gay male lifestyle, the fear of AIDS tapped into a reservoir of existing moral fear of homosexuals. It was a catalyst to the reemergence of a latent "homophobia" that had never really disappeared. Now there was a new reason to discriminate against gays. Thus AIDS has led to a restigmatization of homosexuality. Every avowed male homosexual is a suspected carrier of AIDS and deemed potentially dangerous. This, of course, has pushed many gay men back into the closet, living their lives with new fears and anxieties. It is clear that AIDS threatens two decades of social advances for the gay community.

Concern about AIDS has also become the overriding social and political concern of the gay community, consuming energy that previously went toward other types of social and political work. The gay community was the first to bring the AIDS problem into the public arena and to urge the media, medicine, and government to take action. Action groups in the gay community have engaged in extensive AIDS educational campaigns. This was done out of concern, but not without a fear of government

surveillance and invasion of privacy. There was also apprehension that the images of "bad blood" and depictions of gays as health risks might lead to new exclusions of gays.[10]

The scourge of AIDS in the gay community has led, on the one hand, to divisions among gays (e.g., should bathhouses be closed) and, on the other, to unprecedented changes in sexual behavior (e.g., witness the dramatic drop in the number of sex partners and types of sexual encounters reported in several studies and indexed by the large decrease in new cases of rectal gonorrhea).[11]

There is also a great emotional toll from the AIDS epidemic in the gay community. Nearly everyone in the community has friends or acquaintances who have died from the disease. As one gay activist recently put it, many people in the gay community were suffering a "grief-overload" as a result of the losses from AIDS.[12]

The social image of AIDS has affected medical care and scientific research as well. In general, the medical voice concerning AIDS, at least in terms of describing it to the public and outlining its perils, has on the whole been cautious and even-handed. The tenor of information has been factual and not unduly emotional. The Center for Disease Control (CDC) has again and again declared that AIDS is not transmitted by casual contact and, although it is a major epidemic and a public health threat, it is one with specific risk groups.

However, some medical scientists have placed the dangers of AIDS in a highly negative light either to raise the public's concern or to elicit private or governmental research funds. For example, "Dr. Alvin Friedman-Kein, an AIDS researcher who saw the first cases, said that AIDS will probably be the plague of the century."[13] Dr. Mathilde Krim was quoted in *The New York Post* last September as saying that "it is only a matter of time before it afflicts heterosexuals on a large scale" while presenting no evidence or data to support the claim.[14] The media, of course, pick up these assertions, often highlighting them in headlines, which reinforces the public fear.

The stigma of AIDS in a few cases has affected medical practice. There have been some reports of doctors, health workers, or hospitals who have refused to treat AIDS patients. But fortunately, these extreme examples are rare and, for the most part, AIDS sufferers seem to have received at least adequate care from most medical facilities. But a mistrust of the ramifications of the public attitudes toward AIDS may well keep some "high risk" individuals from seeking medical diagnosis or care. The fear of being found seropositive and becoming a social pariah might well keep carriers of the AIDS virus from medical attention.

Finally, stigmatized attitudes toward a disease can constrain medical progress. As Allen Brandt points out, the negative social meanings attached to VD actually obstructed medical efforts. He noted that research funding was somewhat limited because the issue was thought to be best dealt with behaviorally. Among many VD researchers the discovery of penicillin was treated with ambivalence, since they were afraid a cure of syphilis would promote promiscuity.[15]

While medical scientists have recently gained a great deal of knowledge about AIDS, including isolating the virus, describing the modes of transmission, and developing a test for screening HTLV-III antibodies in blood (although it is imperfect for screening people[16]), the stigma AIDS presents has probably limited public funding for AIDS research and deterred some types of community research on AIDS natural history. Several commentators have noted that federal funding for research and prevention of AIDS was slow in emerging because AIDS was seen as a "gay disease." It was only when it threatened blood transfusions and blood products that public consciousness was aroused and federal support was forthcoming. Unfortunately, this increased support for research and education was "misinterpreted as an indicator that AIDS was a universal threat destined to work its way inexorably through all segments of society."[17]

One of the most striking aspects about the social reaction to AIDS is how fear and stigma have led to a resistance to information about AIDS. While at times the media have sensationalized AIDS, there has also been a great a deal of information communicated concerning AIDS, its characteristics, and its modes of transmission. Yet study after study finds a small but substantial and consistent proportion of the population that exhibits profound misinformation about AIDS. An October 1985 Harris Poll reported that 50 percent of those asked believed one could get AIDS from living in the same house with someone who had it or from "casual contact," and one-third of the respondents thought that one can catch it from "going to a party where someone with AIDS is."[18]

Another study of high school students in San Francisco found that 41.9 percent believed you could get AIDS if kissed by someone with the disease; 17.1 percent thought if you touched someone with the disease you could get AIDS; 15.3 percent believed just being around someone with AIDS can give you the disease; and 11.6 percent thought all gay men have AIDS.[19] In a study of adolescents in Ohio, fully 60 percent believed that touching or coming near a person with AIDS might transmit the disease.[20] These authors contend that low knowledge of AIDS is correlated with high perceived susceptibility.

In a survey in San Francisco, New York, and London, the researchers found that "more knowledge was significantly negatively correlated with general fear of AIDS and with anti-gay attitudes among risk groups."[21] It appears that rather than low knowledge creating fear, the social meaning of AIDS creates resistance and barriers to taking in accurate information about AIDS.

Such misinformation is also prevalent among health-care providers. In a Massachusetts study of the effect of AIDS educational programs on health-care providers, the researchers reported that before the program, "20.5 percent of providers thought AIDS could be transmitted by shaking hands and 17.2 percent thought it could be acquired simply by being in the same room with a patient."[22] Many of these beliefs seem resistant to change. In the Massachusetts study, "after the [educational] programs, 15 percent of the providers still thought AIDS could be transmitted by sneezing or coughing, and 11.3 percent thought it could be transmitted by shaking hands. [In addition] after the . . . programs, the majority (66.2 percent) still thought that gowns were always necessary and a substantial minority (46.3 percent) still considered quarantine necessary."[23]

While the educational programs affected some change in knowledge about AIDS, the researchers found a strong resistance to changing knowledge and attitudes among a substantial minority of health-care providers. Such misinformation among health-care providers can only have negative effects on AIDS patients.

One of the social tragedies of the fear and stigma is that it has constrained compassion for AIDS sufferers. In our culture, we generally show caring and compassion for severely and terminally ill patients. The social meaning of AIDS mutes this compassion in families, among health-care providers, and with the public at large. It is a shame that a victim of any disease in our society must suffer the plight of Robert Doyle of Baltimore. After discovering he had pneumonia brought on by AIDS, no nursing home or hospice would take him. His family rejected him and his lover demanded that he move out of the apartment. With only months to live, he had no support, resources, or place to die. He finally rented a room in a run-down hotel, where the staff refused to enter the room and left food for him in the hallway. After a newspaper story, a stranger took him into her home, only to ask him to leave in a few days; next an elderly couple took him in, until threatening telephone calls and vandalism forced him to move again. He finally found a home with three other adults, one also an AIDS victim. Soon he was returned to the hospital where he died.[24] The fear of AIDS turned this sick and dying man into a social outcast.

CONCLUSION

The social meaning of AIDS has added to the victim-blaming response common to sexually and behaviorally related diseases a powerful victim-fearing component. This has engendered an overreaction to the perils of AIDS and fueled the public fears of the disease. Some dangers and threats are, of course, very real, but the triple stigma of AIDS presents a frightening picture to the public, which leads to misguided attempts at "protection" and to resistance to contrary information. This only makes managing life more difficult for the sufferers and does not make the world "safer" from AIDS.

Since a medical cure or prevention for AIDS in the near future is unlikely, it is important that efforts be made to reduce the "hysteria" and overreaction surrounding this disease. We need to redouble our efforts to diffuse the unwarranted aspects of the fear of AIDS and to reduce its stigma. There are several strategies for attempting to accomplish this.

AIDS appears to be "out of control." If some type of medical intervention emerged that could limit the spread and/or symptoms of the disease, this sense of lack of control might be decreased and the public expectations of medicine's protective function might be somewhat restored. But given the historical examples of epilepsy and syphilis, available and efficacious medical treatments do not in themselves alter the image of a disorder. The stigmas of these diseases, while perhaps reduced, are still prevalent in our society.

Activists, policymakers, and medical personnel must directly attempt to change the image of the disease. Sometimes a disease's stigmatized image is reinforced by incorrect information. A classic example is the notion that leprosy was highly contagious and sufferers needed to be placed in isolated colonies. We know now that leprosy is not easily communicable. With epilepsy, myths developed that both emerged from and sustained the stigma, including notions like epilepsy is an inherited disease or it causes crime. These myths often gained professional support and led to misguided public policies such as forbidding marriage or immigration.[25] Such incorrect information and mythology must be unmasked and not be allowed to become the basis for social policies.

Another strategy to reduce stigma is to "normalize" the illness; that is, to demonstrate that not only "deviants" get the disease. It is important to show that conventional people can suffer the disease and, to the extent possible, lead normal lives. For example, Rock Hudson's belated public disclosure of his AIDS was an important symbol. He was identified as a solid, clean-cut American man, almost an ideal. He was also a movie hero with whom many people had made some kind of vicarious relationship.

To a certain extent Rock Hudson helped bring AIDS out of the closet. An important public policy strategy should be to "normalize" AIDS as much as possible—to present exemplars of people who still can live relatively normal, if difficult, lives, with positive antibodies, ARC, or even AIDS. The media has done this to a degree with children—depicted as innocent victims of the disease—but we need to bring other AIDS sufferers back into our world and recreate our compassion for them.

We need to develop policies that focus on changing the image of AIDS and confront directly the stigma, resistance to information, and the unnecessary fears of the disease. Given the social meaning of AIDS, this won't be easy. While studies have shown us how difficult it is to change public attitudes toward illnesses,[26] images of diseases like leprosy (Hanson's disease) and, to a lesser degree, epilepsy have changed. We must develop the professional and public resolve to change the social meanings and response to AIDS and make this a high priority, along with the control, treatment, and eventual eradication of the disease. It is incumbent upon us to reduce the social as well as the physical suffering from AIDS.

NOTES

1. Susan Sontag, *Illness as Metaphor* (New York: Farrar, Straus and Giroux, 1978).

2. Merle A. Sande, "The Transmission of AIDS: The Case Against Casual Contagion," *New England Journal of Medicine,* vol. 314 (1986), pp. 380–82. See also, June E. Osborn, "The AIDS Epidemic: An Overview of the Science," *Issues in Science and Technology* (Winter, 1986), pp. 40–55.

3. Jacques Liebowitch, *A Strange Virus of Unknown Origin* (New York: Ballantine, 1985), pp. 3–4.

4. Cited in Matt Clark et al., "AIDS." *Newsweek* (October 12, 1984), pp. 20–24, 26–27.

5. Allen M. Brandt, *No Magic Bullet* (New York: Oxford University Press, 1985), p. 92.

6. Erving Goffman, *Stigma* (Englewood Cliffs, NJ: Prentice-Hall, 1963), pp. 30–31.

7. Sontag, 1978. See also, Anselm Strauss and Barney Glaser, *Awareness of Dying* (Chicago: Aldine, 1965).

8. Paul D. Cleary et al., "Theoretical Issues in Health Education about AIDS Risk." Unpublished paper, Department of Social Medicine and Health Policy, Harvard Medical School, 1986.

9. Peter Conrad and Joseph W. Schneider, *Deviance and Medicalization: From Badness to Sickness* (St. Louis: C. V. Mosby, 1980).

10. Ronald Bayer, "AIDS and The Gay Community: Between the Specter and the Promise of Medicine," *Social Research* (Autumn, 1985), pp. 581–606.

11. Donald E. Riesenberg, "AIDS-Prompted Behavior Changes Reported," *Journal of the American Medical Association* (January 10, 1986), pp. 171–72; Ronald Stall, "The Behavioral Epidemiology of AIDS: A Call for Anthropological Contributions," *Medical Anthropology Quarterly* (February, 1986), pp. 36–37; Jonathan Lieberson, "The Reality of AIDS," *New York Review of Books* (January 16, 1986), p. 47.

12. Christopher Collins, "Homosexuals and AIDS: An Inside View." Paper presented to the American Society of Law and Medicine conference on "AIDS: A Modern Plague?" Boston, April, 1986.

13. Lieberson, 1986, p. 45.

14. Ibid., p. 46.

15. Brandt, 1985, p. 137.

16. Carol Levine and Ronald Bayer, "Screening Blood: Public Health and Medical Uncertainty," *Hastings Center Report* (August, 1985), pp. 8–11.

17. George F. Grady, "A Practitioner's Guide to AIDS," *Massachusetts Medicine* (January/February, 1986), pp. 44–50. See also, Kenneth W. Payne and Stephen J. Risch, "The Politics of AIDS," *Science for the People* (September/October, 1984). pp. 17–24.

18. Cited in Lieberson, 1986, p. 44.

19. Ralph J. DiClemente, Jim Zorn, and Lydia Temoshok, "A Large-Scale Survey of Adolescents' Knowledge, Attitudes, and Beliefs About AIDS in San Francisco: A Needs Assessment." Paper presented at the meetings of the Society for Behavioral Medicine, March, 1986.

20. Cited in Ibid., p. 4.

21. Lydia Temoshok, David M. Sweet, and Jane Zich, "A Cross-Cultural Analysis of Reactions to the AIDS Epidemic." Paper presented at the meetings of the Society for Behavioral Medicine, March, 1986.

22. Dorothy C. Wertz et al., "Research on the Educational Programs of the AIDS Action Committee of the Fenway Community Health Center: Final Report." Submitted to the Massachusetts Department of Public Health, AIDS Research Program, 1985, p. 11.

23. Ibid., p. 12.

24. Jean Seligman and Nikki Fink Greenberg, "Only Months to Live and No Place to Die," *Newsweek* (August 12, 1985), p. 26.

25. Joseph W. Schneider and Peter Conrad, *Having Epilepsy: The Experience and Control of Illness* (Philadelphia: Temple University Press, 1983), pp. 22–46.

26. Elaine Cumming and John Cumming, *Closed Ranks* (Cambridge: Harvard University Press, 1957).

Problems of
Mental Health

Social Relationships and Health

JAMES S. HOUSE

KARL R. LANDIS

DEBRA UMBERSON

> *. . . my father told me of a careful observer, who certainly had heart-disease and died from it, and who positively stated that his pulse was habitually irregular to an extreme degree; yet to his great disappointment it invariably became regular as soon as my father entered the room.*
>
> —Charles Darwin (*1*)

Scientists have long noted an association between social relationships and health. More socially isolated or less socially integrated individuals are less healthy, psychologically and physically, and more likely to die. The first major work of empirical sociology found that less socially integrated people were more likely to commit suicide than the most integrated (*2*). In subsequent epidemiologic research age-adjusted mortality rates from all causes of death are consistently higher among the unmarried than the married (*3–5*). Unmarried and more socially isolated people have also manifested higher rates of tuberculosis (*6*), accidents (*7*), and psychiatric disorders such as schizophrenia (*8, 9*). And as the above quote from Darwin suggests, clinicians have also observed potentially health-enhancing qualities of social relationships and contacts.

The causal interpretation and explanation of these associations has, however, been less clear. Does a lack of social relationships cause people to become ill or die? Or are unhealthy people less likely to establish and maintain social relationships? Or is there some other factor, such as a misanthropic personality, which predisposes people both to have a lower quantity or quality of social relationships and to become ill or die?

Such questions have been largely unanswerable before the last decade for two reasons. First, there was little theoretical basis for causal explanation. Durkheim (*2*) proposed a theory of how social relationships affected suicide, but this theory did not generalize to morbidity and mortality from other causes. Second, evidence of the association between social relationships and health, especially in general human populations, was almost entirely retrospective or cross-sectional before the late 1970s. Retrospective studies from death certificates or hospital records ascertained the nature of a person's social relationships after they had become ill or died, and cross-sectional surveys of general populations determined whether people who reported ill health also reported a lower quality or quantity of relationships. Such studies used statistical control of potential confounding variables to rule out third factors that might produce the association between social relationships and health, but could do this only partially. They could not determine whether poor social relationships preceded or followed ill health.

In this article, we review recent developments that have altered this state of affairs dramatically: (i) emergence of theoretical models for a causal effect of social relationships on health in humans and animals; (ii) cumulation

J. S. House is professor and chair of sociology and a research scientist in the Survey Research Center of the Institute for Social Research, Institute of Gerontology, and Department of Epidemiology at the University of Michigan, Ann Arbor, MI 48109. K. R. Landis is a doctoral candidate in the Department of Sociology and research assistant in the Survey Research Center. D. Umberson is a postdoctoral fellow in the Survey Research Center at the University of Michigan and assistant professor-designate of sociology at the University of Texas, Austin.

From *Science*, Vol. 241 (29 July 1988); 540–545. Copyright 1988 by the American Association for the Advancement of Science.

of empirical evidence that social relationships are a consequential predictor of mortality in human populations; and (iii) increasing evidence for the causal impact of social relationships on psychological and physiological functioning in quasi-experimental and experimental studies of humans and animals. These developments suggest that social relationships, or the relative lack thereof, constitute a major risk factor for health—rivaling the effects of well-established health risk factors such as cigarette smoking, blood pressure, blood lipids, obesity, and physical activity. Indeed, the theory and evidence on social relationships and health increasingly approximate that available at the time of the U.S. Surgeon General's 1964 report on smoking and health (*10*), with similar implications for future research and public policy.

THE EMERGENCE OF "SOCIAL SUPPORT" THEORY AND RESEARCH

The study of social relationships and health was revitalized in the middle 1970s by the emergence of a seemingly new field of scientific research on "social support." This concept was first used in the mental health literature (*11, 12*), and was linked to physical health in separate seminal articles by physician-epidemiologists Cassel (*13*) and Cobb (*14*). These articles grew out of a rapidly developing literature on stress and psychosocial factors in the etiology of health and illness (*15*). Chronic diseases have increasingly replaced acute infectious diseases as the major causes of disability and death, at least in industrialized countries. Consequently, theories of disease etiology have shifted from ones in which a single factor (usually a microbe) caused a single disease, to ones in which multiple behavioral and environmental as well as biologic and genetic factors combine, often over extended periods, to produce any single disease, with a given factor often playing an etiologic role in multiple diseases.

Cassel (*13*) and Cobb (*14*) reviewed more than 30 human and animal studies that found social relationships protective of health. Recognizing that any one study was open to alternative interpretations, they argued that the variety of study designs (ranging from retrospective to experimental), of life stages studied (from birth to death), and of health outcomes involved (including low birth weight, complications of pregnancy, self-reported symptoms, blood pressure, arthritis, tuberculosis, depression, alcoholism, and mortality) suggested a robust, putatively causal, association. Cassel and Cobb indicated that social relationships might promote health in several ways, but emphasized the role of social relationships in moderating or buffering potentially deleterious health effects of psychosocial stress or other health hazards. This idea of "social support," or something that maintains or sustains the organism by promoting adaptive behavior or neuroendocrine responses in the face of stress or other health hazards, provided a general, albeit simple, theory of how and why social relationships should causally affect health (*16*).

Publications on "social support" increased almost geometrically from 1976 to 1981. By the late 1970s, however, serious questions emerged about the empirical evidence cited by Cassel and Cobb and the evidence generated in subsequent research. Concerns were expressed about causal priorities between social support and health (since the great majority of studies remained cross-sectional or retrospective and based on self-reported data), about whether social relationships and supports buffered the impact of stress on health or had more direct effects, and about how consequential the effects of social relationships on health really were (*17–19*). These concerns have been addressed by a continuing cumulation of two types of empirical data: (i) a new series of prospective mortality studies in human populations and (ii) a broadening base of laboratory and field experimental studies of animals and humans.

PROSPECTIVE MORTALITY STUDIES OF HUMAN POPULATIONS

Just as concerns began to surface about the nature and strength of the impact of social relationships on health, data from long-term, prospective studies of community populations provided compelling evidence that lack of social relationships constitutes a major risk factor for mortality. Berkman and Syme (*20*) analyzed a probability sample of 4775 adults in Alameda County, California, who were between 30 and 69 in 1965 when they completed a survey that assessed the presence or extent of four types of social ties—marriage, contacts with extended family and friends, church membership, and other formal and informal group affiliations. Each type of social relationship predicted mortality through the succeeding 9 years. A combined "social network" index remained a significant predictor of mortality (with a relative risk ratio for mortality of about 2.0, indicating that persons low on the index were twice as likely to die as persons high on the index) in multivariate analyses that controlled for self-reports in 1965 of physical health, socioeconomic status, smoking, alcohol consumption, physical activity, obesity, race, life satisfaction, and use of preventive health services. Such adjustment or control for baseline health and other risk factors provides a conservative estimate of the predictive power of social relationships, since some of their impact may be mediated through effects on these risk factors.

The major limitation of the Berkman and Syme study was the lack of other than self-reported data on health at baseline. Thus, House et al. (*21*) sought to replicate and extend the Alameda County results in a study of 2754 adults between 35 and 69 at their initial interview and physical examinations in 1967 through 1969 by the Tecumseh (Michigan) Community Health Study. Composite indices of social relationships and activities (as well as a number of the individual components) were inversely associated with mortality during the succeeding 10- to 12-year follow-up period, with relative risks of 2.0 to 3.0 for men and 1.5 to 2.0 for women, after adjustment for the effects of age and a wide range of biomedically assessed (blood pressure, cholesterol, respiratory function, and electrocardiograms) as well as self-reported risk factors of mortality. Analyzing data on 2059 adults in the Evans County (Georgia) Cardiovascular Epidemiologic Study, Schoenbach et al. (*22*) also found that a social network index similar to that of Berkman and Syme (*20*) predicted mortality for an 11- to 13-year follow-up period, after adjustment for age

and baseline measures of biomedical as well as self-reported risk factors of mortality. The Evans County associations were somewhat weaker than those in Tecumseh and Alameda County, and as in Tecumseh were stronger for males than females.

Studies in Sweden and Finland have described similar results. Tibblin, Welin, and associates (*23, 24*) studied two cohorts of men born in 1913 and 1923, respectively, and living in 1973 in Gothenburg, Sweden's second largest city. After adjustments for age, baseline levels of systolic blood pressure, serum cholesterol, smoking habits, and perceived health status, mortality in both cohorts through 1982 was inversely related to the number of persons in the household and the men's level of social and outside home activities in 1973. Orth-Gomer et al. (*25*) analyzed the mortality experience through 1981 of a random sample of 17,433 Swedish adults aged 29 to 74 at the time of their 1976 or 1977 baseline interviews. Frequency of contact with family, friends, neighbors, and co-workers in 1976–77 was predictive of mortality through 1981, after adjustment for age, sex, education, employment status, immigrant status, physical exercise, and self-reports of chronic conditions. The effects were stronger among males than among females, and were somewhat nonlinear, with the greatest increase in mortality risk occurring in the most socially isolated third of the sample. In a prospective study of 13,301 adults in predominantly rural eastern Finland, Kaplan et al. (*26*) found a measure of "social connections" similar to those used in Alameda County, Tecumseh, and Evans County to be a significant predictor of male mortality from all causes during 5 years, again after adjustments for other biomedical and self-reported risk factors. Female mortality showed similar, but weaker and statistically nonsignificant, effects.

These studies manifest a consistent pattern of results, as shown in Figs. 1 and 2, which show age-adjusted mortality rates plotted for the five prospective studies from which we could extract parallel data. The report of the sixth study (*25*) is consistent with these trends. The relative risks (*RR*) in Figs. 1 and 2 are higher than those reported above because they are only adjusted for age. The levels of mortality

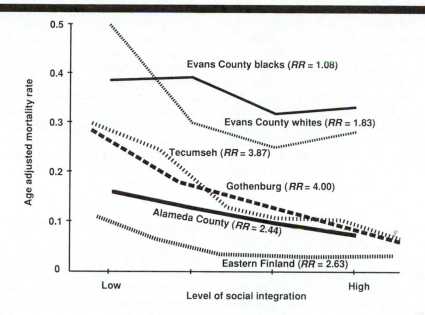

FIGURE 1. Level of social integration and age-adjusted mortality for males in five prospective studies. *RR,* the relative risk ratio of mortality at the lowest versus highest level of social integration.

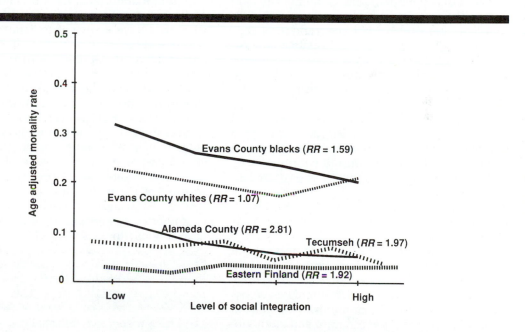

FIGURE 2. Level of social integration and age-adjusted mortality for females in five prospective studies. *RR,* the relative risk ratio of mortality at the lowest versus highest level of social integration.

in Figs. 1 and 2 vary greatly across studies depending on the follow-up period and composition of the population by age, race, and ethnicity, and geographic locale, but the patterns of prospective association between social integration (that is, the number and frequency of social relationships and contacts) and mortality are remarkably similar, with some variations by race, sex, and geographic locale.

Only the Evans County study reported data for blacks. The predictive association of social integration with mortality among Evans County black males is weaker than among white males in Evans County or elsewhere (Fig. 1), and the relative risk ratio for black females in Evans County, although greater than for Evans County white females, is smaller than the risk ratios for white females in all other studies (Fig. 2). More research on blacks and other minority populations is necessary to determine whether these differences are more generally characteristic of blacks compared to whites.

Modest differences emerge by sex and rural as opposed to urban locale. Results for men and women are strong, linear, and similar in the urban populations of Alameda County (that is, Oakland and environs) and Gothenburg, Sweden (only men were studied in Gothenburg). In the predominantly small-town and rural populations of Tecumseh, Evans County, and eastern Finland, however, two notable deviations from the urban results appear: (i) female risk ratios are consistently weaker than those for men in the same rural populations (Figs. 1 and 2), and (ii) the results for men in more rural populations, although rivaling those in urban populations in terms of risk ratios, assume a distinctly nonlinear, or threshold, form. That is, in Tecumseh, Evans County, and eastern Finland, mortality is clearly elevated among the most socially isolated, but declines only modestly, if at all, between moderate and high levels of social integration.

Explanation of these sex and urban-rural variations awaits research on broader regional or national populations in which the same measures are applied to males and females across the full rural-urban continuum. The current results may have both substantive and methodological explanations. Most of the studies reviewed here, as well as others (*27–29*), suggest

that being married is more beneficial to health, and becoming widowed more detrimental, for men than for women. Women, however, seem to benefit as much or more than men from relationships with friends and relatives, which tend to run along same-sex lines (*20, 30*). On balance, men may benefit more from social relationships than women, especially in cross-gender relationships. Small communities may also provide a broader context of social integration and support that benefits most people, except for a relatively small group of socially isolated males.

These results may, however, have methodological rather than substantive explanations. Measures of social relationships or integration used in the existing prospective studies may be less valid or have less variance in rural and small town environments, and for women, thus muting their relationship with mortality. For example, the data for women in Fig. 2 are similar to the data on men if we assume that women have higher quality relationships and hence that their true level of social integration is moderate even at low levels of quantity. The social context of small communities may similarly provide a moderate level of social integration for everyone except quite isolated males. Thus measures of frequency of social contact may be poorer indices of social integration for women and more rural populations than for men and urban dwellers.

Variations in the results in Figs. 1 and 2 should not, however, detract from the remarkable consistency of the overall finding that social relationships do predict mortality for men and women in a wide range of populations, even after adjustment for biomedical risk factors for mortality. Additional prospective studies have shown that social relationships are similarly predictive of all-cause and cardiovascular mortality in studies of people who are elderly (*31–33*) or have serious illnesses (*34, 35*).

EXPERIMENTAL AND QUASI-EXPERIMENTAL RESEARCH

The prospective mortality data are made more compelling by their congruence with growing evidence from experimental and clinical research on animals and humans that variations in exposure to social contacts produce psychological or physiological effects that could, if prolonged, produce serious morbidity and even mortality. Cassel (*13*) reviewed evidence that the presence of a familiar member of the same species could buffer the impact of experimentally induced stress on ulcers, hypertension, and neurosis in rats, mice, and goats, respectively; and the presence of familiar others has also been shown to reduce anxiety and physiological arousal (specifically secretion of free fatty acids) in humans in potentially stressful laboratory situations (*36, 37*). Clinical and laboratory data indicate that the presence of or physical contact with another person can modulate human cardiovascular activity and reactivity in general, and in stressful contexts such as intensive care units (*38*, pp. 122–141). Research also points to the operation of such processes across species. Affectionate petting by humans, or even their mere presence, can reduce the cardiovascular sequelae of stressful situations among dogs, cats, horses, and rabbits (*38*, pp. 163–180). Nerem et al. (*39*) found that human handling also reduced the arteriosclerotic impact of a high fat diet in rabbits. Recent interest in the potential health benefits of pets for humans, especially the isolated aged, is based on similar notions, although the evidence for such efforts is only suggestive (*40*).

Bovard (*41*) has proposed a psychophysiologic theory to explain how social relationships and contacts can promote health and protect against disease. He reviews a wide range of human and animal studies suggesting that social relationships and contacts, mediated through the amygdala, activate the anterior hypothalamic zone (stimulating release of human growth hormone) and inhibit the posterior hypothalamic zone (and hence secretion of adrenocorticotropic hormone, cortisol, catecholamines, and associated sympathetic autonomic activity). These mechanisms are consistent with the impact of social relationships on mortality from a wide range of causes and with studies of the adverse effects of lack of adequate social relationships on the development of human and animal infants (*42*). This theory is also consistent with sociobiological processes which, due to the survival benefit of social relationships and

collective activity, would promote genetic selection of organisms who find social contact and relatedness rewarding and the lack of such contact and relatedness aversive (*43*).

The epidemiologic evidence linking social relationships and supports to morbidity in humans is limited and not fully consistent. For example, although laboratory studies show short-term effects of social relationships on cardiovascular functioning that would, over time, produce cardiovascular disease, and prospective studies show impacts of social relationships on mortality from cardiovascular disease, the link between social relationships and the incidence of cardiovascular morbidity has yet to be firmly demonstrated (*19, 44*). Overall, however, the theory and evidence for the impact of social relationships on health are building steadily (*45, 46*).

SOCIAL RELATIONSHIPS AS A RISK FACTOR FOR HEALTH: RESEARCH AND POLICY ISSUES

The theory and data reviewed above meet reasonable criteria for considering social relationships a cause or risk factor of mortality, and probably morbidity, from a wide range of diseases (*10; 46; 47*, pp. 289–321). These criteria include strength and consistency of statistical associations across a wide range of studies, temporal ordering or prediction from cause to effect, a gradient of response (which may in this case be nonlinear), experimental data on animals and humans consistent with nonexperimental human data, and a plausible theory (*41*) of biopsychosocial mechanisms explaining the observed associations.

The evidence on social relationships is probably stronger, especially in terms of prospective studies, than the evidence which led to the certification of the Type A behavior pattern as a risk factor for coronary heart disease (*48*). The evidence regarding social relationships and health increasingly approximates the evidence in the 1964 Surgeon General's report (*10*) that established cigarette smoking as a cause or risk factor for mortality and morbidity from a range of diseases. The age-adjusted relative risk ratios shown in Figs. 1 and 2 are stronger than the relative risks for all cause mortality reported for cigarette smoking (*10*). There is, however, less specificity in the associations of social relationships with mortality than has been observed for smoking, which is strongly linked to cancers of the lung and respiratory tract (with age-adjusted risk ratios between 3.0 and 11.0). Better theory and data are needed on the links between social relationships and major specific causes of morbidity and mortality.

Although a lack of social relationships has been established as a risk factor for mortality, and probably morbidity, three areas need further investigation: (i) mechanisms and processes linking social relationships to health, (ii) determinants of levels of "exposure" to social relationships, and (iii) the means to lower the prevalence of relative social isolation in the population or to lessen its deleterious effects on health.

MECHANISMS AND PROCESSES LINKING SOCIAL RELATIONSHIPS TO HEALTH

Although grounded in the literature on social relationships and health, investigators on social support in the last decade leaped almost immediately to the interpretation that what was consequential for health about social relationships was their supportive quality, especially their capacity to buffer or moderate the deleterious effects of stress or other health hazards (*13, 14*). Many recent studies have reported either a general positive association between social support and health or a buffering effect in the presence of stress (*49*), but these studies are problematic because the designs are largely cross-sectional or retrospective and the data usually self-reported. The most compelling evidence of the causal significance of social relationships on health has come from the experimental studies of animals and humans and the prospective mortality studies reviewed above—studies in which the measures of social relationships are merely the presence or absence of familiar other organisms, or relative frequency of contact with them, and which often do not distinguish between buffering and main

effects. Thus, social relationships appear to have generally beneficial effects on health, not solely or even primarily attributable to their buffering effects, and there may be aspects of social relationships other than their supportive quality that account for these effects.

We now need a broader theory of the biopsychosocial mechanisms and processes linking social relationships to health than can be provided by extant concepts or theories of social support. That broader theory must do several things. First, it must clearly distinguish between (i) the existence or quantity of social relationships, (ii) their formal structure (such as their density or reciprocity), and (iii) the actual content of these relationships, such as social support. Only by testing the effects on health of these different aspects of social relationships in the same study can we understand what it is about social relationships that is consequential for health.

Second, we need better understanding of the social, psychological, and biological processes that link the existence, quantity, structure, or content of social relationships to health. Social support—whether in the form of practical help, emotional sustenance, or provision of information—is only one of the social processes involved here. Not only may social relationships affect health because they are or are not supportive, they may also regulate or control human thought, feeling and behavior in ways that promote health, as in Durkheim's (*2*) theory relating social integration to suicide. Current views based on this perspective suggest that social relationships affect health either by fostering a sense of meaning or coherence that promotes health (*50*) or by facilitating health-promoting behaviors such as proper sleep, diet, or exercise, appropriate use of alcohol, cigarettes, and drugs, adherence to medical regimens, or seeking appropriate medical care (*51*). The negative or conflictive aspects of social relationships need also to be considered, since they may be detrimental to the maintenance of health and of social relationships (*52*).

We must further understand the psychological and biological processes or mechanisms linking social relationships to health, either as extensions of the social processes just discussed [for example, processes of cognitive appraisal and coping (*53*)] or as independent mechanisms. In the latter regard, psychological and sociobiological theories suggest that the mere presence of, or sense of relatedness with, another organism may have relatively direct motivational, emotional, or neuroendocrine effects that promote health either directly or in the face of stress or other health hazards but that operate independently of cognitive appraisal or behavioral coping and adaptation (*38*, pp. 87–180; *42*, *43*, *54*).

DETERMINANTS OF SOCIAL RELATIONSHIPS: SCIENTIFIC AND POLICY ISSUES

Although social relationships have been extensively studied during the past decade as independent, intervening, and moderating variables affecting stress or health or the relations between them, almost no attention has been paid to social relationships as dependent variables. The determinants of social relationships, as well as their consequences, are crucial to the theoretical and causal status of social relationships in relation to health. If exogenous biological, psychological, or social variables determine both health and the nature of social relationships, then the observed association of social relationships to health may be totally or partially spurious. More practically, Cassel (*13*), Cobb (*14*), and others became interested in social support as a means of improving health. This, in turn, requires understanding of the broader social, as well as psychological or biological, structures and processes that determine the quantity and quality of social relationships and support in society.

It is clear that biology and personality must and do affect both people's health and the quantity and quality of their social relationships. Research has established that such factors do not, however, explain away the experimental, cross-sectional, and prospective evidence linking social relationships to health (*55*). In none of the prospective studies have controls for biological or health variables been able to explain away the predictive association between social relationships and mortality. Efforts to explain away the association of social

relationships and supports with health by controls for personality variables have similarly failed (*56, 57*). Social relationships have a predictive, arguably causal, association with health in their own right.

The extent and quality of social relationships experienced by individuals is also a function of broader social forces. Whether people are employed, married, attend church, belong to organizations, or have frequent contact with friends and relatives, and the nature and quality of those relationships, are all determined in part by their positions in a larger social structure that is stratified by age, race, sex, and socioeconomic status and is organized in terms of residential communities, work organizations, and larger political and economic structures. Older people, blacks, and the poor are generally less socially integrated (*58*), and differences in social relationships by sex and place of residence have been discussed in relation to Figs. 1 and 2. Changing patterns of fertility, mortality, and migration in society affect opportunities for work, marriage, living and working in different settings, and having relationships with friends and relatives, and can even affect the nature and quality of these relations (*59*). These demographic patterns are themselves subject to influence by both planned and unplanned economic and political change, which can also affect individuals' social relationships more directly—witness the massive increase in divorce during the last few decades in response to the women's movement, growth in women's labor force participation, and changing divorce law (*60, 61*).

In contrast with the 1950s, adults in the United States in the 1970s were less likely to be married, more likely to be living alone, less likely to belong to voluntary organizations, and less likely to visit informally with others (*62*). Changes in marital and childbearing patterns and in the age structure of our society will produce in the 21st century a steady increase of the number of older people who lack spouses or children—the people to whom older people most often turn for relatedness and support (*59*). Thus, just as we discover the importance of social relationships for health, and see an increasing need for them, their prevalence and availability may be declining. Changes in other risk factors (for example, the decline of smoking) and improvements in medical technology are still producing overall improvements in health and longevity, but the improvements might be even greater if the quantity and quality of social relationships were also improving.

REFERENCES AND NOTES

1. C. Darwin, *Expression of the Emotions in Man and Animals* (Univ. of Chicago Press, Chicago, 1965 [1872]).
2. E. Durkheim, *Suicide* (Free Press, New York, 1951 [1897]).
3. A. S. Kraus and A. N. Lilienfeld, *J. Chronic Dis.* 10, 207 (1959).
4. H. Carter and P. C. Glick, *Marriage and Divorce: A Social and Economic Study* (Harvard Univ. Press, Cambridge, MA, 1970).
5. E. M. Kitagawa and P. M. Hauser, *Differential Mortality in the United States: A Study in Socio-Economic Epidemiology* (Harvard Univ. Press, Cambridge, MA, 1973).
6. T. H. Holmes, in *Personality, Stress and Tuberculosis,* P. J. Sparer, Ed. (International Univ. Press, New York, 1956).
7. W. A. Tillman and G. E. Hobbs, *Am. J. Psychiatr.* 106, 321 (1949).
8. R. E. L. Faris, *Am. J. Sociol.* 39, 155 (1934).
9. M. L. Kohn and J. A. Clausen, *Am. Sociol. Rev.* 20, 268 (1955).
10. U.S. Surgeon General's Advisory Committee on Smoking and Health, *Smoking and Health* (U.S. Public Health Service, Washington, DC, 1964).
11. G. Caplan, *Support Systems and Community Mental Health* (Behavioral Publications, New York, 1974).
12. President's Commission on Mental Health, *Report to the President* (Government Printing Office, Washington, DC, 1978), vols. 1 to 5.
13. J. Cassel, *Am. J. Epidemiol.* 104, 107 (1976).
14. S. Cobb, *Psychosomatic Med.* 38, 300 (1976).
15. J. Cassel, in *Social Stress,* S. Levine and N. A. Scotch, Eds. (Aldine, Chicago, 1970), pp. 189–209.
16. J. S. House, *Work Stress and Social Support* (Addison-Wesley, Reading, MA, 1981).
17. K. Heller, in *Maximizing Treatment Gains: Transfer Enhancement in Psychotherapy,* A. P. Goldstein and F. H. Kanter, Eds. (Academic Press, New York, 1979), pp. 353–382.
18. P. A. Thoits, *J. Health Soc. Behav.* 23, 145 (1982).
19. D. Reed et al., *Am. J. Epidemiol.* 117, 384 (1983).
20. L. F. Berkman and S. L. Syme, ibid. 109, 186 (1979).
21. J. S. House, C. Robbins, H. M. Metzner, ibid. 116, 123 (1982).
22. V. J. Schoenbach et al., ibid. 123, 577 (1986).
23. G. Tibblin et al., in *Social Support: Health and Disease,* S. O. Isacsson and L. Janzon, Eds. (Almqvist & Wiksell, Stockholm, 1986), pp. 11–19.
24. L. Welin et al., *Lancet* i, 915 (1985).
25. K. Orth-Gomer and J. Johnson, *J. Chron. Dis.* 40, 949 (1987).
26. G. A. Kaplan et al., *Am. J. Epidemiol.,* in press.
27. M. Stroebe and W. Stroebe, *Psychol. Bull.* 93, 279 (1983).
28. W. R. Gove, *Soc. Forces* 51, 34 (1972).
29. K. J. Helsing and M. Szklo, *Am. J. Epidemiol.* 114, 41 (1981).
30. L. Wheeler, H. Reis, J. Nezlek, *J. Pers. Soc. Psychol.* 45, 943 (1983).
31. D. Blazer, *Am. J. Epidemiol.* 115, 684 (1982).
32. D. M. Zuckerman, S. V. Kasl, A. M. Ostfeld, ibid. 119, 410 (1984).
33. T. E. Seeman et al., ibid. 126, 714 (1987).
34. W. E. Ruberman et al., *N. Engl. J. Med.* 311, 552 (1984).
35. K. Orth-Gomer et al., in *Social Support: Health and Disease,* S. O. Isacsson and L. Janzon, Eds. (Almqvist & Wiksell, Stockholm, 1986), pp. 21–31.
36. L. S. Wrightsman, Jr., *J. Abnorm. Soc. Psychol.* 61, 216 (1960).
37. K. W. Back and M. D. Bogdonoff, *Behav. Sci.* 12, 384 (1967).
38. J. J. Lynch, *The Broken Heart* (Basic Books, New York, 1979).
39. R. M. Nerem, M. J. Levesque, J. F. Cornhill, *Science* 208, 1475 (1980).
40. J. Goldmeier, *Gerontologist* 26, 203 (1986).
41. E. W. Bovard, in *Perspectives on Behavioral Medicine,* R. B. Williams (Academic Press, New York, 1985), vol. 2.
42. J. Bowlby, in *Loneliness: The Experience of Emotional and Social Isolation,* R. S. Weiss, Ed. (MIT Press, Cambridge, MA, 1973).
43. S. P. Mendoza, in *Social Cohesion: Essays Toward a Sociophysiological Perspective,* P. R. Barchas and S. P. Mendoza, Eds. (Greenwood Press, Westport, CT, 1984).
44. S. Cohen, *Health Psychol.* 7, 269 (1988).
45. L. F. Berkman, in *Social Support and Health,* S. Cohen and S. L. Syme, Eds. (Academic Press, New York, 1985), pp. 241–262.
46. W. E. Broadhead et al., *Am. J. Epidemiol.* 117, 521 (1983).
47. A. M. Lilienfeld and D. E. Lilienfeld, *Foundations of Epidemiology* (Oxford Univ. Press, New York, 1980).
48. National Heart, Lung and Blood Institute, *Circulation* 63, 1199 (1982).
49. S. Cohen and S. L. Syme, *Social Support and Health* (Academic Press, New York, 1985).
50. A. Antonovsky, *Health, Stress and Coping* (Jossey-Bass, San Francisco, 1979).
51. D. Umberson, *J. Health Soc. Behav.* 28, 306 (1987).
52. K. Rook, *J. Pers. Soc. Psychol.* 46, 1097 (1984).
53. R. S. Lazarus and S. Folkman, *Stress, Appraisal, and Coping* (Springer, New York, 1984).
54. R. B. Zajonc, *Science* 149, 269 (1965).
55. J. S. House, D. Umberson, K. Landis, *Annu. Rev. Sociol.,* in press.
56. S. Cohen, D. R. Sherrod, M. S. Clark, *J. Pers. Soc. Psychol.* 50, 963 (1986).
57. R. Schultz and S. Decker, ibid. 48, 1162 (1985).
58. J. S. House, *Socio. Forum* 2, 135 (1987).
59. S. C. Watkins, J. A. Menken, J. Bongaarts, *Am. Sociol. Rev.* 52, 346 (1987).
60. A. Cherlin, *Marriage, Divorce, Remarriage* (Harvard Univ. Press, Cambridge, MA, 1981).
61. L. J. Weitzman, *The Divorce Revolution* (Free Press, New York, 1985).
62. J. Veroff, E. Douvan, R. A. Kulka, *The Inner American: A Self-Portrait from 1957 to 1976* (Basic Books, New York, 1981).
63. Supported by a John Simon Guggenheim Memorial Foundation Fellowship and NIA grant 1-PO1-AG05561 (to J.S.H.), NIMH training grant 5-T32-MH16806-06 traineeship (to K.R.L.), NIMH training grant 5-T32-MH16806-05 and NIA 1-F32-AG05440-01 postdoctoral fellowships (to D.U.). We are indebted to D. Buss, P. Converse, G. Duncan, R. Kahn, R. Kessler, H. Schuman, L. Syme, and R. Zajonc for comments on previous drafts, to many other colleagues who have contributed to this field, and to M. Klatt for preparing the manuscript.

Community Mental Health Myths and the Fate of Former Hospitalized Patients

STUART A. KIRK

MARK E. THERRIEN

For fifteen years mental health workers in this country have been grappling with the consequences of a fundamental policy change in the mental health field. This reform was initiated primarily by the federal government but adopted by most states and communities with responsibilities for the care of the mentally ill. Although the implementation of community mental health programs has varied widely depending on fiscal and administrative arrangements, community needs and resources, and professional ideologies and methods, one thrust of the community mental health movement has been unmistakably clear: the de-emphasis of the state hospital and long-term custodial care, and the support given to a more decentralized, short-term treatment-oriented system of mental health services available in the local community. The refocusing of mental health services has not been without its problems and critics, but for the most part, the innovations were welcomed by a majority of mental health professionals and their professional organizations. This reform in mental health service delivery is now completed or at least under way in many states and lessons from it are beginning to emerge. This paper addresses one of these important emerging problems—the fate of former hospitalized patients—and the policy issues that the problem raises. The discussion is derived from observations of the experience of the mental health system in the State of Hawaii, but the issues raised are of relevance to other states as well.

The State of Hawaii moved rather late into community mental health. Although catchment areas had been formed and wards at the state's only mental hospital had been allocated to each catchment area in the mid-1960s, it was not until 1971 that a concerted effort was made to reduce the hospital's resident population and that hospital personnel were assigned to staff the community mental health centers. By the end of 1973, the changes in the mental health system were apparent. The number of patients in residence, which had been declining since the late 1950s, declined sharply in the late 1960s and early 1970s. For example, prior to 1960, Hawaii State Hospital had over 1000 resident patients, but by 1968 the number had decreased to 625. And from fiscal year 1968–69 to fiscal year 1972–73 the number of patients in the hospital further declined to 230, a 63 percent decrease. This occurred despite the fact

Dr. Kirk (DSW Univ. of Calif., Berkeley 73), formerly on the faculty at the University of Hawaii, is Associate Professor, College of Social Professions, University of Kentucky.

Mr. Therrien (MSW Univ. of Hawaii 74) was a graduate student at the University of Hawaii when this paper was written.

The authors want to thank Ethel L. Fleming and Daniel J. Myers for their participation in the development of the ideas contained in this paper.

A modified version of this paper was presented at the Annual Forum of the National Conference on Social Welfare, San Francisco, May 1975.

that the number of annual admissions remained relatively high, growing steadily from fewer than 600 in the late 1950s to over 1200 by the early 1970s. Patients were being kept in the hospital for shorter periods of time and long-term patients were being moved out of the hospital to community placements. At the same time, on the Island of Oahu, where approximately 80 percent of the state's population resides, five mental health centers were established, each with its own catchment area, staff, spectrum of services, and satellite clinics. Certainly at the level of the organization of services and the number of hospitalized patients, Hawaii has moved rapidly into community mental health programs. But what has happened to those patients who were hospitalized for long periods of time, or to similar patients who now enter and are discharged from the state hospital very rapidly? What happens to the severely disordered patient who in the past would have been a prime candidate for long-term custodial care?

Perhaps an early clue to the fate of these patients can be found in the original philosophy of community mental health programs. Although community mental health programs were established to supplant the traditional state mental hospital, both their ideology and their most common services are not directed at the needs of those who have traditionally resided in state psychiatric institutions. The ideology of community mental health has been primarily concerned with primary prevention, the importance of early diagnosis and treatment, consultation, social action, crisis intervention, short-term outpatient care, and time-limited, brief inpatient care. Preferred target populations for such services are clearly normal populations who are at risk, persons with mild, acute, treatable disorders, who can be handled in office practice, or severely disordered persons suffering from their first psychiatric crisis. Community mental health programs do, of course, have services for other patient populations, specifically for patients with a long history of severe psychiatric disorder, but these programs are not meant to constitute the core of community mental health practice and are usually the least prestigious of services offered, have the fewest and least trained staff, and are often viewed as undesirable but necessary services.

The transition from state hospital-based mental health services to community mental health services has not been a smooth or complete one. Nevertheless, it is becoming apparent that the needs of former hospital patients and the direction of most community mental health programs are disjointed. This disjunction, however, is not readily apparent because the ideology of community mental health serves to obscure the reality of this problem. To the extent that the belief system of the community mental health movement does not accurately reflect the fate of former patients, the beliefs may be considered as myths, collective beliefs that are built up in response to the wishes of mental health personnel rather than to the facts of the matter.

This paper will argue that there are four such myths developing in community mental health: the myth of rehabilitation, the myth of reintegration, the myth of monetary savings, and the myth of continuity of care. Each of these will be described and analyzed in terms of information obtained through various public documents, recent publications, and dozens of interviews with mental health and welfare officials in Hawaii, and also on the basis of the authors' personal observations and experiences with mental health facilities in six states.

THE MYTH OF REHABILITATION

The community mental health movement, although resulting from changes in community attitudes and psychiatric opinion and from legal changes, was in part a response to the growing belief that hospitalization of the mentally ill was more harmful than helpful. Numerous studies of mental hospitals and, perhaps most persuasively, Goffman's description and analysis of mental institutions in his widely cited book *Asylums* (1961), suggested that mental hospitals were as much the cause of chronic mental illness as the place to cure it. There was the prevalent belief, backed by numerous studies, that admission to a mental hospital, particularly if one's residence there lasted more than several months, would eventually become a lifetime of incarceration (Zusman, 1966; Stuart, 1970). The precise validity of the observation is not as crucial as the fact that it was believed by increasing numbers of mental health professionals.

At the same time, mental health professionals and social scientists concerned with mental disorders were paying increasing attention to the importance of the social environment of the patient. Within hospitals there were moves to develop therapeutic communities on psychiatric wards and to harness group and social forces in the treatment of mental disorder. The emerging implicit belief was that the patient would be better off in the community than subject to the routines of the hospital.

As mental health policies changed, patients were discharged from hospitals in large numbers. The official ideology of the mental health enterprise encouraged this trend as an important policy reform which would facilitate the rehabilitation of mental patients. The official image of the decline of state hospitals was that patients who had been locked in back wards for decades, neglected and institutionalized, would, with the help of drugs and the new community-based mental health programs and the healthful influences of community living, be able to manage themselves better and begin to attain some minimum level of normal functioning. Both the treatment offered by community mental health programs and the avoidance of the dehumanizing forces of the state mental hospitals would together contribute to the rehabilitation of the severely disturbed patient.

This constituted the official or publicly announced objective. The implementation of such a rehabilitation program ran square into several major obstacles: (1) the lack of decent community living facilities; (2) the treatment preferences and attitudes of community mental health staff toward these ex-hospital patients and the difficulty of resocializing hospital staff assigned to community mental health programs; and (3) the lack of sufficient effective treatment methods for these patients.

The first obstacle faced by every state hospital system which wants to close down is what to do with the large number of patients currently hospitalized, some of them hospitalized for many years. Many of these patients have neither family who want them nor financial or social resources to secure adequate housing. The most immediate problem then is one of quality

placement (Weiner et al., 1974). In Hawaii, this entailed the placement of hundreds of patients per year, but the number of licensed boarding homes available was limited and not readily accessible to the state hospital. Furthermore, the steady growth in the number of licensed boarding and care homes was not sufficient to house the increasing number of ex-hospitalized patients because these facilities also had to provide housing for the disabled, aged, and physically ill. The partial resolution of this problem was the proliferation, with the explicit encouragement of the state mental health division, of unlicensed boarding homes for the placement of ex-hospitalized patients. For example, between 1970 and 1973 the number of licensed care homes on Oahu rose from 149 to 195, a 31 percent increase, and by 1972 it was estimated that 68 percent of all the care home beds were occupied by psychiatric patients. Similarly, during those same years the number of licensed boarding homes in the state increased from 99 to 140, a 41 percent increase. Thus, from 1970 to 1973, approximately 87 new licensed care and boarding homes were established, although not all of them exclusively for psychiatric patients. But during that same time on Oahu the number of unlicensed boarding homes with discharged psychiatric patients is estimated to have risen from almost none to 66. For every licensed facility established for the care of the former patients, nearly one unlicensed facility was also created. Thus, initially at least, aftercare planning for the mentally ill did not consist of rehabilitation planning, but merely of ensuring that ex-patients would not have to sleep in the streets (see Lazure, 1974). Aftercare consisted, then, not in mustering new sources of help for the ex-patient, but simply in trying to *replace* the minimum life supports that were ensured in the hospital.

A second obstacle in developing a rehabilitation program for former hospital patients in community mental health centers is quite simply the fact that for the most part the staff of community mental health programs do not think very much can be done with the former hospital patients. Interviews with mental health personnel in Hawaii, for example, found that these patients are routinely referred to as "chronics," a term which connotes that the patient is hopeless, cannot be helped, and will not get better. There is a pervasive belief among staff that nothing very useful can be done for these patients, except perhaps to maintain them on high doses of antipsychotic drugs if they request help.

The belief system regarding these patients is reinforced by the fact that in Hawaii, as in other states undergoing similar reforms, many of the community mental health staff were formerly staff in the state mental hospital, many of them aides or orderlies, and they, as much as the former patients, have become deeply socialized into the values, beliefs, and attitudes fostered by that total institution environment. A repeated complaint made by the more "progressive" community-oriented mental health personnel in Hawaii is that they cannot get the former hospital staff to behave toward patients any differently than they did in the hospital environment. Nevertheless, even the more progressive and better-trained staff members of community mental health settings rarely choose to work with "chronics." They prefer the less disturbed clientele where there is a better prognosis. Consequently, chronics—if they do apply or are referred for service—are usually assigned to ex-state hospital staff who run a "day program," usually consisting of activities similar to those they would have engaged in on the hospital wards. Consequently, many ex-hospital patients involved in community mental health programs are placed in "ward-like" environments where they are supervised by ex-state hospital staff, and they participate in a state hospital routine, albeit, now "in the community." But many of these former patients do not even have the limited involvement provided by a day hospital. They spend the majority of their time in a boarding home, which promotes dependency, passivity, isolation, and inactivity, qualities which formerly the state hospitals have been chided for encouraging (Lamb and Goertzel, 1971; Allen, 1974).

The third obstacle in implementing a full rehabilitation program involves the lack of knowledge about what would constitute an effective and inexpensive treatment for these patients. The only partially effective treatments available are the psychotropic drugs, but these are clearly only a first step. The patients have long-standing and severe problems, have few if any social, financial, or employment resources, and have many social and medical needs. But in the face of these massive problems the mental health system does not have an efficient or effective method of meeting these needs or of transforming backward patients into "normal" citizens. This may account for the fact that half of the schizophrenic patients discharged will be rehospitalized within two years (Gunderson et al., 1974).

The ideology of community mental health has obscured the fate of these patients and the scope of their problems by the rhetoric of rehabilitation, which has functioned to facilitate the discharge of these patients from mental hospitals, but has not provided a qualitatively different program than they had in their former institutions. The return of patients to the community has, in many ways, extended the philosophy of custodialism into the community rather than ending it at the gates of the state hospital; rehabilitation has unfortunately become more a myth than a reality.

THE MYTH OF REINTEGRATION

An integral component of the ex-hospital patient's rehabilitation was to be his reintegration into the community. Instead of being isolated and segregated in a state mental hospital, typically located miles from home, family, and social contacts, the patients who absolutely required hospitalization were to be hospitalized in the community and to be returned as quickly as possible to previous sources of support and previous social responsibilities. By keeping the patient *out* of the hospital, it was assumed that he would be kept *in* the community and that his tenure in the community, if it did not immediately cure him, would at least avoid the dehumanizing processes of institutionalization. This belief, which is still widely held in mental health circles and which undoubtedly has a certain plausibility, is based on a rather vague notion of what constitutes a "community" and a naive view of the patient's life "in the community."

The concept of community has been defined by the federal guidelines in terms of the artificially delineated catchment area—i.e., a circumscribed geographical area which may or may not bear any relationship to political, administrative, racial, or cultural boundaries (Connery, 1968). This has not helped mental health personnel critically appraise the important elements of a patient's relevant community (Panzetta, 1971). Furthermore, many hospitalized patients were formerly transient persons not long identified with a given location (Dunham, 1965) or have lost such identification and social ties in the course of a long hospitalization. The belief in the value of reintegration has been devoid of any systematic analysis of what constitutes a relevant community.

This lack of a critical understanding of the nature of "community" has led to a number of unfortunate developments (Kellert, 1971). First, the emphasis on the catchment area as the community has failed to distinguish separate ethnic and cultural communities. In Hawaii, for example, many neighborhoods are strongly identified as Filipino, Hawaiian, Japanese, or Chinese and vary accordingly in language, customs, and so forth. Placement of ex-hospitalized patients, however, has not taken these cultural variations into consideration. One reason for this has been the fact that almost all boarding homes in Honolulu, both licensed and unlicensed, are run by Filipinos and are located predominantly in Filipino areas—although Filipinos constitute only 14 percent of the population of Hawaii. Thus, a boarding home placement for a Japanese patient is likely to mean both a neighborhood relocation and a cultural one as well. Other states have had similar experiences in the ghettoization of former patients, particularly in the poorer and more deteriorated areas of the city. This seems to have occurred in California (Aviram and Segal, 1973; Chase, 1973) and is apparently taking place in such diverse areas as Long Beach, N.Y., the Uptown section of Chicago, the Times Square and Bowery areas of Manhattan, and in the District of Columbia (Trotter and Kuttner, 1974).

But the segregation of former patients in certain areas of the community is only an indication of another, perhaps more serious, problem of reintegration—that of the social rejection of the mentally disordered, who are likely to possess multiple negative social attributes in addition to their illness: they may be poor, from a minority group, aged, etc. It has long been recognized both by mental health professionals (Joint Commission, 1961; Sarbin and Mancuso, 1970) and by sociologists who have studied deviant behavior (Scheff, 1966; Phillips, 1963) that the former patient often faces rejection by those who know of his hospitalization. There is a well-established, although slowly changing, pattern of public fear, anxiety, and revulsion in response to the mentally ill that has been evident for hundreds of years, albeit in various guises. Placing the hospitalized patient back in the community often runs the risk of subjecting the patient to these negative attitudes. Hence, former patients are not welcomed back into communities with open arms; instead they are often confronted by formal and informal attempts to exclude them from the community by using city ordinances, zoning codes, and police arrests (Aviram and Segal, 1973). They may end up residing in a relatively foreign section of the catchment area, one that is not only deteriorated, but also inhospitable to them. The belief in reintegration, then, is certainly laudable and humane, but it would be unfortunate if the belief in the benefits of community placement inhibited a recognition of the limits and dangers of the forced attempts at reintegration. Residence "in the community" can be just as disabling, frightening, dehumanizing, and isolating as living in the back wards of more formally structured institutions.

THE MYTH OF MONETARY SAVINGS

One of the factors that contributed to the shift from a hospital-centered mental health system to an outpatient community-based one was the realization of the tremendous financial cost involved in maintaining thousands of people inside a hospital. In addition to the expenses of treatment-related activities—e.g., salaries of clinical personnel, drugs, etc.—the hospitals were burdened with the costs of providing 24-hour supervision of the patients and all life support, such as shelter, food and clothing, as well as the costs of maintaining the physical plant. Obviously, many of these costs were required by the nature of residential facilities and not primarily because of the treatment provided. Indeed, state mental hospitals are often cited for the utter lack of treatment given to patients. The concern over the costs of hospital care for the mentally disordered, in tandem with the belief that community-based treatment programs would more effectively rehabilitate these patients, made the transition to community mental health programs seem not only humane, but fiscally sound as well.

But community mental health programs, as has been mentioned previously, neither catered to these former patients exclusively nor even gave them high service priority. Instead, because of the ideology and service biases, a new, hitherto unserviced, clientele is attracted, consisting of less disordered and more acute patients than those traditionally found in mental hospitals (Chu and Trotter, 1974). This is not to say that community mental health programs have totally ignored these patients, but simply that many former hospital patients are not given adequate care by these programs.

Perhaps more to the point of the myth of savings is the fact that total costs for mental health services have *not* declined. In Hawaii, for example, there is certainly a definite trend to increase the relative amount of money allocated to the Preventive and Clinical Services (the community mental health programs) and decrease the percent of the total mental health budget allocated for the one state hospital. Since the mid-1960s the percent of the total state mental health budget allocated to the state hospital had declined from 82 percent to 41 percent in 1973–74 and the amount allocated for the community health programs has risen from 17 percent to 57 percent. However, in terms of the total absolute amount of money allocated for mental health services, there has been a steady increase, especially since 1970. Furthermore, the amount of money allocated for the state hospital also steadily increased until the early 1970s, despite the fact that the number of resident patients had markedly decreased.

Elsewhere a similar pattern has emerged. In California, the state's appropriation for county-operated community mental health programs is four times greater than the funds currently expended for the state hospitals (Aviram and Segal, 1973). But it is not apparent that a community-based program is actually cheaper. The California Department of Finance's study of the mental health program found that in contrast to the $28 average cost per day for each patient at a state hospital, the patient cost per day at the county-level community mental health program was $98—a 250 percent increase (Chase, 1973)! Thus not only is the total expenditure for mental health increasing, but the cost per patient may also be increasing under the new service delivery system. The actual costs of state hospital versus community treatment, however, must await more sophisticated cost-benefit studies.

Of greater fiscal significance in the move to community mental health programs has been the transfer of major fiscal responsibility for these patients from the mental health facilities to the public welfare enterprise—e.g., to Aid to the Totally Disabled programs. The budget figures cited above do not include the increased costs assumed by other agencies for these patients. The shelter, clothes, and meals that had been provided to former patients by the state hospital now are provided by numerous care and boarding homes and paid for not by the mental health department but by other state departments. As far as the authors are aware, no one knows the magnitude of these hidden costs of community mental health or how they compare with the costs of hospitalization.

This shift in fiscal responsibility for former patients makes these patients vulnerable to the policies of public welfare bureaucracies. One rather well-recognized objective of most state welfare bureaucracies is to reduce costs, reduce caseloads, and discourage dependency on welfare. Operationally, for former hospital patients, this means that in addition to their psychiatric disorders, they must contend with a hostile bureaucracy to meet their basic needs. In Hawaii, for example, the state payments to former patients residing in licensed board and care homes are controlled by a point system in which each recipient is evaluated in terms of disability and the payment his boarding or care home operators are given is based on this assessment. The more disabled or disturbed the patient, the more money the boarding home operator receives. The patient is caught between a welfare system that provides minimum suppor and attempts to exclude persons from receiving aid and the boarding home operators, who have no incentive to help the patient get better and in fact may receive a financial reward if the patient deteriorates. Thus, this arrangement may produce increased human suffering as well as increased expenditures by welfare agencies to replace life supports which had been provided by the hospital.

In addition to these direct costs for the community care of the former patients, there are the indirect costs incurred by other community agencies that are called upon to deal with the patients. For example, the police and courts may be increasingly called upon to handle these patients, as has apparently happened in California (Aviram and Segal, 1973). Moreover, other community agencies (emergency rooms, medical clinics, family agencies, fire departments) may have increased demands for their services from this group of patients. But here, also, sound data are not available.

The myth of monetary savings has served to facilitate the transition from state hospitals to community mental health programs by allowing people to believe that community care of former patients would be much less costly. This simply may not be true, especially if total costs, direct and indirect, are considered. This possibility should not serve as an impetus to reopen or enlarge state hospitals at the expense of community mental health programs, but as an indication that care for the severely disturbed is *expensive* and that adequate care for these patients whether provided in the hospital or the community requires an enormous social and fiscal commitment.

THE MYTH OF CONTINUITY OF CARE

It has long been recognized that the delivery of human services, including mental health services, has been fragmented. This is evident in the numerous discussions of gaps in services, duplication of services, and lack of coordination, and the recurrent reports of patients who get "lost in the system." Recognizing these shortcomings, the promoters of community mental health programs place great emphasis on the idea of "continuity of care." Continuity of care refers to the idea that patients needing mental health services should be able to receive the services they need at the time they need them, regardless of the fact that the services required over the course of treatment may be offered by administratively separate agencies. A premium has been placed on the coordination of services among a variety of community service providers so that persons in need of services could move more easily among them. For example, ideally a patient being discharged from the state hospital would be followed up by the local community mental health clinic, which, if necessary, would be able to work closely with the public welfare department, the vocational rehabilitation program, or the boarding home operator.

The goal of continuity of care, however, has been more difficult to achieve than at first expected. In part, this stems from the fact that former hospitalized patients, especially those with a long history of hospitalization, are viewed as an undesirable clientele both by staff members in public agencies not directly concerned with mental health problems and by many of those in mental health agencies. These difficult patients often make little or no headway in psychotherapy, often fail to keep regular appointments, may be physically and socially unattractive, can make enormous demands on staff time and morale, and, at the end, offer the staff little sense of satisfaction or accomplishment. Patients with histories of numerous hospitalizations are simply among the most unwanted clients of health, mental health, and social agencies, and their undesirability may prevent them from receiving appropriate services (Chu and Trotter, 1974). It has been estimated that as few as 10 percent of discharged patients receive treatment at local community mental health centers (Weiner et al., 1974). This is by no means a problem specific to former patients of mental health agencies. A recent study revealed that among a variety of community service agencies over 50 percent of applicants for their services never even begin to receive help from the agencies (Kirk and Greenley, 1974).

Given that former patients may not make the most welcome clients of community agencies, the transfer of patient care from the state hospital to other community agencies becomes problematic. Agencies receiving a large number of such referrals are likely to feel that they are being burdened with a disproportionate share of the responsibility for these patients. Thus, in Hawaii, as the state hospital attempted to place its patients in the few boarding homes licensed and supervised by the state's public welfare department, it found that the public welfare officials were reluctant to accept these patients and that the lists of available boarding homes would not even be shared with the hospital. Public welfare officials felt that the limited number of boarding homes had to serve a range of diverse needs and that they were never intended to be facilities primarily for the mentally disabled. The response of the mental health organizations was to encourage the development of new boarding homes, but the public welfare agency refused to license them. These unlicensed homes, the result of inter-agency conflict, now approximately equal the licensed homes in total bed capacity.

Another source of conflict between the welfare and the psychiatric agencies in Hawaii is the "point system" by which the welfare department assesses the needs of former patients residing in boarding homes. As mentioned, the welfare department assesses each former patient who resides in one of its licensed boarding homes; residents of unlicensed homes receive a substantially lower flat rate. The organizational conflict develops because the welfare department wants to keep expenditures as low as possible and tends to under-assess the disabilities of former psychiatric patients, while mental health personnel push for higher payments to boarding home operators, assuming that it will lead to better patient care. But, as will be recalled, boarding home operators are given no incentive by either the welfare or the mental health department to help patients become more independent. Thus, the transfer of responsibility for patients from the state hospital to other community agencies has resulted not in greater continuity of care but rather in greater inter-organizational conflict.

What appears to be lacking in the attempt to achieve continuity of care is a single agency or person acting as sole agent or advocate for the patient or having primary responsibility for seeing that the former patient's many needs are adequately met. In place of the state hospital's centralized care, the continuity of care program has produced fragmented responsibility for patient care. The state hospital was responsible for food, shelter, medical care, psychiatric therapy, vocational rehabilitation, and more. The hospital may not have adequately met these needs, of course, but at least the failure was attributable to a given institution. Continuity of care in the community for former hospital patients has partially failed, not because the idea is wrong, but because these patients are not highly valued as clientele by many community agencies.

CONCLUSION

In its bold new approach to the delivery of psychiatric services, the community mental health movement held out a number of promises about the likely fate of state hospital patients. The belief was that former patients would be rehabilitated by a well-integrated, coordinated system of services in the community and that the costs of this more humane and more effective program would be less than the costs of institutionalization.

These promises have been partially unfulfilled. Certainly, community mental health programs have reached their goals in relation to some patient populations and indeed have reduced the number of patients in state hospitals. The concern of this paper has been the fate of a specific group of patients: those who have been or would be likely candidates for long-term hospitalization but who, because of the decline of the state mental hospital, are now residing elsewhere. Some of the beliefs about them appear to be taking on the status of myths, reflecting more the intentions and hopes of community health than the uncomfortable realities.

REFERENCES

Allen, P. "A Consumer's View of California's Mental Health Care System," *Psychiatric Quart.* (1974) 48:1–13.

Aviram, U., and Segal, S. P. "Exclusion of the Mentally Ill," *Arch. Gen. Psychiatry* (1973) 29:126–131.

Chase, J. "Where Have All the Patients Gone?," *Human Behav.,* Oct. 1973, pp. 14–21.

Chu, F., and Trotter, S. *The Madness Establishment;* Grossman, 1974.

Connery, R. H. *The Politics of Mental Health;* Columbia Univ. Press, 1968.

Dunham, E. *Community and Schizophrenia;* Wayne State Univ. Press, 1965.

Goffman, E. *Asylums;* Doubleday Anchor, 1961.

Gunderson, J. "Special Report: Schizophrenia, 1974," *Schiz. Bull.,* Summer 1974, pp. 16–54.

Joint Commission on Mental Illness and Health. *Action for Mental Health;* Wiley, 1961.

Kellert, S. R. "The Lost Community in Community Psychiatry," *Psychiatry* (1971) 34:168–179.

Kirk, S., and Greenley, J. "Denying or Delivering Services?," *Social Work* (1974) 19:439–447.

Lamb, H. R., and Goertzel, V. "Discharged Mental Patients—Are They Really in the Community?," *Arch. Gen. Psychiatry* (1971) 24:29–34.

Lazure, L. "Mental Patients' Release Is Hailed, Hit in Gardner," *Worcester Sunday Telegram,* Worcester, Mass., Oct. 13, 1974.

Panzetta, A. *Community Mental Health: Myth and Reality;* Lea & Febiger, 1971.

Phillips, D. "Rejection: A Possible Consequence of Seeking Help for Mental Disorders," *Amer. Sociol. Rev.* (1963) 28:963–972.

Sarbin, T., and Mancuso, J. "Failure of a Moral Enterprise: Attitudes of the Public Toward Mental Illness," *J. Consult. and Clin. Psychol.* (1970) 35:159–173.

Scheff, T. *Being Mentally Ill;* Aldine, 1966.

Stuart, R. *Trick or Treatment;* Champaign, Ill.: Research Press, 1970.

Trotter, S., and Kuttner, B. "The Mentally Ill: From Back Wards to Back Alleys," *Washington Post,* Feb. 24, 1974.

Weiner, S., et al. "A Report on the Closing of a State Hospital," *Admin. in Mental Health,* Summer 1974, pp. 13–20.

Zusman, J. "Some Explanations of the Changing Appearance of Psychotic Patients," *Milbank Memorial Fund Quart.* (1966) 44:363–394.

The Crime Problem

New Alternatives for Fighting Crime

WILLIAM KORNBLUM

VERNON BOGGS

Americans are fed up with street crime. We may be fascinated by high-tech computer crime or international embezzlement schemes, and Mafia sagas are big at the box office, but we are sickened by the crimes that hit us at home. Who among us in the big cities, and increasingly in the suburbs, has not been victimized or had a loved one attacked? At times we seem to be numbed into inaction by overburdened law enforcement institutions, plea-bargained sentencing, and marauding punks. But there are hopeful stirrings in the communities and halls of justice. Citizens are taking constructive action against crime, and a new consensus on the role of employment and community development in preventing crime is fitfully emerging.

For at least the past fifteen years the citizenry has been subject to appeals by aspiring political leaders who claim to have solutions to the "crime problem" or who promise to "get tough" on crime. Yet there must be a good deal of doubt and confusion in the public mind about what are the best strategies for combatting crime. If there were not such confusion, the appeals of politicians who run predominantly on the crime issue should have been more successful than they have been to date. It appears that crime is a dominant issue for the American public, but there is a deep vein of skepticism among significant segments of the electorate. The promises of single-minded approaches to street crime, and crime more generally, come increasingly into conflict with more realistic, emerging efforts of concerned citizens and law enforcement officials at the local level who are developing approaches to their specific crime problems. Therefore, a main objective of the federal government's approach to crime should be to encourage and support the most successful local efforts at crime prevention and victim assistance. Single-minded approaches to the complexities of street crime may have some merit, but they need to be incorporated into a more comprehensive governmental approach to developing anticrime strategies.

Demographics offer hope. Because of the general aging of the population, the number of potential young offenders is decreasing. Most recent statistics show a 2 to 3 percent decrease in violent street crime and burglaries from 1980 to 1983, decreases which may continue through the decade. It also appears that in some communities a decrease in crime can be attributed to greater involvement of neighbors in their own anticrime programs.

But recent decreases are not sufficient. We will always have crime, but it must be reduced to the more tolerable levels that existed prior to the 1960s. Between 1970 and 1980, for example, the annual number of reported violent crimes in the United States increased from about eight million to well over 12 million. Robberies rose from 203,000 to over 450,000, and rape went from 27,000 to over 77,000. And these dramatic increases were by no means explained simply by population growth. Thus the rates of reported violent crime per 100,000 population increased from 253 in 1970 to over 550 in 1980; rape rates went from about eight per 100,000 persons to over 10; robbery rates increased from 172 to over 215. So while we may take heart in recent declines, the overall rates

William Kornblum is professor of sociology at the Graduate School and University Center, City University of New York. Vernon Boggs is assistant professor of sociology at York College, City University of New York.

From *Social Policy* 14 (3), Winter 1984: 24–28. Published by Social Policy Corporation, New York. Copyright 1984 by Social Policy Corporation.

continue to reflect our failure as a society to successfully address the crime problem.

The first assumption of the anticrime policy proposed here is that every level of government must be maximally committed to crime prevention but with different roles at each level. Strategies that shift the financial burden of crime prevention to states and municipalities are an abdication of national leadership. The need to promote comprehensive local approaches to crime will require national-level funding and guidelines. Secondly, we assume that the challenge of fighting street crime requires that we build on recent experiences with the most promising experiments in community crime prevention and employment for "high risk" populations. In this regard it is worthwhile to examine some of the most popular unidimensional proposals for reducing or preventing street crime with an eye toward incorporating the best elements of each in a more systematic approach to fighting street crime, even at the risk of doing some injustice to the complexities of anticrime approaches.

GETTING TOUGH ON CRIME

"Get tough" strategies are by far the most popular approaches recommended by conservatives and anticrime politicians. They seem to address best the public's outrage over "revolving door" justice that allows criminals to escape severe punishment and resume lives of crime and predation. At first glance the "get tough" recommendations may seem effectively to take on the serious increases in street crimes in ways more liberal approaches apparently have not.

Harvard political scientist James Q. Wilson and Stanford economist Thomas Sowell are among the most articulate and widely read advocates of "get tough" strategies. In *Thinking About Crime* Wilson succinctly summarizes the overall impact of violent crime on American community life:

> Predatory crime does not merely victimize individuals . . . it impedes and, in the extreme case, even prevents the formation and maintenance of community. By disrupting the delicate nexus of ties, formal and informal, by which we

are linked with our neighbors, crime atomizes society. . . . Common undertakings become difficult or impossible except for those motivated by a shared desire for protection.[1]

These and other extremely negative effects of crime justify for Wilson a set of stiff, and in some instances rather costly, recommendations: more criminals should be incapacitated through more severe sentencing; prisons should be expanded and improved through better facilities and more vocational programs; criminals should receive mandatory sentences; there should be more judges and prosecutors; and greater efforts should be made to stem the illegal flow of drugs into this country.

While economist Thomas Sowell generally agrees with Wilson's recommendations for stiffer and surer sentencing, he finds greatest fault with the criminal justice system itself. He is especially unhappy with fads in judicial activism resulting commonly, he believes, from "intellectual fashions" that have persuaded the courts to bend over backwards in protecting the constitutional rights of defendants at the expense of the rights of victims. "One man's right to appeal," he notes, "means a sacrifice of someone else's right to a speedy trial and/or the sacrifice of innocent third parties victimized by the backlog of other criminals free on bail while awaiting trial in a congested court system."[2] This orientation to the problems of criminal justice in America would lend support to more narrow interpretations of the rights of due process. Sowell is somewhat vague on specific recommendations in this vein, but others, who share his views in the U.S. Senate and elsewhere, have advocated "stop and frisk" and the abrogation of exclusionary-evidence rules as examples of steps toward higher rates of arrest, conviction, and sentencing.

Although they currently have much support in the Senate, the "get tough" advocates run into serious problems in implementing their proposals. Much opposition predictably comes from segments of the citizenry who are concerned with any weakening of constitutional safeguards. But there also appears to be quite a bit of public resistance to anticrime strategies that promise to significantly increase the total prison population and the costs of law enforcement more generally. Part of the public's reluctance to fund ambitious prison-building programs may stem from lingering doubts about the effect of prison sentences on individual criminals, as well as the fear of high costs, as evidenced, for example, in New York voters' rejection of a prison-bond issue in 1981. More liberal recommendations for criminal justice reform also face the same kinds of public resistance.

THE DECRIMINALIZATION OPTION

On the more liberal end of the anticrime policy spectrum are a variety of voices calling for reform of criminal codes and penal policies. One of the most widely cited is Norvall Morris' *The Honest Politician's Guide to Crime Control.*[3] Morris, a University of Chicago law professor and criminologist, is perhaps the nation's most forceful advocate for decriminalization of "status offenses" and "victimless crimes." In general, advocates of decriminalization wish to reduce or eliminate penalties for offenses ranging from prostitution and pornography to heroin and other drug use. They reason that these crimes hurt only the individual consumer of these now illegal goods or services. Their continuing illegality, it is further argued, only promotes the development of illegal markets and highly inflated prices, which, in turn, spawns a criminal establishment devoted to supplying the illegal demand.

Many of the crimes associated with heroin addiction, for example, would be unnecessary if the United States adopted the English model for decriminalization of addictive drugs that allows addicts to receive drug doses from physicians once they have declared their addiction. For Morris and many other theorists these are persuasive reasons for taking decriminalization seriously as a strategy for criminal-code reform. And if these crimes, said to be mainly detrimental to the perpetrator, were stricken from our criminal codes, Morris believes that almost half of the funds now spent for law enforcement would become available to fight far more serious crimes against persons and property.

Needless to say, decriminalization has not yet won many advocates nor has it become a particularly strong movement for criminal justice reform. There appear to be too many lay citizens and law enforcement officials who continue to feel that legalization of gambling, prostitution, drug traffic, and other so-called victimless crimes would leave a residue of criminal establishments, just as legalization of gambling in Las Vegas and Atlantic City has not eliminated organized crime in those cities. More importantly, voters might feel that reduction of criminal penalties would be tantamount to legitimizing behavior that most Americans do not want to condone.

PRAGMATIC TRENDS

These representative policy recommendations from conservative "get tough" proponents and liberal "decriminalization" lobbyists generally commit the same error. Each attempts to decrease violent crime by reforming the criminal justice system, but neither deals adequately with the issues of crime prevention.

Since neither approach has resulted in significant decreases in crime or increases in perceived public safety, we must look elsewhere for policies that do not place all their emphasis on the already overburdened criminal justice system. As criminologist Elliot Currie notes:

A decade of self-consciously "tough" legislation and of ever stiffer prison sentences has left us in the unenviable position of having both the highest rate of incarceration for "street" crimes [as opposed to political crimes] in the world and, simultaneously, the highest levels of serious violent crimes outside some parts of . . . the "developing" world.[4]

This does not mean there is a consensus anywhere in favor of abandoning efforts at improving the criminal justice system. Rather, in looking beyond criminal justice reform, criminologists like Currie and others believe that the failure of conservative deterrence policies raises once again the need to look carefully at the main tenets of the much-maligned liberal anticrime policies.

These policies tend to deny the depth of social pathology criminal lives engender; they rely on "human capital" solutions (in the form of therapy and training), which assume an ever-expanding availability of social goods; and, above all, they develop massive national social programs with little thought to the need to enhance the networks of supportive institutions at the local level.

The family, the larger kin networks, and local support groups of all kinds form the first line of crime prevention in most communities. In going beyond both old-fashioned liberal and conservative policy orientations, today's most effective anticrime activists accept some of both positions while insisting on the vital importance of community development and community empowerment in pragmatic crime prevention strategies.

There is a consensus from all quarters that the courts and the police need help. They require greater material support in carrying out their direct mandates and, equally important, they need help in preventing cases from ever reaching the formal judiciary process. Exciting strategies for achieving these prevention goals are emerging throughout the United States and in the main they are based on local initiatives to address concrete crime problems community residents face.

As Charles Silberman notes in his monumental book, *Criminal Violence, Criminal Justice,* "the development of more effective social controls in poor communities can provide a far larger payoff in reduced crime and improved order than can the development of more effective means of policing, more efficient courts, or improved correctional programs."[5] This is not an argument against funding judiciary reform and the police. It is rather an argument in favor of giving serious attention to successful models of community development and crime control. Thus Silberman concludes, "I have looked at what is; from Puerto Rico to New York to California, I have seen evidence that it is possible to infuse poverty-stricken neighborhoods with a sense of community and purpose, and thus to develop the internal controls that help reduce or [prevent] crime."[6] Increasingly, we see these "internal controls" emerging out of local experience at two very closely related efforts— employment interventions in the lives of teenagers and young adults and community

problem-solving programs, ranging from local dispute settlement to crime-stop patrols.

EMPLOYMENT INTERVENTION

Employment is the most promising strategy for directing juveniles and young adults in poor communities away from crime. Pragmatists within the law enforcement establishment who take a hard look at the effects of incarceration generally see the prisons as schools for professional crime. Criminal rehabilitation programs based on counseling or psychotherapy in its many forms are viewed with even greater pessimism. Employment and vocational training are seen as having the most potential for reducing recidivism rates and thus reducing crime by ex-offenders.

The late Robert Martinson, a criminologist at the City University of New York, studied over 2000 penal programs and their corresponding recidivism rates. His findings were that the only "treatment" modality which made a significant statistical difference in reducing recidivism was employment during, after, or in lieu of incarceration. This finding strongly supports efforts to develop effective employment alternatives to crime. And there is a good deal of encouraging corroboration from specific employment and support programs.

Beginning in the 1960s and continuing through the 1970s, there were a number of important demonstrations of the effect of employment and training on reducing recidivism. Many new programs are developing now. Since almost 70 percent of violent crimes are committed by ex-offenders, efforts to develop programs directed at the population of those with some penal backgrounds are particularly important. It is difficult, however, to group these experiments together since they often take differing approaches and involve somewhat different populations.

In general, the programs are either small-scale, community-based approaches or large-scale, state or federally funded and designed programs. Some emphasize the pretrial diversion of first offenders into work or training; others are designed to take high-risk juveniles out of their peer groups for skills development and supported work; and still others provide ex-offenders and newly released inmates with monetary and educational incentives for avoiding crime. Reams of evaluation studies are available about these efforts, but Silberman's conclusion may best summarize their broader lessons:

> If a community development program is to have any chance of success, those in charge must understand that the controls that lead to reduced crime cannot be imposed from the outside; they must emerge from changes in the community itself, and in the people who compose it. Hence the emphasis must be on enabling poor people to take charge of their own lives—on helping them gain a sense of competence and worth, a sense of being somebody who matters.[7]

The House of Umoja in Philadelphia is one such successful program. In a ghetto neighborhood where youth groups were once responsible for over 40 deaths a year and hundreds of injuries, there is now an inner-city Boys Town. Run by Sister Falaka Fattah, the program's founder, this neighborhood organization has virtually eliminated gangs and street violence. The House of Umoja effectively combines surrogate family relationships with job opportunities and placement counseling for youth.

Another successful program, the "best example of community regeneration" that Charles Silberman found anywhere in his travels, is the Centro de Orientación y Servicios in the most impoverished section of Ponce, Puerto Rico's second largest city. Silberman notes that the Centro has

> originated several programs for adults as well as juveniles—programs that are reshaping the tone and fabric of the entire community; in the process, the delinquency rate has been cut in half, despite an exploding teenage population.[8]

The key to this program's success is that it attacks the problems of crime and dependency on a broad front, beginning with basic, low-cost health care, and extending to individual advocacy and employment placement. A corps of ten full-time, paid "advocates" from the community, with their own backgrounds in crime, are trained to look out for, protect, represent, and help youngsters in trouble. The essence of the project is that all work together to find common solutions to youth and adult problems. This strategy preserves dignity while it builds self-confidence.

The great advantage of Umoja and the Ponce Centro, and of many other similar community action programs, is that they approach the crime issue within a framework of community development. Another approach, one which complements rather than replaces these invaluable efforts, is found in the larger-scale efforts to meet the needs of thousands of ex-offenders and juvenile delinquents. Some of these, like the Job Corps, are federally funded, but increasingly they are developed through local initiatives and leadership even if they require public subsidies in order to survive.

The Job Corps is designed to reach juveniles who are school dropouts or otherwise likely candidates for penal institutions. In this regard, it can almost be considered as a type of pretrial intervention program because it tends to be used by judges as an alternative to locking teenagers in houses of detention or jails. And the Job Corps is the only large-scale training and work program that actually gives poor youths a chance to get out of their neighborhoods to experience the wider world of people and opportunities. Thus, Job Corps evaluations find that success in the program "increases participants productivity and economic motivation to work."[9]

The Job Corps increased in size from about 20,000 in the early 1970s to over 35,000 by 1980. While somewhat reduced under Reagan, the Corps' success and its special place in the nation's array of anticrime employment programs indicates that it should be at least tripled in size. After all, it costs far less to maintain a young man or woman in the Job Corps than in a penal institution, and evaluations show that the cost of Job Corps enrollment is paid back in employee taxes within five to ten years after graduation.

Supported work programs differ from pretrial interventions in that they generally begin during or just after incarceration. An early demonstration model for rehabilitation through supported work was the Youth Development and Research Center run by the University of North Carolina during the 1960s. Although a small-scale program, this pioneering example of work release for juvenile offenders showed the desirability of developing "new careers for the poor" in employment training just as it demonstrated success in preventing recidivism.

Not all supported work programs have had uniform success, including one of the most ambitious—the Manpower Demonstration and Research Corporation's supported work program, described in numerous evaluation reports as well as in Ken Auletta's informative book, *The Underclass.*[10] This nationwide demonstration of training and job placement involved 10,043 persons. It was more successful for ex-drug addicts and welfare mothers than it was for its ex-offender population, and some observers of employment programs designed to prevent crime use this example to play down the promise of all such programs.

But there is always fresh evidence that the supported work approach is successful when it is developed at the community level and draws on the talents of a street-wise, dedicated staff. The Safer Foundation, for example, has helped about 42,000 ex-offenders in Iowa and Illinois since 1970. It offers a full range of material assistance, health care and counseling, combined with excellent job readiness training and job placement. Only about 11 percent of its clients in some of the toughest Midwestern neighborhoods became repeat offenders within two years, about one-third the national recidivism rate.

COMMUNITY EMPOWERMENT

Another fast-developing anticrime model stresses maximum participation and empowerment of local residents. The Ponce Centro embodies most of these innovative features, as do a number of extremely imaginative programs specializing in community dispute resolution and crime prevention. The general approach that distinguishes these politically sophisticated programs is that local social control agencies need to be strengthened or developed. This goal, in turn, usually requires the development of a rather wide range of crime control approaches, from simple "whistle stop" crime prevention to ambitious efforts at victim-offender reconciliation.

Community crime-stop programs instruct neighbors in the best techniques for alerting the police and in protecting each other's property. Auxiliary police patrols, taxi radio networks, and other voluntary patrol approaches increase the "eyes on the street" making it harder for criminals. These efforts have generally had success where they have developed with the cooperation and support of professional law enforcement agencies. They have contributed to lower crime rates and greater public confidence. But invaluable as these programs are, they are only partial solutions in the absence of more far-reaching efforts in the same communities to enlist citizens in the more difficult aspects of dispute resolution and crime prevention.

The Community Boards Program now in effect in six of San Francisco's inner-city communities is one of the best available examples of citizen empowerment through anticrime activities. Founded in 1976 by a highly imaginative community organizer, Ray Shonholtz, this citizen-run program takes on a wide range of simple and complex local mediations. Issues brought before the volunteer mediation forums range from simple nuisance disputes to resolution of gang and racial conflicts. The forums routinely deal with neighbors' desire to rid their area of drug pushers and similar local social-control issues, but severe unsolved crimes, of course, remain the province of the professional police and courts. The forums also pay a great deal of attention to remedying conditions that can lead to victimization. The program covers almost one-third of San Francisco's population. Although at its inception this model for neighborhood justice forums was staffed primarily by professionals, it was privately funded and developed independently of official law enforcement institutions.

The Victim Offender Reconciliation Program (VORP) pioneered by PACT, Inc., a nonprofit community-corrections organization that has organized operating programs in ten Midwestern cities, is another good example of the community empowerment model. VORP specializes in alternatives to incarceration through face-to-face encounters between victim and offender. Most of the cases mediated by its trained community volunteers are referred by the courts, but an offender cannot replace conventional sentencing with mediation until the victim and the state agree to a restitution plan. In this model, the encounters themselves are so delicate that the VORP program tends to remain focused on reconciliation, restitution, and reintegration of the offender in the community. It does not necessarily develop into other crime-stop activities unless community activists themselves choose to do so. But in communities which have developed such high levels of volunteer experts, it is extremely likely that a wide array of self-help anticrime programs will be developed.

In summary, empowerment increases the probability that people will take it upon themselves to develop various local strategies for dealing with their specific crime problems. More complex and costly programs, especially in the area of employment and training, will require outside support, as will the initiation of the more sophisticated mediation models. Evidence to date from communities across the United States indicates that once they become involved in their own anticrime programs through community development approaches, local citizen-activists not only develop more programs for themselves, but commonly assist neighboring communities to do the same. And the more experience they gain in local anticrime entrepreneurism, the better community activists are equipped to work with government agencies in program designs for court reform and employment programs.

Recognizing these positive trends, a wise government would encourage them with seed money, planning assistance, and resources to promote even greater and more widespread local social-control efforts. Communities in high-crime areas have higher birth rates, so are likely to experience increases in adolescent and young adult populations despite overall decreases in these higher-risk age groups in the national population. And these population increases for young, poor people are hitting us at a time when employment opportunities for new labor-force entrants are at record lows.

Clearly we must support community efforts at crime control and victim assistance with far more resources for youth workers and youth programs oriented toward anticrime programs. Employment, especially for juveniles and the less crime-hardened ex-offenders, when combined with greater efforts at local crime prevention, are the most promising initiatives on the anticrime scene.

It seems very likely, as more Americans become involved in positive local anticrime programs, there will be more support for court reform and other urgently needed institutional change. Before we do damage to precious constitutional rights or invest in vastly increased prison capacities, let us develop national-level policies that hit hardest at crime prevention and the diversion of our juvenile population away from crime.

NOTES

1. James Q. Wilson, *Thinking About Crime* (New York: Vintage Press, 1977), p. 23.

2. Thomas Sowell, *Knowledge and Decisions* (New York: Basic Books, 1980), p. 278.

3. Norvall Morris, *The Honest Politician's Guide to Crime Control* (Chicago: University of Chicago Press, 1970).

4. Elliot Currie, "Crime and Politics," in Walter Truett Anderson (ed.), *Rethinking Liberalism* (New York: Avon Books, 1983), p. 113.

5. Charles Silberman, *Criminal Violence, Criminal Justice* (New York: Random House, 1978), p. 582.

6. Ibid., p. 582.

7. Ibid., p. 583.

8. Ibid., p. 590.

9. Charles Mallar, et al., *Evaluation of the Economic Impact of the Job Corps Program: Second Follow-Up Report* (Princeton, N.J.: Mathematica Policy Research, April 1980) cited in James W. Thompson, et al., *Employment and Crime* (Washington, D.C.: National Institute of Justice, October, 1981), p. 179.

10. Ken Auletta, *The Underclass* (New York: Random House, 1982).

The Proven Key to Crime Control

EUGENE H. METHVIN

New York City Deputy Police Inspector John J. Hill was fuming as he studied the map of his new command, a two-square-mile, 130,000-population precinct in Brooklyn. He saw hundreds of red pins, each one denoting a robbery.

In October 1981, Hill ordered 90th Precinct officers to collect photographs and records of everyone arrested in the previous two years for robbery, or any other serious felony, who was now back "on the street." To focus more effectively on these criminals, the officers divided their rogues' gallery into seven neighborhood albums and added indexes of physical characteristics, aliases and residences.

Analyzing these data, officers realized they were arresting the same offenders repeatedly, usually in the same neighborhoods. Soon robbery victims, instead of waiting days to view thousands of photos at the central police headquarters, were whisked to the 90th Precinct to study a few dozen pictures. Almost overnight, the precinct's officers were making arrests in an astounding *half* of all reported robberies, 2½ times the New York Police Department's average.

Within six months, the 90th Precinct's robberies dropped over 40 percent. The plunge has now continued for four straight years, from 2223 in 1981 to 1187 in 1985. Burglaries and rapes have also declined sharply.

Nationwide, America experienced an 11.5-percent drop in serious crime reported in the three years 1982–84—believed to be the largest decrease since FBI uniform crime reporting began more than 50 years ago. Several factors are involved in this decline. One is the Neighborhood Watch program in which citizens throughout the country are helping police fight crime. Another is that the crime-prone population of 15- to 19-year-olds has declined in the last decade. Most important, however, is our increasing attention to career criminals—identifying them as early as possible and locking them up. We have almost doubled our prison population in the last ten years.

But crime is still outrageously high. The rate per 100,000 people is nearly 50-percent greater than it was 20 years ago. Why? Because our legislators and law-enforcement officials have been slow to respond to new and proven methods of crime control. The nation has learned a number of strategic lessons about coping with lawlessness, and evidence suggests that we can achieve even greater reductions if we act vigorously.

Nasty, brutal. Ten years ago, little was known about the rates at which individual criminals commit crimes. Since then, research has revealed that far more crime is committed by a smaller fraction of offenders than anyone had suspected. This knowledge has helped police, prosecutors and judges sharpen methods for nailing these violent predators.

In 1978, University of Pennsylvania criminologist Marvin Wolfgang completed a first-of-a-kind study of virtually the entire population of 9945 males born in 1945 and raised in Philadelphia. Wolfgang's findings electrified the law-enforcement world: 627 of these young men, just under seven percent of the group, had collected at least five arrests before age 18, and they accounted for nearly two-thirds of all the violent crimes committed by the "Class of '45." Worse, these hard-core criminals admitted that, for each arrest, they got away with from 8 to 11 other serious crimes. Incredibly, even the 14 murderers among them averaged only four years behind bars.

When Wolfgang repeated the study on the 13,160 Philadelphia males born in 1958, the proportion of chronic offenders was virtually

Reprinted with permission from the May 1986 *Reader's Digest*. Copyright © 1986 by The Reader's Digest Assn., Inc.

the same: 982 young men, 7.5 percent, collected five or more arrests before age 18. But there was a difference. The "Class of '58" was far more violent. Compared with the Class of '45, these youths had almost double the offense rate for rape and aggravated assault, triple for murder and a whopping five-fold for robbery. They are, says Wolfgang, "a very violent criminal population of a small number of nasty, brutal offenders. They begin early in life and should be controlled equally early."

Superfelons. It would seem simple to say, "Lock 'em up," but the fact is the nation cannot afford to put them *all* away. If the Philadelphia ratios hold for the entire nation, we would have to keep 1.23 million young men in prison—more than double the present crowded population.

But research by the Rand Corporation indicates a way out of this dilemma, by providing a further breakdown of the crime-prone minority. Of 2190 prisoners questioned by Rand researchers, nearly all admitted to many more crimes than those for which they were convicted. But a tiny fraction of these career criminals proved to be *extraordinarily* high-rate offenders—superfelons. Half the burglars averaged fewer than six burglaries a year, while ten percent committed more than 230. Half the robbers committed five robberies a year, but ten percent averaged 87. Drug dealing was the most radically skewed: half the offenders averaged 100 deals a year; the upper tenth averaged 3251.

Thus, even chronic criminals are not a homogeneous lot; locking up one high-rate burglar for a year will prevent as many crimes as locking up 40 of the intermittent burglars.

Can we tell them apart? Experts say yes. The age at which offenders enter a life of crime and their use of drugs are two keys to identifying superfelons.

Males under age 18 commit perhaps as much as half of all serious crime in the United States. Arrest-record analyses and prisoner surveys demonstrate that high-rate predators begin by age 13 and hit their peak rates as robbers and burglars around 16. To Wolfgang, the factor that jumps out is the age at which these high-rate offenders commit their second serious offense. If they do it before 15, the probability is high they will commit dozens of offenses by age 30.

He concludes: "After the third conviction, serious juvenile offenders should be considered adult criminals and treated accordingly."

Add Jan and Marcia Chaiken, who researched criminal behavior for Rand, "Offenders who support $50-a-day heroin addictions or who use both alcohol and barbiturates heavily are especially likely to be persistent, serious, high-rate criminals."

Criminologists from Temple and Maryland universities agree. They found that 243 Baltimore addicts committed about half a million crimes over 11 years, averaging 2058 apiece, 187 a year.

Using the inmate responses from the Rand survey, criminologist Peter W. Greenwood has refined the superfelon profile. He believes that a convicted robber or burglar should draw long-term imprisonment if he matches any four of these seven variables: 1. Convicted prior to age 16. 2. Committed to a juvenile facility. 3. Used heroin or barbiturates within two years before the current arrest. 4. Used heroin or barbiturates as a juvenile. 5. Held a job less than one of the two years before his current arrest. 6. Had a prior robbery or burglary conviction. 7. Spent more than half the preceding two years in jail.

Greenwood tested the validity of his seven-point profile against the sentences judges had given the 781 convicted robbers and burglars among Rand interviewees in California. His scale miscast as high-rate offenders only four percent of the intermittent offenders (who averaged five robberies a year) and mislabeled as low-rate offenders only three percent of the superfelons (who averaged 87 robberies a year).

The judges, however, gave many more low-rate offenders long terms and superfelons short terms. Greenwood argues that his strategy of "selective incapacitation" would have allowed California in 1981 to keep 700 fewer convicted robbers behind bars, while reducing street crime by 27,150 robberies and saving $10 million.

Encouraging results. Impressed by the Rand and Wolfgang studies, many police departments and prosecutors are intensifying their efforts to arrest and convict young "heavies" who fit the violent-predator profile. Though some are resisting the idea, legislators in 20 states and the District of Columbia have made it easier to try young criminals as adults, subjecting them to tougher prosecution and longer incarceration. The new emphasis is paying off. Consider these successes:

Washington State legislators, infuriated by cases such as the Seattle youngster released by juvenile judges 35 times after felony arrests, enacted a strict code in 1978. They ordered youngsters fingerprinted and photographed at each felony arrest, opened juvenile-arrest records to adult-court prosecutors and judges, and imposed stern sentences for repeaters. Before the 1978 reform, juveniles ran up an average of 7.5 felony arrests before incarceration. Now they go to prison after 3.5 arrests, and the number behind bars has doubled.

In 1983 the Justice Department's Office of Juvenile Justice and Delinquency Prevention (OJJDP) enlisted five police departments and 13 prosecutors in a campaign to identify and incarcerate high-rate juvenile offenders. Police interview school authorities and social workers, then consolidate police, court and probation records, and identify teen-agers who have multiple arrests but so far have managed to slip through the revolving-door juvenile-court and family-services systems. The preliminary results are encouraging.

The five police departments—ranging from Oxnard, Calif. (pop. 121,000), to Jacksonville, Fla. (pop. 578,000)—find they are repeatedly arresting a tiny minority of very active young criminals: only about 30 per 100,000 population. These individuals average just under 16 years old, generally have their first police contact at age 9, and rarely go three months without some collision with police. More than half commit violent crimes. A majority come from "crime families," in which parents and siblings have criminal records, and a large proportion are on drugs.

In Oxnard, for example, crime-analyst Lynne Thayer traced robberies, burglaries and assaults for three months on a map of a 35-block high-crime neighborhood, using orange dots to represent residences of five identified high-rate juvenile offenders. Toward the end of the period, four of the five repeaters were jailed; the fifth went to jail two months later. In the second three months, the neighborhood's robberies, burglaries and assaults plummeted from 69 to 27.

Prison works. City College of New York sociologist Robert Martinson tracked 400,000 criminals who went through special rehabilitation programs over a 25-year period. His stunning finding: seven out of ten who are convicted and then imprisoned or put on probation will never be arrested again; but none of the rehabilitation programs themselves curbed recidivism.

A century ago, Americans sent virtually every felon to prison. Today, even with our increasing use of imprisonment, only nine out of a hundred who are caught and convicted land behind bars. Declared Martinson: "That's where we went wrong. We abandoned a largely successful system of certain punishment in favor of all kinds of happy experiments where we told ourselves we did not have to be so nasty as to punish anybody."

More and more, studies like Martinson's are showing that while prisons may not rehabilitate, they do work as a deterrent. They also reduce crime by keeping the worst criminals away from society.

Concludes Alfred Regnery, administrator of the OJJDP: "The criminologists have given us important knowledge about who commits crime. If police, prosecutors and judges put it to work, we can vastly improve the fairness and effectiveness of our criminal-justice system, ease prison crowding and enjoy safer streets and homes."

Second Thoughts about Gun Control

JAMES D. WRIGHT

Gun control, it has been said, is the acid test of liberalism. All good liberals favor stricter gun controls. After all, doesn't the United States have the most heavily armed population on earth? Are we not the world's most violent people? Surely these facts must be causally connected. The apparently desperate need to "do something" about the vast quantity of firearms and firearms abuse is, to the good liberal, obvious.

At one time, it seemed evident to me, we needed to mount a campaign to resolve the crisis of handgun proliferation. Guns are employed in an enormous number of crimes in this country. In other countries with stricter gun laws, gun crime is rare. Many of the firearms involved in crime are cheap handguns, so-called Saturday Night Specials, for which no legitimate use or need exists. Many families buy these guns because they feel the need to protect themselves; eventually, they end up shooting one another. If there were fewer guns around, there would also be less crime and less violence. Most of the public also believes this, and has supported stricter gun control for as long as pollsters have been asking the question. Yet Congress has refused to act in a meaningful way, owing mainly to the all-powerful "gun lobby" headed by the National Rifle Association. Were the power of this lobby somehow effectively countered by the power of public opinion, stricter gun laws would follow quickly, and we would begin to achieve a safer and more civilized society.

When I first began research on the topic of private firearms, in the mid-1970s, I shared this conventional and widely held view of the issue. Indeed, much of it struck me as self-evidently true. My initial interest in the topic resulted from a life-long fascination with the bizarre:

I certainly did not own a gun (I still don't), and neither, as far as I knew, did many of my friends. Still, readily available survey evidence showed that half the families in the United States did own one, and I wondered what unspeakable oddities or even pathologies an analysis of this half of the American population would reveal.

My first scholarly paper on the topic, "The Ownership of the Means of Destruction," appeared in 1975. This demographic comparison between gun-owning and non-gun-owning households revealed no shocking information. Gun owners, it turned out, were largely small-town and rural Protestants of higher-than-average income. Fear of crime, interestingly enough, did not seem to be related to gun ownership. The general tone of my piece remained unmistakably "anti-gun," but the findings did not provide much new information to strengthen the "anti-gun" lobby's arguments. At about the same time, I prepared a more polemical version of the paper, which was eventually published in the *Nation.* The General Counsel of the National Rifle Association described the piece as "emotionally supercharged drum-beating masquerading as scholarly analysis." Clearly, I was on the right track; I had managed to offend the right people.

The *Nation* article was abridged and reprinted in the Sunday Chicago *Tribune,* a newspaper read by about two million people, many of whom saw fit to write me after the piece appeared. Almost all the letters I received were provocative; some were very favorable, but most were vitriolic attacks from gun nuts. I was accused of being "incredibly biased," "strange and contradictory," of telling "many outright 100% lies," of being "sophistic" and "intellectually

James D. Wright is Professor of Sociology at the University of Massachusetts, Amherst.

Reprinted with permission of the author from *The Public Interest,* No. 91 (Spring 1988), pp. 23–39. © 1988 by National Affairs, Inc.

dishonest," of being "unable to grasp truth," and of taking "thousands of words to say *nothing* constructive." I answered every letter I received. In a few cases, a long and profitable correspondence developed. The first wave of correspondence over the *Tribune* piece affirmed my assumption that many gun owners were crazy. Subsequent waves, however, convinced me that many were indeed thoughtful, intelligent, often remarkably well-read people who were passionately concerned about their "right to keep and bear arms," but were willing, nonetheless, to listen to reason.

Two years later, in 1977, my colleague Peter Rossi and I received a grant from the National Institute of Justice to undertake a comprehensive, critical overview of the research literature on guns, crime, and violence in America. The results of this overview were published in 1981 in a three-volume government report and in 1983 as a commercial monograph, entitled *Under the Gun*. Subsequent to this work, we received another grant to gather original data on gun acquisition, ownership, and use from about 2000 men doing felony time in ten state prisons all over the United States. We assembled this information in a government report and later in a monograph, *Armed and Considered Dangerous*. The felon survey marked the temporary end of my firearms research program, one that ran roughly from 1974 through 1986, when *Armed and Considered Dangerous* was finally published.

As I have already suggested, at the outset of the research program I had a strong feeling that the pro-gun-control forces had never marshalled their evidence in the most compelling way, that they were being seriously undercut by the more artful polemics of the National Rile Association and related pro-gun groups. That the best available evidence, critically considered, would eventually prove favorable to the pro-control viewpoint was not in serious doubt—at least not to me, not in the beginning.

In the course of my research, however, I have come to question nearly every element of the conventional wisdom about guns, crime, and violence. Indeed, I am now of the opinion that a compelling case for "stricter gun control" *cannot be made,* at least not on empirical grounds. I have nothing but respect for the various pro-gun-control advocates with whom I have come into contact over the past years. They are, for the most part, sensitive, humane, and intelligent people, and their ultimate aim, to reduce death and violence in our society, is one that every civilized person must share. I have, however, come to be convinced that they are barking up the wrong tree.

WHAT IS "GUN CONTROL"?

Before I describe the intellectual odyssey that led to my change in thinking, it is critical to stress that "gun control" is an exceedingly nebulous concept. To say that one favors gun control, or opposes it, is to speak in ambiguities. In the present-day American political context, "stricter gun control" can mean anything from federal registration of firearms, to mandatory sentences for gun use in crime, to outright bans on the manufacture, sale, or possession of certain types of firearms. One can control the manufacturers of firearms, the wholesalers, the retailers, or the purchasers; one can control the firearms themselves, the ammunition they require, or the uses to which they are put. And one can likewise control their purchase, their carrying, or their mere possession. "Gun control" thus covers a wide range of specific interventions, and it would be useful indeed if the people who say they favor or oppose gun control were explicit about what, exactly, they are for and against.

In doing the research for *Under the Gun,* I learned that there are approximately 20,000 gun laws of various sorts already on the books in the United States. A few of these are federal laws (such as the Gun Control Act of 1968), but most are state and local regulations. It is a misstatement to say, as pro-gun-control advocates sometimes do, that the United States has "no meaningful gun control legislation." The problem is not that laws do not exist but that the regulations in force vary enormously from one place to the next, or, in some cases, that the regulations carried on the books are not or cannot be enforced.

Much of the gun legislation now in force, whether enacted by federal, state, or local statutes, falls into the category of reasonable social precaution, being neither more nor less stringent than measures taken to safeguard against abuses of other potentially life-threatening objects, such as automobiles. It seems reasonable, for example, that people should be required to obtain a permit to carry a concealed weapon, as they are virtually everywhere in the United States. It is likewise reasonable that people not be allowed to own automatic weapons without special permission, and that felons, drug addicts, and other sociopaths be prevented from legally acquiring guns. Both these restrictions are in force everywhere in the United States, because they are elements of federal law. About three-fourths of the American population lives in jurisdictions where the registration of firearms purchases is required. It is thus apparent that many states and localities also find this to be a useful precaution ragainst something. And many jurisdictions also require "waiting periods" or "cooling off" periods between application and actual possession of a new firearms purchase. These too seem reasonable, since there are very few legitimate purposes to which a firearm might be put that would be thwarted if the user had to wait a few days, or even a few weeks, to get the gun.

Thus, when I state that "a compelling case for 'stricter gun control' cannot be made," I do not refer to the sorts of obvious and reasonable precautions discussed above, or to related precautionary measures. I refer, rather, to measures substantially more strict than "reasonable precaution," and more specifically, to measures that would deny or seriously restrict the right of the general population to own a firearm, or that would ban the sale or possession of certain kinds of firearms, such as handguns or even the small, cheap handguns known colloquially as "Saturday Night Specials."

EFFECTS OF GUN LAWS

One wonders, with some 20,000 firearms regulations now on the books, why the clamor continues for even more laws. The answer is obvious: none of the laws so far enacted has significantly reduced the rate of criminal violence. *Under the Gun* reviewed several dozen research studies that had attempted to measure the

effects of gun laws in reducing crime; none of them showed any conclusive long-term benefits.

As it happens, both sides of the gun-control debate grant this point; they disagree, though, as to why there is no apparent connection between gun-control laws and crime rates. The NRA maintains that gun laws don't work because they can't work. Widely ignored (especially by criminals) and unenforceable, gun-control laws go about the problem in the wrong way. For this reason, the NRA has long supported mandatory and severe sentences for the use of firearms in felonies, contending that we should punish firearms abusers once it is proven that an abuse has occurred, and leave legitimate users alone until they have actually done something illegal with their weapon.

The pro-control forces argue that gun laws don't work because there are too many of them, because they are indifferently enforced, and because the laws vary widely from one jurisdiction to the next. What we need, they would argue, are federal firearms regulations that are strictly enforced all across the nation. They would say that we have never given gun control a fair test, because we lack an aggressive *national* firearms policy.

This example illustrates an important point that I have learned and relearned throughout my career in applied social research: the policy consequences of a scientific finding are seldom obvious. On this particular point, the science is reasonably clear-cut: gun control laws do not reduce crime. But what is the implication? One possible implication is that we should stop trying to control crime by controlling guns. The other possible implication is that we need to get much more serious than we have been thus far about controlling guns, with much stricter, nationally standardized gun-control policies. There is little or nothing in the scientific literature that would allow one to choose between these possibilities; either could well be correct.

GUNS, CRIMES, AND NUMBERS

What is the annual firearms toll in this country? Our review of the data sources revealed that some components of the toll, especially the annual fatality count, are well known, whereas other components are not. In recent years, the total number of homicides occurring in the United States has been right around 20,000. Of these, approximately 60 percent are committed with firearms. There are somewhat fewer than 30,000 suicides committed in an average recent year, of which about half involve a firearm. Deaths from firearms accidents have represented about 2 percent of the total accidental deaths in the nation for as long as data have been collected, and add about 2000 deaths per year to the toll. Taken together, then, there are about 30,000 deaths from firearms in an average year; this amounts to some 1–2 percent of all deaths from any cause.

Both camps in the gun control war like to spew out exaggerated rhetoric. In the case of gun deaths, the anti-control forces shout that the total deaths due to firearms in a year are less than the deaths due to automobile accidents (about 50,000)—"but nobody wants to ban cars!" To counter, the pro-control people express the gun toll as a number of deaths per unit of time. The resulting figure is dramatic: on average, someone in the United States dies from a firearm every seventeen or eighteen minutes.

Death is not the whole story, of course. One must also include non-fatal but injurious firearms accidents, crimes other than homicide or suicide committed with guns, unsuccessful suicide attempts involving firearms, and so on. None of these things is known with much precision, and the lack of firm data is an invitation to exuberant formulations on both sides. Still, reasonable compromise values for the various components suggest a total incident count of fewer than a million per year—that is, incidents in which a firearm of some sort was involved in some way in some kind of violent or criminal incident (intentional or accidental, fatal or not). Pro-gun people have dismissed this estimate as much too high, and anti-gun people have dismissed it as much too low, so I figure it can't be too far off.

When we shift to the guns side of the "guns and crime" equation, the numbers jump by a few orders of magnitude, although here, too, some caution is needed. In the course of the twentieth century, so far as can be told, some 250 million total firearms (excluding military weapons) have been manufactured in or imported into the United States. Published guesses about the number of guns in private hands in this country run upwards to a billion—an absurd and inconceivably large estimate. Most of the published estimates are produced by advocates and thus are not to be trusted, most of all since both sides have vested interests in publishing the largest possible numbers: the pro-gun people, to show the vast number of people whose rights would be infringed by stricter gun controls; the anti-gun people, to show the obvious urgency of the situation.

It is not known for certain how many of the 250 million guns of the twentieth century remain in private hands; 150 million is a sensible guess. Survey evidence dating from at least 1959 routinely shows that about 50 percent of all American households possess at least one firearm, with the average number owned (among those owning at least one) being just over three. Whatever the exact number, it is obvious that there are lots and lots of guns out there—many tens of millions at the very least.

Both sides trumpet these large numbers with relish. To the NRA, these big numbers show clearly that "nothing can be done." The vast size of the private U.S. arsenal renders any effort to control it utterly futile. To the pro-control forces, these same numbers demonstrate, with equal clarity, that "something must be done." The vast size of the private U.S. arsenal makes the effort to control it essential.

The numbers do speak clearly to at least one point: if we are going to try to "control" guns as a means of controlling crime, then we are going to have to deal with the guns already in private hands; controls over new purchases alone will not suffice. Taking the highest plausible value for the number of gun incidents—1 million per year—and the lowest plausible value for the number of guns presently owned—say, 100 million—we see rather quickly that the guns now owned exceed the annual incident count by a factor of at least a hundred; in other words, the existing stock is adequate to supply all conceivable nefarious purposes for at least the next century.

These figures can be considered in another way. Suppose we did embark on a program of firearms confiscation, with the ultimate aim of achieving a "no guns" condition. We would have to confiscate at least a hundred guns to get just one gun that, in any typical year, would be involved in any kind of gun incident; several hundred to get just one that would otherwise be involved in a chargeable gun crime; and several thousand to get just one that would otherwise be used to bring about someone's death. Whatever else one might want to say about such a policy, it is not very efficient.

DEMAND CREATES ITS OWN SUPPLY

One of the favorite aphorisms of the pro-gun forces is that "if guns are outlawed, only outlaws will have guns." Sophisticated liberals laugh at this point, but they shouldn't. No matter what laws we enact, they will be obeyed only by the law-abiding—this follows by definition. If we were to outlaw, say, the ownership of handguns, millions of law-abiding handgun owners would no doubt turn theirs in. But why should we expect the average armed robber or street thug to do likewise? Why should we expect felons to comply with a gun law when they readily violate laws against robbery, assault, and murder?

For the average criminal, a firearm is an income-producing tool with a consequent value that is several times its initial cost. According to data published by Phillip Cook of Duke University, the average "take" in a robbery committed with a firearm is more than $150 (in 1976 dollars) and is three times the take for a robbery committed with any other weapon; the major reason for the difference is that criminals with guns rob more lucrative targets. Right now, one can acquire a handgun in any major American city in a matter of a few hours for roughly $100. Even if the street price of handguns tripled, a robber armed with a handgun could (on the average) recoup his entire capital outlay in the first two or three transactions.

As long as there are *any* handguns around (and even "ban handgun" advocates make an exception for police or military handguns), they will obviously be available to anyone *at some price*. Given Cook's data, the average street thug would come out well ahead even if he spent several hundred—perhaps even a few thousand—on a suitable weapon. At those

prices, demand will always create its own supply: just as there will always be cocaine available to anyone willing to pay $200 a gram for it, so too will handguns always be available to anyone willing to pay a thousand dollars to obtain one.

The more militant "ban handgun" advocates urge what is easily recognized as the handgun equivalent of Prohibition. Why would we expect the outcome of "handgun prohibition" to differ from its 1920s predecessor? A black market in guns, run by organized crime, would almost certainly spring up to service the demand. It is, after all, no more difficult to manufacture a servicable firearm in one's basement than to brew up a batch of homemade gin. Afghani tribesmen, using wood fires and metal-working equipment much inferior to what can be ordered from a Sears catalogue, hand-manufacture rifles that fire the Russian AK-47 cartridge. Do we ascribe less ability to the Mafia or the average do-it-yourselfer?

A recent poll of the U.S. adult population asked people to agree or disagree with this proposition: "Gun control laws affect only law-abiding citizens; criminals will always be able to find guns." Seventy-eight percent agreed. There is no reasonable doubt that the majority, in this case, is right.

CRIMES OF PASSION

Sophisticated advocates on both sides by now grant most of the preceding points. No one still expects "stricter gun control" to solve the problem of hard-core criminal violence, or even make a dent in it. Much of the argument has thus shifted toward violence perpetrated not for economic gain, or for any other good reason, but rather in the "heat of the moment"—the so-called "crimes of passion" that turn injurious or lethal not so much because anyone intended them to, but because, in a moment of rage, a firearm was at hand. Certainly, we could expect incidents of this sort to decline if we could somehow reduce the availability of firearms for the purpose. Or could we?

Crimes of passion certainly occur, but how often? Are "heat of the moment" homicides common or rare? The fact is, nobody knows.

The assumption that they are very common, characteristic of the pro-control world view, is derived from the well-known fact that most homicides involve persons known to one another before the event—typically family members, friends, or other acquaintances. But ordinarily, the only people one would ever have any good reason to kill would be people known intimately to oneself. Contrary to the common assumption, prior acquaintance definitely does *not* rule out willful, murderous intent.

The "crime of passion" most often discussed is that of family members killing one another. One pertinent study, conducted in Kansas City, looked into every family homicide that occurred in a single year. In 85 percent of the cases examined, the police had previously (within the prior five years) been called to the family residence to break up a domestic quarrel; in half the cases, the police had been there five or more times. It would therefore be misleading to see these homicides as isolated and unfortunate outbursts occurring among normally placid and loving individuals. They are, rather, the culminating episodes of an extended history of violence and abuse among the parties.

Analysis of the family homicide data reveals an interesting pattern. When women kill men, they often use a gun. When men kill women, they usually do it in some more degrading or brutalizing way—such as strangulation or knifing. The reason for the difference seems obvious: although the world is full of potentially lethal objects, almost all of them are better suited to male than to female use. The gun is the single exception: all else held constant, it is equally deadly in anyone's hands. Firearms equalize the means of physical terror between men and women. In denying the wife of an abusive man the right to have a firearm, we may only be guaranteeing her husband the right to beat her at his pleasure. One argument against "stricter gun control" is thus that a woman should have as much right to kill her husband as a man has to kill his wife.

Some will gasp at this statement; no one, after all, has a "right" to kill anyone. But this, of course, is false: every jurisdiction in the United States recognizes justifiable homicides in at least some extenuating circumstances, and increasingly a persistent and long-standing pattern of physical abuse is acknowledged to be one of them. True, in the best of all possible worlds, we would simply do away with whatever gives rise to murderous rage. This is not, regrettably, the world in which we live.

INTERNATIONAL COMPARISONS

Comparing the United States with other civilized nations in terms of guns, crime, and violence is the "service revolver" in the pro-control armament, the first line of defense against all disputation. The essentials are well-known: there are, in the United States, no strict federal controls over civilian arms, vast numbers of firearms in private hands, and an enormous amount of gun crime and violence. In other nations (England and Japan, for example), there are strict national controls, few guns, and little or no gun crime. Is this not conclusive evidence that strong gun laws reduce gun violence? One would be hard-pressed to find a single example of pro-control writing in which these points are not featured prominently.

It does not take advanced training in research methods to see that in the absence of more detailed analyses, such comparisons are vacuous. Any two nations will differ along many dimensions—history, culture, social structure, and legal precedent, to name a few—and any of these differences (no less than the difference in gun laws or in the number of guns available) might well account for the difference in violent crime rates. Without some examination of these other potentially relevant factors, attributing the crime difference to the gun-law or gun-availability difference begs the question.

The English case is commonly cited. It is quite clear, however, that the rates of firearm ownership and violent crime were both extremely low in England for decades *before* that nation's strict gun law was passed, and also that the gun laws have not prevented a very sharp increase in gun crime in England in the past decade. Japan is also commonly cited. In fact, the rate of *non-gun* homicide in the United States is many times higher than the total homicide rate of Japan, so there is also much more to the U.S.–Japan difference than meets the eye.

What is true of comparisons among nations is equally true of other geographic aggregates—for example, regions, states, or counties. Any two aggregates, like any two countries, will have any number of differences—differences that must somehow be held constant in order to make any sense of the differences in crime rates. The methodological point is easy to demonstrate with a single example: it is well known that gun ownership is much more widespread in small towns and rural areas than in big cities. Violent crime, in contrast, is disproportionately a big-city problem. Should we therefore conclude from this evidence alone that guns are not the cause of crime, or that high rates of gun ownership actually reduce crime? Probably not: rather, we should demand something more from the analysis. Without that "something more," nothing of value can be inferred; this is also the case with crude comparisons between the United States and other countries.

PUBLIC OPINION

Public opinion has always played a key role in the case for stricter gun control. If the effectiveness of "gun control" in reducing crime is in some doubt, as it obviously is, at least little apparent harm would be done by such controls, and the public clearly favors them. If majority sentiment has counted for little or nothing, it is only because of the Machiavellian workings of the gun lobby.

The first "gun control" question in a national poll was apparently asked in the 1930s. Even at that early date, large majorities responded favorably. In 1959, Gallup instituted what is now the standard "gun control" question, asking whether one would favor or oppose a law that required a person to acquire a police permit before purchasing a gun. In the original study, and in many subsequent studies, the proportions favoring such a law have seldom dropped below 70 percent.

These large majorities are interpreted by gun-control advocates as evidence of wide popular demand for stricter gun controls, but the fact is that two-thirds to three-quarters of the American population resides in political jurisdictions in which something similar to the Gallup "police permit" mechanism is *already* in force. The majority sentiment may only represent an endorsement of the status quo, not a demand for bold new gun-control initiatives.

Other gun-control measures that are sometimes asked about—those substantially more stringent than registration or permit requirements—are not, in general, received with much popular enthusiasm. Bans on the manufacture, sale, or ownership of handguns, for example, are rejected by good-sized majorities; government use of public funds to buy back guns and destroy them is rejected by an even larger majority. Mandatory sentencing for the criminal use of a firearm is enormously popular; mandatory sentencing for the illegal carrying or possession of a firearm is less so. In general, the poll evidence suggests that most people support most of the "reasonable social precautions" I discussed earlier, but do not wish to see government go much further. Not incidentally, immense majorities of the population, approaching 90 percent, believe that the Constitution guarantees them the right to own a gun. Pro-control advocates who effusively cite "public opinion" as a principal rationale for stricter gun control rarely comment on this finding.

THE SATURDAY NIGHT SPECIAL

The notorious Saturday Night Special has received a great deal of attention. The term is used loosely: it can refer to a gun of low price, inferior quality, small caliber, short barrel length, or some combination of these. The attention is typically justified on two grounds: first, these guns have no legitimate sport or recreational use, and secondly, they are the firearms preferred by criminals. Thus, the argument goes, we could just ban them altogether; in doing so, we would directly reduce the number of guns available to criminals without restricting anyone's legitimate ownership rights.

The idea that the Saturday Night Special is the criminal's gun of choice turns out to be wrong. Our felon survey showed, overwhelmingly, that serious criminals both prefer to carry and actually do carry relatively large, big-bore, well-made handguns. Indeed, not more than about one in seven of these criminals' handguns would qualify as small and cheap. Most of the felons wanted to be and actually were at least as well armed as their most likely adversaries, the police. There may well be good reason to ban Saturday Night Specials, but the criminal interest in such weapons is not one of them. Most serious felons look on the Saturday Night Special with considerable contempt.

It is too early to tell how these data will be interpreted among "Ban Saturday Night Special" advocates. The most recent wrinkle I have encountered is that they should be banned not because they are preferred or used by criminals, but because, being cheap, they tend to be owned by unknowledgeable, inexperienced, or irresponsible people. One may assume that cheap handguns, like cheap commodities of all sorts, tend to be owned by poor people. The further implication—that poor gun owners are less knowledgeable, experienced, or responsible than more affluent owners—has, however, never been researched; it is also the sort of "elitist" argument that ordinarily arouses liberal indignation.

What about the other side of the argument— that these guns have no legitimate use? It is amazing how easily people who know little about guns render such judgments. When I commenced my own research, it occurred to me that I ought to find out what gun owners themselves had to say on some of these matters. So I picked up the latest issues of about a half-dozen gun magazines. It is remarkable how informative this simple exercise turned out to be.

One magazine that surfaced is called *Handgunning,* which is specifically for devotees of handgun sports. Every issue of the magazine is full of articles on the sporting and recreational uses of handguns of all kinds. I learned, for example, that people actually hunt game with handguns, which never would have occurred to me. In reading a few articles, the reason quickly became obvious: it is more sporting than hunting with shoulder weapons, and it requires much more skill, which makes a successful handgun hunt a much more satisfying accomplishment.

In my journey through this alien turf, I came upon what are called "trail guns" or "pack guns." These are handguns carried outdoors, in the woods or the wilds, for no particular reason except to have a gun available "just in case" one encounters unfriendly fauna, or gets lost and needs small game for food, or is injured and needs to signal for help. The more I read about trail guns, the more it seemed that people who spend a lot of time alone in the wilds, in isolated and out-of-the-way places, are probably being pretty sensible in carrying these weapons.

One discussion went on in some detail about the characteristics to look for in a trail gun. It ought to be small and light, of course, for the same reason that serious backpackers carry nylon rather than canvas tents. "Small and light" implies small caliber (a .22 or .25), a short barrel, and a stainless-steel frame (to afford greater protection from the elements). The article mentioned that some of the finest weapons of this sort were being manufactured in Europe, and at very reasonable prices. And suddenly it dawned on me: the small, low-caliber, short-barreled, imported, not-too-expensive guns the article was describing were what are otherwise known as Saturday Night Specials. And thus I came to learn that we cannot say that Saturday Night Specials have "no legitimate sport or recreational use."

It would be sophistic to claim that most Saturday Night Specials are purchased for use as trail guns; my point is only that some are. Most small, cheap handguns are probably purchased by persons of modest means to protect themselves against crime. It is arguable whether protection against crime is a "legitimate" or "illegitimate" use; the issues involved are too complex to treat fairly in this article. It is worth stressing, however, that poor, black, central-city residents are by far the most likely potential victims of crime; if self-protection justifies owning a gun, then a ban on small, cheap handguns would effectively deny the means of self-protection to those most evidently in need of it.

There is another argument against banning small, cheap handguns: a ban on Saturday Night Specials would leave heavy-duty handguns available as substitute weapons. It is convenient to suppose that in the absence of small, cheap handguns, most people would just give up and not use guns for whatever they had in mind. But certainly some of them, and perhaps many of them, would move up to bigger and better handguns instead. We would do well to remember that the most commonly owned handgun in America today is a .38-caliber double-action revolver, the so-called Police Special that functions as the service revolver for about 90 percent of American police. If we somehow got rid of all the junk handguns, how many thugs, assailants, and assassins would choose to use this gun, or other guns like it, instead? And what consequences might we then anticipate?

The handgun used by John Hinckley in his attack on President Reagan was a .22-caliber revolver, a Saturday Night Special. Some have supported banning the Saturday Night Special so as to thwart psychopaths in search of weapons. But would a psychopath intent on assassinating a President simply give up in the absence of a cheap handgun? Or would he, in that event, naturally pick up some other gun instead? Suppose he did pick up the most commonly owned handgun available in the United States, the .38 Special. Suppose further that he got off the same six rounds and inflicted the same wounds that he inflicted with the .22. A .38 slug entering Jim Brady's head where the .22 entered would, at the range in question, probably have killed him instantly. The Washington policeman would not have had a severed artery but would have been missing the larger part of his neck. The round deflected from its path to President Reagan's heart might have reached its target. One can readily imagine at least three deaths, including the President's, had Hinckley fired a more powerful weapon.

REACTIONS

The preceding does not exhaust my skepticism about gun-control doxology; it merely illustrates some of the doubts I have come to entertain. As far as I can tell, the arguments in favor of "stricter gun control" fail nearly every empirical test, although in many cases, I hasten to add, the "failure" is simply that the appropriate research is not available.

There is an interesting asymmetry in the gun-control debate. For rather obvious reasons,

the pro-control people want to change things, and the anti-control people are happy enough with the status quo. This implies that the burden of proof typically rests on the pro-control side; they have to show that the suggested changes, whatever they are, would improve conditions. Thus, the pro-control argument is far more commonly advanced via recitation of research findings, statistics, and the like; in many cases, the anti-control argument involves nothing more complicated than a reference to the Second Amendment.

My gun research has been more enthusiastically received in anti-control circles than among pro-control advocates. One prominent pro-control luminary described some of the research in *Under the Gun* as "constructed on an incomplete and misconceived reading of the relevant research, an unwillingness to cumulate circumstantial evidence, and standards of proof that inherently rule out nonexperimental conclusions." The NRA reaction was more positive although not uncritical; the entry on *Under the Gun* in the *American Rifleman* read: "Although the authors' anti-gun bias leads them to exaggerate the amount of gun abuse and to praise too readily some poor research, this book is fairly objective and probably the best summary of scholarly research on the issue." Much to my relief, however, the reactions of putatively neutral outsiders were neither harsh nor guarded. Thus the review in *Contemporary Sociology* described it as "the most comprehensive review of gun control research yet published," and noted later that "it is the highest compliment to say that this book should have something to offend, or at least annoy, everyone. Both 'gun nuts' and 'gun control nuts' will be discomfited."

Armed and Considered Dangerous came out several years later, in 1986, so all the returns are not yet in. I have taken some fairly hard knocks from pro-control people for believing too literally what the felons in the survey told me—a criticism I accept. And in general, the reaction in pro-gun circles was along the lines of "we told you so," with a subtext that, once again, the sociologists had spent hundreds of thousands of dollars belaboring some very obvious points. But here, too, the reaction in the professional social-science community was largely favorable. The review in *Contemporary Sociology* called it "a must for those interested in firearms, crime, or policy research" and concluded that "the gun control debate will never be the same again."

Grateful though I am for this last comment, it is assuredly wrong. In the "Great American Gun War," as B. Bruce-Briggs has described it in this journal (Fall 1976), as in most other areas of public policy, relatively little turns on factual matters that could be resolved through more and better research; most of what is at issue turns on values, ideologies, and world views that are remarkably impervious to refutation by social-science research. No one who believes deeply that gun control would make this a better world—or that it wouldn't—will be persuaded otherwise by any of the research I or anyone else has done.

Applied social research can often describe a problem well, but it can seldom suggest a viable solution. Most of the implications I have seen fit to draw from my gun research are negative in character: this won't work for this reason, that won't work for that reason, and so on. What to do about guns, crime, and violence in America is a question that has occupied many intelligent and capable people for decades, and no one has yet come up with a compelling, workable, legal answer. It is unlikely that "research" will provide that answer. As for social scientists with an interest in the topic, I think we ought simply to resign ourselves to doing what we do best—capable, informative research—and leave the search for "solutions" to the political process itself. Few of us will be entirely satisfied with the outcome; but a political process that proceeds in ignorance of or contempt for the best information we can provide is undesirable. On the other hand, to make too much of the "policy implications" of our research is to suggest that we command an expertise that is not usually at our disposal.

Into the Mouths of Babes

JAMES TRAUB

It is well within the reach of most white-collar criminals to assume an air of irreproachable virtue, especially when they're about to be sentenced. But there was something unusually compelling about the bearing of Niels L. Hoyvald and John F. Lavery as they stood before Judge Thomas C. Platt of the United States District Court in Brooklyn last month—especially in light of what they were being sentenced for. As president and vice president of the Beech-Nut Nutrition Corporation, Hoyvald and Lavery had sold millions of bottles of "apple juice" that they knew to contain little or no apple juice at all—only sugars, water, flavoring and coloring. The consumers of this bogus product were babies.

One prosecutor of the case, Thomas H. Roche, had summed up Beech-Nut's behavior as "a classic picture of corporate greed and irresponsibility." The company itself had pleaded guilty the previous fall to 215 counts of violating Federal food and drug laws, and had agreed to pay a $2 million fine, by far the largest ever imposed in the 50-year history of the Food, Drug and Cosmetic Act. Beech-Nut had confessed in a press release that it had broken a "sacred trust."

Yet here was Niels Hoyvald, 54 years old, tall, silver-haired, immaculately dressed, standing before Judge Platt with head bowed, as his attorney, Brendan V. Sullivan Jr., described him as "a person we would be proud to have in our family." When it was Hoyvald's turn to address the judge, he spoke firmly, but then his voice cracked as he spoke of his wife and mother: "I can hardly bear to look at them or speak to them," he said. "I ask for them and myself, please don't send me to jail."

Judge Platt was clearly troubled. He spoke in a semiaudible mutter that had the crowd in the courtroom craning forward. Though it was "unusual for a corporate executive to do time for consumer fraud," he said, he had "no alternative" but to sentence Hoyvald to a prison term of a year and a day, plus fines totaling $100,000. He then meted out the same punishment to the 56-year-old Lavery, who declined to speak on his own behalf. He received his sentence with no show of emotion.

The combination of babies, apple juice and a well-known name like Beech-Nut makes for a potent symbol. In fact, apple juice is not especially nutritious (bottlers often fortify it with extra vitamin C), but babies love it and find it easy to digest. Parents are pleased to buy a product that says "no sugar added" and "100% fruit juice"—as Beech-Nut advertised—and seem to regard it as almost as pure and natural as mother's milk. That, of course, was the sacred trust Beech-Nut broke, and is now struggling to repair. The company's share of the $760 million United States baby-food market has dropped from a high of 20 percent in 1986, when Beech-Nut and the two executives were indicted, to 17 percent this year. Its losses in the fruit-juice market have been even more dramatic. Richard C. Theuer, the company's president since 1986, still gets a stream of letters from outraged parents "who don't realize that it was a long time ago." Some of them, he says, are "almost obscene."

If parents are outraged by Beech-Nut's actions, many people are also baffled. Even after the trial and the verdict, the question of motive lingers: why would two men with impeccable records carry out so cynical and reckless a fraud? Except for Theuer, no current Beech-Nut employee who was involved in the events of the trial agreed to be interviewed for this article,

James Traub writes frequently on legal issues.

From *The New York Times Magazine,* July 24, 1988. Copyright © 1988 by The New York Times Company. Reprinted by permission.

nor did Hoyvald or Lavery. But a vivid picture of the economic and psychological concerns that impelled the company along its ruinous course emerges from court documents and a wide range of interviews. The Beech-Nut baby-food scandal is a case study in the warping effects of blind corporate loyalty.

For three-quarters of a century after its founding in 1891 as a meat-packing company, Beech-Nut expanded steadily into a large, diversified food concern, eventually including Life Savers, Table Talk pies, Tetley tea, Martinson's coffee, chewing gum and, of course, baby food. The company had an image straight from Norman Rockwell—pure, simple, healthful. In 1969, Beech-Nut was taken over by the Squibb Corporation. Only four years later, a remnant of the old company was spun off and taken private by a group led by a lawyer, Frank C. Nicholas. The company that emerged from the Squibb umbrella sold only baby food, and, as in earlier years, regularly divided with Heinz the third or so of the market not controlled by Gerber. It was a completely new world for Beech-Nut's newly independent owners, and an extremely precarious one. Beech-Nut was in a continuous financial bind.

After an expensive and unsuccessful effort in the mid-1970's to market Beech-Nut as the "natural" baby food, the imperative to reduce costs became overwhelming. In 1977, when a Bronx-based supplier, who would later take the name Universal Juice, offered Beech-Nut a less-expensive apple-juice concentrate, the company abandoned its longtime supplier for the new source. The savings would never amount to much more than $250,000 a year, out of a $50 million-plus manufacturing budget, but Beech-Nut was under the gun.

At the time, the decision may have seemed insignificant. Ira Knickerbocker, head of agricultural purchasing at the main Beech-Nut plant, in Canajoharie, N.Y., who has since retired, says that in 1977 the new concentrate was only slightly less expensive than the competition's. "There was never a question about the quality or anything else," he insists. Yet no other baby-food company, and no large apple-juice manufacturer, ever bought significant quantities of concentrate from Universal. In early 1981, Heinz would return the product to Universal after samples had failed to pass conventional laboratory tests and the supplier refused to let company officials visit the plant.

Another Federal prosecutor, John R. Fleder, contends that the low price of the Universal concentrate, which eventually reached 25 percent below the market, "should have been enough in itself to tip off anybody" that the concentrate was diluted or adulterated. Jack B. Hartog, a supplier who had sold Beech-Nut much of its apple concentrate until 1977, agrees with Fleder: "There was no question about it in the trade."

John Lavery, Beech-Nut's vice president of operations and manager of the plant in Canajoharie, did not question the authenticity of the concentrate. After spending his entire career at Beech-Nut, Lavery had risen to a position in which he managed almost 1,000 employees. In the small hamlets around Canajoharie, a company town in rural Montgomery County, northwest of Albany, Lavery was known as a figure of propriety and rectitude. "He was as straight and narrow as anything you could come up with," says Ed Gros, an engineer who worked with Lavery at Beech-Nut. Lavery was a fixture in the Methodist church, on the school board and in community organizations.

In 1978, after initial testing indicated the presence of impurities in the new concentrate, Lavery agreed to send two employees to inspect the "blending facility" that Universal's owner, Zeev Kaplansky, claimed to operate in New Jersey. The two reported that all they could find was a warehouse containing a few 55-gallon drums. The bizarre field trip aroused further suspicions among executives at the Canajoharie plant, but only one, Jerome J. LiCari, head of research and development, chose to act on them.

LiCari sent samples of the concentrate to an outside laboratory. The tests, he reported to Lavery, indicated that the juice was adulterated, probably with corn syrup. Rather than return the concentrate, or demand proof of its authenticity, as Heinz would do three years later, Lavery sent down the order that Kaplansky sign a "hold-harmless agreement," indemnifying Beech-Nut against damages arising from consumer and other complaints. (Ironically, in May 1987 Beech-Nut settled a class-action suit against it totaling $7.5 million.)

LiCari, however, was scarcely satisfied by Lavery's legalistic approach. Like Lavery, LiCari was also every bit the local boy. Born and raised in neighboring Herkimer County, he had worked in the Beech-Nut plant during summers home from college, and, after 14 years with Beech-Nut, he had achieved his greatest ambitions. Yet it was LiCari who accepted the solitary role of institutional conscience. In April 1979, and again in July, he sent samples of the concentrate to a second laboratory, in California. The April test again found signs of adulteration, but the July test did not. LiCari concluded that Kaplansky had switched from corn syrup to beet sugar, an adulterant that current technology could not detect. Once again he approached Lavery, suggesting that Beech-Nut require Kaplansky to repurchase the concentrate. This time, Lavery instructed that the concentrate be blended into mixed juices, where adulteration is far harder to detect. Lavery's attorney, Steven Kimelman, says that his client does not recall his rationale for the decision, but argues that on this matter, as on others, he acted in concert with other executives, including LiCari.

Lavery and LiCari were locked in a hopeless conflict of roles, values, and personality. Steven Kimelman characterizes Lavery as "more like a general. He's the kind of guy who gives orders, and he has no trouble making up his mind; LiCari was too much of a scientist type to him, and not practical enough." LiCari had become consumed by the issue of the concentrate. By the spring of 1981 he was working almost full time on tests to determine its purity. Finally, on Aug. 5, LiCari circulated a memo to executives, including Lavery. "A tremendous amount of circumstantial evidence," he wrote, makes for "a grave case against the current supplier" of apple concentrate. No matter what the cost, LiCari concluded, a new supplier should be found.

Several days later, LiCari was summoned to Lavery's office, where, as he told the jury, "I was threatened that I wasn't a team player, I wasn't working for the company, threatened to be fired." The choice could not have been more stark: capitulate, or leave.

Many of those who know Lavery find this picture of him simply unbelievable. The Canajoharie view is that Lavery was victimized. Ed Gros, Lavery's former colleague, speculates that LiCari "had a personal vendetta" against Lavery. Ira Knickerbocker blames the Government. Yet even Lavery's friends admit to a kind of moral bafflement. "I've lost a lot of sleep over this," says a former company vice president, Bill Johnsey.

Steven Kimelman denies that Lavery threatened LiCari, but concedes that his client made a "mistake in judgment." The mistake was in not kicking the matter up to Hoyvald when he received the Aug. 5 memo. Kimelman insists that Lavery "thought that LiCari tended to overreact," and in any case felt that there was no other concentrate whose purity he could entirely trust. In fact, LiCari's tests showed no signs of adulteration in several other, more expensive, concentrates. A harsher view is that Lavery acted quite consciously. "He just didn't care," says Thomas Roche, one of the prosecutors. "He showed an extraordinary amount of arrogance. I think his sole objective was to show Beech-Nut and Nestlé [since 1979, the corporate parent] that he could do well."

Or perhaps Lavery had simply blinded himself to the consequences of his acts. The apple juice had become merely a commodity and the babies merely customers. One exchange between another prosecutor, Kenneth L. Jost, and an executive at the Canajoharie plant, Robert J. Belvin, seemed to sum up Lavery's state of mind:

"Mr. Belvin, what did you do when you found that Beech-Nut had been using a product in what it called apple juice that was not in fact apple juice?"

"I—I became very upset."

"Why were you very upset?"

"Because we feed babies. . . ."

"Did you ever hear Mr. Lavery express a sentiment similar to that you have just described to the jury?"

"No."

By 1979, Beech-Nut's financial condition had become so precarious that Frank Nicholas admitted failure and sold the company to Nestlé S.A., the Swiss food giant. Nestlé arrived with $60 million in working capital and a commitment to restore a hallowed brand name to health. The view in the food industry was that

Beech-Nut had been rescued from the brink. Yet evidence presented at the trial gives the exact opposite impression—of a Procrustean bed being prepared for nervous managers. Hoyvald, who chose to testify on his own behalf, admitted that in 1981, his first year as chief executive, he had grandiosely promised Nestlé that Beech-Nut would earn $700,000 the following year, though there would be a negative cash flow of $1.7 million. Hoyvald had arrived at Nestlé only a year before, but he was a seasoned executive in the food business. The answer nevertheless shot back from Switzerland: the cash flow for Beech-Nut, as for all other Nestlé subsidiaries, would have to be zero or better. "The pressure," as he conceded, "was on."

Hoyvald testified that he knew nothing about adulterated concentrate until the summer of 1982. In January 1981, however, LiCari had sent to both Lavery and Hoyvald a copy of an article in a trade magazine discussing signs of adulteration in apple juice, and had written and attached a memo noting, among other things, that "Beech-Nut has been concerned over the authenticity of fruit juice products." LiCari also told the jury that in August of that same year, several weeks after his disastrous confrontation with Lavery, he went to Beech-Nut's corporate headquarters in Fort Washington, Pa., to appeal to Hoyvald—an uncharacteristic suspension of his faith in the chain of command. Hoyvald had been appointed president only four months earlier, and LiCari testified that he liked and trusted his new boss, whom he felt had a mandate from Nestlé to restore Beech-Nut's prestige. The meeting in Fort Washington persuaded LiCari that he had finally found an ally. Hoyvald, LiCari testified, "appeared shocked and surprised" at LiCari's report, and left him feeling "that something was going to be done and they would stop using it."

Then, month after month, nothing happened. Finally, at a late-fall company retreat at a ski resort in Vermont, LiCari raised the issue with Hoyvald one last time. Hoyvald told him, he testified, that he was unwilling to fire Lavery. (In his own testimony, Hoyvald denied that either meeting had taken place.)

LiCari was now convinced that the company was bent on lawbreaking, as he later testified, and rather than acquiesce, he quit, in January 1982. His allies concerned with quality control remained behind, but evidently none was stubborn or reckless enough to press his point.

Hoyvald, like Lavery, was a man with an exemplary background, though one that was a good deal more varied and sophisticated than his subordinate's. Born and raised in a provincial town in Denmark, he had relocated to the United States and received his Master of Business Administration degree from the University of Wisconsin in 1960. An ambitious man, Hoyvald had hopscotched across five companies before joining Beech-Nut as head of marketing in 1980, with the promise that he would be promoted to president within a year. Throughout his career, Hoyvald's watchword had been "aggressively marketing top quality products," as he wrote in a three-page "Career Path" addendum to a 1979 résumé. He had turned around the faltering Plumrose Inc., a large food company, by emphasizing quality, and he viewed the job at Beech-Nut as a chance to do just that.

In June 1982, Hoyvald's principles were abruptly tested when the quality of his own product was decisively challenged. A trade association, the Processed Apples Institute, had initiated an investigation into longstanding charges of adulteration throughout the apple-concentrate business. By April 1982, an investigator working for the institute, a former New York City narcotics detective named Andrew Rosenzweig (who is now chief investigator for the Manhattan District Attorney's office), was prowling around the Woodside, Queens, warehouse of a company called Food Complex, which was Universal's manufacturing arm. By diligent questioning, and searching by flashlight through a dumpster in the middle of many nights, Rosenzweig discovered that Food Complex omitted apples from its recipe altogether, and that its biggest customer was Beech-Nut. On June 25, Rosenzweig tracked a tanker truck full of sugar water out of the Food Complex loading dock and up the New York State Thruway to Canajoharie, where he planned to confront management with his findings. He was hoping to persuade the company to join a civil suit being prepared against Universal and Food Complex; but, expecting the worst, he secretly tape-recorded the ensuing conversation.

At the trial, the tape proved to be a damning piece of evidence. In the course of the discussion, Lavery and two other executives, instead of disputing Rosenzweig's claim that Beech-Nut was making juice from suspect concentrate, unleashed a cascade of tortuous rationalizations. When Rosenzweig explained that the trade association had made new strides in lab testing, Lavery, obviously panicking, suddenly announced: "At this point, we've made our last order from" Universal. But despite considerable pressure, Lavery refused to give Rosenzweig samples of the concentrate, and declined to join the suit. The one anxiety he expressed was over the possibility of bad publicity.

On June 28, Paul E. Hillabush, the head of quality assurance at Canajoharie, called Hoyvald to tell him of Rosenzweig's visit. Hillabush testified that he suggested Beech-Nut recall the product. But Beech-Nut would not only have had to switch to a new and more expensive concentrate, it would have had to admit publicly that the product it had been selling since 1978 was bogus. The cover-up, which Lavery had begun three years earlier with the order to blend the concentrate in mixed juices, was attaining an irresistible momentum.

Hoyvald made the fateful decision to reject Hillabush's advice, and to devote the next eight weeks to moving the tainted products as fast as possible. It would be aggressive marketing, though not of a quality product.

The Apple Institute's suit, as it turned out, was only the first wave to hit the beach. Federal and state authorities had been investigating suppliers of adulterated concentrate since the spring, and the trail led them, too, to Canajoharie. On July 29, an inspector from the United States Food and Drug Administration arrived at the plant, announced that samples taken from supermarket shelves had proved to be adulterated, and took away cases of apple juice ready to be shipped. On Aug. 11, Paul Hillabush received a call from an old friend, Maurice Guerrette, an assistant director with the New York State Department of Agriculture and Markets, who reported much the same conclusion. Guerrette recalls receiving one of the great shocks of his life when Hillabush tried to laugh the whole thing off. It was only then that he realized—as would each investigator in his turn—that Beech-Nut was not the victim of a crime, but its conscious perpetrator.

Guerrette's phone call persuaded Lavery and others—incorrectly, as it turned out—that a seizure action was imminent. After consulting with Hoyvald, executives in Canajoharie decided to move the entire inventory of tainted juice out of the state's jurisdiction. And so, on the night of Aug. 12, nine tractor-trailers from Beech-Nut's trucking company were loaded with 26,000 cases of juice and taken in a ghostly caravan to a warehouse in Secaucus, N.J. One of America's most venerable food companies was fleeing the law like a bootlegger.

By the late summer of 1982, Beech-Nut was racing to unload its stock before regulators initiated a seizure action. On Sept. 1, Hoyvald managed to unload thousands of cases of juice from the Secaucus warehouse to Puerto Rico, despite the fact that the Puerto Rican distributor was already overstocked. Two weeks later, Hoyvald overruled his own lawyers and colleagues, who again suggested a recall, and ordered a feverish "foreign promotion"; under certain circumstances, American law does not prohibit the selling abroad of products banned at home. Within days, 23,000 cases were trucked at great expense from the company's San Jose, Calif., plant to Galveston, Tex., where they were off-loaded onto the first boat bound for the Dominican Republic, where they were sold at a 50 percent discount.

While Beech-Nut's sales staff shipped the evidence out to sea, its lawyers were holding Federal and state agencies at bay. On Sept. 24, lawyers scheduled a meeting with F.D.A. officials that was designed to placate their adversaries. It worked. Three more weeks passed before the F.D.A. Administrator, Taylor M. Quinn, threatened to seize the juice, and thus finally wrung from the company a pledge to begin a nationwide recall. New York State authorities, less patient, threatened a seizure before Beech-Nut hurriedly agreed to a state recall. But the delay allowed Niels Hoyvald to virtually complete his master plan.

By the middle of November Hoyvald could boast, in a report to his superior at Nestlé: "The recall has now been completed, and due to our many delays, we were only faced with having to destroy approximately 20,000 cases. We received adverse publicity in only one magazine." As it turned out, of course, Hoyvald's self-congratulation was premature.

Further Federal and state investigations exposed details of the cover-up, as well as the fact that Beech-Nut had continued to sell the juice in its mixed-juice product for six months after the recall. New York State sued Beech-Nut for selling an adulterated and misbranded product, and imposed a $250,000 fine, by far the largest such penalty ever assessed in the state for consumer violations. In November 1986, the United States Attorney obtained indictments of Hoyvald, Lavery, Beech-Nut, Zeev Kaplansky and Kaplansky's colleague Raymond H. Wells, the owner of Food Complex. Beech-Nut eventually settled by agreeing to pay a $2 million fine. Kaplansky and Wells, who had earlier settled the apple-institute suit with a financial agreement and by ceasing production of their concentrate, also pleaded guilty, and await sentencing. The F.D.A. referred the case to the Justice Department for criminal prosecution.

The case against Hoyvald and Lavery seemed overwhelming—so overwhelming that Lavery's first attorney suggested he plead guilty. Why did Lavery and Hoyvald insist on standing trial? Because both men, by most reports, are still convinced that they committed nothing graver than a mistake in judgment.

Hoyvald and Lavery seem to think of themselves as corporate patriots. Asked by one of the prosecutors why the entire inventory of concentrate was not destroyed once it came under suspicion, Hoyvald shot back testily: "And I could have called up Switzerland and told them I had just closed the company down. Because that is what would have been the result of it."

The question of what Nestlé would have said, or did say, was not resolved by the trial. Jerome LiCari testified that in 1980 and 1981 he had expressed his concerns to six different Nestlé officials, including Richard Theuer, who was then a vice president of Nestlé and would become Beech-Nut's president in 1986. In an extraordinary effort to clear its reputation, Nestlé brought all six officials to court, mostly from Switzerland, and each one either contradicted LiCari's account or stated he had no memory of the alleged conversation. Nestlé is acutely sensitive to its public image, which was tarnished in the 1970's and early 80's when it aggressively promoted infant formula in third-world countries despite public health concerns, sparking international controversy and boycott campaigns.

Nestlé has defended its subsidiary's acts as vigorously as it defended its own in the past. The company has spent what sources close to the case estimate as several million dollars in defending the two executives, and has agreed to keep both men on the payroll—at annual salaries of $120,000 and $70,000—until their current appeals are exhausted.

In a memo sent to Canajoharie employees after the verdict, James M. Biggar, president of Nestlé's American operations, claimed that LiCari had confused "what he wished he had said" with "what he actually said or did," and faulted management only for failing to keep an "open door."

Richard Theuer, the man Nestlé chose to replace Hoyvald, promises to keep that door open. He hopes to convince the public that at "the new Beech-Nut" decisions will be taken, as he says, "on behalf of the babies."

CHAPTER

5

Alcohol and Drug Abuse

Smoke Gets in Your Eyes: Cigarette Smoking As Deviant Behavior

GERALD E. MARKLE

RONALD J. TROYER
Western Michigan University

This article focuses on the long-standing, but recently intensified controversy over cigarette smoking. In the late 1960s and the 1970s a variety of laws and regulations were implemented to regulate smoking and the smoker. Initially these strictures were what Gusfield terms assimilative, but more recently they have become coercive. In 1978, for example, a California referendum to ban smoking in most public places was narrowly defeated. Many view this controversy using a medical model or emphasizing the conflicting rights of smokers and nonsmokers. We analyze it as a status battle between pro and antismoking vested interests. Using data from a variety of primary and secondary sources such as government statistics, corporate reports, state codes, marketing reports and public opinion polls, we focus on the political, economic and organizational forces which have militated for or against changes. At stake is the symbolic definition of a behavior as socially approved or illegitimate and the consequent denigration of the losers. We predict more and increasingly militant confrontations between pro and antismoking forces, both at the individual and collective level.

For the past fifteen years most sociological studies of deviance have focused on individuals and their subcultures and neglected the process of the social definition and redefinition of deviant categories:[1] how, under what conditions, and by whom are deviant categories created, maintained or abolished? Our investigation of cigarette smoking will address these questions. . . .

Gusfield's (1963) work on the American temperance movement, particularly its creation of deviant and criminal labels, is our exemplar. His analysis is causal, focusing on status politics and the symbolic nature of the crusade. This focus remains unchanged, though the initial winner of the conflict became the eventual loser. Moreover, the validity of his argument is independent of truth claims about alcohol; whether the drug is actually an aphrodisiac, a depressant or a tool of the devil is largely irrelevant. Finally, his investigation is symmetrical because it considers the motives and actions of both sides, and indeed the interaction of dominant and deviant groups, necessary to understand the conflict.

From Gusfield's work, we identify two dynamic processes by which deviant categories may be created or redefined. In the assimilative model, the violator admits deviance, and thus the reformer views that person with pity and sympathy:

While legislation may be sought . . . the major activities are efforts to persuade the sufferer to

We would like to thank Doris Cubbernuss and Rogert Nemeth for their assistance in this research. We also thank Roland Chilton, Stanley Robin, James Petersen and Ronald Kramer for reading earlier drafts of this article.

[1]Recent exceptions are studies on deviant drinking (Levine, 1978; Schneider, 1978), hyperactivity (Conrad, 1975), child abuse (Pfohl, 1977) and rape (Rose, 1977). See Spector and Kitsuse (1977) for a theoretical rationale of this type of study.

From the article originally published in *Social Problems*, Vol. 26, No. 5 (June 1979): 611–625. Used with permission
© 1979 by the Society for the Study of Social Problems.

remake his habits and customs. The orientation of the movement . . . is toward the welfare of the potential abstainer by his conversion to the habits of abstinence (1963:69).

In the coercive model, on the other hand, the reformer's exhortations "fall on deaf and angry ears. The expected homage is not paid; the act of deference is absent" (1963:69). The violator must be approached and engaged in political and legal battle as an enemy. As its name implies, the temperance movement began in the assimilative mode, but understanding and education failed to produce penitence. It was coercive measures in [the] form of power politics that eventually led to prohibition.

Cigarette smoking, as a social phenomenon, provides an opportunity to examine the creation of deviant categories. Like alcohol and other drugs which are common to everyday life, cigarette smoking has a long history of changing normative definitions. In an earlier article (Nuehring and Markle, 1974), we demonstrated that cigarette smoking was reemerging as a deviant behavior, and argued that this reemergence was a status battle between nonmedical (primarily political and economic) interests. Furthermore, recent and significant changes in smoking attitudes and behaviors seemed to reflect those social conflicts. We characterized the anticigarette rules and legislation of the late 1960s and early 1970s as assimilative, but speculated that those forces might soon turn to coercive tactics. In this paper we continue that analysis and show that the antismoking movement has kept growing and now has coercive, as well as assimilative, tactics. Looking at both sides of the controversy, we examine the role of vested interests in this process. In showing the conflict between pro and antismoking forces we also show how the image of the smoker has become more deviant in the mid and late 1970s.

RECENT HISTORY

In our first paper (Nuehring and Markle, 1974) we reviewed the convoluted history of cigarette smoking in the United States. Banned by 14 states early in this century, cigarette smoking became an acceptable, perhaps even desirable, behavior by the 1950s. In the late 1960s and

early 1970s, however, a number of antismoking regulations were enacted. These reforms were almost exclusively assimilative: educational campaigns were launched, advertising was regulated and products were labeled as dangerous. As in the temperance movement some of these reforms had moral overtones. In 1965, for example, the State of Florida passed a law (Code 233.09) stipulating that public schools must "teach efficiently and faithfully . . . the adverse health effects of cigarette smoking [and] kindness to animals" along with "proper flag salute."

Attacks on smoking and tobacco have continued, but with different emphasis, during the mid and late 1970s. Now coercive rather than assimilative tactics characterize the antismoking movement. New regulations, which treat the smoker more as enemy than friend, focus on the protection of minors, air and food pollution and fire prevention.

Thirty-seven states now have laws which prevent the sale or gift of cigarettes to minors (for a review see Brody and Brody, 1977: Appendix 1). Most of these laws are designed to punish adult offenders and protect youth. But a few such laws take a less charitable view of the juvenile. A 1976 California law (Code 10602.5), for example, states that smoking or having tobacco on school premises is cause for suspension or expulsion, while a 1975 Florida law (Code 859.07) may compel a minor to testify in court where, and from whom, he obtained cigarettes. That these statutes are seldom (if ever) enforced shows that, as in Gusfield's analysis, their purpose is essentially symbolic.

Smokers have been officially labeled as polluters of our food and air. Nine states prohibit smoking in places where certain foods (e.g., baked goods, milk, ice) are produced or canned. More importantly, twenty-six states have recently passed laws which prohibit smoking in various places (such as elevators, concert halls, museums and physicians' offices). Increasingly smokers are finding the legal pursuit of their habit restricted, with the possibility of even stricter measures in the near future. In 1978, for example, more than 40 percent of California voters supported the most coercive antismoking measure yet proposed: a ban on smoking "in any enclosed public place, enclosed place of employment, enclosed educational facility and in any enclosed health facility" (Hill, 1978). Smoking, it appears, may become an activity permissible only for those of legal age in the privacy of their home. Finally, smokers have been characterized as involuntary arsonists. Thirty-six states selectively ban smoking or the disposal of burned cigarettes to protect structures or woodlands from fire hazards.

During the 1960s the federal government was at the center of the cigarette controversy, then the dispute decentralized and state and local issues predominated. By the late 1970s, however, the federal government again began to dominate the cigarette news. In May 1976, the FTC announced another investigation into the tobacco industry's advertising practices and recommended stronger warnings on cigarette packs and advertisements (*New York Times,* 1976). In the same year, Congress considered measures prohibiting use of any funds in the agricultural appropriation for tobacco programs (*Congressional Quarterly Almanac,* 1976:729) and a graduated tax on cigarettes with the heaviest fees on those with high tar and nicotine content (*Congressional Quarterly Almanac,* 1976:61). Although neither of these measures passed, antitobacco forces were more successful in 1977 when the House of Representatives approved an amendment to a foreign economic aid bill that made tobacco products ineligible for Food for Peace sales. However, the Senate approved a substitute amendment, which eventually became law, merely giving priority to food and fiber commodities (*Congressional Quarterly Weekly Report,* 1977:1206). The same session of Congress saw another attempt to bar use of federal funds for tobacco subsidy programs but the amendment was defeated by a voice vote (*Congressional Quarterly,* 1977:1300).

In 1978 the cigarette controversy intensified, reaching levels of polemic and public coverage which had not been seen since the 1960s. In the spring of 1978, for example, Senator Kennedy held hearings on "the Disease Prevention and Health Protection Act of 1978" S. 3115, which proposes new taxes on high-tar cigarettes, an antismoking resource center, and modification of cigarette pack labeling (*ASH Newsletter,* 1978, VIII:3). But the most significant development in the controversy has been the conversion of Joseph Califano, Secretary of the Department of Health, Education and Welfare. A former smoker himself, Califano has recently taken a strong position against smoking and tobacco. On January 11, 1978, he announced a federal program urging voluntary increases in antismoking announcements on broadcast media (Califano, 1978).[2]

These recent activities are potentially significant and symbolically important. Yet the battle over the redefinition of smoking norms is hardly concluded. The resources of the forces for the status quo, though not easily seen by the public, are nevertheless impressive. As a National Cancer Institute report notes, "More than 150 bills affecting the cigarette industry have been introduced since 1966, but none has been passed by congress since 1970" (U.S. Department of Health, Education and Welfare, 1977:78).

PROSMOKING FORCES

There are enormous vested interests in maintaining cigarette smoking as an approved behavior. In this section we consider the involvement, particularly that relating to finances, of three groups: the tobacco industry, advertising and government. In some cases (e.g., tobacco manufacturers) we show specific political linkages between vested interest and behavior;

---

[2]As shown in the following press conference exchange, support from President Carter has been less than enthusiastic (*Congressional Quarterly,* 1978:141):

   Q: *Your Secretary of HEW wants to spend $23 million to persuade Americans to stop smoking, while there are people on your staff, Mr. President, who smoke in public like chimneys. Could you explain this apparent contradiction? [Laughter]*

   A: *I don't see the contradiction there. I can't deny that the Secretary of HEW, who is responsible for the nation's health, points out as have his predecessors for 15 or 20 years, that smoking is a danger to health. The U.S. Surgeon General, as you know, years ago confirmed this in tests. I happen to think that that is his responsibility. It is not his responsibility to tell a particular American citizen whether they can or cannot smoke.*

for others (e.g., the federal government) we show contrary and ambiguous linkages; most often, however, we merely correlate behavioral outcomes with financial interests.

Tobacco farming plays an important role in the American economy. In 1977 there were some 400,000 farms in the United States which harvested 2.3 billion dollars worth of tobacco (U.S. Department of Agriculture, 1978a:10). Tobacco is currently the fifth largest crop for the entire United States, representing 2.5 percent of the total cash receipts from all farm commodities; moreover tobacco may be the best farm investment of all crops, averaging $2375 per acre.[3] In three states (North Carolina, Kentucky and South Carolina) tobacco is a major agricultural product (USDA, 1978a:17; Tobacco Institute, 1978).

Tobacco manufacturing interests are much more concentrated than farming interests. In 1977 R. J. Reynolds alone accounted for one-third of all sales in the domestic cigarette market. Its 1977 sales and earnings reached "record levels": sales were $6.36 billion, up 10.6 percent from 1976; net earnings were $423 million, up 19.9 percent from 1976. Return on the average common stockholders equity was 18.8 percent. Interestingly, only 44 percent of all net sales came from domestic tobacco: international sales of tobacco added another 20 percent while transportation, energy, foods and beverages (e.g., Hawaiian Punch, ChunKing food) and aluminum products made up the balance (R. J. Reynolds, 1978). Other major tobacco manufacturers have also diversified their operations. For example, the Miller Brewing Company is owned by Phillip Morris and accounts for 26 percent of the operating revenues of the parent company (Phillip Morris, 1978).

In order to promote and defend these interests, the eleven companies which manufacture cigarettes have created the Tobacco Institute, located in Washington, D.C. The Institute seeks to "promote a better public understanding of the tobacco industry and its place in the nation's economy" (*Encyclopedia of Associations,* 1978). Much of the activity of the Institute has been in the political arena, channeling tens of thousands of dollars into the election campaigns of national leaders. A former congressman from North Carolina heads the Institute and employs three lobbyists with extensive political experience. Senator Kennedy is quoted as claiming that: "hour for hour and dollar for dollar, they're probably the most effective lobby on Capitol Hill" (Jensen, 1978).

Tobacco companies and their executives have also acted on their own to further the interests of cigarettes. The National Information Center on Political Finance places direct and indirect contributions by executives of the six largest tobacco companies to 1972 campaigns at $278,000. And in May 1976 three directors at R. J. Reynolds resigned when it was disclosed the company had illegally funneled $65,000 to $90,000 in corporate funds to domestic political campaigns (Jensen, 1976:1).

The role of the federal government in the tobacco controversy is ambiguous and contrary. Certainly it appears to have a vested interest in promoting tobacco sales, since it collected $2.3 billion in cigarette excise taxes in 1977.[4] Moreover, the U.S. leads the world in tobacco exports: in 1977 the net balance of tobacco trade contributed $1.33 billion to the U.S. balance of payments (Tobacco Institute, 1978).

Within the Federal government, congressional representatives of major tobacco states

---

[3]This compares very favorably to such crops as corn and wheat which yield an average of less than $400 per acre. Despite these data, tobacco farmers are not a wealthy group. According to Mann (1975:89):

Comparing commercial tobacco farms with other types of commercial farms, we find that tobacco farms are smaller in size (128 acres vs. 530) and have a lower value of land and buildings ($36,000 vs. $104,000), and lower value of farm products sold ($10,470 vs. $25,680).

In fact some writers have argued that most tobacco farmers could not survive without the high return from this crop and that the allotment program should be considered as "an important social welfare program in the traditionally poor south" (Bradford and Infanger, 1978).

[4]Other governmental units also benefit from the smoking habit. In 1977, state and local governments collected approximately $4 billion through taxes on tobacco products (U.S. Department of Agriculture, 1978a:26).

and the U.S. Department of Agriculture have influenced tobacco production. Since 1933, USDA has controlled supplies, supported prices, subsidized exports and provided marketing assistance to tobacco farmers. The importance and impact of this program may be assessed by its size: as of March 1, 1978, 621 million pounds of flue-cured tobacco, valued at $629 million, were held under guaranteed government loan (U.S. Department of Agriculture, 1978b). Since tobacco allotments are tied to specific farms, they increase land values: in 1967 the program added as much as $6000 to an acre of burley tobacco (Shuffett and Hoskins, 1969) while by 1975 an allotment was probably worth $10,000 per acre (Mann, 1975).

The financial impact of the cigarette controversy has filtered through the American economy. Aside from the direct combatants, the sector with the greatest vested interest in the dispute is the advertising industry and media. After cigarette advertising was banned from the broadcast media in 1971, cigarette sales increased for three successive years. This irony has an explanation: with the ban on cigarette commercials, powerful antismoking commercials—with their enormous public impact—were sharply curtailed. To fill this void, advertisers switched to the print media; by 1971 manufacturers had tripled their expenditures for newspaper, magazine and outdoor advertising (Morris, 1972:43), and in 1975 R. J. Reynolds spent $31.7 million to advertise its top-selling Winston cigarettes (*Advertising Age,* 1976). The total expenditures are vast: in 1977 the tobacco companies spent an estimated $400 million on advertising (Jensen, 1978).

The strength of the prosmoking forces was vividly demonstrated during the battle over Proposition 5 in California. One month before the election a poll showed Californians favoring the measure by a 58–38 margin. But by election eve the situation had changed dramatically. As Walter Cronkite (1978) reported:

> Californians are used to expensive campaigns for their votes on ballot initiatives. But they've never been wooed so lavishly to vote against anything as they are on Proposition 5, the measure regulating their indoor smoking. . . . The opponents have blitzed the airwaves with a nearly $5 million campaign, more than the combined expenditures of all the candidates for governor. Most of the money is coming from four giants of the tobacco industry. Two of them, Phillip Morris and R. J. Reynolds, have spent well over a million dollars apiece. . . . The campaign has turned around Proposition 5 from an almost sure winner in August to a 16 point underdog in one poll this week. And it's become an issue in public debate.

With tobacco interests eventually spending $5.6 million compared to an outlay of $578,000 by their opponents (Rood, 1978), Proposition 5 was handily defeated.

ANTISMOKING FORCES

There is no strong well-financed national antismoking group but there are many interest groups with diverse motives who are opposed to cigarette smoking. In this section we consider the involvement of the federal government, voluntary action citizen groups and private entrepreneurs in the antismoking movement.

While some departments of the federal government have promoted tobacco interests, others have been at the forefront of the antismoking campaign. The Public Health Service, for example, has been actively involved in anticigarette activities for a number of years. One of its offices, The National Clearinghouse for Smoking and Health, publishes and distributes materials urging people to quit smoking. Its efforts have been somewhat limited in recent years because of budget reductions and relegation to virtual obscurity. From its inception in 1966 to 1972, the budget of the Clearinghouse was $2.5 million per year. In 1973 the allocation dropped to $900,000 and in 1974 it was moved out of Washington to the Center for Disease Control in Atlanta with no budget of its own. However, HEW Secretary Califano has reinvigorated the office. He changed its name to the Office for Smoking and Health, moved it back to Washington, and requested $6 million for its 1978 budget.

Federal regulatory agencies such as the Civil Aeronautics Board, the Federal Trade Commission and the Interstate Commerce

Commission have all issued rulings favorable to the antismoking position. Not only have these agencies been willing to act, but the rulings have become increasingly coercive, such as the increasingly stringent restrictions on smoking on interstate transportation. The reasons for this regulatory militancy are not clear. However we previously (Nuehring and Markle, 1974) speculated that internal organizational needs for role definition and power influenced agency behavior.

An additional reason for the antismoking actions by the regulatory agencies appears to be the pressure applied by antismoking citizen groups. ASH (Action on Smoking and Health), for example, has filed numerous petitions with agencies seeking anticigarette decisions. Headed by John Banzhaf, the man who persuaded the FCC to issue its "equal time" ruling on anticigarette commercials in 1967, ASH serves as the legal arm of the antismoking movement. Among its activities in 1977, for example, ASH filed two petitions with the CAB, one each with FAA and FDA, convinced the Food and Drug Administration that a special warning about smoking be included in birth control pill packages, and assisted in a law suit filed by a nonsmoker (ASH, 1978).

Other citizen groups exerting pressure on government bodies include GASP (Group Against Smokers Pollution) and NIC (National Interagency Council on Smoking). GASP, which has members in every state, promotes the rights of nonsmokers and seeks antismoking laws and regulations (GASP, n.d.). GASP chapters, for example, have been involved in promoting the California antismoking referendum and the New Jersey attempt to ban smoking in public places. The NIC has concentrated more on education against smoking but does favor prohibition of cigarette advertising (*Encyclopedia of Associations,* 1978:801).

Health organizations such as the American Cancer Society, the American Heart Association and the American Lung Association initially endorsed assimilative reform of the smoker. Recently, however, they have approved more coercive tactics. Since 1974, the American Cancer Society, for example, has called for elimination of all cigarette advertising (Brody, 1974), an end to the tobacco subsidy program (*New York Times,* 1977), state and local restriction of smoking in public places, and strict enforcement of the ban on cigarette sales to minors (Brody, 1978). And all of those health groups appear to have rejuvenated their antismoking campaign by again making antismoking spots available to the mass media.[5]

Other vested interests benefiting from and sometimes encouraging the antismoking movement include profit-making enterprises. A check of the 1977–1978 *Books in Print,* for example, reveals 17 monographs with stop or quit smoking in the title. Insurance companies have found that they can profit as well as attract new customers by offering discounts as high as 20 and 25 percent to nonsmokers (Cole, 1973). Organized crime has benefited from the antismoking movement support of "sin taxes." The vast tax differential, for example 26¢ a pack in New York to 2¢ a pack in North Carolina, has made cigarette smuggling a lucrative business estimated to net $800 million annually (*Time,* 1977).

Several commercial enterprises, including Smoke No More, The Schick Treatment, Damon Hypothesis and Fresh Start, are in the quit smoking business (Condon, 1976). The two largest organizations are Smokewatchers, with franchises in 17 states, and SmokEnders, which claims to have graduated 100,000 people from its course. Founded in 1969 SmokEnders claims that smokers can "unlearn their habit . . . comfortably, intelligently, pleasantly, even joyfully" (SmokEnders, 1977). In fact an independent retrospective study claims that SmokEnders has a 70 percent success rate (Condon, 1976). It is difficult to evaluate SmokEnders' methods: everyone in the program signs a statement that he or she will refrain from talking about the course and

---

[5]The antismoking campaigns waged by these health groups show some ambivalence. Epstein (1978), for example, points out that the American Cancer Society has endorsed several restrictive antismoking measures but never launched the well-organized lobbying effort needed to insure their enactment and implementation.

will not teach SmokEnders' course without the company's permission. What is known is that these methods are profitable: in 1976 the company grossed $5 million, up from $4.1 million in 1975 (Condon, 1976).

SMOKING ATTITUDES AND PATTERNS

So far we have suggested that the antismoking strictures of the seventies are becoming more coercive in spite of the opposition of powerful vested interests. At first glance this appears to be explained by the public's acceptance of the health argument. Table 1[6] indicates that by 1975 four out of five smokers agreed that "smoking is harmful to health." Yet in 1949, long before the current antismoking movement began, Gallup (1972:874) reported that 52 percent of cigarette smokers and 66 percent of noncigarette smokers responded yes to "Do you think cigarette smoking is harmful or not?" However, this sentiment did not result in social control measures regulating smoking or smokers.

We have previously argued (Nuehring and Markle, 1974) that a simple medical model is inadequate to explain smoking attitudes and behavior: normative considerations are probably the crucial factor. In addition to being seen as harmful to health, smoking came to be seen as undesirable, deviant behavior, and smokers as social misfits. In fact data now show that people increasingly view smoking as socially reprehensible.

As smokers have labeled themselves as deviant, the social undesirability of the habit has grown. As Table 1 indicates, three-fourths of all nonsmokers and about a third of all current smokers agree that "it's annoying to be near someone who is smoking." Further, smoking has come to be seen as inappropriate behavior for several traditionally esteemed occupations.

In 1964, less than half of both current smokers and nonsmokers said that doctors should not smoke. By 1975, almost six out of ten said so. The same pattern holds for teachers with better than 80 percent of never smokers and more than 60 percent of current smokers agreeing. Singling out teachers even more than health professionals would seem to indicate a strong normative component in antismoking sentiment.

Table 1 also shows that support for coercive control measures has grown.[7] By 1975 nine out of ten never smokers, and almost three of every four current smokers, agree that smoking "should be allowed in fewer places than it is now"; a decade ago only one-third of all smokers agreed with that item. More than two of every five smokers, double the proportion from the mid 1960s, agree that cigarette advertising "should be stopped completely." Among never smokers, support for limiting smoking and its advertising has also grown much stronger.

Smoking attitudes, then, have become more anticigarette and more coercive. Smoking behavior has also altered in recent years, especially with respect to per capita consumption, quitting patterns and differentials according to age and sex. [USDA (1971, 1978a) figures show that] per capita sales, measured as cigarettes consumed per year, declined sharply as a result of the Surgeon General's Report in 1964. Thereafter sales cycled, rising again and then declining steeply, presumably because of the effectiveness of antismoking commercials. In the early 1970s per capita sales increased sharply, in part because of the cessation of antismoking media activities. Since the mid 1970s, however, sales have leveled off. Despite continued antismoking activities, there seems to be a residual or "steady state" population of smokers.

A medical model would suggest that people smoke cigarettes in order to ingest nicotine. However . . . cigarette consump-

---

[6]See Nuehring and Markle (1974) for a description of the 1964 and 1966 survey methodology. The same techniques were employed in the 1975 study except that a majority of the interviews were conducted by telephone with supplemental interviews of nontelephone households (U.S. Department of Health, Education and Welfare, 1976c).

[7]However, support for one coercive statement has an ambiguous pattern. In 1964, approximately one-third of the never smokers and slightly more than 55 percent of the smokers agreed that "Nothing more should be done about cigarettes until the cigarette manufacturers are given a reasonable amount of time to come up with a safer cigarette." Curiously, smokers' support for the statement declined to just under 50 percent in 1975 while support among never smokers rose to about 40 percent.

TABLE 1

*Percentage Who "Strongly Agree" or "Agree" with the Following Statements by Year, Sex and Smoking Habits of the Respondent**

Statement	Sex	1964 Never	1964 Current	1966 Never	1966 Current	1970 Never	1970 Current	1975 Never	1975 Current
Smoking is harmful to health	M	85.9	68.6	86.4	71.3	92.1	79.9	93.6	81.7
	F	89.8	70.6	89.1	73.2	92.2	77.8	95.0	80.5
It is annoying to be near a person who is smoking	M	62.6	19.2	66.3	24.2	75.2	32.4	77.0	35.0
	F	70.3	20.3	71.3	27.2	79.2	36.5	80.6	34.6
Doctors should set a good example by not smoking cigarettes	M	74.8	48.3	74.0	56.2	79.7	56.9	82.8	58.9
	F	76.8	47.1	82.5	52.8	87.4	58.3	90.0	58.6
People in the health professions should set a good example by not smoking cigarettes	M	**	**	80.9	62.9	81.1	61.7	84.8	63.2
	F	**	**	85.7	58.4	87.9	60.7	90.9	62.6
Teachers should set a good example by not smoking cigarettes	M	**	**	84.2	69.3	75.8	59.3	83.8	65.0
	F	**	**	88.2	65.4	84.2	56.6	87.2	59.1
Cigarette smoking is enough of a health hazard for something to be done about it	M	85.0	63.9	80.9	65.1	89.0	78.7	89.0	72.6
	F	83.9	66.5	82.7	72.2	91.1	79.6	91.7	70.7
Smoking of cigarettes should be allowed in fewer places than it is now	M	61.1	32.4	62.2	35.5	58.0	40.4	79.2	49.9
	F	69.4	35.1	68.7	33.8	72.7	43.2	83.0	52.4
Cigarette advertising should be stopped completely	M	43.1	21.2	34.2	21.2	60.6	49.3	56.9	42.6
	F	47.4	24.6	44.7	24.6	71.4	50.6	68.3	42.5

*See Nuehring and Markle (1974) for sample distributions for the 1964 and 1966 surveys. In the 1975 sample there were 1,795 males and 3,580 females who had never smoked, and 2,243 males and 1,828 females who were current smokers.

**This question was not asked in 1964.

Sources: U.S. Department of Health, Education, and Welfare, Adult Use of Tobacco-1970. See Tables 2d, 2f, 2i, 2j, 2k, 2o, 2q, and 2r. Adult Use of Tobacco-1975: Tables. See tables on pages II-2, II-5, II-7, II-8, II-11, II-13, II-14, and II-17.

tion, measured as pounds of tobacco per year, has declined steadily over the past two decades despite the fact that the length of cigarettes has been increased three times during the same period. The reason is that although the average cigarette is longer today than it was ten years ago, it contains less tobacco. From 1939 to 1943, some 319 cigarettes were produced per pound of tobacco leaf. In 1976, 489 cigarettes were produced per pound of tobacco leaf[8] (U.S. Department of Agriculture, 1978a:22). Thus, people seem to measure smoking satisfaction not only physiologically, but also in social psychological or normative ways not related to nicotine consumption.

Related to the pattern of less tobacco per cigarette is the increased popularity of low-tar varieties containing less tobacco per cigarette

[8]The decreasing amount of tobacco per cigarette is due to greater use of reconstituted leaf (stems, scraps, and dust reprocessed into a sheet), by a process called "Fluffing" or "Puffing" much the way wheat and rice are puffed as breakfast cereals, and to reducing the circumference (Brody, 1975, 1976).

(King, 1976:8). The low-tars commanded 8 percent of the market in 1974 (Hammer, 1975:7), but by 1978 they comprised 23 percent of all cigarettes sold (Fletcher, 1978). This change seems to represent a behavioral response to the emphasis antismoking forces have put on the health risks of smoking, since low-tar cigarettes have been identified as safer than other cigarettes. Here again, though, it may be more important to smoke a constant number of cigarettes per day than it is to ingest a constant amount of nicotine per day.

Another behavioral pattern that reflects the success of the antismoking movement is the large number of people who have quit smoking. The U.S. Department of Health, Education and Welfare, for example, estimates (1977:57) that 29 million Americans stopped smoking between 1965 and 1975. If correct,[9] this represents a dramatic behavioral change, especially considering the reputed difficulty of breaking the habit.

This change in cigarette consumption is dramatically illustrated when the proportion of smokers in the adult male population is examined. In 1955, 56.9 percent of all males 18 years old smoked cigarettes (HEW, 1970) but by 1975, only 39.3 percent of all males 21 years old did. The decline has been steady and present in almost all age groups. Health professionals have led this trend: from 1967 to 1975 smoking among physicians declined from 30 percent to 21 percent, among dentists from 34 percent to 23 percent, and among pharmacists from 35 percent to 28 percent (U.S. Department of Health, Education and Welfare, 1977).

Cigarette smoking has not declined among women, it has remained constant. In both 1955 and 1975, some 28 percent of all women 18 years and older smoked cigarettes. While fewer women than men smoke, this difference between the sexes is disappearing.

Differences in smoking trends by sex are most dramatic among teenagers. There seems to be a consensus in the literature that smoking among teenage boys rose until 1969 but has remained around the 30 percent level since then. However, cigarette smoking among teenage girls has continued to increase, both in proportion smoking and number of cigarettes smoked. In 1969, for example, 22 percent of all teenage girls smoked with 10 percent of the smokers consuming a pack a day. By 1975, 27 percent of all teenage girls smoked with 39 percent consuming a pack a day. As the U.S. Department of Health, Education and Welfare (1977:1) notes, ". . . girls' behavior has simply caught up with that of boys, and smoking among teenage boys is not on the increase."

As a way of explaining these data, we speculate that cigarette smoking has been symbolically associated with the liberation of women. Using a Madison Avenue version of feminism, for example, Phillip Morris advertises Virginia Slims cigarettes with the ironic verse:

> You've come a long way baby
> To get where you've got to today
> You've got your own cigarette now, baby
> You've come a long, long way

As evidence for this linkage, the highest proportion of women who smoke are those employed outside the home in white-collar jobs. For males, white-collar workers are less likely to be current smokers than males in all other occupations. But, while smoking has declined among male-dominated health professionals, the proportion of smokers among nurses has remained constant over the past decade (U.S. Department of Health, Education and Welfare, 1977:13). Apparently, the antismoking campaign has had less impact on females because of the symbolic meaning of smoking for women.

EMERGING CONFRONTATIONS

As antismoking forces shift from an assimilative attack on the product to a coercive attack on the smoker, there have been recent attempts to label the smoker as a psychological misfit. As a psychiatrist, in a letter to *The New York Times,* has proposed:

> What we need is a national campaign that results in stigmatization rather than glorification of the

---

[9]While there has been a substantial decrease in the proportion of Americans smoking, the numbers quitting and not smoking may be overstated, given the emerging undesirability of the act (Warner, 1978).

smoker. This in my opinion, would be the most effective way of reducing the number of smokers and confining their smoking to the privacy of their homes (Gardner, 1978).

Behavioral scientists have contributed to this stigmatization, perhaps inadvertently, with studies exploring the personality configuration of the smoker. Perhaps most influential has been Eysenck's (1965) contention that smokers are more extroverted and neurotic than nonsmokers. Rae (1975) and Cherry and Kiernan (1976) claimed support for this theory in their studies of British college students and adults. In the United States, Smith (1970) reported smokers scoring higher on extroversion.

More negative evaluative characteristics have been attributed to smokers by some authors. Studies of both adults and college students indicated that smokers scored lower on agreeableness and strength of character, and higher on antisocial tendencies, impulsiveness, crudeness and orality; in addition, they were more externally oriented and happy-go-lucky (Smith, 1969, 1970). Another study of college students reported that smokers demonstrated personality traits of defiance, impulsivity and danger seeking; showed more oral preoccupations and stress; and had perceptions of having experienced minimal warmth, protection and affection while growing up (Jacobs and Spilkin, 1971). Reynolds and Nichols (1976) claimed that the smokers, among the 885 students they examined, were less well-adjusted and more likely to engage in antisocial activities. Finally, studies in both the United States (Borland and Rudolph, 1975) and Canada (Hanley and Robinson, 1976) purport that smokers are academic underachievers.

Some authors have directly questioned the mental health of smokers (Smith, 1970; Srole and Fischer, 1973); Fisher (1976), for example, claimed that female smokers are preoccupied with power because of penis envy. Dr. Jerome H. Jaffe, the top White House drug abuse official in the Nixon Administration suggested that people who smoke more than a pack of cigarettes a day be described as suffering from a "compulsive smoking disorder" (Brody, 1975:38). And a new term—compulsive smoking syndrome—has been proposed as a disorder to be listed in the Diagnostic and Statistical Manual of the American Psychiatric Association.

These attempts to stigmatize the smoker have not gone unchallenged. For years the industry has portrayed the smoker as a desirable person (e.g., the "Marlboro Man"). And recent and heavy advertising in soft pornographic magazines[10] is clearly an attempt to pair smoking with erogenous behavior. Nationally syndicated columnist William Safire (1974) has also protested that government attempts to lower the social status of smokers is an abuse of power. Other citizens have similarly complained:

> I am particularly sick of being issued the lousiest seat on a plane (although I have paid the same) because I might want a smoke during flight; of getting "kitchen" tables in the non-smoking sections of restaurants (although my bill will be just as high) (Murphy, 1978).

As attempts to restrict and label the smoker continue, and as nonsmokers become more militant, interpersonal relations between users and abstainers may become strained. In fact one study found that nonsmokers rated persons more negatively when they smoked and that smokers greatly underestimated the extent to which their smoking was considered discourteous (Bleda and Sandman, 1977). If this study of Army and Air Force personnel is indicative of the general population, further confrontations and conflicts will follow.[11] As the Secretary of Health, Education and Welfare has noted:

> . . . the etiquette of smoking has changed, slowly but perceptibly. Once the smoker asked, "Would you like a cigarette?" Today the question is, "Do you mind if I smoke?" And more and

[10]In 1976, cigarette advertising accounted for an astounding 38 percent of all advertising revenue for *Oui* and 21 percent for *Playboy* (ASH Newsletter, 1977).

[11]When, on a Western Airlines flight, a man complained about cigarette smoke coming from the smoking section, six smokers, including two in the nonsmoking section, lit up and began to blow smoke at him (Salpukas, 1975). Nonsmokers are showing similar militance. Several incidents on commuter trains are reported including a nonsmoker breathing garlic on other commuters who ignored the no smoking sign, and that several nonsmokers have equipped themselves with battery operated fans to blow smoke back in smokers' faces (1975).

more nonsmokers are finding the courage to answer with a polite but emphatic, "Yes, I do mind" (Califano, 1978).

CONCLUSION

Our first paper concluded with the statement: "Activities of the past few years and the next few years may show that, once again, the sale and possession of cigarettes is emerging as a deviant behavior" (Nuehring and Markle, 1974:525). In fact in the mid and late 1970s the antismoking movement has become more active, more politically effective and more coercive. Cigarette smokers, who in increasing numbers see themselves as deviant actors, have been labeled as drug addicts and neurotics as well as air polluters and fire hazards. Smokers who do not accept these labels face increasing confrontations with militant nonsmokers. These battles may be interpersonal or highly organized political campaigns such as the 1978 vote in California—The Clean Indoor Air Act—which would have banned smoking in nearly all public facilities and private businesses.

Most commentators interpret the smoking controversy from a medical framework. Scientists have demonstrated that smoking causes cancer and a host of other diseases. Therefore abstention is seen as a rational response to a health danger, while smoking is labeled as an irrational behavior. We do not deny that the health issue has played a role in the controversy. However, we have shown that since the early 1900s, and particularly since the 1950s, people have been informed about the health risks of smoking. To think of smoking behavior as irrational leads to a scientific dead end. Our task is to understand the phenomenon, not to place it beyond the scope of systematic investigation.

We might attribute the smoking controversy, and its resultant coercive regulations and laws, to the defensive behavior of the nonsmoker. Convinced that smoking is a health hazard for all people, abstainers are simply asserting their right to health and long life. This explanation is fine as far as it goes. But it does not account for the recent escalation of the smoking controversy. We maintain that individual opposition to

smoking is only effective, or even allowable, within a collective context. Only by examining the institutional and organizational forces involved in the dispute can the dynamics of the controversy be appreciated.

Thus we maintain that sociopolitical rather than health factors have been decisive in shaping the smoking controversy. Increasingly smokers and nonsmokers may be seen as members of two status groups in conflict. At stake is the collective conferral of legitimacy and consequent prestige. If the norms of the nonsmoker are officially endorsed, the smoker clearly will drop in status ranking.

Enormous vested interests are attempting to define and redefine the social status of the smoker. For years cigarette advertising has glorified the smoker. Recent increases in smoking among teenagers, particularly women, demonstrate the vigor of this campaign. On the other hand the antismoking movement has inspired a multitude of new laws and regulations which restrict the smokers' habit. Because strictures are rarely enforced their actual impact on public smoking is difficult to assess. However the important effect of these measures is that they constantly stigmatize the smoker.

Our investigation of cigarette smoking is a case study of how deviant categories are created. But our findings can be linked to those on a variety of other social problems. For example, the antismoking movement has much in common with the temperance movement. Both issues involve human health, but both social movements have strong political and symbolic components. Both were initially characterized by assimilative tactics which later developed into coercive tactics. The battles over smoking are not as identified with clear regional, ethnic and religious boundaries as were those over drinking. However the link between vested interests and public opinion is easier to document in the smoking controversy than it was for temperance.

Smoking, like many other emerging social problems, is characterized by a conflict of vested interests over the collective definition of individual behavior. We have shown how each side of the conflict has tried, and continues to try, to get its definition as the accepted public definition. Whether cigarette smoking again becomes more desirable or more deviant is contingent on the outcome of the current status battles between pro and antismoking interests.

REFERENCES

Advertising Age. "Costs of cigarette advertising: 1968–1975." Advertising Age 47 (November 22): 36, 38. (1976).

ASH (Action on Smoking and Health). "Smoking and health: History of the battle, 1964–1975." Washington, D.C.: ASH. (1975).

———. "History of the war against smoking: 1964–1978." Washington, D.C.: ASH. (1978).

ASH Newsletter. "News you should know." ASH 7 (January–February): 6. (1977).

———. "Senate hearings on health bill and teenage smoking." ASH 8 (May–June): 3. (1978).

Bleda, Paul R. and Paul H. Sandman. "In smokes way: Socioemotional reactions to another's smoking." Journal of Applied Psychology 62 (4): 452–458. (1977).

Bloor, David. Knowledge and Social Imagery. London: Routledge and Kegan Paul. (1976).

Borland, Barry L. and Joseph P. Rudolph. "Relative effects of low socioeconomic status, parental smoking and poor scholastic performance on smoking among high school students." Social Science and Medicine 9 (1): 27–30. (1975).

Bradford, Garnett L. and Craig L. Infanger. "The tobacco industry and health: Understanding a contradiction." Intellect 106 (February): 318–321. (1978).

Brody, Alvan and Betty Brody. The Legal Rights of Non Smokers. New York: Avon. (1977).

Brody, Jane E. "Cancer society steps up drive on growing smoking problems." New York Times, February 8: 32. (1974).

———. "Heavy smoking called disorder." New York Times, June 5: 38. (1975).

———. "Massive drive urged to combat smoking." New York Times, February 1: A-10. (1978).

Califano, Joseph A., Jr. Address before the National Interagency Council on Smoking and Health, Shoreham Hotel, Washington, D.C., January 11. (1978).

Cherry, Nicola and Kathy Kierman. "Personality scores and smoking behaviour." British Journal of Social Preventive Medicine 30 (2): 123–31. (1976).

Cole, Robert J. "Insurance discounts for nonsmokers spread from life to care policies." New York Times, November 1: 63. (1973).

Condon, James C. "Tobacco is a dirty word-they loved it." New York Times, December 5, Section III: 5. (1976).

Congressional Quarterly Weekly Report. "Tobacco." 35 (June 25): 1300. Washington, D.C.: Congressional Quarterly, Inc. (1977).

———. "Tobacco Issue." 35 (June 18): 1206. Washington, D.C.: Congressional Quarterly, Inc. (1977).

———. "Text of President Carter's January 12, News Conference." 36 (January 21): 138–141. Washington, D.C.: Congressional Quarterly, Inc. (1978).

Congressional Quarterly Almanac. "Cigarette taxes." 32:61 Washington, D.C.: Congressional Quarterly, Inc. (1976).

———. "Tobacco subsidies." 32:729–730. Washington, D.C.: Congressional Quarterly, Inc. (1976).

Conrad, Peter. "The discovery of hyperkinesis: Notes on the medicalization of deviant behavior." Social Problems 23 (October): 12–21. (1975).

Cronkite, Walter. CBS-TV Evening News, November 2. (1978).

Dullea, Georgia. "And as the gaspers of the world unite, nonsmokers become fashionably cool." New York Times, November 5: 51. (1975).

Encyclopedia of Associations. Encyclopedia of Associations, 12th edition, Volume 11. Detroit: Gale Research Company. (1978).

Eysenck, Hans Jurgen. Smoking, Health, and Personality. Basic Books: New York. (1965).

Epstein, Samuel. The Politics of Cancer. San Francisco: Sierra Club Books. (1978).

Fisher, Jerid M. "Sex differences in smoking dynamics." Journal of Health and Social Behavior 17 (2): 145–150. (1976).

Fletcher, Elaine. "He'd rather switch (brands) than quit." Detroit Free Press, August 2:1-C. (1978).

Gallup, George Horace. The Gallup Poll: Public Opinion, 1935–1971, Vol. I. New York: Random House. (1972).

Gardner, Richard A. "Letter to the editor." New York Times, July 30: 18. (1977).

GASP (Group Against Smokers' Pollution). "Does tobacco smoke turn you off?" GASP: College Park, Maryland. (n.d.).

Glasnick, Jack. "Letter to the editor." New York Times, April 6: 30. (1974).

Gusfield, Joseph R. Symbolic Crusade: Status Politics and the American Temperance Movement. Urbana, Illinois: University of Illinois Press. (1963).

Hammer, Alexander R. "Low-tar cigarettes taking increasingly higher share of market." New York Times, December 27:7. (1975).

Hanley, J. A. and J. C. Robinson. "Cigarette smoking and the young: A national survey." Canadian Medical Association Journal 114 (March 20): 511–517. (1976).

Hill, Galdwin. "Californians will vote on whether to restrict smoking in public." New York Times, March 16: C-11. (1978).

Jacobs, Martin A. and Aron Z. Spilkin. "Personality patterns associated with heavy cigarette smoking in male college students." Journal of Consulting and Clinical Psychology 37 (3): 428–432. (1971).

Jensen, Michael C. "3 directors out at R. J. Reynolds." New York Times, May 29:1. (1976).

———. "Tobacco: A potent lobby." New York Times, February 19, Section III: 1. (1978).

King, Wayne. "Low-tar cigarettes creating a 'revolution'." New York Times, October 30: 8. (1976).

Lear, Martha Weinman. "All the warnings, gone up in smoke." New York Times, March 10: 18–19, 86, 91. (1974).

Levine, Harry Gene. "The discovery of addiction: Changing conceptions of habitual drunkenness in America." Journal of Studies on Alcohol 39 (January): 143–174. (1978).

Mann, Charles Kellogg. Tobacco: The Ants and the Elephants. Salt Lake City, Utah: Olympus Publishing Company. (1975).

Morris, John D. "Cigarette ads up in publications." New York Times, January 19:43. (1972).

Murphy, Phyllis. "Letters to the editor." Christian Science Monitor, February 10:19. (1978).

New York Times. "F.T.C., citing rise in smoking, to look into cigarette ads." May 18:16. (1976).

———. "Cancer group opens drive to end tobacco subsidy." January 15: A-8. (1977).

Newsweek. "The new issues." Newsweek, October 2: 56–61. (1978).

Nuehring, Elaine and Gerald E. Markle. "Nicotine and norms: The re-emergence of a deviant behavior." Social Problems, 21 (April): 513–526. (1974).

Pfohl, Stephen J. "The discovery of child abuse." Social Problems 24 (February): 310–323. (1977).

Phillip Morris Incorporated. Annual Report—1977. New York: Phillip Morris Incorporated. (1978).

Rae, Gordon. "Extraversion, neuroticism and cigarette smoking." British Journal of Social and Clinical Psychology 14 (November): 429–430. (1975).

Reynolds, Carl and Robert Nichols. "Personality and behavioral correlates of cigarette smoking: One-year follow-up." Psychological Reports 38 (1): 251–258. (1976).

R. J. Reynolds Industries, Inc. 1977 Annual Report. Winston-Salem, North Carolina: R. J. Reynolds Industries. (1978).

Rood, W. B. "Tobacco firms pour more money into proposition 5 fight." Los Angeles Times, November 5: Part I, 3. (1978).

Rose, Vicki McNickle. "The rise of the rape problem." Pages 167–195 in Armand L. Mauss and Julie Camile Wolfe (eds.), This Land of Promises. Philadelphia: J. B. Lippincott. (1977).

Safire, William. "On puffery." New York Times, May 16: 41. (1974).

Salpukas, Agis. "Smokers facing new strictures." New York Times, May 16:41. (1975).

Schneider, Joseph W. "Deviant drinking as disease: Alcoholism as a social accomplishment." Social Problems 25 (4): 361–372. (1978).

Shuffett, D. M. and J. Hoskins. "Capitalization of burley tobacco allotment rights." American Journal of Agricultural Economics 51 (May): 471–474. (1969).

Simon, William E. and Louis H. Primavera. "The personality of the cigarette smoker: Some empirical data." The International Journal of the Addictions 11 (1): 81–94. (1976).

Smith, Gene M. "Relations between personality and smoking behavior in preadult subjects." Journal of Consulting and Clinical Psychology 33: 710–715. (1969).

_____. "Personality and smoking: A review of the empirical literature." In William A. Hunt (ed.), Learning Mechanisms in Smoking. Chicago: Aldine. (1970).

SmokEnders. "The easy way." Phillipsburg, New Jersey: SmokEnders, Inc. (1977).

Spector, Malcolm and John I. Kitsuse. Constructing Social Problems. Menlo Park, California: Cummings Publishing Company. (1977).

Srole, Leo and Anita Kassen Fischer. "The social epidemiology of smoking behavior 1953 and 1970: The Midtown Manhattan study." Social Science and Medicine 7 (May):341–358. (1973).

Time. "The Mafia: Big, bad, and booming." Time, May 16: 32–42. (1977).

Tobacco Institute. "Tobacco industry profile." Tobacco Institute: Washington, D.C. (1978).

U.S. Department of Agriculture. Annual Report on Tobacco Statistics, 1968. Statistical Bulletin No. 450, Agricultural Marketing Service. Washington, D.C.: Government Printing Office. (1969).

_____. Annual Report on Tobacco Statistics, 1970. Statistical Bulletin No. 454, Agricultural Marketing Service. Washington, D.C.: Government Printing Office. (1971).

_____. Annual Report on Tobacco Statistics, 1977. Statistical Bulletin No. 605, Agricultural Marketing Service. Washington, D.C.: Government Printing Office. (1978a).

_____. "ASCS commodity fact sheet: Flue cured tobacco." Agricultural Stabilization and Conservation Service. Washington, D.C.: Government Printing Office. (1978b).

U.S. Department of Health, Education and Welfare. Changes in smoking habits between 1955 and 1966. Washington, D.C.: Government Printing Office. (1970).

_____. Adult use of tobacco—1970. Washington, D.C.: Government Printing Office. (1973).

_____. "Adult use of tobacco—1975: Summary." Washington, D.C. (1976a).

_____. "Adult use of tobacco—1975: Tables." Washington, D.C. (1976b).

_____. "Adult use of tobacco—1975: Methodology." Washington, D.C. (1976c).

_____. The Smoking Digest: Progress Report on a Nation Kicking the Habit. Washington, D.C.: Government Printing Office. (1977).

Warner, Kenneth E. "Possible increases in the underreporting of cigarette consumption." Journal of the American Statistical Association 73 (June): 314–318. (1978).

Alcoholism: The Mythical Disease

HERBERT FINGARETTE

The idea that alcoholism is a disease is a myth, and a harmful myth at that. The phrase itself—"alcoholism is a disease"—is a slogan. It lacks definite medical meaning and therefore precludes one from taking any scientific attitude toward it, pro or con. But the slogan has political potency. And it is associated in the public consciousness with a number of beliefs about heavy drinking that do have meaning, and do have important consequences for the treatment of individuals and for social policy. These beliefs lack a scientific foundation; most have been decisively refuted by the scientific evidence.

This assertion obviously conflicts with the barrage of pronouncements in support of alcoholism's classification as a disease by health professionals and organizations such as the American Medical Association, by the explosively proliferating treatment programs, and by innumerable public-service organizations. So it may seem that a sweeping challenge to the disease concept can only be hyperbole, the sensationalist exaggeration of a few partial truths and a few minor doubts.

To the contrary: the public has been profoundly misled, and is still being actively misled. Credulous media articles have featured so many dramatic human-interest anecdotes by "recovering alcoholics," so many "scientific" pronouncements about medical opinion and new discoveries, that it is no wonder the lay public responds with trusting belief.

Yet this much is unambiguous and incontrovertible: the public has been kept unaware of a mass of scientific evidence accumulated over the past couple of decades, evidence familiar to researchers in the field, which radically challenges each major belief generally associated in the public mind with the phrase "alcoholism is a disease." I refer not to isolated experiments or off-beat theories but to massive, accumulated, mainstream scientific work by leading authorities, published in recognized journals. If the barrage of "public service" announcements leaves the public wholly unaware of this contrary evidence, shouldn't this in itself raise grave questions about the credibility of those who assure the public that alcoholism has now been scientifically demonstrated to be a disease?

One may wonder why it is important whether or not alcoholism is a disease. To begin with, "disease" is the word that triggers provision of health-insurance payments, employment benefits such as paid leave and workmen's compensation, and other government benefits. The direct cost of treatment for the "disease" of alcoholism is rapidly rising, already exceeding a billion dollars annually. Add in all related health costs and other kinds of benefits, and the dollar figure is well into the tens of billions annually. Alcoholism is, of course, profoundly harmful, both to the drinkers themselves and to others. But if it ceased to be characterized as a disease, all the disease-oriented methods of treatment and resulting expenditures would be threatened; this in turn would threaten the material interests of hundreds of thousands of alcoholics and treatment staffers who receive these billions in funds. The other side of the coin would be many billions in savings for taxpayers and those who pay insurance premiums.

It is not surprising that the disease concept of alcoholism is now vigorously promoted by a vast network of lobbies, national and local, professional and volunteer, ranging from the most prestigious medical associations to the most crassly commercial private, profit-making providers of treatment. This is big politics and big business.

Use of the word "disease" also shapes the values and attitudes of society. The selling of the disease concept of alcoholism has led courts, legislatures, and the populace generally to view damage caused by heavy drinkers as a product of "the disease and not the drinker." The public remains ambivalent about this, and the criminal

Reprinted with permission of the author from *The Public Interest*, 91 (Spring 1988): 3–22. © 1988 by Herbert Fingarette. This article is a summary of material from the author's book *Heavy Drinking: The Myth of Alcoholism as a Disease* (Berkeley: University of California Press, 1989).

law continues to resist excusing alcoholics for criminal acts. But the pressure is there, and, of more practical importance, the civil law has largely given in. Civil law now often mandates leniency or complete absolution for the alcoholic from the rules, regulations, and moral norms to which non-diseased persons are held legally or morally accountable. Such is the thrust of a current appeal to the U.S. Supreme Court by two veterans, who are claiming certain benefits in spite of their having failed to apply for them at any time during the legally specified ten-year period after discharge from the army. Their excuse: alcoholism, and the claim that their persistent heavy drinking was a disease entitling them to exemption from the regulations. The Court's decision could be a bellwether.

What seems compassion when done in the name of "disease" turns out, when the facts are confronted, to subvert the drinker's autonomy and will to change, and to exacerbate a serious social problem. This is because the excuses and benefits offered heavy drinkers work psychologically as incentives to continue drinking. The doctrine that the alcoholic is "helpless" delivers the message that he might as well drink, since he lacks the ability to refrain. As for the expensive treatments, they do no real good. Certainly our current disease-oriented policies have not reduced the scale of the problem; in fact, the number of chronic heavy drinkers reported keeps rising. (It is currently somewhere in the range of ten to twenty million, depending on the definitions one uses.)

In the remainder of this discussion I will set out the major beliefs associated with the disease concept of alcoholism, and then summarize the actual evidence on each issue. I will also sketch an alternative perspective on chronic heavy drinking that is warranted by the evidence we have today.

CONVENTIONAL WISDOM

Science, according to the conventional view, has established that there is a specific disease that is triggered by drinking alcoholic beverages. Not everyone is susceptible; most people are not. But (the argument continues) a significant minority of the population has a distinctive biological vulnerability, an "allergy" to alcohol. For these people, to start drinking is to start down a fatal road. The stages are well defined and develop in regular order, as with any disease, with the symptoms accumulating and becoming increasingly disabling and demoralizing. First comes what looks like normal social drinking, but then, insidiously and inevitably, come heavier and more frequent drinking, drunken bouts, secret drinking, morning drinking, and, after a while, "blackouts" of memory from the night before. It begins to take more and more liquor to get the same effect—physical "tolerance" develops—and any attempt to stop drinking brings on the unbearable and potentially life-threatening "withdrawal" symptoms. Eventually, the crucial symptom develops: "loss of control." At that point, whenever the person takes a drink, the alcohol automatically triggers an inability to control the drinking, and drunken bouts become the rule. There follows an inevitable, deepening slavery to alcohol, which wrecks social life, brings ruin, and culminates in death. The only escape—according to this elaborate myth—is appropriate medical treatment for the disease.

The myth offers the false hope that as a result of recent "breakthroughs" in science we now basically understand what causes the disease—a genetic and neurophysiological defect. But fortunately, it is claimed, medical treatment is available, and generally produces excellent results. However, the argument continues, even after successful treatment the alcoholic can never drink again. The "allergy" is never cured; the disease is in remission, but the danger remains. The lifelong truth for the alcoholic is, as the saying goes, "one drink—one drunk." The possibility of a normal life depends on complete abstinence from alcohol. There are no "cured" alcoholics, only "recovering" ones.

That is the classical disease concept of alcoholism. As I have said, just about every statement in it is either known to be false or (at a minimum) lacks scientific foundation.

ORIGINS OF THE MYTH

Before turning to the substance of the specific claims, it helps to be aware of the historical context. For it is important to recognize that the disease concept of alcoholism not only has no basis in current science: it has *never* had a scientific justification.

The understanding of alcoholism as a disease first surfaced in the early nineteenth century. The growing popularity of materialistic and mechanistic views bolstered the doctrine that drinking problems stemmed from a simple malfunctioning of the bodily machinery. The new idea was popularized by Benjamin Rush, one of the leading medical theorists of the day.

Rush's claim was ideological, not scientific, since neither Rush nor anyone else at that time had the experimental facilities or the biological knowledge to justify it. It seemed plausible because of its compatibility with the crude biological theories of the time, assumptions that we now know to be erroneous. Nevertheless, the idea seized the public imagination, in part because it appealed to the growing mercantile and manufacturing classes, whose demand for a disciplining "work ethic" (especially among the working class) was supported by this new "scientific" indictment of drinking. We should realize that the nineteenth-century version of the doctrine, as advanced by the politically powerful temperance movement, indicted *all* drinking. Alcohol (like heroin today) was viewed as inherently addictive. The drinker's personal characteristics and situation were considered irrelevant.

The nineteenth-century temperance movement crested in 1919 with the enactment of the Prohibition Amendment; but by 1933 the idea of total prohibition had lost credibility, and the amendment was repealed. For one thing, the public no longer accepted the idea that no one at all could drink alcohol safely. In addition, the costs of prohibition—such as gangsterism and public cynicism about the law—had become too high. Most people wanted to do openly and legally, in a civilized way, what large numbers of people had been doing surreptitiously.

For the temperance impulse to survive, it had to be updated in a way that did not stigmatize all drinking on moral or medical grounds. Any new anti-alcohol movement had to be more selective in its target, by taking into account the desires of drinkers generally, as well as the interests of the now legal (and growing) alcoholic beverage industry.

A new sect arose with just the right formula. Alcoholics Anonymous, founded in 1935, taught that alcohol was not the villain in and of itself, and that most people could drink safely. (In this way the great majority of drinkers and the beverage industry were mollified.) A minority of potential drinkers, however, were said to have a peculiar biological vulnerability; these unfortunates, it was held, are "allergic" to alcohol, so that their drinking activates the disease, which then proceeds insidiously along the lines outlined earlier.

This contemporary version of the disease theory of alcoholism, along with subsequent minor variants of the theory, is often referred to now as the "classic" disease concept of alcoholism. Like the temperance doctrine, the new doctrine was not based on any scientific research or discovery. It was created by the two ex-alcoholics who founded A.A.: William Wilson, a New York stockbroker, and Robert Holbrook Smith, a physician from Akron, Ohio. Their ideas in turn were inspired by the Oxford religious movement, and by the ideas of another physician, William Silkworth. They attracted a small following, and a few sympathetic magazine articles helped the movement grow.

What A.A. still needed was something that would serve as a scientific authority for its tenets. After all, the point of speaking of a "disease" was to suggest science, medicine, and an objective malfunction of the body. The classic disease theory of alcoholism was given just such an apparent scientific confirmation in 1946. A respected scientist, E. M. Jellinek, published a lengthy scientific article, consisting of eighty-plus pages impressively filled with charts and figures. He carefully defined what he called the "phases of alcoholism," which went in a regular pattern, from apparently innocent social drinking ever downward to doom. The portrait, overall and in its detail, largely mirrored the A.A. portrait of the alcoholic. Jellinek's work and A.A. proselytizing generated an unfaltering momentum; the disease concept that they promulgated has never been publicly supplanted by the prosaic truth.

Jellinek's portrait of the "phases of alcoholism" was not an independent scientific confirmation of A.A. doctrine. For as Jellinek explicitly stated, his data derived entirely from a sampling of A.A. members, a small fraction of whom had answered and mailed back a questionnaire that had appeared in the A.A. newsletter. The questionnaire was prepared by A.A. members, not by Jellinek; Jellinek himself criticized it, finding it scientifically inadequate. In addition, many A.A. members did not even subscribe to the newsletter, and so had no opportunity to respond. Jellinek obtained only 158 questionnaires, but for various reasons could actually use just 98 of them. This was a grossly inadequate set of data, of course, but it was all Jellinek had to work with.

Predictably, the data from these ninety-eight questionnaires generated a portrait of alcoholism that coincided with the A.A. portrait. Since Jellinek was a reputable scientist, it is not surprising that he pointed to the various limitations of the data base and the highly tentative nature of his conclusions. It is equally unsurprising that A.A. propagandists publicized the impressively charted and statistically annotated portrait drawn by Jellinek, but glossed over his scholarly reservations about the hypotheses and data.

The "alcoholism movement," as it has come to be called among those familiar with the facts, has grown at an accelerating rate. Its growth results from the cumulative effect of the great number of drinkers indoctrinated by A.A., people who passionately identify themselves with the A.A. portrait of "the alcoholic." A.A. has vigorously supported the idea of "treatment" for alcoholics; in turn, the rapidly proliferating "treatment" centers for the "disease of alcoholism" have generally supported A.A. All this has generated a kind of snowballing effect.

By the 1970s there were powerful lobbying organizations in place at all levels of government. The National Council on Alcoholism (NCA), for example, which has propagated the disease concept of alcoholism, has been a major national umbrella group from the early days of the movement. Until 1982 the NCA was subsidized by the liquor industry, which had several representatives on its board. The alliance was a natural one: at the cost of conceding that a small segment of the population is allergic to alcohol and ought not to drink, the liquor industry gained a freer hand with which to appeal to the majority of people, who are ostensibly not allergic.

Health professionals further widened the net, and economic incentives came powerfully into play. Federal and local governments began to open their health budgets to providers of alcoholism treatment, and also to alcoholism researchers. Insurance companies are increasingly required to do the same. Today, treatment aimed at getting alcoholics to stop drinking brings in over a billion dollars a year. Alcoholism researchers now rely on what is probably the second largest funding source after defense—government health funds. And by now there are hundreds of thousands of former heavy drinkers who feel an intense emotional commitment; they supply a large proportion of the staffs of treatment centers.

Large and powerful health-professional organizations (such as the American Medical Association) now have internal constituencies whose professional power and wealth derive from their role as the authorities responsible for dealing with the "disease" of alcoholism. As usual, these interest constituencies lobby internally, and the larger organization is persuaded to take an official stand in favor of the meaningless slogan, "alcoholism is a disease." Thus there are many health organizations that now endorse this slogan.

Judges, legislators, and bureaucrats all have a stake in the doctrine. They can now with clear consciences get the intractable social problems posed by heavy drinkers off their agenda by compelling or persuading these unmanageable people to go elsewhere—that is, to get "treatment." Why should these public officials mistrust—or want to mistrust—this safe-as-motherhood way of getting troublesome problems off their backs while winning popular approval? The ample evidence that these "treatment" programs are ineffective, and waste considerable amounts of money and resources, is ignored.

THE "PHASES OF ALCOHOLISM"

The "phases-of-alcoholism" portrait of the alcoholic has been examined in detail in a number of major studies dating back to the 1960s. A recent summary of the scientific literature on this topic indicates that the typical drinking pattern is characterized by much fluctuating between levels of consumption. Thus, many drinkers with numerous and severe problems are found later to have markedly improved, or to have developed different problems. Some also deteriorate. Individual drinkers do not develop in any consistent pattern, nor do they remain stable in a single pattern. Some claim "loss of control"; others do not. Many report no social problems associated with their drinking (and so, not surprisingly, many heavy drinkers are not recognized as such by friends, colleagues, or even family).

One of the leading scientists in the field, Marc Schuckit, summarizes the evidence as to whether alcoholics drink persistently by pointing out that "in any given month, one half of alcoholics will be abstinent, with a mean of four months of being dry in any one-year to two-year period." In general, as George Vaillant has reported, the cumulative evidence is that during any reasonably long period (ten to twenty years), roughly one-third of alcoholics "mature out" into various forms of moderate drinking or abstinence. The rate of "maturing out" for heavy problem drinkers—including those not diagnosed as alcoholics—is substantially higher.

A number of factors are associated with rates of "natural" improvement (i.e., improvement independent of any formal treatment): higher socioeconomic class, greater education, regular employment, and being married are positively associated with higher improvement rates. Those who "mature out" at lower than average rates tend to be socially deprived and alienated. "None of this," says one specialist on the topic, "fits with the disease model of alcoholism insofar as that model implies keeping early symptoms and early problems and adding others as time passes." Certainly none of this fits with the concept of a disease whose pattern of development is uniform, and essentially independent of individual social and cultural characteristics.

BIOLOGICAL CAUSES?

What does it mean to say that alcoholism is a disease? In public discussions in the news media, it is usually taken to mean that alcoholism has a single biological cause. "I believe [alcoholics] have a genetic predisposition and a certain kind of biochemistry that dooms you to be an alcoholic if you use alcohol." This is a characteristic remark, with what in this domain is a familiar kind of specious authority. The statement was printed in an alcoholism bulletin issued under the aegis of a University of California Extension Division Alcoholism Program. It appears in an interview with Kevin Bellows, a lay activist heading an international organization fighting alcoholism.

Lay activists are not alone in pressing this theme. When I was on a network talk-show recently, the physician on the panel—a man high in government alcoholism advisory councils—devoted most of his time to running through a list of recent research discoveries about the biological peculiarities of alcoholics. His thesis was that alcoholism is unquestionably a disease, and he plainly implied that it has a biological cause. What the lay audience does not realize is that the newly discovered biological phenomena can rarely be regarded as *causes* of chronic heavy drinking; instead, they are merely *associated* with chronic heavy drinking, or with intoxication. Nevertheless, the audience is led to infer that they play a causal role; in fact, we know that there are *no* decisive physical causes of alcoholism.

Long-term heavy drinking is undoubtedly an important contributing cause of bodily ailments—including major organ, nerve, circulatory, and tissue disorders. The illness and mortality rates of heavy drinkers are far higher than those of the population generally. Chronic heavy drinking is rivaled only by habitual smoking as a major contributor to the nation's hospital and morgue populations. But all this is the *effect* of drinking; the drinking behavior itself is the cause. Stop the behavior and you stop its terrible physical effects.

Another abnormal physical condition associated with heavy drinking is the appearance of biological "markers." These metabolic and other physiological conditions—statistically abnormal but not necessarily ailments in and of themselves—may often be present among alcoholics. More significantly, some of them are present in persons who are not and have not been alcoholics, but who have been identified on independent grounds as being at higher-than-average risk of eventually becoming alcoholics. Such "markers" can serve as warning signs for those at higher risk. It has been hypothesized that some of these biological "markers" may play a causal role in bringing about alcoholic patterns of drinking. The question is: What kind and what degree of causality are at issue?

One much discussed metabolic "marker" is the difference in the way those who are independently identified as being at higher risk oxidize alcohol into acetaldehyde and in turn metabolize the acetaldehyde. The toxic effects of acetaldehyde in the brain have led to speculation that it might play a key causal role in inducing alcoholism. Analogous claims have been made about the higher level of morphine-like substances that alcoholics secrete when they metabolize alcohol. As it happens (so often in these matters), there are serious difficulties in measuring acetaldehyde accurately, and the reported results remain inadequately confirmed. But these confirmation problems are problems of technique, and not of fundamental importance.

The substantive point, generally obscured by the excitement of new discovery, is that even if the existence of any such metabolic processes were confirmed, they still would not cause alcoholic behavior, because the metabolism of alcohol takes place only when there is alcohol in the body. Therefore, these metabolic products cannot be present in alcoholics who have not been drinking for a period of time, and in whom the total metabolic process in question is not presently taking place. Yet by definition, these individuals return to drinking and do so recurrently, in spite of the intermittent periods of sobriety. The metabolic phenomena bear only on drinking that is done while in a state of intoxication; the key question about alcoholism, however, is why a sober person, with no significant toxic product remaining in the body, should resume drinking when it is known to have such harmful effects.

The story of biological discoveries concerning alcoholism is always the same: many unconfirmed results are unearthed, but no causal link to repetitive drinking is ever established. There is one exception, however: the recent discoveries in genetics. A study of these, and of how they have been reported to the public, is revealing.

ALCOHOLISM AND GENES

Several excellently designed genetic studies of alcoholism have recently come up with credible positive results; thus we have been hearing from activists, treatment-center staff members, and physicians that "alcoholism is a genetic disease." The reality—as revealed by the data—is very different from what this slogan suggests.

The course followed in these recent "decisive" studies has been simple: find children who were born of an alcoholic mother or father, who were put up for adoption very shortly after birth, and who thus spent little time with their biological parents. Then see whether this group of children shows a higher rate of alcoholism in later life than a comparable group of adoptees whose biological parents were not alcoholics. Controlling all other relevant conditions so that they are the same for both groups, one can infer that any eventual differences in the group rates of alcoholism are attributable to their heredity, the one respect in which they differ. In all these studies, the prevalence of alcoholism was significantly greater among the biological sons of alcoholics, especially the sons of alcoholic fathers. Doesn't this suggest that alcoholism is hereditary?

To answer this question, let us consider the first of these reports, a 1973 article by Donald Goodwin and his colleagues. They concluded that about 18 percent of the biological sons of an alcoholic parent themselves became alcoholics, whereas only 5 percent of the biological sons of non-alcoholic parents became alcoholics—a statistically significant ratio of almost four to one, which in all probability is ascribable to heredity. This is what we typically hear about in the media, with or without the precise numbers.

Now let's look at the same data from a different angle, and in a more meaningful context. As simple arithmetic tells us, if 18 percent of the sons of alcoholics do become alcoholics, then 82 percent—more than four out of five—do *not*. Thus, to generalize from the Goodwin data, we can say that the odds are very high—better than four to one—that the son born of an alcoholic parent will *not* become an alcoholic. Put differently, it is utterly false, and perniciously misleading, to tell people with a parental background of alcoholism that their heredity "dooms" them to become alcoholics, or even that their heredity makes it probable that they will become alcoholics. Quite the contrary. Their alcoholic heredity does make it more probable that they'll become alcoholics than if they had non-alcoholic parents, but the probability is still low. This is to say that life circumstances are far more important than genes in determining how many people in any group will become heavy drinkers.

There is yet another important implication: since 5 percent of the sons of non-alcoholic parents become alcoholics, and since there are far more non-alcoholic parents than alcoholic ones, that 5 percent ends up representing a far larger total number of alcoholic sons. This is consistent with what we know anyway—the great majority of alcoholics do not have alcoholic parents.

The most recent (and influential) adoptee genetic study, reported by Cloninger and his colleagues, concludes with these words: "The demonstration of the critical importance of sociocultural influences in most alcoholics suggests that major changes in social attitudes about drinking styles can change dramatically the prevalence of alcohol abuse regardless of genetic predisposition."

Given the possibly dramatic effect of social attitudes and beliefs, the media emphasis on genes as the cause of alcoholism has a pernicious, though unremarked, effect. As we have noted, only a minority of alcoholics have an alcoholic parent. Emphasis on heredity as the "cause" of alcoholism may give a false sense of assurance to the far greater number of people who are in fact in danger of becoming alcoholics, but who do not have an alcoholic parent. These potential alcoholics may feel free to drink heavily, believing themselves genetically immune to the "disease."

The Special Committee of the Royal College of Psychiatry put the matter in perspective by saying the following in its book-length statement on alcoholism: "It is common to find that some genetic contribution can be established for many aspects of human attributes or disorders (ranging from musical ability to duodenal ulcers), and drinking is unlikely to be the exception."

CAUSES OF ALCOHOLISM

There is a consensus among scientists that no single cause of alcoholism, biological or otherwise, has ever been scientifically established. There are many causal factors, and they vary from drinking pattern to drinking pattern, from drinker to drinker. We already know many of the predominant influences that evoke or shape patterns of drinking. We know that family environment plays a role, as does age. Ethnic and cultural values are also important: the Irish, Scandinavians, and Russians tend to be heavy drinkers; Jews do not. The French traditionally drank modest amounts at one sitting, but drank more regularly over the course of the day. Cultural norms have changed in France in recent decades and so have drinking styles.

We have interesting anthropological reports about the introduction of European styles of drinking into non-European tribal societies. Among the Chichicastenango Indians of Guatemala, for example, there are two different ways of drinking heavily. When drinking ceremonially, in the traditional way, men retain their dignity and fulfill their ceremonial duties even if they have drunk so much that they cannot walk unassisted. When they drink in the bars and taverns where secular and European values and culture hold sway, the men dance, weep, quarrel, and act promiscuously.

The immediate social setting and its cultural meaning are obviously important in our own society. The amount and style of drinking typically vary according to whether the drinker is in a bar, at a formal dinner party, a post-game party, or an employee get-together. It is known that situations of frustration or tension, and the desire for excitement, pleasure, or release from feelings of fatigue or social inhibitions, often lead people to drink. Much depends on what the individual has "learned" from the culture about the supposed effects of alcohol, and whether the person desires those particular effects at a particular moment.

But does any of this apply to alcoholics? The belief in a unique disease of alcoholism leads many to wonder whether the sorts of influences mentioned above can make much of a difference when it comes to the supposedly "overwhelming craving" of alcoholics. Once one realizes that there is no distinct group of "diseased" drinkers, however, one is less surprised to learn that no group of drinkers is immune to such influences or is vulnerable only to other influences.

DO ALCOHOLICS LACK CONTROL?

In fact, alcoholics do have substantial control over their drinking, and they do respond to circumstances. Contrary to what the public has been led to believe, this is not disputed by experts. Many studies have described conditions under which diagnosed alcoholics will drink moderately or excessively, or will choose not to drink at all. Far from being driven by an overwhelming "craving," they turn out to be responsive to common incentives and disincentives, to appeals and arguments, to rules and regulations. Alcohol does not automatically trigger uncontrolled drinking. Resisting our usual appeals and ignoring reasons we consider forceful are not results of alcohol's chemical effect but of the fact that the heavy drinker has different values, fears, and strategies. Thus, in their usual settings alcoholics behave without concern for what others regard as rational considerations.

But when alcoholics in treatment in a hospital setting, for example, are told that they are not to drink, they typically follow the rule. In some studies they have been informed that alcoholic beverages are available, but that they should abstain. Having decided to cooperate, they voluntarily refrain from drinking. More significantly, it has been reported that the occasional few who cheated nevertheless did not drink to excess but voluntarily limited themselves to a drink or two in order to keep their rule violation from being detected. In short, when what they value is at stake, alcoholics control their drinking accordingly.

Alcoholics have been tested in situations in which they can perform light but boring work to "earn" liquor; their preference is to avoid the boring activity and forgo the additional drinking. When promised money if they drink only moderately, they drink moderately enough to earn the money. When threatened with denial of social privileges if they drink more than a certain amount, they drink moderately, as directed. The list of such experiments is extensive. The conclusions are easily confirmed by carefully observing one's own heavy-drinking acquaintances, provided one ignores the stereotype of "the alcoholic."

Some people object that these experiments take place in "protected" settings and are therefore invalid. This gets things backwards. The point is that it is precisely settings, circumstances, and motivations that are the crucial influences on how alcoholics choose to drink. The alcohol per se—either its availability or its actual presence in the person's system—is not decisive.

Indeed, the alcohol per se or its ready availability seems to be irrelevant to how the alcoholic drinks. Among the most persuasive experiments demonstrating the irrelevance of alcohol to the alcoholic's drinking are several studies in which alcoholic subjects were deceived about whether they were drinking an alcoholic or non-alcoholic beverage. Alan Marlatt and his colleagues, for example, asked a group of alcoholics to help them "taste-rate" three different brands of the same beverage. Each individual subject was installed in a private room with three large pitchers of beverage, each pitcher supposedly containing a different brand of the same beverage. Their task, of course, was phony. Unknown to them, the subjects had been assigned to one of four groups. One group was told that the beverage in the three pitchers was tonic water—which was true. But a second group was told that the beverage was a tonic-and-vodka mix—though in fact it, too, was pure tonic water. Those in the third group were told that the beverage was tonic-and-vodka—which in fact it was. Those in the fourth group were told that it was simply tonic water—whereas in fact it too was tonic-and-vodka. The subjects were left alone (actually observed through a one-way window) and allowed to "taste" the drinks at will, which they did. The total amount drunk and the rapidity of sips were secretly recorded.

The results of this study (and several similar ones) were illuminating. First, none of the alcoholic subjects drank all the beverage—even though, according to the disease theory, those who were actually drinking vodka ought to have proceeded to drink uncontrollably. Second, all of those who believed they were drinking vodka—whether they really were or had been deceived—drank more and faster. Conversely, all of those who believed they were drinking pure tonic—though some were actually drinking vodka—drank less and more slowly. The inference is unambiguous: the actual presence or absence of alcohol in the system made no difference in the drinking pattern; what the alcoholics *believed* was in the beverage did make a difference—in fact, all the difference.

These results fit into a more general pattern revealed by similar experiments on other aspects of alcohol-related behavior in both alcoholics and non-alcoholics: change the beliefs about the presence of alcohol (or the effect it is supposed to have), and the behavior changes. But the alcohol itself plays no measurable role.

Mark Keller, one of the early leaders of the alcoholism movement, has responded to such evidence by redefining (or as he would say, "reexplaining") the key concept of "loss of control." We are now told that this concept never connoted an automatically induced inability to stop drinking. Like other sophisticated advocates of the disease concept, Keller now means that one "can't be sure." The alcoholic who has resolved to stop drinking may or may not stand by his resolution. We are told that "loss of control" is compatible, though unpredictably, with temporary, long-term, or indefinite remission. Here medical terms such as "remission" provide a facade of scientific expertise, but the substance of what we are told is that "loss of control" is consistent with just about anything. This precludes prediction, and of course explains nothing. If it retains any empirical content at all, it amounts to a platitude: someone who for years has relied on a certain way of handling life's stresses may resolve to change, but he or she "can't be sure" whether that promise will be fully kept. This is reasonable. But it is not a scientific explanation of an inner process that causes drinking.

Similarly, the idea that "craving" causes the alcoholic to drink uncontrollably has been tacitly modified. It was plausible in its original sense, which is still the popular understanding: an inordinately powerful, "overwhelming," and "irresistible" desire. But the current experimental work regards "mild craving" as a form of "craving." Of course the whole point of "craving" as an explanation of a supposed irresistible compulsion to drink is abandoned here. But the *word* is retained—and the public is misled.

There have been other adjustments in response to new evidence, designed to retain the "disease" terminology at whatever cost. We now read that "of course alcoholism is an illness that consists of not just one but many diseases, having different forms and causes." We also hear—in pronouncements addressed to more knowledgeable audiences—that alcoholism is a disease with biological, psychological, social, cultural, economic, and even spiritual dimensions, all of them important. This is a startling amplification of the meaning of "disease," to the point where it can refer to *any* human problem. It is an important step toward expanding the medicalization of human problems—a trend that has been deservedly criticized in recent years.

A USEFUL LIE?

Even if the disease concept lacks a scientific foundation, mightn't it nevertheless be a useful social "white lie," since it causes alcoholics to enter treatment? This common—and plausible—argument suffers from two fatal flaws.

First, it disregards the effects of this doctrine on the large number of heavy drinkers who do not plan to enter treatment. Many of these heavy drinkers see themselves (often correctly) as not fitting the criteria of "alcoholism" under some current diagnostic formula. The inference they draw is that they are therefore not ill, and thus have no cause for concern. Their inclination to deny their problems is thus encouraged. This can be disastrous, since persistent heavy drinking is physically, mentally, and often socially destructive.

Furthermore, since most people diagnosable as alcoholics today do not enter treatment, the disease concept insidiously provides an incentive to keep drinking heavily. For those many alcoholics who do not enter treatment and who (by definition) want very much to have a drink, the disease doctrine assures them that they might as well do so, since an effort to refrain is doomed anyway.

Moreover, a major implication of the disease concept, and a motive for promoting it, is that what is labeled "disease" is held to be excusable because involuntary. Special benefits are provided alcoholics in employment, health, and civil-rights law. The motivation behind this may be humane and compassionate, but what it does functionally is to reward people who continue to drink heavily. This is insidious: the only known way to have the drinker stop drinking is to establish circumstances that provide a motivation to stop drinking, not an excuse to continue. The U.S. Supreme Court currently faces this issue in two cases before it. And the criminal courts have thus far resisted excusing alcoholics from criminal responsibility for their misconduct. But it's difficult to hold this line when the AMA insists the misconduct is involuntary.

The second flaw in the social "white lie" argument is the mistaken assumption that use of the word "disease" leads alcoholics to seek a medical treatment that works. In fact, medical treatment for alcoholism is ineffective. Medical authority has been abused for the purpose of enlisting public faith in a useless treatment for which Americans have paid more than a billion dollars. To understand why the treatment does no good, we should recall that many different kinds of studies of alcoholics have shown substantial rates of so-called natural improvement. As a 1986 report concludes, "the vast majority of [addicted] persons who change do so on their own." This "natural" rate of improvement, which varies according to class, age, socioeconomic status, and certain other psychological and social variables, lends credibility to the claims of success made by programs that "treat" the "disease" of alcoholism.

Many of the clients—and, in the expensive programs, almost all of the clients—are middle-class, middle-aged people, who are intensely motivated to change, and whose families and social relations are still intact. Many, often most,

are much improved by the time they complete the program. They are, of course, delighted with the change; they paid money and went through an emotional ordeal, and now receive renewed affection and respect from their family, friends, and co-workers. They had been continually told during treatment that they were helpless, and that only treatment could save them. Many of them fervently believe that they could never have been cured without the treatment.

The sound and the fury signify nothing, however; for the rates of improvement in these disease-oriented treatment programs do not significantly differ from the natural rates of improvement for comparable but untreated demographic groups. That is to say, these expensive programs (which cost between $5000 and $20,000) contribute little or nothing to the improvement. Even so, the claims that patients leave their programs improved are true; to the layman such claims are impressive. The reality, however, is less impressive, since over half a dozen major studies in the past two decades have concluded that the money, time, and trust expended on these treatments are badly spent.

There is some disagreement about the effectiveness of more modest forms of treatment. Some reports—for example, a major study done by Saxe and his colleagues for the Congressional Office of Technology Assessment—conclude that no single method of treatment is superior to any other (a judgment made by all the major studies). But according to the Saxe study, the data appear to show that "treatment seems better than no treatment." That is, some help-oriented intervention of any kind—it doesn't matter which—may contribute modestly to improvement. The now classic British experiment led by Griffith Edwards showed that an hour or so of firm and sensible advice produced overall results as good as those produced by a full year of the most complete and sophisticated treatment procedures in a first-class alcoholism hospital and clinic. Such conclusions have led a number of authorities (including a World Health Organization committee in 1980) to argue for brief informal counseling on an outpatient basis as the preferred method in most cases.

Note, however, that what is now recommended is not really *medical* treatment. Physicians may still control it, and the institutional setting may be "outpatient," but the assistance provided is merely brief, informal, common-sense advice. The medical setting merely adds unnecessary expense.

So much for the optimistic view about "treatment." A British report concludes that "it seems likely that treatment may often be quite puny in its powers in comparison to the sum of [non-treatment] forces."

The more pessimistic reading of the treatment-outcome data is that these elaborate treatments for alcoholism as a disease have no measurable impact at all. In a review of a number of different long-term studies of treatment programs, George Vaillant states that "there is compelling evidence that the results of our treatment were no better than the natural history of the disease." Reviewing other major treatment programs with long-term follow-ups, he remarks that the best that can be said is that these programs do no harm.

NEW APPROACHES

In recent years, early evaluation studies have been reexamined from a non-disease perspective, which has produced interesting results. For example, it appears that the heaviest and longest-term drinkers improve more than would be expected "naturally" when they are removed from their daily routine and relocated, with complete abstinence as their goal. This group is only a small subset of those diagnosable as alcoholics, of course. The important point, though, is that it is helpful to abandon the one-disease, one-treatment approach, and to differentiate among the many different patterns of drinking, reasons for drinking, and modes of helping drinkers.

Indeed, when we abandon the single-entity disease approach and view alcoholism pluralistically, many new insights and strategies emerge. For example, much depends on the criteria of success that are used. The disease concept focuses attention on only one criterion—total, permanent abstinence. Only a small percentage of alcoholics ever achieve this abolitionist goal. But a pluralistic view encourages us to value other achievements, and to measure success by other standards. Thus, marked improvement is quite common when one takes as measures of success additional days on the job, fewer days in the hospital, smaller quantities of alcohol drunk, more moderate drinking on any one occasion, and fewer alcohol-related domestic problems or police incidents. The Rand Report found that about 42 percent of heavy drinkers with withdrawal symptoms had reverted to somewhat more moderate drinking with no associated problems at the end of four years. Yet, as non-abstainers, they would count as failures from the disease-concept standpoint.

The newer perspective also suggests a different conception of the road to improvement. Instead of hoping for a medical magic bullet that will cure the disease, the goal here is to change the way drinkers live. One should learn from one's mistakes, rather than viewing any one mistake as a proof of failure or a sign of doom. Also consistent with the newer pluralistic, non-disease approach is the selection of specific strategies and tactics for helping different sorts of drinkers; methods and goals are tailored to the individual in ways that leave the one-disease, one-treatment approach far behind.

Much controversy remains about pluralistic goals. One of the most fiercely debated issues is whether so-called "controlled drinking" is a legitimate therapeutic goal. Some contend that controlled drinking by an alcoholic inevitably leads to uncontrolled drinking. Disease-concept lobbies, such as the National Council on Alcoholism, have tried to suppress scientific publications reporting success with controlled drinking, and have excoriated them upon publication. Some have argued that publishing such data can "literally kill alcoholics." Authors of scientific studies, such as Mark and Linda Sobell, have been accused of fraud by their opponents (though expert committees have affirmed the scientific integrity of the Sobells' work). Attacks like these have been common since 1962, when D. L. Davies merely reviewed the literature and summarized the favorable results already reported in a number of published studies—and was severely criticized for doing so. But since that time hundreds of similar reports have appeared. One recent study concludes that most formerly heavy drinkers who are now socially adjusted become social drinkers rather than abstainers.

In any case, the goal of total abstinence insisted upon by advocates of the disease concept is not a proven successful alternative, since only a small minority achieves it. If doubt remains as to whether the controversy over controlled drinking is fueled by non-scientific factors, that doubt can be dispelled by realizing that opposition to controlled drinking (like support for the disease concept of alcoholism) is largely confined to the U.S. and to countries dominated by American intellectual influence. Most physicians in Britain, for example, do not adhere to the disease concept of alcoholism. And the goal of controlled drinking—used selectively but extensively—is widely favored in Canada and the United Kingdom. British physicians have little professional or financial incentive to bring problem drinkers into their consulting rooms or hospitals. American physicians, in contrast, defend an enormous growth in institutional power and fee-for-service income. The selling of the term "disease" has been the key to this vast expansion of medical power and wealth in the United States.

What should our attitude be, then, to the long-term heavy drinker? Alcoholics do not knowingly make the wicked choice to be drunkards. Righteous condemnation and punitive moralism are therefore inappropriate. Compassion, not abuse, should be shown toward any human being launched upon a destructive way of life. But compassion must be realistic: it is not compassionate to encourage drinkers to deny their power to change, to assure them that they are helpless and dependent on others, to excuse them legally and give them special government benefits that foster a refusal to confront the need to change. Alcoholics are not helpless; they can take control of their lives. In the last analysis, alcoholics must *want* to change and *choose* to change. To do so they must make many difficult daily choices. We can help them by offering moral support and good advice, and by assisting them in dealing with their genuine physical ailments and social needs. But we must also make it clear that heavy drinkers must take responsibility for their own lives. Alcoholism is not a disease; the assumption of personal responsibility, however, is a sign of health, while needless submission to spurious medical authority is a pathology.

Shifts and Oscillations in Deviant Careers: The Case of Upper-Level Drug Dealers and Smugglers

PATRICIA A. ADLER

PETER ADLER
University of Tulsa

This is the first study of drug trafficking in the United States to penetrate the upper echelons of the marijuana and cocaine business—the smugglers and their primary dealers. We spent six years observing and interviewing these traffickers and their associates in southwestern California and examining their typical career paths. We show how drug traffickers enter the business and rise to the top, how they become disenchanted due to the rising social and legal costs of upper-level drug trafficking, how and why they either voluntarily or involuntarily leave the business, and why so many end up returning to their deviant careers, or to other careers within the drug world.

The upper echelons of the marijuana and cocaine trade constitute a world which has never before been researched and analyzed by sociologists. Importing and distributing tons of marijuana and kilos of cocaine at a time, successful operators can earn upwards of a half million dollars per year. Their traffic in these so-called soft[1] drugs constitutes a potentially lucrative occupation, yet few participants manage to accumulate any substantial sums of money, and most people envision their involvement in drug trafficking as only temporary. In this study we focus on the career paths followed by members of one upper-level drug dealing and smuggling community. We discuss the various modes of entry into trafficking at these upper levels, contrasting these with entry into middle- and low-level trafficking. We then describe the pattern of shifts and oscillations these dealers and smugglers experience. Once they reach the top rungs of their occupation, they begin periodically quitting and re-entering the field, often changing their degree and type of involvement upon their return. Their careers, therefore, offer insights into the problems involved in leaving deviance.

Previous research on soft drug trafficking has only addressed the low and middle levels of this occupation, portraying people who purchase no more than 100 kilos of marijuana or single ounces of cocaine at a time (Anonymous, 1969; Atkyns and Hanneman, 1974; Blum et al.,

An earlier version of this paper was presented at the annual meetings of the American Society of Criminology, Denver, Colorado, November 1983. Correspondence to: Department of Sociology, University of Tulsa, Tulsa, Oklahoma 74104.

The term "soft" drugs generally refers to marijuana, cocaine and such psychedelics as LSD and mescaline (Carey, 1968). In this paper we do not address trafficking in psychedelics because, since they are manufactured in the United States, they are neither imported nor distributed by the group we studied.

From the article originally published in *Social Problems*, Vol. 31, No. 2 (December 1983): 195–207. © 1983 by the Society for the Study of Social Problems. Used with permission.

1972; Carey, 1968; Goode, 1970; Langer, 1977; Lieb and Olson, 1976; Mouledoux, 1972; Waldorf et al., 1977). Of these, only Lieb and Olson (1976) have examined dealing and/or smuggling as an occupation, investigating participants' career developments. But their work, like several of the others, focuses on a population of student dealers who may have been too young to strive for and attain the upper levels of drug trafficking. Our study fills this gap at the top by describing and analyzing an elite community of upper-level dealers and smugglers and their careers.

We begin by describing where our research took place, the people and activities we studied, and the methods we used. Second, we outline the process of becoming a drug trafficker, from initial recruitment through learning the trade. Third, we look at the different types of upward mobility displayed by dealers and smugglers. Fourth, we examine the career shifts and oscillations which veteran dealers and smugglers display, outlining the multiple, conflicting forces which lure them both into and out of drug trafficking. We conclude by suggesting a variety of paths which dealers and smugglers pursue out of drug trafficking and discuss the problems inherent in leaving this deviant world.

SETTING AND METHOD

We based our study in "Southwest County," one section of a large metropolitan area in southwestern California near the Mexican border. Southwest County consisted of a handful of beach towns dotting the Pacific Ocean, a location offering a strategic advantage for wholesale drug trafficking.

Southwest County smugglers obtained their marijuana in Mexico by the ton and their cocaine in Colombia, Bolivia, and Peru, purchasing between 10 and 40 kilos at a time. These drugs were imported into the United States along a variety of land, sea, and air routes by organized smuggling crews. Southwest County dealers then purchased these products and either "middled" them directly to another buyer for a small but immediate profit of approximately $2 to $5 per kilo of marijuana and $5000 per kilo of

cocaine, or engaged in "straight dealing." As opposed to middling, straight dealing usually entailed adulterating the cocaine with such "cuts" as manitol, procaine, or inositol, and then dividing the marijuana and cocaine into smaller quantities to sell them to the next-lower level of dealers. Although dealers frequently varied the amounts they bought and sold, a hierarchy of transacting levels could be roughly discerned. "Wholesale" marijuana dealers bought directly from the smugglers, purchasing anywhere from 300 to 1000 "bricks" (averaging a kilo in weight) at a time and selling in lots of 100 to 300 bricks. "Multi-kilo" dealers, while not the smugglers' first connections, also engaged in upper-level trafficking, buying between 100 to 300 bricks and selling them in 25 to 100 brick quantities. These were then purchased by middle-level dealers who filtered the marijuana through low-level and "ounce" dealers before it reached the ultimate consumer. Each time the marijuana changed hands its price increase was dependent on a number of factors: purchase cost; the distance it was transported (including such transportation costs as packaging, transportation equipment, and payments to employees); the amount of risk assumed; the quality of the marijuana; and the prevailing prices in each local drug market. Prices in the cocaine trade were much more predictable. After purchasing kilos of cocaine in South America for $10,000 each, smugglers sold them to Southwest County "pound" dealers in quantities of one to 10 kilos for $60,000 per kilo. These pound dealers usually cut the cocaine and sold pounds ($30,000) and half-pounds ($15,000) to "ounce" dealers, who in turn cut it again and sold ounces for $2000 each to middle-level cocaine dealers known as "cut-ounce" dealers. In this fashion the drug was middled, dealt, divided and cut—sometimes as many as five or six times—until it was finally purchased by consumers as grams or half-grams.

Unlike low-level operators, the upper-level dealers and smugglers we studied pursued drug trafficking as a full-time occupation. If they were involved in other businesses, these were usually maintained to provide them with a legitimate front for security purposes. The profits to be made at the upper levels depended on an individual's style of operation, reliability, security, and the amount of product he or she consumed. About half of the 65 smugglers and dealers we observed were successful, some earning up to three-quarters of a million dollars per year.[2] The other half continually struggled in the business, either breaking even or losing money.

Although dealers' and smugglers' business activities varied, they clustered together for business and social relations, forming a moderately well-integrated community whose members pursued a "fast" lifestyle, which emphasized intensive partying, casual sex, extensive travel, abundant drug consumption, and lavish spending on consumer goods. The exact size of Southwest County's upper-level dealing and smuggling community was impossible to estimate due to the secrecy of its members. At these levels, the drug world was quite homogeneous. Participants were predominantly white, came from middle-class backgrounds, and had little previous criminal involvement. While the dealers' and smugglers' social world contained both men and women, most of the serious business was conducted by the men, ranging in age from 25 to 40 years old.

We gained entry to Southwest County's upper-level drug community largely by accident. We had become friendly with a group of our neighbors who turned out to be heavily involved in smuggling marijuana. Opportunistically (Riemer, 1977), we seized the chance to gather data on this unexplored activity. Using key informants who helped us gain the trust of other members of the community, we drew upon snowball sampling techniques (Biernacki and Waldorf, 1981) and a combination of overt and covert roles to widen our network of contacts. We supplemented intensive participant-observation, between 1974 and 1980,[3] with unstructured, taped interviews. Throughout, we employed extensive measures to cross-check the reliability of our data, whenever

possible (Douglas, 1976). In all, we were able to closely observe 65 dealers and smugglers as well as numerous other drug world members, including dealers' "old ladies" (girlfriends or wives), friends, and family members.

BECOMING A DRUG TRAFFICKER

There are three routes into the upper levels of drug dealing and smuggling. First, some drug users become low-level dealers, gradually working their way up to middle-level dealing. It is rare, however, for upper-level dealers to have such meager origins. Second, there are people who enter directly into drug dealing at the middle level, usually from another occupation. Many of these do extremely well right away. Third, a number of individuals are invited into smuggling because of a special skill or character, sometimes from middle-level drug trafficking careers and other times from outside the drug world entirely. We discuss each of these in turn.

Low-Level Entry

People who began dealing at the bottom followed the classic path into dealing portrayed in the literature (Anonymous, 1969; Blum et al., 1972; Carey, 1968; Goode, 1970; Johnson, 1973). They came from among the ranks of regular drug users, since, in practice, using drugs heavily and dealing for "stash" (one's personal supply) are nearly inseparable. Out of this multitude of low-level dealers, however, most abandoned the practice after they encountered their first legal or financial bust, lasting in the business for only a fairly short period (Anonymous, 1969; Carey, 1968; Lieb and Olson, 1976; Mandel, 1967). Those who sought bigger profits gradually drifted into a full-time career in drug trafficking, usually between the ages of 15 and 22. Because of this early recruitment into

---

This is an idealized figure representing the profit a dealer or smuggler could potentially earn and does not include deductions for such miscellaneous and hard-to-calculate costs as: time or money spent in arranging deals (some of which never materialize); lost, stolen, or unpaid money or drugs; and the personal drug consumption of a drug trafficker and his or her entourage. Of these, the single largest expense is the last one, accounting for the bulk of most Southwest County dealers' and smugglers' earnings.

We continued to conduct follow-up interviews with key informants through 1983.

dealing as an occupation, low-level entrants generally developed few, if any, occupational skills other than dealing. One dealer described his early phase of involvement:

> I had dealt a limited amount of lids [ounces of marijuana] and psychedelics in my early college days without hardly taking it seriously. But after awhile something changed in me and I decided to try to work myself up. I probably was a classic case—started out buying a kilo for $150 and selling pounds for $100 each. I did that twice, then I took the money and bought two bricks, then three, then five, then seven.

This type of gradual rise through the ranks was characteristic of low-level dealers; however, few reached the upper levels of dealing from these humble beginnings. Only 20 percent of the dealers we observed in Southwest County got their start in this fashion. Two factors combined to make it less likely for low-level entrants to rise to the top. The first was psychological. People who started small, thought small; most had neither the motivation nor vision to move large quantities of drugs. The second, and more critical factor, was social. People who started at the bottom and tried to work their way up the ladder often had a hard time finding connections at the upper levels.[4] Dealers were suspicious of new customers, preferring, for security reasons, to deal with established outlets or trusted friends. The few people who did rise through the ranks generally began dealing in another part of the country, moving to Southwest County only after they had progressed to the middle levels. These people were lured to southwestern California by its reputation within drug circles as an importation and wholesale dealing market.

Middle-Level Entry

About 75 percent of the smugglers and dealers in Southwest County entered at the middle level. Future big dealers usually jumped into transacting in substantial quantities from the outset, buying 50 kilos of "commercial" (low-grade) marijuana or one to two ounces of cocaine. One dealer explained this phenomenon:

> Someone who thinks of himself as an executive or an entrepreneur is not going to get into the dope business on a small level. The average executive just jumps right into the middle. Or else he's not going to jump.

This was the route taken by Southwest County residents with little or no previous involvement in drug trafficking. For them, entry into dealing followed the establishment of social relationships with local dealers and smugglers. (Naturally, this implies a self-selecting sample of outsiders who become accepted and trusted by these upper-level traffickers, based on their mutual interests, orientation, and values.) Through their friendships with dealers, these individuals were introduced to other members of the dealing scene and to their "fast" lifestyle. Individuals who found this lifestyle attractive became increasingly drawn to the subculture, building networks of social associations within it. Eventually some of these people decided to participate more actively. This step was usually motivated both by money and lifestyle. One dealer recounted how he fell in with the drug world set:

> I used to be into real estate making good money. I was the only person at my firm renting to long hairs and dealing with their money. I slowly started getting friendly with them, although I didn't realize how heavy they were. I knew ways of buying real estate and putting it under fictitious names, laundering money so that it went in as hot cash and came out as spendable income. I slowly got more and more involved with this one guy until I was neglecting my real estate business and just partying with him all the time. My spending went up but my income went down and suddenly I had to look around for another way to make money fast. I took the money I was laundering for him, bought some bricks from another dealer friend of his, and sold them out of state before I gave him back the cash. Within six months I was turning [selling] 100 bricks at a time.

---

[4]The exception to this was where low-level dealers rose on the "coattails" of their suppliers: as one dealer increased the volume of his or her purchases or sales, some of his or her customers followed suit.

People who entered drug dealing at these middle levels were usually between the ages of 25 and 35 and had been engaged in some other occupation prior to dealing seriously. They came from a wide range of occupational backgrounds. Many drifted into the lifestyle from jobs already concentrated in the night hours, such as bartender, waiter, and nightclub bouncer. Still others came from fields where the working hours were irregular and adaptable to their special schedules, such as acting, real estate, inventing, graduate school, construction, and creative "entrepreneurship" (more aptly called hand-to-mouth survival, for many). The smallest group was tempted into the drug world from structured occupations and the professions.

Middle-level entrants had to learn the trade of drug trafficking. They received "on-the-job training" (Miller and Ritzer, 1977:89) in such skills as how to establish business connections, organize profitable transactions, avoid arrest, transport illegal goods, and coordinate participants and equipment. Dealers trained on-the-job refined their knowledge and skills by learning from their mistakes. One dealer recalled how he got "burned" with inferior quality marijuana on his first major "cop" [purchase] because of his inexperience:

I had borrowed around $7000 from this friend to do a dope deal. I had never bought in that kind of quantity before but I knew three or four guys who I got it from. I was nervous so I got really stoned before I shopped around and I ended up being hardly able to tell about the quality. Turned out you just couldn't get high off the stuff. I ended up having to sell it below cost.

Once they had gotten in and taught themselves the trade, most middle-level entrants strove for upward mobility. About 80 percent of these Southwest County dealers jumped to the upper levels of trafficking. One dealer described her mode of escalation:

When I started to deal I was mostly looking for a quick buck here or there, something to pay some pressing bill. I was middling 50 or 100 bricks at a time. But then I was introduced to a guy who said he would front me half a pound of coke, and if I turned it fast I could have more, and on a regular basis. Pretty soon I was turning six,

seven, eight, nine, 10 pounds a week—they were passing through real fast. I was clearing at least 10 grand a month. It was too much money too fast. I didn't know what to do with it. It got ridiculous, I wasn't relating to anyone anymore, I was never home, always gone. . . . The biggest ego trip for me came when all of a sudden I turned around and was selling to the people I had been buying from. I skipped their level of doing business entirely and stage-jumped right past them.

Southwest County's social milieu, with its concentration of upper-level dealers and smugglers, thus facilitated forming connections and doing business at the upper levels of the drug world.

Smuggling

Only 10 percent of Southwest County drug smugglers were formerly upper-level dealers who made the leap to smuggling on their own; the rest were invited to become smugglers by established operators. About half of those recruited came directly from the drug world's social scene, with no prior involvement in drug dealing. This implies, like middle-level entry into dealing, both an attraction to the drug crowd and its lifestyle, and prior acquaintance with dealers and smugglers. The other half of the recruits were solicited from among the ranks of middle-level Southwest County dealers.

The complex task of importing illegal drugs required more knowledge, experience, equipment, and connections than most non-smugglers possessed. Recruits had some skill or asset which the experienced smuggler needed to put his operation together. This included piloting or navigating ability, equipment, money, or the willingness to handle drugs while they were being transported. One smuggler described some of the criteria he used to screen potential recruits for suitability as employees in smuggling crews:

Pilots are really at a premium. They burn out so fast that I have to replace them every six months to a year. But I'm also looking for people who are cool: people who will carry out their jobs according to the plan, who won't panic if the load arrives late or something goes wrong, 'cause this happens a lot. . . . And I try not to get people who've been to prison before, because they'll be more likely to take foolish risks, the kind that I don't want to have to.

Most novice smugglers were recruited and trained by a sponsor with whom they forged an apprentice-mentor relationship. Those who had been dealers previously knew the rudiments of drug trafficking. What they learned from the smuggler was how to fill a particular role in his or her highly specialized operation.

One smuggler we interviewed had a slightly larger than average crew. Ben's commercial marijuana smuggling organization was composed of seven members, not including himself. Two were drivers who transported the marijuana from the landing strip to its point of destination. One was a pilot. The dual roles of driver and co-pilot were filled by a fourth man. Another pilot, who operated both as a smuggler with his own makeshift crew and as a wholesale marijuana dealer who was supplied by Ben, flew runs for Ben when he wasn't otherwise occupied. The sixth member was Ben's enforcer and "stash house" man; he lived in the place where the marijuana was stored, distributed it to customers, and forcibly extracted payments when Ben deemed it necessary. The seventh member handled the financial and legal aspects of the business. He arranged for lawyers and bail bondsmen when needed, laundered Ben's money, and provided him with a legitimate-looking business front. Most of these family members also dealt drugs on the side, having the choice of taking their payment in cash ($10,000 for pilots; $4000 for drivers) or in kind. Ben arranged the buying and selling connections, financed the operation, provided the heavy equipment (planes, vans, radios) and recruited, supervised, and replaced his crew.

Relationships between smugglers and their recruits were generally characterized by a benign paternalism, leading apprentices to form an enduring loyalty to their sponsor. Once established in a smuggling crew, recruits gained familiarity with the many other roles, the scope of the whole operation, and began to meet suppliers and customers. Eventually they branched out on their own. To do so, employees of a smuggling crew had to develop the expertise and connections necessary to begin running their own operations. Several things were required to make this move. Acquiring the technical knowledge of equipment, air routes, stopovers, and how to coordinate personnel was relatively easy; this could be picked up after working in a smuggling crew for six months to a year. Putting together one's own crew was more difficult because skilled employees, especially pilots, were hard to find. Most new smugglers borrowed people from other crews until they became sufficiently established to recruit and train their own personnel. Finally, connections to buy from and sell to were needed. Buyers were plentiful, but securing a foreign supplier required special breaks or networks.

Another way for employees to become heads of their own smuggling operations was to take over when their boss retired. This had the advantage of keeping the crew and style of operation intact. Various financial arrangements could be worked out for such a transfer of authority, from straight cash purchases to deals involving residual payments. One marijuana smuggler described how he acquired his operation:

> I had been Jake's main pilot for a year and, after him, I knew the most about his operation. We were really tight, and he had taken me all up and down the coast with him, meeting his connections. Naturally I knew the Mexican end of the operation and his supplier since I used to make the runs, flying down the money and picking up the dope. So when he told me he wanted to get out of the business, we made a deal. I took over the set-up and gave him a residual for every run I made. I kept all the drivers, all the connections—everything the guy had—but I found myself a new pilot.

In sum, most dealers and smugglers reached the upper levels not so much as a result of their individual entrepreneurial initiative, but through the social networks they formed in the drug subculture. Their ability to remain in these strata was largely tied to the way they treated these drug world relationships.[5]

---

[5]For a more thorough discussion of the social networks and relationships in Southwest County's drug world see Adler and Adler (1983).

SHIFTS AND OSCILLATIONS

We have discussed dealers and smugglers separately up to this point because they display distinct career patterns. But once individuals entered the drug trafficking field and rose to its upper levels, they became part of a social world, the Southwest County drug scene, and faced common problems and experiences. Therefore, we discuss them together from here on.

Despite the gratifications which dealers and smugglers originally derived from the easy money, material comfort, freedom, prestige, and power associated with their careers, 90 percent of those we observed decided, at some point, to quit the business. This stemmed, in part, from their initial perceptions of the career as temporary ("Hell, nobody wants to be a drug dealer all their life"). Adding to these early intentions was a process of rapid aging in the career: dealers and smugglers became increasingly aware of the restrictions and sacrifices their occupations required and tired of living the fugitive life. They thought about, talked about, and in many cases took steps toward getting out of the drug business. But as with entering, disengaging from drug trafficking was rarely an abrupt act (Lieb and Olson, 1976:364). Instead, it more often resembled a series of transitions, or oscillations,[6] out of and back into the business. For once out of the drug world, dealers and smugglers were rarely successful in making it in the legitimate world because they failed to cut down on their extravagant lifestyle and drug consumption. Many abandoned their efforts to reform and returned to deviance, sometimes picking up where they left off and other times shifting to a new mode of operating. For example, some shifted from dealing cocaine to dealing marijuana, some dropped to a lower level of dealing, and others shifted their role within the same group of traffickers. This series of phase-outs and re-entries, combined with career shifts, endured for years, dominating the pattern of their remaining involvement with the business. But it also represented the method by which many eventually broke away from drug trafficking, for each phase-out had the potential to be an individual's final departure.

Aging in the Career

Once recruited and established in the drug world, dealers and smugglers entered into a middle phase of aging in the career. This phase was characterized by a progressive loss of enchantment with their occupation. While novice dealers and smugglers found that participation in the drug world brought them thrills and status, the novelty gradually faded. Initial feelings of exhilaration and awe began to dull as individuals became increasingly jaded. This was the result of both an extended exposure to the mundane, everyday business aspects of drug trafficking and to an exorbitant consumption of drugs (especially cocaine). One smuggler described how he eventually came to feel:

> It was fun, those three or four years. I never worried about money or anything. But after awhile it got real boring. There was no feeling or emotion or anything about it. I wasn't even hardly relating to my old lady anymore. Everything was just one big rush.

This frenzy of overstimulation and resulting exhaustion hastened the process of "burnout" which nearly all individuals experienced. As dealers and smugglers aged in the career they became more sensitized to the extreme risks they faced. Cases of friends and associates who were arrested, imprisoned, or killed began to mount. Many individuals became convinced that continued drug trafficking would inevitably lead to arrest ("It's only a matter of time before you get caught"). While dealers and smugglers generally repressed their awareness of danger, treating it as a taken-for-granted part of their daily existence, periodic crises shattered their casual attitudes, evoking strong feelings of fear. They temporarily intensified security precautions and retreated into near-isolation until they felt the "heat" was off.

---

[6] While other studies of drug dealing have also noted that participants did not maintain an uninterrupted stream of career involvement (Blum et al., 1972; Carey, 1968; Lieb and Olson, 1976; Waldorf et al., 1977), none have isolated or described the oscillating nature of his pattern.

As a result of these accumulating "scares," dealers and smugglers increasingly integrated feelings of "paranoia"[7] into their everyday lives. One dealer talked about his feelings of paranoia:

> You're always on the line. You don't lead a normal life. You're always looking over your shoulder, wondering who's at the door, having to hide everything. You learn to look behind you so well you could probably bend over and look up your ass. That's paranoia. It's a really scary, hard feeling. That's what makes you get out.

Drug world members also grew progressively weary of their exclusion from the legitimate world and the deceptions they had to manage to sustain that separation. Initially, this separation was surrounded by an alluring mystique. But as they aged in the career, this mystique became replaced by the reality of everyday boundary maintenance and the feeling of being an "expatriated citizen within one's own country." One smuggler who was contemplating quitting described the effects of this separation:

> I'm so sick of looking over my shoulder, having to sit in my house and worry about one of my non-drug world friends stopping in when I'm doing business. Do you know how awful that is? It's like leading a double life. It's ridiculous. That's what makes it not worth it. It'll be a lot less money [to quit], but a lot less pressure.

Thus, while the drug world was somewhat restricted, it was not an encapsulated community, and dealers' and smugglers' continuous involvement with the straight world made the temptation to adhere to normative standards and "go straight" omnipresent. With the occupation's novelty worn off and the "fast life" taken-for-granted, most dealers and smugglers felt that the occupation no longer resembled their early impressions of it. Once they reached the upper levels of the occupation, their experience began to change. Eventually, the rewards of trafficking no longer seemed to justify the strain and risk involved. It was at this point that the straight world's formerly dull ambiance became transformed (at least in theory) into a potential haven.

Phasing-Out

Three factors inhibited dealers and smugglers from leaving the drug world. Primary among these factors were the hedonistic and materialistic satisfactions the drug world provided. Once accustomed to earning vast quantities of money quickly and easily, individuals found it exceedingly difficult to return to the income scale of the straight world. They also were reluctant to abandon the pleasures of the "fast life" and its accompanying drugs, casual sex, and power. Second, dealers and smugglers identified with, and developed a commitment to, the occupation of drug trafficking (Adler and Adler, 1982). Their self-images were tied to that role and could not be easily disengaged. The years invested in their careers (learning the trade, forming connections, building reputations) strengthened their involvement with both the occupation and the drug community. And since their relationships were social as well as business, friendship ties bound individuals to dealing. As one dealer in the midst of struggling to phase-out explained:

> The biggest threat to me is to get caught up sitting around the house with friends that are into dealing. I'm trying to stay away from them, change my habits.

Third, dealers and smugglers hesitated to voluntarily quit the field because of the difficulty involved in finding another way to earn a living. Their years spent in illicit activity made it unlikely for any legitimate organizations to hire them. This narrowed their occupational choices considerably, leaving self-employment as one of the few remaining avenues open.

Dealers and smugglers who tried to leave the drug world generally fell into one of four

---

[7]In the dealers' vernacular, this term is not used in the clinical sense of an individual psychopathology rooted in early childhood traumas. Instead, it resembles Lemert's (1962) more sociological definition which focuses on such behavioral dynamics as suspicion, hostility, aggressiveness, and even delusion. Not only Lemert, but also Waldorf et al. (1977) and Wedow (1979) assert that feelings of paranoia can have a sound basis in reality, and are therefore readily comprehended and even empathized with others.

patterns.[8] The first and most frequent pattern was to postpone quitting until after they could execute one last "big deal." While the intention was sincere, individuals who chose this route rarely succeeded; the "big deal" too often remained elusive. One marijuana smuggler offered a variation of this theme:

> My plan is to make a quarter of a million dollars in four months during the prime smuggling season and get the hell out of the business.

A second pattern we observed was individuals who planned to change immediately, but never did. They announced they were quitting, yet their outward actions never varied. One dealer described his involvement with this syndrome:

> When I wake up I'll say, "Hey, I'm going to quit this cycle and just run my other business." But when you're dealing you constantly have people dropping by ounces and asking, "Can you move this?" What's your first response? Always, "Sure, for a toot."

In the third pattern of phasing-out, individuals actually suspended their dealing and smuggling activities, but did not replace them with an alternative source of income. Such withdrawals were usually spontaneous and prompted by exhaustion, the influence of a person from outside the drug world, or problems with the police or other associates. These kinds of phase-outs usually lasted only until the individual's money ran out, as one dealer explained:

> I got into legal trouble with the FBI a while back and I was forced to quit dealing. Everybody just cut me off completely, and I saw the danger in continuing, myself. But my high-class tastes never dwindled. Before I knew it I was in hock over $30,000. Even though I was hot, I was forced to get back into dealing to relieve some of my debts.

In the fourth pattern of phasing-out, dealers and smugglers tried to move into another line of work. Alternative occupations included: (1) those they had previously pursued; (2) front businesses maintained on the side while dealing or smuggling; and (3) new occupations altogether. While some people accomplished this transition successfully, there were problems inherent in all three alternatives.

(1) Most people who tried resuming their former occupations found that these had changed too much while they were away. In addition, they themselves had changed: they enjoyed the self-directed freedom and spontaneity associated with dealing and smuggling, and were unwilling to relinquish it.

(2) Those who turned to their legitimate front business often found that these businesses were unable to support them. Designed to launder rather than earn money, most of these ventures were retail outlets with a heavy cash flow (restaurants, movie theaters, automobile dealerships, small stores) that had become accustomed to operating under a continuous subsidy from illegal funds. Once their drug funding was cut off they could not survive for long.

(3) Many dealers and smugglers utilized the skills and connections they had developed in the drug business to create a new occupation. They exchanged their illegal commodity for a legal one and went into import/export, manufacturing, wholesaling, or retailing other merchandise. For some, the decision to prepare a legitimate career for their future retirement from the drug world followed an unsuccessful attempt to phase-out into a "front" business. One husband-and-wife dealing team explained how these legitimate side businesses differed from front businesses:

> We always had a little legitimate "scam" [scheme] going, like mail-order shirts, wallets, jewelry, and the kids were always involved in that. We made a little bit of money on them. Their main purpose was for a cover. But [this business] was different; right from the start this was going to be a legal thing to push us out of the drug business.

---

[8]At this point, a limitation to our data must be noted. Many of the dealers and smugglers we observed simply "disappeared" from the scene and were never heard from again. We therefore have no way of knowing if they phased-out (voluntarily or involuntarily), shifted to another scene, or were killed in some remote place. We cannot, therefore, estimate the numbers of people who left the Southwest County drug scene via each of the routes discussed here.

About 10 percent of the dealers and smugglers we observed began tapering off their drug world involvement gradually, transferring their time and money into a selected legitimate endeavor. They did not try to quit drug trafficking altogether until they felt confident that their legitimate business could support them. Like spontaneous phase-outs, many of these planned withdrawals into legitimate endeavors failed to generate enough money to keep individuals from being lured into the drug world.

In addition to voluntary phase-outs caused by burnout, about 40 percent of the Southwest County dealers and smugglers we observed experienced a "bustout" at some point in their careers.[9] Forced withdrawals from dealing or smuggling were usually sudden and motivated by external factors, either financial, legal, or reputational. Financial bustouts generally occurred when dealers or smugglers were either "burned" or "ripped-off" by others, leaving them in too much debt to rebuild their base of operation. Legal bustouts followed arrest and possibly incarceration: arrested individuals were so "hot" that few of their former associates would deal with them. Reputational bustouts occurred when individuals "burned" or "ripped-off" others (regardless of whether they intended to do so) and were banned from business by their former circle of associates. One smuggler gave his opinion on the pervasive nature of forced phase-outs:

> Some people are smart enough to get out of it because they realize, physically, they have to. Others realize, monetarily, that they want to get out of this world before this world gets them. Those are the lucky ones. Then there are the ones who have to get out because they're hot or someone else close to them is so hot that they'd better get out. But in the end when you get out of it, nobody gets out of it out of free choice; you do it because you have to.

Death, of course, was the ultimate bustout. Some pilots met this fate because of the dangerous routes they navigated (hugging mountains, treetops, other aircraft) and the sometimes ill-maintained and overloaded planes they flew.

However, despite much talk of violence, few Southwest County drug traffickers died at the hands of fellow dealers.

Re-Entry

Phasing-out of the drug world was more often than not temporary. For many dealers and smugglers, it represented but another stage of their drug careers (although this may not have been their original intention), to be followed by a period of reinvolvement. Depending on the individual's perspective, re-entry into the drug world could be viewed as either a comeback (from a forced withdrawal) or a relapse (from a voluntary withdrawal).

Most people forced out of drug trafficking were anxious to return. The decision to phase-out was never theirs, and the desire to get back into dealing or smuggling was based on many of the same reasons which drew them into the field originally. Coming back from financial, legal, and reputational bustouts was possible but difficult and was not always successfully accomplished. They had to re-establish contacts, rebuild their organization and fronting arrangements, and raise the operating capital to resume dealing. More difficult was the problem of overcoming the circumstances surrounding their departure. Once smugglers and dealers resumed operating, they often found their former colleagues suspicious of them. One frustrated dealer described the effects of his prison experience:

> When I first got out of the joint [jail], none of my old friends would have anything to do with me. Finally, one guy who had been my partner told me it was because everyone was suspicious of my getting out early and thought I made a deal [with police to inform on his colleagues].

Dealers and smugglers who returned from bustouts were thus informally subjected to a trial period in which they had to re-establish their trustworthiness and reliability before they could once again move in the drug world with ease.

---

[9]It is impossible to determine the exact percentage of people falling into the different phase-out categories: due to oscillation, people could experience several types and thus appear in multiple categories.

Re-entry from voluntary withdrawal involved a more difficult decision-making process, but was easier to implement. The factors enticing individuals to re-enter the drug world were not the same as those which motivated their original entry. As we noted above, experienced dealers and smugglers often privately weighed their reasons for wanting to quit and wanting to stay in. Once they left, their images of and hopes for the straight world failed to materialize. They could not make the shift to the norms, values, and lifestyle of the straight society and could not earn a living within it. Thus, dealers and smugglers decided to re-enter the drug business for basic reasons: the material perquisites, the hedonistic gratifications, the social ties, and the fact that they had nowhere else to go.

Once this decision was made, the actual process of re-entry was relatively easy. One dealer described how the door back into dealing remained open for those who left voluntarily:

> I still see my dealer friends, I can still buy grams from them when I want to. It's the respect they have for me because I stepped out of it without being busted or burning someone. I'm coming out with a good reputation, and even though the scene is a whirlwind—people moving up, moving down, in, out—if I didn't see anybody for a year I could call them up and get right back in that day.

People who relapsed thus had little problem obtaining fronts, re-establishing their reputations, or readjusting to the scene.

Career Shifts

Dealers and smugglers who re-entered the drug world, whether from a voluntary or forced phase-out, did not always return to the same level of transacting or commodity which characterized their previous style of operation. Many individuals underwent a "career shift" (Luckenbill and Best, 1981) and became involved in some new segment of the drug world. These shifts were sometimes lateral, as when a member of a smuggling crew took on a new specialization, switching from piloting to operating a stash house, for example. One dealer described how he utilized friendship networks upon his re-entry to shift from cocaine to marijuana trafficking:

> Before, when I was dealing cocaine, I was too caught up in using the drug and people around me were starting to go under from getting into "base" [another form of cocaine]. That's why I got out. But now I think I've got myself together and even though I'm dealing again I'm staying away from coke. I've switched over to dealing grass. It's a whole different circle of people. I got into it through a close friend I used to know before, but I never did business with him because he did grass and I did coke.

Vertical shifts moved operators to different levels. For example, one former smuggler returned and began dealing; another top-level marijuana dealer came back to find that the smugglers he knew had disappeared and he was forced to buy in smaller quantities from other dealers.

Another type of shift relocated drug traffickers in different styles of operation. One dealer described how, after being arrested, he tightened his security measures:

> I just had to cut back after I went through those changes. Hell, I'm not getting any younger and the idea of going to prison bothers me a lot more than it did 10 years ago. The risks are no longer worth it when I can have a comfortable income with less risk. So I only sell to four people now. I don't care if they buy a pound or a gram.

A former smuggler who sold his operation and lost all his money during phase-out returned as a consultant to the industry, selling his expertise to those with new money and fresh manpower:

> What I've been doing lately is setting up deals for people. I've got foolproof plans for smuggling cocaine up here from Colombia; I tell them how to modify their airplanes to add on extra fuel tanks and to fit in more weed, coke, or whatever they bring up. Then I set them up with refueling points all up and down Central America, tell them how to bring it up here, what points to come in at, and what kind of receiving unit to use. Then they do it all and I get 10 percent of what they make.

Re-entry did not always involve a shift to a new niche, however. Some dealers and smugglers returned to the same circle of associates, trafficking activity, and commodity they worked with prior to their departure. Thus, drug dealers' careers often peaked early and then displayed a variety of shifts, from lateral mobility, to decline, to holding fairly steady.

A final alternative involved neither completely leaving nor remaining within the deviant world. Many individuals straddled the deviant and respectable worlds forever by continuing to dabble in drug trafficking. As a result of their experiences in the drug world they developed a deviant self-identity and a deviant modus operandi. They might not have wanted to bear the social and legal burden of full-time deviant work but neither were they willing to assume the perceived confines and limitations of the straight world. They therefore moved into the entrepreneurial realm, where their daily activities involved some kind of hustling or "wheeling and dealing" in an assortment of legitimate, quasi-legitimate, and deviant ventures, and where they could be their own boss. This enabled them to retain certain elements of the deviant lifestyle, and to socialize on the fringes of the drug community. For these individuals, drug dealing shifted from a primary occupation to a sideline, though they never abandoned it altogether.

LEAVING DRUG TRAFFICKING

This career pattern of oscillation into and out of active drug trafficking makes it difficult to speak of leaving drug trafficking in the sense of a final retirement. Clearly, some people succeeded in voluntarily retiring. Of these, a few managed to prepare a post-deviant career for themselves by transferring their drug money into a legitimate enterprise. A larger group was forced out of dealing and either didn't or couldn't return; their bustouts were sufficiently damaging that they never attempted re-entry, or they abandoned efforts after a series of unsuccessful attempts. But there was no way of structurally determining in advance whether an exit from the business would be temporary or permanent. The vacillations in dealers' intentions were compounded by the complexity of operating successfully in the drug world. For many, then, no phase-out could ever be definitely

assessed as permanent. As long as individuals had the skills, knowledge, and connections to deal they retained the potential to re-enter the occupation at any time. Leaving drug trafficking may thus be a relative phenomenon, characterized by a trailing-off process where spurts of involvement appear with decreasing frequency and intensity.

SUMMARY

Drug dealing and smuggling careers are temporary and fraught with multiple attempts at retirement. Veteran drug traffickers quit their occupation because of the ambivalent feelings they develop toward their deviant life. As they age in the career their experience changes, shifting from a work life that is exhilarating and free to one that becomes increasingly dangerous and confining. But just as their deviant careers are temporary, so too are their retirements. Potential recruits are lured into the drug business by materialism, hedonism, glamor, and excitement. Established dealers are lured away from the deviant life and back into the mainstream by the attractions of security and social ease. Retired dealers and smugglers are lured back in by their expertise, and by their ability to make money quickly and easily. People who have been exposed to the upper levels of drug trafficking therefore find it extremely difficult to quit their deviant occupation permanently. This stems, in part, from their difficulty in moving from the illegitimate to the legitimate business sector. Even more significant is the affinity they form for their deviant values and lifestyle. Thus few, if any, of our subjects were successful in leaving deviance entirely. What dealers and smugglers intend, at the time, to be a permanent withdrawal from drug trafficking can be seen in retrospect as a pervasive occupational pattern of mid-career shifts and oscillations. More research is needed into the complex process of how people get out of deviance and enter the world of legitimate work.

REFERENCES

Adler, Patricia A., and Peter Adler. "Criminal commitment among drug dealers." Deviant Behavior 3:117–135. (1982).

————. "Relations between dealers: The social organization of illicit drug transactions." Sociology and Social Research 67(3):260–278. (1983).

Anonymous. "On selling marijuana." Pp. 92–102 in Erich Goode (ed.), Marijuana. New York: Atherton. (1969).

Atkyns, Robert L., and Gerhard J. Hanneman. "Illicit drug distribution and dealer communication behavior." Journal of Health and Social Behavior 15(March):36–43. (1974).

Biernacki, Patrick, and Dan Waldorf. "Snowball sampling." Sociological Methods and Research 10(2):141–163. (1981).

Blum, Richard H., and Associates. The Dream Sellers. San Francisco: Jossey-Bass. (1972).

Carey, James T. The College Drug Scene. Englewood Cliffs, NJ: Prentice-Hall. (1968).

Douglas, Jack D. Investigative Social Research. Beverly Hills, CA: Sage. (1976).

Goode, Erich. The Marijuana Smokers. New York: Basic. (1970).

Johnson, Bruce D. Marijuana Users and Drug Subcultures. New York: Wiley. (1973).

Langer, John. "Drug entrepreneurs and dealing culture." Social Problems 24(3):377–385. (1977).

Lemert, Edwin. "Paranoia and the dynamics of exclusion." Sociometry 25(March):2–20. (1962).

Lieb, John, and Sheldon Olson. "Prestige, paranoia, and profit: On becoming a dealer of illicit drugs in a university community." Journal of Drug Issues 6(Fall):356–369. (1976).

Luckenbill, David F., and Joel Best. "Careers in deviance and respectability: The analogy's limitations." Social Problems 29(2):197–206. (1981).

Mandel, Jerry. "Myths and realities of marijuana pushing." Pp. 58–110 in Jerry L. Simmons (ed.), Marijuana: Myths and Realities. North Hollywood, CA: Brandon. (1967).

Miller, Gale, and George Ritzer. "Informal socialization: Deviant occupations." Pp. 83–94 in George Ritzer, Working: Conflict and Change. 2nd edition. Englewood Cliffs, NJ: Prentice-Hall. (1977).

Mouledoux, James. "Ideological aspects of drug dealership." Pp. 110–122 in Ken Westhues (ed.), Society's Shadow: Studies in the Sociology of Countercultures. Toronto: McGraw-Hill, Ryerson. (1972).

Redlinger, Lawrence J. "Marketing and distributing heroin." Journal of Psychedelic Drugs 7(4):331–353. (1975).

Riemer, Jeffrey W. "Varieties of opportunistic research." Urban Life 5(4):467–477. (1977).

Waldorf, Dan, Sheigla Murphy, Craig Reinarman, and Bridget Joyce. Doing Coke: An Ethnography of Cocaine Users and Sellers. Washington, DC: Drug Abuse Council. (1977).

Wedow, Suzanne. "Feeling paranoid: The organization of an ideology." Urban Life 8(1):72–93. (1979).

CHAPTER

6

Problems
of the
Economy

The Worthy and Unworthy Homeless

JAMES D. WRIGHT

Americans have always found it necessary to distinguish between the "deserving" and "undeserving" poor—the former, victims of circumstances beyond their control who merit compassion; the latter, lazy, shiftless bums who could do better for themselves "if they wanted to" and who therefore merit contempt. The ensuing tension in our collective attitude toward the poor is reflected both in public policy and in public opinion surveys. A 1984 survey asked people to agree or disagree that "most people who do not get ahead in life probably work just as hard as people who do." Forty-seven percent agreed with this sentiment, 44 percent disagreed, and the remainder were neutral or had no opinion. In the same survey, 84 percent agreed that "any person who is willing to work hard has a good chance of succeeding" but 80 percent also agreed that "even if people try hard they often cannot reach their goals."

Poverty in America has become visible again, both as a phenomenon and as a public policy issue. I refer specifically to the apparently dramatic increase in homelessness that has occurred in the past several years and to the media and political attention that the problem of homelessness has received. These days, homeless and destitute people can be found wandering the streets of any large urban area; no one can possibly remain oblivious to their existence. What to do about or for the homeless has likewise become an important political issue, with some thirty-two separate bills introduced in the Hundredth Congress that deal with one or another aspect of the homelessness problem.

So far, the homeless seem to be included among the "deserving poor," at least by the general public. A recent national survey by the Roper Organization reported by *Newsweek* on September 21, 1987, asked what problems we should be spending more money on. "Caring for the homeless" was the top priority item, favored by 68 percent. (In contrast, foreign aid was mentioned by only 5 percent, and "military, armaments, and defense" by only 17 percent.) Thus, most people seem to feel that the homeless deserve our help, if not our compassion. But an opposite, more mean-spirited view has also begun to surface. On December 1, 1986, Stuart Bykofsky wrote a "My Turn" column for *Newsweek* magazine entitled "No Heart for the Homeless." The analysis turned on the division of the homeless into three groups: "(1) the economically distressed, who would work if they could find work; (2) the mentally ill, who can't work; (3) the alcoholic, the drug-addicted, and others who won't work." His solution to the problem was workfare for the first group, mental institutions for the second, and indifference to (or outright hostility toward) the third.

Bykofsky's simplistic categorization was unburdened by numbers or percentages, and so we

James D. Wright is the Charles and Leo Favrot Professor of Human Relations in the Department of Sociology at Tulane University. He has written thirteen books, including: The State of the Masses, *with Richard Hamilton*; Under the Gun, *with Peter Rossi and Kathleen Daly; and, most recently,* Homelessness and Health, *with Dee Weber.*

From *Society,* July/August 1988. Published by permission of Transaction Publishers, from *Society,* Vol. 25, No. 5. Copyright © 1988 by Transaction Publishers.

are not told how many of the homeless fit his various types. Concurrent with the increased media and political attention being given to the problem, there has also been an outpouring of research studies that provide reliable guides to the relative proportions of "worthy" and "unworthy" homeless. My aim here is to review the findings of some of these studies, to see if we cannot be more precise about how many homeless deserve our sympathies and how many do not.

The many recent studies available for our use are uneven in coverage and quality. The largest and most geographically dispersed sample of homeless people available is that contained in *Homelessness and Health,* my study of clients seen in the National Health Care for the Homeless Program (HCH). Data for the first year of the HCH program describe nearly 30,000 homeless people seen in health clinics in sixteen large cities all over the country. Because of its size, geographical dispersion, and my familiarity with the results, I use the findings from this study extensively in the following discussion.

A second study upon which I have drawn is the Peter H. Rossi et al. survey of homeless people in Chicago, *The Condition of the Homeless in Chicago.* One problem faced by many studies is that they are based exclusively on shelter users; it has long been recognized that the shelter users are only one of two important components of the homeless population, the other being "street homeless" who, for whatever reason, rarely or never use the shelter system. One among many virtues of the Rossi et al. survey is its extremely thorough and systematic sampling of the street homeless. This fact, coupled with the breadth of topics covered and the general degree of sophistication in the conduct of the research, make the Chicago survey especially useful.

Neither of the above sources provides answers to all the important questions, and so in some cases I have relied on other research. In all cases, I have sacrificed technical niceties for completeness of coverage, knowing full well that new and better research will no doubt change the picture, at least in small details.

For convenience, it is useful to begin by imagining a sample of 1000 homeless people,

drawn at random, let us say, from the half million or so homeless people to be found in America on any given evening. Based on the research I have sketched, we can then begin to cut up this sample in various ways, so as to portray as graphically as possible the mosaic of homelessness in this country. Our strategy is to work from "more deserving" to "less deserving" subgroups, ending with the absolutely least deserving—the lazy, shiftless bums. Along the way, I call attention to various characteristics of and problems encountered by each of the subgroups we consider.

HOMELESS FAMILIES

Among the many tragedies of homelessness, there is none sadder than the homeless family—often an intact family unit consisting of a wife, her husband, and one or more dependent children, victims of unemployment and other economic misfortune, struggling in the face of long odds to maintain themselves as a unit and get back on their feet again. How many members of homeless families can we expect to find among our sample of 1000 homeless people?

Although the rising number of homeless families has become a matter of considerable policy concern, evidence on their proportion in the larger homeless population is hard to come by. Most of the pertinent research has been done in homeless family shelters, or in facilities for homeless women and children; and while this material is useful for descriptive purposes, it does not tell us anything about relative proportions.

Some useful information appears in my HCH study. Across the sixteen cities covered in the study, 16 percent of all clients seen were described as members of homeless family groups. In six of the sixteen cities, family status was not systematically reported; among the 18,842 clients seen in the remaining ten cities, 28 percent were members of homeless family groups. Thus, somewhere between 160 and 280 of our 1000 homeless people will be members of homeless families—whether male or female, adult or child. Let us take the midpoint of the range, 220 members of homeless families, as our best and final estimate, consistent with most other studies of the topic. The remainder are lone individuals.

The HCH study further suggests that among the 220 members of homeless families, 99 will be children (under age sixteen) and 121 will be adults; among the adults will be 83 adult women and 38 adult men. One important conclusion, then, is that nearly a tenth of the homeless on the streets of American cities today are homeless children in the care of their adult parent or parents.

A second important conclusion, one that follows from the relative preponderance of women to men among the adult family members, is that most homeless families consist of single mothers with their children rather than intact nuclear families. (There would also be a few single fathers with children, but their numbers are minuscule in all studies.) If each of the 38 adult men is coupled with one of the 83 adult women, then we get 38 male-female pairs and 45 single females among the total of 121 adult family members in our hypothetical sample of 1000. Somewhat more than half of the homeless families are single-parent (typically, single-mother) units, somewhat less than half are intact nuclear families.

Most of the intact nuclear families have children of dependent age, but only about half of them actually have their children with them. The most common arrangement among the remainder is that the children are living with other relatives; in some cases, the children are in foster care. Thus, only 17 or 18 of the intact male-female pairs would also include children as part of the family unit. The 99 children would thus be distributed among, say, 18 mother-father pairs and 45 single parents (mostly mothers). Thus, most homeless children live in broken families, one among the many problems homeless children face.

Studies of the effects of homelessness on children paint a uniformly shocking and depressing picture. According to Ellen Bassuk, in the *American Journal of Public Health* in 1986, developmental delays of varying severity are observed in more than half. My research has confirmed that homeless children suffer various physical disorders at rates two to ten times those

seen among children in general. Some of the problems encountered by homeless children are depression, anger, anxiety, low self-esteem, and uncertainty about life (at a psychological level); and inadequate nutrition, dangerous living conditions, violence and abuse, a lack of parental authority, no quiet place to do homework, and so on (at a more concrete, palpable level). One homeless child that I have met—she lives with her mother and siblings in a welfare hotel in New York City—described her "dream" as "a clean apartment and a safe place to play out of doors." This does not seem like too much to ask. We might wonder what kind of world it is where this can only be a dream to some children.

As for the adult members of homeless family units, the picture is somewhat brighter; among both men and women, rates of alcohol and drug abuse, and mental illness, are lower than they are among lone homeless individuals. The adult family members also suffer fewer chronic physical disorders, are more likely to be short-term (or situationally) homeless, and are rated as having better housing and employment prospects than the lone homeless are. In general, their prospects for the future are much brighter; compared to the lone homeless, the adult family members are simply more intact. Many of these families need little more than a "helping hand" to get them through a rough stretch. Many of the single mothers with dependent children need little more than an expedited Aid to Families with Dependent Children (AFDC) process. Helping hands and more efficient AFDC processing would certainly not solve all the problems these families face, but it would make a considerable dent.

Members of homeless families constitute a significantly large fraction of the homeless population; my guess is that we would find 220 of them in a sample of a thousand homeless people, nearly half of them homeless children. Not only would most people look on homeless families as most deserving of help, there is also reason to believe that they need the least help (in that they appear to have the fewest disabling problems and tend generally to be the most intact), and that even relatively modest assistance would make a substantial difference in their life chances and circumstances. If the available resources are such as to require triage, then homeless families should be the top priority.

LONE WOMEN AND CHILDREN

By these calculations, there remain in our hypothetical sample of 1000 some 780 lone homeless persons—single individuals on the streets by themselves. Based on the HCH study, some 6 percent of these 780 are children or adolescents age nineteen or less (which amounts to 47 additional children in the sample of 1000), 20 percent are adult women (156 additional women), and 74 percent are adult men (which leaves, from the original sample of 1000, only 580 adult males not members of homeless family groups). Adding these to the earlier results, we get two significant conclusions: First, among the total of a thousand homeless persons, $99 + 47 = 146$ will be children or youth aged nineteen or less, approximately one in every seven. Second, among the remaining 854 adults, $156 + 83 = 229$ will be women, which amounts to 229/854 or 27 percent of all adults. Combining all figures, homeless children and homeless adult women themselves comprise $146 + 229 = 375$ of the original 1000—three of every eight. Adult men comprise the majority of the homeless, but not the overwhelmingly majority; a very sizable minority—nearly 40 percent of the total—are women and children.

Most of the lone children found in these calculations are teenagers, which is also to say that nearly all homeless preteen children are still living with one or both of their parents. Still, children as young as twelve or thirteen will be found in sizable numbers in these data. Although men predominate among homeless adults, boys and girls are found in equal numbers among homeless children and teenagers; in the HCH data that form the basis for the preceding calculations, 51 percent of the lone homeless aged nineteen or less are boys, and 49 percent are girls; among all children (under age sixteen) in these data (whether lone individuals or members of homeless family groups), the split is also nearly 50:50. The heavy preponderance of males to females is observed only among the adults.

Although precise numbers are hard to come by, there is little doubt that many of these homeless teenagers are runaway or throwaway children fleeing abusive family situations. Among the girls, the rate of pregnancy is astonishing: 9 percent of the girls ages thirteen to fifteen, and 24 percent of the girls ages sixteen to nineteen, were pregnant at or since their first contact with the HCH clinic system; the rate for sixteen-to-nineteen-year-olds is the highest observed in any age group. There is impressionistic evidence, but no hard evidence, to suggest that many of these young girls are reduced to prostitution in order to survive; many will thus come to possess lengthy jail records as well. Drug and alcohol abuse are also common problems. Indeed, the rate of known drug abuse among the sixteen-to-nineteen-year-old boys—some 16 percent—is the highest rate recorded for any age group in our data.

I am discussing a time in life when the average adolescent's biggest worries are acne, or whom to invite to the high school prom, or where to go to college—a time of uncertainty, but also a time of hope and anticipation for the future. In contrast, homeless adolescents must worry about where to sleep tonight, or where the next meal is coming from, or who is going to assault them next. What hope for the future can be nourished under these conditions? Many of these kids—tough kids on mean streets, but kids nonetheless—face an unending downward spiral of booze, drugs, crime, and troubles with the law. They too must surely be counted among the "deserving" homeless; indeed, anything that can be done should be done to break the spiral and set them back on a path to an independent and productive adult existence.

Among the 854 adults remaining in our initial sample of 1000 homeless will be 229 adult women, or 27 percent of all adults. Again, this is very close to the figure reported in most studies. In the Chicago survey, 24 percent were women, and no recent study has reported a figure of less than 20 percent. Homeless women are not a new phenomenon; studies by D. L. Jones in Massachusetts, published in the 1974 *Journal of Social History,* and by P. F. Clements in Philadelphia confirm sizable fractions of women among the homeless, at least since colonial times. (Clements' work is published in E. H. Monkkonen's *Walking to Work: Tramps in America*.) Compared to homeless adult men, homeless women are younger by about two years on the average; 42 percent of the adult HCH women, but only 30 percent of the adult men, are under thirty. Compared to the men, the women are much more likely to have psychiatric impairments, but much less likely to abuse alcohol and drugs.

There are many different kinds of homeless women, and it is a mistake to think of "the" problems of homeless women as though all homeless women faced the same problems. One large and important subgroup is comprised of the lone mentally impaired women from whom the "bag lady" stereotype has been derived. This is the subset of homeless women that in some sense has been created by deinstitutionalization and related changes in our mental health treatment system. A reasonable guess is that they constitute about a third of all homeless women. Compared to other homeless women, they are much older (the median age of the group is forty) and predominantly white (58 percent); their principal need is for vastly improved community mental health services.

A second group, accounting for more than a quarter of the total, are mothers with dependent children in their care. These women tend to be young (the median age is twenty-seven), and their rates of mental disorder and substance abuse are relatively low. Only about half receive AFDC; many would presumably be employable if day care were available. Yet a third group are the homeless teenage girls, some of whose problems I have already discussed. The remainder of the women fall into a residual "other" category; the distinctive feature of this group is that alcohol and drug abuse is much more widespread than among the other women, rivaling the rates found generally among homeless men.

Most people would feel comfortable counting the adult women among the "deserving" homeless as well. Just as women and children are the first to be evacuated from a sinking ship, so too should women and children be the first to be rescued from the degradations of street life or a shelter existence. If we add to the group of "deserving" homeless the relatively small number of adult men in homeless family groups, then our initial cut leaves but 580 persons from the original 1000 yet to account for.

LONE ADULT MEN

What is to be said about those who remain—the 580 lone adult males, not members of homeless families? A small percentage of them, much smaller than most people would anticipate, are elderly men, over age sixty-five; in the HCH data, the over-sixty-fives comprise about 3 percent of the group in question, which gives us 17 elderly men among the remaining 580. In fact, among all HCH adults, just about 3 percent are over age sixty-five; the lone adult men are not exceptional in this respect.

Since, in the national population as a whole, about 12 percent are over sixty-five, our 3 percent figure means that there are many fewer elderly homeless than would otherwise be expected—a "shortage" or "deficit" of elderly homeless that has been remarked upon in several studies. What explains the apparent shortage of homeless persons over sixty-five? First, a number of entitlements become available to persons once they turn sixty-five, chief among them Medicare and Social Security payments. It is possible that these benefits are adequate to get most older homeless persons off the streets or out of the shelters and into some sort of reasonably stable housing situation. A second possibility is premature mortality; homeless persons, that is, may only rarely survive to age sixty-five in the first place.

Little research has been done on mortality among the homeless, but the few studies that are available suggest that the mortality hypothesis is not to be taken lightly. Alstrom and his colleagues, in a study reported in the *British Journal of Addictions* in 1975, followed 6032 homeless Swedish men for a three-year period. Observed mortality during the study period (n = 327 deaths) exceeded the age-adjusted expected mortality (n = 87 expected deaths) by a factor of approximately four; the average age at death among the 327 men was about fifty-three years. My own study of the topic has produced a similar result; among 88 deaths occurring among clients seen in the HCH program, the average age at death was fifty-one. Based on these findings, we can conclude that homeless men die some twenty or so years earlier than they "should." Thus, premature death must certainly account for at least some portion of the elderly "deficit."

The shortage of over-sixty-fives is not the only striking aspect of the age distribution of the homeless; the fact is, homeless people are surprisingly young. The median age of HCH adults is thirty-four years; all recent demographic studies of homeless populations have remarked on the low average age, perhaps because the stereotype is that the homeless tend to be old. Today, the average homeless adult male is somewhere in his early to middle thirties.

The low average age of the homeless sustains an important and often overlooked conclusion, namely, that the rise of the "new homeless" is in some sense a result of the so-called baby boom, the immensely large generations born in the United States between 1947 and 1964. As a cohort, the average age of the baby boom is now in the early thirties, almost identical to the average age of homeless people.

The baby boom has posed serious problems for virtually every institution it has touched in the course of its life span, beginning with the crisis in elementary education that commenced in the early 1950s, continuing through to a serious national housing shortage today, and ending ultimately with what will be a serious shortage of burial space around the year 2020 and thereafter. The more affluent members of the baby boom generation have come to be known as "Yuppies" (young urban professionals), whose housing preferences and purchasing power are in many respects responsible for the current housing crisis. What is often overlooked in discussions of the Yuppies is that they sit at the upper end of an income distribution, the other end of which reaches down into the poverty population. In the lowest reaches of this income distribution one finds the "new homeless," whose numbers have clearly begun to strain the capacity of the existing social welfare system.

As for the elderly, those over sixty-five, surely they are to be included within the "deserving" group. As it happens, only about half of them receive Social Security benefits. Many of those who do receive Social Security payments find that no housing can be purchased or rented within their means. Well over half have chronic physical health problems that further contribute to their hardships. Certainly, no one will object if we include the elderly homeless among those deserving our sympathies.

LONE VETERANS

We are now left with, let us say, 563 nonelderly lone adult men. If we inquire further among this group, we will discover another surprising fact: at least a third of them are veterans of the United States Armed Forces. Indeed, over a number of recent studies, reviewed by M. Robertson in Bingham, Green, and White's *The Homeless in Contemporary Society,* the percentage of veterans among the men varies from a low of 32 percent to a high of 47 percent. The one-third figure is clearly conservative; the true figure might be as high as one-half. As a point of comparison, 41 percent of all adult men in the United States are also veterans; in this respect, the homeless are not much different.

The studies reviewed by Robertson show the homeless veterans to be slightly older and proportionally more white than homeless nonveteran men; compared to the national veteran population, Vietnam-era veterans are overrepresented. About one in five have service-related disabilities sufficiently serious to prevent them from working; service-related psychiatric difficulties, while not always disabling, are also widespread. Among the Vietnam-era veterans, posttraumatic stress syndrome may be the most common psychiatric problem. Most of the veterans, especially the younger ones, report chronic unemployment problems as well. No more than about a third receive any form of assistance from the Veteran's Administration.

Most homeless veterans are drawn from the lower socioeconomic strata, having enlisted to obtain, as Robertson has put it, "long term economic advantages through job training as well as postmilitary college benefits and preferential treatment in civil service employment," only to find that their economic and employment opportunities remain limited after they have mustered out. The lure of military service proves to have been a false promise for many of these men: "Despite recruitment campaigns that promote military service as an opportunity for maturation and occupational mobility, veterans continue to struggle with postmilitary unemployment and mental and physical disability without adequate assistance from the federal government." One of the Vietnam veterans in Robertson's study summed up the stakes involved: "If they expect the youth of America to fight another war, they have to take care of the vets."

Many of the homeless veterans are alcoholic or drug abusive, and many are also mentally ill; the same could be said for other subgroups that we have considered. Whatever their current problems and disabilities, these men were there when the nation needed them. Do they not also deserve a return of the favor?

LONE DISABLED MEN

Sticking with the admittedly conservative one-third estimate, among the 563 adult men with whom we are left, 188 will be veterans; 375 nonelderly, nonveteran adult men are all that remain of the initial 1000. Sorting out this subgroup in the HCH data, we find that a third are assessed by their care providers as having moderate to severe psychiatric impairments—not including alcohol or drug abuse. Many among this group have fallen through the cracks of the community mental health system. In the vast majority of cases, they pose no immediate danger to themselves or to others, and thus they are generally immune to involuntary commitment for psychiatric treatment; at the same time, their ability to care for themselves, especially in a street or shelter environment, is at best marginal. Compassion dictates that they too be included among the "deserving" group.

Just what they "deserve" is hotly contested; I cannot do justice here to the many complex issues involved. Some, for example New York's Mayor Ed Koch, think that they deserve involuntary commitment if their lives or well-being are imperiled by the material conditions of their existence; civil libertarians think they deserve the

right to die on the streets if they want to. Many mental health professionals seem to feel that reopening the large state mental institutions is the only viable solution; others think that coming through on the promise of community-based mental health care—the explicit promise upon which deinstitutionalization was justified—is the only morally defensible approach. All agree that for many of the mentally ill homeless, the least restrictive treatment has meant a life of scavenging food from street sources and sleeping in alleys and gutters—and this, no one intended.

Subtracting the 125 or so mentally disabled men from the remaining group of 375 leaves 250 of the original 1000. Among these 250 will be some 28 or so men who are physically disabled and incapable of working. This includes the blind and the deaf, those confined to wheelchairs, the paraplegic, those with amputated limbs, and those with disabling chronic physical illnesses such as heart disease, AIDS, obstructive pulmonary disease, and others. Like the mentally disabled, these too can only be counted among the "deserving" group. Subtracting them leaves a mere 222 remaining—nonelderly, nonveteran adult males with no mental or physical disability.

Of these 222, a bit more than half—112 men—will be found to have some sort of job: my data suggest that 7 will have full-time jobs, 27 will have part-time jobs, and 78 will be employed on a sporadic basis (seasonal work, day labor, odd jobs, and the like). Rossi's Chicago data show largely the same pattern. The remainder—110 men—are unemployed, and among these some 61 will be looking for work. All told, then, among the 222 will be 173 who are at least making the effort: looking for work, but so far with no success, or having a job but not one paying well enough to allow them to afford stable housing. This then leaves us with 49 people from the initial 1000 who are not members of homeless families, not women, not children, not elderly, not veterans, not mentally disabled, not physically disabled, not currently working, and not looking for work. Call these the "undeserving homeless," or, if you wish, lazy shiftless bums. They account for about 5 percent of the total—a mere one in every twenty.

NO EASY SOLUTION

There are many different kinds of homeless people, and it is pointless even to think of "the" homeless as though they were a homogeneous, undifferentiated group. Many of them—some 40 percent by my estimates—are alcohol abusive; a tenth abuse other drugs; a third are mentally ill; many have long-term chronic employment problems; most are estranged from their families and disaffiliated from the larger society. But very few of them are "homeless by choice" (to adopt a most unfortunate, although characteristic, phrase of Ronald Reagan), and all but a residual fraction merit our compassion on one or more counts.

There are no cheap or easy solutions to the problems of homelessness. At varying levels of analysis, homelessness is a housing problem, an employment problem, a demographic problem, a problem of social disaffiliation, a mental health problem, a substance abuse problem, a family violence problem, a problem created by cutbacks in social welfare spending, a problem resulting from the decay of the traditional nuclear family, and a problem intimately connected to the recent increase in persons living below the poverty level, as well as others.

In puzzling through the complex array of factors that cause homelessness, in the hopes of finding some solutions, coldheartedness is not the proper sentiment. Should we, as Bykofsky suggests, have "no heart" for a disabled thirty-three-year-old Vietnam veteran suffering from posttraumatic stress syndrome, or for a pregnant fifteen-year-old runaway girl whose father has raped and beaten her once too often, or for a feverish infant in the arms of her homeless mother, or for an entire family that has been turned out because the factory where the father worked was shut down, or for an arthritic old gentleman who has lost his room in the "welfare hotel" because he was beaten savagely and relieved of his Social Security check? These are very much a part—a large part—of today's homeless population, no less than the occasional "shiftless bum." Indifference to the plight of "shiftless bums" comes all too easily in an illiberal era; but indifference to the plight of homeless families, women, children, old people, veterans, and the disabled comes easily only to the cruel.

Joblessness versus Welfare Effects: A Further Reexamination

WILLIAM J. WILSON

with ROBERT APONTE

and KATHRYN NECKERMAN

[Elsewhere] we pointed out that the extraordinary rise in female-headed families, particularly among the black poor, is now being viewed in policy circles as a reflection of the failure of federal antipoverty programs. According to this view, liberal welfare policies, especially those associated with the Great Society program (which expanded eligibility for income transfer payments, increased benefit levels, and created or expanded programs such as Medicaid and food stamps), have reduced the incentive to work and to create or maintain stable families. We also attempted to show that much of the empirical research on changing family structure has provided only limited support for this argument. It retains great appeal, nonetheless, because the logic of the association between welfare and family/work disincentives is intuitively compelling and appears largely consistent with aggregate trends in social welfare spending and changes in family structure over time. However, it was not until Charles Murray developed the thesis in his controversial critique of the Great Society, *Losing Ground,* that the welfare thesis was widely discussed in the popular media.[1]

Murray argues that welfare generosity is the fundamental cause of black family disintegration in the inner city and contributes substantially to joblessness among younger black men as well. He contends that in 1970, a poor urban family with one worker literally could improve its financial situation by dissolving its marriage, withdrawing its members from the labor market, and subsisting on welfare. Indeed, Murray implies that by 1970 the monetary value of the full welfare benefit package available to unmarried mothers exceeded the minimum-wage earnings from a full forty-hour work week.

Murray illustrates this argument by presenting the case of a fictitious young unmarried couple, Harold and Phyllis, in an "average" city at two points in time—1960 and 1970. Phyllis is pregnant, and the couple must decide between remaining unmarried and thus qualifying for Aid to Families with Dependent Children (AFDC) or marrying and subsisting on Harold's minimum-wage earnings. In 1960, the welfare package would have barely supported Phyllis and her child. Moreover, the law did not permit payment of welfare benefits if the couple were to cohabit, regardless of their marital status. In that situation, Murray argues, Harold and Phyllis would very likely decide to marry and live on his earnings. However, by 1970 the situation had changed—the income from the welfare package would not only exceed Harold's minimum-wage earnings, but it could be collected while the couple cohabited as a family unit provided they were not legally married. Thus, Murray concludes, the couple would tend to eschew marriage and minimum-wage employment in favor of welfare.

There are a number of problems with this presentation. First, Murray's calculations were based on welfare benefits from the state of Pennsylvania, where AFDC payments rose at twice the national average over the 1960s.[2] Hence the example of "shift in incentives" that Murray presents as "typical" was likely to be far greater than that confronted by most poor families.

Of greater importance is Murray's inadequate attention to trends in the relative advantages of welfare versus work *after 1970.* He

Chapter 4 from William J. Wilson, *The Truly Disadvantaged* (Chicago: University of Chicago Press, 1987), pp. 93–106, 204–209. Reprinted with permission of author and publisher.

states that real AFDC payments, which had risen sharply during the 1960s, continued to grow during the 1970s until about mid-decade, after which average payments "increased little if at all in most states."[3] Real benefit levels, in fact, have fallen dramatically since the early 1970s. Danziger and Gottschalk reveal that by 1980 the real value of AFDC plus food stamps had been reduced by 16 percent from their 1972 levels. By 1984 the combined payments were only 4 percent higher than their 1960 levels and 22 percent less than in 1972.[4] In the words of Greenstein, "no other group in American society experienced such a sharp decline in real income since 1970 as did AFDC mothers and their children."[5]

Finally, the 1975 enactment of the Earned Income Tax Credit further increased the incentives for members of low-income households to work. Thus, Greenstein estimates that Harold's 1980 minimum-wage income plus in-kind transfers would have been one-third higher in Pennsylvania (and higher still in other states) than the family's welfare payments and other benefits. Accordingly, he concludes, "if perverse welfare incentives in the late 1960s actually led to family dissolution and black unemployment, as Murray contends, then these trends should have reversed themselves in the 1970s, when the relative advantage of work over welfare increased sharply. They didn't. The number of female-headed households continued to surge, and black employment declined."[6]

As shown [elsewhere], much research supports Greenstein's claim that changes in welfare benefit levels alone cannot explain family disintegration. Although Murray does not discuss much of this literature, he does cite the Income Maintenance Experiments as evidence of strong welfare effects on family structure. The Seattle/Denver experiments (which were the most comprehensive and best administered) indicated that guaranteed incomes significantly reduced the stability or frequency of marriage. The effects were not consistent across payment levels, however: at the highest income level, the payments (or guarantees) had no effect on marital stability. In addition, the experimental conditions differed substantially from those under which states actually dispense AFDC payments (the primary source of public assistance to families), thereby jeopardizing generalizations from one to the other. For example, the experiments provided income support to two-parent as well as one-parent families, but, unlike the AFDC program, adjusted payments (or guarantees) were also provided to *both* adults (and the children) in cases of marital splits. Finally, as Cain notes, the effects of the income transfers were confounded with those of the experimental training program, which was shown to have increased marital instability; thus the magnitude and direction of the effects of income transfers alone are unclear.[7]

Thus, neither Murray's comparisons nor the empirical literature establishes the claim that liberal welfare policies are the major cause of changing family structure among blacks. An alternative hypothesis on the role of joblessness was presented [elsewhere].

THE FAMILY, JOBLESSNESS, AND CHANGES IN ECONOMIC ORGANIZATION: "THE MALE MARRIAGEABLE POOL" AND FAMILY STRUCTURE BY REGION

[We have] argued that when jobless figures among black men are combined with the men's relatively high rates of incarceration and premature mortality,[8] it becomes clear that the ability of black men to provide economic support is even lower than official employment statistics convey. The full dimensions of the problem were depicted with an index that showed the ratio of employed men to women of the same age and race. Designated as a "male marriageable pool index" (MMPI), this measure is intended to reveal the marriage market conditions facing women, on the assumption that to be marriageable a man needs to be employed.[9] The men and women are matched by age and race, since most people marry within their own race and near their own age. If it is correct to assume that most of the black men escaping census coverage are jobless, then their omission from the MMPI exerts little bias on the analyses.

Trends in the MMPI for the nation as a whole showed that unlike white women, black women, particularly younger black women, are confronting a shrinking pool of economically stable, or "marriageable," men. This finding supports the hypothesis that the rise of black female-headed families is directly related to increasing black male joblessness. Data presented below on both MMPI and family status by region over the 1960–80 period afford a more direct test of this hypothesis.

The trends in the MMPI reveal that changes in the ratios of employed men to women among whites have been minimal, with modest declines only among Northern whites (see table 4.1). On the other hand, the ratios for blacks have declined substantially in all regions but the West. The Northern regions averaged losses of more than 11 employed black men per 100 women among persons aged twenty to forty-four, with even greater losses if the youngest men (ages sixteen to forty-four) are included.[10] The South averaged a loss of more than 6 employed men per 100 women in the twenty to forty-four age category, and almost as many when the youngest men are included. The

"marriageable pool" of black men in the West, however, declined only by about the same amount as that of Northern whites. On the basis of these trends, we would expect growth in female-headed families to be greatest among blacks in the Northern regions, followed by the South, and to be least among whites and Western blacks.

Table 4.2 presents figures on female family headship by race and region for women under age forty-five in 1960 and 1980. We focus on female family heads under age forty-five because that group is the fastest growing and it is economically the most disadvantaged of women householders.[11] They are also more likely to have borne their children outside of marriage and therefore have more difficulty obtaining child support.[12] Two measures describe changes in female headship: the proportion of all family heads under age forty-five who are women and the proportion of all women under age forty-five

TABLE 4.1

Male Marriageable Pool Index (employed men per 100 women) by Race, Age, and Region, 1960 and 1980

	Northeast				North-Central			
	White		Black		White		Black	
	1960	1980	1960	1980	1960	1980	1960	1980
16–19	43.8	45.1	31.2	22.7	50.5	51.4	27.4	25.5
20–24	77.9	74.1	59.1	48.1	81.6	77.4	58.0	49.0
25–34	89.5	87.9	67.7	57.8	93.4	90.3	69.0	57.6
35–44	88.1	88.4	71.4	60.4	92.2	90.4	73.8	61.3
16–44	80.8	78.1	63.0	50.3	84.5	81.0	63.0	50.7
20–44	86.9	84.7	67.5	56.3	90.6	87.0	68.8	56.3

	South				West			
	White		Black		White		Black	
	1960	1980	1960	1980	1960	1980	1960	1980
16–19	44.2	50.7	38.9	29.2	48.1	51.3	NA	29.6
20–24	75.9	78.7	70.5	58.0	77.8	76.6	57.7	57.3
25–29	85.8	89.6	71.1	68.2	90.0	88.9	69.1	69.0
35–44	87.0	89.3	71.6	67.7	90.0	91.8	76.2	73.1
16–44	78.1	81.1	65.2	59.7	82.0	81.4	NA	60.5
20–44	84.4	86.8	71.2	65.1	87.7	86.8	69.7	67.0

Note: The 1960 figures for 16- to 19-year-olds refer to nonwhites rather than to blacks. This has a sizable effect only for Western blacks. In 1960, blacks made up only 49 percent of all Western nonwhites, while in all other regions, blacks comprised over 95 percent of all nonwhites.

Sources: U.S. Bureau of the Census, *U.S. Census of Population, 1960: Characteristics of the Population*, pt. 1, U.S. Summary (Washington, D.C.: Government Printing Office, 1961); and idem, *Census of Population: Detailed Characteristics of the Population*, pt. 1, U.S. Summary (Washington, D.C.: Government Printing Office, 1980).

TABLE 4.2

Indicators of Family Status by Race and Region, 1960 and 1980, Family Heads, and Women Ages Fifteen to Forty-four

	Proportion of Families Headed by Women		Proportion of Women Heading Families	
	Black	White	Black	White
Northeast				
1960	24.2	6.1	13.4	3.5
1980	48.6	12.3	25.4	6.5
Change 1960–80	+24.4	+ 6.2	+12.0	+3.0
North Central				
1960	22.7	4.8	13.4	2.9
1980	49.0	10.6	25.5	6.2
Change 1960–80	+26.3	+ 5.8	+12.1	+3.3
South				
1960	21.6	6.1	10.0	3.7
1980	37.2	10.0	19.1	6.1
Change 1960–80	+15.6	+ 3.9	+ 9.1	+2.4
West				
1960	21.5	7.5	14.1	4.7
1980	39.5	16.9	22.9	7.9
Change 1960–80	+18.0	+ 9.4	+ 8.7	+3.2

Sources: U.S. Bureau of the Census, *U.S. Census of Population, 1960: Characteristics of the Population,* pt. 1, U.S. Summary (Washington, D.C.: Government Printing Office, 1961); and idem, *Census of Population: Detailed Characteristics of the Population,* pt. 1, U.S. Summary (Washington, D.C.: Government Printing Office, 1980).

who head families. While the first measure (which describes trends in family type by sex of head) is useful because it is the conventional index of female headship, the second measure (which describes trends in family headship among women) is important as well because it does not vary with changes in the number of male-headed families.

Trends in joblessness and family structure by race and region largely conform to our expectations: as table 4.3 shows, a large drop in the MMPI tends to be associated with a sizable increase in female-headed families. The proportion of black women under forty-five heading families grew most substantially in the Northeastern and North-Central regions (+12.0 and +12.1), followed by the South (+9.1), and then the West (+8.7). On the other hand, the smaller proportions of younger white women heading families varied little by region.

TABLE 4.3

Change in the Male Marriageable Pool Index and Indicators of Family Status by Race and Region, 1960–1980

	MMPI	Families Headed by Women	Proportion of Women Heading Families
Northeast			
Black	−11.2	+24.4	+12.0
White	− 2.2	+ 6.2	+ 3.0
North Central			
Black	−12.5	+26.3	+12.1
White	− 3.6	+ 5.8	+ 3.3
South			
Black	− 6.1	+15.6	+ 9.1
White	+ 2.4	+ 3.9	+ 2.4
West			
Black	− 2.7	+18.0	+ 8.7
White	− 0.9	+ 9.4	+ 3.2

Source: See table 4.1.

Data based on the first measure, the proportion of families headed by women, also largely conformed to our expectations among blacks in the Northern regions and the South. We did not expect, however, the West to show a faster rate of growth in the proportion of black families headed by women than did the South (+18 and +15.6, respectively), nor did we expect so sharp a rise in the proportion of black women heading families in the West.

A number of characteristics unique to Western blacks, four-fifths of whom live in California, may help to explain these findings. Representing less than 9 percent of the total black population, Western blacks are far more likely to be recent migrants and to have higher levels of income and education than blacks in other regions of the country. Beyond that, the social and economic characteristics of black women who head families in California are closer to those of white female heads than to those of other black female heads. For instance, they become family heads more frequently through divorce than through separation and out-of-wedlock births, and have higher average incomes and lower rates of poverty. They also receive less welfare than women heading families in Northern regions (in the South, AFDC eligibility levels are low and welfare recipiency is restricted), despite the fact that AFDC payment guarantees in California are the highest in the continental United States.[13]

If the social and economic traits of California's black female family heads are more like those of white female heads, the reasons for their respective high rates of marital dissolution may be similar. In their landmark study of female-headed families, Ross and Sawhill suggested that the relatively high rates of marital dissolution among Western whites could be a function of selective migration.[14] Divorce is also significantly higher among blacks in the West than among blacks in other regions; indeed, the differential exceeds that between Western and non-Western white women.[15] Trends in female family headship among whites as well as among blacks in the West, moreover, appear to be unrelated to changes in the MMPI. The proportion of white families headed by women grew significantly higher in the West than in the other three regions, despite the fact that the white MMPI rose in the West and declined in the other three regions (see tables 4.1 and 4.2). It therefore seems quite reasonable to hypothesize that female family headship among Western blacks, as among Western whites, is significantly bolstered by the influx of relatively well-off migrants among whom marital dissolution is relatively high.

Nonetheless, although the MMPIs for blacks in the West changed only slightly from 1960 to 1980, they are still significantly lower than those of Western whites. While deterioration of employment conditions cannot explain the growth of black female-headed families in the West, the substantial black-white difference in male employment is quite plausibly one of the major reasons for the racial gap in female headship in the West. Moreover, in the three regions in which more than 90 percent of the nation's blacks reside, the MMPI remains a powerful predictor of the phenomenal rise of black female-headed families.

CHANGING ECONOMIC ORGANIZATION AND BLACK MALE JOBLESSNESS

If we have good reason to believe that black male joblessness is strongly related to changes in black family structure, it is also reasonable to hypothesize that the rapid contraction of the black "male marriageable pool" is related to basic changes in economic organization that have occurred in recent decades. The shift in economic activity from goods production to services has been associated with changes in the location of production: first, an interregional movement of industry from the North to the South and West; and second and more important, a movement of certain industries away from the older central cities where blacks are concentrated.

We have shown that the ratio of employed black men per one hundred black women of the same age decreased most rapidly in the two Northern regions. As table 4.4 reveals, these areas have experienced substantially less employment growth than the rest of the country.[16] Moreover, these trends are concentrated in sectors where "employment conditions typically do not require substantial education: manufacturing, retail, and wholesale trade." Between

TABLE 4.4

Employment Growth by Region

Region	Time Period	
	1950–77	1970–77
Northwest		
New England	44.6	6.3
Middle Atlantic	28.4	−1.1
North Central		
East North Central	52.8	8.5
West North Central	71.8	15.6
South		
South Atlantic[a]	128.1	20.1
East South Central	107.5	21.9
West South Central	133.0	29.8
West		
Mountain	185.5	36.8
Pacific	155.0	21.0
U.S. Total	70.3	8.6

[a]Between 1970 and 1977, all southern states experienced job growth of at least 10 percent while the District of Columbia had a loss of 16.1 percent.
Source: Bernard L. Weinstein and Robert E. Firestine, *Regional Growth and Decline in the United States* (New York: Praeger, 1978), table 1.5.

1970 and 1980, for example, 701,700 manufacturing jobs were lost from the economies of these regions.[17]

Data on the decrease in manufacturing, wholesale, and retail employment by region, however, do not reveal another pattern that appears especially relevant to the drop in the black MMPI ratios across the country: the decline of these jobs in the nation's largest cities, where blacks are heavily concentrated. Between 1947 and 1972, the central cities of the thirty-three most populous metropolitan areas (according to 1970 figures) lost 880,000 manufacturing jobs, while manufacturing employment in their suburbs grew by 2.5 million. The same cities lost 867,000 jobs in retail and wholesale trade at the same time that their suburbs gained millions of such positions.[18] While the black populations of these central cities were growing substantially, white and middle-class residents migrated to the suburbs. Between 1950 and 1980, populations in these central cities lost more than 9 million whites and added more than 5 million blacks,[19] many of them from the rural South.[20]

The decline in demand for the designated types of unskilled labor has been most severe in the older central cities of the North. The four largest (New York, Chicago, Philadelphia, and Detroit), which in 1982 accounted for more than one-quarter of the nation's central-city poor, lost more than a million jobs in manufacturing, wholesale, and retail enterprises between 1967 and 1976 alone,[21] at the same time that their populations were rapidly becoming minority dominant. By 1980, blacks and Hispanics accounted for virtually half of New York City's population, 57 percent of Chicago's, 67 percent of Detroit's, and 43 percent of Philadelphia's. The major portion of this minority population, especially in the latter two cities, is black.

The decline in blue-collar employment in the central city has been partly offset by expansion in "knowledge-intensive" fields such as advertising, finance, brokering, consulting, accounting, and law. For example, between 1953 and 1984 New York City lost about 600,000 jobs in manufacturing but gained nearly 700,000 jobs in white-collar service industries; Philadelphia lost 280,000 jobs in manufacturing but added 178,000 jobs in white-collar service industries; Baltimore lost 75,000 jobs in manufacturing but gained 84,000 jobs in white-collar service industries; and St. Louis lost 127,000 jobs in manufacturing but added 51,000 jobs in white-collar service industries.[22]

However, the research on the decline of entry-level jobs in the inner city (reported [elsewhere]) provides more direct evidence that these demographic and employment trends have produced a serious mismatch between the skills of inner-city blacks and the opportunities available to them. As pointed out earlier, substantial job losses have occurred in the very industries in which urban minorities have the greatest access, and substantial employment gains have occurred in the higher-education-requisite industries that are beyond the reach of most minority workers. If one examines recent data presented by Kasarda on central-city educational attainment by race, the extent to which inner-city blacks are poorly matched for these employment trends is readily apparent. Trichotomizing attainment into less than high school, high school completion only, and some college, Kasarda finds that whereas a plurality of central-city white men (ages sixteen to sixty-four) have attended at least some college, the modal category among black men is less than high school for all regions of the country except the West.[23] "This mismatch is one major reason why both unemployment rates and labor-force dropout rates among central city blacks are much higher than those of central city white residents," states Kasarda, "and why black unemployment rates have not responded well to economic recovery in many northern cities."[24]

However, Kasarda's measure of "lower education requisite" jobs and "higher education requisite" jobs does not address the question of the actual relevance of levels of education to real job performance. Many jobs identified as "higher education" jobs because of the average level of education of the workforce may not really require "higher educational" training. For example, a number of people have observed that the new high technology is "user friendly" and can be operated in most cases by people who have mastered the "3Rs."[25] Nonetheless, if jobs in the high growth industry depend on a mastery of the 3Rs, and if employers tend to associate such skills with higher levels of formal education, then they will tend to favor those with more, not less, formal education, thereby institutionalizing "job requirements." Moreover, many inner-city minorities face an additional problem when access to jobs is increasingly based on education criteria. Samuel Bowles and Herbert Gintis, in a provocative study of the history of education in the United States, have argued that consignment to inner-city schools helps guarantee the future economic subordinacy of minority students.[26] More specifically, inner-city schools train minority youth so that they feel and appear capable of only performing jobs in the low wage sector. Citing a recent study of disadvantaged workers which indicated that appearance was between two and three times as important to potential employees as previous work experience, high school diplomas or test scores, Bowles and Gintis contend that students in ghetto schools are not encouraged to develop the levels of self-esteem or the styles of presentation which employers perceive as evidence of capacity or ability. Secondly, schools adopt patterns of socialization which reflect the background and/or future social position of their students. Those schools with a high concentration of poor and minorities have radically different internal environments, methods of teaching and attitudes toward students than predominantly white, upper middle class suburban schools. Bowles and Gintis state that:

> Blacks and minorities are concentrated in schools whose repressive, arbitrary, generally chaotic internal order, coercive authority structures and minimal possibilities for advancement mirror the characteristics of inferior job situations. Similarly, predominantly working-class schools tend to emphasize behavioral control and rule following, while schools in well-to-do suburbs employ relatively open systems that favor greater student participation, less direct supervision, more electives and in general a value system stressing internalized standards of control.[27]

If the characteristics of inferior job situations are mirrored in the internal order of ghetto schools, then the transformation of the urban economy from jobs perceived to require lower education to those perceived to require higher education or the mastery of the 3Rs is even more problematic for inner-city residents.

The change in the MMPI of younger black men presents a particular problem of interpretation. Although the overall decline in the proportion of black marriageable men in the South is not nearly so great as that in the Northern regions, the shrinkage in the "male marriageable pool" for ages sixteen to twenty-four is actually greater there than in the North. In a recent study of the decline in black teenage employment from 1950 to 1970, Cogan argues that "the decline in the demand for low-skilled agricultural labor" was "the driving force behind the sizable reductions in the aggregate black teenage employment ratio during the period 1950–1970."[28] If the primary source of employment for black teenagers in the South was drastically reduced by mechanization of agricultural production, it is reasonable to assume that many Southern black men aged twenty to twenty-four suffered the same fate.

The substantial decline in the MMPI for black youth outside the South cannot be explained by the mechanization of agriculture, since the vast majority of non-Southern blacks are living in metropolitan areas. However, the changes in economic organization affecting central cities, where more than three-quarters of all metropolitan blacks reside, are likely to have had a significant impact on the employment of black youth. Research has shown that youth employment problems are concentrated among the less educated as well as among blacks.[29] In turn, central-city and poverty-area or ghetto residence has also been found to depress youth employment.[30] These findings are consistent with the implications of Kasarda's research: shifts in employment mix should have their greatest impact on low-skilled workers in the central cities. Finally, evidence suggests that these declines in employment of low-skilled workers accelerated during the 1970s.[31] Decennial employment ratios of black youth show that while joblessness among Southern youth increased more rapidly during the 1960s than the 1970s, among Northern youth the increase was more substantial over the latter decade. The timing of these two trends is consistent with the interpretation that changes in economic organization have had an impact on the employment of black youth.

CONCLUSION: RACE, FAMILY STRUCTURE, AND PUBLIC POLICY

We have attempted [here] to show that Murray's thesis in *Losing Ground* does not begin to come to grips with the complex problem of the rising number of female-headed families and out-of-wedlock births because he overemphasizes the role of liberal welfare policies and plays down what is perhaps the most important factor in the rise of black female-headed families—the extraordinary rise in black male joblessness. We have shown here that the decline in the incidence of intact marriages among blacks is associated with the declining economic status of black men. [Elsewhere] we demonstrated that black women nationally, especially young black women, are facing a shrinking pool of "marriageable" (i.e., employed) black men. This finding supports the hypothesis that the sharp rise of black female-headed families is directly related to increasing black male joblessness. Regional longitudinal data on female headship and the "male marriageable pool" were presented [here] to provide a further test of this hypothesis.

The trends in the MMPI reveal that whereas changes in the ratios of employed men to women among whites have been minimal for all age categories and in all regions of the country from 1960 to 1980, the ratios for blacks have declined substantially in all regions except the West. On the basis of these trends, we expected the most rapid growth in the number of black female heads to be in the Northern regions, followed by the South and the West. The data conformed to our expectations, except for the larger-than-expected increase in black female-headed families in the West. Our explanation of this latter finding focused on the pattern of selective black migration to the West. The smaller proportions of white women heading families varied little by region.

The MMPI can be constructed only on the basis of aggregate racial data, rather than by race and income class as we would prefer. Nevertheless, as we have shown, the rise of the female-headed family has had its major impact on the impoverished. Work cited [elsewhere] indicated that black female-headed families were poorer, more permanent, and more welfare-dependent than families led by white women. In a similar vein, recent work by Bane with the Michigan Panel Study of Income Dynamics showed that unlike whites, the majority of blacks experiencing a transition into a female-headed family were poor afterward.[32] Around two-thirds of those were in poverty, however, even *before* experiencing such a transition. Such findings increase our confidence that the incidence of female-headed families among blacks, more so than among whites, is related to conditions of economic deprivation.

We conclude, therefore, that the problem of joblessness should be a top-priority item in any public policy discussion focusing on enhancing the status of families. Unfortunately, in recent years joblessness has received very little attention among policymakers concerned about the plight of families in the United States. Even the perceptive Daniel Patrick Moynihan, an early advocate of this point of view, failed to emphasize this issue in his Harvard University Godkin lectures on the family and nation.[33] Instead he chose to focus on measures to aid poor families, such as establishing a national benefit standard for child welfare aid, indexing benefits to inflation, and enlarging personal and dependent tax exemptions. These are all constructive suggestions, but they need to be included in a more comprehensive reform program designed to create a tight labor market that enhances the employment opportunities of both poor men and women. Such an undertaking will, we believe, do far more in the long run to enhance the stability and reduce the welfare dependency of low-income black families than will cutting the vital provisions of the welfare state.

We emphasize the need to create employment opportunities for both sexes, even though our focus [here] is on the problem of black male joblessness. To identify black male joblessness as a major source of black family disintegration is not to suggest that policymakers should ignore the problems of joblessness and poverty among current female heads of families. Rather we underline the point that the tragic decline of intact black households cannot be divorced from the equally tragic decline in the black male "marriageable pool" in any serious policy deliberations on the plight of poor American families.

NOTES

1. Charles Murray, *Losing Ground: American Social Policy, 1950–1980* (New York: Basic Books, 1984).

2. See, e.g., Robert Kuttner, "A Flawed Case for Scrapping What's Left of the Great Society," *Washington Post Book World,* November 25, 1984, p. 4; and Robert Greenstein, "Losing Faith in 'Losing Ground,'" *New Republic,* March 25, 1985, pp. 12–17.

3. Murray, *Losing Ground,* p. 165.

4. Sheldon Danziger and Peter Gottschalk, "The Poverty of Losing Ground," *Challenge,* May/June 1985, p. 36.

5. Greenstein, "Losing Faith in 'Losing Ground,'" p. 16.

6. Ibid., p. 14.

7. Glen Cain, "Comments on August 18th Version of Marital Stability Findings, Chapter Three," mimeo, 1981.

8. Alfred Blumstein, "On the Racial Disproportionality of United States' Prison Populations," *Journal of Criminal Law and Criminology* 73 (Fall 1982): 1259–81; Reynolds Farley, "Homicide Trends in the United States," *Demography* 17 (May 1980): 177–88.

9. The MMPI figures include estimates of the number of men in the armed forces by region. The census enumerates men in the armed forces as part of the population of the area in which they are stationed; in these figures, however, they are reallocated among the regions according to the proportion of the total population (by race) residing in each region.

Region	Black		White	
	1960	1980	1960	1980
Northeast	16.0	18.3	26.1	22.5
North Central	18.2	20.1	30.2	27.7
South	60.0	53.0	27.4	31.3
West	5.7	8.5	16.3	18.6

If enlistment rates varied systematically by region, this allocation formula would be biased; unfortunately, the *Selected Manpower Statistics,* published by the Department of Defense, provides no information on enlistment rates by state or region.

While there are slight differences by age and sex in the regional distribution of the population, they are not great enough to distort the index. For instance, of the age-groups with a high proportion of servicemen, the civilian black males ages twenty to twenty-four show the greatest deviation from the distribution of the total black population in 1980.

Region	Total Population	20- to 24-Year-Old Civilian Males
Northeast	18.3	16.9
North Central	20.1	20.8
South	53.0	53.2
West	8.5	9.1

However, the MMPI values based on allocation of the servicemen according to this alternative distribution show very little difference from those based on the total population; for the Northeast, the region showing the greatest deviation, the MMPI based on this alternative allocation is 47.4, very close to the 48.1 reported in table 4.1. For the sake of simplicity and comparability, then, an allocation based on total population was chosen.

10. We stress the MMPI for men over nineteen years of age for a number of reasons. First, data for 1960 for black men between the ages of sixteen and nineteen are unavailable. Use of 1960 data for nonwhite males is acceptable only for the three regions where well over 90 percent of young nonwhite males were black. In the West in 1960 only about half of all nonwhite males were black. Also, the majority of teenagers are in school, and it is more difficult to suggest that they join the labor force full time to support a family than it is to suggest that older men do so.

11. For instance, poverty rates in 1982 for white and black families headed by women under the age of forty-five were 33 percent and 53 percent respectively, compared to 11 percent and 35 percent for white and black families headed by women ages forty-five and over. U.S. Bureau of the Census, *Current Population Reports,* Series P-60, no. 144, "Characteristics of the Population below Poverty Level, 1982" (Washington, D.C.: Government Printing Office, 1983).

12. One-quarter of all women under forty-five heading families were never married, compared to 8 percent of those forty-five and over. Never-married women have more difficulty getting child support than other women; according to Garfinkel and Uhr, only about 10 percent of all single mothers received child support awards in 1978, compared to half of all separated women and four-fifths of all divorced women. Irwin Garfinkel and Elizabeth Uhr, "A New Approach to Child Support," *Public Interest* 75 (Spring 1984): 111–22.

13. Both blacks and whites in the West are significantly more likely to be recent migrants than blacks and whites elsewhere. According to the 1980 census, for women ages twenty-five to thirty-nine, for example, more than 15 percent of Western blacks and about 14 percent of Western whites were migrants (the California proportion was about 13 percent for both groups), compared to less than 7 percent in other regions.

While educational attainment by white women was not always greater in the West or in California than in other areas, for blacks in the West greater attainment held consistently for women ages twenty-five to thirty-nine. For example, 85 percent of Western black women of those ages were high school graduates, and 13 percent were college graduates (the same as California), compared to 75 percent or fewer in other regions. Less than 12 percent of Southern black women and less than 11 percent of Northern black women of the same age-group were college graduates.

Western black families had higher incomes than families elsewhere, but more important, this was true for the female-headed families. For example, the median family incomes of black families led by women ages twenty-five to thirty-four and thirty-five to forty-four were $7,543 and $10,596 respectively in the West (in California, incomes were slightly higher). In the North Central region, the region with the second highest average income among black female-headed families, the comparable figures were only $6,488 and $9,922.

Poverty rates were unavailable for the age breakdowns most appropriate to our arguments, but the pattern of lower poverty in the West among black families headed by women under the age of sixty-five holds nevertheless. Among such families with heads ages fifteen to twenty-four years, nearly 70 percent of those in the South, more than 70 percent of those in the Northern regions, but only 65 percent of those in the West were poor. Among black families headed by women under age sixty-five, Westerners' poverty rates were 39 percent (only 36 percent in California), compared to 45 percent in the Northeast, 46 percent in the North-Central, and 48 percent in the South.

Black female family heads in California tend to resemble white female heads more than other black women heading families in their levels of income and education, as noted above. But even from a purely demographic perspective, the relative similarity between these groups of women is apparent. Like the well-established pattern of white female heads (Heather L. Ross and Isabelle Sawhill, *Time of Transition: The Growth of Families Headed by Women* [Washington, D.C.: Urban Institute, 1975]; and Mary Jo Bane and David T. Ellwood, "Single Mothers and Their Living Arrangements," working paper supported by U.S. Department of Health and Human Services grant, contract no. HHS-82-0038, 1983), black women heading families in California are more likely to head families because of a divorce than a separation or illegitimate birth. Not only are black women in California far more prone to divorce than elsewhere, but a far smaller proportion of never-married black California women had ever borne children than was the case among never-married women elsewhere. Never-married black women ages fifteen to forty-four in the West had borne some 52 children per 100 women, compared to 64 in the South and Northeast, and 70 in the North-Central region.

The California AFDC program has the highest payment guarantee in the continental United States. (Over 84 percent of Western black female-headed families live in California.) Despite this, only 53 percent of Western black families headed by women under twenty-five (usually the poorest group) reported any public assistance income in 1979, while 60 percent of such families in the Northeastern and North-Central regions reported welfare income.

14. Ross and Sawhill, *Time of Transition.*

15. For instance, among ever-married women between the ages of twenty-five and thirty-nine, 37 percent of both California and Western blacks, but only 28 percent of all such black women nationwide, ever divorced. Among white women of the same ages, the respective percentages are 33%, 32%, and 26%. U.S. Bureau of the Census, *1980 Census of Population: Detailed Characteristics of the Population,* pt. 1, U.S. Summary (Washington, D.C.: Government Printing Office, 1983).

16. John D. Kasarda, "The Implications of Contemporary Redistribution Trends for National Urban Policy," *Social Science Quarterly* 61 (1980): 303–22; and Bernard L. Weinstein and Robert E. Firestine, *Regional Growth and Decline in the United States* (New York: Praeger, 1978).

17. Kasarda, "Implications of Contemporary Redistribution Trends," p. 384.

18. Ibid.

19. Of the thirty-three largest Standard Metropolitan Statistical Areas in 1970, data on the 1950 population by race were unavailable for three (San Jose; San Bernardino-Riverside-Ontario; and Anaheim, Santa Ana-Garden Grove, in California) and part of one additional SMSA (Everett of Seattle). All of these areas are in the West. We have not argued here that central cities in the West have experienced much loss of low-skilled jobs. Indeed Kasarda ("Urban Change and Minority Opportunities," in *The New Urban Reality,* ed. Paul E. Peterson [Washington, D.C.: Brookings Institution, 1985]) has argued that Sunbelt cities, especially in the West, have tended to experience job growth even in low-skilled jobs. Moreover, as of 1980, these central cities contained only 1.2 million whites and about 74,000 blacks. Finally, the figures we present in the text understate the shifts in population of the other central cities. This is because the 1950 data for blacks are based on counts for nonwhites, thus inflating their 1950 population count, while the data for whites include most Hispanics, another socially disadvantaged group. Hence, the extent of population decline among non-Hispanic whites in the big cities is quite understated. U.S. Bureau of the Census, *U.S. Census Population,* vol. 2: *Characteristics of the Population,* pt. 1, U.S. Summary (Washington, D.C.: Government Printing Office, 1953); idem, *1970*

Census of Population: Detailed Characteristics of the Population, pt. 1, U.S. Summary (Washington, D.C.: Government Printing Office, 1973); and idem, *1980 Census of Population.*

20. C. Horace Hamilton, "The Negro Leaves the South," *Demography* 1 (1964): 273–95; and Neil Fligstein, *Going North: Migration of Blacks and Whites from the South, 1900–1950* (New York: Academic Press, 1981).

21. John D. Kasarda, "Caught in the Web of Change," *Society* 21 (1983): 44.

22. Kasarda, "Regional and Urban Redistribution of People and Jobs in the U.S.," paper prepared for the National Research Council Committee on National Urban Policy, National Academy of Science, 1986. "White-collar service industries" are "defined as those service industries where executives, managers, professionals, and clerical employees exceed more than 50% of the industry workforce." Ibid., pp. 18–19.

23. Ibid.

24. Ibid., p. 27.

25. I would like to thank Sar Levitan for bringing this point to my attention.

26. Samuel Bowles and Herbert Gintis, *Schooling in Capitalist America: Education and the Contradictions of Economic Life* (New York: Basic Books, 1976).

27. Ibid., p. 132.

28. John Cogan, "The Decline in Black Teenage Employment, 1950–70," *American Economic Review* 72 (September 1982): 621–38, quote on p. 635.

29. Martin Feldstein and David T. Ellwood, "Teenage Employment: What Is the Problem?" in *The Youth Labor Market Problem: Its Nature, Causes, and Consequences,* ed. Richard B. Freeman and David A. Wise (Chicago: University of Chicago Press, 1982); and David T. Ellwood and David A. Wise, "Youth Employment in the Seventies: The Changing Circumstances of Young Adults," working paper no. 1055, National Bureau of Economic Research, Cambridge, Mass., 1983.

30. D. N. Wescott, "Youth in the Labor Force: An Area Study," *Monthly Labor Review* 99 (1976): 3–9; B. Magnum and R. Seniger, *Coming of Age in the Ghetto* (Baltimore: Johns Hopkins University Press, 1978); S. L. Friedlander, *Unemployment in the Urban Core: An Analysis of Thirty Cities with Policy Recommendations* (New York: Praeger, 1972); Richard B. Freeman, "Economic Determinants of Geographic and Individual Variation in the Labor Market Position of Young Persons," in Freeman and Wise, *Youth Labor Market Problem;* and Albert Rees and Wayne Gray, "Family Effects in Youth Employment," in Freeman and Wise, *Youth Labor Market Problem.*

31. Black male youth employment-to-population ratios by age for the Northeast, North-Central, and South for the years 1960–80 are shown here.

	16–19 Years			20–24 Years		
	1960	1970	1980	1960	1970	1980
Northeast	31.4	26.1	19.6	67.3	61.2	48.5
North Central	26.5	27.8	22.3	62.3	62.2	48.0
South	36.0	27.4	25.8	68.3	60.8	55.6

32. Mary Jo Bane, "Household Composition and Poverty: Which Comes First?" revised paper prepared for the conference on Poverty and Policy: Retrospect and Prospects, Williamsburg, Va., December 6–8, 1984.

33. Daniel Patrick Moynihan, *Family and the Nation* (New York: Harcourt Brace Jovanovich, 1986).

Work Satisfaction and Industrial Trends in Modern Society

ROBERT BLAUNER

In 1880 that famous pioneer of survey research, Karl Marx, drew up a questionnaire of 101 items, 25,000 copies of which were sent to various workers' societies and socialist circles. This long schedule, which exhorts workers to describe "with full knowledge the evils which they endure," is composed entirely of questions of *objective fact* relating to size of plant, working conditions, wages, hours, strikes and trade unions. What appears strange in contrast with present-day surveys is the lack of questions concerning the *feelings* of the workers about their work, employers, and place in society.[1]

It is not that Marx believed that the subjective beliefs of workers were automatic and immediate reactions to their objective material conditions. He knew that workers might experience "false consciousness" instead of the "correct" awareness of their class position. But whereas the development of political class consciousness was problematic for Marx (in the short run, although not over the long haul), there seemed nothing problematic about the subjective reactions of the working class to the wretched conditions of factory labor in the early industrial society of the nineteenth century. Marxists assumed that the *alienation* of labor (which referred to an objective relationship between the employee and the social organization of the work process) would have as its subjective consequence the *estrangement* of the laborers from the factory system. The worker's lack of control, epitomized in his social status as a "wage slave" and his psychotechnic status as an "appendage of the machine,"

would result in *feelings of dissatisfaction,* which, along with the development of the more problematic consciousness of shared class interests, would be powerful enough to launch revolutionary movements and sustain them to victory.

Two recent students of Marx have stated that "the Marxian theory of why men under capitalism would revolt was based on an assumption of what prompts men to be satisfied or dissatisfied with their work."[2] And since these expected revolts of industrial workers did not occur in many Western countries, even Marxist intellectuals in recent years have begun to look more closely at workers' subjective dispositions and attitudes. While socialists and general intellectuals were writing about the proletariat in an impressionistic fashion, sometimes without direct contact with the working classes, more empirical social researchers in industry and in the academic disciplines began to question workers directly. Systematic surveys of employee attitudes, begun in the early 1920's, developed so rapidly that in the bibliography of a recent review of research and opinion on job attitudes more than 1500 items are listed.[3]

The present paper surveys research on attitudes of workers toward their work, especially those investigations commonly called job satisfaction studies. To assess the absolute level of job satisfaction in the working population is not my aim, for this is an impossible task, but rather, my purposes are (1) to locate differences in the incidence and intensity of work satisfaction among those in diverse occupations and work

This paper was originally prepared as a research memorandum for a survey of workers' attitudes being conducted by the Fund for the Republic's Trade Union Project, in cooperation with the Institute of Industrial Relations of the University of California, Berkeley. I am especially grateful to Seymour Martin Lipset both for general intellectual stimulation and for detailed criticism of an earlier draft of the paper.—AUTHOR'S NOTE.

From Galenson & Lipset (eds.), *Labor and Trade Unionism* (New York: Wiley, 1960), pp. 339–360. Reprinted with permission of Professor Blauner.

settings and (2) to discern the factors that, in accounting for these differences, seem to indicate the important preconditions of satisfaction in work. Further, the paper considers the implications of these findings for theories of work and workers in modern society, in the light of industrial and social trends.

EXTENT OF SATISFACTION: A REVIEW OF GENERAL RESEARCH

Before considering occupational differences and the factors that account for them, I shall briefly consider evidence on the general extent of job satisfaction by looking at the results of six representative sample studies. In Table 1 the figure in the extreme right-hand column indicates the percentage of workers who gave the dissatisfied response to such a question as "Taking into consideration all the things about your job (work), how satisfied or dissatisfied are you with it?"[4]

In the 1946 issue of the *Personnel and Guidance Journal*, Robert Hoppock began summarizing the results of all published studies of job satisfaction, most of which were nonrepresentative samples of individual companies or occupations. When, by 1958, 406 percentages of the proportion of persons dissatisfied with their jobs in these several hundred studies had been averaged out, they yielded a median percentage of 13 per cent dissatisfied.[5] This figure is quite similar to the summary percentages of dissatisfaction resulting from more representative labor force samples.

Thus the most recent American research on satisfaction attitudes seems to support the generalization that: "Even under the existing conditions, which are far from satisfactory, most workers like their jobs. Every survey of workers' attitudes which has been carried out, no matter in what industry, indicates that this is so."[6]

But a caveat should be inserted at this point. Many of these studies, which seek to determine the proportion of workers who are satisfied or dissatisfied with their jobs, fail to specify sufficiently an inherently vague concept and ignore the cultural pressures on workers to exaggerate the degree of actual satisfaction. Despite this, the evidence shows that in the numerous samples of the labor force which have been interviewed, more than 80 per cent indicate general job satisfaction.[7] Even though the methodological limitations make it hard to accept the findings of any one of these studies by itself, it is much harder to reject the weight of their cumulative evidence.

TABLE 1

Proportion of Dissatisfied Workers in Major Job Satisfaction Studies

Researchers	Scope of Sample	Composition of Study	Date	Per Cent Dissatisfied
Morse and Weiss*	Random national	401 employed men	1955	20
Centers†	Representative national	811 men	1949	17
Palmer‡	Norristown, Pa.	517 labor force members	1957	10
Shister and Reynolds§	New England city	800 manual workers	1949	12 21**
Hoppock‖	New Hope, Pa.	309 labor force members	1935	15
Kornhauser¶	Detroit area	324 employed persons	1952	11

*Nancy C. Morse and Robert S. Weiss, "The Function and Meaning of Work and the Job," *American Sociological Review,* 20 (1955), pp. 191–198.

†Richard Centers, *The Psychology of Social Classes* (Princeton: Princeton University Press, 1949), p. 172.

‡Gladys L. Palmer, "Attitudes toward Work in an Industrial Community," *American Journal of Sociology,* 63 (1957), pp. 17–26.

§Joseph Shister and L. G. Reynolds, *Job Horizons: A Study of Job Satisfaction and Labor Mobility* (New York: Harper, 1949). p. 33.

‖Robert Hoppock, *Job Satisfaction* (New York: Harper, 1935), p. 246.

¶Arthur Kornhauser, *Detroit as the People See It* (Detroit: Wayne University Press, 1952), p. 54.

**Two separate samples.

Although it is difficult, therefore, not to accept the proposition that at least the majority (and possibly a very large majority) of American workers are moderately satisfied in their work, such a finding is neither particularly surprising nor sociologically interesting. Under "normal" conditions there is a natural tendency for people to identify with, or at least to be somewhat positively oriented toward, those social arrangements in which they are implicated. Attitude surveys show that the majority of employees like their company, that the majority of members are satisfied with their unions, and undoubtedly research would show a preponderance of positive over negative attitudes toward one's own marriage, family, religion, and nation-state. It is the presence of marked occupational *differences* in work attitudes to which I turn in the next section that is of more theoretical interest.

OCCUPATIONAL DIFFERENCES IN WORK SATISFACTION

Work satisfaction varies greatly by occupation. Highest percentages of satisfied workers are usually found among professionals and businessmen. In a given plant, the proportion satisfied is higher among clerical workers than among factory workers, just as in general labor force samples it is higher among middle-class than among manual working class occupations. Within the manual working class, job satisfaction is highest among skilled workers, lowest among unskilled laborers and workers on assembly lines.

When a scale of relative job satisfaction is formed, based on general occupational categories, the resulting rank order is almost identical with the most commonly used occupational status classification—the Edwards scale of the Bureau of the Census. For example, the mean indexes of satisfaction in Table 2 resulted from a survey of all New Hope, Pa., jobholders in 1935.

A similar rank order resulted in a national survey when the proportions of workers in each occupational group who would continue the same kind of work in the event they inherited enough money to live comfortably were computed[8] (Table 3).

TABLE 2

Occupational Group	Mean Index[9]	Number in Sample
Professional and managerial	560	23
Semiprofessional, business, and supervisory	548	32
Skilled manual and white collar	510	84
Semiskilled manual workers	483	74
Unskilled manual workers	401	55

TABLE 3

Occupational Group	Percent Who Would Continue Same Kind of Work	Number in Sample
Professionals	68	28
Sales	59	22
Managers	55	22
Skilled manual	40	86
Service	33	18
Semiskilled operatives	32	80
Unskilled	16	27

The generally higher level of job satisfaction of white-collar over blue-collar workers is confirmed by a study of twelve different factories in 1934, in which the scores of clerical workers on job satisfaction were considerably higher than those of factory workers;[10] by the Centers national sample, which found that only 14 per cent of workers in middle-class occupations were dissatisfied with their jobs, compared to 21 per cent of those in working class occupations;[11] and by a 1947 *Fortune* poll, which revealed that the proportion of employees who said their jobs were interesting was 92 per cent among professionals and executives, 72 per cent among salaried employees and 54 per cent among factory workers.[12] However, a study of the Detroit area population found that only among such upper white-collar employees as secretaries, draftsmen, and bookkeepers was the incidence of job satisfaction greater than among manual workers; such lower white-collar employees as clerks, typists, and retail salespeople were somewhat less satisfied than blue-collar workers.[13]

Further evidence of the relation of job satisfaction to occupational status is provided by studies of retirement plans. Although there are a number of factors which affect the retirement decision, it is plausible to argue that the more satisfying a job is to the worker, the more likely he will choose not to retire. In a study of work and retirement in six occupations it was found that the proportion of men who wanted to continue working or had actually continued working after age sixty-five was more than 67 per cent for physicians, 65 per cent for department store salesmen, 49 per cent for skilled printers, 42 per cent for coal miners, and 32 per cent for unskilled and semiskilled steelworkers.[14]

As has been shown in the preceding section of this paper, the majority of workers in all occupations respond positively when asked whether or not they are satisfied with their jobs. But that does not mean they would not prefer other kinds of work. The average worker in a lower-status occupation says that he would choose another line of work if he had the chance to start his working life anew. This question then, is perhaps a more sensitive indicator of latent dissatisfactions and frustrations; the occupational differences it points to, though forming the same pattern as the other, are considerably greater. For example, when a survey of 13,000 Maryland youths was made during the depression it was found that 91 per cent of professional-technical workers preferred their own occupation to any other, compared to 45 per cent of managerial personnel and farm owners, 41 per cent of skilled manual workers, 37 per cent of domestic workers, 36 per cent of office and sales personnel, 14 per cent of unskilled, and 11 per cent of semiskilled manual workers.[15]

More detailed data for a number of professional and manual working class occupations strongly confirms these general findings. Note how for six different professions, the proportion of satisfied persons ranges from 82 per cent to 91 per cent, whereas for seven manual occupations it varies from 16 per cent for unskilled automobile workers to 52 per cent for skilled printers. (See Table 4.)

To some extent, these findings on occupational differences in job satisfaction reflect not only differences in the objective conditions of

TABLE 4

Proportion in Various Occupations Who Would Choose Same Kind of Work If Beginning Career Again

Professional Occupations, %		Working Class Occupations,§ %	
Mathematicians*	91	Skilled printers	52
Physicists*	89	Paper workers	52
Biologists*	89	Skilled automobile workers	41
Chemists*	86	Skilled steelworkers	41
Lawyers†‡	83	Textile workers	3
Journalists‡	82	Unskilled steelworkers	2
		Unskilled automobile workers	16

Sources:
*"The Scientists: A Group Portrait," *Fortune*, October 1948, pp. 106–112.
†"The U.S. Bar," *Fortune*, May 1939, p. 176.
‡Leo Rosten, *The Washington Correspondents* (New York: Harcourt, Brace and Company, 1938), p. 347.
§These are unpublished data which have been computed from the IBM cards of a survey of 3000 factory workers in 16 industries, conducted by Elmo Roper for *Fortune* magazine in 1947. A secondary analysis of this survey is being carried out by the Fund for the Republic's Trade Union Project. The general findings of the original study appeared in "The Fortune Survey, *Fortune*, May 1947, pp. 5–12, and June 1947, pp. 5–10.

work for people in various jobs, *but also occupational differences in the norms with respect to work attitudes.*[16] The professional is expected to be dedicated to his profession and have an intense intrinsic interest in his area of specialized competence; the white-collar employee is expected to be "company" oriented and like his work; but the loyalty of the manual worker is never taken for granted and, more than any other occupational type, cultural norms permit him the privilege of griping. In fact, it has been asserted that "the natural state of the industrial worker . . . is one of discontent."[17] The same point has been clearly made in an analysis of the latent function of the time clock:

> The office staff does not "clock-in"—ostensibly because they are not paid by the hour, but it seems likely that at least part of the reason for this is the supposition that, unlike labourers, they do not necessarily dislike work and can be placed on their honour to be punctual. The working classes, as we have seen, are supposed to dislike work and therefore need "discipline" to keep them in order. Since "clocking-in" has been abolished in many firms, it cannot be accepted as absolutely necessary.[18]

FACTORS THAT ACCOUNT FOR OCCUPATIONAL DIFFERENCES IN SATISFACTION

The literature on work is filled with numerous attempts to list and often to estimate the relative importance of the various components, elements, or factors involved in job satisfaction. These lists do not correspond neatly with one another; they bear a large number of labels, but they all are likely to include, in one way or another, such variables as the income attached to a job, supervision, working conditions, social relations, and the variety and skill intrinsic in the work itself. The classification of these items is quite arbitrary and the number of factors considered relevant can be broken down almost indefinitely.[19]

Whereas most studies attempt to explain variations in job satisfaction among individual employees in the same company or occupation, the interest of the present paper is to explain the gross differences in work attitudes that exist among those in *different* occupations and industries. Four factors that seem useful in accounting for these differences are discussed: occupational prestige, control, integrated work groups, and occupational communities.[20]

Occupational prestige. Occupational prestige is the one best explanatory factor in the sense that if all occupations (for which sufficient data are available) were ranked in order of extent of typical job satisfaction, and these ranks were compared with the rank order in which they partake of public esteem, the rank-order correlations would be higher than those resulting from any other factor. This is because the prestige of any occupation depends on the level of skill the job entails, the degree of education or training necessary, the amount of control and responsibility involved in the performance of the work, the income which is typically received—to mention the most readily apparent factors. Since occupational prestige as a kind of composite index partly subsumes within itself a number of factors which contribute heavily to differences in satisfaction, it is not surprising that it should be itself the best individual measure of satisfaction.

In addition, jobs that have high prestige will tend to be valued for their status rewards even when "objective" aspects of the work are undesirable; similarly, low-status jobs will tend to be undervalued and disliked.

> . . . the lowliness or nastiness of a job are subjective estimates. . . . A doctor or a nurse, for example, or a sanitary inspector, have to do some things which would disgust the most unskilled casual laborer who did not see these actions in their social context. Yet the status and prestige of such people is generally high. . . . Above all, it is the prestige of his working group and his position in it which will influence the worker's attitude to such jobs.[21]

That the actual findings on differences in job satisfactions correspond quite closely to the scale of occupational prestige has been shown in the previous section. Professionals and business executives have the highest prestige in our society; they also consistently report the highest degree of work satisfaction. According to the most thorough occupational prestige study, doctors are the most esteemed major occupational group in the United States.[22] It is not surprising therefore that this public esteem is an important source of their satisfaction with their work:

> [For] physicians . . . work is a source of prestige. Some doctors stated that to be a physician meant that one belonged to an elite class. It meant that one associated with important people and was in a position of leadership in the community.[23]

Among non-professional or managerial employees, white-collar workers are generally more satisfied with their jobs than manual workers. Again status considerations play an important role. Even when white-collar work does not outrank manual jobs in income or skill, office workers are accorded higher social prestige than blue-collar personnel.[24]

Although this is so, manual work seems to be viewed with greater respect in America, with its democratic frontier traditions, than in many other nations.[25] The historic "social inferiority complex," the "sense of social subordination" of the European industrial worker, to use the words of Henri DeMan,[26] has never been well developed in the United States. We might expect, therefore, that the level of work satisfaction among manual workers would be higher in this country than in Europe.[27] With the rapidly increasing number of attitude surveys of European workers since the war, such a comparison would be of considerable interest.

Within the world of manual work, occupational differences in satisfaction are also related to the differences in prestige that exist among various working class jobs. The higher incidence of positive work attitudes consistently found among skilled workers is not only caused by the skill factor per se; the craftsman takes pride in the fact that he is looked on with more respect in the community than the factory operative or the unskilled laborer.[28] Moreover, those manual workers in occupations which are particularly looked down on will find difficulty in deriving overall positive satisfactions in their work. Interviewers of coal miners have remarked on the great pride with which they are shown various home improvements made possible by the higher wages of a period of prosperity, and on the sensitivity with which some miners react to the public image of the occupation, which has been, in part, created by the hostility of the mass media to the militancy of the union.

> I don't like to strike, because people all get mad at the miners then. I wish the people would realize that the miner has to live too, and not hate him when he tries to better conditions for himself. It bothers me the way people say bad things about the miners, and makes me ashamed of my job.[29]

An attempt has been made to illustrate the manner in which variations in work satisfaction among different occupations tend to follow variations in occupational prestige. Although this generalization is, to an impressive extent, supported by the evidence, it does not hold unfailingly. We can note occupations with relatively high prestige whose general level of satisfaction is lower than would be expected, whereas some low-status jobs seem to be highly satisfying. This suggests that in certain cases other factors play a role even more important than status. A good test of the approach applied here is to see whether the other factors which

have been advanced as critical ones can indeed account for discrepancies in the generally marked association between occupational prestige and job satisfaction.

Control. In a perceptive passage, the Belgian socialist Henri DeMan remarks that "all work is felt to be coercive."[30] The fact that work inherently involves a surrender of control, a "subordination of the worker to remoter aims," is probably what makes the relative degree of control in work so important an aspect of job attitudes. As Max Weber, the German sociologist, suggested long ago, "no man easily yields to another full control over the effort, and especially over the amount of physical effort he must daily exert."[31]

There seem to be significant cultural as well as individual differences in the need for control and independence in work. In America, where individual initiative has long been a cultural ideal, we would expect strong pressures in this direction. And we do find that surprising proportions of manual workers in this country have attempted to succeed in small business,[32] and that for many others the idea of running a gas station or a number of tourist cabins is a compelling dream.[33]

Lack of control over the conditions of work is most pronounced for industrial workers.

> The very evidence of his daily work life brings home to the manual worker the degree to which he is directed in his behavior with only limited free choices available. From the moment of starting work by punching a time clock, through work routines that are established at fixed times, until the day ends at the same mechanical time recorder, there is impressed upon the industrial worker his narrow niche in a complex and ordered system of interdependency . . . a system over which he, as an individual, exercises little direct control.[34]

The factory worker is at the bottom of the bureaucratic hierarchy; he is a person for whom action is constantly being originated, but who himself originates little activity for others.[35]

At the same time, diverse factory jobs and working class occupations vary greatly in the degree of control they permit over the conditions of work: it is these variations, of which workers are keenly aware, that are most interesting for the purpose of accounting for differences in satisfaction.

The notion of control in work, as I am using it, is, of course, a vague, *sensitizing* concept which covers a wide range of phenomena rather than a concept which is precisely delimited and identifiable by precise indicators. Among its most important dimensions are control over the use of one's *time* and physical *movement,* which is fundamentally control over the *pace* of the work process, control over the *environment,* both technical and social, and control as the *freedom* from *hierarchal authority.* Naturally, these dimensions are highly interrelated; a business executive high on the occupational ladder will tend to be high in each, whereas an unskilled laborer will have little control from any of these viewpoints. *It is possible to generalize on the basis of the evidence that the greater the degree of control that a worker has (either in a single dimension or as a total composite) the greater his job satisfaction.*[36]

Control Over Time, Physical Movement and Pace of Work. Assembly line work in the automobile industry is a good example of the almost complete absence of this aspect of control.

Its coerced rhythms, the inability to pause at will for a moment's rest, and the need for undeviating attention to simple routines made it work to be avoided if possible and to escape from if necessary. So demanding is the line that one worker, echoing others, complained: "You get the feeling, everybody gets the feeling, whenever the line jerks everybody is wishing, 'break down, baby!' "[37]

The consensus of the work literature is that assembly line work, especially in the automobile industry, is more disliked than any other major occupation, and the prime factor in dissatisfaction with the assembly line is the lack of control over the pace of production.[38] Workers in assembly line plants have strong preferences for jobs off the line. A study of the job aspirations of 180 men on the line found that the 'workers' motivations were not what might normally be expected. It was not promotion or transfer in order to improve one's economic

status. Rather, it was primarily a desire 'to get away from the line.' " *Only 8 per cent* were satisfied, in the sense of not preferring to get an off-line job.[39] The difference between line and off-line jobs has been clearly stated by the sociologist Ely Chinoy who worked in an automobile plant and studied automobile workers:

Work at a machine may be just as repetitive, require as few motions and as little thought as line assembly, but men prefer it because it does not keep them tied as tightly to their tasks. "I can stop occasionally when I want to," said a machine-operator. "I couldn't do that when I was on the line." Production standards for a particular machine may be disliked and felt to be excessive, but the machine operator need only approximate his production quota each day. The line-tender must do all the work that the endless belt brings before him. . . .[40]

The greater dissatisfaction with mass production assembly line jobs is confirmed by the findings in an automobile plant that "men with highly repetitive jobs, conveyor paced, and so forth, were far more likely to take time off from work than those whose jobs did not contain such job characteristics," and that quit rates were almost twice as high among men on the assembly line as among men off the line.[41] In a study of Maryland youth during the depression, it was found that the occupation most disliked by female workers was that of operator on cannery conveyor belts. Every one of the fifty-three cannery operatives in the sample expressed a preference for different work![42] The control of these workers over the pace of production is at least as minimal as that of automobile workers, and in addition they lack even the protection of a strong union.

A machine operator may go all out in the morning to produce 100 pieces, take it easy in the afternoon, only putting out 50; at any rate, it is his own decision. In similar fashion a few assembly line workers may be able to build up a "bank" of automobile seats which they assemble to the oncoming bodies; a few try to get ahead and gain time for rest by working up the line, but for the great majority it is hopeless. Assembly line workers are "alienated," according to the researchers who have studied them. In their work they "can secure little significant experience of themselves as productive human beings." As one automobile worker put it a little wistfully:

> You understand, if you get a job that you're interested in, when you work you don't pay attention to the time, you don't wait for the whistle to blow to go home, you're all wrapped up in it and don't pay attention to other things. *I don't know one single job like that.*[43]

According to David Riesman, what these wage earners are deprived of is "any chance to extend themselves, to go all-out." A stark example is the worker on the packinghouse assembly line who goes home after his day's work in order to "try to accomplish something for that day."[44] How do these workers stand it? Here is the deadly answer of a Hormel meat worker: "The time passes."

> Most workers are so busily engaged in pushing the flow of work that they do not *consciously* suffer from the inherent monotony of their work. They are well adjusted, because they have reduced their level of aspirations to the rather low level of the job. They coast along, keeping busy, visiting, talking, making time go by, and getting the work done in order to get "out of there" in order to get home![45]

The great dissatisfaction with automobile assembly work is an example of a discrepancy between occupational status and job satisfaction. The status of the automobile worker is not lower than that of other semiskilled American factory workers; in fact, the level of wages would suggest that it is higher than manual workers in many other industrial occupations, especially those in non-durable goods manufacturing. But the control of the automobile assembly line worker over the work process is considerably less than in other major industrial occupations, and this is a big factor in accounting for the prevalence of job discontent.

It is interesting to contrast automobile manufacturing with mining, an occupation which, though considered lower in prestige,[46] seems to provide marked work satisfaction. Alvin Gouldner, in his study of a gypsum plant, found that although the miners had considerably less status in the community than surface workers, they showed much greater work

motivation. He attributed this high job satisfaction to the fact that miners

> were not "alienated" from their machines: that is, they had an unusually high degree of control over their machines' operation. The pace at which the machines worked, the corners into which they were poked, what happened to them when they broke down, was determined mainly by the miners themselves. On the surface, though, the speed at which the machines worked and the procedures followed were prescribed by superiors.[47]

Finally, the higher job satisfaction of skilled workers (documented in the preceding sections of this paper) is related to the fact that they have a large measure of control over the pace of their work. The fact that craftsmen themselves largely determine the speed at which they work gives them a marked advantage over most factory workers.[48]

Control Over the Technical and Social Environment. In those occupations in which the physical environment or the technological work process is particularly challenging, control over it seems to be an important aspect of job satisfaction. Coal-miners have "a very personal sense of being pitted against their environment" and express "feelings of accomplishment and pride at having conquered it."[49] That steel production is found fascinating is suggested by a mill worker: "It's sort of interesting. Sometimes you have a battle on your hands. You have to use your imagination and ability to figure out what move to make."[50] Similarly, it has been noted that railroad workers derive a sense of power in "the manipulation of many tons of railroad equipment." Engineers derive more pleasure in running large engines rather than small ones; switchmen and brakeman "give the signals that move fifty or so freight cars back and forth like so many toys."[51]

A further source of the dissatisfaction with automobile assembly, then, is the fact that these jobs provide so little scope for control over the technical environment; there is little that is challenging in the actual work operation. As a man on the line puts it:

> There is nothing more discouraging than having a barrel beside you with 10,000 bolts in it and using them all up. Then you get a barrel

with another 10,000 bolts, and you know that every one of those 10,000 bolts has to be picked up and put in exactly the same place as the last 10,000 bolts.[52]

Paralleling the control of industrial workers over the technical environment is the satisfaction derived by professional and white-collar employees from control over a social environment, namely, clients and customers. A study of salespeople concluded that "the completion of the sale, the conquering of the customer, represents the challenge or the 'meaningful life-experience' of selling."[53] As one salesclerk, contemplating the import of his retirement, said: "I think to be perfectly truthful about it, the thing I miss most is being able to project myself into a sphere, conquer it, and retire with a pleased feeling because I have conquered it."[54]

Control as the Freedom from Direct Supervision. On a slightly different level of analysis is this third dimension, which refers not to the aspects of the work process under control, but rather to the locus of control. One of the most consistent findings of work research is that industrial workers consider light, infrequent supervision, "foremen who aren't drivers," a crucial element in their high regard for particular jobs and companies.

The absence of close supervision in the mines has been considered an important determinant of the miners' high level of satisfaction.[55] And truck drivers and railroad workers, in explaining their preference for their own trades, stress the independence they experience in these jobs where the contact between employees and supervisor is so much less frequent than in factory work. As two railroad engineers put it:

> I'd work anywhere except at a shop or in the factory. Just don't like a place where someone is watching you do your work all the time. That's why I like my job on the railroad now.
>
> I wouldn't last three days working in a shop with a foreman breathing down my neck. Here I'm my own boss when I run the trains, nobody tells me what to do. . . .[56]

Such impressionistic evidence is confirmed by the more systematic comparisons of Hoppock, who found that the mean job satisfaction index of railroad employees ranked only below professional men and artists; it was higher than managers, clerical workers, small business proprietors, salesmen, and storeclerks! Although railroading is a high-status industrial occupation—railroaders have historically been part of the labor aristocracy—its occupational prestige is below most white-collar occupations. On the other hand, truck driving is a lower-status manual occupation (truck drivers are classified as semi-skilled operatives by the census, and the popular stereotypes of this occupation are somewhat derogatory), and yet in the Hoppock survey the satisfaction of truck drivers outranked all industrial occupations except railroading and was approximately the same level as that of salesmen.[57]

It is plausible that the marked discrepancy between job satisfaction and occupational status in these industries can be explained by the high degree of control, especially as reflected in freedom from supervision, which the workers enjoy.

If control in the work process is a crucial determinant of a worker's subjective feelings of well-being on the job, as I am trying to demonstrate, the question whether industrial trends are increasing or decreasing these areas of control becomes quite significant. It is interesting that Faunce's recent study of an *automated* engine plant shows that various dimensions of control may not change in the same direction. Compared to work in a non-automated, non-assembly line engine plant, automation greatly decreased the worker's direct control over his machine and pace of work, and this was felt to be a source of serious dissatisfaction. On the other hand, the increased responsibility and control over a complex technical environment of automated equipment was seen as a source of greater satisfaction and heightened status. Thus, while Faunce was able to locate the elements which made for satisfaction and those which made for dissatisfaction in these jobs (his analysis seems very congruent with the present discussion), it was rather difficult to assess the overall effect of the change on work satisfaction.[58]

Integrated Work Groups. A third factor that is important in explaining occupational differences in work satisfaction is the nature of on-the-job social relations. The technological structure of certain industries such as steel production and mining requires that the work be carried out by *teams* of men working closely together, whereas in industries such as automobile assembly the formation of regular work groups is virtually prohibited by the organization of production. There is much evidence to support the proposition that the greater the extent to which workers are members of integrated work teams on the job, the higher the level of job satisfaction.

In a steel mill in which 85 per cent of sixty-two workers interviewed were satisfied with their jobs, Charles Walker found that "the source of satisfaction most often articulated or implied was that of being part of, or having membership in, the hot mill crew." As three steel workers express it:

(A heater helper) We work for a while, it's like playing baseball. First one fellow is up and then you have your turn at bat. We can knock off every so often and take a smoke and talk. I like working with men I know and working like a team.

(A piercer plugger) The crew I am in is very good. Our foreman likes to see his men on top and he does everything to help us . . . this attitude makes a lot of people put out more steel. . . . Over here it's teamwork. . . . You can have a lot of Hank Greenbergs on the team but if you don't work together, it isn't a team at all. And we like our work because we carry on a lot of conversation with signs and the men laugh and joke and the time passes very quick.

(A piercer dragout worker) There's nothing like working here in this mill. Everybody cooperates. Every man works as a member of a team and every man tries to turn out as much steel as they possibly can. We work hard and get satisfaction out of working hard.[59]

While recognizing that close kinship ties and a small town atmosphere encouraged such cooperative spirit, Walker attributed the principal cause of the integrated work teams to the basic technological process of making steel, which requires small group operations. He compared this technology and its results with that of the automobile assembly plants in which the technological structure is such that the majority of workers perform their operations individually. There,

the pattern of social interaction produced by the moving line is such that although workers will talk to the man in front of them, behind them, and across from them, no worker will interact with exactly the same group of men as any other worker will; therefore, no stable work groups are formed. Walker considered this a major element in the greater dissatisfaction he found among automobile workers compared to steel workers.

Mining is another occupation where technological conditions seem to favor the development of closely knit work groups. Since, as one miner expressed it, "the mines are kind of a family affair," where "the quality of the sentiment is of a depth and complexity produced only by long years of intimate association," it is not surprising that many miners feel that the loss of social contacts at work is a major disadvantage of retirement. The dangerous nature of the work is another factor that knits miners together:

To be an old-timer in the mines means something more than merely knowing the technique of a particular job; it also means awareness and acceptance of the responsibility which each man has for his fellow-workers. The sense of interdependence in relation to common dangers is undoubtedly an important factor in the spirit of solidarity which has characterized miners in all countries for many generations.[60]

Within the same factory, departments and jobs vary considerably in the extent to which the work is carried out by individuals working alone or by groups; the consequences of these differences have been a major interest of the "human relations in industry" movement. A recent study of one department in a factory manufacturing rotating equipment found that the employees who were integrated members of informal work groups were, by and large, satisfied with both the intrinsic characteristics of their jobs, and such "extended characteristics" as pay, working conditions, and benefits, whereas the non-group members tended to be dissatisfied. Sixty-five per cent of "regular" group members were satisfied, compared to 43 per cent of members of groups which were deviant in accepting less fully the values of the factory community, and compared to only 28 per cent of isolated workers.[61]

The classic investigations of the functions of informal work groups in industry have been produced by the "human relations in industry" school, associated most directly with the Harvard Business School and the writings of Elton Mayo, and represented by the pioneering experiments at the Hawthorne plant of the Western Electric Company.[62] These studies have demonstrated that informal work groups establish and enforce norms which guide the productive and other behavior of workers on the job, and that such management problems as absenteeism, turnover, and morale can often be dealt with through the manipulation of work groups and supervisorial behavior. But it is striking that the human relations school has concerned itself so little with the job itself, with the relation between the worker and his work, rather than the relation between the worker and his mates.[63] A typical human relations discussion of the conditions of employee morale is likely to give all its emphasis to matters of communication, supervision, and the personality of workers and ignore almost completely intrinsic job tasks.[64] In a recent study by the Harvard Business School entitled *Worker Satisfaction and Development,* the only sources of work satisfaction discussed are those which directly concern workers' integration in work groups and cliques. Although creativity is a major concern of the author, it is the creativity of the *work group* to adapt to new circumstances, rather than the creative expression of an individual in his work, that he is interested in.[65]

In its emphasis on the importance of integrated work groups the human relations approach has made an important contribution. But "a way of seeing is a way of not seeing," and its neglect of the other factors imposes serious limitations on the usefulness of this approach, at least in providing an adequate theory of the conditions of work satisfaction.[66]

Occupational Communities. The nature of the association among workers *off-the-job* is also a factor in work satisfaction. The evidence of the work literature supports the notion that levels of work satisfaction are higher in those industries and in those kinds of jobs in which workers make up an "occupational community." One such industry is mining. Not only is the actual work carried out by solitary work groups, but, in addition, miners live in a community made up largely of fellow workers. This kind of "inbreeding" produces a devotion to the occupation which is not characteristic of many other working class jobs:

> Somehow when you get into mining and you like the men you work with, you just get to the place after a while that you don't want to leave. *Once that fever gets hold of a man, he'll never be good for anything else.*
> A fellow may quit the mines, but when they whistle, he goes back. I've had a lot better jobs, but I've always liked to work in the mines. I can't explain it, except I like being with the gang; I never could just sit around much.[67]

Such occupational communities are likely to develop in occupations that are isolated, either spatially or on the basis of peculiar hours of work. Coal mining and textile industries characteristically have grown up in *isolated small communities;* sailors, cowboys, and long-distance truck drivers are also isolated from contact with persons in other jobs. Similarly, *off-hours shifts* favor the development of occupational communities; this is the case with printers, a large proportion of whom work nights,[68] steelworkers, who often rotate between day, swing, and graveyard shifts, firemen, and, of course, railroad men.

The essential feature of an occupational community is that workers in their off-hours socialize more with the persons in their own line of work than with a cross section of occupational types. Printers generally go to bars, movies, and baseball games with other printers.[69] In a small town steel mill, 87 per cent of the workers had spent "in the last week," at least some time off the job with other workers in their department; almost half said they had seen many or almost all of their fellow workers.[70] However, in a large tractor plant of 20,000 people only 41 per cent of the employees said that they got together socially outside the plant with employees from their own work groups.[71] *Occupational communities rarely exist among urban factory workers.*

A second characteristic of an occupational community is that its participants "talk shop" in their off-hours. That this is true of farmers, fishermen, miners, and railroaders has been described far more by novelists than by social scientists. The significance of talking about work off the job has been well expressed by

Fred Blum, who notes that the assembly line workers in the meat packing plant he studied rarely do so.

> Whether they are with their family or their friends, rare are the occasions when workers feel like talking about their work. In response to the question: "Do you talk with your friends about the work you are doing?" only a very small number indicated that they do talk with their friends—or their wife—about their work. Quite a few said that they "only" talk with their friends "if they ask me" or that they talk "sometimes" or "seldom." Some workers are outspoken in saying that they do not like to talk about their work. "If we get out of there, we are through with that to the next day." Another worker said, "When I leave down there, I am through down there. I like to talk about something else." *He adds to this with some astonishment: "Railroadmen always want to talk about their work."*[72]

Third, occupational communities are little worlds in themselves. For its members the occupation itself is the reference group; its standards of behavior, its system of status and rank, guide conduct.[73]

> Railroading is something more than an occupation. Like thieving and music, it is a world by itself, with its own literature and mythology, with an irrational system of status which is unintelligible to the outsider, and a complicated rule book for distributing responsibility and rewards.[74]

We can suggest a number of mechanisms by means of which occupational communities increase job satisfaction.[75] First, when workers know their co-workers off the job, they will derive deeper social satisfactions on the job. In the second place, an effect of the isolation of the occupation is that workers are able to develop and maintain a pride in and devotion to their line of work; at the same time, isolation insulates them from having to come to grips with the general public's image of their status, which is likely to be considerably lower than their own. Participation in an occupational community means not only the reinforcement of the group's sense of general prestige; in such worlds one's skill and expertise in doing the actual work becomes an important basis of individual status and prestige. Finally, unlike the "alienated" assembly line worker, who is characterized by a separation of his work sphere from his non-work sphere—a separation of work from life as Mills and Blum put it—the work and leisure interests of those in occupational communities are highly integrated. If the integration of work and non-work is an important element in general psychic adjustment, as some assert, then these workers should exhibit higher job satisfaction, since satisfaction with life in general seems to be highly related to satisfaction in work.[76]

CONCLUSIONS

When we read modern accounts of what work and workers were like before the industrial revolution, we continually find that the dominant image of the worker of that period is the craftsman. Viewed as an independent producer in his home or small shop with complete control over the pace and scheduling of his work, making the whole product rather than a part of it, and taking pride in the creativity of his skilled tasks, his traits are typically contrasted with those of the alienated factory worker—the allegedly characteristic producer of modern society.[77]

It is remarkable what an enormous impact this *contrast* of the craftsman with the factory hand has had on intellectual discussions of work and workers in modern society, *notwithstanding its lack of correspondence to present and historical realities*. For, indeed, craftsman, far from being typical workers of the past era, accounted for less than 10 per cent of the medieval labor force, and the peasant, who was actually the representative laborer, was, in the words of the Belgian socialist Henri DeMan, "practically nothing more than a working beast."[78] Furthermore, the real character of the craftsman's work has been romanticized by the prevalent tendency to idealize the past, whereas much evidence suggests that modern work does not fit the black portrait of meaningless alienation. In fact, it has been asserted "that in modern society there is far greater scope for skill and craftsmanship than in any previous society, and that far more people are in a position to use such skills."[79]

For intellectuals, it seems to be particularly difficult to grasp both the subjective and relative character of monotony and the capacity of workers to inject meaning into "objectively meaningless" work. Their strong tendency to view workers as dissatisfied suggests the idea that the alienation thesis, though a direct descendant of Marxist theory and related to a particular political posture, also reflects an intellectual perspective (in the sociology of knowledge sense) on manual work.

Surprisingly enough, business executives also tend to view manual workers as alienated. Perhaps this attitude reflects in part the growing influence of intellectual ideas including neo-Marxist ones, on the more progressive business circles; perhaps, more importantly, this stems again, as in the case of the intellectual, from the middle-class businessman's separation and distance from the workaday world of his industrial employees. At any rate, such industrial spokesmen as Peter Drucker and Alexander Heron are likely to generalize much as does James Worthy of Sears, Roebuck, who, in discussing "overfunctionalization," has written:

> The worker cannot see that total process, he sees only the small and uninteresting part to which he and his fellows are assigned. In a real sense, the job loses its meaning for the worker— the meaning, that is, in all terms except the pay envelope.
>
> Thus a very large number of employees in American industry today have been deprived of the sense of performing interesting, significant work. In consequence, they have little feeling of responsibility for the tasks to which they are assigned.[80]

But, *work has significant positive meanings to persons who do not find overall satisfaction in their immediate job.* A still viable consequence of the Protestant ethic in our society is that its work ethic (the notion of work as a calling, an obligation to one's family, society, and self-respect, if no longer to God), retains a powerful hold. This is most dramatically seen in the reactions of the retired and unemployed. The idea is quite common to American workers at all occupational levels that soon after a worker retires, he is likely to either "drop dead" or "go crazy" from sheer inactivity.[81] An English industrial psychiatrist states that this is actually a common calamity in British industry.[82] Similarly, the studies made in the 1930's of unemployed people show that the disruption of the work relationship often leads to the disruption of normal family relations, to political apathy, and to a lack of interest in social organizations and leisure-time activities.[83]

The studies of job satisfaction reviewed in this paper further question the prevailing thesis that most workers in modern society are alienated and estranged. There is a remarkable consistency in the findings that the vast majority of workers, in virtually all occupations and industries, are moderately or highly satisfied, rather than dissatisfied, with their jobs.

However, the marked occupational differences in work attitudes and the great significance which workers impute to being, at least to some extent, masters of their destiny in the work process, along with the fact that surrender of such control seems to be the most important condition of strong dissatisfaction are findings at least as important as the overall one of general satisfaction. Perhaps the need for autonomy and independence may be a more deep-seated human motive than is recognized by those who characterize our society in terms of crowdlike conformity and the decline of individualism.

These findings also have clear implications for industrial engineering. If industry and society have an interest in workers' experiencing satisfaction and pride in their work, a major effort must be made to increase the areas of control which employees have over the work process, especially in those industries and occupations where control is at a minimum. Charles Walker, who has written perceptively of the automobile worker's lack of control, has advocated two major solutions for humanizing repetitive assembly line work: job rotation and job enlargement. Where job rotation was introduced in one section of the automobile plant he studied, job satisfaction increased without loss of efficiency or production. The idea of recombining a number of jobs into one enlarged job seems especially to appeal to the line workers: as one man said, "I'd like to do a whole fender myself from the raw material to the finished product."[84] But such radical job enlargement would be a negation of the assembly line method of production. Therefore, we must anticipate the day when the utopian solution of eliminating assembly line production entirely will be the practical alternative for a society which is affluent and concerned at the same time that its members work with pride and human dignity.

Finally, the findings of this paper indicate a need for considerable further research on industrial statistics and industrial trends. If the evidence shows that extreme dissatisfaction is concentrated among assembly line workers, it becomes terribly important, for a total assessment of the conditions of work in modern America, to know what proportion of the labor force works on assembly lines or in other job contexts involving little control over their work activities. It is startling, considering the importance of such data, that such figures do not exist. This situation helps maintain the conventional belief that the mechanized assembly line worker is today's typical industrial worker in contrast to the craftsman of the past.

An indication that the actual proportion of assembly line workers is quite small is suggested by figures of the automobile industry, the conveyor belt industry par excellence. If we consider total employment in the industrial groupings involved in the manufacturer, sales, repair, and servicing of automobiles, we find that assembly line workers make up less than 5 per cent of all workers in this complex. There are approximately 120,000 automobile workers who are line assemblers, yet the number of skilled repair mechanics in all branches of the industry, a job which in many ways resembles the craft ideal, exceeds 500,000. In addition, the 120,000 assemblers are outnumbered by 400,000 managers who own or operate gas stations, garages, new and used car lots, and wrecking yards, and by 200,000 *skilled* workers in automobile plants.[85] Recent developments, especially automation, have served further to decrease the proportion of assembly line operatives in the industry.

If the situation in the automobile industry is at all typical, research might well show that those kinds of job contexts which are associated with high work satisfaction and control over one's time and destiny, such as skilled repair work and self-employment, are more representative than is commonly believed, and are even increasing over the long run. Such a prospect should bring considerable satisfaction to all those in the diverse intellectual traditions who have been concerned with what happens to human beings in the course of their major life activity, their work. And yet, this would not necessarily mean that the problem of the lack of fulfillment in work had become less serious. For as one industrial sociologist has suggested, this problem *may become more acute,* not because work itself has become more tedious, fractionated, and meaningless, but because the ideal of pride in creative effort is shared by an increasingly large proportion of the labor force as a result of the rise of democratic education and its emphasis on individualism and occupational mobility.[86]

Note on Methodological Problems in Job Satisfaction Research

By far the most common technique employed in job satisfaction studies is the poll-type questionnaire in which workers are asked directly, "How satisfied are you with your occupation?" or, "Do you like your job?" These questions have a number of advantages. They are quite straightforward and, in general, are easily understood in a common-sense fashion. Research costs are relatively economical, and what may be the guiding consideration is that the data are quantifiable and easily expressed in a form which can both indicate the total distribution of work satisfaction and dissatisfaction in a given population, and can readily locate differences among workers according to occupation, industry, educational level, sex, etc.

However, such a direct questionnaire runs certain risks which are common to all opinion polls. The respondent may not want, or may not be able, to answer honestly. In this case we suggest a cultural bias toward indicating contentment; the meaning of the question may not always be the same to the worker as it is to the interviewer; and simply the manner in which the question is phrased or asked may favor one response rather than another. For example, it has been suggested that dichotomizing responses into only "satisfied" and "dissatisfied" categories has the effect of overestimating the actual degree of satisfaction by pushing those who are in a middle category toward the satisfied alternative.[87]

There are further problems which stem from the special character of work attitudes. There is a certain naïvete in expecting frank and simple answers to job satisfaction questions in a society where one's work is so important a part of one's self that to demean one's job is to question one's very competence as a person. In addition, even if a person could be as honest in reporting about his job satisfaction as in reporting the number of children in his family, this problem is as inherently vague and nebulous as the latter question is precise. While most empirical investigators in this field operate with a common-sense notion of satisfaction, a few writers have been aware of the problem of conceptualization. In the first full-length book on job satisfaction, Hoppock wrote in 1935:

> The problem is complicated by the ephemeral and variable nature of satisfaction. Indeed, there may be no such thing as *job* satisfaction independent of the other satisfactions in one's life. Family relationships, health, relative social status in the community, and a multitude of other factors may be just as important as the job itself in determining what we tentatively choose to call job satisfaction. A person may be satisfied with one aspect of his job and dissatisfied with another. Satisfactions may be rationalized, and the degree of satisfaction may vary from day to day. A person may never be wholly satisfied.[88]

Assuming that we are able to arrive at some kind of definition or delimitation of the concept, the problem then arises as to who is to judge a person's satisfaction in work. Are people really satisfied because they say they are satisfied: since Freud this question has become standard currency. If they are honest with the interviewer, can they be honest with themselves? And if people who say they are satisfied are actually so, is this not on a superficial level, a kind of normal adjustment to reality? What about the depth of satisfaction? How many people derive profound, creative fulfillment in work? And does not the existence of general satisfaction reflect a generally low level of aspiration; an adaptation to what Marx called an *animal,* rather than a *human,* level of living?[89]

The above considerations suggest the extent to which the study and analysis of work satisfaction is fraught with problems not only of conceptualization, but of differences in ideals and value premises. At the heart of the question is the philosophic controversy between those who uphold an objective, and those who advocate a subjective theory of values. For the latter, people are satisfied in work if they truly feel themselves satisfied. The former approach, however, organizes a set of objective standards of behavior which individuals must meet. True fulfillment involves meeting the standards of the observer (an intellectual), rather than the standards of the individuals themselves. This is the characteristic approach of the critics of mass culture who do not find reassurance in the fact that most viewers today actually like the movies and television fare.

Although the above discussion indicates the enormous difficulties involved in getting a fair estimate of the absolute level of job satisfaction, we can speak with far greater assurance about relative levels of satisfaction experienced by members of different occupational groups. It is difficult to interpret a finding that 70 per cent of factory workers report satisfaction with their jobs because we do not know how valid and reliable our measuring instrument is. But when 90 per cent of printers compared to only 40 per cent of automobile workers report satisfaction, the relative difference remains meaningful. For this reason, the present paper has concentrated on interpreting differences in work satisfaction among people in different occupations and work settings, rather than attempting to assess absolute levels of job attitudes.

NOTES

1. One could argue that Marx was not only half a century ahead of his time in the use of the survey technique, but that he understood, even in 1880, the methodological difficulties in getting at subjective feelings. But then it might be retorted that he still had something to learn about eliminating bias in his questions: for example, item 59: "Have you noticed that the delay in paying your wages makes it necessary for you to resort frequently to the pawn-broker, paying a high rate of interest, and depriving yourself of things which you need; or to fall into debt to shopkeepers, becoming their victim because you are their debtor?" The entire questionnaire which was first published on April 20, 1880 in the *Revue Socialiste* appears in English in T. B. Bottomore and Maximilien Rubel, *Karl Marx, Selected Writings in Sociology and Social Philosophy* (London: Watts and Company, 1956), pp. 204–212. Bottomore and Rubel mention that very few workers took the trouble to return Marx' extremely long and difficult questionnaire and that no results were ever published.

2. Reinhard Bendix and Seymour Martin Lipset, "Karl Marx' Theory of Social Classes," in R. Bendix and S. M. Lipset, *Class, Status and Power* (Glencoe: The Free Press, 1953), p. 32 ff.

3. Frederick Herzberg, Bernard Mausner, Richard O. Peterson, and Dora P. Capwell, *Job Attitudes: Review of Research and Opinion* (Psychological Service of Pittsburgh, 1957).

4. This is the question used in the Morse and Weiss study.

5. H. Alan Robinson, "Job Satisfaction Researches of 1958," *Personnel and Guidance Journal,* 37 (1959), p. 670.

6. J. C. Brown, *The Social Psychology of Industry* (Baltimore: English Pelican Edition, 1954), pp. 190–191. He proceeds to give supporting evidence from British studies.

7. Of course, as the industrial psychologist Arthur Kornhauser has written, "Simple summary conclusions of this kind are dangerously inadequate. Feelings of satisfaction or dissatisfaction are complicated and varied. Working people may be satisfied with many of the conditions of their employment and still be markedly dissatisfied about other features of the job or of their working lives. The number considered dissatisfied will depend in large measure upon the arbitrary method of defining what the term dissatisfaction refers to in the given case." "Psychological Studies of Employee Attitudes," in S. D. Hoslett, ed., *Human Factors in Management* (Parkville, Mo.: Park College Press, 1946), p. 304. In this extensive critique of the methodology of job satisfaction research, Kornhauser also points out that respondents may not want or even be able to answer such questions honestly. There is a certain naïvete in expecting frank and simple answers to job satisfaction questions in a society where one's work is so important a part of one's self that to demean one's job is to question one's own competence.

8. Morse and Weiss, *op. cit.,* p. 197.

9. In this index, the figure 100 would indicate extreme dissatisfaction, 400 indifference, and 700 extreme satisfaction. Hoppock, *op. cit.,* p. 255. A rather similar rank order was found by Donald Super. In his study, the percentages of satisfied workers were 85.6 for professionals, 74.2 for managerial, 41.9 for commercial (lowest white collar), 55.9 for skilled manual and 47.6 for semiskilled. However, Super's study has serious weaknesses: the sample was not chosen randomly but taken from members of hobby groups, and it overrepresented workers with high education and in high status occupations. D. Super, "Occupational Level and Job Satisfaction," *Journal of Applied Psychology,* 23, (1939), pp. 547–564.

10. R. S. Uhrbock, "Attitudes of 4430 Employees," *Journal of Social Psychology,"* 5 (1934), pp. 365–377, cited in Hoppock, *op. cit.,* p. 141.

11. Centers, *op. cit.,* p. 134.

12. Alexander R. Heron, *Why Men Work* (Stanford: Stanford University Press, 1948), pp. 71–72. A 1948 *Fortune* poll which asked the same question to *youth* between the ages of 18 to 25 found that the proportion of those who found their work interesting or enjoyable "all of the time" was 85 per cent for professionals and executives, 64 per cent for white collar workers, 59 per cent for non-factory manual labor and 41 per cent for factory labor. Cited in Lawrence G. Thomas, *The Occupational Structure and Education* (Englewood Cliffs, N.J.: Prentice-Hall, 1956), p. 201, whose summary of studies on the extent of, and occupational differences in, job satisfaction is one of the best in the literature.

13. Kornhauser, *Detroit . . .,* p. 55.

14. E. A. Friedmann and R. J. Havighurst, *The Meaning of Work and Retirement* (Chicago: University of Chicago Press, 1954), p. 183.

15. Howard M. Bell, *Youth Tell Their Story* (Washington: American Council on Education, 1938), p. 134.

16. Theodore Caplow has pointed to the importance of this factor in his *The Sociology of Work* (Minneapolis: University of Minnesota Press, 1954), p. 133.

17. F. H. Harbison, "Collective Bargaining and American Capitalism," in A. W. Kornhauser, Robert Dubin, and Arthur Ross, eds., *Industrial Conflict* (New York: McGraw-Hill, 1954), p. 278.

18. Brown, *op. cit.,* pp. 98–99.

19. A summary of the findings of the hundreds of job factor studies is found in Chapter 3 of F. Herzberg, et al., *op. cit.,* pp. 37–94. A critical discussion of the methodological problems involved in the attempt to assess the relative saliency of various factors is A. W. Kornhauser, "Psychological Studies of Employee Attitudes," *op. cit.,* pp. 305–319.

20. Omission of other factors, such as skill, variety of operations, wages, and job security, does not suggest their lack of importance. But these are at once highly related to occupational prestige and control, and, at the same time, they do not seem as useful in explaining gross occupational differences.

21. Brown, *op. cit.,* pp. 149–150. One's prestige *within* an occupation or work group is paramount for job satisfaction; I ignore it in my discussion because it explains individual rather than group differences in satisfaction.

22. When a national sample rated 90 occupations, doctors were second only to Supreme Court justices. National Opinion Research Center, "Jobs and Occupations: A Popular Evaluation," in Bendix and Lipset, eds., *Class, Status and Power* (Glencoe: The Free Press, 1953), p. 412.

23. Friedmann and Havighurst, *op. cit.,* p. 161. Thus "to be a doctor was to be doing the best of all possible jobs in the best of all possible professions." A consequence of the high satisfaction received from identifying oneself with a profession in such public esteem is that the doctor is reluctant to give up such identity: the authors found that, "except on rare occasions, physicians do not retire while they are in reasonably good physical condition."

24. See Lipset and Bendix, *Social Mobility in Industrial Society* (Berkeley: University of California Press, 1959), pp. 14–17.

25. Now a rather stock generalization, Werner Sombart was evidently one of the first to state it.

26. H. DeMan, *Joy in Work* (London: George Allen and Unwin, 1929), pp. 59–60, 208–209.

27. On the other hand when the norms of an "open society" encourage *all* to strive for upward advancement, large numbers of people who do not succeed will feel dissatisfied and frustrated, as the sociologist Robert Merton has emphasized in his "Social Structure and Anomie." See Merton, *Social Theory and Social Structure* (Glencoe: The Free Press, 1957), pp. 131–160. In Europe, manual workers have more distinctive class cultures and reference groups than in America; therefore they are probably much less likely to subscribe to the advancement norms of the whole society. Consideration of this factor alone would suggest *less* dissatisfaction with jobs and occupational status in Europe.

28. Friedmann and Havighurst found this to be true among the printers they studied, *op. cit.,* pp. 176–177. It has been noted that Chicago plumbers, who express a high level of work satisfaction, often stress their function of "protecting public sanitation" and compare their contribution to community health with that of doctors. Joel Seidman, et al., *The Worker Views His Union* (Chicago: University of Chicago Press, 1958), pp. 52–53.

29. Quotation from an interview with a coal miner in Friedmann and Havighurst, *op. cit.,* pp. 73–76. I do not intend to give the impression that the above is a representative quotation; the typical reaction seems to be an overt rejection of the anti-union media and public image. However, it seems likely that such feelings as the above might still haunt the average worker who would never express them. The role of the coal miner's "occupational community" in insulating him from these derogatory evaluations is discussed later in this paper.

30. DeMan, *op. cit.,* p. 67. "Even the worker who is free in the social sense, the peasant or the handicraftsman, feels this compulsion, were it only because while he is at work, his activities are dominated and determined by the aim of his work, by the idea of a willed or necessary creation. Work inevitably signifies subordination of the worker to remoter aims, felt to be necessary, and therefore involving a renunciation of the freedoms and enjoyments of the present for the sake of a future advantage."

31. E. C. Hughes, *Men and Their Work* (Glencoe: The Free Press, 1959), pp. 47–48. William Foote Whyte has put it in more general terms, "No normal person is happy in a situation which he cannot control to some extent." *Money and Motivation* (New York: Harper, 1955), p. 94.

32. Twenty-three per cent of the manual workers in a labor force sample in Oakland, California, had been in business at some time during their work history. Lipset and Bendix, *Social Mobility in Industrial Society*, p. 179. Cultural differences in aspirations for independence and control in work as well as differing economic opportunities are suggested in the contrast between British and American opinion poll data. Fifty-one per cent of the Americans questioned wanted to start their own businesses compared to only 33 per cent of the Britons; Americans were also considerably more likely to say they would actually do so. Hadley Cantril, *Public Opinion 1935–1946* (Princeton: Princeton University Press, 1951), p. 528.

33. See especially Ely Chinoy, *Automobile Workers and the American Dream* (Garden City: Doubleday, 1955). He quotes a machine operator: "The main thing is to be independent and give your own orders and not have to take them from anybody else. That's the reason the fellows in the shop all want to start their own business. Then the profits are all for yourself. When you're in the shop there's nothing for yourself in it. So you just do what you have to in order to get along. A fellow would rather do it for himself. If you expend the energy, it's for your own benefit then," pp. xvi–xvii.

34. Dubin, "Constructive Aspects of Industrial Conflict," in Kornhauser, Dubin, and Ross, *op. cit.*, p. 43.

35. W. F. Whyte, *op. cit.*, p. 234.

36. Control, of course, is not independent of the other factors. The relationship between occupational status and control is particularly marked; in fact, the (status) "hierarchy is a direct reflection of freedom from control. . . ." Edward Gross, *Work and Society* (New York: Crowell, 1958), p. 428. The relationship of control to skill is intimate; in fact, skill may be conceived as a form of control over the technological process of work. Finally, control is related to integrated work teams. An important result of the pioneering research of Elton Mayo and his colleagues was the increased awareness that the informal work group, in setting and enforcing informal production standards, gives many industrial workers some control over their job situations.

37. Chinoy, *op. cit.*, p. 71.

38. C. R. Walker and Robert H. Guest, *Man on the Assembly Line* (Cambridge: Harvard University Press, 1952), p. 62.

39. *Ibid.*, pp. 113, 110.

40. Chinoy, *op. cit.*, pp. 71–72.

41. Walker and Guest, *op. cit.*, pp. 120, 116–117.

42. Bell, *op. cit.*, p. 135.

43. Chinoy, *op. cit.*, p. 70.

44. Fred H. Blum, *Toward a Democratic Work Process* (New York: Harper, 1953), p. 96.

45. *Ibid.*, p. 85.

46. In the North-Hatt occupational prestige study, "Machine operator in a factory" (the category closest in social meaning to an auto worker) ranked 65th in prestige among 90 occupations, considerably higher than "coal miner" which was ranked 77th. Most people ranked machine operator in a factory as "average" in general standing, and coal miners as "somewhat below average" or "poor."

47. Alvin W. Gouldner, *Patterns of Industrial Bureaucracy* (Glencoe: The Free Press, 1954), pp. 140–141.

48. Seidman, et al., *op. cit.*, p. 55.

49. Friedmann and Havighurst, *op. cit.*, p. 176.

50. C. R. Walker, *Steeltown* (New York: Harper, 1950), p. 61.

51. John Spier, "Elements of Job Satisfaction in the Railroad Operating Crafts," unpublished paper, Berkeley, California, 1959.

52. Walker and Guest, *op. cit.*, p. 54.

53. Friedmann and Havighurst, *op. cit.*, p. 178.

54. *Ibid.*, p. 106.

55. Gouldner, *op. cit.*, pp. 55 ff. Seidman, et al., *op. cit.*, p. 23.

56. Reynolds and Shister, *op. cit.*, pp. 13–14.

57. Hoppock, *op. cit.*, pp. 225 ff. In Bell's Maryland youth survey the majority in all occupational categories except professionals preferred a different kind of job. However, the proportion of truck drivers who were so "discontented" was less than that of clerks, salespersons, farm laborers and operatives in clothing and textiles. Bell, *op. cit.*, p. 135.

58. William A. Faunce, "Automation and the Automobile Worker," pp. 370–379 in this volume.

59. Walker, *op. cit.*, pp. 66–67.

60. Friedmann and Havighurst, *op. cit.*, pp. 65, 90–91.

61. A. Zaleznik, C. R. Christensen, and F. J. Roethslisberger, *The Motivation, Productivity and Satisfaction of Workers: A Prediction Study* (Cambridge: Harvard University, 1958), pp. 258–277. In this factory the most important thing in accounting for group membership was ethnicity: the Irish workers tended to be the integrated members of "regular groups," while the non-Irish employees were by and large isolates or in deviant groups.

62. The most complete account of this study appears in F. J. Roethslisberger and W. J. Dickson, *Management and the Worker* (Cambridge: Harvard University Press, 1939). Other accounts of the research of the Mayo school may be found in Elton Mayo and George F. Lombard, *Teamwork and Labor Turnover in the Aircraft Industry of Southern California* (Cambridge: Harvard University Graduate School of Business Administration, 1944); Elton Mayo, *The Human Problems of an Industrial Civilization* (New York: The Macmillan Co., 1933); and *The Social Problems of an Industrial Civilization* (Cambridge: Graduate School of Business Administration, Harvard University, 1946).

63. It is difficult to determine whether this neglect stems from an implicit assumption that work tasks are sufficiently challenging for basically "non-rational" workers, or conversely, from a view that the alienation of the worker from his work is so immutable that one must concentrate instead on engineering work groups and supervision, since these are amenable to change. From a history of ideas point of view the most important source of this neglect is probably the intellectual heritage of Elton Mayo, who was greatly influenced by Emile Durkheim's theory of the increasing atomization of modern society and the consequent growth of *anomie*. Whereas Marx saw the solution to the modern social problem in the "restoration" to the worker of control over his conditions of work, Durkheim rather saw it in the reintegration of individuals into solitary social groups which could buttress the individual from the pressures of the mass state and, in addition, provide personal equilibrium and security. Mayo, in following Durkheim rather than Marx, ignores almost completely the relation of the worker to his work and concentrates instead on his integration into small work groups as a condition of industrial harmony and social health.

64. For example, Robert N. McMurray, "Management Mentalities and Worker Reactions," in Hoslett, *op. cit.*, especially his discussion of the morale study of J. D. Houser.

65. A. Zaleznik, *Worker Satisfaction and Development* (Cambridge: Harvard University Business School, 1956). A similar case in point is the excellent study of an Indian textile mill by A. K. Rice of the London Tavistock Institute. In his theoretical discussion, Rice gives equal weight to three dimensions of work satisfaction: psychological closure or the doing of a complete task, responsibility and control over the task, and work group integration. But in presenting his findings, Rice ignores almost completely the first two intrinsic job dimensions and concentrates on the work group factor. *Productivity and Social Organization: The Ahmedabad Experiment* (London: Tavistock Publications, 1958).

66. For a summary of the major theoretical and ideological criticisms that have been made of the Mayo School, see Henry

A. Landsberger, *Hawthorne Revisited* (Ithaca: Cornell University Press, 1958), especially Chapter III.

67. Friedmann and Havighurst, *op. cit.,* pp. 70–71.

68. The most thorough analysis of an occupational community is the study of the printers by S. M. Lipset, M. Trow, and J. Coleman, *Union Democracy* (Glencoe: The Free Press, 1956). This section is considerably indebted to the insights of these authors. An important discussion of occupational communities in another context is C. Kerr and A. Siegel, "The Inter-Industry Propensity to Strike," in Kornhauser, Dubin, and Ross, *op. cit.,* pp. 189–212. They argue that the fact that workers in these occupations form an "isolated mass" and are not integrated into the society as a whole encourages militant strike activity.

69. Lipset, Trow, and Coleman, *op. cit.*

70. Walker, *op. cit.,* pp. 111–112.

71. Daniel Katz, "Satisfactions and Deprivations in Industrial Life," in Kornhauser, Dubin, and Ross, *op. cit.,* p. 102.

72. Blum, *op. cit.,* pp. 96–97. My emphasis.

73. The French sociologist Emile Durkheim felt that occupational communities which he termed "corporations" were the one agency which could provide stable norms for individuals living in an essentially normless society. See the preface to the second edition, *The Division of Labor in Society* (Glencoe: The Free Press, 1949).

74. Caplow, *op. cit.,* p. 96.

75. The reverse process, high job satisfaction leading to high participation in an occupational community, has been described by Lipset and his colleagues in their study of union printers. Lipset, et al., *op. cit.,* pp. 124–126.

76. Evidence on this point is reviewed in Herzberg, et al., *op. cit.,* pp. 17–20.

77. Marx's classic characterization is the best known: "Owing to the extensive use of machinery and to the division of labor, the work of the proletarians has lost all individual character, and consequently, all charm for the workman. He becomes an appendage of the machine, and it is only the most simple, most monotonous, and most easily acquired knack, that is required of him." But almost identical accounts abound in the writings of non-Marxist intellectuals. Compare Adriano Tilgher, *Work: What It Has Meant to Men Through the Ages* (New York: Harcourt Brace and Co., 1930), p. 151, and Henry Durant, *The Problem of Leisure* (London: George Routledge and Sons, 1938), pp. 6 ff.

78. DeMan, *op. cit.,* p. 146. The 10 per cent estimate is from Brown, *op. cit.,* p. 24.

79. Brown, *op. cit.,* p. 207. A leading advocate of the alienation thesis, the French industrial sociologist Georges Friedmann, was unable to find any decline in the proportion of skilled workers in selected German, French, and English industries during the early years of the twentieth century. *Industrial Society* (Glencoe: The Free Press, 1955), p. 200. Statistics of the American labor force show that the proportion of skilled workers has risen considerably since 1940 and is expected to continue rising; the proportion of unskilled laborers has been declining consistently since 1920. Semiskilled operatives, the largest manual category, increased the fastest until 1940. The increase since then has been negligible and it is expected that this group will decline in the future. *The most striking change in occupational composition, reflecting a general upgrading in skill, is the increase in the proportions of clerical and professional workers.* U. S. Department of Labor, Bureau of Labor Statistics, Bulletin 1215, *Occupational Outlook Handbook, 1957,* pp. 34–35.

80. James C. Worthy, "Organizational Structure and Employee Morale," *American Sociological Review,* 15 (1950), p. 175. Cf. Peter Drucker, *Concept of the Corporation* (John Day Co., 1946), p. 179, and Heron, *op. cit.*

81. Morse and Weiss, *op. cit.,* p. 192; Friedmann and Havighurst, *op. cit.,* pp. 89, 162, 36 ff. Eric Hoffer notes that death rates increased among older longshoremen when a retirement plan was put into effect. A convention of general practitioners recently advised against compulsory retirement on this basis. See *SF Chronicle,* October 7, 1958. That this may be more of a stereotyped notion than a fact is suggested by the directors of the Cornell Study of Occupational Retirement who found in a panel of more than 1000 males of the same age that those who retired were more likely to *improve* in health, while those who remained working were more likely to decline in health. Wayne E. Thompson and Gordon F. Streib, "Situational Determinants: Health and Economic Deprivation in Retirement," *Journal of Social Issues,* XIV (1958), pp. 18–34.

82. Brown, *op. cit.,* p. 190.

83. See E. W. Blake, *Citizens Without Work* (New Haven: Yale University Press, 1940), and *The Unemployed Man* (New York: Dutton, 1934); M. Jahoda-Lazarsfeld and H. Zeisel, *Die Arbeitslosen von Marienthal* (Leipzig: Psychologische Monographien: 1933); Mirra Komarovsky, *The Unemployed Man and His Family* (New York: Dryden Press, 1940). Daniel Bell in considering the possibilities of automation has raised the question: "Work, said Freud, was the chief means of binding an individual to reality. What will happen, then, when not only the worker but work itself is displaced by the machine?" *Work and Its Discontents* (Boston: Beacon Press, 1956), p. 56.

84. Walker and Guest, *op. cit.,* p. 154.

85. The source for the estimate of 120,000 assembly line workers is a statement on page 426 of the U. S. Department of Labor's *Occupational Outlook Handbook, 1957,* which says that assembly line workers "in mid-1956 represented approximately 15 per cent of all the automobile workers." In this context all automobile workers refers to the 800,000 employed in manufacturing, 15 per cent of which is 120,000. The total employment in automobile manufacturing, automobile sales, automobile garage and repair shops, and gasoline service stations, according to 1950 census figures, is almost 2.5 million. This total was used as the base to compute the estimate of 5 per cent as the proportion of assembly line workers among all employees in the complex of automobile industries. The other figures are from the 1950 Census.

86. Moore, *op. cit.,* p. 231.

87. Herzberg, et al., *op. cit.,* p. 4.

88. Hoppock, *Job Satisfaction* (New York: Harper, 1935), p. 5.

89. See K. Marx, "On Alienated Labor," translated by Johnson, et al. (dittoed). This is the position of Fred Blum, *Toward a Democratic Work Process.*

The Welfare State As Workplace

MICHAEL LIPSKY

One of the subtler failures of the modern welfare state is its defeat of the ideal of service, to convert it to careerism or cynicism, or to hurry the departure of committed workers from public service. This not only exacts a personal toll, but stunts an important potential force for change.

Workers on the front lines of the welfare state find themselves in a corrupted world of service. The worker is continually torn between mobilizing client energies and rendering the client docile, between advocating on a client's behalf and minimizing client services. The contradictory bureaucratic need to manipulate people in order to "help" them mirrors the more fundamental ambiguities in the way society views its poor. It is the front-line worker who is called upon to broker these contradictions and rationalize them to the client and to her or himself.

While much has been written about the contradictions in social welfare programs, relatively little attention has been paid to the welfare state as a place of work, and the conditions experienced by its workforce. Those who directly carry out social welfare policy or apply public sanctions range from highly respected (and paid) physicians staffing health clinics to harried CETA counselors who are just one jump ahead of their clients in status and income. But the workplace conditions and limitations are interestingly similar.

First, resources are chronically inadequate in relation to the tasks workers are asked to perform. This alone differentiates street-level public employment from most other kinds of labor. High caseloads, limited time to obtain information, and inadequate training and methods for the tasks frustrate workers' human impulses to treat people as individuals.

Public defenders committed to the ideal of providing the indigent with legal representation find themselves in court without time even to interview the client, let alone prepare adequately. Teachers find that the more pressing the need for creative classroom instruction, the more likely is the school to be overcrowded, and the more inundated the teacher is with disciplinary and housekeeping chores. When welfare workers in Massachusetts are assigned the statutory maximum of 180 cases (and others stack up, uncovered), or when judges have dozens of cases to dispose of daily, the possibility of personalized assessment becomes submerged in the need to process the work.

This scarcity, however, is *inherent,* not only because the available financial resources reflect an ambivalent commitment to social welfare programs, but because the demand for services tends to increase with the supply. One of the better kept secrets of the welfare state is how wide and deep is the reservoir of demand for human services generally. For example, it has long been recognized that middle class people use doctors more frequently than poor people. But when quality health care is made available at reasonable cost, poor people frequent doctors and psychotherapists just as eagerly as rich ones.

Michael Lipsky teaches political science at M.I.T. This article explores themes also treated in his Street-Level Bureaucracy: Dilemmas of the Individual in Public Services *(Russell Sage Foundation, 1980).*

From *Working Papers for a New Society,* May/June 1980, pp. 33–38. Reprinted with permission of The Commonwealth Foundation.

The equalization of the distribution of health professionals across racial and class lines would overwhelm the resources of health training institutions. Opinions to the contrary fail to take into account the additional demand that would be expressed were decent services universally available.

Thus, workers find that the best way to keep demand within manageable proportions is to deliver a consistently inaccessible or inferior product. Public programs often cannot charge fees, but they can set "prices" by inflicting indignities such as requiring long waits, or limiting information.

Obviously, these techniques contradict the ostensible program goals. Yet a worker who provides superior service will be rewarded only with additional clients. Greater availability or quality of services like health care, or greater accessibility of effective counseling to families in crisis, simply attracts more customers and harder cases. Adding capacity fails to solve the worker's perennial problem of inadequate resources (although it may in fact extend mediocre service to more people).

The worker in public welfare programs confronts the dilemma of the fabled highway planner of the congested Long Island Expressway. The engineers kept adding additional lanes on the theory that this would alleviate traffic jams. However, the increased capacity only attracted more drivers, so that congestion was perpetuated, albeit at higher traffic levels.

This effect operates in a wide variety of settings. Neighborhood multiservice centers invariably abandon "outreach" plans, for response to services soon overwhelms capacity. Whenever cities make emergency calls easier by introducing 911 numbers, they find an untapped backlog of demand for public safety assistance. Indeed, New York City at one point conducted a campaign to encourage *less* use of 911. Similarly, the legal services program originally envisioned providing a few thousand attorneys for the poor. By 1970, when the program had become fairly well accepted on the street and in Congress, it was estimated that some 50,000 lawyers would have to be employed to meet the *known* needs of the poor.

To deal with such excess demand, social welfare bureaucracies have developed their own Peter Principle: services expand until they reach the point of mediocrity. This promotes the day-to-day functioning of the agency, but it also puts the provider in the demoralizing position of being unable to serve anybody adequately.

This means that social service agencies often present classic examples of "goal displacement," that is, the substitution of the organization's bureaucratic needs for the original agency mission. Job agencies change their objectives from placement to counseling when jobs for clients don't exist. The day-to-day objective of social service agencies becomes managing the caseload rather than providing the service. In this way the immediate organizational need to set priorities collides with the legal mandate for open entitlement and multiple objectives.

Ostensibly, official policy is a matter of statutory law, but what workers actually do in the work-place effectively *becomes* the policy. Frequently, workers actually pursue policies that are at odds with the nominal objectives of agency managers.

Not long ago, New York City welfare planners resorted to a variety of devices to reduce the people on the welfare rolls. One tactic that was rejected involved restricting intake hours. Managers decided against this for fear that welfare workers would go out of the centers and take applications from people at home, on the street, etc., since application may be made (under existing Federal law) "at agency office, in own home, by telephone, by mail, or in any suitable place." The managers knew that the front-line workers could easily undercut the policy.

Similarly, for years the Veterans' Administration hospital system got around Congress's prohibition against paying for outpatient treatment by resorting to the fiction that the patients were really not outpatients at all, but potential inpatients receiving "Pre-Bedcare." When treatment rules were finally changed to permit outpatient care for the first time, the number of "Pre-Bedcare" patients mysteriously dropped.

Sometimes front-line workers can modify nominal policies to further client interests, as in the case of the VA doctors who insisted on bending the rules to treat outpatients or the New York welfare workers who could threaten to enroll poor people on the street if intake hours were cut.

But more often, the pressures and contradictions of work are such that policy is established by the accretion of routines. This sort of policy by default cannot possibly work in favor of social change, because the conditions of work create relations between workers and clients that are fundamentally alienating to both. This is an inevitable result of work that involves people-processing, with its implicit need to deny human interaction. Dehumanization lies at the core of the people-processing business, for the work has its basis in human complexity, and yet requires workers to disregard most of that complexity.

Street-level workers for the welfare state are alienated from their clients (and thus from their work) because they work only on portions of the client's needs. By its very nature, their work does not permit them to respond to people individually or get at underlying causes. The institutional imperative to process people into the correct category of client tends to overwhelm both professional obligations to treat the whole person, as well as the commonsense recognition that responding only to present situations may result in ignoring the most important dimensions of the problem.

Recent reforms have sought to recognize that treating only parts of people in need is a recipe for frustration and failure. For example, social workers and psychologists have been employed in hospitals, schools, and courts in efforts to respond holistically to the citizen-client. Reformers recognize that a health problem such as lead poisoning may be a problem of income and law. A legal problem (e.g., needing a divorce) may be rooted in a problem of poverty. This aspect of work in the welfare state will remain alienating as long as we seek the causes of social problems in their victims rather than in the social and economic structure.

In the name of efficiency, convenience, or optimal utilization of resources, the world of social services has become more and more specialized, which means that street-level bureaucrats tend to work only on segments of the process.

In recent years specialization in welfare has been promoted as a way to save money or to introduce cost-conscious workers into the process. However, division between intake and casework means that interviews and fact-gathering either must be repeated or communication failures will cause even more slippage.

In addition, the front line workers in social agencies often do not control the outcome of their work. Specialization means that they only participate in a fraction of the work with clients. They do not control all of the resources of the agency they work for. Sometimes they process people for other bureaucracies, which ultimately disposes of cases. Often, clients' problems are simply not subject to closure. That is what turns many public service agencies into revolving doors. The solutions agencies offer are not adequate. People do not stay "fixed." To the extent that this causes workers severe dissonance between objectives and capabilities, they develop coping mechanisms to shield them from the gap between expectations and accomplishment. They are alienated to the extent they experience this discrepancy as loss of control over situations they are supposed to control.

Most of the social workers, teachers, legal aid lawyers or health care workers who survive the frustrating first months of employment rationalize the contradictions and the alienation by simply adjusting to the limitations of their job. They develop conceptions of their work and of their clients that narrow the gap between their own workplace limitations and the service ideal. But often these compromises undermine the service ideal or put the worker in the position of manipulating citizens on behalf of agencies from which citizens seek help.

At best, street-level workers develop techniques for salvaging some degree of service within the structural constraints. They invent relatively benign versions of mass processing that more or less permit them to deal with their publics fairly, appropriately and even successfully. At worst, they give in to favoritism, stereotyping, and routinizing, which moderate the frustrations of the workday and serve primarily the institutional needs of the agencies.

Compromises in work habits and attitudes are rationalized as reflecting workers' greater maturity and keener appreciation of practical realities. But these rationalizations merely summarize the prevailing constraints on human service bureaucracies. They are certainly not "true," in any absolute sense. People with seemingly insurmountable problems may be hopeless cases only within the assumptions of the present social system.

These compromises and limitations are not restricted to social institutions that deal only with the poor. Many of them apply to bureaucracies for such broad public services as education and law enforcement. The teacher who subjectively abandons his or her aspirations to help children to read has succumbed to a private assessment about the status quo in public education. But this personal compromise says nothing about the potential of individual children to learn, or the capacity of a gifted teacher to instruct. This potential remains intact. It is rather the system of schooling and the organizational constraints of the schooling bureaucracy that teaches that children are dull or unmotivated and that teachers must abandon their personal commitments to teach.

In the same way, the judicial system teaches that offenders are incorrigible, that police officers must be impersonal and highly reactive to any hints of disobedience among youth, and that judges are not able to make informed determinations about where to send offenders. Although the potential for thoughtful and useful intervention is not contradicted by the limitations of individual ingenuity, the system teaches that the juvenile crime problem is intractable.

In short, the social welfare workplace teaches the most committed among us that their commitment is naive or futile and at odds with the way the world really operates. These lessons are likely to be underscored as the fiscal crisis deepens. Budget cutbacks exacerbate the conflict between the street-level roles of advocate for the poor and protector of the bureaucracy. Public demands for increased public sector productivity insist on quantitative achievements, but erode the quality of service.

As two California psychiatrists explained after conducting workshops for state workers victimized by Proposition 13: "Either their jobs are at stake, or their job is to make the cuts, or they must accomplish their jobs despite the cuts, because we, the public, won't accept any reduction in services." Workers, in short, must live within the public's ambivalence about paying the welfare state's bill.

Consider the alarm public officials display when they discover that a benefit program turns out to be far more open-ended than they had previously assumed. Many programs accurately identify a social need, but fail to incorporate society's actual political commitment to serve the need. Once again, the street-level worker bears the brunt of the ambiguities and must navigate the contradictions on behalf of a political structure that names pressing needs but limits commitment to meet the needs. Perhaps the baldest expressions of this contradiction are welfare grants that provide a fraction of officially established *minimal* requirements.

The food stamp program caused a great deal of official consternation because it entitled far more people to benefits than was originally anticipated, resulting in costs that were extremely difficult to control except through categorical cutbacks. In welfare programs constant harping on the error rate, "chislers," or alleged medicaid fraud reflects not so much evidence that these abuses are widespread as ambivalent public commitment to the program. As a result, front line workers in the bureaucracy are under continuous pressure to realize the simultaneous—and contradictory—objectives of service and cost control.

As the fiscal crisis deepens, it is likely also to exacerbate the tensions between provider and consumer of services. Workers who have been set up to fail may be so alienated from their work that it becomes difficult to make common cause with their clients, especially at a time of growing competition for resources.

Furthermore, since social service workers operate in a workplace in which performance quality is difficult to measure and there is seldom recognition for qualitatively outstanding work, the safest course in career terms is usually adherence to bureaucratic rather than human standards. At best, workers are forced to hoard their chips, measuring them out carefully when a favored client or desperate situation requires responsive intervention.

Thus the conditions that give rise to alienation in work may cumulatively contribute to separating the client from the public service worker. This is significant since in earlier periods public service workers have championed client rights and benefits. In the past fledgling public service unions and worker associations bargained for clients as well as for themselves (social workers and teachers are two examples). This sense of common struggle has diminished as the connection between workers and clients has dissipated.

The current direction of the American welfare state as workplace is toward greater specialization and professionalism, but at the same time toward more automation and dependence on technological solutions. Generalists and people skilled in putting coalitions together are replaced by the new generation of policy analysts. Information processing is increasingly handled by computers, and there is some tendency to transform work into something computers can handle.

In general, these developments, in whole or in part, increase client dependency, make service work less understandable to citizens, define human services as work only highly trained people can do, and decrease or distort accountability. No doubt, these tendencies are welcomed by many people of good will for their apparent sophistication of method. But great care must be taken to explore whether these developments actually contribute to the needs of citizens, or whether they contribute instead to the aggrandizement of professions or the need of public officials to manage their agencies and their client populations.

Accountability is demanded (not unreasonably) in the name of service provision and cost control. However, workers who cannot be held accountable through collection and assessment of hard measures may have their work transformed so that they end up doing tasks that *are* measurable. The lower the status of workers the more bureaucratic are the controls. Social workers get quality control; physicians get peer review.

Some critics of social welfare bureaucracy, both on the left and right, argue that providing assistance through traditional social services is inherently paternalistic, inflexible, inefficient, and conducive to the creation of a permanently dependent welfare class. These critics often favor replacing social programs with direct income-support schemes that would use market-like mechanisms to create greater efficiency and

freedom of choice. The Family Assistance Plan, housing allowances, and education vouchers all promised to replace categorical, bureaucratic programs with more efficient innovations.

But despite the theoretical appeal of this approach, these schemes in practice have encountered revealing political fates. Those conservatives who think they support income transfer approaches invariably shy away from the size of the bill necessary to provide properly for the need; they often side with those whose primary motivation is to cut costs. Moreover, chronic inefficiencies in natural markets (as in housing) or the need to create new markets (as in voucher-supported schools) fatally distort this approach. In low income communities, it rarely works as advertised when government simply provides funds and invites recipients to go out and bargain for services in the marketplace.

Other critics, primarily on the liberal side, try to deal with problems of welfare bureaucracies by increasing their accountability to communities. For example, the new Department of Social Services in Massachusetts proposes to develop service policies through forty citizen councils spread across the state. While decentralized structures do produce greater responsiveness, this reform fails to alter fundamentally the casework approach or workplace stress. In addition, it may weaken central financial support as the locus of responsibility shifts to localities.

One must also be careful not to dismiss change out of hand and celebrate the status quo. Information processing innovations, for example, may free citizens from dependence on paternalistic and manipulative workers (and free workers from the need to manipulate). Citizen-empowering developments invest clients with resources, but may also circumscribe their actions. Case-by-case analysis is necessary in order to assess the advantages or disadvantages of various approaches.

Ultimately, political and economic structures must be changed to obviate the need for compensatory services in the first place. A cut in the unemployment rate often does more than adding new services. But there will always be some services in education and health for example, which are not compensatory, but simply fundamental to a decent society. To the extent that these service needs remain, the service milieu should promote a society in which people take care of themselves, look after one another, and have the resources and the environmental supports to prosper without the intervention of public agents. Measures that advance these objectives—those that train people to support each other, navigate the channels of public agencies, and provide income to alleviate need—point in the right direction.

American liberals have fallen into the habit of defining social pathology as a condition in need of a social program. The client-processing model based on unequal power relationships may be so intrinsically degrading to both client *and* provider that it should be avoided wherever possible. Nonetheless, despite the attractiveness of self-help approaches and proposals for fundamental structural changes that would eliminate the need for social services, there remains a great residual need for people-to-people activities—public education, public safety, legal assistance, health care, and counseling come immediately to mind.

An essential condition for transformation of the welfare state workplace is for workers to recognize the need for alliances with their clients. Both are threatened by budget cuts; both can benefit from flexible structuring of assignments and activities. Instead of hiding behind the defense of bureaucratic constraints, public workers must take responsibility for developing the discretionary aspects of their jobs.

Friendly critics of the welfare state should reject both Olympian disdain or uncritical support of public employees. We should look hard to identify those circumstances in which workers have been able to modify the people-processing approach in favor of more humane relations with clients.

Ultimately, the structure of the welfare state workplace reflects political, not technical, constraints. Prevailing approaches to social services flow from the priorities of dominant political forces. To change these underlying realities, it will take new coalitions of public workers, clients, and citizens who can address the entirely valid taxpayer concerns about efficiency, but at the same time respect client needs and the human dimension of the street-level agencies—where the fate of innovation will finally rest.

Problems of Family Life

Coming Apart: Radical Departures Since 1960

STEVEN MINTZ

SUSAN M. KELLOGG

A generation ago Ozzie, Harriet, David, and Ricky Nelson epitomized the American family. Over 70 percent of all American households in 1960 were like the Nelsons: made up of dad the breadwinner, mom the homemaker, and their children. Today, less than three decades later, "traditional" families consisting of a breadwinner father, a housewife mother, and one or more dependent children account for less than 15 percent of the nation's households. As American families have changed, the image of the family portrayed on television has changed accordingly. Today's television families vary enormously, running the gamut from traditional families like "The Waltons" to two-career families like the Huxtables on "The Cosby Show" or the Keatons on "Family Ties"; "blended" families like the Bradys on "The Brady Bunch", with children from previous marriages; two single mothers and their children on "Kate and Allie"; a homosexual who serves as a surrogate father on "Love, Sidney"; an unmarried couple who cohabit in the same house on "Who's the Boss?"; and a circle of friends, who think of themselves as a family, congregating at a Boston bar on "Cheers." [1]

Since 1960 U.S. families have undergone a historical transformation as dramatic and far reaching as the one that took place at the beginning of the nineteenth century. Even a casual familiarity with census statistics suggests the profundity of the changes that have taken place in family life. Birthrates plummeted. The average number of children per family fell from 3.8 at the peak of the baby boom to less than 2 today. At the same time, the divorce rate soared. Today the number of divorces each year is twice as high as it was in 1966 and three times higher than in 1950. The rapid upsurge in the divorce rate contributed to a dramatic increase in the number of single-parent households, or what used to be known as "broken homes." The number of households consisting of a single woman and her children has doubled since 1960. A sharp increase in female-headed homes was accompanied by a steep increase in the number of couples cohabiting outside marriage; their numbers have quadrupled since 1960. [2]

Almost every aspect of family life seems to have changed before our eyes. Sexual codes were revised radically. Today only about one American woman in five waits until marriage to become sexually active, compared to nearly half in 1960 who postponed intercourse. Meanwhile, the proportion of births occurring among unmarried women quadrupled. At the same time, millions of wives entered the labor force. The old stereotype of the breadwinner-father and housewife-mother broke down as the number of working wives climbed. In 1950, 25 percent of married women living with their husbands worked outside the home; in the late 1980s the figure is nearly 60 percent. The influx of married women entering the labor force was particularly rapid among mothers of young children. Now more than half of all mothers of school-age children hold jobs. As a result, fewer young children can claim their mother's exclusive attention. What Americans have witnessed since 1960 are fundamental challenges to the forms, ideals, and role expectations that have defined the family for the last century and a half. [3]

Profound and far-reaching changes have occurred in the American family—in behavior and in values. Contemporary Americans are much more likely than their predecessors to postpone or forgo marriage, to live alone outside familial units, to engage in intercourse prior to marriage, to permit marriages to end in divorce, to permit

Reprinted with permission of The Free Press, a division of Macmillan, Inc. from *Domestic Revolutions: A Social History of American Family Life* by Steven Mintz and Susan M. Kellogg. Copyright © 1988 by The Free Press.

mothers of young children to work outside the home, and to allow children to live in families with only one parent and no adult male present. Earlier family norms—of a working father, a housewife, and children—have undergone major alterations. The term "family" has gradually been redefined to include any group of people living together, including such variations as single mothers and children, unmarried couples, and gay couples.[4]

All these changes have generated a profound sense of uncertainty and ambivalence. Many Americans fear that the rapid decline in the birthrates, the dramatic upsurge in divorce rates, and the proliferation of loose, non-contractual sexual relationships are symptoms of increasing selfishness and self-centeredness incompatible with strong family attachments. They also fear that an increased proportion of working mothers has caused more children to be neglected, resulting in climbing rates of teenage pregnancy, delinquency, suicide, drug and alcohol abuse, and failure in school.[5]

Today fear for the family's future is widespread. In 1978 author Clare Boothe Luce succinctly summarized fears about the fragility of the family that continue to haunt Americans today:

> Today 50% of all marriages end in divorce, separation, or desertion. . . . The marriage rate and birth rate are falling. The numbers of one-parent and one-child families are rising. More and more young people are living together without benefit of marriage. . . . Premarital and extra-marital sex no longer raises parental or conjugal eyebrows. . . . The rate of reported incest, child molestation, rape, and child and wife abuse is steadily mounting. . . . Runaway children, teenage prostitution, youthful drug addiction and alcoholism have become great, ugly, new phenomena.[6]

What are the forces that lie behind these changes in family life? And what are the implications of these transformations?

NEW MORALITY

The key to understanding the recent upheavals in family life lies in a profound shift in cultural values. Three decades ago most Americans shared certain strong attitudes about the family. Public opinion polls showed that they endorsed marriage as a prerequisite of well-being, social adjustment, and maturity and agreed on the proper roles of husband and wife. Men and women who failed to marry or who resented their family roles were denigrated as maladjusted or neurotic. The message conveyed by the broader culture was that happiness was a by-product of living by the accepted values of hard work and family obligation.[7]

Values and norms have shifted. The watchwords of contemporary society are "growth," "self-realization," and "fulfillment." Expectations of personal happiness have risen and collided with a more traditional concern (and sacrifice) for the family. At the same time, in addition to its traditional functions of caring for children, providing economic security, and meeting its members' emotional needs, the family has become the focus for new expectations of sexual fulfillment, intimacy, and companionship.[8]

Today a broad spectrum of family norms that prevailed during the 1950s and early 1960s is no longer widely accepted. Divorce is not stigmatized as it used to be; a large majority of the public now rejects the idea that an unhappily married couple should stay together for their children's sake. Similarly, the older view that anyone who rejected marriage is "sick," "neurotic," or "immoral" has declined sharply, as has the view that people who do not have children are "selfish." Opinion surveys show that most Americans no longer believe that a woman should not work if she has a husband who can support her, that a bride should always be a virgin when she marries, or that premarital sex is always wrong.[9]

Economic affluence played a major role in the emergence of a new outlook. Couples who married in the 1940s and 1950s had spent their early childhood years in the depression and formed relatively modest material aspirations. Born in the late 1920s or 1930s, when birthrates were depressed, they faced little competition for jobs at maturity and were financially secure enough to marry and have children at a relatively young age. Their children, however, who came of age during the 1960s and 1970s, spent their childhoods during an era of unprecedented affluence. Between 1950 and 1970, median family income tripled. Increased affluence increased opportunities for education, travel, and leisure, all of which helped to heighten expectations of self-fulfillment. Unlike their parents, they had considerable expectations for their own material and emotional well-being.[10]

In keeping with the mood of an era of rising affluence, philosophies stressing individual self-realization flourished. Beginning in the 1950s, "humanistic" psychologies, stressing growth and self-actualization, triumphed over earlier theories that had emphasized adjustment as the solution to individual problems. The underlying assumptions of the new "third force" psychologies—a name chosen to distinguish them from the more pessimistic psychoanalytic and behaviorist psychologies—of Abraham Maslow, Carl Rogers, and Erich Fromm, is that a person's spontaneous impulses are intrinsically good and that maturity is not a process of "settling down" and suppressing instinctual needs but of achieving one's potential.[11]

Even in the early 1960s, marriage and family ties were regarded by the "human potential movement" as potential threats to individual fulfillment as a man or a woman. The highest forms of human needs, contended proponents of the new psychologies, were autonomy, independence, growth, and creativity, all of which could be thwarted by "existing relationships and interactions." Unlike the earlier psychology of adjustment, associated with Alfred Adler and Dale Carnegie, which had counseled compromise, suppression of instinctual impulses, avoidance of confrontations, and the desirability of acceding to the wishes of others, the new humanistic psychologies advised individuals to "get in touch" with their feelings and freely voice their opinions, even if this generated feelings of guilt.[12]

The impulse toward self-fulfillment and liberation was further advanced by the prophets of the 1960s counterculture and New Left, Norman O. Brown and Herbert Marcuse. Both Brown and Marcuse transformed Sigmund Freud's psychoanalytic insights into a critique of the constraints of liberal society. They were primarily concerned not with political or economic repression but rather with what they perceived as the psychological repression of the individual's instinctual needs. Brown located the source of repression in the ego mechanisms that

controlled each person's instincts. Marcuse, in a broader social critique, believed that repression was at least partially imposed by society.[13]

For both Brown and Marcuse, the goal of social change was the liberation of eros, the agglomeration of an individual's pleasure-seeking life instincts, or, as Marcuse put it, the "free gratification of man's instinctual needs." Brown went so far as to challenge openly the basic tenets of "civilized sexual morality," with its stress on genital, heterosexual, monogamous sex, and extolled a new ideal of bisexualism and "polymorphous perversity" (total sexual gratification). For a younger affluent, middle-class generation in revolt against liberal values, the ideas of Brown and Marcuse provided a rationale for youthful rebellion.[14]

An even more thoroughgoing challenge to traditional family values was mounted by the women's liberation movement, which attacked the family's exploitation of women. Feminists denounced the societal expectation that women defer to the needs of spouses and children as part of their social roles as wives and mothers. Militant feminist activists like Ti-Grace Atkinson called marriage "slavery," "legalized rape," and "unpaid labor" and denounced heterosexual love as "tied up with a sense of dependency." The larger mainstream of the women's movement articulated a powerful critique of the idea that child care and housework was the apex of a woman's accomplishments or her sole means of fulfillment. Feminists uncovered unsettling evidence of harsher conditions behind conventional familial togetherness, such as child abuse and wife beating, wasted lives and exploited labor. Instead of giving the highest priority to their families, women were urged to raise their consciousness of their own needs and abilities. From this vantage point, marriage increasingly came to be described as a trap, circumscribing a woman's social and intellectual horizons and lowering her sense of self-esteem. Homemaking, which as recently as the early 1960s had been celebrated on such television shows as "Queen for a Day," came under attack as an unrecognized and unpaid form of work in contrast to more "serious" occupations outside the home. And, as for marital bliss forevermore, feminists warned that divorce—so common and so economically difficult for women—was an occurrence for which every married woman had to be prepared. In general the feminists awakened American women to what they viewed as the worst form of social and political oppression—sexism. The introduction of this new awareness would go far beyond the feminists themselves.[15]

The challenge to older family values was not confined to radical members of the counterculture, the New Left, or the women's liberation movement. Broad segments of society were influenced by, and participated in, this fundamental shift in values.

Although only a small minority of American women ever openly declared themselves to be feminists, there can be no doubt that the arguments of the women's movement dramatically altered women's attitudes toward family roles, child care, marital relationships, femininity, and housework. This is true even among many women who claim to reject feminism. Polls have shown a sharp decline in the proportion of women favoring large families and a far greater unwillingness to subordinate personal needs and interests to the demands of husbands and children. A growing majority of women now believe that both husband and wife should have jobs, both do housework, and both take care of children. This represents a stunning shift of opinion in a decade and a half. A new perception of woman in the family has taken hold. In extreme imagery she is a superwoman, doing a full-time job while managing her home and family well. The more realistic image is of the wife and mother who works and struggles to manage job and family with the help of spouse, day care, and employer. Thus, as women increasingly seek employment outside the home, the family itself shifts to adjust to the changing conditions of its members while striving to provide the stability and continuity it has traditionally afforded.[16]

During the 1960s a sexual revolution that predated the counterculture swept the nation's literature, movies, theater, advertising, and fashion. In 1962, Grossinger's resort in New York State's Catskill mountains introduced its first singles-only weekend, thereby publicly acknowledging couples outside marriage. That same year Illinois became the first state to decriminalize all forms of private sexual conduct between consenting adults. Two years later, in 1964, the first singles bar opened on New York's Upper East Side; the musical *Hair* introduced nudity to the Broadway stage; California designer Rudi Gernreich created the topless bathing suit; and bars featuring topless waitresses and dancers sprouted. By the end of the decade, a growing number of the nation's colleges had abolished regulations specifying how late students could stay outside their dormitories and when and under what circumstances male and female students could visit with each other.[17]

One of the most important aspects of this latter-day revolution in morals was the growth of a "singles culture"—evident in a proliferation of singles bars, apartment houses, and clubs. The sources of the singles culture were varied and complex, owing as much to demographic shifts as to the ready availability of birth control, cures for venereal diseases, and liberalized abortion laws. The trend toward postponement of marriage, combined with increased rates of college attendance and divorce, meant that growing numbers of adults spent protracted periods of their sexually mature lives outside marriage. The result was that it became far easier than in the past to maintain an active social and sex life outside marriage. It also became more acceptable, as its patterns became grist for the popular media and imagination.[18]

Sexually oriented magazines started to display pubic hair and film-makers began to show simulated sexual acts. *I Am Curious (Yellow)* depicted coitus on the screen. *Deep Throat* released in the 1970s, showed cunnilingus and fellatio. Other manifestations of a relaxation of traditional mores included a growing public tolerance of homosexuality, a blurring of male and female sex roles, increasing public acceptance of abortion, the growing visibility of pornography, a marked trend away from female virginity until marriage, and a sharp increase in the proportion of women engaging in extramarital sex. Within one decade the cherished privacy of sexuality had been overturned and an era of public sexuality had been ushered in.[19]

Increasingly, values championed by the women's movement and the counterculture were adopted in a milder form by large segments of the American population. A significant majority of Americans adopted permissive attitudes on such matters as premarital sex, cohabitation outside of marriage, and abortion. Fewer women aspired to motherhood and homemaking as a full-time career and instead joined the labor force as much for independence and self-fulfillment as from economic motives. The preferred number of children declined sharply, and to limit births, the number of abortions and sterilizations increased sharply. A revolution had occurred in values and behavior.[20] . . .

THE FEMINIZATION OF POVERTY

Today families headed by women are four and a half times as likely to be poor as families headed by males. Teenagers who have children out of wedlock are seven times as likely to be in poverty. Although female-headed families constitute only 15 percent of the U.S. population, they account for over 50 percent of the poor population. Teenagers and women in their early twenties who bear illegitimate children constitute a large segment of the population that remains poor and dependent on welfare for long periods of time.[21]

And yet the picture is not quite so bleak as it might seem at first glimpse. Although a majority of poor families are female-headed, it is no longer true that most female-headed families are poor. Over the past two decades, the poverty rate of female-headed families has declined steeply, as women have succeeded in obtaining better-paying jobs in the labor force. Back in 1960 50 percent of all female-headed families lived in poverty. By 1970 the figure had fallen to 38 percent and down to 19 percent in 1980. Meanwhile, few female-headed families remain in poverty for very long. Most mothers who receive public assistance are self-supporting individuals who have recently experienced a sudden divorce or separation. Most of these women leave the welfare rolls within two years. And finally, many poor women eventually marry, leaving poverty. Nearly three-quarters of young black women who bear a child out of wedlock marry by the age of twenty-four, usually ending their poverty.[22]

Still, there can be little doubt that the nation's welfare policies actually provide incentives to the poor to avoid marriage. Under present law, if an AFDC mother marries, the stepfather assumes financial responsibility for supporting her children, which may deter the couple from marrying. In twenty-nine states, unemployed fathers are ineligible for assistance, which may encourage an unemployed father to desert his family so that his wife and children can obtain AFDC benefits. The discouragement of marriage in American welfare law contrasts sharply with European policies. In such countries as France, Hungary, Sweden, and East and West Germany, which have adopted explicit "family policies," the national government subsidizes families in a variety of ways, including the provision of family allowances to supplement parents' income and direct cash payments to parents when they have children.[23]

CHILDREN IN A NEW AGE

Along with a mounting federal commitment to shore up the nation's poor families came another domestic revolution, a radical new self-consciousness about child rearing. Over the past quarter century, Americans have grown progressively more concerned about the plight of the nation's young people. Alarmed by sharp increases in delinquency, alcohol and drug abuse, pregnancy, and suicides among children and adolescents, parents became uneasy about the proper way to raise children. They also worried about the effects of day care, the impact of divorce, and the consequences of growing up in a permissive society in which premarital sex, abortion, and drugs are prevalent.

The past two decades have witnessed significant changes in the experience of childhood and adolescence. Since 1960 the proportion of children growing up in "traditional families" in which the father is the breadwinner and the mother is a full-time homemaker has fallen dramatically while the number growing up in single-parent, female-headed households or in two-worker, two-parent households has risen steeply. Before 1960 divorce was an occurrence experienced by relatively few children. Of children born during the 1970s, in contrast, 40 percent will experience a divorce before their sixteenth birthdays, and nearly 50 percent will spend at least part of their childhood in a single-parent home.[24]

At the same time as marriages grew less stable, unprecedented changes took place within families. The proportion of married women with preschoolers who were in the labor force jumped from 12 percent in 1950 to 45 percent in 1980. Families grew smaller and, as a result, children have fewer siblings. Families also became more mobile, and hence children have less and less contact with relatives outside the immediate family. According to one estimate, just 5 percent of American children see a grandparent regularly. Young children spend more of their time in front of the television set or in the care of individuals other than their parents—in day-care centers, preschool programs, or the homes of other families—and more and more teenagers take part-time work.[25]

Each of these changes has evoked anxiety for the well-being of children. Many adults worry that a high divorce rate undermines the psychological and financial security of children. Others fear that children who live with a single female parent will have no father figure with whom to identify or to emulate and no firm source of guidance. Many are concerned that two-career parents with demanding jobs substitute money for affection, freedom for supervision, and abdicate their parental roles to surrogates. Still others fret that teenage jobs undermine school attendance and involvement and leave young people with too much money to spend on clothing, records, a car, or drugs. Today's children and adolescents, many believe, are caught between two difficult trends—decreasing parental commitment to child nurture and an increasingly perilous social environment saturated with sex, addictive drugs, and alcohol—that make it more difficult to achieve a well-adjusted adulthood.[26]

According to many Americans, children have paid a high price for the social transformations of the 1960s and 1970s—spiraling divorce rates, the rapid influx of mothers into the work force, a more relaxed attitude toward sex, and the widespread use of television as a form of child care. They are afraid that these patterns have eroded an earlier ideal of childhood as a special, protected state—a carefree period of innocence—and that today's permissive culture encourages a "new precocity" that thrusts children into the adult world before they are mature enough to deal with it. They worry about the deleterious effects of divorce, day care, and overexposure—through television, movies, music, and advertisement—to drugs, violence, sex, and pornography. They are concerned that parents have absorbed a far too egalitarian view of their relationship with their children and have become incapable of exercising authority and discipline.[27]

Giving credence to these fears are a variety of social indicators that appear to show an erosion in the parent-child bond and a precipitous decline in children's well-being. Public opinion polls indicate that two-thirds of all parents believe that they are less willing to make sacrifices for their children than their parents were. Other social statistics—ranging from college entrance examination results to teenage suicide rates—suggest that the decline in parental commitment to children has been accompanied by a sharp increase in problems among young people. Since 1960 the high-school dropout rate has increased until roughly one student in four drops out before graduation; juvenile delinquency rates have jumped 130 percent; the suicide rate for young people fifteen to nineteen years old has more than tripled; illegitimate births among white adolescent females have more than doubled; and the death rate from accidents and homicides has grown sixteenfold. Half a million adolescent females suffer from such eating disorders as anorexia nervosa or bulimia. American teenagers have the highest pregnancy rate of any industrialized nation, a high abortion rate and a high incidence of such venereal diseases as syphilis, gonorrhea, and genital herpes.[28]

Of course, it is easy to exaggerate the depravity of today's youth. Such problems as drug abuse, illegitimacy, and suicide affect only a small fraction of young people, and millions of others are raised in strong, caring homes by supportive and loving parents. Despite this, however, there is a widespread perception that American society is experiencing great difficulty in preparing children for adulthood.[29]

To a growing number of Americans, parenthood has become an increasingly frightening prospect. Fathers who once drag raced in hot rods and guzzled beer illegally are frightened by the idea of their children using drugs. Mothers who once made out with their boyfriends in parked cars are alarmed by statistics showing that teenage girls run a 40 percent chance of becoming pregnant and run three times the risk of contracting venereal disease than they did. One result is that parents have become progressively more self-conscious, anxious, and guilt-ridden about child rearing; fearful that even a single mistake in parenting might inflict scars that could last a lifetime. To address parents' mounting anxiety, a veritable torrent of child-rearing manuals has appeared.[30]

Although most discussions of child rearing in the 1960s and 1970s dwell on Dr. Benjamin Spock, his era of influence was even then coming to an end. Until 1960, American child-rearing literature was dominated by a handful of manuals, notably Spock's *Baby and Child Care* and the publications of Dr. Arnold Gesell and the Yale Child Development Clinic, which traced the stages of children's physical, cognitive, and emotional development. The arena rapidly grew more crowded and confused during the 1960s with the publication of a spate of new child-rearing books. By 1981 more than 600 books were in print on the subject of child development. These new manuals tended to convey a sense of urgency absent in earlier child care books, rejecting the easy going approach championed by Dr. Spock. One child care expert, Dr. Lee Salk, addressed the subject in words typical of the new child-rearing literature: "Taking parenthood for granted can have disastrous results."[31]

As the number of child-rearing books multiplied during the 1960s, a fundamental schism became increasingly apparent. At one pole were those echoing concerns voiced by Vice President Spiro T. Agnew that overpermissiveness—that is, too much coddling of children and overresponsiveness to their demands—resulted in adolescents who were anarchic, disrespectful and undisciplined. An extreme example of this viewpoint could be found in James Dobson's *Dare to Discipline,* which called on parents to exercise firm control of their children through the use of corporal punishment. At the other pole were writers like Mark Gerzon, author of *A Childhood for Every Child,* who took the position that the characteristic American child-rearing techniques

stifled creativity, generated dependence, instilled sexist biases, and produced repressed and conformist personalities. Authors like Gerzon called on parents to reject control through power and authority and to foster an environment based on warmth and understanding. Most child-rearing books, however, fell between the two, calling on parents to balance firmness and love and to adapt their methods to the unique temperament, needs, and feelings of each child.[32]

Although the authors of the burgeoning new child-rearing literature disagreed vehemently on such specific issues as the desirability of day care or whether mothers of young children should work outside the home, they did agree that successful child raising presents a much more difficult challenge today than it did in the past, noting that even parents with a deep commitment to their offspring confront difficulties that their parents did not have to face.[33]

Among the most potent new forces that intrude between parents and children is television. The single most important caretaker of children in the United States today is not a child's mother or a baby-sitter or even a day-care center but the television set in each child's home. Young children spend more time watching television than they do in any other activity other than sleep. The typical child between the ages of two and five spends about thirty hours a week viewing television, nearly a third of the child's waking time. Older children spend almost as much time in front of the TV. Indeed, children aged six to eleven average twenty-five hours a week watching TV, almost as much time as they spend in school. Since 1960 the tendency has been for children to become heavier and heavier television viewers.[34]

The debate about television's impact on children has raged furiously since the early 1950s. Critics are worried about parents' use of the television set as a baby-sitter and pacifier and as a substitute for an active parental role in socialization. They argue that excessive television viewing is detrimental because it encourages passivity and inhibits communication among family members. They express concern that children who watch large amounts of television tend to develop poor language skills, an inability to concentrate, and a disinclination to read. Moreover, they feel that television viewing tends to replace hours previously devoted to playtime either alone or with others. And, most worrisome, they believe that violence on TV provokes children to emulate aggressive behavior and acquire distorted views of adult relationships and communication.[35]

Research into the impact of television on children has substantiated some of these concerns and invalidated others. Television does appear to be a cause of cognitive and behavioral disturbances. Heavy television viewing is associated with reduced reading skills, less verbal fluency, and lower academic effort. Exposure to violence on television tends to make children more willing to hurt people and more aggressive in their play and in their methods of resolving conflicts. Time spent in front of the TV set does displace time previously spent on other activities and, as a result, many games and activities—marbles, jacks and trading cards, for example—are rapidly disappearing from American childhood.[36]

However, television also introduces children to new experiences easily and painlessly and stimulates interest in issues to which they might not otherwise be exposed. For many disadvantaged children, it provides a form of intellectual enhancement that deprived homes lacking books and newspapers could not afford. And, for many children, television programs provide a semblance of extended kinship attachments and outlets for their fantasies and unexpressed emotions.[37]

While some television shows, such as "Sesame Street" and "Mr. Rogers' Neighborhood", do appear to improve children's vocabularies, teach them basic concepts, and help them verbalize their feelings, overwhelming evidence suggests that most television programs convey racial and sexual stereotypes, desensitize children to violence, and discourage the kinds of sustained concentration necessary for reading comprehension. On balance, it seems clear that television cannot adequately take the place of parental or adult involvement and supervision of children and that the tendency for it to do so is a justifiable reason for increased public concern.[38]

The single most profound change that has taken place in children's lives since 1960 is the rapid movement of millions of mothers into the labor force. In the space of just twelve years, the number of mothers of children five or under who work outside the home tripled. Today nearly half of all children under the age of six have a mother who works. Many factors have contributed to this trend, including a rising cost of living and a declining rate of growth in real family income; increased control of fertility through contraception and abortion, which has meant that careers are less likely to be disrupted by unplanned pregnancies; and women's rising level of educational achievement, which has led many women to seek work not only as a way of getting a paycheck but as a way of obtaining personal independence and intellectual stimulation.[34]

The massive movement of mothers into the work force presented a major social problem: How should young children be cared for when their mothers work outside the home? This question gave rise to more controversy than almost any other family-related issue during the late 1960s and early 1970s.[40]

The event that first precipitated this debate was the publication in 1964 of a Department of Labor study that found almost one million latchkey children in the United States, unsupervised by adults for significant portions of the day. As the number of working mothers climbed in the late 1960s, many family experts advocated day care as a necessary response to the large number of mothers who had gone to work. At first the national debate focused on the child care problems of single mothers—widowed, divorced, and unmarried—and on whether they should be encouraged to enter the labor force.[41]

Liberals, led by Senator Walter Mondale, argued on behalf of a national system of comprehensive child development and day-care centers. Building on the model of the Head Start program, Mondale proposed in 1971 that the federal government establish a national system of services that included day-care programs, nutritional aid for pregnant mothers, medical and dental care, and after-school programs for teenagers. President Richard Nixon vetoed the bill in a stinging message that called the proposal fiscally irresponsible, administratively unworkable, and a threat to "diminish both parental authority and parental involvement with children." The president warned against committing "the vast authority of the national government to the side of communal approaches to child rearing over against the family-centered approach."[42]

Following the presidential veto, congressional support for a federally funded system of day care evaporated. Nevertheless the actual number of children enrolled in nursery schools or group day-care centers grew dramatically. At the time of the president's veto, less than one-third of all mothers with children one year old or younger held jobs. Today half of such women work, three-quarters of them full-time. As a result a majority of all children now spend some of their preschool years in the care of someone other than their mother.[43]

The trend is toward formal group day-care programs. Back in 1970 just 21 percent of all three- and four-year-olds were cared for in day-care centers or nursery schools. But between 1970 and 1983 the proportion virtually doubled, climbing to 38 percent. Today over two-thirds of all three- to four-year-olds are in a day-care, nursery school, or prekindergarten program.[44]

The single largest provider of day care now is the federal government, which offers child care, health, and educational services to some 400,000 low-income children through the Head Start program and which subsidizes private day-care facilities through child care tax credits, state block grants, and tax breaks for employers who subsidize day-care services. Nonetheless, the great majority of preschool child care arrangements in the United States are private, ranging from informal baby-sitting arrangements to private day-care centers run by national chains. Today two-thirds of all children are cared for in private facilities, and day care is an eleven-billion-dollar industry. The largest private corporation, Kinder-Care, has more than a thousand centers licensed to care for as many as a hundred thousand children.[45]

The drive for expanded day-care programs has its principal roots in the growing number of working mothers, the proliferation of single-parent homes, and the belief that access to day care is necessary to guarantee women's equal right to pursue a career. But the trend has also been fueled by new theories of child development, which emphasize the psychologically beneficial effects of a stimulating peer environment, by mounting evidence that children

can assimilate information earlier than previously thought, and by research that has shown that disadvantaged children who participated in Head Start were more likely to graduate from high school, enroll in college, and obtain self-supporting jobs and were less likely to be arrested or register for welfare than were other children from low-income families.[46]

As formal child care programs proliferated, parents, educators, and social scientists began to examine the impact of day care on children's social and psychological growth, their intellectual development, and their emotional bond with their mother. The effects of day care remain the subject of intense controversy. Expert opinion varies widely, from those who fear that such programs provide an inadequate and unsatisfactory substitute for the full-time care and devotion of a mother to those who stress the resilience and adaptability of children. On one side, Jerome Kagan, a Harvard developmental psychologist, concludes that recent research reveals "that group care for young children does not seem to have much effect, either facilitating or debilitating, on the cognitive, social or affective development of most children." On the other side of the debate, Michael Rutter, a child psychologist at London's Institute for Psychiatry, states that "although day care for very young children is not likely to result in serious emotional disturbance, it would be misleading to conclude that it is without risks or effects."[47]

At present, knowledge about the impact of day care in children's intellectual, social, and emotional development remains limited. Research has suggested that quality day care has "neither salutary nor adverse effects on the intellectual development of most children"; that early entry into full-time day care may interfere with "the formation of a close attachment to the parents"; and that children in group day care are somewhat more aggressive, more independent, more involved with other children, more physically active, and less cooperative with adults than mother-raised children.[48]

The most pressing problem for parents at the moment is an inadequate supply of quality day care. The quality of day-care centers varies widely. The nature of care ranges from family day care, in which a woman takes children into her home for a fee, and cooperatives staffed or administered by parents, to on-site company nurseries, instituted by approximately one hundred corporations, and child care chains. High-quality centers, which can charge as much as $500 a month to care for a child, usually enroll only a small group of children and provide a great deal of individual attention. Low-quality centers, in contrast, tend to have a high ratio of children to caretakers, a high level of staff turnover, a low level of parental involvement, and a high noise level.[49]

Another serious problem is the lack of access to day care on the part of poorer children. Access to day care varies enormously according to family income. Seventy-five percent of all children from families with incomes of more than $25,000 a year participate in day-care or preschool programs by the age of six, compared to just a third of children from families with incomes of less than $15,000. Today, as a result of limited public funding, just a fifth of all eligible children are enrolled in Head Start. Children from poorer families are also less likely to participate in programs with an educational component.[50]

The United States lags far behind major European nations in assuming public responsibility for children's welfare. Today most European countries offer a variety of programs designed to assist working mothers, including paid maternity and paternity leaves for mothers and fathers who hold jobs, financial allowances for families with children, and subsidized public nurseries and kindergartens. Finland and Hungary go even further, paying mothers who stay at home with their children. The United States, with its long tradition of private-sector approaches to public problems and ingrained hostility toward state intervention in the family, has yet to come to terms with the problems presented by the massive influx of mothers into the workplace. The burden of coping with child care remains with the individual family.[51]

Of all the dramatic changes that have taken place in children's lives in recent years, the one that has aroused the deepest public concern is the spiraling divorce rate. Since 1960 the number of children involved in divorce has tripled, and in every year since 1972, more than a million children have had their homes disrupted

by divorce. Of the children born in the 1970s, 40 percent will experience the dissolution of their parents' marriage before they themselves are sixteen. As one expert noted, "Children are becoming less and less of a deterrent to divorce."[52]

As divorce became a more pervasive part of the American scene, researchers began to ask penetrating questions about the psychological and emotional implications of divorce for children. Back in the 1920s, authorities on the family, using the case-study method, had concluded that children experienced the divorce of their parents as a devastating blow that stunted their psychological and emotional growth and caused maladjustments that persisted for years. Beginning in the late 1950s and continuing into the early 1970s, a new generation of researchers argued that children were better off when their parents divorced than when they had an unstable marriage; that divorce disrupted children's lives no more painfully than the death of a parent, which used to break up families just as frequently; and that the adverse effects of divorce were generally of short duration.[53]

Recent research has thrown both of these points of view into question. On the one hand, it appears that conflict-laden, tension-filled marriages have more adverse effects on children than divorce. Children from discordant homes permeated by tension and instability are more likely to suffer psychosomatic illnesses, suicide attempts, delinquency, and other social maladjustments than are children whose parents divorce. As of now, there is no clear-cut empirical evidence to suggest that children from "broken" homes suffer more health or mental problems, personality disorders, or lower school grades than children from "intact" homes.[54]

On the other hand, it is clear that divorce is severely disruptive, at least initially, for a majority of children, and a significant minority of children continue to suffer from the psychological and economic repercussions of divorce for many years after the breakup of their parents' marriage. It is also apparent that children respond very differently to a divorce and to a parent's death. When a father dies children are often moody and despairing. During a divorce, many children, and especially sons, exhibit anger, hostility, and conflicting loyalties.[55]

Children's reactions to divorce vary enormously, depending on their age and gender and, most important of all, their perception of their parents' marriage. Children who viewed their parents' marriage as unhappy tend to adjust more easily to divorce than those who regarded their home life as basically happy.[56]

For many children initial acceptance of their parents' separation is followed by a deep sense of shock. Although some children react calmly on learning that their parents are divorcing, a majority of children of all ages are vulnerable to feelings of pain, anger, depression, and insecurity. Family breakups often result in regressive behavior and developmental setbacks that last at least a year.[57]

Studies that followed children five years after a divorce found that a majority of children show resilience and increased maturity and independence. But, for a significant minority, the emotional turmoil produced by divorce proves to be long standing, evident in persistent feelings of hostility, depression, sexual anxiety, and concern about being loved. Among a minority of children, the apparent consequences of divorce include alcohol and drug abuse, outward-directed despair and aggression, and sexual promiscuity.[58]

Clearly, divorce is an extremely stressful experience for children, whose economic and emotional costs continue to run high long after the parents' separation. Economic disruption is the most obvious consequence of a divorce. In the immediate aftermath of a divorce, the income of the divorced woman and her children falls sharply, by 73 percent in the year following divorce, while the father's income rises by 42 percent. Adding to the financial pressures facing children of divorce is the fact that a majority of divorced men evade court orders to support their children. Recent surveys indicate that only 40 percent of support orders are fully complied with during the first year after a divorce and that by the tenth year after separation, the figure falls to 13 percent.[59]

Other sources of stress result from the mother's new financial responsibilities as her family's breadwinner, additional demands on her time as she tries to balance economic and child-rearing responsibilities, and, frequently, adjustment to unfamiliar and less comfortable living arrangements. Burdened by her new responsibilities as head of her household, a mother often devotes less time to child rearing, forcing her to rely more heavily on neighbors, relatives, and older children.[60]

The emotional and psychological upheavals caused by divorce are often aggravated by a series of readjustments children must deal with, such as loss of contact with the noncustodial parent. Many children of divorce have to deal with feelings of abandonment by their natural fathers. More than nine of every ten children are placed in their mother's custody, and recent studies have found that two months following a divorce fewer than half the fathers see their children as often as once a week and, after three years, half the fathers do not visit their children at all.[61]

Further complicating children's adjustment to their parents' divorce is the impact of remarriage. Roughly half of all mothers are remarried within approximately two years of their divorce, thus many children of divorce live only briefly in single-parent homes. Today there are over 4 million households—one of every seven with children—in which one parent has remarried and at least one child is from a previous union. These reconstituted families often confront jealousies and conflicts of loyalty not found in families untouched by divorce, leading a number of investigators to conclude that "homes involving steprelationships proved more likely to have stress, ambivalence, and low cohesiveness" than did two-parent homes. At the same time, other researchers have found that most children of divorce favored remarriage.[62]

Today's children are growing up in an unstable and threatening environment in which earlier sources of support have eroded. They live in a permissive culture that exposes them from an early age to drugs, sex, alcohol, and violence. The increasing divorce rate, the entry of many mothers into the full-time work force, high rates of mobility, and the declining importance of the extended family all contribute to a decline in support and guidance. As a society, the United States has largely failed to come to grips with the major issues facing children, such as the need for quality care while parents work and the need for a stable emotional environment in which to grow up.[63]

NOTES

1. The statistics on changes in family composition can be found in Daniel Yankelovich, *New Rules: Search for Self-Fulfillment in a World Turned Upside Down* (New York, 1981), xiv–xv.

2. Stephen L. Klineberg made a similar argument in a public lecture, "American Families in Transition: Challenges and Opportunities in a Revolutionary Time," delivered at Rice University, February 15, 1983. Also see Andrew Hacker, *The End of the American Era* (New York, 1971), 174; James J. Lynch, *The Broken Heart: The Medical Consequences of Loneliness* (New York, 1977), 8–10; *Time* (December 2, 1985), 41; *NYT,* June 27, 1979, I, 1; *NYT,* May 26, 1981, I, 1.

It must be emphasized that despite the dramatic changes that have taken place, the institution of the family is not an endangered species. Today, commitment to marriage remains strong and 90 percent of young Americans marry. Despite rising divorce rates, the majority of marriages do not end in divorce, most divorced individuals remarry, and only a small percentage marry more than twice. Even when divorces occur, they do not necessarily produce grave social problems. Forty percent of all divorces occur within four years of marriage and usually involve no children. At the same time, the desire to have children remains as high as ever. Today only 1 percent of American women say that the ideal number of children in a family is none. And despite concern about the fragility of family ties, the increase in the divorce rate has been largely offset by a decline in death rates. As a result, marriages today are only slightly more likely to be disrupted by divorce, desertion, or death than they were earlier in the century. Indeed, even with the rising divorce rate, fewer children today are raised in institutions or by relatives or by mothers barely able to support them than formerly. In spite of the rising divorce rate, the prevalence of single-parent households has not increased markedly among the middle class because women today are much more likely to remarry after a divorce.

Even in the controversial areas of child care and sexuality, behavior has changed less than newspaper headlines suggest. Today most preschoolers are cared for by full-time mothers or mothers who work part-time. Most mothers of young children accommodate their work schedules to the needs of their children. Continuity is also apparent in sexual behavior. Despite the increasing incidence of premarital sex and widespread public discussion of swinging, wife swapping, and illegitimacy, the overwhelming majority of women who have premarital sex have just one or two partners, usually a fiance or a steady date. Nor has the proportion of unmarried white women having babies increased dramatically. In 1950, 99.5 percent of white teenage women did not have illegitimate births; thirty years later, 98.1 percent of this group did not. See Mary Jo Bane, *Here to Stay: American Families in the Twentieth Century* (New York, 1976), 12–13, 30; Sar A. Levitan and Richard S. Belous, *What's Happening to the American Family?* (Baltimore, 1981), 21, 63; Mary Jo Bane et al., "Child Care Settings in the United States" in *Child Care and Mediating Structures,* eds. Brigitte Berger and Sidney Callahan (Washington, D.C., 1979), 19; Carol Tavris and Carole Offir, *The Longest War: Sex Differences in Perspective* (New York, 1977), 64–69.

3. Tavris and Offir, *The Longest War,* 64–69; Peter Uhlenberg and David Eggebeen, "Declining Well-Being of American Adolescents," *The Public Interest* (Winter 1986), 32–33; Lynch, *Broken Heart,* 8–10; *Time* (December 2, 1985), 41; *NYT,* June 27, 1979, I, 1; *NYT,* May 26, 1981, I, 1; *NYT,* March 16, 1986, I, 18.

4. The impact of these changes is most readily apparent in the lives of a key "pace-setting" segment of the population: educated career women. These women are four times less likely to marry than women of lower economic and educational status and 50 percent more likely to divorce. See Andrew Hacker, "Goodbye to Marriage," *New York Review of Books* (May 3, 1979), 23–27. Peter Clecak, *America's Quest for the Ideal Self: Dissent and Fulfillment in the 60s and 70s* (New York, 1983), 93–94.

5. Yankelovich, *New Rules,* 104, 184. It is easy to exaggerate the significance of rising rates of divorce, working mothers, and single parent households and to conclude that these changes are bad for the family. But it is also possible to view these developments in a more favorable light. Declining birthrates mean that Americans are less likely to bear children by accident or because it is socially expected than earlier Americans, while rising divorce rates mean that people today are less willing to tolerate unhappy and empty marriages. See Klineberg, "American Families in Transition."

6. Ben J. Wattenberg, *The Good News Is the Bad News Is Wrong* (New York, 1985), 290–91.

7. Joseph Veroff, Elizabeth Douan, and Richard A. Kulka, *The Inner American: A Self Portrait from 1957 to 1976* (New York, 1981), 191, 192, 194, 196; Yankelovich, *New Rules,* 5, 68, 97, 99.

8. Yankelovich, *New Rules,* 5. The rapid rise in the divorce rate is clearly a legacy of changing social values. When individuals are asked why they have decided to get a divorce, a new set of reasons predominates. A survey conducted by the Family Service Association found that the major source of conflict in marriages involved "communications." Conflict over sex was another reason commonly cited in explanations of divorce. More traditional areas of conflict, such as disputes over children and family finances, lagged far behind. See *NYT,* January 3, 1974, I, 16.

It should be noted, however, that the best predictors of a marital breakup remain what they have always been: a teenage marriage, a wife pregnant before marriage, and a low level of family income. Psychological stress continues to be a leading cause of divorce, since many marriages fail following an acutely stressful experience, such as an unexpected death in the family, revelation of an infidelity, or loss of a job. See Arthur J. Norton and Paul C. Glick, "Marital Instability in America: Past, Present, and Future," in *Divorce and Separation: Context, Causes, and Consequences,* eds. George Lebinger and Oliver C. Moles (New York, 1979), 6–19; Bane, *Here to Stay,* 22, 32–33, 36.

Traditional causes of marital stress were aggravated by social and legal changes during the 1970s. Economic instability produced conditions conducive to high divorce rates. Instability in a husband's employment or earnings is a major source of strain in the marriages of poorer couples, producing friction because of the husband's inability to fulfill his family's expectations. Divorce is more likely as well when a wife's earnings are higher than her husband's, in part because independent earnings add to a woman's sense of self-esteem and in part because this contributes to the husband's sense of insecurity. As more wives entered the labor force after 1970, this factor became a growing source of marital strain. Increased rates of social mobility across ethnic, religious, and geographical lines also contributed to the rising rates of marital instability. Census statistics disclose that more and more people are marrying partners who come from outside their ethnic or religious group or their area of birth. After marriage an increasing number of couples pull up stakes and move to new parts of the country, particularly to the Sunbelt, disrupting ties with family and friends. Divorce statistics show that the twelve metropolitan areas with the highest divorce rates are all located in Southern and Western states. Victor R. Fuchs, *How We Live* (Cambridge, Mass., 1983), 147–50; *NYT,* November 13, 1981, I, 12.

Changes in law also contributed to the rising number of divorces. Legal changes that made it easier to obtain a divorce included enactment of no-fault divorce laws in every state except South Dakota, "do-it-yourself" divorce kits that allow couples to dissolve a marriage without the help of a lawyer, a tendency toward lower alimony awards, and a trend toward making property settlements less contingent on who was at fault in breaking up the marriage. *NYT,* January 5, 1974, I, 16; *NYT,* March 19, 1975, I, 33; *NYT,* February 7, 1983, I, 1; Joan Anderson letter, *NYT,* December 5, 1981, I, 24; Lenore J. Weitzman and Ruth B. Dixon, "The Transformation of Legal Marriage Through No-Fault Divorce: The Case of the United States," in *Marriage and Cohabitation in Contemporary Societies; Areas of Legal, Social, and Ethical*

Change, eds. John M. Eekelaar and Sanford N. Katz (Toronto, 1979), 143–53; Lynne Carol Halem, *Divorce Reform: Changing Legal and Social Perspectives* (New York, 1980), 233–83.

Finally, the current upsurge in divorces may be a product of the early marriages contracted during World War II and the early postwar period, when an unprecedented number of very young couples were joined together in wedlock. The high number of divorces during and after the World War II may have contributed to the high divorce rate during the 1970s, because the children of divorce face a substantially higher risk than others of having their own marriages fail. Norton and Glick, "Marital Instability in America," 6–19; *NYT,* November 27, 1977, I, 1; *NYT,* April 13, 1982, C1.

9. Veroff, Douan, and Kulka, *The Inner American,* 191, 192, 194, 196; Yankelovich, *New Rules,* 5.

10. Richard A. Easterlin, "The American Baby Boom in Historical Perspective" Occasional Paper No. 79 (Washington, D.C., National Bureau of Economic Research, 1962); "Relative Economic Status and the American Fertility Swing," in *Social Structure, Family Life Styles, and Economic Behavior,* ed. Eleanor B. Sheldon (Philadelphia, 1972); Easterlin, "The Conflict Between Aspirations and Resources," *Population and Development Review,* 2 (September/December 1972), 417–26; Arthur A. Campbell, "Baby Boom to Birth Dearth and Beyond," *Annals,* 435 (January 1978), 52–53.

11. Russell Jacoby, *Social Amnesia: A Critique of Conformist Psychology from Adler to Laing* (Boston, 1975); Ehrenreich, *Hearts of Men,* 89–98, 122, 147, 164–65; Yankelovich, *New Rules,* 235.

12. Refer to note 11. For an example of the new viewpoint on marriage and divorce, see a popular textbook, *Essentials of Life and Health* (New York, 1972): "Far from being a wasting illness, divorce is a healthful adaptation, enabling monogamy to survive in a time when patriarchal powers, privileges and marital systems have become unworkable; far from being a radical change in the institution of marriage, divorce is a relatively minor modification of it. . . ."; quoted in Lynch, *The Broken Heart,* 10.

13. Allen J. Matusow, *The Unraveling of America: A History of Liberalism in the 1960s* (New York, 1984), 277–80, 321–23.

14. Refer to note 13. If a single term gave expression to the growing influence of young people during the 1960s, it was the phrase the "generation gap." It referred to the appearance among the young of a separate culture, a distinct language, and a distinctive outlook, apart from the world of adults. A shift in generational experience may have contributed to the perceived gulf between old and young. Young people of the 1960s, unlike their parents, had escaped the years of hardship, austerity, and sacrifice of the depression and World War II. Also contributing to a generation gap was the rising level of education attained by younger Americans. Many studies conducted during the 1960s concluded that those who had attended college were generally more liberal in their social, religious, and moral attitudes than those who had not.

It would be a mistake, however—a mistake made by many social commentators—to exaggerate the dimensions of the generation gap during the 1960s. Little persuasive evidence was uncovered during the sixties showing extensive alienation between adolescents and their parents. Survey research found a deep cleavage within the younger generation itself, dividing young college students from those who had entered blue collar jobs directly from high school, who were reportedly appalled "by the collapse of patriotism and respect for the law." Altogether, little evidence was found to indicate that younger Americans had abandoned traditional moral frameworks. Even in the most controversial and highly publicized areas of change—sex and drug-taking—truly dramatic shifts would have to wait for the 1970s. Studies of sexual behavior in the late 1960s detected only a modest liberalization in sexual practices compared to findings of twenty years before, while surveys of drug use found that only about 10 percent of young Americans had experimented with marijuana.

A number of influential studies of college students also argued that younger people's rejection of the strict norms that prevailed in the 1950s did not constitute a generation gap. According to these studies, students were simply giving expression to suppressed elements in their parents' lives. See Yankelovich, *New Rules,* 174; Kenneth Keniston, *Young Radicals* (New York, 1968); *NYT,* February 4, 1971, I, 1; *NYT,* January 17, 1972, I, 33; *NYT,* August 18, 1977, C13; *NYT,* December 1, 1968, VI, 129; *NYT,* November 2, 1969, VI, 32ff.; *NYT,* January 18, 1970, VI, 10.

15. Manchester, *Glory and the Dream,* 1221, 1355, 1463–68. The literature on the women's movement is vast. A useful introduction is William H. Chafe, *Women and Equality: Changing Patterns in American Culture* (New York, 1977). On the ideology of feminism, see Barbara Sinclair Deckard, *The Women's Movement: Political, Socioeconomic, and Psychological Issues* (New York, 1975); Sara Evans, *Personal Politics: The Roots of Women's Liberation in the Civil Rights Movement and the New Left* (New York, 1979); Jo Freeman, *The Politics of Women's Liberation: A Case of an Emerging Social Movement and Its Relation to the Public Policy Process* (New York, 1975); Judith Hole and Ellen Levine, *Rebirth of Feminism* (New York, 1971); *Radical Feminism,* eds. Anne Koedt, Ellen Levine, and Anita Rapone (New York, 1973); Gayle Graham Yates, *What Women Want: The Ideas of the Movement* (Cambridge, Mass., 1971).

16. On the impact of feminism, see Judith M. Bardwick, *In Transition: How Feminism, Sexual Liberation, and the Search for Self-Fulfillment Have Altered America* (New York, 1979); Chafe, *Women and Equality,* ch. 5; Cynthia Fuchs Epstein, "Ten Years Later: Perspectives on the Women's Movement," *Dissent,* 22 (Spring 1975), 169–76; Janet Giele, *Women and the Future: Changing Sex Roles in Modern America* (New York, 1978); Elinor Lenz and Barbara Myerhoff, *The Feminization of America: How Women's Values are Changing Our Public and Private Lives* (Los Angeles, 1985); Jane de Hart Mathews, "The New Feminism and the Dynamics of Social Change," in *Women's America: Refocusing the Past,* eds. Linda Kerber and Jane de Hart Mathews (New York, 1981), 397–421.

17. Manchester, *Glory and the Dream,* 1035–36. On the sexual revolution, see "Sex and the Contemporary American Scene," *Annals of the American Academy of Political and Social Science,* 376 (March 1968).

18. *NYT,* February 10, 1971, I, 48. On the growth of a "singles culture," see *NYT,* January 3, 1974, I, 16; *NYT,* April 21, 1977, C1. Homosexual rights ordinances were adopted in Ann Arbor, Michigan; Berkeley, California; Columbus, Ohio; Detroit, Michigan; Minneapolis, Minnesota; San Francisco, California; Seattle, Washington; and Washington, D.C., between 1972 and 1974. In 1973, the American Psychiatric Association removed homosexuality from its list of mental disorders.

19. Manchester, *Glory and the Dream,* 1035–36; "Sex and the Contemporary American Scene," *Annals of the American Academy of Political and Social Science,* 376 (March, 1968); *NYT,* February 10, 1971, I, 48; *NYT,* January 3, 1974, I, 16; *NYT,* April 21, 1977, C1.

20. Yankelovich, *New Rules,* xiv, 88, 97, 99, 100, 103, 104.

21. Sar A. Levitan, *Programs in Aid of the Poor,* 5th ed. (Baltimore, 1985), 13–14, 34–38, 94–95.

22. Welfare mothers divide into at least two identifiable groups. Most single women on welfare are older women seeking temporary assistance while recovering from the loss of a spouse through divorce, desertion, or death. These women account for 85 to 90 percent of all single women who ever go on welfare. Another group of single women on welfare are younger, less-educated mothers, particularly those who bore an illegitimate child during their teens or early twenties, who are more likely to remain dependent on public assistance for long periods. Roughly 10 to 15 percent of the people who ever go on welfare remain on public assistance for eight years or more; they constitute more than half of the people on welfare at any one time. See Mickey

Kaus, "Welfare and Work: A Symposium," *New Republic* (October 6, 1986), 22; *NYT,* September 25, 1986, I, 26. Ben J. Wattenberg, *The Good News Is the Bad News Is Wrong* (New York, 1985), 191, 240, 243.

23. Sar A. Levitan, *Programs in Aid of the Poor for the 1970s* (Baltimore, Md., 1969), 29; Sheila B. Kamerman and Alfred J. Kahn, eds., *Family Policy: Government and Families in Fourteen Countries* (New York, 1978), 428–503.

24. Sheila B. Kamerman and Cheryl D. Hayes, eds., *Families That Work: Children in a Changing World* (Washington, D.C., 1982), 12–36; Joan Beck, "Growing Up in America is Tough," *Houston Chronicle* (April 2, 1986), A10; Glazer, "Rediscovery of the Family," 50.

Growing anxiety over children and adolescents was, of course, related to the postwar baby boom. Census statistics showed an explosion in the number of young Americans during the 1960s. The number of young people aged fourteen to twenty-four jumped 47 percent in a decade, reaching forty million in 1970. At the end of the 1960s, young people accounted for 20 percent of the American population, a third more than in 1960. Because teenagers and young adults constituted a growing proportion of the population, as a result of depressed birthrates during the 1930s followed by the postwar baby boom, young people exerted a disproportionate influence on public opinion.

The 1960s witnessed major gains in income, education, and employment by teenagers. Teenagers were far more likely to finish high school or attend college than were their parents. The proportion of young Americans receiving college degrees tripled in the three decades after 1940—climbing from 6 to 16 percent—while the proportion receiving high school diplomas doubled—from 38 percent to 75 percent. *NYT,* February 4, 1971, I, 1; *NYT,* January 17, 1972, I, 33; *NYT,* August 18, 1977, C13.

25. Today, as many as two-thirds of all American high school junior and seniors hold part-time paying jobs. See Ellen Greenberger and Laurence Steinberg, *When Teenagers Work: The Psychological and Social Costs of Adolescent Employment* (New York, 1986), 3–46.

26. Joan Beck, "Growing Up in America Is Tough," *Houston Chronicle* (April 2, 1986), A10.

27. Marie Winn, *Children Without Childhood* (New York, 1983); David Elkind, *The Hurried Child: Growing Up Too Soon* (Reading, Mass., 1981); Vance Packard, *Our Endangered Children: Growing Up in a Changing World* (Boston, 1983). Similar fears were already being voiced in the 1950s. See Eda LeShan, *The Conspiracy Against Childhood* (New York, 1967).

28. Peter Uhlenberg and David Eggebeen, "The Declining Well-Being of American Adolescents," *Public Interest,* no. 85 (Winter 1986), 25–38.

29. While it is true that the suicide rate for white male adolescents increased 260 percent between 1950 and 1976, the illegitimacy rate of illegitimate births among white adolescent females increased 143 percent over the same period, and the rate of death by homicide among white adolescent males increased 77 percent between 1959 and 1976, actual rates remained at low levels. The white male adolescent homicide rate rose from 3 per 100,000 in 1959 to 8 per 100,000 in 1976; the white male adolescent suicide rate climbed from 4 per 100,000 in 1950 to 13 per 100,000 in 1976; and illegitimacy among white teenage women rose from 5.1 per 1,000 to 12.4 per 1,000. It is also easy to exaggerate drug usage. Seventeen percent of all high school seniors have tried cocaine once in their life; 54 percent have tried marijuana at least once. See Ira S. Steinberg, *The New Lost Generation: The Population Boom and Public Policy* (New York, 1982), 7–19; Adam Paul Weisman, "I Was a Drug-Hype Junkie," *New Republic* (October 6, 1986), 14–17.

30. *NYT,* October 26, 1969, I, 57; *NYT,* April 2, 1967, VI, 112ff.

31. *NYT,* September 11, 1973, I, 50; *NYT,* December 25, 1969, 37.

32. *NYT,* April 14, 1974, VII, 3; *NYT,* November 8, 1968, I, 54; *NYT,* January 7, 1973, I, 22, 23; *NYT,* February 16, 1969, VII, Pt. 2,

4; *NYT,* June 27, 1976, VI, 26ff.; *NYT,* December 3, 1973, I, 54; *NYT,* March 16, 1981, II, 8; *NYT,* September 11, 1973, I, 50.

33. *NYT,* December 3, 1973, I, 54; *NYT,* March 16, 1981, II, 8; *NYT,* September 11, 1973, I, 50.

34. Fuchs, *How We Live,* 51, 55–56, 69–71; Bane, *Here to Stay,* 15; John P. Murray, *Television and Youth: 25 Years of Research and Controversy* (Stanford, Wash., 1980), 67.

35. Marie Winn, *The Plug-In Drug* (New York, 1977); Murray, *Television and Youth,* 18–57.

36. Murray, *Television and Youth,* 18–57; *NYT,* January 6, 1959, March 2, 1969, September 18, 1969, September 28, 1969, September 4, 1971, January 11, 1972, April 20, 1980, reprinted in *Childhood, Youth and Society,* ed. Gene Brown (New York, 1980), 70–94.

37. Refer to note 36.

38. Refer to note 36.

39. Fuchs, *How We Live,* 126–33, 150, 166, 169, 173–74, 190, 204; *NYT,* November 30, 1977, I, 1. One set of factors that propelled married women into the labor force was a rising cost of living and a declining rate of growth in real family income. Income, adjusted for inflation, rose 38 percent during the 1950s and 33 percent in the 1960s, but dropped 9.2 percent between 1973 and 1982. At the same time that real income fell, other costs, especially for housing, climbed steeply. Back in 1971, it took an income of just $6,770 to afford a median-price house, which then cost just $24,800. Actual median income that year was $10,300, 51.9 percent more than was required. A decade later, the median price of a house had climbed to over $70,000 and a family that earned the median family income was unable to afford such a house. Other economic factors that led many married women to seek a paycheck included rising real wages for women workers, which increased the attractiveness of work outside the home and the growth of service industries, such as retail trade, education, and health. Such service jobs have traditionally offered more opportunities to women than other occupations because they do not rely on physical strength, their work hours are usually flexible, and the workplace is often located in residential areas.

40. Sheila Kamerman and Alfred Kahn, "The Day-Care Debate: A Wider View," *Public Interest,* no. 54 (1979), 76–93.

41. *NYT,* November 30, 1970, I, 1; *NYT,* April 1, 1973, IV, 9; *NYT,* January 9, 1976, I, 18.

42. Edward B. Fiske, "Early Schooling Is Now the Rage," *NYT,* April 13, 1986, XII, 24–30; *NYT,* December 10, 1971, and April 30, 1972, in *The Family,* ed. Gene Brown, 337–43.

43. Fiske, "Early Schooling," 25; Kamerman and Kahn, "The Day-Care Debate," 76–93.

44. Fiske, "Early Schooling," 25.

45. Ibid., 25–26. A 1985 Conference Board study estimated that 120 companies and 400 hospitals and public agencies sponsored daycare centers at or near their facilities. Another 2500 firms provide financial support for child care. *NYT,* June 21, 1985, 25: 2.

46. Fiske, "Early Schooling," 25–26.

47. Packard, *Our Endangered Children,* 137–38; Jerome Kagan, "The Effects of Infant Day Care on Psychological Development," *The Growth of the Child* (New York, 1978), 78.

48. Packard, *Our Endangered Children,* 139–41, 146, 166–72; Jay Belsky and Laurence D. Steinberg, "The Effects of Day Care: A Critical View," *Child Development,* 49 (1978), 929–49; Belsky and Steinberg, "What Does Research Teach Us About Day Care?" *Children Today* (July-August, 1979); Sally Provence, Audrey Naylor and June Patterson, *The Challenge of Day Care* (New Haven, 1977).

49. Packard, *Our Endangered Children,* 144–58.

50. Fiske, "Early Schooling," 30.

51. Sheila B. Kamerman and Alfred J. Kahn, eds., *Family Policy: Government and Families in Fourteen Countries* (New York, 1978), 428–503; *NYT,* June 9, 1979, 17: 2; Packard, *Our Endangered Children,* 162–66; *Houston Chronicle,* March 2, 1987, A7.

Ten states—California, Connecticut, Hawaii, Illinois, Kansas, Massachusetts, Minnesota, New Hampshire, Ohio, and Washington—currently require employers to grant special leaves to pregnant women and to reinstate them in their jobs or comparable positions when they return. In all other states, maternity policies are governed by the 1978 federal Pregnancy Discrimination Act, which made it illegal to discriminate on the basis of pregnancy or childbirth in hiring, reinstatement, termination, and disability benefits.

Five states—California, Hawaii, New Jersey, New York, and Rhode Island—provide temporary disability insurance, which provides half the wage the female worker earned during a six to ten week maternity leave.

52. Packard, *Our Endangered Children,* 185; Uhlenberg and Eggebeen, "The Declining Well-Being of American Adolescents," 37.

53. Levitan and Belous, *What's Happening to the American Family?,* 69–72; Halem, *Divorce Reform,* 191–93.

54. Packard, *Our Endangered Children,* 189–210; Halem, *Divorce Reform,* 174–81; Levitan and Belous, *What's Happening to the American Family?,* 69–72; Judith S. Wallerstein and Joan B. Kelley, *Surviving the Breakup: How Children and Parents Cope With Divorce* (New York, 1980); Cynthia Longfellow, "Divorce in Context: Its Impact on Children" in *Divorce and Separation,* 287–306.

55. Refer to note 54.

56. Refer to note 54.

57. Refer to note 54.

58. Refer to note 54.

59. Fuchs, *How We Live,* 73–75, 149–50, 214; Levitan and Belous, *What's Happening to the American Family?,* 72–75; *NYT,* April 2, 1974, I, 34; Lenore Weitzman, *The Divorce Revolution: The Unexpected Social and Economic Consequences for Women and Children* (New York, 1985).

60. Refer to note 59.

61. *NYT,* May 22, 1983, VI, 48–57; *NYT,* November 23, 1980, I, 28.

62. Packard, *Our Endangered Children,* 294; Halem, *Divorce Reform,* 187–91; Levitan and Belous, *What's Happening to the American Family?,* 70, 74.

63. Winn, *Children Without Childhood;* Elkind, *The Hurried Child;* Packard, *Our Endangered Children.*

The Economic Consequences of Divorce

LENORE J. WEITZMAN

Divorce has radically different economic consequences for men and women. While most divorced men find that their standard of living improves after divorce, most divorced women and the minor children in their households find that their standard of living plummets. This [discussion] shows that when income is compared to needs, divorced men experience an average 42 percent rise in their standard of living in the first year after the divorce, while divorced women (and their children) experience a 73 percent decline.

These apparently simple statistics have far-reaching social and economic consequences. For most women and children, divorce means precipitous downward mobility—both economically and socially. The reduction in income brings residential moves and inferior housing, drastically diminished or nonexistent funds for recreation and leisure, and intense pressures due to inadequate time and money. Financial hardships in turn cause social dislocation and a loss of familiar networks for emotional support and social services, and intensify the psychological stress for women and children alike. On a societal level, divorce increases female and child poverty and creates an ever-widening gap between the economic well-being of divorced men, on the one hand, and their children and former wives on the other.

The data reviewed in this [analysis] indict the present legal system of divorce: it provides neither economic justice nor economic equality.

The economic consequences of the current system of divorce emerge from two different types of analysis. In the first analysis we focus on income. Here we compare men's and women's *incomes* before and after divorce. The second analysis focuses on *standards of living*. Here we ask how the husbands' postdivorce standards of living compare with that of their former wives.

Since it is reasonable to expect postdivorce incomes and standards of living to vary with the length of marriage and the family income level before divorce, these two factors are controlled in the following analyses.

POSTDIVORCE INCOME: RELATIVE DEPRIVATION FOR WOMEN AND CHILDREN

To compare the experiences of men and women after divorce, each spouse's postdivorce income is measured against the "baseline" figure of the family's predivorce income.

In this analysis, we assume full compliance with court-ordered alimony and child support awards. This means the wife's postdivorce income has been "adjusted" by adding the amount of alimony and child support she was awarded to her income from other sources, such as wages or welfare payments. Similarly, the husband's income has been adjusted by deducting the amount of alimony and child support he was ordered to pay from his postdivorce income.

In view of the high rate of noncompliance with support orders, this method of calculation obviously underestimates husbands' incomes and overestimates wives'. (Since many husbands do not comply with court orders for support, husbands will have *more* income than these calculations assume and wives will have *less*—and the real income difference between the two spouses *will be greater* than these figures suggest.) Thus, if there is an error in these calculations it is that the income differences between men and women have been *minimized*.

The data were collected in interviews that took place about a year after the legal divorce. In many cases the year brought additional income for one or both parties—from new jobs,

Reprinted with permission of The Free Press, a division of Macmillan, Inc., from *The Divorce Revolution: The Unexpected Social and Economic Consequences for Women and Children in America* by Lenore J. Weitzman. Copyright © 1985 by Dr. Lenore J. Weitzman.

increased working hours, supplementary income or aid from the government, and (among some women and a large number of men) salary raises and cost-of-living increases. Thus the combined postdivorce income of the two former spouses is often greater than the family income at the time of the divorce.

Here we compare postdivorce incomes for three groups of couples: those divorced after shorter marriages (under 10 years), after mid-length marriages (11 to 17 years), and after long marriages (18 years or more).

Shorter Marriages

For couples married less than ten years, we found a striking disparity between the postdivorce income levels of former husbands and wives (see Table 26). One year after the divorce, husbands had postdivorce incomes equivalent to at least three-quarters of the family's total income before the divorce. Most wives, in contrast, lived on a fraction of the family's predivorce income—a half, or a third, or a quarter.

Only wives from low-income families had close to three-quarters (71 percent) of the family's predivorce income—but they too had less income than their former husbands. In middle- and higher-income families, the wives had much less. For example, in families with predivorce incomes between $30,000 and $40,000 a year, the wife's income was reduced to 39 percent of the former family standard, while her husband maintained 75 percent.

The contrast is most pronounced among families with predivorce incomes of $40,000 or more. Relative to other divorced women, these wives appear to be moderately well off: they had mean support awards of close to $8000 a year and total yearly incomes of $18,000. But compare them to their former husbands: the wives' income is only 29 percent of the former family income, while the husbands' is three-quarters of that standard, or more than twice as much dollar income ($18,000 vs. $46,550 per year).

In short, as family income goes up, divorced wives experience greater "relative deprivation." That is, they are relatively worse off

TABLE 26

Postdivorce Incomes of Couples Married Less Than Ten Years

Predivorce Yearly Family Income	Mean Yearly Support Awarded to Wife[1,2]	Median Postdivorce Income		Median Postdivorce Income As Percentage of Predivorce Family Income	
		Wife's (Adjusted)[3]	Husband's (Adjusted)[4]	Wife (Adjusted)	Husband (Adjusted)
Under $20,000 (n = 41)[5]	$ 550	$ 9,050	$10,750	71%	94%
$20–29,999 (n = 24)	$1,350	$13,000	$18,100	56%	78%
$30–39,999 (n = 19)	$1,750	$15,000	$30,000	39%	75%
$40,000+ (n = 21)	$7,750	$18,000	$46,550	29%	75%

[1] All dollar figures are rounded to nearest $50.
[2] Court-ordered alimony and child support, including zero and one dollar awards.
[3] Wife's adjusted income calculated by adding court-ordered alimony and child support awarded plus income from any other source (such as wages or welfare).
[4] Husband's adjusted income calculated by subtracting court-ordered alimony and child support from husband's total income.
[5] n refers to the number of cases on which the percentages are based.

This table is based on data from interviews with divorced men and women, Los Angeles County, California, 1978.

than their former husbands, and they are relatively worse off than they were during marriage. Thus wives in families with incomes of less than $20,000 before divorce had 71 percent of that income after divorce, but this dropped to 56 percent for wives in families with between $20,000 to $30,000 incomes before divorce, to 39 percent for wives in families with incomes of $30,000 to $40,000, and to a mere 29 percent for wives in families with incomes of $40,000 and more before the divorce.

PER CAPITA INCOME

The foregoing discussion treats the postdivorce households of men and women as if each contained only one person. However, women are more likely than men to have dependent children in their households and more likely to share their postdivorce income with them. One way of building this factor into the analysis is to calculate the *per capita income* in the two households by dividing the adjusted income of each spouse by the number of people in each household.

Before discussing these data, however, it is important to note two methodological decisions that were made. First, we have once again assumed full compliance with alimony and child support orders. Second, although we have included new spouses and permanent cohabitors in calculating the number of persons in each postdivorce household, we have not included the income these adults may bring into the household. (Rather, we have assumed that *none* of these new members is contributing to the family's income.)

Again, both of these decisions are likely to lead us to underestimate the husbands' income after divorce. Not only does noncompliance result in more income being left in the husbands' households, so does remarriage—since men were more likely than women to remarry or cohabit within the first year after divorce and most second spouses and cohabitors were employed. Among couples married less than 10 years, 19 percent of the husbands had remarried within one year of the divorce, in contrast to only 4 percent of their former wives.

Table 27 shows the *per capita* income for the same group of families examined in Table 26. It reveals that the presence of children in the wife's postdivorce household makes a major difference: it diminishes the amount of money available to each member. As a result, the wife and each member of her household have far less *per capita* income than the husband (and each member of his household).

Table 27 highlights three major findings. First, divorced men at every income level who were married less than ten years had a much higher *per capita* income—that is, they have much more money to spend on themselves—than their former wives. Second, the disparity between former husbands and wives is much greater when we compare *per capita* income rather than household income because the *per capita* measure takes into account the additional needs of the children. And third, the children and wives of upper-middle-class men experience the greatest relative deprivation. When we compare *household* income for the average divorcing couple (in Table 26), we see a 22 percent discrepancy between husbands' and wives' postdivorce incomes (78 percent vs. 56 percent), but when we compare *per capita* income, the discrepancy increases to 83 percent (164 percent vs. 81 percent). Similarly, for lower-income couples, a household discrepancy of 23 percent is a *per capita* discrepancy of 56 percent. For the highest income couples, a household discrepancy of 44 percent becomes a *per capita* discrepancy of enormous proportions—144 percent difference between the *per capita* incomes of former husbands and wives.

These comparisons show how the presence of children in the wife's household increases demands on her income. When a mother shares her smaller portion of the pie with the couple's children, both she and the children end up with significantly less money than the father.

It seems somewhat ironic to note that judges often explain their higher awards to the husband by saying that he will soon have to support a second family. Yet these data show that it is more typically women who are supporting other family members. When men do remarry, the court awards allow them to support their new families at a much higher level. In this subsample, for

TABLE 27

Median Postdivorce Per Capita Incomes of Couples Married Less Than Ten Years

Predivorce Yearly Family Income	Predivorce Per Capita Family Income[1]	Postdivorce Per Capita Income		Postdivorce Per Capita Income As Percentage of Predivorce Family Per Capita Income	
		Wife (Adjusted)[2,4]	Husband (Adjusted)[3,4]	Wife (Adjusted)	Husband (Adjusted)
Under $20,000 (n = 41)[5]	$ 6,050	$ 7,000	$10,450	116%	172%
$20–29,999 (n = 24)	$11,000	$ 8,900	$18,050	81%	164%
$30–39,999 (n = 19)	$17,500	$13,050	$27,000	75%	154%
$40,000+ (n = 21)	$23,500	$12,000	$45,700	51%	195%

[1]All dollar figures are rounded to nearest $50.
[2]Wife's postdivorce adjusted per capita family income was calculated by taking the wife's total income (from all sources including alimony and child support) and dividing by the number of people in her postdivorce family (including children in her custody).
[3]Husband's postdivorce adjusted per capita income was calculated by taking the husband's total income, subtracting any alimony and child support awarded to his ex-wife, and dividing the remaining amount by the number of people in his postdivorce family (including any new spouse, permanent cohabitant, or children in his custody).
[4]These figures *do not* include any additional income provided by the new spouse for the 19% of the divorced men and the 4% of the divorced women in this subsample who had remarried by the time of the interview (approximatley one year after the legal divorce), or by a permanent cohabitant.
[5]n refers to the number of cases on which the percentages are based.
This table is based on data from interviews with divorced men and women, Los Angeles County, California, 1978.

example, the 19 percent of the men who remarried were supporting their new families at per capita levels well above those of their former wives and children.

Paralleling the findings in Table 26 on household income, we find that the discrepancy between the husbands' and wives' postdivorce *per capita* income is smallest among low- and average-income families. In the average-income range, for example, the husband has about *twice* as much money as his former wife and each of his children. In the higher-income range, the ratio is closer to four times as much. Thus among families with predivorce incomes of $40,000 a year or more, the wives and children are left with half of their former *per capita* level, while the husband's *per capita* income is close to 200 percent above his former level.

The result is that most wives experience rapid *downward* mobility after divorce, while most husbands' economic status is substantially

improved. Indeed, our interviews reveal that it is the *discrepancy* between the two households, a discrepancy that is largest among middle-class and upper-middle-class couples, that engenders the resentment that so many divorced women express. The injustice, in their eyes, is that she is forced to live so poorly when he is allowed to live so well.

Marriages of Eleven to Seventeen Years

The same discrepancies in postdivorce incomes are evident among couples divorced after marriages of 11 to 17 years. Here the data (tables not shown) follow the patterns in Tables 26 and 27. Again, analysis of postdivorce *household* incomes reveals men to be relatively better off after divorce than their former wives. And again, analysis of *per capita* income intensifies the differences because many wives are still sharing their smaller household incomes with minor children. Since the costs of raising children increase with the age of the child and are highest in the teenage years, the older children in these families fully consume their *per capita* share of the family budget.

As with couples in shorter marriages, the greatest gap between men and women's postdivorce incomes among those married 11 to 17 years occurs in the higher-income groups. In families with predivorce incomes of $40,000 or more, the wife's postdivorce *per capita* income is 64 percent of the family's former standard, while that of the husband is 222 percent.

One implication of these findings is that a man can substantially improve his standard of living by getting a divorce. In addition, the richer he is, the more he has to gain. The parallel implication, of course, is that women have a lot to lose—economically—from divorce, and those married to well-to-do men have the most to lose. Instead of living the life of the mythical alimony drone surrounded by luxury, the wife of fifteen years is more likely to find herself deprived of virtually all the benefits she enjoyed as the wife of a relatively well-to-do man. For this reason, she suffers a much greater financial loss by divorce than does a divorced woman from a lower-income family.

Long-married Couples and Displaced Homemakers

Economically, older and longer-married women suffer the most after divorce. Their situation is much more drastic—and tragic—than that of their younger counterparts because the discrepancy between men's and women's standards of living after divorce is much greater than for younger couples, and few of these women can ever hope to recapture their loss.

Once again, among this group the discrepancy between former husbands and wives is evident at all income levels, and most pronounced—and severe—for those with predivorce family incomes of $40,000 or more a year.

When the courts project the postdivorce prospects for women after shorter marriages, they assume that most of these women will be able to build new lives for themselves.[1] They reason that a woman in her twenties or early thirties

is young enough to acquire education or training and thus has the potential to find a satisfying and well-paid job. To be sure, such women will probably have a hard time catching up with their former husbands, but most of them will be able to enter or re-enter the labor force. In setting support for these younger women, the underlying assumption is that they will become self-sufficient. (I am not questioning that assumption. What has been questioned is the court's optimism about the ease and speed of the transition. Younger divorced women need more generous support awards for training and education to maximize their long-run job prospects.[2] But their potential for some level of "self-sufficiency" is not questioned.)

But what about the woman in her forties or fifties—or even sixties at the point of divorce? What are her prospects? Is it reasonable for judges to expect her to become self-sufficient? This woman's problems of job placement, retraining, and self-esteem are likely to be much more severe.[3] Her divorce award is likely to establish her standard of living for the rest of her life.

The hardest case is that of the long-married woman who has devoted her life to raising children who are now grown. Consider, for example, the hypothetical Ann Thompson, age fifty-three, who was formerly married to a wealthy corporate executive. She is much better off after divorce than the vast majority of divorced women her age because her former husband earns $6000 a month net. The average Los Angeles judge would award Ann Thompson $2000 a month in spousal support, giving her a total income of $24,000 a year in contrast to her husband's $48,000 a year (after alimony payments are deducted from his income). Her former husband will be able to maintain his comfortable standard of living on his $48,000 income (which is likely to rise) and the tax benefits he gets from paying alimony. But Ann, with her house sold, no employment prospects, and the loss of her social status and social networks, will not be able to sustain anything near her former standard of living.

Since Ann Thompson's three children are over eighteen, she is not legally entitled to any child support for them.[4] She is likely, however, to be contributing to their college expenses. In addition, one or more of them is likely to still be living with her, and all probably return from time to time for extended visits. Thus she may well be providing as much if not more for their support than their well-to-do father.*

The combined effects of a less than equal income and a greater than equal share of the children's expenses invariably result in extreme downward mobility for long-married divorced women in California. They are both absolutely and relatively worse off than their former husbands. Although the courts are supposed to aim at balancing the resources of the two postdivorce households, the data reveal that they do not come near this goal.

Household income. Because the data comparing household income of long-married couples are similar to the patterns in shorter marriages, they are not discussed in the same detail here. They reveal (tables not shown) that the postdivorce income of men in all income

groups is substantially higher than that of their former wives. On the average (i.e., considering all predivorce income levels), courts allow long-married divorced men to retain twice as much disposable income as they award to the women with whom these men shared the building years of long marriage.

Per capita income. Data on the *per capita* incomes of ex-husbands and wives after eighteen years or more of marriage are presented in Table 28. These data follow the pattern observed in short marriages (Table 27) and reveal a wider gap between men and women than the comparison of household income reveals. They also show lower incomes and greater deprivation for long-married women when compared with their younger counterparts.

Table 28 indicates that men married more than eighteen years have a much higher *per*

TABLE 28

Median Postdivorce Per Capita Incomes of Couples Married Eighteen Years or More

Predivorce Yearly Family Income	Per Capita Family Income[1]	Postdivorce Per Capita Income		Postdivorce Per Capita Income As Percentage of Predivorce Family Per Capita Income	
		Wife (Adjusted)[2,4]	Husband (Adjusted)[3,4]	Wife (Adjusted)	Husband (Adjusted)
Under $20,000 (n = 12)[5]	$ 5,750	$6,500	$11,950	113%	208%
$20–29,999 (n = 13)	$11,500	$6,100	$11,500	53%	100%
$30–39,999 (n = 16)	$12,306	$9,100	$18,000	74%	146%
$40,000 or more (n = 22)	$20,162	$8,500	$28,640	42%	142%

[1] All dollar figures are rounded to nearest $50.
[2] Wife's postdivorce adjusted per capita family income was calculated by taking the wife's total income (from all sources including alimony and child support) and dividing by the number of people in her postdivorce family (including children in her custody).
[3] Husband's postdivorce adjusted per capita income was calculated by taking the husband's total income, subtracting any alimony and child support awarded to his ex-wife, and dividing the remaining amount by the number of people in his postdivorce family (including any new spouse, permanent cohabitant, or children in his custody).
[4] These figures *do not* include any additional income provided by the new spouse for the 36 percent of the divorced men and the 6 percent of the divorced women who had remarried by the time of the interview (approximately one year after the legal divorce).
[5] n refers to the number of cases on which the percentages are based.

This table is based on data from interviews with divorced men and women, Los Angeles County, California, 1978.

*When Stanford University students from divorced families were interviewed for a class research project most reported that they first asked their mother for money, even though they knew she had less than their father, because they found her more sympathetic and willing to support them.[5]

capita income—that is, they have much more money to spend on themselves—than their former wives at every level of (predivorce family) income. Even where the discrepancy is smallest, in lower-income families, the husband and every member of this postdivorce family have *twice* as much money as his former wife and his children. In higher-income families, the discrepancy is enormous. The husband and each person in his postdivorce household—his new wife, cohabitor, or child—have three times as much disposable income as his former wife and the members of her postdivorce household. When we realize that the "other members" of the wife's postdivorce household are almost always the husband's children, the discrepancy between the two standards of living seems especially unjust.

Table 28 shows only one group of women who maintain the standard of living of their marriage: those with predivorce family incomes of less than $20,000. However, even these women are worse off than their former husbands, who are living on over 200 percent of their former per capita income after they divorce.

Since the contrast between husbands and wives follows the pattern observed above, and increases as we go up the income scale, the wives who experience the most relative deprivation are, here again, those who shared a median family income of over $40,000 a year before divorce. They are expected to live at less than half (42 percent) of their former *per capita* standard, while their former husbands advance to 142 percent.

Although considerable concern has been expressed about the plight of the wife after a lengthy marriage,[6] and California courts have explicitly held that the parties' incomes should *not* be sharply disparate after long marriages,[7] it is nevertheless clear that *the pattern of support and property awards tends to impoverish the long-married woman* while it provides the long-married man with an ongoing comfortable standard of living.

The women in this group are much worse off than their younger counterparts because they not only face a severely diminished income, they also have less potential for supplementing the money they receive from their ex-husbands with money from employment or other sources. They thus remain more dependent on their former husbands, and are more likely than any other group of women to suffer from the courts' unequal allocation of the husband's income at divorce.

In light of these data, it is not surprising to find that the group of divorced women who report the most distress with their financial loss and who express the strongest feelings of outrage and injustice, are the longer-married middle- and upper-middle-class women we interviewed. These relatively well-to-do women—those who shared family incomes of $40,000 or $50,000 or more before the divorce—experience the *greatest downward mobility* after divorce.

Accompanying their loss of income are the secondary effects of downward mobility: the moves to less comfortable housing and poorer neighborhoods, the loss of neighborhood and friendship networks, the need to establish credit and find services in new communities, and the need to help out with the financial problems of children who are legally grown but not financially self-sufficient.

Not inconsiderable among these secondary effects of economic deprivation is the woman's estrangement from established social activities and social networks. Newly restricted income often precludes her participation in activities that her friends take for granted but she can no longer afford. When she declines their invitations they soon stop asking her and she becomes increasingly isolated from both friends and social community.

In addition, when a woman's friendship networks have been built around her husband's job or profession, she usually loses her place after divorce and finds herself on the outside looking in. While most divorced women retain a few married friends who remain supportive, social activities with the old "circle" usually decline. Within a year, the dissociation from marital friends is typically much greater for women than for men.[8]

For the women whose social life has been husband-centered, the postdivorce losses often entail more than friends and social networks. Being the wife of a doctor or corporate executive, for example, can be the anchor of one's identity and the major source of one's self-esteem. It can also be the basis for one's social acceptability, as well as a full-time career in its own right. Many women who have lived through and for their husbands say that the loss of the role of wife is tantamount to "losing a part of myself." As one woman put it, "it was like cutting me out of my life." Many women expressed both terror and anger at the "total and irrevocable loss of status" because their entire lives had been built around and sustained by their involvement in their husbands' work.[9]

Psychologists Judith Wallerstein and Joan Kelly report the experiences of divorced upper-middle-class women in Marin County, California, as one of losing the moorings of their identity:

> The decline in the standard of living was made more troublesome for some women by the way it brought them into a lower socioeconomic class. Women who had been in the highest and most prosperous socioeconomic group, in particular, faced an entirely changed life. For these women, all of them left by their husbands, the moorings of their identification with a certain social class, and with it the core of their self-esteem—formerly exclusively determined by the husband's education, occupation, and income—were shaken loose.[10]

It should not be surprising to find that women feel more socially and psychologically dislocated by divorce than men. In general, women are far more likely than men to define the family not only as the anchor of their identity, but also as the source of their continuity. Work typically fulfills these functions for men. As sociologist Robert Weiss states it, "The occupational role affords a man structure, an opportunity to engage with others socially, and a self-definition to which his marital status is largely irrelevant."[11] Since divorced men maintain their occupational roles after divorce, they are less likely than women to feel a disjuncture between their former and present selves.

In addition to the emotionally jarring effects of lost identity and status, divorce for middle- and upper-class homemakers commonly means an abrupt career cessation. Women who have filled their days with activities that demand considerable competence—whether as volunteer members of hospital boards, or charitable fund-raisers, or more directly as their husbands' advisors, editors, or speech writers—suddenly find their skills unwanted and devalued when no longer enhanced by a husband's prestigious name. Furthermore, skills developed in the course of such a partnership career are usually not transferable to the marketplace because employers consider an employment history legitimate only if it has been *paid* employment.

Inevitably, some of these women feel regret at having relinquished earlier career opportunities. But many more feel that they and their husbands made conscious choices about the type of relationship they would share, and they are proud of the role they played as wives and mothers. Their only regret is the way their contributions have been devalued or ignored entirely at divorce.

In this context, it is significant that both the men and the women who had been married over eighteen years said they believed in partnership and sharing principles. (One hundred percent of the wives and 99 percent of the husbands agreed with the following statement: "I assumed that we would share all of the property and income we would acquire.") But, as the data in Table 28 so clearly show, the divorce courts do not honor their implicit contract.

Instead, the rules have been changed in the middle of the game. And the current rules—or rather the way the current rules are being interpreted—suggest that when the marriage dissolves, the property they have acquired and the income the husband earns are treated as "his" rather than "theirs," and he alone reaps the lion's share of the benefits from the partnership that she helped to build.

No wonder many of these long-married women feel betrayed by a society that encouraged them to believe their husbands would support them for life, and frustrated by discovering the importance of forgone options only when they are past a point where they can easily choose a different course. Betty Friedan has aptly described this kind of disillusionment: "It is growing up and believing that love and *marriage will take care of everything,* and then one day waking up at thirty, forty, fifty, and facing the world alone and facing the responsibility [alone]."[12]

POSTDIVORCE STANDARDS OF LIVING: IMPOVERISHMENT OF WOMEN AND CHILDREN

The income disparity between men and women after divorce profoundly affects their relative standards of living.

To examine this effect we rely on an index of economic well-being developed by the U.S. government. The model for our analysis was constructed by Michigan researchers who followed a sample of 5000 American families, weighted to be representative of the U.S. population.[13] Economists Saul Hoffman and John Holmes compared the incomes of men and women who stayed in intact families with the incomes of divorced men and divorced women over a seven-year period.*

A comparison of the married and divorced couples yielded two major findings. First, as might be expected, the dollar income of both divorced men and divorced women declined, while the income of married couples rose. Divorced men lost 19 percent in income while divorced women lost 29 percent.[14] In contrast, married men and women experienced a 22 percent rise in income.[15] These data confirm our commonsense belief that both parties suffer after a divorce. They also confirm that women experience a greater loss than their former husbands.

The second finding of the Michigan research is surprising. To see what the income loss meant in terms of family purchasing power, Hoffman and Holmes constructed an index of family income in relation to family needs.[16] Since this income/need comparison is adjusted for family size, as well as for the each member's age and sex, it provides an individually tailored measure of a family's economic well-being in the context of marital status changes.

The Michigan researchers found that the experiences of divorced men and women were strikingly different when this measure was used. Over the seven-year period, the economic position of divorced men actually improved by 17 percent.[17] In contrast, over the same period divorced women experienced a 29 percent decline in terms of what their income could provide in relation to their needs.[18]

To compare the experiences of divorced men and women in California to those in Michigan, we devised a similar procedure to calculate the basic needs of each of the families in our interview sample. This procedure used the living standards for urban families constructed by the Bureau of Labor Statistics of the U.S. Department of Labor.[19] First, the standard budget level for each family in the interview sample was calculated in three different ways: once for the predivorce family, once for the wife's postdivorce family, and once for the husband's postdivorce family. Then the income in relation to needs was computed for each family. (Membership in postdivorce families of husbands and wives included any new spouse or cohabitor and any children whose custody was assigned to that spouse.) These data are presented in Figure 3.

Figure 3 reveals the radical change in the standards of living to which we alluded earlier. Just one year after legal divorce, *men experience a 42 percent improvement in their postdivorce standard of living, while women experience a 73 percent decline.*

These data indicate that *divorce is a financial catastrophe for most women:* in just one year they experience a dramatic decline in income and a calamitous drop in their standard of living. It is hard to imagine how they deal with such severe deprivation: every single expenditure that one takes for granted—clothing, food, housing, heat—must be cut to one-half or one-third of what one is accustomed to.

It is difficult to absorb the full implications of these statistics. What does it mean to have a 73 percent decline in one's standard of living? When asked how they coped with this drastic

---

*Detailed information from the interviews provided the researchers with precise income data, including income from employment, intra-family transfers, welfare, and other government programs. Alimony and/or child support paid by the husband was subtracted from his income and added to the wife's postdivorce income. Finally, to facilitate direct comparisons, all income was calculated in constant 1968 dollars so that changes in real income could be examined without the compounding effect of inflation.

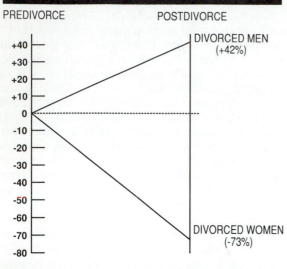

PREDIVORCE   POSTDIVORCE

DIVORCED MEN
(+42%)

DIVORCED WOMEN
(-73%)

*Income in relation to needs with needs based on U.S. Department of Agriculture's low standard budget.

Based on weighted sample of interviews with divorced persons, Los Angeles County, California, 1978.

FIGURE 3. Change in standards of living* of divorced men and women (approximately one year after divorce).

decline in income, many of the divorced women said that they themselves were not sure. It meant "living on the edge" and "living without." As some of them described it:

> We ate macaroni and cheese five nights a week. There was a Safeway special for 39 cents a box. We could eat seven dinners for $3.00 a week. . . . I think that's all we ate for months.

> I applied for welfare. . . . It was the worst experience of my life. . . . I never dreamed that I, a middle class housewife, would ever be in a position like that. It was humiliating . . . they make you feel it. . . . But we were desperate, and I *had* to feed my kids.

> You name it, I tried it—food stamps, soup kitchens, shelters. It just about killed me to have the kids live like that. . . . I finally called my parents and said we were coming . . . we couldn't have survived without them.

Even those who had relatively affluent lifestyles before the divorce experienced a sharp

reduction in their standard of living and faced hardships they had not anticipated. For example, the wife of a dentist sold her car "because I had no cash at all, and we lived on that money—barely—for close to a year." And an engineer's wife:

> I didn't buy my daughter any clothes for a year—even when she graduated from high school we sewed together two old dresses to make an outfit.

The wife of a policeman told an especially poignant story about "not being able to buy my twelve-year-old son Adidas sneakers." The boy's father had been ordered to pay $100 a month child support but had not been paying. To make up that gap in her already bare-bone budget, she had been using credit cards to buy food and other household necessities. She had exceeded all her credit limits and felt the family just could not afford to pay $25 for a new pair of Adidas sneakers. But, as she said a year later,

> Sometimes when you are so tense about money you go crazy . . . and you forget what it's like to be twelve years old and to think you can't live without Adidas sneakers . . . and to feel the whole world has deserted you along with your father.

Others spoke of cutting out all the non-essentials. For one woman it meant "no movies, no ice cream cones for the kids." For another it meant not replacing tires on her son's bike "because there just wasn't the money." For another woman it meant not using her car—a real handicap in Los Angeles—and waiting for two buses in order to save the money she would have to spend for gas. In addition to scaled-down budgets for food ("We learned to love chicken backs") and clothing ("At Christmas I splurged at the Salvation Army—the only 'new' clothes they got all year"), many spoke of cutting down on their children's school lunches ("I used to plan a nourishing lunch with fruit and juice; now she's lucky if we have a slice of ham for a sandwich") and school supplies and after-school activities ("he had to quit the Little League and get a job as a delivery boy").

Still, some of the women were not able to "make it." Fourteen percent of them moved onto the welfare rolls during the first year after the divorce, and a number of others moved back into their parents' homes when they had "no money left and nowhere to go and three children to feed."

EXPLAINING THE DISPARITY BETWEEN HUSBANDS' AND WIVES' STANDARDS OF LIVING

How can we explain the strikingly different economic consequences of divorce for men and women? How could a law that aimed at fairness create such disparities between divorced men and their former wives and children?

The explanation lies first in the inadequacy of the court's awards, second in the expanded demands on the wife's resources after divorce, and third in the husband's greater earning capacity and ability to supplement his income.

Consider first the court awards for child support (and in rarer cases, alimony). Since judges do not require men to support either their children or their former wives as they did during marriage, they allow the husband to keep most of his income for himself. Since only a few wives are awarded alimony, the only supplementary income they are awarded is child support and the average child support award covers less than half of the cost of raising a child. Thus, the average support award is simply inadequate: even if the husband pays it, it often leaves the wife and children in relative poverty. The custodial mother is expected to somehow make up the deficit alone even though she typically earns much less than her former husband.

In this regard, it is also important to note the role that property awards play in contributing to—rather than alleviating—the financial disparities between divorced women and men. Under the old law, when the wife with minor children was typically awarded the family home, she started her postdivorce life on a more equal footing because the home provided some stability and security and reduced the impact of the income loss suffered at divorce. Today, when the family home is more commonly sold to allow an "equal" division of property, there is no cushion to soften the financial devastations that low support awards create for women and children. Rather, the disruptive costs of moving and establishing a new household further strain their limited income—often to the breaking point.

The second explanation for the disparity between former husbands and wives lies in the greater demands on the wife's household after divorce, and the diminished demands on the husband's. Since the wife typically assumes the responsibility for raising the couple's children, her need for help and services increases as a direct result of her becoming a single parent. Yet at the very time that her need for more income and more financial support is greatest, the courts have drastically reduced her income. Thus the gap between her income and her needs is wider after divorce.

In contrast, the gap between the husband's income and needs narrows. Although he now has fewer absolute dollars, the demands on his income have diminished: he often lives alone and he is no longer financially responsible for the needs of his ex-wife and children. While he loses the benefits of economies of scale, and while he may have to purchase some services (such as laundry and cooking) that he did not have to buy during marriage, he is nevertheless much better off because he has so much more money to spend on himself. Since he has been allowed to retain most of his income for himself, he can afford these extra expenses and still have more surplus income than he enjoyed during marriage.

The final explanation for the large income discrepancy between former husbands and wives lies in the different earning capacities and starting points of the two adults at the time of the divorce. Not only do men in our society command higher salaries to begin with, they also benefit from the common marital pattern that gives priority to their careers. Marriage gives men the opportunity, support, and time to invest in their own careers. Thus marriage itself builds and enhances the husband's earning capacity. For women, in contrast, marriage is more likely to act as a career liability. Even though family roles are changing, and even though married women are increasingly working for pay during marriage, most of them nevertheless subordinate their careers to their husbands' and to their family responsibilities. This is especially true if they have children. Thus women are often doubly disadvantaged at the point of divorce. Not only do they face the "normal" 60 percent male/female income gap that affects all working women, they also suffer from the toll the marital years have taken on their earning capacity.

Thus marriage—and then divorce—impose a differential disadvantage on women's employment prospects, and this is especially severe for women who have custody of minor children. The responsibility for children inevitably restricts the mother's job opportunities by limiting her work schedule and location, her availability for overtime, and her freedom to take advantage of special training, travel assignments, and other opportunities for career advancement.

Although the combined income of the former spouses typically increases after divorce, most of the rise is a result of the husband's increased income. Even though women who have not been employed during marriage seek jobs after divorce, and part-time workers take full-time jobs, neither of these factors accounts for as much as the rise in male wages in the first year after divorce.

It is, in fact, surprising to see how many divorced men receive salary increases (and bonuses) immediately after divorce. While some of these are probably routine raises, and others may be the result of more intense work efforts or overtime work, it is also evident that some men manage to delay a bonus or commission or raise until after the divorce is final. This allows them to minimize the income they have to report to the court when child support (or alimony) awards are being made.

While the courts have long been aware of the control that self-employed men can exercise over the amount and timing of the income they receive, our data suggest that many salaried employees may exercise similar control over their income since many of them manage to obtain salary increases soon after their divorces become final. Whether or not this is coincidence, the fact remains that the income of divorced men often increases substantially in the first year after the divorce.

During the same period, the obligations that these men have for alimony and child support typically remain fixed or diminish: some support obligations have been reduced or terminated by terms of the divorce settlement (and others have been reduced or stopped without

the courts' permission). The result, once again, is that divorced men have more "surplus income" for themselves.

The discrepancy between divorced men and women has been corroborated by other research. Sociologist Robert Weiss and economist Thomas Espenshade found parallel disparities in the standards of living of former husbands and wives after divorce, and Weiss corroborates the finding that the greatest reduction in post-divorce income is experienced by women who shared higher family incomes before the divorce.[20] Census Bureau data also document the disparities in both income and standards of living of men and women after divorce. In 1979, the median *per capita* income of divorced women who had not remarried was $4152, just over half of the $7886 income of divorced men who had not remarried.[21]

The situation of divorced women with young children is even more grim. The median income in families headed by women with children under six years of age was only 30 percent of the median income for all families whose children were under six.[22] Thus, for the United States as a whole, the "income of families headed by women is at best half that of other families; the income of families headed by women with young children is even less, one-third of that of other families."[23]

SOCIAL CONSEQUENCES: STRESS, ISOLATION, COMPETENCE, AND HEALTH

The economic disparity that divorce creates between former husbands and wives not only brings economic hardships for most divorced women and their children, it is also one of the major causes of economic inequality between men and women in the larger society. But before we move to these larger societal consequences, let us first look at some of the more immediate social effects on the participants themselves.

It is not surprising to find that the financial hardships generated by the present system of divorce create greater pressures on women than on divorced men at all income levels. Many middle-class women who "manage to survive" nonetheless report that they are in a constant state of financial crisis after divorce.[24] More women than men at all class levels in our sample reported that they were "more concerned about money now than when they were married," "more careful about budgeting," and "spending their money on necessities, not extras."

Nor is it surprising to find that 70 percent of the divorced women we interviewed reported being perpetually worried about "making ends meet" and "not being able to pay their bills." They worried about obtaining court-ordered support, terrified of large unexpected expenses, anxious about mounting costs, frustrated by their own inability to earn enough or to find a better job, and overwhelmed by their steadily diminishing standard of living in an inflationary economy. (In contrast, most divorced men say they *never* worry about being able to meet their bills.)

In fact, in a national survey of the quality of American life, divorced women were more likely to report that they feel "frightened," that "life is hard," that they "always feel rushed," "worry about a nervous breakdown," and "worry . . . about bills" than were *any* other group of American men and women.[25]

Since financial worries cannot help affecting their social and emotional lives, it is not surprising that divorced women report more stress and less satisfaction with their lives than any other group of Americans. As the authors of a national survey report:

> Our data demonstrate . . . that divorce has a different meaning to women than to men. We have pointed out the great dissatisfaction divorced women feel with the economic circumstances of their lives, a feeling not shared by divorced men. [There are numerous] other evidences that the life of a divorced woman is more stressful than that of a divorced man. . . . Divorced women report far more stress in answer to these questions than any of the other groups of women. Divorced men, on the contrary, are somewhat *less* likely to report stress than the other groups of men . . . [they] do not find their lives strained or disturbing. The life of divorced women is unrelievedly negative. . . . [T]hey find their lives less satisfying than other women do and marked by much psychological stress.[26]

Since divorced women tend to be more readily excluded from former social networks, they are likely to become more isolated after divorce. Although most of the women we interviewed maintained one or two close friends, their larger circle of friends gradually dissolved. Divorced men were much more likely to report being invited to dinner by old friends, being included in social activities, and "maintaining most of my old friends after the divorce."

The demands of being a single working parent severely limits the time, energy, and money the divorced woman has to devote to her own life,[27] and many report feeling "locked into the world of their children and obligations" with little time for themselves.[28]

Although sociologists have long known that adults who live alone have generally lower levels of well-being than those who are married, until recently no one considered the single-parent family as a distinct living arrangement. But a 1984 University of Michigan study found major differences in social isolation between "singles" and single parents.[29] They report that single adults who live alone are not socially isolated because most of them "compensate" by establishing many more contacts outside the household (than do people who live with others). But the women who are single parents turn out to be "true isolates": "even though they have contact with some neighbors and relatives, their lives are severely restricted in terms of opportunities for much social contact with friends."[30] The authors conclude that "these patterns of living appear to have detrimental consequences" and that "these women reveal significantly negative feelings about their life circumstances."[31]

Competence and Self-esteem

One ironic result of the fact that most divorced women begin their postdivorce lives with a long list of negatives—less money, inadequate vocational skills, low self-esteem, heightened anxiety and stress, and great fear about the future—is that they are likely to find their lives after divorce better and more satisfying than they anticipated. Thus most divorced women, along with most divorced men, report a rise in competence and self-esteem at some time during the first year after divorce. The majority of respondents (83 percent of both sexes) reported they were now functioning better than during the marriage. They also felt better about themselves (82 percent of the men, 88 percent of the women) and considered themselves more competent in their work (47 percent of the men, 68 percent of the women), more physically attractive (45 percent of the men, 50 percent of the women), and possessed of better parenting skills (48 percent of the men, 62 percent of the women with minor children).

Thus, in spite of the pervasive economic difficulties that divorce brings, a portrait of resilience and resourcefulness also emerges from these data. While the postdivorce period is obviously one of many contrasts and many possibilities, and while there is obviously a great deal of variation in reactions to divorce among different individuals (and, as we found, within the same individual at different points in time), a surprisingly large percentage of divorced persons of both sexes report that they are functioning better and are more competent than they were during marriage. Although those who are younger, richer, and male tend to report less stress and relatively greater well-being after a divorce, even those who suffer economically report that they have "grown" from the experience of divorce and feel better about themselves.

The implicit comparison, is, of course, a marriage that has failed and the turmoil of the breakup. Since both men and women report their greatest trauma and psychological distress (as well as their greatest physical distress) occurred in the final stages of the marriage, it is not surprising to find that the divorce itself comes as something of a relief.

These positive feelings not only suggest the depressant effect of an unsatisfying marriage; they also reveal underlying expectations about life after divorce. Here it is significant that women often exceed men in their reports of postdivorce competence and self-esteem. This may reflect the fact that women had greater fears about the future and thus took greater pride in coping and surviving.

Thus even the longer-married older housewives who suffer the greatest financial hardships after divorce (and who feel most economically deprived, most angry, and most "cheated" by the divorce settlement) say they are "personally" better off than they were during marriage. They are proud of the skills they used to deal with the crisis, to marshal a support network, to manage their finances, and to take control of their lives. They also report improved self-esteem, more pride in their appearance, and greater competence in all aspects of their lives.

These dramatic reactions expose the extent to which the self-confidence and self-esteem of so many women are stifled during marriage, leaving them with the most minimal expectations for themselves and their lives after divorce. For women who have defined themselves in terms of their husbands and children, this may be the first time in their lives that they have felt free to focus on themselves and develop their own interests. As one woman put it, "I have been there for others all my life. Now I can be for me." Said another: "It's important to have my own identity. When I was a doctor's wife I lost my whole identity, even my name was his—first and last."

It is perhaps significant that many women expressed particular pride in their ability to cope with the economic hardships they had confronted. The double message of pride and economic hardship pervades the interviews. Consider for example the following responses to these two questions: "What has been the best thing about your life since the divorce? What has been the worse?" A fifty-six year-old divorcee replied,

> [The best:] The change in me, I am a whole person. I like myself better. The children like me better. I am happier. I am my own person to make my own mistakes for the first time in my life.

> [The worst:] I had absolutely no concept of the legal and financial aspects or expectations of the world. I had to find out about taxes, paying bills, etc., the hard way—no kidding. It scared me. . . . I'm more careful and pinch pennies. I cut down everywhere and cut out all the luxuries in my life. I'm not financially as well off and balancing my checkbook is quite a problem for me.

And a forty-six-year-old woman:

> [The best:] I learned how strong I am. I've been through hell and back and I know that I can make it.

[The worst:] I don't have any money. I can't afford a lot of things I need . . . and I probably rely on my kids too much.

And a sixty-two-year-old woman:

[The best:] My children and the friends who were there for me . . . and that I was able to get myself back on my feet after the emotional trauma . . . that I survived and am in control.

[The worst:] I'm still very bitter about losing everything. . . it still eats at me to hear about my husband's lifestyle and vacations when I have to count every dollar . . . and I worry a lot about my future—about money and medical bills and all that.

Similarly, a thirty-three-year-old woman said:

[The best:] I feel much better about myself because I'm doing things that I want to do, that are making me grow as a person. I've become a lot more independent. I've learned how to do things that I depended upon other people to do before.

[The worst:] Before I was divorced I had absolutely no concern with how I spent money, where it came from or how much I spent. I spent what I wanted and needed, and now I have to be very careful not to spend more than I have. I've had to save and cut down on everything. I do not spend money on entertainment, do not join my group to go out for dinner. I have fewer clothes, have given up [domestic] help, am more careful at the market—money is my biggest problem.

The composite portrait that emerges from these data is one of divorced women who are generally relieved to be rid of the stress of the end-of-the-marriage tensions and to have the divorce process itself completed; who are proud of the strength and resourcefulness they have discovered within themselves; who enjoy their new-found sense of control over their lives; and who are nevertheless stressed and anxious about their precarious financial situation and the hardships the divorce has created for their children. Their positive attitudes are thus qualified by and mitigated by financial tensions in their lives.

While men and women alike perceive the financial disparity in their postdivorce circumstances, they do not agree on their relative well-being in all other respects. When asked, "Who do you think is financially better off since the divorce?" both sexes reported that the man was. However, when asked, "Who do you think is better off in nonfinancial terms?" the majority of each sex saw themselves as better off since the divorce (60 percent of the men and 69 percent of the women). In fact, a third of the women and a quarter of the men said that the divorce "helped me realize my true potential."

It is indicative that what women say they miss most about marriage is the husband's income (and this is especially true of those from higher-income, longer-married families), while men report that they most miss having a sexual partner (especially younger men), and having a partner in life.

In this context, it is important to note one important difference in the strategies used by men and women to adjust after divorce. Divorced women appear to be much more skilled than their former husbands in calling upon one or two friends or relatives to help them weather the transition. Thus even though divorced women are more likely to report that they have lost "a community" of friends through the divorce, they are more likely to have one person they can call on if they have a problem (most typically a mother, a female friend, a male friend, even the ex-spouse). Divorced men in contrast are more likely to say there is "no one" they can call on. While they say they have many friends, they are not as likely to ask them for help.

These findings may reflect male-female differences in willingness to ask for help, or willingness to admit they got help, or both. They certainly also reflect women's greater lifetime reliance on others for support: they do not expect to be able to handle their problems alone, nor does society generally expect them to do so. All the greater the irony, then, that the law now effectively demands that they summon forth self-sufficiency in just one sphere: finances.

Mental and Physical Health

Data from national samples consistently document the disruptive effects of divorce on the mental and physical health of both sexes.

This is not surprising, since divorce and marital separation consistently rank second and third in a list of 42 stressful life events: the death of a spouse is the only event considered to require greater readjustment.[32]

The psychological distress engendered by divorce is revealed by the fact that divorced men and women exhibit more symptoms (such as "nervous breakdown" and "inertia"), and in more serious degree, than do persons of other marital statuses.[33] Divorced and separated people have the highest admission rates to psychiatric facilities (compared to married, widowed, and never married people), and this holds true across different age groups, for both sexes, and for blacks and whites alike.[34]

Divorce also takes a toll on the physical well-being of both sexes. Divorced people have more illness, higher mortality rates (in premature deaths), higher suicide rates, and more accidents than those who are married.[35] In fact, the marital status of a person is one of the best predictors of his or her health, disease, and death profile.[36]

While both sexes "share" some of the psychic and physical distress of divorce, women seem to experience the greater stress and their stress seems to take a higher toll. Beyond question, much of the women's stress is attributable to their economic condition. This is to be expected in light of the well-known relationship between low socioeconomic status and both mental and physical illness.

Three decades of research have shown a strong correlation between low income and both stress and psychiatric disability.[37] Having a low socioeconomic status and being a single mother is "additively and cumulatively associated with physical morbidity among mothers."[38]

When present low income is combined with the prospect of continuing low income, stress is intensified. Anticipated income for the coming year is related to both physical and mental health following divorce: the lower the anticipated income, the less favorable the individual's physical and psychological well-being.[39]

Clearly the sex-linked differences in stress and mental health are not a direct or necessary result of divorce itself. Rather, they are created in large measure by the present legal system which, through inadequate property awards and low and poorly enforced support awards, drastically reduces the standard of living of divorced women and their children.

SOCIETAL CONSEQUENCES

The rise in divorce has been the major cause of the increase in female-headed families,[40] and that increase has been the major cause of the feminization of poverty. Sociologist Diana Pearce, who coined the phrase "feminization of poverty," was one of the first to point to the critical link between poverty and divorce for women.[41] It was, she said, the mother's burden for the economic and emotional responsibility for child-rearing that often impoverished her family.

Contrary to popular perception, most female-headed single parent families in the United States are *not* the result of unwed parenthood: they are the result of marital dissolution.[42] Only 18 percent of the nearly ten million female-headed families in the United States are headed by an unwed mother: over 50 percent are headed by divorced mothers and the remaining 31 percent by separated mothers.[43]

When a couple with children divorces, it is probable that the man will become single but the woman will become a single parent. And poverty, for many women, begins with single parenthood. More than half of the poor families in the United States are headed by a single mother.[44]

The National Advisory Council on Economic Opportunity estimates that if current trends continue, the poverty population of the United States will be composed solely of women and children by the year 2000.[45] The Council declares that the "feminization of poverty has become one of the most compelling social facts of the decade."[46]

The Rise in Female Poverty

The well-known growth in the number of single-parent, female-headed households has been amply documented elsewhere. (The 8 percent of all children who lived in mother-child families in 1960, rose to 12 percent by 1970,[47] and to 20 percent by 1981.[48]) Also well-documented is the fact that these mother-headed families are the fastest growing segment of the American poor.[49]

What has not been well documented, and what appears to be relatively unknown—or unacknowledged—is the direct link between divorce, the economic consequences of divorce, and the rise in female poverty. The high divorce rate has vastly multiplied the numbers of women who are left alone to support themselves and their minor children. When the courts deny divorced women the support and property they need to maintain their families, they are relying, they say, on the woman's ability to get a job and support herself. But with women's current disadvantages in the labor market, getting a job cannot be the only answer—because it does not guarantee a woman a way out of poverty.[50] Even with full-time employment, one-third of the women cannot earn enough to enable them and their children to live above the poverty level.[51] The structure of the job market is such that *only half* of all full-time female workers are able to support two children without supplemental income from either the children's fathers or the government.[52]

In recent years there have been many suggestions for combating the feminization of poverty. Most of these have focused on changes in the labor market[53] (such as altering the sex segregation in jobs and professions, eliminating the dual labor market and the disparity between jobs in the primary and secondary sectors, eradicating the discriminatory structure of wages, and providing additional services, such as child care,[54] for working mothers) and on expanding social welfare programs (such as increasing AFDC benefits to levels above the poverty line, augmenting Medicaid, food stamp, and school lunch programs, and making housewives eligible for Social Security and unemployment compensation).[55]

A third possibility, which has not received widespread attention, is to change the way that courts allocate property and income at divorce. If, for example, custodial mothers and their children were allowed to remain in the family home, and if the financial responsibility for children were apportioned according to the means of the two parents, and if court orders for support

were enforced, a significant segment of the population of divorced women and their children would not be impoverished by divorce.

The Rise in Child Poverty and Economic Hardships for Middle-class Children of Divorce

Beyond question, the present system of divorce is increasing child poverty in America. From 1970 to 1982, the percentage of American children living in poverty rose form 14.9 percent to 21.3 percent.[56] According to demographer Samuel Preston, most of the growth in the number of children in poverty occurred in the category of female-headed families.[57]

While the vast majority (82 percent) of all children born in the United States today are born into two-parent families, more than half of these children are likely to experience the disruption of their parents' marriage before they reach age eighteen. As noted above, U.S. Census Bureau data show that close to 60 percent of the children born in 1983 *would not* spend their entire childhood living with both natural parents,[58] while Sandra Hofferth of the National Institute of Child Health and Human Development, projected that two-thirds of the children born in wedlock in 1980 would experience a parental divorce before they reach age seventeen.[59]

Whichever figures we use, the statistics suggest that we are sentencing a significant proportion of the current generation of American children to lives of financial impoverishment.

Clearly, living in a single-parent family does not have to mean financial hardship. The economic well-being of many of these children is in jeopardy only because their mothers bear the whole responsibility for their support. That jeopardy would end if courts awarded more alimony, higher amounts of child support, and a division of property that considered the interests of minor children. It would also be greatly reduced if the child support awards that the courts have already made were systematically enforced. Under the present legal system, however, the financial arrangements of divorce foster the financial deprivation of millions of children.

Although the deprivation is most severe below the poverty level, it affects children at every income level. In fact, middle-class children, like their mothers, experience the greatest relative deprivation. The economic dislocations of divorce bring about many changes which are particularly difficult for children: moving to new and less secure neighborhoods, changing schools, losing friends, being excluded from activities that have become too expensive for the family's budget, and having to work after school or help care for younger siblings.

Not surprisingly, the children of divorce often express anger and resentment when their standard of living is significantly less than that in their father's household.[60] They realize that their lives have been profoundly altered by the loss of "their home" and school and neighborhood and friends, and by the new expectations their mother's reduced income creates for them. It is not difficult to understand their resentment when fathers fly off for a weekend in Hawaii while they are told to forgo summer camp, to get a job, and to earn their allowance. That resentment, according to psychologists Judith Wallerstein and Joan Kelly, is "a festering source of anger":

> When the downward change in the family standard of living followed the divorce and the discrepancy between the father's standard of living and that of the mother and children was striking, this discrepancy was often central to the life of the family and remained as a festering source of anger and bitter preoccupation. The continuation of this discrepancy over the years generated continuing bitterness between the parents. Mother and children were likely to share in their anger at the father and to experience a pervasive sense of deprivation, sometimes depression, accompanied by a feeling that life was unrewarding and unjust.[61]

The middle-class children of divorce may also feel betrayed by their disenfranchisement in their parents' property settlement. Since the law divides family property between the husband and wife and makes no provision for a child's share of the marital assets, many children feel they have been unfairly deprived of "their" home, "their" piano, "their" stereo set, and their college education. The last item is indicative, for children's taken-for-granted expectations about the future are often altered by the divorce. For example, one mother reported that the most upsetting thing about the divorce

was her son's loss of the college education he'd been promised. His father, who had always pressed him to follow in his footsteps at Dartmouth, told him that a private college was now out of the question; he would have to stay home and take advantage of the low tuition at the state college. While this father could still "afford" to send his son to Dartmouth, his priorities had changed.

The loss of an education at a private college is symbolic of the changed fortunes of children of divorce at all class levels. Recall the U.S. Census Bureau data on child support which indicated that even though child support awards are quite modest, less than half of all fathers comply fully with court orders for child support. Another quarter make some payment, and close to 30 percent do not pay anything at all.[62]

Inasmuch as about 1.2 million children's parents divorce each year, the 30 percent who receive no support from their fathers adds up to 360,000 new children each year. Over a ten-year period, this amounts to 4 million children. If we add to these the approximately 3 million over the years who receive only part of their child support (or receive it only some of the time), we find a ten-year total of 7 million children deprived of the support to which they are entitled. Remembering that fewer than 4 million children are born each year helps to put all these figures in perspective.[63]

The failure of absent parents to provide child support has taken an especially severe toll in recent years because of sharp cutbacks in public programs benefiting children since 1979. The Children's Defense Fund shows that children's share of Medicaid payments dropped from 14.9 percent in 1979, to 11.9 percent in 1982, despite a rise in the child proportion among the eligible.[64] The Aid to Families with Dependent Children (AFDC) program has also been sharply cut back. In 1979, there were 72 children in AFDC for every 100 children in poverty, but only 52 per 100 in 1982.[65]

It is not surprising to find a strong relationship between the economic and psychological effects of divorce on children. Economic deprivation following divorce has been linked to increased anxiety and stress among American children.[66] Mounting evidence also shows that children of divorce who experience the most psychological stress are those whose post-divorce lives have been impaired by inadequate income. For example, Hodges, Tierney, and Buchsbaum find "income inadequacy" the most important factor in accounting for anxiety and depression among preschool children in divorced families.[67] When family income is adequate, there are no differences in anxiety-depression levels between children in divorced families and those in intact families. However, "children of divorced families with inadequate income had substantially higher levels of anxiety-depression."[68] Hodges, Wechsler, and Ballantine also find significant correlations between income and adjustment for preschool children of divorce (but not, interestingly, for preschool children of intact families).[69]

In summary, the accumulating evidence shows that children in divorced families are likely to suffer a variety of adjustment problems if they experience greater geographic mobility, lower income, and poorer adequacy of income. Unfortunately, these experiences are common to most children of divorce.

CONCLUSION:
THE TWO-TIER SOCIETY

The economic consequences of the present system of divorce reverberate throughout our society. Divorce awards not only contribute heavily to the well-documented income disparity between men and women, they also lead to the widespread impoverishment of children and enlarge the ever-widening gap between the economic well-being of men and women in the larger society. Indeed, if current conditions continue unabated we may well arrive at a two-tier society with an underclass of women and children.

Thrust into a spiral of downward mobility by the present system of divorce, a multitude of middle-class women and the children in their charge are increasingly cut off from sharing the income and wealth of former husbands and fathers. Hampered by restricted employment opportunities and sharply diminished income, these divorced women are increasingly expected to shoulder alone the burden of providing for both themselves and their children.

Most of the children of divorce share their mother's financial hardships. Their presence in her household increases the strains on her meager income at the same time that they add to her expenses and restrict her opportunities for economic betterment.

Meanwhile, divorced men increasingly are freed of the major financial responsibility for supporting their children and former wives. Moreover, these men retain more than higher incomes. They experience less day-to-day stress than their ex-wives, they enjoy relatively greater mental, physical, and emotional well-being, and have greater freedom to build new lives and new families after divorce.

The economic disparities between men and women after divorce illuminate the long-standing economic disparities between the incomes of men and women during marriage. In theory, those differences did not matter in marriage, since they were partners in the enterprise and shared the husband's income. As Christopher Jencks observes, "As long as most American men and women married and pooled their economic resources, as they traditionally did, the fact that men received 70 percent of the nation's income had little effect on women's material well being."[70] But with today's high divorce rate, the ranks of unmarried women are vastly increased, and the relative numbers of women who share a man's income are greatly diminished.

The result is that the economic gulf between the sexes in the larger society is increasing. Some of this would have occurred even if the traditional divorce law remained everywhere in force. But the new divorce laws—and the way these laws are being applied—have exacerbated the effects of the high divorce rate by assuring that ever greater numbers of women and children are being shunted out of the economic mainstream.

The data on the increase in female poverty, child poverty, and the comparative deprivation of middle-class women and children suggest that we are moving toward a two-tier society in which the upper economic tier is dominated by men (and the women and children who live with them). The former wives of many of these men, the mothers of their children, and the children themselves are increasingly found in the lower economic tier. Those in the first tier enjoy a comfortable standard of living; those in the lower tier are confined to lives of economic deprivation and hardship.

Obviously the two tiers are not totally segregated by sex: professional women for example, whether married or divorced, are more likely to be found in the first tier, and members of many minority groups, both men and women, are more likely to fall into the second. Yet among these groups, and among all families at the lower income levels, divorce brings a better economic future for men than for their former wives.

The concept of a two-tier society does not imply a static model. There is movement between the two tiers. But the structural conditions of the lives of women in the lower tier make it extremely difficult for them to improve their economic fortunes by hard work or any of the other traditional routes to economic mobility. The divorced women in the lower tier face not merely the sex-segregated job market and the male-female wage gap that confront all women, but also the responsbilities and restrictions that devolve upon heads of one-parent families. For these women, the discrepancy between earnings and need is typically too large to allow them to provide even the bare necessities of life for themselves and their families.

Obviously, membership in the second tier is not necessarily permanent. Some women will find jobs or return to school or obtain training that will enable them to improve their status. Many of those who are under thirty and some of those who are under forty will accomplish the same result by remarrying. But even those women who manage eventually to improve their financial situation will typically spend their early postdivorce years in acute economic hardship. The fact that they are poor only temporarily does not mean that they and their children suffer any the less[71] or that they can ever recapture the losses of those wasted years.

NOTES

1. These assumptions are discussed in Lenore J. Weitzman, *The Divorce Revolution*, N.Y.: The Free Press, 1985, Chapters 6 and 7 on alimony awards, pp. 157–158, 165–166, 176–177 in Chapter 6, and pp. 184–187, 197, 204–206, in Chapter 7.

2. See Weitzman, L.J. *op. cit.* Chapter 7, pp. 206, 209, and Chapter 6, 165–169.

3. The special problems that older women face at divorce are discussed in Weitzman, L.J. *op. cit.* Chapter 7, pp. 187–194, 198–201, 209–212.

4. The issue of support for dependent children over eighteen is discussed in Weitzman, L.J. *op. cit.* Chapter 9, pp. 278–281.

5. The study is discussed in Chapter 9, p. 279.

6. *In re Marriage of Rosan,* 24 Cal. App. 3d 855, 101 Cal. Rptr. 295 (1972); *In re Marriage of Brantner,* 67 Cal. App. 3d 416, 136 Cal. Rptr. 635 (1977); *In re Marriage of Morrison,* 20 Cal. 3d 437, 143 Cal. Rptr. 139, 573 P.2d 41 (1978). See also Lillian B. Rubin, *Women of Certain Age* (New York: Harper and Row, 1979) and Janet Zollinger Giele, *Women in the Middle Years* (New York: Wiley, 1982).

7. *In re Marriage of Andreen,* 76 Cal. App. 3d 667, 143 Cal. Rptr. 94 (1978).

8. This finding is also reported by E. Mavis Hetherington, Martha Cox, and Roger Cox, "The Aftermath of Divorce," in *Mother–Child, Father–Child Relations,* J.H. Stevens, Jr. and M. Mathews, eds. (Washington, D.C.: NAEYC, 1977) (hereafter cited as Hetherington et al., "Aftermath of Divorce").

9. Prudence Brown and Hanna Fox, "Sex Differences in Divorce," in *Gender and Disordered Behavior: Sex Differences in Psychopathology,* Edith S. Gomberg and Violet Franks, eds. (New York: Brunner/Mazel, 1979), pp. 113–114.

10. Judith Wallerstein and Joan Kelly, *Surviving the Breakup: How Parents and Children Cope with Divorce* (New York: Basic Books, 1980), p. 23 (hereafter cited as Wallerstein and Kelly, *Surviving the Breakup*).

11. Robert S. Weiss, *Marital Separation* (New York: Basic Books, 1975).

12. "Report of NOW Conference on Marriage and Divorce," *New York Times,* Jan. 21, 1974, p. 232, cols 7–8. See also Betty Friedan, *It Changed My Life* (New York: Random House, 1976).

13. Saul Hoffman and John Holmes, "Husbands, Wives, and Divorce," in *Five Thousand American Families—Patterns of Economic Progress* (Ann Arbor, Mich.: Institute for Social Research, 1976), p. 24 (hereafter cited as Hoffman and Holmes, "Divorce").

14. Ibid., p. 27 (Table 2.1), p. 31 (Table 2.2). Hoffman and Holmes are frequently cited as showing that divorced men have only a 10 percent decline in real money income. While this figure is shown in Table 2.1, it is based on the husband's total postdivorce income before any alimony and/or child support is paid. Once these support payments are deducted from the husband's income, husbands experience a 19 percent decline in real income.

15. Ibid., p. 27 (Table 2.1).

16. This index, which is based on the Department of Agriculture's "Low-Cost Food Budget," adjusted for the size, age, and sex composition of the family, is described in note 19, below.

17. Hoffman and Holmes, "Divorce," p. 27 (Table 2.1). This is closer to the rate of improvement of married couples who improved their standard of living by 21 percent. (Note that their income rose 22 percent, but their income in relation to needs rose 21 percent.)

18. Ibid., p. 31 (Table 2.2).

19. We assumed that the basic needs level for each family was the Lower Standard Budget devised by the Bureau of Labor Statistics, U.S. Department of Labor, *Three Standards of Living for an Urban Family of Four Persons* (1967). This budget is computed for a four-person urban family (husband and wife and two children) and kept current by frequent adjustments. See, e.g., McCraw, "Medical Care Costs Lead Rise in 1976–77 Family Budgets," *Monthly Labor Review,* Nov. 1978, p. 33. A Labor Department report devised a method for adjusting this standard budget to other types of families, depending on family size, age of oldest child, and age of head of household. Bureau of Labor Statistics, U.S. Department of Labor, *Revised Equivalence Scale for Estimating Equivalent Incomes or Budget Costs by Family Type,* Bulletin No. 1570-2 (1968). For example, the needs of a family of two persons (husband and wife) with the head of household of age thirty-five was calculated at 60 percent of the base figure for a Lower Standard Budget.

A Lower Standard Budget was calculated for each family in our interview sample three different ways: once for the predivorce family, once for the wife's postdivorce family, and once for the husband's postdivorce family. The income over needs for each family was then computed. Membership in postdivorce families of husbands and wives included a new spouse or cohabitor (where applicable), and any children whose custody was assigned to that spouse. I am indebted to my research assistant, David Lineweber, for programming this analysis.

20. Robert S. Weiss, "The Impact of Marital Dissolution on Income and Consumption in Single-Parent Households," *Journal of Marriage and the Family* Vol. 46, February 1984, pp. 115–127; Thomas Espenshade, "The Economic Consequences of Divorce," *Journal of Marriage and the Family,* Vol. 41, August 1979, pp. 615–625.

Similar results in California are reported by Marilyn Little, "Divorce and the Feminization of Poverty," paper presented at the meetings of Sociologists for Women in Society, American Sociological Association, August 30, 1983. See also Ruth A. Brandwein, Carole A. Brown, and E. M. Fox, "Women and Children Lost: The Social Situation of Divorced Mothers and Their Families," *Journal of Marriage and the Family* Vol. 36, 1974, pp. 498–514.

21. Bureau of the Census, U.S. Dept. of Commerce, "Money Income of Families and Persons in the United States: 1979," *Current Population Reports* Series P–60, No. 129, 1981, p. 23.

22. Bureau of the Census, U.S. Dept. of Commerce, "Families Maintained by Female Householders 1970–79," *Current Population Reports* Series P–23, No. 107, 1980, p. 36.

23. National Center on Women and Family Law, "Sex and Economic Discrimination in Child Custody Awards," *Clearinghouse Review* Vol. 16, no. 11, April 1983, p. 1132.

24. Angus Campbell, Philip E. Converse, and Willard L. Rodgers, *The Quality of American Life: Perceptions, Evaluations, and Satisfactions* (New York: Russell Sage Foundation, 1976), pp. 420 and 404, Table 12–5.

25. Ibid., p. 404, Table 12–5.

26. Ibid., p. 398, Table 12–2, pp. 420, 421.

27. Ann Goetting, "Divorce Outcome Research: Issues and Perspectives," in *The Family In Transition,* Fourth Edition, Arlene S. Skolnick and Jerome H. Skolnick, eds. (Boston: Little Brown & Co., 1983), p. 369 (reprinted from *Journal of Family Issues* Vol. 2, no. 3, Sept. 1981), pp. 350–378. (hereafter cited as Goetting, "Divorce Outcomes," with page citations to the Skolnick volume).

28. Hetherington et al., "Aftermath of Divorce."

29. "Living Alone: Do Today's Independent Lifestyles Reflect A Trend Toward Social Isolation And A Consequent Threat to Health And Well-being?" *Institute for Social Research Newsletter* (Ann Arbor, Mich.: University of Michigan, August 1984), pp. 3–4.

30. Ibid., pp. 3–4.

31. Ibid., p. 4.

32. T. Holmes and R. Rahe, "The Social Readjustment Rating Scale," *Journal of Psychosomatic Research* Vol. 11, 1967, pp. 213–218. See generally, Bruce Dohrenwend, "Social Status and Stressful Life Events," *Journal of Personality and Social Psychology* Vol. 28, 1973.

33. D. Landbrook, "The Wealth and Survival of the Divorced," *Conciliation Courts Review* Vol. 14, 1976, pp. 21–33.

34. Bernard L. Bloom, Shirley J. Asher, and Stephen W. White, "Marital Disruption as a Stressor: A Review and Analysis," *Psychological Bulletin* Vol. 85, 1978, pp. 867–894.

35. Goetting, "Divorce Outcomes," pp. 370–72.

36. James J. Lynch, *The Broken Heart: The Medical Consequences of Loneliness in America* (New York: Basic Books, 1977).

Ann Goetting cautions that a lot of this research does not control for social class: "Since both poor health and high mortality on the one hand, and divorce on the other, are more common among

the lower than the higher socioeconomic classes, the relationship between health and divorce may be at least partly due to factors associated with social class." Goetting, "Divorce Outcomes," p. 370.

37. Bruce P. Dohrenwend and Barbara S. Dohrenwend, *Social Status and Psychological Disorder* (New York: Wiley, 1969); Jerome Myers, Jacob Lindenthal, and M. Pepper, "Social Class, Life Events and Psychiatric Symptoms: A Longitudinal Study." Paper presented at Conference on Stressful Life Events, New York, June 1973.

38. P. Berkman, "Spouseless motherhood, psychological stress, and physical morbidity," *Journal of Health and Social Behavior* Vol. 10, 1969, p. 330.

39. Prudence Brown, "Psychological Distress and Personal Growth among Women Coping with Marital Dissolution," doctoral dissertation, University of Michigan, 1976. *Dissertation Abstracts International* Vol. 37, 1976, pp. 947–8. Gay Kitson and Marvin M. Sussman, "The Process of Marital Separation and Divorce: Male and Female Similarities and Differences," Unpublished paper, Case Western Reserve University, Cleveland, Ohio, November 1976.

40. Jane R. Chapman and Gordon Chapman, "Poverty Viewed as a Woman's Problem—the U.S. Case," in *Women and the World of Work,* Anne Hoiberg, ed. (New York: Plenum, 1982).

41. Diana Pearce, "The Feminization of Poverty: Women, Work and Welfare," *Urban and Social Change Review,* Feb. 1978; and Diana Pearce and Harriette McAdoo, "Women and Children: Alone and in Poverty" (Washington, D.C.: National Advisory Council on Economic Opportunity, September 1981), p. 1 (hereafter cited as Pearce and McAdoo, "Women and Children in Poverty").

42. House Hearings on Child Support Enforcement legislation before the sub-committee on Public Assistance and Unemployment Compensation of the Committee on Ways and Means of the U.S. House of Representatives on July 14, 1983, p. 13. (Washington, D.C.: U.S. Government Printing Office, 1984) (hereafter cited as House Hearings 1983).

43. Ibid.

44. Barbara Ehrenreich and Francis Fox Piven, "The Feminization of Poverty: When the Family Wage System Breaks Down," *Dissent,* 1984, p. 162 (hereafter cited as Ehrenreich and Piven, "Feminization of Poverty").

45. National Advisory Council on Economic Opportunity, *Critical Choices for the '80s,* August 1980, p. 1 (Washington, D.C.: National Advisory Council, 1980).

46. Ibid.

47. Christopher Jencks, "Divorced Mothers, Unite," *Psychology Today,* November 1982, pp. 73–75 (hereafter cited as Jencks, "Divorced Mothers").

48. Ehrenreich and Piven, "Feminization of Poverty," p. 163.

49. Ibid., p. 162; Pearce and McAdoo, "Women and Children in Poverty"; Heather L. Ross and Isabel V. Sawhill, *Time of Transition: The Growth of Families Headed by Women* (Washington, D.C.: The Urban Institute Press, 1975).

50. Pearce and McAdoo, "Women and Children in Poverty," pp. 6, 18.

51. Briefing paper prepared for California Assemblyman Thomas H. Bates for hearings on "The Feminization of Poverty," San Francisco, Calif., April 8, 1983, mimeo, p. 6 (hereafter cited as Bates brief).

52. Ibid. Pearce and McAdoo, "Women and Children in Poverty."

53. See generally, Pearce and McAdoo, "Women and Children in Poverty," and Ehrenreich and Piven, "Feminization of Poverty."

54. Child care is clearly one of the most fundamental needs of single mothers, and yet, in 1983, fully 84 percent of the working mothers were *not* able to obtain government-licensed child care for their children. California Commission on the Status of Women, Briefing Paper for hearings on the Feminization of Poverty conducted by California Assemblyman Thomas H. Bates, April 8, 1983.

55. Ehrenreich and Piven, "Feminization of Poverty."

56. Samuel H. Preston, "Children and the Elderly: Divergent Paths for American's Dependents," Presidential address to the Population Association to be published in *Demography* Vol. 21, no.4, forthcoming, citing Bureau of the Census, U.S. Dept. of Commerce, "Money Income and Poverty Status 1982," *Current Population Reports* Series P–60, No. 140, 1983. Citations that follow are to pages in the Preston manuscript.

57. Ibid., p.15.

58. Interview with Dr. Arthur Norton, March, 1984.

59. Sandra Hofferth, "Updating Children's Life Course," Center for Population Research, National Institute for Child Health and Development, 1983.

60. Wallerstein and Kelly, *Surviving the Breakup,* p. 231.

61. Ibid.

62. See Chapter 9, pp. 283–284, citing Bureau of the Census, "Child Support and Alimony, 1981," *Current Population Reports,* Series P–23, No. 124.

63. House Hearings 1983, p. 27.

64. Children's Defense Fund, *American Children in Poverty* (Washington, D.C.: Children's Defense Fund, 1984).

65. Ibid.

66. Goetting, "Divorce Outcomes," and Nicholas Zil and James Peterson, "Trends in the Behavior and Emotional Well-Being of U.S. Children," Paper given at the 1982 Annual Meeting of the Association for the Advancement of Science, Washington, D.C., 1982.

67. William F. Hodges, Carol W. Tierney, and Helen K. Bushbaum, "The Cumulative Effect of Stress on Preschool Children of Divorced and Intact Families," *Journal of Marriage and the Family* Vol. 46, no. 3, August 1984, pp. 611–629, 614.

68. Ibid.

69. Ibid., citing their earlier work.

70. Jencks, "Divorced Mothers."

71. Ibid.

Sex
Deviance

Entering Male Prostitution

DAVID F. LUCKENBILL

One of the central problems in the investigation of male prostitution is entry, an individual's movement into the life. Although there has been a fair amount of research on the problem, studies of entry suffer from one or two drawbacks that preclude a sound understanding of the process. First, they gloss over the context of entry. Researchers generally explain entry in terms of one or more background conditions that predispose individuals to prostitution. These include a defective home life (Craft, 1966; Ginsburg, 1967; Marlowe, 1964; Russell, 1971), homosexual seduction in childhood (Boyer and James, 1983; Coombs, 1974; Freyhan, 1947), poor academic and vocational training (Deisher et al., 1969; Gandy and Deisher, 1970), and poverty coupled with limited prospects for making money legitimately (Allen, 1980; Harris, 1973; MacNamara, 1965; Reiss, 1961). Although these conditions may be related to entry, researchers generally ignore the ways in which they lead to entry. Indeed, unlike those who study female prostitution (Davis, 1978; Gray, 1973; Prus and Irini, 1980), researchers gloss over the contextual conditions that mediate entry, channeling predispositions toward male prostitution.[1]

Second, studies focus on one facet of entry at the expense of another. For analytic purposes, entry can be divided into initial involvement and the outset of regular involvement. Most studies focus on regular involvement, possibly on the assumption that the two facets are synonymous, with initial participation marking the onset of regular participation. This assumption is unwarranted. Life histories reveal that although some individuals move into regular involvement promptly after their first "trick," others abstain for a time or turn tricks occasionally, moving into regular involvement months or even years later (Wells, n.d.). Clearly, the first trick may hasten the move to regular participation, but the conditions that are causally related to regular participation may differ from those related to the first trick. Thus, by focusing on regular involvement, researchers overlook the conditions leading to initial involvement and the way in which initial involvement can facilitate regular involvement.[2]

To acquire a sound understanding of entry, it would be useful to view involvement in male prostitution as a career. From this standpoint, entry occurs in a sequence of steps, each of which may be the outcome of a somewhat different set of conditions (Becker, 1963: 22–25; Luckenbill and Best, 1981). Accordingly, to understand entry, attention would center on the context of entry as well as on the background conditions that predispose an individual to prostitution. Furthermore, attention would focus on an individual's initial involvement as well as on his movement into regular involvement. Each point of analysis reflects an aspect of the development of a prostitute, and each offers some understanding of that process.

This article considers how a number of boys entered prostitution. First, it examines their initial involvement, specifying the conditions leading to their first sexual sale. Second, it examines their movement into a level of regular involvement. It considers why some moved into regular participation shortly after their first trick while others abstained for a time or turned

David F. Luckenbill is Assistant Professor of Sociology at Northern Illinois University. His research interests include interpersonal criminal violence and careers in deviance.

AUTHOR'S NOTE: I want to thank Harold E. Smith for his assistance in carrying out the interviews. I also want to thank Joel Best and Robert M. Emerson for their helpful comments. This report is based on research supported by the Center for Research on Law and Justice, University of Illinois, Chicago.

From *Urban Life* 14 (2), July 1985: 131–153. Copyright © 1985 Sage Publications, Inc. Reprinted by permission of Sage Publications, Inc.

tricks occasionally before moving into regular participation.

SAMPLE AND METHOD

The data derive from interviews with 26 male prostitutes or "hustlers" in Chicago. It is impossible to know whether this sample is representative, as the population of male prostitutes is unknown. But an effort was made to acquire a heterogeneous sample. The subjects ranged from 18 to 34 years of age. Three were black, 2 were Hispanic, and the rest were white. Five had fathers who held white-collar jobs, 5 had fathers who were unemployed or absent from the home, and the remainder had fathers who held blue-collar jobs. Whereas 18 subjects did not complete high school, 8 finished high school, and 3 of them completed two or more years of college. Nine were raised in the Chicago area; the rest grew up elsewhere, typically in small midwestern cities. When they turned their first trick, 10 subjects regarded themselves as homosexual, 12 identified themselves as bisexual, and 4 regarded themselves as heterosexual. At the time of interviewing, 3 had been hustling for less than two years, 16 had been hustling for more than two years, and 7 had been retired for less than two years after careers ranging from four to eleven years. Five subjects operated as street hustlers, and 21 worked as bar hustlers.

The subjects were not incarcerated at the time of interviewing; most were involved in prostitution on a regular basis. As a consequence, finding and interviewing hustlers was difficult. They were leery of outsiders and reluctant to spend time talking when they could be hustling. The subjects were contacted by a graduate student whose research ties with Chicago's gay community earned him a trustworthy reputation. He located the subjects, and we interviewed them in settings they found convenient, including the offices in two bars, the graduate student's apartment, and their residences. Interviews lasted from 45 to 90 minutes and were tape-recorded. Five subjects were interviewed twice. The process of contacting and interviewing subjects spanned 28 months.

Each interview covered a variety of matters relating to the subject's career in prostitution.

One set of open-ended questions focused on entry. Questions centered on such matters as the events leading to his first trick, the character of his first sale, the length of time between his first trick and regular involvement, and the events leading to regular involvement.

INITIAL INVOLVEMENT

How boys get involved in male prostitution has been a topic of general concern. Popular accounts indicate that coercion and trickery are typical paths to initial involvement. Here, an older man uses force or deception to compel or lure an innocent, often troubled boy into prostitution in order to obtain a share of his earnings (Lindecker, 1981: 167–181; Lloyd, 1976: 2–23; *Newsweek,* 1973; Palmquist, 1978: 126–127). Although coercion and trickery may be paths to prostitution, none of the subjects in this study entered through them. They described two other paths to initial involvement. In one, the boy turns to prostitution in order to manage what he regards as a situation of financial desperation. In the second, the boy turns to prostitution in order to take advantage of an attractive opportunity to earn some spending money and acquire sexual satisfaction. Each path will be examined in turn.

Defensive Involvement

One path to initial involvement may be called "defensive." The boy is embedded in a situation of financial need and limited prospects. Given his circumstances, he searches for a way to make ends meet. Through association with an experienced hustler or an older man who proposes a sexual sale, he learns about prostitution. Defining the activity as an acceptable means for survival, he closes on his first trick. Thus, initial involvement reflects a practical solution to a "threatening" situation—a pattern that resembles Lofland's (1969: 39–103) conception of the "defensive deviant act."

Fifteen hustlers moved into prostitution in order to manage what they regarded as a desperate situation. At the time of their first trick these boys were destitute. They could not rely on their families for support, as they left home in their adolescent years (a mean of 15 years). Many of them grew up in homes broken by divorce or desertion, and all of them claimed to have strained, often embittered relations with their parents. For 12 boys this situation led to their departure. Most ran away, but some, like Don,[3] were thrown out: "I left home when I was 16 because I had problems with my mother. Actually, I got the boot the first of that year. I got disowned." The other 3 boys were placed in foster homes or state institutions, which they ultimately left. John recalled:

> I didn't like my mother too well after a few things that she done. We never really talked. I was always last on the totem pole, so to speak. . . . I was kicked out when I was 14, and I was placed into a halfway house until I was of age to be on the street, of age to be out on my own, and that was until 16. And they kicked me out of there. At 16 I was on the street, on my own.

After leaving home these boys drifted for a short time, living day to day on the street. Eventually, they got rooms in cheap hotels or rooming houses, often sharing them with similarly situated peers, or they were taken in by sympathetic older men.

These boys did not have a steady or sufficient source of income. Twelve were unemployed. Although 5 of them received modest state assistance, usually in the form of rent subsidies and food stamps, they generally lived a hand-to-mouth existence, taking odd jobs and relying on the limited support of friends and acquaintances. The other 3 held low-paying jobs; one cleaned air vents in buildings, the second cars, and the third bused tables.

In addition, their economic prospects were dim. They could not return home because their home life was too unbearable, or their parents had asked them not to return, or they had no home to which they could return. And their chances of securing steady, well-paying jobs were poor because they lacked the necessary qualifications. They were too young and inexperienced to get good jobs. Moreover, all of them quit high school, dropping out for any of several reasons. For some, their homosexual reputations engendered hostile relations with other students, and this made

school unpleasant. For others, school was difficult or boring, and they decided to quit rather than endure further difficulty or boredom. For still others, school was pleasant and they received good grades but their home life was unpleasant, so they quit school and left town. Given their youth, lack of work experience, and poor education, these boys were restricted to unskilled labor. In short, they were desperate, facing serious financial need and limited opportunities for coping with it.

Financial need and limited opportunities cannot sufficiently explain entry, as many individuals faced with the same sort of situation probably do not turn to prostitution. The move to prostitution was hastened by two conditions: association with experienced hustlers or prospective customers, who presented prostitution as a good way to make ends meet; and definition of prostitution as acceptable in light of their circumstances.[4]

Anywhere from one week to six months after striking out on their own, these boys met other members of the world of prostitution. Nine associated with experienced hustlers. Four encountered hustlers while "cruising" avenues or parks for partners for sexual trades; 3 met hustlers while patronizing arcades or cafes; and 2 observed hustlers standing on the street talking with older men, approached one or more of the hustlers, and asked them what was happening. At some point in their association, the hustlers presented prostitution as a good source of income. In some cases, they explicitly recommended prostitution. Jerry indicated, "You see, I used to go out with hustlers, and they used to tell me I could be out there making money myself." Mike's friend, a veteran hustler, not only recommended prostitution but also gave him a short orientation and arranged his first trick:

> An older friend of mine took me to a park, Washington Square, which is called Bughouse Square, a hustling spot since after the war. He took me down there, and we were walking around there. And he was explaining about drag queens and gay life and tricks and this and that, and money and all of this. And a friend of his, a guy that he had tricked with before, came around. And he set the whole thing up. I was just there. He did all the talking about the money and everything. The guy took me to a hotel It was easy.

In other cases, hustlers served as models—persons who seemed to make good money with minimal effort. John had a job cleaning air vents and lived in a rooming house in a predominantly gay area of Chicago. During his daily rounds, he came into contact with various street people. His realization that some of them were hustlers was pivotal:

> I'm sitting here and I got an 8-hour-a-day job, and I didn't want it. And these people (hustlers) are making more money than I am, and they got an easier job. So I quit my job and turned around to hustling.

Six boys learned about prostitution from their first customers, who proposed to pay them for fleeting sexual relations. They met these men in different settings, including avenues, parks, and bus stations. Whereas the customers entered the setting to find a hustler, the boys entered for other reasons, such as to find someone for a sexual trade or to use the rest room. After they met, the customers engaged the boys in casual conversation and subsequently offered to pay them for sex. Sometimes, this occurred quickly. Dennis was cruising a street corner when the customer approached him. The man inquired, "How old are you?" Dennis stated, "Sixteen" (he was 13). The man asked, "Do you know what goes on down here?" "Yeah, I'm aware of what's going on," thinking the man meant that the place was one where men arranged sexual trades. The man followed up, "How would you like to make some money?" Dennis answered, "What do I have to do for it?" The man said, "Let's go for a ride and we'll talk about it."

Other times, the process was more complex. After arriving in the city by bus, Eddie was standing in the bus terminal, "getting my bearings," when the customer approached. The man asked, "What's going on?" "I don't know," Eddie answered. "Did you just get into town?" "Yeah." The man inquired, "Where are you staying?" "No place. Actually, I'm looking for my uncle" (this was a lie). The man suggested that they go to his place so they could look in the telephone book for the uncle's address. Eddie agreed, unaware that the man planned to have sex with him: "I just thought he was a nice guy trying to help a poor kid out." Shortly after they arrived at the customer's home, the man asked, "Have you ever had your dick sucked?" Eddie replied, "What? No!" He was shocked by the query, for "that was something I never heard of down in Selma, Alabama." The man replied, "Well, how would you like to make $100 and impress your uncle when you find him?" Eddie accepted the offer, thinking "If you want to suck my dick, fruit, for $100, go ahead."

On learning about prostitution, these boys eagerly pursued their first trick. Their decision was based on their definition of prostitution as an acceptable activity. Conceivably, when experienced hustlers or prospective customers present prostitution as a good way to make money, some individuals may reject it as wrong or repulsive. However, these 15 boys defined prostitution as acceptable in light of their circumstances. Eleven saw it as a means for survival. Reflecting on his decision to hang around a bus station in order to attract a customer, Marty said:

> I did it more as a forced, survival thing. I had no job. I was on the streets, and I had been giving sex just for a place to stay. And that's because I didn't know any better. I wasn't old enough to rent a room. I fell into it because I needed it. It was a means of surviving.

When a man approached him in the park and offered to pay him $20 for a brief sexual relationship, Rod recognized the opportunity as a blessing not to be taken lightly and quickly agreed: "It was a surprise, but I took it. I was broke. I took it just for the money." Four other boys viewed prostitution as a superior way to make a living. Compared with the respectable jobs for which they were qualified, hustling offered a means for making more money with less effort.

Some researchers argue that homosexual contact makes the individual's decision to hustle difficult (Hoffman, 1972; Reiss, 1961).[5] They argue that many hustlers are heterosexual. As a consequence, before these individuals can engage in an act of prostitution, they must justify the sexual contact, employing a rationale that allows them to have sex with a man and maintain a heterosexual self-image. This involves defining the act as a money-making venture, limiting oneself to a masculine sex role, and remaining affectively neutral during contact. For most of those interviewed in this research who turned to prostitution out of desperation, homosexual contact posed no problem. Thirteen considered themselves homosexual or bisexual, and they had had prior homosexual relations for pleasure. Such experience provided them with the skills prostitution required. And, importantly, having found homosexual relations pleasurable, they were favorably disposed to such contacts.

For the other two boys, however, the thought of engaging in homosexual relations was problematic. They regarded themselves as heterosexual, and they had confined themselves to heterosexual relations. Yet they accepted the proposition, justifying the exchange as a money-making rather than a sexual transaction. Thus, although Eddie was shocked by the customer's offer, the opportunity to make an easy $100 was simply too good to pass up. They also performed a masculine role, permitting the customers to fellate them but shunning additional contact.[6]

After deciding to pursue prostitution, these boys closed on their first trick. For those who learned about prostitution from experienced hustlers and elected to try their hand at it, closure took time. Eight boys went to an avenue, park, or bus station thought to contain customers.[7] Some learned of the settings through observation: John moved to a particular street corner because he had seen hustlers getting picked up there. Others learned of the setting through conversation with hustlers; Rick's lover (a hustler) told him about a "cruisy street" in Detroit where men picked up boys. Once there, they waited for customers to contact them and arrange a sexual sale. Although these boys knew how to engage in homosexual relations, they were naive about the complexities of the transaction—how to meet customers, what to charge, where to have sex, and so on. As a result, their customers had substantial control over the transaction, directing the boys' participation. Marty's first trick provides a good example. He went to the bus station and stood near a stairway, hoping that a customer would contact him. After about 45 minutes, a man in his 50s approached and opened conversation. Early in the conversation, the man offered to pay him "a few bucks" for sex. Unaware of the "going rate,"

he accepted. Then the customer asked if he had a place where they could have sex; Marty said he did not. The customer suggested that they go to the hotel across the street; Marty agreed. They went to the hotel, had sex, and the customer paid him $15. For those boys who learned about prostitution from their first customers, closure on their first trick took little time, for they already had been contacted and propositioned by customers. Yet, although most knew how to engage in sex, they were naive about the intricacies of the sale and, as a consequence, followed their customers' directions.

Adventurous Involvement

A second path to initial involvement may be called "adventurous." The individual is embedded in a situation of relative comfort. In the course of everyday life, he inadvertently meets an older man who proposes to pay him for sexual relations. Defining the transaction as an acceptable way to make a little spending money and perhaps acquire sexual satisfaction, he agrees to participate. Thus, involvement reflects a decision to take advantage of an attractive situation—a pattern resembling Lofland's (1969: 104–117) conception of the "adventurous deviant act."

Eleven hustlers turned to prostitution more as a lark than as a means to survive. At the time of their first tricks, their circumstances differed from those of the hustlers who moved into prostitution out of desperation. Admittedly, their chances of acquiring steady, well-paying jobs were poor, for they lacked the necessary qualifications. They were too young (a mean of 15 years) and too inexperienced to get good jobs. Also, although they were in school, most of them disliked school and received below-average grades. However, these boys were not destitute. Some characterized their financial situations as wanting, but all of them enjoyed the support of their parents. Ten lived at home, and many of them received allowances in addition to the necessities of life. One boy who left home received regular financial assistance from his parents. Thus, these boys did not view their situation as desperate despite limited prospects, they were not financially pressed.

During their daily rounds, these boys inadvertently made contact with their first customers.[8] They met these men in various settings, including avenues, parks, cafes, and movie theaters. Whereas the customers entered the settings to find a hustler, the boys entered or passed through for different reasons, such as to find a partner for a sexual trade, to get a soft drink, or to see a movie. After they met, the customer engaged the boy in casual conversation and subsequently offered to pay him for sexual relations. In some cases, this occurred quickly; the customer made an offhand statement and then broached the sale. In other cases, the process was complex; the customer approached the boy, engaged him in casual conversation, took him to a private place (such as the man's residence), probed his sexual preference, and then made the proposal.

Whether the proposal was straightforward or not, it presented the boys with a dilemma: whether to accept or reject it. Some individuals probably decline such proposals, opposed to the idea of receiving payment for something they enjoy or repelled by the thought of homosexual contact. However, these 11 boys agreed to the offer, although many did so with some reluctance. As Bob recalled, "I didn't feel right taking his money because I enjoyed it, you know I just couldn't see why I should take money for it. But I needed it, so I did." Their agreement was based on their definition of the transaction as acceptable, as financially and, in many cases, sexually rewarding. Although these boys did not regard themselves as desperate, neither did they regard themselves as affluent. As a consequence, they were open to ways to supplement meager allowances and finance movies, nice clothes, jewelry, and the like. As Bob noted:

I had no idea anybody would pay me to go home with them. So when it came up, it was a nice surprise, because I needed the money. I didn't get much from my parents or anything. It was a way to earn a few extra bucks.

Similarly, Jim accepted the proposal in order to make some spending money:

The main thing that made me [accept] was the flash of the money. You know, when you're brought up in a poor environment, where you can't get much money from your family and here comes this guy and all he wants to do is play with your dick for a few minutes, and he gives you $50, shit you'll do that all day long for $50.

Seven boys also expected the sale to be sexually satisfying, and this, in addition to payment, made their participation acceptable. Speaking of his first customer, Jaime said, "I met him at the show and things just clicked. He was good looking, and he asked me if I'd go to bed with him for money." He agreed, in large part, "because he was good looking."

For 9 boys, homosexual contact posed no problem. They considered themselves homosexual or bisexual, and they had participated in homosexual relations prior to their first trick. Given such experience, they not only had the knowledge and skill to perform the sexual services, they also were amenable to homosexual contact. For 2 boys, however, the thought of engaging in homosexual relations was problematic. Jim and Tom considered themselves heterosexual and had limited themselves to heterosexual relations. Yet they agreed to participate, finding the money too good to pass up. Jim recalled:

He came over to me and just said, "Well, can I see it [penis]?" And I didn't know how to act. I just looked at him, you know. Wow! And he came over and touched it, and it felt good, obviously. But I didn't know how to act. So I just stood there. Then he says, "If I give you this, would you let me suck it?" And I looked at him, and it was $40. And I said, "Sure," you know. Why not, $40!

For these boys, closure on their first trick took little time. They did not need to move to a setting housing prospective customers, as they had already happened onto such a site. They did not need to attract customers, for they had inadvertently done so. And they did not need to arrange sales, as they already had been propositioned. Still, as with those who turned to prostitution out of desperation, these boys knew little about the nature of the sexual sale. Although most of them had the knowledge and skill to engage in homosexual relations, they were naive about the complexities of the sale.

As a result, their customers had substantial control over the transaction, determining the place where they had sex, setting the price and time of payment, and delivering the payment whenever they wanted.

REGULAR INVOLVEMENT

The first trick did not always mark the onset of regular involvement. Many boys immersed themselves in prostitution immediately after their first trick, but some abstained or hustled on rare occasions, moving into regular participation months or years later. This section examines the conditions leading to a level of regular involvement, looking in particular at why some boys immediately turned to regular involvement and others did not.[9]

Fifteen hustlers moved into what they considered full-time involvement shortly after their first tricks. Eight boys, on their own initiative, went to a street setting (typically the same setting in which they met their first customers) in hopes of arranging sales with other men. Dennis recalled:

> Hustling became a steady, full-time thing. I knew then, after the first trick. It took me about a week to get up enough nerve to go back down there. But then I did. [Did you go to the same corner?] Yeah. I actively sought out the money, and I got the tricks.

The other 7 boys moved into full-time involvement with the assistance of their first customers. In some cases, the first customer told the boy about popular hustling sites or introduced the boy to other customers who told him about such sites. In discussing his first trick, Eddie stated:

> I ended up staying with the guy for three or four days, and he introduced me to some other people. They weren't $100 tricks. Back then the going price was $10, $15. And they told me about some good places to hustle.

In other cases, the boy enjoyed a brief yet exclusive relationship with his first customer. The customer not only paid for additional sexual services, he also provided the boy with food, shelter, and other amenities. Jaime developed a steady relationship with his first customer, and moved into street hustling only after the relationship ended. Although Jim had a similar relationship, his first customer also acquainted him with the street scene: "I asked him, 'Where can I go if I want to make more money?' And he showed me the streets. He showed me through the city of New York, showed me 42nd Street, this and that."

Regardless of the way these hustlers move into regular participation, three conditions hastened the move. First, they found hustling financially and sometimes sexually rewarding. The first trick revealed that sexual sales yielded good money with little effort. As Rick pointed out:

> I got a thrill out of it. As soon as I got out of the car, I wanted to go do another one. Having the money in my hand, it seemed so nice. I just wanted to do it again, to get some more money.

Similarly, Marty said, "That was more money than I was used to having in a long time, and I wanted more. So I went out and made more." Compared with his respectable job, John found hustling superior:

> It was a lot better than my regular job. And back then you could get a lot of tricks. There wasn't no heat from the cops. And it was a hell of a lot better than going to work, cleaning air vents.

For some, hustling also was sexually satisfying. Rod maintained, "I hustled because I liked hustling. . . . I needed the money, but I also liked sex. So why not make a living at something like?"

Second, they defined prostitution as an acceptable pursuit. These boys varied in their views of the public's acceptance of male prostitution. Some thought the gay world accepted hustling but the straight world rejected it. When asked if he thought hustling was accepted, Rod said, "By the gay people, yes. By the straight people, well most straight people don't know about it, but they'd probably look down on it." Other boys believed that even the gay world objected to prostitution. Ben observed:

> It just seems as if everybody looks down so much on hustlers. Male and female, whatever they may be. It's like society looks down on them for what they do for their living.

Yet all 15 boys viewed prostitution as a personally acceptable pursuit. Many of them justified their continued participation in terms of survival. Tom believed that hustling is widely condemned, "but when it comes down to it, I ain't got no job, I ain't got no permanent place to stay, I got to get out and hustle, for the shirt on my back." Marty argued, "In the beginning, it was a means for survival. Otherwise, I would have starved to death on the streets." Some of the boys also justified their continued involvement in terms of ease. Hustling seemed easier than the other jobs for which they were qualified. George said, "To me, it was just easy money. I didn't feel guilty about doing anything. It was just an easy way to make money."

Defining prostitution as a rewarding and acceptable enterprise cannot sufficiently account for the immediate shift to regular participation. This is so because those boys who abstained or hustled occasionally after their first trick also defined hustling as rewarding and acceptable. What appears to distinguish the two groups is perceived financial need. Of the 15 boys who immediately turned to regular involvement, 14 viewed themselves as desperate, with minimal support and limited prospects. Their first trick not only showed that prostitution was rewarding, it also indicated that prostitution could be used to make ends meet. Given this recognition, they immersed themselves in the life. Speaking of his first trick, Mike said:

> I got $20 for it. After I got it, I thought "Wow, people just pay you for this." And it just all fell into place. This was it! I felt kind of uncomfortable about it being a guy, but that just wore off. It disappeared and I never thought about it anymore.

George first turned to prostitution as a lark, yet he moved into full-time involvement soon after his first trick on the assumption that hustling would free him from an unpleasant home life.

In contrast, 10 of the 11 boys who did not immediately move into regular involvement did not view themselves as desperate. Bob, David, and Joe, among others, enjoyed the support of their parents. Gordon joined the navy a few weeks after his first trick, and he engaged in only two or three tricks during his tour of duty.

Wayne left home soon after his first trick, but he did not turn to hustling because he had a "sugar daddy" who supported him:

> He gave me everything I wanted. You know, like everything I wanted I got. I always had money. I had a car. I always had pot. Everything. [Did you hustle during this time?] No, I didn't need to.

Although Richard first turned to prostitution out of desperation, he did not immediately move into regular involvement because, only days after his first trick, he acquired a sugar daddy who supported him.

Of the 11 boys who abstained or hustled occasionally after their first trick, 9 eventually turned to full-time involvement. They made the move after their main sources of support waned. Their loss of support took different forms: for some support ended when they finished or dropped out of school and left home; for others support ended when their relationships with sugar daddies terminated; for still others support ended when they left their respectable jobs. With little money and few immediate prospects, they turned to hustling, an activity that had been profitable in the past. Two boys decided to pursue hustling and picked the site in which to hustle independently of others. Max recalled:

> I heard [in my hometown] that Chicago is a great place to go because the faggots give you money. So, when I came to the city, I had no job. I had nothing. So I figured on hustling. . . . I started in Bughouse Square because that's where a lot of the kids were.

But the rest acted on the advice of friends or acquaintances. When Gordon finished his military tour, he returned to Chicago and began to work. After two years of employment, he was laid off. During his layoff, he met some hustlers who suggested that he try bar hustling:

> I ran into some dudes, some hustlers, in the bar. And they told me about this place. I learned about [a hustler bar]. And they told me I could be hustling there. And that's when I really started heavy, three or four times a week.

The two remaining boys shifted from occasional hustling into part-time involvement. Unlike those who hustled full-time, these boys had a stable and sufficient source of income. Bill worked as a hospital custodian and Carlos worked in construction. They hustled not to survive, but to make some extra money. Bill pointed out, "I don't hustle as a job. I just use it as extra money, and I only do it when I want extra money." Carlos said:

> I hustle once in a while, to make a little money, but only when the guy's good looking. And when there's a lot of money involved! I go for the big money, the big cash. If I don't get that, I don't hustle, period. They look for me. I don't look for them.

The desire for extra money cannot account for their move to regular, albeit part-time, involvement because they did not seek out customers. A condition that helps to explain the shift is opportunity. Although they did not seek out customers, they spent a fair amount of their leisure time in well-known hustler bars drinking and socializing. As a result, they were in a position to attract a steady number of prospective customers and to select from those men customers who were attractive, seemingly affluent, and so on. It is not surprising, then, that these boys moved into part-time involvement shortly after they began to frequent the hustler bars on a regular basis.

CONCLUSION

This analysis indicates that contextual conditions play a significant role in entering male prostitution. Certainly, background conditions are important. They can provide an individual with a set of circumstances that make prostitution a viable activity. Strained parental relations, little or no work experience, and a poor education can present a boy with a set of circumstances that make hustling a good way to survive or earn extra money. Background conditions also can shape an individual's orientations toward dealing with situations. Early homosexual experience can predispose a boy to the sexual contact his first trick entails, and a rewarding first trick can predispose him to a level of regular participation given the need or opportunity. However, background conditions cannot sufficiently account for an

individual's course of action, as individuals with similar backgrounds deal with situations differently. Social contacts mediate entry, channeling movement into both initial and regular involvement. Through association with experienced hustlers or prospective customers, a boy learns that prostitution is a good way to make ends meet, earn extra money, or enjoy himself. He also learns some of the popular sites in which to ply the trade. By talking with and observing other hustlers, he learns how to contact customers and arrange sexual sales. And by following the directions of his first few customers, he learns how to carry out sales with a minimum of risk.

This analysis is consistent with some analyses of female prostitution (Boyer and James, 1983; Davis, 1978; Decker, 1979: 145–214; Gray, 1973; Prus and Irini, 1980: 26–74, 245–249). Research indicates that a girl generally turns to prostitution out of financial desperation, due to lack of support and limited prospects, or disenchantment with her life, due to a turbulent home life, failure in school, or a tedious job, or a combination of the two. Yet most researchers agree that these circumstances do not necessarily lead girls to prostitution. Prior to "turning out," a girl typically establishes contact with someone involved in the world of prostitution—a prostitute or pimp, or a bartender or hotel clerk. Through such association, she learns about the world—the main characters, the fast pace, the social and material rewards, and the unpleasantries. In light of her circumstances, familiarity with sex, and fascination with the life, she decides to enter. And given strong economic motivation, attachment to particular members of the world, and adequate knowledge to ply the trade, she turns to full-time involvement. Therefore, entering female prostitution, like entering male prostitution, is hastened by contextual as well as background conditions.

In some respects, however, the process of entering male prostitution differs from that of entering female prostitution, and these differences seem to stem from differences between the two worlds. In general, the world of female prostitution is more complex, featuring a larger cast of characters, a greater number of expectations, and a wider variety of rewards; these features serve to shape the course of entry and commit a girl to a level of full-time involvement. Prior to or shortly after entry, a girl typically develops a strong relationship with a pimp. Among other things, he expects her to pursue prostitution intensively, and he rewards her for turning over large sums of money on a routine basis and punishes her for failing to do so (Gray, 1973: 414–415). As a consequence, a girl's regular involvement is likely to follow immediately after initial involvement, and it is likely to be at a full-time level (Prus and Irini, 1980: 30–33). In order to earn as much money as possible, a novice is subject to some training and supervision (Bryan, 1965; Heyl, 1979). She is instructed in how to carry out various sexual activities, how to protect herself from disease, dangerous customers, and police officers, and how to get the most money from a customer with the least amount of work. Finally, prostitution offers a variety of social and material rewards that attract and commit a girl to the life. In considering girls' reasons for moving into prostitution, researchers report that liking her pimp, being attracted to the "fast life," seeing a way to be "somebody," or becoming admired are as likely to be mentioned as the money (Gray, 1973: 411; Prus and Irini, 1980: 54).

The world of male prostitution is less complex. A hustler ordinarily does not have a pimp (Barry, 1979: 9–10; but see Allen, 1980). Consequently, the time at which he turns to regular involvement and the level at which he pursues regular involvement are a function of his financial circumstances, not the pressure exerted on him by a third party. Furthermore, a novice is not trained or supervised in the trade. He learns how to hustle by observing and talking with other hustlers and by dealing with customers. John noted:

> Everything I learned, I learned from doing. Nobody ever sat down and told me anything. Everybody compares notes, so to speak. But to know what you want to do, and how you want to do it, and how you want to make your money, you work that out on your own.

Finally, male prostitution offers relatively few social rewards. A boy may be flattered by the fact that men are willing to pay for sex, and he may find exchanges with attractive men sexually satisfying. But he pursues the life largely for the money.

Thus, the process of entry varies with the complexity of the world in which deviants operate. Nevertheless, whether one looks at careers in male prostitution, female prostitution, or some other world, the context of entry holds some important answers to the problem of entry. Clearly, background conditions can predispose individuals to deviance by means of shaping their circumstances and orientations. But, as Cullen (1984) contends, contextual conditions channel individuals' predispositions toward concrete activities. Therefore, researchers who wish to acquire a sound understanding of entry need to focus on the context as well as the background of entry.

NOTES

1. Three exceptions are Allen (1980), Harris (1973: 29–35), and Reiss (1961). Although they consider the context of entry and note the importance of a boy's circumstances and contacts with other prostitutes to the process of entry, their accounts are rather brief and superficial. These researchers are concerned with other matters, such as the characteristics and lifestyles of male prostitutes and the way in which prostitutes cope with homosexuality.
Whereas most researchers gloss over the context of entry in explaining movement into prostitution, popular writers focus almost exclusively on the context of entry (see Lloyd, 1976; Palmquist, 1978).

2. Also, by focusing on regular involvement, researchers overlook those cases in which individuals do *not* move into regular involvement.

3. All names are pseudonyms.

4. Here, I am using "prostitution" loosely. Those boys who associated with experienced hustlers were presented with the practice of hustling, and they defined that practice as acceptable in light of their circumstances. Those boys who associated with prospective customers were presented with the idea of an exchange of sex for money, and they defined that transaction as acceptable.

5. A principal issue in the study of male prostitution is the hustler's sexual preference. Researchers differ over what proportion of hustlers are homosexual, heterosexual, and bisexual, as well as over how sexual preference is determined (see, for example, Hoffman, 1972). In general, recent studies reveal smaller proportions of heterosexual hustlers than older studies (see Boyer and James, 1983).

6. These cases are consistent with Reiss's (1961) findings. But, unlike Reiss's subjects, these two boys (and two boys discussed below) did not seem to close on the sale by virtue of the teachings of their peer groups.

7. Whereas 8 boys sought out customers on their own, Mike's friend took him to a park, introduced him to a customer, and arranged the sale.

8. Although these boys turned to prostitution given an offer to engage in a sexual sale, there is no reason why boys in situations of relative comfort should not seek out customers. It is plausible that homosexual or bisexual boys with a steady and sufficient source of support may want to earn extra money and, learning about prostitution, seek out customers or mechanisms for meeting customers. The observations of a former escort agency operator,

who was interviewed during the project, are instructive in this regard. Lonnie claimed that all of the boys who entered his agency did so by answering the want ads he placed in the gay newspapers. Most of these boys were gainfully employed and used prostitution to augment their respectable income, and some of them had never engaged in prostitution prior to entering his agency.

9. The numbers of hours per day and days per week that correspond to regular or "full-time" as opposed to "part-time" levels of involvement are variable and close to overlapping. Hence, one hustler characterizing his involvement as full-time may hustle six to eight hours a day, five to six days a week, whereas another characterizing his involvement as full-time may hustle three to four hours a day, four to five days a week. Similarly, one claiming to work part-time may hustle one to three hours a day, one to two days a week, whereas another claiming to work part-time may hustle two to three hours a day, two to three days a week. In this analysis, I distinguish between full-time and part-time involvement on the basis of the hustlers' own perceptions of these matters.

REFERENCES

Allen, D. (1980) "Young male prostitutes: a psychosocial study." Archives of Sexual Behavior 9: 399–426.

Barry, K. (1979) Female Sexual Slavery. Englewood Cliffs, NJ: Prentice-Hall.

Becker, H. (1963) Outsiders. New York: Free Press.

Boyer, D. K. and J. James (1983) "Prostitutes as victims," pp. 109–146 in D. MacNamara and A. Karmen (eds.) Deviants: Victims or Victimizers? Beverly Hills, CA: Sage.

Bryan, J. (1965) "Apprenticeships in prostitution." Social Problems 12: 287–297.

Coombs, N. R. (1974) "Male prostitution: a psychosocial view of behavior." Amer. J. of Orthopsychiatry 44: 782–789.

Craft, M. (1966) "Boy prostitutes and their fate." British J. of Psychiatry 112: 1111–1114.

Cullen, F. (1984) Rethinking Crime and Deviance Theory. Totowa, NJ: Rowman & Allanheld.

Davis, N. (1978) "Prostitution," pp. 195–222 in J. Henslin and E. Sagarin (eds.) The Sociology of Sex. New York: Schocken.

Decker, J. (1979) Prostitution. Littleton, CO: Fred B. Rothman.

Deisher, R., V. Eisner, and S. Sulzbacher (1969) "The young male prostitute." Pediatrics 43: 936–942.

Freyhan, F. (1947) "Homosexual prostitution." Delaware State Medical J. 19: 92–94.

Gandy, P. and R. Deisher (1970) "Young male prostitutes: the physician's role in social rehabilitation." J. of the Amer. Medical Assoc. 212: 1661–1666.

Ginsburg, K. N. (1967) "The 'meat rack': a study of the male homosexual prostitute." Amer. J. of Psychotherapy 2: 170–185.

Gray, D. (1973) "Turning out: a study of teenage prostitution." Urban Life and Culture 1: 401–425.

Harris, M. (1973) The Dilly Boys. Rockville, MD: New Perspectives.

Heyl, B. (1979) The Madam as Entrepreneur. New Brunswick, NJ: Transaction.

Hoffman, M. (1972) "The male prostitute." Sexual Behavior 2: 19–21.

Lindecker, C. L. (1981) Children in Chains. New York: Everest House.

Lloyd, R. (1976) For Money or Love. New York: Ballantine.

Lofland, J. (1969) Deviance and Identity. Englewood Cliffs, NJ: Prentice-Hall.

Luckenbill, D. and J. Best (1981) "Careers in deviance and respectability: the analogy's limitations." Social Problems 29: 197–206.

MacNamara, D. (1965) "Male prostitution in American cities: a socioeconomic or pathological phenomenon?" Amer. J. of Orthopsychiatry 35: 204.

Marlowe, K. (1964) "The life of the homosexual prostitute." Sexology 31: 24–26.

Newsweek (1973) "The chickenhawks." April 30: 42.

Palmquist, A. (1978) The Minnesota Connection. Van Nuys, CA: Bible Voice.

Prus, R. and S. Irini (1980) Hookers, Rounders, and Desk Clerks. Toronto: Gage.

Reiss, A. J. (1961) "The social integration of queers and peers." Social Problems 9: 102–120.

Russell, D. H. (1971) "From the Massachusetts court clinics: on the psychopathology of boy prostitutes." Int. J. of Offender Therapy 15: 49–52.

Wells, J. W. (n.d.) The Male Hustler. New York: Lancer.

Exposure to Pornography and Aggression toward Women: The Case of the Angry Male

SUSAN H. GRAY
Fordham University at Lincoln Center

This paper reviews research since 1970 into the effects of pornography on men's treatment of, and underlying attitudes toward, women. There is little evidence that exposure to hard-core pornography produces aggressive behavior in men. However, levels of aggression in already angered men are increased by exposure to hard-core materials. I also discuss research into the long-term effects of exposure to pornography and the difference between laboratory-induced anger and deeper anger which is a product of psycho-sexual development. I conclude that anger is a greater social problem than pornography, particularly in men who are unable to resolve that anger and to distinguish it from sexual arousal and control over women.

More than a decade after President Johnson's Commission on Obscenity and Pornography (1970) published its report in the United States, the debate continues over the effects of pornography on men's treatment of, and attitudes toward, women. What, if anything, should be done about pornography? Those opposed to it are divided. Some believe protection of the First Amendment, which guarantees freedom of speech and the press, takes precedence over the suppression of pornography. Others believe pornography leads to violence and support actions to reduce its market. For example, Women Against Pornography, an organization founded in New York City in 1979, tries to educate people about the harmful effects of pornographic images of women and encourages boycotts (Kaminer, n.d.; Lederer, 1980). Brownmiller (1975), an active member of the group, and other feminists such as Dworkin (1981), equate pornography with rape, viewing both as male tactics for expressing and ideologically encouraging hostility towards women.

Civil libertarians, on the other hand, argue that any idea can be considered obscene and that it is difficult, and therefore dangerous, to try to draw lines. Suppression of one form of expression, such as pornography, could pave the way for suppression of other unpopular forms of expression and ultimately stifle dissent. . . .

The differing ideological positions on pornography have encouraged researchers to study what harmful effects, if any, result from pornography. The president's commission, examining the effects of a variety of sexually explicit materials, concluded that they were not harmful either to individuals or to society, but could even be educational. The commission recommended the repeal of anti-pornography statutes. Because the commission did not distinguish between portrayals of genital intercourse between consenting adults and violent and more explicit depictions of sado-masochism and rape, it was later criticized (Davis and Braucht, 1973). These criticisms led to new research on the effects of pornography, which I review in this paper.

WHAT IS PORNOGRAPHY? AND WHO CONSUMES IT?

Defining pornography is the key problem in the debate over, and study of, its effects. Neither

From the article originally published in *Social Problems*, Vol. 29, No. 4 (April 1982): 387–398. © 1982 by the Society for the Study of Social Problems. Used with permission.

the president's commission nor the U.S. courts have come up with a definition acceptable to all. The president's commission examined all sexually explicit materials, including books, manuscripts, photographs and films. The mildest material it considered was depictions of nudity. Believing that the word "pornography" denoted disapproval, the president's commission preferred the words "obscenity" or "sexually explicit materials." Court definitions of obscenity, the legal term for pornography, have ranged from material which on the whole appeals to prurient interests and has no redeeming social value (*Roth v. United States,* 1957) to a reluctance to define obscenity and a delegation of that task to local communities (*Miller v. California,* 1973). Women Against Pornography targets any materials depicting violence towards women, and has included under this broad category *Vogue* magazine fashion spreads by photographer Richard Avedon and a Warner Brothers billboard advertisement, later discontinued, which read: "I'm black and blue from the Rolling Stones and I love it."[1] Most contemporary research on pornography studies both soft-core and hard-core materials. Although the distinction between soft-core and hard-core is sometimes fuzzy, "soft-core" generally refers to depictions of nudity or semi-nudity, or depictions of sexual activity without explicit photographs or descriptions of genitals. "Hard-core" generally refers to depictions of nudes engaged in implied sexual activity with a focus upon the genitals. For the purpose of this paper, I define pornography as both soft-core and hard-core depictions of sexual behavior, be they found in magazines, books, films or audiotapes.

Most consumers of pornography are young, married men. They are college educated, politically liberal, high consumers of the mass media in general, and had an average annual income of $12,000 in 1970 (Nawy, 1973; Wilson and Abelson, 1973). About a quarter of all men have been exposed to sado-masochistic materials. Men use pornography most often as means of enhancing the responsiveness and enjoyment of sexual intercourse with a stable partner. Younger consumers without a stable partner usually use pornography to masturbate (Nawy, 1973; Wilson and Abelson, 1973).

Malamuth and Spinner (forthcoming) analyzed the content of photographs, drawings and cartoons in *Playboy* and *Penthouse* magazines from 1973 to 1977 to see if there had been changes in the number of portrayals of violence against women. They found that violent portrayals have been increasing in both of these periodicals, although they never exceeded 10 percent of all the cartoons and five percent of the photographs and drawings. One of Malamuth and Spinner's criteria of sexual violence was scenes that depicted sado-masochism, a form of sexual expression which can take place between consenting adults and is not necessarily exploitative or violent against women. Changing fashions in sexual expression may account for the increase that Malamuth and Spinner found. On the other hand, Diamond (1980) suggests an increasing violence in pornography represents a patriarchal response to increases in the social power of women.

Smith (1976) studied "adults only" paperback fiction available in "adult" bookstores in the United States and found violent themes in about one third of the 428 books he reviewed. The violence was not always physical, but included blackmail and mental coercion, usually committed by men against women. Typically, the woman was forced to participate in an initially unwanted sexual act and began by protesting but ended up pleading for more, her sexual passion unleashed. . . .

ANGER, HARD-CORE PORNOGRAPHY, AND AGGRESSION

Several studies show that aggression levels in previously angered males are raised by exposure to hard-core pornography, but that aggression is not raised in non-angered males (Meyer, 1972; Baron, 1974, 1978; Donnerstein *et al.,* 1975). Pornography facilitates the expression of anger if anger toward a particular target already exists. Violence is facilitated either through

---

[1]See Bullough and Bullough (1977) for further discussion of the problem of defining pornography.

teaching an angered man to view women poorly (the behaviorist model) or through encouraging a cathartic release of anger.

Portrayals of violence without sexual content can facilitate the expression of anger as well as can portrayals of sexually-related violence. In Meyer's (1972) study, undergraduate male students were angered by painful electric shocks, which they thought were the result of negative evaluations by another student (gender unspecified) of their performance on a task. The angered students were then shown a violent film segment (a knife fight scene in *From Here to Eternity*), a segment from a hard-core "stag" movie, an exciting but non-violent and sexually neutral film segment (a cowboy saddling and riding a half-broken horse), or not shown any film. Subjects who viewed the violent film clip gave the most electric shocks to the person that had angered them. Viewers of the "stag" film gave more shocks than did viewers of the cowboy clip or those who saw no film. A difficulty of experiments such as this is that retaliatory behavior toward a specific person is different from displaced retaliation toward a more general target. Hurting a known or an unknown person because a woman aroused your anger in a pornographic novel or film is different from hurting the specific person who hurt you. The relationship between these two expressions of anger is not clear from the data available.

Angered men need not be exposed to explicit sexual materials to interpret them sexually. An early study of male sex offenders shown drawings with ambiguous sexual connotations found that the offenders were capable of producing their own pornographic content (Linder, 1953). A more recent study of undergraduates found that angered men rated cartoons with both exploitative and non-exploitative sexual themes from *Playboy* as higher in sexual content than did non-angered men (Baron, 1978). Angered men can easily attribute their arousal to sexual stimuli, rather than to their anger. Where there is no explicit sexual stimuli in the immediate environment, an angered man will conjure up some, if necessary.

The strength of the pornographic stimulus affects whether an angered man acts aggressively. When angered and then subsequently

aroused by hard-core pornography, men have difficulty distinguishing between anger and sexual arousal. Soft-core pornography is less likely to trigger subsequent aggression in angered men. Sexual arousal through soft-core pornography either distracts attention from previous anger or defuses anger through recognition of the incompatibility of sexual arousal with aggression (Baron, 1974; Donnerstein *et al.,* 1975).

Men can be distracted from their anger by hard-core as well as soft-core pornography. Zillman and Sapolsky (1977) angered male college students and then exposed them to either neutral photographs (furniture, scenery and abstract art), soft-core pornography, or hard-core pornography. Both soft-core and hard-core materials defused anger, and subjects exposed to either were no more likely to retaliate against the researcher than were the subjects exposed to neutral photographs.

Baron and Bell (1977) found that aggression by angered men was inhibited after exposure to strongly arousing pornography. They point out that it is not just a question of whether pornography is soft-core or hard-core, but whether the themes are tenderness (aggression-inhibiting) or wildness and impulsivity (aggression-facilitating). The issue is further complicated by studies which examine anger and exposure to pornography in reverse order. Men who are shown hard-core pornography and then angered attribute their arousal to anger, rather than sexuality, thus facilitating their aggression (Donnerstein *et al.,* 1975). Anger can also be increased because men are distracted by their anger from a source of sexual stimulation. As the studies reviewed here show, men who are not previously or subsequently angered usually do not become aggressive when exposed to hard-core or soft-core pornography.

In a society in which responses to anger other than aggression are permitted (e.g. seduction), aggression need not be the main response of angered men. Laboratory research subjects sitting in front of a machine which they believe they can use to administer electric shocks to victims do not have many other behavioral options for discharging arousal. Yet, as the studies discussed above show, even with behavioral options curtailed, men confronted with highly arousing pornography usually remain non-aggressive in front of such machines—provided they have not been angered. For angered men, sexuality and aggression are more compatible, particularly where there is difficulty distinguishing anger from sexual arousal and where the sexual arousal does not distract from or diffuse the anger.

PORNOGRAPHY AND AGGRESSION: THE LONG-TERM EFFECTS

Studies of pornography usually measure its effects immediately or 10 minutes after exposure, though some attention has also been given to long-term effects.

People exposed to hard-core pornography who are not angered do not become aggressive over time. In a study of married couples over a 12-week period, Mann *et al.,* (1973) found that viewing weekly hard-core pornographic films with themes including sado-masochism produced no significant changes in sexual behavior, other than an increase in sexual behavior on film-viewing nights. Pornography can also become boring over time, resulting in lowered interest and response to it (Howard *et al.,* 1973).

There is evidence that pornography gradually erodes inhibitions against aggression toward both men and women. Male subjects in Baron and Bell's (1973) study initially gave weaker electric shocks to female victims than to male victims. When Donnerstein and Hallam (1978) gave men a second opportunity to shock a woman who had angered them, the men's inhibitions decreased drastically after a 10-minute

wait in which they sat quietly, if they had previously been shown hard-core films.[2] There has been too little research on the long-term effects of exposure to pornography in potentially deviant or already deviant men. However, there is some evidence that long-term exposure is not detrimental to men who are chronically angry towards, or incompetent with, adult women.

Goldstein and Kant have studied rapists and pedophiles (child molesters) admitted to a state hospital in California (Goldstein, 1973; Goldstein and Kant, 1974; Kant and Goldstein, 1970).[3] Rapists and pedophiles reported less exposure to pornography during adolescence and adulthood than the general male population. Not only did rapists report that the pornography they found most exciting was the portrayal of non-violent heterosexual intercourse, but they had less exposure to these portrayals and to photographs or movies of fully-nude women, oral sex, or sado-masochistic activity than the general male population. Rapists had more exposure than the general male population to photographs of explicit sexual acts while they were six to 10 years old, but these photographs did not necessarily portray violence. Goldstein and Kant (1974) theorized that pornography performs an educational function for men during their formative years; deprived of information about sex, rapists and pedophiles have few stimuli which portray society's definition of the "normal sex act." The rapists and pedophiles studied found it more difficult to talk about sex and had fewer sources of sexual information, such as parental explanations.

Goldstein and Kant found that rapists and pedophiles did not initiate the postures or acts they found most exciting in pornography, but

[2]In a contradictory study by Jaffe *et al.* (1974), men were not initially inhibited in their aggression toward women, but gave more intense electric shocks to women than to men. These were research subjects who had *not* been previously angered, but had been strongly aroused. However, a further study by Donnerstein (1980) revealed that when men are exposed to *both* pornography and violence in the same film, more aggression is exhibited toward men than toward women, both on the first and second opportunity. Even with previously angered men, therefore, aggression toward women may still be inhibited under highly arousing conditions, although not consistently so. Men who are aggressive toward other men, after exposure to pornography and violence, may be acting because of the way they see men treat women in violent pornographic materials. This aggressive behavior would indirectly benefit, rather than harm, women.

[3]Another way to gauge the long-term effects of the wide-spread availability of pornography on sexually deviant men is to examine statistical information from Denmark. Since the Danish ban on pornographic literature was repealed in 1967, sex offenses have been decreasing in Copenhagen (Kutchinsky, 1973). However, prosecutions have also decreased as a greater tolerance has developed for behavior such as "peeping" or verbal indecency. Rape has remained fairly stable over the last few decades, with only several dozen cases reported in Copenhagen each year. Child molestation has decreased. These statistics reveal no harmful social consequences of the repeal.

used portrayals of these acts for more general sexual arousal and masturbation. Hard-core pornography was not an incitement to rape or child molestation. But violence and brutality, *whether associated with sex or not,* were often mentioned as disturbing—particularly to rapists. Violence and brutality—not sexuality—were the stimuli for aggression.

> We must consider that sex offenders are highly receptive to suggestions of sexual behavior congruent with their previous formed desires and will interpret the material at hand to fit their needs. . . . [The question becomes] whether the stimulus most likely to release anti-social behavior is one representing sexuality or one representing aggression (Goldstein and Kant, 1974:109).[4]

A related study by Kercher and Walker (1973) found that convicted rapists exposed to slides containing non-rape sexual cues were not aroused any more than were men from the general population. Moreover, the rapists rated the slides less appealing than the general population. Abel, Blanchard, Barlow and Mavissakian (1975) and Abel, Barlow, Blanchard and Guild (1977) studied the relationship between exposure to audiotaped narration of rape scenes and arousal patterns in rapists. Although they concluded that arousal patterns are idiosyncratic, the rapists they studied did become more sexually aroused by narrations of rape and aggression than did non-rapists. Both Abel, Barlow, Blanchard and Guild (1977) and Barbaree *et al.,* (1979) suggest that narrations of violent sex do not arouse rapists any more than do narrations of sex between mutually consenting partners. Rather, narrations of violent sex fail to inhibit arousal to the extent that force inhibits the arousal of normal males, or enables them to suppress their arousal.

TYPES OF ANGER, FANTASY, AND IMAGES OF WOMEN

Research to date suggests that anger is a greater social problem than pornography, especially when anger is directed toward those less powerful. Anger is most dangerous in men who are unable to effectively distinguish between aggression, the control of women, and sexual arousal. The goals of social change might be better served by focusing on the source of anger in men, and by helping men to deal with that anger, than by focusing on pornography. Anger not validated by pornography will be validated elsewhere if supported by cultural values. Recent "horror" films such as *I Spit On Your Grave* depict violence against "liberated," independent women (Ebert, 1981).

It is unrealistic to hope to eliminate all anger in men toward women; it is equally unrealistic to hope to eliminate pornography. A complex relationship exists between sex and anger. Both sex and anger involve one person who has less power than the other or others. Relationships between men and women in western culture are generally power relationships. The struggle between men and women for power is often arousing to both, but most people do not translate that arousal into violence.

Nevertheless, the relationship between sex and anger is an important one. What many researchers have not considered is that anger takes different forms. Studies on pornography and aggression in angered men often view anger superficially as a factor leading to erosion of self-esteem in the laboratory. This superficial anger may be a different kind of anger than the anger manifested by chronically disturbed men. The deep anger in disturbed men is a potentially

---

[4]Groth and Birnbaum (1979) also conclude that rape is related more to the need to express anger than to consumption of pornography. However, a study of sexual offenders by Davis and Braucht (1973) did find a small relationship between childhood exposure to pornography and later rape, statutory rape or homosexual prostitution (r = + 0.26). Part of the control population in Davis and Braucht's research consisted of members of religious organizations, men who are probably less likely to consume or to admit to the consumption of pornography, thereby affecting the comparative statistic on the general male population's use of pornography. In addition, in any retrospective study, it is unclear whether or not there is a direct causal relationship between early exposure to pornography and sexual deviance. The amount of early exposure to pornography may be a reflection of a character already likely to become involved in sexual offenses. Finding that sexual offenders are consumers of pornography is like finding that many heroin addicts at one point also smoked marijuana. It does not demonstrate that one is an outgrowth of the other.

unresolved component of psychoanalytic development (Stoller, 1975). Deep anger may stimulate more socially destructive behavior than the superficial anger stimulated in experimental laboratories. To view the effects of pornography on this deep anger we have only the indirect evidence from studies of sex offenders. An important question is whether those with unresolved deep anger are those more likely to attack women when their superficial anger is stimulated in the laboratory or in everyday life. To stimulate superficial anger in the laboratory, I feel, could help those with deep anger to quickly get in touch with their feelings. The routine insults of everyday life, including the thwarting of expectations derived from pornography, perhaps provide this stimulus for the rapist. More information is needed on the process, and the extent, to which everyday incidents put people in touch with their deep anger.

It has been argued that the consumption of pornography is a cathartic device to discharge momentary aggressive impulses (English, 1980). But pornography can also be a tool for validating a deeper anger toward women. This may be one reason why soft-core pornography generally distracts men who are angry, but hard-core pornography is less likely to do so. If superficially induced anger puts men in touch with a deeper anger, partially validated by pornography, then pornography becomes more dangerous than we might otherwise believe. The process by which men are put in touch with deep anger must become a central question in the debate over pornography.

I believe that non-angered men perceive both soft-core and hard-core pornography as fantasy. Most people can distinguish between fantasy and reality. For those who cannot, it is the unresolved anger and not the pornography which creates the fundamental problem. Artistic media, such as films, novels or even advertising, often employ fantasy, and its creators expect it to be recognized as such. That a particular portrayal is not realistic, or expresses anger toward a group of people, is usually not an effective argument for the portrayal's danger to society. In situations in which lack of realism is a danger to society (e.g. propaganda or racist literature and films), it is usually because

consumers cannot easily separate reality from fiction. Both soft-core and hard-core pornography may often be crude—a form of low culture rather than high culture—but they are nevertheless, I believe, folk art forms. Like comic books or murder mysteries, pornography is a manifestation of popular culture, created by members of a society. Should we ask that pornography be more realistic than other forms of fiction? That some of the literature previously labelled pornographic is now regarded as quality literature, rather than pornography, makes the answer to this question particularly difficult. The dividing line between low-brow and high-brow art can be vague.

I believe that the content of most sexual fantasies is not inherently bad simply because it is silly, or angry, or not representative of the "real" sex life of most people—or even because it may shape reality. In sex, there can be elements of objectification, of dominance and submission, of competition, lovelessness and pain. Some people may prefer to repress these in their sex lives; others may take delight in expressing them. But pornography reveals the options, both exploitative and non-exploitative—options which are there independent of the existence of pornography. Often revealing to consumers what they like, pornography is equally capable of demonstrating what they do not like.

If pornographic images of women are often derogatory, and validate anger, the images of consumers of pornography are often equally so. Consumers are portrayed as tragic figures involved in the exploitation of male sexual desire by female workers in the pornography industry who seek avenues for economic upward mobility. This exploitation is degrading to both the seller and the buyer, as are many other forms of commercial enterprise when the business ethic takes precedence over all else.

If some people nevertheless find the images of women in pornography repulsive, it is futile to try to change images of women by reducing the amount of pornography available. Suppression rarely changes social images over time; more often it drives them underground, thereby giving them a tantalizing flavor. Suppression could even encourage a more extreme pornographic genre.

THE FUTURE OF PORNOGRAPHY

Future research on pornography should endeavor to: (1) provide a more uniform definition of pornography; (2) investigate systematically the link between sexual arousal, anger and aggression when a greater range of behavioral options are presented; (3) decide whether to focus on the general male population or a population with greater pathology when investigating angered men; and (4) create unobtrusive measures of arousal and a mechanism for the male subject to differentiate between specific women and unknown and unseen female targets. Greater coordination of research efforts in these ways would help clarify the extent to which angered men are dangerous when exposed to pornography. At present, the move towards suppression of extreme forms of pornography is not supported by solid empirical evidence of the harmful effects of pornography.

Johnson and Goodchilds (1973) suggest an alternative to suppression: a pornography more clearly in line with both feminist and humanist values. In this genre, neither sex would be manipulated or used as an object, as they are in conventional pornography. English (1980) has speculated on a pornography in which older women pair with younger men, body types become more variable, and sexual expression becomes less phallocentric, thereby making pornography more appealing to female consumers. Some would argue that this would no longer be pornography.

Faust (1980) has argued that women have their own distinct pornographic genre in escapist romantic fiction whose heroines are often alternately raped and seduced. Brownmiller (1975), on the other hand, insists that there can be no female equivalent of pornography, a male invention. In Brownmiller's sense of pornography as domination, escapist romantic fiction is an exercise in masochism and contrary to humanist and/or feminist values. The content of

pornography might be changed if those with humanist and feminist values became involved in its production, thereby creating a new market among feminist and humanist consumers. There is no reason to expect, however, that traditional pornography would not continue to be in demand as well.

If the relationship between exposure to pornography and the degree of violence against women is the key issue in the debate over pornography, it must be recognized that themes of violence have become an integral part of most of our media. A disturbed mind will find exciting stimuli wherever it looks. The amount of violence depicted in pornography is less than the amount of violence shown on television in the United States (Dienstbier, 1977). Dienstbier has pointed out the irony in U.S. society's massive exposure to violence in the media with lower exposure to violence in real life, coupled with society's lower exposure to pornography in the media and higher exposure to sex in real life.

We are not likely to eliminate the anger underlying male violence against women completely. To the extent which we do not, pornography can always evoke that anger. Psychoanalysts claim that a certain amount of frustration and anger is necessary to create a separate ego identify. Without that frustration and developmental anger, normal forms of loving and normal expressions of sexuality would not occur (Stoller, 1975). If we view these expressions as desirable, but if that same anger, when unresolved, produces violence against women,[5] we need cultural mechanisms to encourage socially acceptable forms of resolving this anger or directing it more appropriately: better communication in interpersonal relations, changes in the rigid role expectations and notions of masculinity which lead to pain and anger when they cannot be lived up to, and improved education for men about the nature of being a woman and about female sexuality. Without these, violence toward women can find its expression with or without pornography. With these mechanisms, pornography may once again be viewed as just another form of fantasy,

[5]As Chodorow (1978) points out, contemporary family organization contributes to lack of respect for women as well.

probably not dangerous and maybe no longer attractive to men who are no longer angry.

REFERENCES

Abel, Gene G., David H. Barlow, Edward B. Blanchard and Donald Guild "The components of rapists' sexual arousal." Archives of General Psychiatry 34: 895–903. (1977).

Abel, Gene G., Edward B. Blanchard, David H. Barlow and Matig Mavissakian "Identifying specific erotic cues in sexual deviations by audiotaped descriptions." Journal of Applied Behavior Analysis 8: 247–260. (1975).

Amoroso, Donald M. and Marvin Brown "Problems in studying the effects of erotic material." Journal of Sex Research 9: 187–195. (1973).

Barbaree, H. E., W. L. Marshall and R. D. Lanthier "Deviant sexual arousal in rapists." Behaviour Research and Therapy 17: 215–222. (1979).

Baron, Robert A. "Aggression-inhibiting influences of heightened sexual arousal." Journal of Personality and Social Psychology 30: 318–322. (1974).

———. "Aggression-inhibiting influences of sexual humor." Journal of Personality and Social Psychology 36: 189–197. (1978).

———. "Heightened sexual arousal and physical aggression: An extension to females." Journal of Research in Personality 13: 91–102. (1979).

Baron, Robert A. and Paul A. Bell "Effects of heightened sexual arousal on physical aggression." Paper presented to the annual convention of the American Psychological Association, Montreal, August. (1973).

———. "Sexual arousal and aggression by males: Effects of type of erotic stimuli and prior provocation." Journal of Personality and Social Psychology 35: 79–87. (1977).

Brownmiller, Susan Against Our Will: Men, Women and Rape. New York: Bantam. (1975).

Bullough, Vern and Bonnie Bullough Sin, Sickness and Sanity: A History of Sexual Attitudes. New York: New American Library. (1977).

Chodorow, Nancy The Reproduction of Mothering: Psychoanalysis and the Sociology of Gender. Berkeley: University of California Press. (1978).

Commission on Obscenity and Pornography The Report of the Commission on Obscenity and Pornography. Washington, D.C.: U.S. Government Printing Office. (1970).

Davis, Keith and G. Nicholas Braucht "Exposure to pornography, character and sexual deviance: A retrospective survey." Journal of Social Issues 29: 183–196. (1973).

Diamond, Irene "Pornography and repression: A reconsideration." Signs 5: 686–701. (1980).

Dienstbier, Richard A. "Sex and violence: Can research have it both ways?" Journal of Communication 27: 176–188. (1977).

Donnerstein, Edward "Pornography and violence against women: Experimental studies." Annals of the New York Academy of Science 347: 277–288. (1980).

Donnerstein, Edward and John Hallam "Facilitating effects of erotica on aggression against women." Journal of Personality and Social Psychology 36: 1270–1277. (1978).

Donnerstein, Edward, Marcia Donnerstein and Ronald Evans "Erotic stimuli and aggression: Facilitation or inhibition?" Journal of Personality and Social Psychology 32: 237–244. (1975).

Dworkin, Andrea Pornography: Men Possessing Women. New York: Putnam. (1981).

Ebert, Roger "Why movie audiences aren't safe anymore." American Film 6 (March): 54–56. (1981).

English, Deidre "The Politics of Porn." Mother Jones 5 (April): 44–45. (1980).

Faust, Beatrice Women, Sex and Pornography: A Controversial Study. New York: Macmillan. (1980).

Goldstein, Michael J. "Exposure to erotic stimuli and sexual deviance." Journal of Social Issues 29: 197–219. (1973).

Goldstein, Michael J. and Harold S. Kant Pornography and Social Deviance. Berkeley: University of California Press. (1974).

Gordon, John "On sex and sexism." Inquiry 3 (May 5): 29–31. (1980).

Groth, A. Nicholas and H. Jean Birnbaum Men Who Rape: The Psychology of the Offender. New York: Plenum. (1979).

Hentoff, Nat "The new legions of erotic decency." Inquiry 3 (December 10): 5–7. (1979).

Howard, James L., Myron B. Liptzin and Clifford B. Reifler "Is pornography a problem?" Journal of Social Issues 29: 133–145. (1973).

Jaffe, Yoran, Neil Malamuth, Joan Feingold and Seymour Feshbach "Sexual arousal and behavioral aggression." Journal of Personality and Social Psychology 30: 759–764. (1974).

Johnson, Paula and Jacqueline D. Goodchilds "Pornography, sexuality and social psychology." Journal of Social Issues 29: 231–238. (1973).

Kaminer, Wendy Women Against Pornography: Where We Stand on the First Amendment. Mimeographed. Women Against Pornography, 358 W. 47 Street, New York, N.Y. (n.d.).

Kant, Harold S. and Michael J. Goldstein "Pornography." Psychology Today 4 (December): 59–61, 76. (1970).

Kercher, Glen A. and C. Eugene Walker "Reactions of convicted rapists to sexually explicit stimuli." Journal of Abnormal Psychology 81: 46–50. (1973).

Kutchinsky, Bert "The effect of easy availability of pornography on the incidence of sex crimes: The Danish experience." Journal of Social Issues 29: 163–181. (1973).

Lederer, Laura (ed.) Take Back the Night: Women on Pornography. New York: William Morrow. (1980).

Lindner, Harold "Sexual responsiveness to perceptual tests in a group of sexual offenders." Journal of Personality 21: 364–374. (1953).

Malamuth, Neil M. and James V. P. Check "Penile tumescence and perceptual responses to rape as a function of victim's perceived reactions." Journal of Applied Social Psychology 10: 528–547. (1980).

Malamuth, Neil N. and Barry Spinner "A longitudinal content analysis of sexual violence in the bestselling erotica magazines." Journal of Sex Research. (Forthcoming).

Malamuth, Neil M., Scott Haber and Seymour Feshbach "Testing hypotheses regarding rape: Exposure to sexual violence, sex differences and the normality of rapists." Journal of Research in Personality 14: 121–137. (1980).

Malamuth, Neil M., Maggie Heim and Seymour Feshbach "Sexual responsiveness of college students to rape depictions: Inhibitory and disinhibitory effects." Journal of Personality and Social Psychology. (Forthcoming).

Malamuth, Neil M., Ilana Reisin and Barry Spinner "Exposure to pornography and reaction to rape." Paper presented to the annual convention of the American Psychological Association, New York City, August. (1979).

Mann, Jay, Jack Sidman and Sheldon Starr "Evaluating social consequences of erotic films: An experimental approach." Journal of Social Issues 29: 113–131. (1973).

Meyer, Timothy "The effects of sexually arousing and violent films on aggressive behavior." Journal of Sex Research 8: 324–331. (1972).

Nawy, Harold "In the pursuit of happiness? Consumers of erotica in San Francisco." Journal of Social Issues 29: 147–161. (1973).

New York Times "Judge in Wisconsin calls rape by boy 'normal' reaction." May 27: sec. A, p. 9. (1977).

Rosen, Raymond C. and Francis J. Keefe "The measurement of human penile tumescence." Psychophysiology 15: 366–376. (1978).

Smith, Don D. "The social content of pornography." Journal of Communication 26: 16–24. (1976).

Stoller, Robert J. Perversion: The Erotic Form of Hatred. New York: Pantheon. (1975).

Wilson, W. Cody and Herbert I. Abelson "Experience with and attitudes toward explicit sexual materials." Journal of Social Issues 29: 19–39. (1973).

Zillman, Dorf and Barry S. Sapolsky "What mediates the effect of mild erotica on annoyance and hostile behavior in males?" Journal of Personality and Social Psychology 35: 587–596. (1977).

Cases cited

Miller v. California, 413 U.S. 15, 1973.
Roth v. United States, 354 U.S. 476, 1957.

Problems
of the
Cities

Caught in the Web of Change

JOHN D. KASARDA

Two fundamental, yet conflicting, transformations mark the recent history and near-term prospects of our older, larger cities. First is a *functional* change: these cities are becoming administration, information, and higher-order service centers, rather than centers for producing and distributing material goods. Secondly, there is *demographic* change: the residents are no longer predominantly whites of European heritage, but are predominantly blacks, Hispanics, and members of other minority groups.

Concomitant with the functional transformation of these cities have been changes both in the composition and the size of their overall employment bases. During the past two decades, most older, larger cities have experienced substantial job growth in occupations associated with knowledge-intensive service industries. However, selective job growth in these high-skill, predominantly white-collar industries has not nearly compensated for post-World War II employment declines in manufacturing, wholesale trade, and other predominantly blue-collar industries, which once constituted the urban economic backbone. As a result, the total number of jobs available in most of these cities has shrunk considerably over the past three decades.

Analogously, concomitant with the ethnic and racial transformations, there have been substantial changes in the socioeconomic composition and total size of the cities' residential populations. As predominantly white, middle-income groups have dispersed (initially to the suburbs and now increasingly to nonmetropolitan areas), they have been only partially replaced by predominantly lower-income minority groups. The result has been dramatic declines both in the aggregate sizes and the aggregate personal-income levels of the cities' resident populations, while concentrations of the economically disadvantaged continue to expand.

The simultaneous transformation and selective decline of the employment and residential bases of the cities have contributed to a number of serious problems, including a widening gap between urban job-opportunity structures and the skill levels of disadvantaged residents (with correspondingly high rates of structural unemployment), spatial isolation of low-income minorities, and intractably high levels of urban poverty. Accompanying these problems have been a plethora of social and institutional ills further aggravating the predicament of people and places in distress: rising crime, poor public schools, and the decay of once-vibrant residential and commercial subareas.

Responsive to the hardships confronting cities and their inhabitants, the federal government has introduced a variety of urban programs over the past fifteen years. Unfortunately, these programs have had little effect in stemming urban decline or improving long-term employment prospects for the underprivileged. Indeed, mounting evidence suggests that the plight of economically distressed cities and their underprivileged residents is worse than before America's urban programs began.

The poor track record of these federal urban programs is attributable primarily to the failure of our policy-makers to appreciate fully the technological and economic dynamics underlying

John D. Kasarda is chairman of the Department of Sociology at the University of North Carolina-Chapel Hill. Coauthor, with Brian J. Berry, of Contemporary Urban Ecology, *his current research includes work on entry-level job loss and minority unemployment in the cities.*

From *Society,* November/December 1983. Published by permission of Transaction Publishers, from *Society,* Vol. 21, No. 1. Copyright © 1983 by Transaction Publishers.

industry's locational choices, on the one hand, and an inadequate consideration of the changing roles of older cities in an advanced service economy, on the other. I will focus on these dynamics and transformations, especially as they have altered the capacity of America's older cities to offer employment opportunities and social mobility for disadvantaged resident groups.

SOCIOECONOMIC SPRINGBOARDS

Cities always have and always will perform valuable social and economic functions, but changing technological and industrial conditions (both national and international) alter such functions over time. Apropos of the assimilation and socioeconomic upgrading of masses of disadvantaged persons historically, it must be remembered that cities performed these functions most effectively during an industrial and transportation age now gone.

During the late nineteenth and early twentieth centuries, America's industrial revolution fostered dramatic national economic development, creating millions of low-skill jobs. Most of this economic development and employment growth occurred in the cities, which possessed comparative advantages over other locations. For firms concentrating in the cities, costs were substantially reduced and efficiency was increased. Among the advantages were superior long-distance transportation and "break in bulk" terminal facilities; abundant and ambitious immigrant labor, willing to work for extremely low wages; essential complementary businesses; and private and public municipal services, such as police and fire protection, sewage systems, and running water.

Territorially restricting transportation technologies and the burgeoning manpower needs of a labor-intensive manufacturing economy generated unprecedentedly high urban concentration. Because the transit and terminal costs of coal were high, manufacturers sought to minimize expenses by clustering together around rail or water terminal sites and sharing bulk carriage costs. Since the main terminal was also where most other raw materials used in the production process were received, and where finished products were shipped, additional cost advantages accrued to factories concentrating near terminal points.

The lack of efficient short-distance transportation technology likewise acted to confine the sites of complementary businesses as well as the residences of the urban labor force. Wholesale establishments, warehouses handling finished goods, and ancillary businesses that serviced the factories or used their byproducts reduced costs by locating close to the factories. Similarly, most workers employed by the factories and related business establishments, unable to afford commuting, were clustered within walking distance of their place of employment. Indeed, as late as 1899, the average commuting distance of workers in New York City was approximately two blocks.

Our industrial cities thus evolved in the late nineteenth century as compact agglomerations of production and distribution facilities and as places where millions of unskilled or semiskilled migrants both lived and worked. Spatially circumscribed by prevailing transportation technologies, industrial development and concentrative migration occurred together, generating explosive urban growth. Chicago, for example, which was incorporated in 1833 with a population of 4100 grew to be a city of more than 2 million residents by 1910, the vast majority of whom lived and worked within a three-mile radius of the city's center.

Spurring the dramatic growth of our industrial cities were a rapidly advancing western resource frontier and burgeoning commercial markets. A powerful entrepreneurial spirit held that individualism, competition, the pursuit of profit, and economic growth were uniformly positive and beneficial. In this political-economic climate, urban industrial development surged, catapulting the entire country into a period of enormous economic expansion. By the dawn of the twentieth century, the output of America's industrial cities had surpassed the *combined* total industrial output of Britain, France, and Germany, the world's leaders in 1860.

It cannot be overemphasized that the employment bases of our early industrial cities were characterized by entry-level job surpluses; today, entry-level job deficits characterize urban employment bases. It was these job surpluses, with few requisites for entry, that attracted the waves of migrants and offered them a foothold in the urban economy. In turn, the rapidly expanding job base that accompanied national economic growth provided ladders of opportunity and social mobility for the migrants, most of whom were escaping areas of economic distress.

Access to opportunity and social mobility was obtained at significant human cost, however. Prejudice, discrimination, hostility, and (frequently) physical violence greeted the new arrivals. Lacking financial resources, unaccustomed to city ways, and often without English language skills, immigrants were given the lowest status and were segregated in overcrowded dwellings in the least desirable areas. A polluted, unsanitary physical environment contributed to high morbidity and mortality, as did the hazardous working conditions found in the factories. Political corruption and exploitation were common, working hours were long, and there was no such thing as a minimum wage. Virtually all immigrants held so-called dead-end jobs.

Nonetheless, there was an abundance of jobs for which the only requisites were a person's desire and physical ability to work. Overall economic growth and this surplus of low-skill jobs gave our older industrial cities a unique historical role as developers of manpower and springboards for social mobility.

During the first half of the twentieth century, numerous advances occurred in transportation, communication, and production-distribution technologies. These served to reduce markedly the previous locational advantages that our older, compactly structured cities had held for manufacturing and warehousing and made uncongested suburban sites more cost-effective. Among these advances were the shift from rail and barge transport to trucking, the spread of peripheral highways and public utilities, and automated assembly-line techniques. By 1960, further advances in transportation and communication technologies, together with growing industrial competition

from nonmetropolitan areas and abroad, made our larger, older cities all but obsolete with respect to manufacturing and warehousing. A massive exodus of blue-collar jobs began—an exodus that accelerated during the past decade.

Exacerbating blue-collar job losses in the cities has been the post–World War II flight of retail trade and consumer services, which followed their traditional middle- and upper-income patrons to the suburbs and exurbs. Between 1954 and 1978, more than 15,000 shopping centers and malls were constructed to serve expanding suburban and exurban populations. By 1975, these shopping centers and malls produced more than one-half of the United States' annual retail sales. As a consequence, central cities have suffered marked job losses in standard retail and consumer-service industries.

Significant countertrends, however, are under way in certain retail and service sectors, as businesses and institutions offering highly specialized goods and services continue to be attracted to downtown areas. The specialized nature of these establishments often makes it advantageous to locate at centralized nodes that maximize accessibility to people and firms in the metropolitan area. Advertising agencies; brokerage houses; consulting firms; financial institutions; luxury goods shops; legal, accounting, and professional complexes—these have been accumulating in the central business districts. Traditional department stores and other establishments—unable to compete effectively or unable to afford the skyrocketing rents—are being replaced.

The past two decades have also witnessed a remarkable growth of high-rise administrative offices in the central business districts of our largest cities. Even with major advances in telecommunications technology, many administrative headquarters still rely on a complement of legal, financial, public relations, and other specialized services that are most readily available in the central business districts. Unlike manufacturing, wholesale trade, and retail trade—which typically have large space-per-employee requirements—most managerial, clerical, professional, and business-service functions are space-intensive. In addition, persons performing these service functions can be "stacked" vertically, layer after layer, in downtown high-rises without losing any productivity. Indeed, office proximity often enhances the productivity of those whose activities entail extensive, non-routinized, face-to-face interaction. The result has been an office-building boom in the central business districts.

EMPLOYMENT-DEMOGRAPHIC DISARTICULATIONS

The growth of administrative, financial, professional, and similar "knowledge class" jobs in the central business districts of our large cities, together with substantial losses of blue-collar jobs, has altered the important role the cities once played as opportunity ladders for the disadvantaged. Aggravating the problems engendered by the deterioration of historical blue-collar job bases has been the flight of middle-income population and traditional retail-trade and consumer-service establishments elsewhere in the city. Further, these movements have combined to erode city tax bases, damage secondary labor markets, and isolate many disadvantaged persons in economically distressed subareas where the opportunities for employment are minimal.

Particularly hard hit by post–World War II declines of middle-income population and blue-collar jobs are our larger, older cities in the northern industrial belt. Unfortunately, it is many of these same cities that have experienced the largest postwar migration inflows of persons whose educational backgrounds and skills are ill-suited for the information-processing jobs which have partially replaced the lost blue-collar jobs. Consequently, inner-city unemployment rates are well above the national average and are inordinately high among educationally disadvantaged minorities, whose numbers continue to grow in our urban centers.

Data presented in Table 1 for our four largest northern cities illustrate the scope of urban employment decline in the postwar period. New York City and Chicago, for example, have each lost more than 300,000 manufacturing jobs since 1947, with the most pronounced employment losses occurring after 1967. Also ravaged have been Philadelphia and Detroit.

Wholesale and retail trade employment in all these cities likewise deteriorated considerably. However, there are temporal differences. Whereas most retail-employment losses occured before 1967, wholesale-employment declines (like those in manufacturing) accelerated after 1967, during which more than two-thirds of the total 1947–77 job declines occurred. The accelerating pace of central-city job losses in the manufacturing and wholesale sectors reflects the

TABLE 1

Employment Changes in Major Northern Cities

	Manufacturing	Wholesale	Retail	Selected Services	Total
New York					
1948–77	−330,535	−122,071	−208,595	153,250	−507,951
1967–77	−285,600	−82,925	−94,053	30,992	−431,586
Chicago					
1948–77	−301,407	−51,827	−100,803	57,874	−396,163
1967–77	−180,900	−41,023	−49,829	45,246	−226,506
Philadelphia					
1948–77	−171,130	−26,573	−63,263	15,263	−245,703
1967–77	−106,400	−19,328	−23,743	2,242	−147,229
Detroit					
1948–77	−185,073	−21,980	−78,804	−4,484	−290,341
1967–77	−56,400	−20,617	−32,632	−10,706	−120,355

Source: Censuses of Manufacturing and Censuses of Business.

technological forces discussed above as well as the growing diseconomies of central-city locations for production and warehousing activities.

The selective nature of job declines in the twelve large cities noted above is indicated by employment-change data for their service industries. Only Detroit showed a net loss in service-industry jobs between 1947 and 1977, and this loss is entirely accountable by service-industry job losses since 1967. Chicago and New York City, on the other hand, have shown substantial vitality in their service industries since World War II. Even in these cities, though, service-industry job growth was overwhelmed by employment declines in manufacturing, wholesale trade, and retail trade. Overall, Chicago lost nearly 400,000 jobs between 1947 and 1977; during the same time period, New York City lost more than 500,000 jobs. In each case, the vast majority of overall job losses are attributable to blue-collar employment declines. Moreover, detailed analysis of sectoral employment change demonstrates that all of the net increase in service employment in New York City, Chicago, and Philadelphia has been in knowledge-intensive industries (e.g., finance, health and legal services, colleges and universities, engineering firms, and such business services as accounting, advertising, data processing, management consulting, and R&D). Conversely, service-sector employment opportunities with lower educational requirements (e.g., in hotels, personal services, and a full range of such consumer services as auto repair) have declined markedly.

Thus, a rather clear picture emerges. Central-city employment in those industries which traditionally sustained large numbers of less-skilled persons has declined precipitously. These employment losses have been partially replaced by newer service industries, which typically have high educational requisites for entry. The dissonant expansion in large northern cities of population groups whose educational backgrounds place them at a serious disadvantage deserves attention.

Obtaining an accurate account of each city's changing demographic composition (by race and ethnicity) is not without its complications. Because Hispanics (most of whom are classified as whites in the census) are typically considered a racial-ethnic minority, one cannot determine actual minority compositional changes in the cities without separating this group from whites, blacks, and others. Published census data do not permit one to do this. However, the 1970 fourth-count summary computer tapes and the 1980 system's File-1A computer tapes both contain information on how the Hispanic/Spanish-origin population was allocated for each city across "white," "black," and "other." With this information, it is possible to reconstruct each city's 1970 and 1980 non-Hispanic white population, non-Hispanic black population, and non-Hispanic "other" (primarily Asian) population in addition to its Hispanic population. These adjustments permit refined analysis of each city's racial-ethnic residential compositional changes and their actual minority demographic transformation. (See Table 2.)

New York City, which experienced an overall population decline of 823,212 during the 1970–80 decade, lost 1,392,718 non-Hispanic whites. Thus, in just ten years, New York's non-Hispanic white population (i.e., its nonminority population) dropped by an amount larger than the *total* population of any other U.S. city with the exception of Los Angeles, Chicago, Philadelphia, and Houston. Approximately 25 percent of the loss of non-Hispanic whites in New York City was replaced by an infusion of more than 200,000 Hispanics during the 1970s and, to a somewhat lesser extent, by the growth of non-Hispanic "others" and non-Hispanic blacks. The transition to minority residential dominance of our nation's largest city seems all but assured.

Chicago's demographic experience during the 1970s was similar to New York City's, but at about one-half the scale. Registering a net population drop of 357,753 residents between 1970 and 1980, Chicago's non-Hispanic white population declined by 699,357, whereas the city's minority population (non-Hispanic blacks, non-Hispanic "others," plus Hispanics) grew by 341,604. More than 50 percent of Chicago's minority population increase during the decade consisted of Hispanics (174,206). By 1980, 57 percent of Chicago's resident population was composed of minorities.

Among the four largest northern cities in the United States (New York, Chicago, Philadelphia, and Detroit), the City of Brotherly Love had the smallest aggregate population decline, losing

TABLE 2

Demographic Changes in Major Northern Cities

	Total Population	Non-Hispanic Whites	Non-Hispanic Blacks	Non-Hispanic Other*	Hispanic Population*	Percent Minority
New York						
1980	7,071,639	3,668,945	1,694,127	302,543	1,406,024	48
1970	7,894,851	5,061,663	1,517,967	112,940	1,202,281	36
CHANGE	−823,212	−1,393,718	176,160	189,603	203,743	
Chicago						
1980	3,005,072	1,299,557	1,187,905	95,547	422,063	57
1970	3,362,825	1,998,914	1,076,483	39,571	247,857	41
CHANGE	−357,753	−699,357	111,422	55,976	174,206	
Philadelphia						
1980	1,688,210	963,469	633,485	27,686	63,570	43
1970	1,948,609	1,246,940	646,015	10,975	44,679	36
CHANGE	−260,399	−283,471	−12,530	16,711	18,891	
Detroit						
1980	1,203,339	402,077	754,274	18,018	28,970	67
1970	1,511,336	820,181	651,847	9,254	30,054	46
CHANGE	−307,997	−418,104	102,427	8,764	−1,084	
Total Change 1970–80	−1,749,361	−2,793,650	377,479	271,054	395,756	

*The term "Hispanic" is used for all those classified as Hispanic or Spanish origin. "Non-Hispanic Other" is used for those classified as Asians, American Indians, and Pacific Islanders.

slightly over a quarter of a million residents during the 1970s. Both the number of non-Hispanic whites and non-Hispanic blacks declined in Philadelphia between 1970 and 1980, while other, non-Hispanic minorities and Hispanics increased. Philadelphia's substantial decline in non-Hispanic whites (283,471) together with its net increase of 23,072 minority residents during the 1970s raised its minority proportion to 43 percent in 1980.

Detroit experienced the highest rate of non-Hispanic-white residential decline of any major city in the country. Between 1970 and 1980, Detroit lost more than one-half of its non-Hispanic white residents (from 820,181 to 402,077). Concurrently, Detroit had the fourth-largest absolute increase of non-Hispanic blacks of any city in the country (102,427), falling just behind Chicago in black population increase. Combined with modest increases in Hispanics and other minorities, Detroit's large increase in black residents and precipitous drop in non-Hispanic white residents transformed the city's residential base from 46

percent minority in 1970 to 67 percent minority in 1980.

Between 1970 and 1980, our four largest northern cities suffered an aggregate loss of 2,793,650 non-Hispanic whites, while their Hispanic residential bases increased by nearly 400,000. Added to the Hispanic increase during the 1970s were substantial cumulative increases of non-Hispanic blacks (377,479) and other non-Hispanic minorities (271,054), resulting in a total increase of more than 1,040,000 minority residents in the four cities. These compositional changes have further implications.

CONSEQUENCES OF MISMATCH

It has been noted that job opportunities matching the educational backgrounds and skills of many minorities have disappeared from major northern cities. Concurrently, as higher-income white-collar workers moved to the suburbs and exurbs, white-collar jobs increased substantially in the central city. One consequence of the residence–job opportunity mismatch is increased commuting in both directions between central cities and outlying nodes. This mismatch manifests itself each weekday morning on the radial urban expressways, where one observes heavy streams of white-collar workers commuting into the central business districts from their suburban residences; simultaneously, in the opposite lanes, streams of inner-city residents are commuting to their blue-collar jobs in outlying areas.

The job opportunity–residential composition mismatch has had especially deleterious consequences for minorities and blue-collar ethnic whites left behind in the inner city. As blue-collar industries have deconcentrated, they have become scattered among suburban, exurban, and nonmetropolitan sites. Their dispersed nature makes public transportation from central-city neighborhoods to most outlying locations impractical, requiring virtually all city residents who work outside the central city to commute by private automobile. The high and increasing costs of inner-city automobile ownership, insurance, and maintenance impose a heavy financial burden on these people. Moreover, a large portion of inner-city residents, particularly low-income minorities, can afford neither the luxury nor the employment necessity of owning an automobile. In Chicago, for example, four out of five inner-city blacks do not own automobiles. The result is rising rates of urban structural

unemployment, especially among disadvantaged minorities who traditionally had found employment in those industries which have relocated in the suburbs, nonmetropolitan areas, and abroad.

In our four largest northern cities, unemployment rates among minorities have risen dramatically. (See Table 3.) With the exception of industrially crippled Detroit, the rise in unemployment rates among whites in these cities between 1971 and 1980 corresponded very closely with the rise in the national unemployment rate. The moderate rise in youth unemployment among whites also echoed national trends. Black and other minority unemployment rates, however, soared. Worst hit was Detroit, where adult-male minority unemployment rates rose to nearly 30 percent in 1980. Recall that Detroit also experienced a major increase in black residents between 1970 and 1980. Youth minority unemployment rates for Detroit, already high in 1971 (44.4 percent), rose to 52.1 percent in 1980.

New York City, with its huge white outmigration, experienced negligible growth in adult white-male unemployment between 1971 and 1980. But unemployment rates for adult black males nearly doubled during the decade, and rates for black youth unemployment rose from 26.3 percent to 40 percent. Chicago lost a much larger proportion of its jobs than New York City during the 1970s and registered significant increases both in its white and black resident-unemployment rates. By 1980, adult black-male

TABLE 3

Changing Unemployment Rates in Major Northern Cities

Race, Sex, and Age	New York		Chicago		Philadelphia		Detroit	
	1971	1980	1971	1980	1971	1980	1971	1980
White								
Men, 20+	5.8	6.6	4.0	8.6	3.4	7.0	6.5	18.2
Women, 20+	5.5	7.1	3.7	6.9	4.4	6.3	5.3	11.8
Both sexes, 16–19	20.4	23.8	14.2	21.0	14.2	19.4	17.5	22.2
Black and other								
Men, 20+	6.2	11.0	6.4	14.3	7.7	19.4	10.4	29.3
Women, 20+	7.4	7.7	7.1	11.5	3.5	15.7	13.6	19.8
Both sexes, 16–19	26.3	40.0	36.3	55.0	22.7	46.4	44.4	52.1

Source: Current Population Surveys and Geographic Profiles of Employment and Unemployment, 1971 and 1980.

unemployment reached 14.3 percent, and black youth unemployment had climbed to 55 percent—nearly triple the unemployment rate for white youths.

The picture in Philadelphia is no brighter, with adult male minority-unemployment rates reaching nearly 20 percent and minority youth unemployment rates exceeding 46 percent in 1980. Diverging from the pattern in other major northern cities, unemployment rates for adult minority women increased *fourfold* in Philadelphia between 1971 and 1980.

The extent of unemployment in these four cities is not fully captured by the rates just cited, for they refer only to those jobless persons actively seeking employment during the month before the survey was taken. Thus these figures exclude workers who have given up searching and others who have dropped out of the labor force but who would work if presented with an opportunity. If such persons were included in the unemployment statistics, central-city jobless rates would, no doubt, be much higher.

WHAT NEXT?

It is certain that chronically high unemployment will plague large portions of the urban underclass so long as the demographic and job-opportunity structures of the cities move in conflicting directions. Despite a variety of public policy efforts to slow the departure of blue-collar jobs from our cities, the exodus continues apace. Government subsidies, tax incentives, and regulatory relief contained in existing and proposed urban programs are not nearly sufficient to overcome the technological and market-driven forces that are redistributing jobs and shaping the economies of our major cities.

Cities that can exploit their emerging service-sector roles may well experience renewed economic vitality and net job increases in the years ahead. However, it is doubtful that those on the bottom rungs of the socioeconomic ladder will benefit, since they lack the appropriate skills for advanced service-sector jobs. Indeed, their employment prospects could further deteriorate. New York City, for instance, capitalizing on its strength as an international financial and administrative center, experienced a net increase of 167,000 jobs between 1977 and 1981. Yet, while the city's overall employment base was expanding, its minority unemployment rates continued to climb. This is because virtually all of New York's employment expansion during the four-year period was concentrated in white-collar service industries, whereas manufacturing employment dropped by 55,000 jobs and wholesale and retail-trade employment declined by an additional 9000 jobs. These figures, together with the other data for New York City presented above, provide dramatic testimony that the urban residence–job opportunity mismatch and corresponding minority unemployment rates can worsen even under conditions of overall central-city employment gains.

The seemingly dysfunctional growth of underprivileged populations in our urban centers at a time when these centers are experiencing serious contractions in lower-skill jobs raises a number of interrelated questions: What is it that continues to attract and hold underprivileged persons in inner-city areas of distress? How are the underprivileged able to stay economically afloat? What, in short, has replaced traditional urban jobs as a means of economic subsistence for the underclass?

Answers to these questions may be found in the dramatic rise since 1960 of two alternative economies that increasingly dominate the livelihood of the urban underclass: the *welfare economy* (public housing, food stamps, aid to families with dependent children, etc.) and the *underground economy* (illegal activities and unreported cash and barter transactions). These alternative economies have mushroomed in our cities, functioning as institutionalized surrogates for the declining production economies that once attracted and sustained large numbers of disadvantaged residents.

Yet, while the burgeoning production economies of our urban past provided substantial numbers of the disadvantaged with a means of entry into the mainstream economy as well as with opportunities for mobility, today's urban welfare and underground economies often have the opposite effects—limiting options and reinforcing the urban concentration of those without access to the economic mainstream. Most urban welfare programs, for example, have been specifically targeted to inner-city areas of greatest distress, thereby providing the subsistence infrastructure that keeps disadvantaged people there. Dependent on place-oriented public housing, nutritional assistance, health care, income maintenance and other such programs, large segments of the urban underclass have become anchored in areas of severe employment decline. Racial discrimination and insufficient low-cost housing in areas of employment growth further obstruct mobility and job acquisition by the underclass, as do deficiencies in the technical and interpersonal skills so necessary to obtain and hold jobs. The upshot is that increasing numbers of potentially productive persons find themselves socially, economically, and spatially isolated in segregated inner-city wastelands, where they subsist on a combination of government handouts and their own informal economies. Such isolation, dependency, and blocked mobility breed hopelessness, despair, and alienation which, in turn, foster drug abuse, family dissolution, and other social malaise disproportionately afflicting the urban underclass.

My comments here should not be interpreted as implying that government aid to people and places in distress is unnecessary or without merit. Most urban welfare programs have had important palliative effects, temporarily relieving some very painful symptoms associated with the departure of blue-collar jobs—poor housing, inadequate nutritional and health care, and so on. Still, while some success has been achieved in relieving these pains, underlying structural disarticulations are growing worse. These disarticulations, to reiterate, are rooted in conflicting demographic and functional transformations in our cities, resulting in a widening gap between their residents' skill levels and new job-opportunity structures.

READINGS SUGGESTED BY THE AUTHOR

Kasarda, J. D. "The Changing Occupational Structure of the American Metropolis: Apropos the Urban Problem." In B. Schwartz, ed., *The Changing Face of the Suburbs*. Chicago: University of Chicago Press, 1976.

Kasarda, J. D. "The Implications of Contemporary Redistribution Trends for National Urban Policy." *Social Science Quarterly* 61 (December 1980):373–400.

Mohl, R. A. "The Industrial City." *Environment* 18 (1976): 28–38.

Muller, P. O. *The Outer City*. Resource Paper no. 75-2. Washington: Association of American Geographers, 1976.

Palen, J. J. *The Urban World*. New York: McGraw-Hill, 1975.

Zimmer, B. "The Urban Centrifugal Drift." In A. H. Hawley and V. P. Rock, eds., *Metropolitan America in Contemporary Perspective*. New York: Halsted, 1975.

Corporate Strategies and the Decline of Transit in U.S. Cities

J. ALLEN WHITT
University of Louisville

GLENN YAGO
State University of New York at Stony Brook

The urban transportation systems that carry us around are not solely the result of technological innovation or efficiency. They are also a product of the rising and sinking political and market power of industrial interest groups, the changing relations among social classes, the politics of urban development struggles, and the inherent dynamics of the economic system. We attempt to show how these factors, particularly corporate control of transportation policy, have profoundly shaped urban streetcar, automobile, bus, and rail transport in the United States during this century. We conclude that this private dominance over urban transportation policy has often led to narrow, profit-seeking behavior that has thwarted the development of more effective public transit.

In the United States two related ideas tend to dominate our thinking about urban transit systems. The overwhelming reliance on private automobile[s] is seen as the result of millions of individual transit consumers freely choosing the mode of transportation that offers them the most satisfaction and efficiency of movement. These conventional ideas of technical efficiency and consumer choice also are used to account for the less successful fate of competing modes of transit. If the streetcar or bus does not attract as many riders as the automobile, it is because these other ways of getting around town have lost out in the transit marketplace in a fair and open contest of efficiency and satisfaction.

These popular explanations of why we rely on the automobile to the virtual exclusion of other modes also are given support by established scholarly authority. For example, following in the long line of such a tradition, Meyer and Gomez-Ibanez (1981) argue that the private automobile is so popular and technically superior that it has been, and will continue to be, the preferred mode of urban transport, and that we must learn to adapt our cities to the automobile.

J. Allen Whitt is Associate Professor of Sociology at the University of Louisville. His major areas of research include urban politics, corporate elites, transportation, and work organization. Recent publications include Urban Elites and Mass Transportation: The Dialectics of Power *(Princeton University Press, 1982) and* Organizational Democracy *(Cambridge University Press, forthcoming) with Joyce Rothschild-Whitt.*

Glenn Yago is Director of the Economic Research Department at the State University of New York at Stony Brook. His research on urban transportation, housing, and economic development has been published in the Annual Review of Sociology, Comparative Social Research, *and the* International Journal of Urban and Regional Research. *His book,* The Decline of Transit, *was published in 1984 by Cambridge University Press.*

From *Urban Affairs Quarterly* 21 (1), September 1985: 37–65. Copyright © 1985 Sage Publications, Inc. Reprinted by permission of Sage Publications, Inc.

In this article we develop an alternative perspective to the technological efficiency/popular choice point of view. We have come to this alternative perspective as a result of our independent research on the history of urban transportation (Yago, 1983; Whitt, 1982). We argue that there is an important, largely neglected dimension to the creation and change of transportation systems. This dimension is the political-economic dimension which profoundly affects the character of urban transit systems, above and beyond simple technological availability, the state of consciousness at city hall, and free public choice. In addition to the classical market forces of supply and demand, there are other important institutions that operate to constrain those forces in significant ways. To understand why particular systems of transport achieve dominance, or wither, it is necessary to understand: (1) the inherent dynamics of the market economic system; (2) the historic rise and fall of the political-economic power of industrial interest groups; (3) changing relations among social classes; and (4) the struggles over urban development and land use schemes.

We cannot review all of these issues here. Our aim will be to demonstrate some of the links among economic development, social class formation, city growth, and transportation. In particular, we wish to show that urban transportation development in the United States in many ways has been under the strong influence or control (directly or indirectly) of profit-seeking corporations. Our point is that corporate control has affected public choices, contributed to transit problems, and retarded the development of more effective public transit.

It is important to point out that we are not arguing the issue of public transportation versus private automobiles. We are not saying that cars should give way to mass transit in our cities because such transit is more efficient. Rather, we are raising the issue of why the United States—almost alone among industrialized countries of the world—relies almost exclusively on automobiles to move people in our cities. We would argue that an effective urban transportation system should consist of a balanced and coordinated system of mass transit, private autos, and other modes; not the present overwhelming dominance of one mode. In other words, how do we account for the peculiar situation evident in American cities? To attempt an answer, we must look at the historical record.

At the close of World War I, Delox Wilcox, the country's earliest and most prominent transportation engineer, recognized how transportation was subordinated to the individual transit operator's interest and how that situation led to the decline of electrical railway systems.

> It must be admitted that in the development of the street railway systems and the corporations that controlled them in this country, *the idea of public service has generally been incidental.* The driving force, the motive that has negotiated franchises, consolidations, and mergers, has been for profit only [Wilcox, 1919: 34; emphasis added].

More than half a century later, Bradford C. Snell, U.S. Senate Antitrust Committee Counsel, noted in his study of U.S. surface transportation that the highly concentrated corporate power of automobile firms and their diversification into various areas of transportation manufacturing "may have retarded the development of mass transportation, and, as a consequence may have generated a reliance on motor vehicles incompatible with metropolitan needs" (Snell, 1974: A47).

Both Wilcox and Snell recognized an underlying force, the corporate profit motive, that we will argue has contributed to the decline of public transportation in the United States. Profit-seeking by both street railway magnates and automobile corporations often has proved damaging to the rational organization of city space for both social and economic needs. State intervention generally has been limited to accommodating the hegemonic interest of particular industrial groups engaged either in transit operation, as in the beginning of the twentieth century, or in transportation equipment production later in the century. Government traditionally has been limited to planning which is local, limited in scope, short range, and ad hoc; it commonly has not addressed the larger issue of the overall relation between transportation and city development. Government, we hold, has been ineffective in defending and advancing the common public interest in transportation. Corporate leaders have been allowed to engage in internal class organization and private planning in order to thrash out their common corporate interests in urban transportation, and to dominate policy and development issues.

Transportation development has been continuously subordinated to large corporate control, but the specific industrial groups exercising that control have changed with the shifting composition and concentration of corporate capital.

What follows is an exploration of the development of national transportation policy as it has been subordinated to the interests of large corporations within the United States. We are concerned with policy changes, corporate intervention in policy formation, and the influence of corporate power on the decline of public transportation, both through direct intervention in planning and through the creation of economic and political institutional frameworks that minimized the opportunities for transit development.

ECONOMIC BACKGROUND AFFECTING NATIONAL TRANSPORTATION POLICY

The historical circumstances of capital accumulation in the United States have played a substantial role in the formation of business interests in transportation.

Before World War I, the capitalist class in the United States on the whole was characterized by intraclass competition, rather than coalition. Although the patterns of industrial development were apparent by the Civil War, the development of legal structures for corporations, the role of state intervention in providing the basis for economic consolidation, and the development of market infrastructure all developed by the turn of the century. This allowed the United States to produce a more competitive manufacturing system with greater technical diversity than in Europe (Averitt, 1968).[1] Corporate financing was primarily internal, with banks entering the industrial stock market only in the late 1870s. In this more competitive situation, the possibilities for innovative transportation technology rose dramatically. Whether in the more rapid electrification of streetcars, or in the motorization

of transportation, the rate at which surplus-absorbing outlets for capital accumulation were provided was very rapid in the United States.[2] Nor was there much reliance on existing corporate giants for technological innovation. The technical convergence of growth in the automobile, oil, and rubber industries, as well as the internal expansion of cities during this period, made capital accumulation highly dynamic, and the realignment of industrial power was profound.

The initial emergence of the auto-oil-rubber nexus as representative of an industrial strategy for economic growth was the outcome of historical circumstances specific to the United States. Auto production began in earnest nearly a decade after the first merger movement in the petroleum, rubber, and steel industries began the process of monopolization (Kennedy, 1941: 135; Bunting, 1972). Auto expansion and the reorganization of corporate growth strategy was financed by the largest U. S. banks during the 1920s (Seltzer, 1928; Chandler, 1968; Edwards, 1966). These economic conditions provided a powerful base for its integration of financial and industrial automotive interests, the market expansion of basic industries (e.g., the indigenous steel and oil industries), and the stimulation of consumer demand. The decline of older rail-linked industrial groups such as coal, electric machinery manufacturing, and utilities lessened competition with auto interests and allowed the close linkage between motorization and economic growth. As contrasted with the European case, the weaker involvement of the state in accumulation at both local and national levels of government and the absence of organized labor and popular demands for transit services allowed the unhindered pursuit of motorization as a corporate strategy for industrial expansion.

The Growth Period of Public Transportation in the United States

After the Civil War, the limitations of horse-drawn trolley systems became readily apparent (Ward, 1971: 131–134). After an initial period of growth, the market for trolley systems became saturated—demand for the geographically limited transit technology was satisfied. Under these conditions the rapid innovation of the electrification of trolley lines with low per unit cost and increasing supply capability became possible and desirable. More important, the electrification of urban transportation corresponded with the growth of the electrical manufacturing industry; the most important industry of the period 1888–1900 (Passer, 1953; McKay, 1976). Urban transportation in the form of electric trolleys became part of the universal growth in public utilities investment during this period.

Electrification meant transit growth. For most of the period between 1890 and 1918, urban transportation ridership grew faster than the urban population. The streetcar network pushed cities toward their peripheries as population and industry expanded. Land speculators and transit owners spoke with one voice (and were sometimes the same person) encouraging this expansion (Wilcox, 1921: 67–100). Urban transportation was viewed by transit owners and city planners as a "moral influence" in removing people from unhealthy environments in inner cities (Tarr, 1973; McShane, 1975; Warner, 1976).[3] Because of the increased cost of investment, electrification encouraged the consolidation and concentration of transit ownership among local companies. A conglomeration of land-owning, public utilities, and financial interests (e.g., transit trusts such as Yerks in Chicago and Doherty or Mellon on the East Coast) came to dominate public transportation.[4] Similarly, the private railroads also attempted to discourage the growth of streetcar lines either by taking ownership of such lines or by developing competitive lines to drive commuter traffic away from the electrics. Rate wars and "line wrecking" were common business strategies that hampered fiscally sound urban transportation (Forbes, 1905: 35). The resulting tendency toward the monopolization of street railways by land and public utility interests and by steam railroads set the stage for electrical transportation's decline.

Although the street railway building booms of 1890–1908 were well financed, the transit monies often were pocketed through overcapitalization, corrupt accounting practices, or overextended transit lines that were unprofitable—except, of course, for land speculation and investment. The combination of corruption and poor management resulted in a total credit collapse between 1916 and 1923, when over a third of the transit companies in the United States went bankrupt (Smerk, 1975: 135). During this period capital moved toward the more profitable, less politically problematic field of automobile investment. As one major transportation financier testified before the Federal Electrical Railway Commission (FERRC) in 1919: "We insiders are selling out just as fast as we can, and when ten years are up, you won't find your Uncle Dudley or any one of us that will own a share of stock or bond in electrical transit" (FERRC, 1920: 1058).

Simultaneously with "cut throat competition," the political activity of the producers and consumers of transportation services also discouraged investment in public transit. Between 1916 and 1920, the transit industry experienced the highest level of strike activity in its history (Kuhn, 1951: 26–27). Labor costs in the transit industry increased faster than average industrial wages (Schmidt, 1935). These higher labor costs, along with wartime inflation affecting material costs, drove the ratio of operation costs to gross income of transit firms from 50% to 77%. As unionized transit workers made gains in their ability to strike, transit lines made less profit. During this early period the right to operate public transportation was granted by local government to private entrepreneurs. In the late nineteenth century citizens and consumers formed popular movements to constrain transit operating companies through their local franchise charters. As a result, the power of those transit companies was curbed and, unintentionally, these restraints helped to establish monopoly barriers to new entrants into public transportation. Franchises often prescribed the use of certain types of equipment, thus restricting innovation, and frequently they required line extensions, street maintenance, and street construction. Such practices usually served to benefit existing firms that were able to meet concomitant costs. Automobiles also benefited by extensive street construction. Finally, flat-rate fares in some franchises subsidized suburban development relative to inner-city travel.

Attempts by transit trusts to circumvent or renegotiate franchise agreements lead to overcrowding and the abandonment of lines due to service cutbacks by operators. This situation eventually lead to popular calls for public ownership. Between 1898 and 1920, every major U. S. city was the scene of legal battles, referenda over rate hikes, public ownership campaigns, and investigations of transit corruption.[5] In this politically volatile climate the corporate liberals of the National Civic Federation (NCF) intervened to consider the transit problem. As reported by August Belmont, owner of New York's transit properties and president of the Federation, the NCF's investigation determined that public ownership would be less efficient than adequate regulation (Jensen, 1956). But regulation for whom?

The government policy that resulted from NCF recommendations was typical of urban reform during the corporate liberal period. Regulation removed the political struggle over transportation from the public sphere of city politics to the forums of appointed, business-oriented, public utility and public service commissions at the state level. This was the first step in insulating transportation decisions from public pressure by the de facto disenfranchisement of the urban population. Transportation planning by appointed state-level organizations was substantially different from direct public participation in transportation policy decision making on local transportation councils and referenda.

Typically, students of urban transportation have attempted to isolate a single cause for the origin of transit's decline, particularly focusing on corruption, poor business practices, the lack of technological innovation, overcrowded service, land use dispersion, and the rise of the automobile.

However, all of these factors are linked in the change from public to private transportation organization. This change involved not merely the technological shift from rail to rubber wheel vehicles; it encompassed basic relations of labor and capital, the production of transportation equipment, and the cost of job-related travel for the working class.

By shifting from public to private transportation technology, business avoided rising labor and construction costs. Organized public transit workers could be left to attrition, and the production of automobiles and streets could be accomplished with unorganized labor. Where private companies were obligated by public franchises to lay track, the federal government would construct roads. The cost of transportation infrastructure could thereby be socialized.

The shift to private transportation would remove the volatile political issue of urban transportation from the political agenda. Consumer movements over rate hikes, public ownership, and transit corruption would be unlikely to form. Finally, the shift from public to private transportation ensured the transfer of capital investment from an increasingly restricted area of local transit operations to a more expansive one, that of national transportation equipment production.

Corporate Strategy and State Policy: The Fall of Mass Transportation

Although the corporate abuse of the "local transit trusts," capital flight from transportation, the movement toward state regulation, and the reorganization and new composition of leading corporate capital did much to start mass transportation's decline, it did not ensure its demise. During the 1920s, when public transit stagnated, an ambiguous relationship between private and public transportation developed. After the initial rash of abandonments and receiverships following World War I, conditions within the transit industry stabilized. Receiverships fell from 9% to 7% annually and remained below 18% until the Depression. Moreover, the reduction in riders and track miles could be interpreted as the first rational shrinkage in railway networks to a more financially viable economic scale (Dewees, 1970: 564–565). In addition, the decline in ridership may well have been the result of new, more honest accounting practices that became dominant as the result of state regulations during the 1920s.

The idea that more autos resulted in less public transit, an idea prominent in Federal Railway Commission testimonials and among modern historians, seems a gross oversimplification. If the ridership between 1918 and 1927 for major U. S. cities is disaggregated, we find an increase in ridership for some major cities (St. Louis saw a 3.1% gain in ridership; Chicago, a 10.1% gain; and New York City, a 37% gain; see Barrett, 1976:

418–419; memo of the effect of the automobile on patronage, APTA File .075.441). Decreases in public transportation were felt mostly by cities with less than 500,000 population (Dewees, 1970: 569).

There was an inverse relationship between automobile density and city size. In cities in which bus and rail modernization were undertaken, traffic surveys showed public transit trips increasing at a higher rate than autogenerated trips—17% compared to 25%. A sharp decline in public transportation had been arrested. Despite financial disasters and rising fares, rail transit was surviving and was cheaper than the operation of buses. Aggregate data from trade sources have shown that comparative costs and profit analysis of motor buses, electric buses, and electric streetcars during this period support the contention that existing transportation operations with bus and streetcar facilities were more economically efficient than solely bus operations (St. Clair, 1981: 579–600).

Even though transit operations retreated from the financial brink, the impact of earlier mismanagement by local transit monopolies was devastating for the equipment manufacturers (Hilton and Due, 1960). The railway equipment industry had peaked, and the absence of significant levels of new private or public investment meant that an already limited market contracted further. Meanwhile, other supplier and related industries also were in eclipse or transformation. The coal, electrical manufacturing, steel, and public utilities industrial complex, which comprised the leading growth sectors of the pre-World War I economy, changed (Duncan and Lieberson, 1970). As a newly regulated industry, public utilities were buffeted by investigations and scandals leading to the Holding Company Act of 1934. Coal and steel reoriented their production toward the growing auto and construction sectors. And electrical machinery manufacturing shifted from capital to consumer goods production. Relatively, the overall position of these industries declined.

Meanwhile, economic centralization and concentration in new growth sectors—auto, oil, and rubber—proceeded. The automobile industry provides a prime example of the concentration and centralization of capital with the rise of market oligopolies. Although the

automobile was initially developed in Germany and France in the late nineteenth century (Flink, 1970: 12), the first successful commercial automobile in the United States was introduced in 1893 (Motor Vehicle Manufacturers Association of the U.S., 1974: 11). At first the industry was small and consisted of a multitude of dynamic, highly competitive firms. For example, Flink (1970: 302) estimates that over 500 companies engaged in the manufacturing of automobiles in the United States between 1900 and 1908. However, some firms lost out while their more success[ful] competitors grew, and the industry soon began to show signs of rising concentration. As early as 1912, only seven companies accounted for over half of the U. S. production of autos. In 1908, there were 253 active automobile manufacturers in the United States; by 1920, there were only 108. Just nine years later there were 44. The industry was characterized by aggressive reorganization and acquisition by key firms such as General Motors (Yago, 1980; other Department of Justice documents on GM Antitrust suit). In the context of increasing concentration within the automobile industry, the resiliency of mass transportation, along with declines in automobile demand, produced a crisis requiring a response in corporate strategy. Although new financing and reorganization within large automotive companies had been achieved (Chandler, 1968), there remained problems of competing transportation modes. From 1923 on, the new car market was saturated (Weiss, 1961; Kennedy, 1941; Seltzer, 1928). Alfred Sloan, Henry Ford, Charles W. Nash, the National Automobile Chamber of Commerce, and others agreed that the problem required a more rapid turnover of automobiles (Flink, 1975: 145–152). General Motors led the way with strategies for frequent style changes, extensive advertising, franchise distribution, and cheap financing. Despite these changes, stabilization of the automobile market remained a threat to the industry and to suppliers associated with it. The oil and rubber industries faced overproduction and falling prices; housing construction went into decline.[6]

Corporations required long-range plans to neutralize public transportation effectively and thereby promote demand. Early automotive industrialists such as Bill Durant and Henry

Ford were incapable of establishing the cross-industrial coalitions that would be necessary to accomplish such a task (Chandler, 1968; Flink 1975). The following scenario seems likely. The spectacular investment in street railways during boom years had created large, "sunk," fixed capital costs that by the 1920s could be used at reduced expense and were thereby more competitive; this aided the mini-recovery of mass transportation in major cities during this period. Simultaneously, capital that was invested in street railways was devalued through lower productivity and use. Although the automobile industry attempted to overcome the old, fixed capital investment in street railways by promoting federally subsidized road investment ("new" fixed capital investment), thereby facilitating automotive traffic, rail transit remained a serious constraint on the expansion of automobiles and related industries, which were the centers of capital accumulation during this period.

The transportation technology that first allowed the decentralization in expansion of cities became a burden to later additional expansion. Continued urban expansion was essential in order for cities to fulfill their function as loci of economic activity and of increased capital accumulation. For this to happen, the U. S. population had to be put in cars.

It soon became obvious that the mere manipulation of conditions internal to the auto industry was insufficient to accomplish this crucial task. Ford was wrong. Solely by producing cheap automobiles, the United States would not be motorized. By 1927, Chevrolet had overtaken Ford due to Sloan's successful strategies of product diversification, marketing, and auto purchase financing (Flink, 1976; Chandler, 1968). But Sloan was also wrong: Refinements in automobile production and distribution could not accomplish full motorization. The competition from public carriers would not disappear. The stagnation of automobile demand, overproduction, and general indicators of economic crisis all led the automobile industry and its partners to develop a new corporate strategy: destruction of urban rail transit. This was accomplished by ripping up rails and replacing streetcars with buses, and by simultaneously displacing thousands of transit passengers into automobiles.[7]

The auto-oil-rubber coalition firms used various methods to promote conversion from electrical transit to buses: direct acquisition of electrical transit operating companies (as in the case of Motor Transit Corporation and National City Lines); the establishment of noncompetitive supply contracts; investments by corporate officers or managers in other transit lines; financial pressure through banks; direct or indirect loans; and trade association activities. The long and complicated history of this transformation of urban transportation is detailed elsewhere (Snell, 1974; Yago, 1980).

The consequences of the conversion were disastrous for mass transportation. In order to finance bus modernization, route abandonment became common as a cost-cutting measure, leaving many riders with no alternative to the automobile. This also hastened declining ridership by shrinking the area served by public transportation. Generally, buses were also less appealing to passengers. Moreover, bus operations were less economically efficient than mixed modal systems (St. Clair, 1981).

Local transit monopolies declined and were supplanted by a national corporate coalition of automobile-oil-rubber oligopolies. The fragmented nature of locally owned transit systems in the United States facilitated the successful penetration of this corporate strategy into local transportation development. The lack of coordination between transit systems nationally and regionally allowed the isolation of key transit systems, their conversion to buses, and the subsequent decline of rail transit. As noted earlier, industrial groups that might have opposed this corporate strategy either were now dependent on this growth coalition or had little remaining power. For example, other transportation equipment producers, such as Dr. Thomas Conway, the Brill Company, Westinghouse, and other streetcar lines, opposed conversions. Throughout the 1930s Conway called meetings to defend rail lines and to popularize the use of modernized streetcars that would reduce operating costs. However, the attempts of equipment producers and users to inform and convince civic associations, city governments and transit groups concerning the merits of modernized streetcar equipment were quashed by the superior economic and political power of

General Motors and its allied companies. The elimination of the competition electric transit posed for buses and private automobiles was a boon for motorization. As auto, truck, and bus dominance was promoted by corporate actions and spread throughout the urban areas of the United States, it became progressively more difficult for transit consumers' preferences to call forth alternatives to motor vehicles. Economist Matthew Edel shows how those persons who do not wish to drive and who would prefer good public transportation are caught in a bind of increasingly restricted choice:

> The relation of each driver to others can be described by what game theorists call the *prisoner's dilemma,* after the case of two suspects, each of whom is told separately by the district attorney that the other will confess, in which case his sentence may be harsh, each will confess to keep his risk small. In any prisoner's dilemma situation, one course can yield everyone the best result, if everyone follows it. But if not everyone follows it, then those who do make the attempt suffer a great loss. Unless there is some mechanism for ensuring that others will make the attempt, it is therefore rational to accept a suboptimal outcome and not try for the best possible result. This is the case with the automobile. For each individual it may be irrational not to drive, unless enough others also stop driving and demand good public transit.

> In this situation, to seek a psychological explanation for why individuals drive is to ask the wrong question. The problem is not why individuals drive, given the options open to them. It is why the options in American cities involve few alternatives to life in residential neighborhoods that require automobiles be used for work, shopping, and other necessary activities [Edel, 1973: 117].

The actions of the auto interests greatly compounded this dilemma, leading to the growth to overwhelming dominance of the private auto. Given restricted effective choice, the insulation of transportation policymaking from mechanisms of citizen participation, it is now difficult if not impossible to determine what the "true" preferences of transit consumers may be. Behavior becomes an unreliable indicator. Although many of us probably would prefer not to drive, we do drive as we no longer have any reasonable alternative.

State Policy: The Gradual Shift toward Motorization

State intervention into transportation policy dates back to World War I. However, until World War II transportation policy was merely an element of other policy areas such as national defense, public service, economic recovery, and urban planning. State intervention before World War I was primarily concerned with decreasing the time and cost of travel for conveying goods to market and people to work. Street railways were supportive of federally aided line extensions. But state subsidization was for construction costs alone. Line extensions, although quite useful for the factories involved, were not financially sound, and streetcar companies were locked into serving these costly and often failing lines through existing franchise agreements.

Other more indirect measures were taken that inhibited public transit, perhaps unintentionally. Restrictive franchise agreements forced streetcar companies to bear heavy tax burdens. In 1917–1918, rail taxes used in road building reached $2.25 million (FERRC, 1920: 425). Similarly, regulatory statutes created an impressive environment for rail transit. Bus companies often required less stringent public franchises or none at all, and thereby were exempt from various tax and imposed arrangements, as they did not need the exclusive access to rights-of-way. State regulatory policies and the beginnings of highway building often led to offsetting the lower operating costs of rail transit, which still had higher land acquisition and fixed investment costs.

It was not until the New Deal, when Roosevelt extended aid to urban highways in 1934 and 1936, that highway policy became an important part of personal transportation and urban planning policy. Although the New Deal was severely constrained in the amount of financial support it could give to highway development, the notion of physical infrastructural support was firmly established. The National Resources Planning Board, the Reconstruction Finance Corporation, and the Bureau of Public Roads all acted to construct constraints and biases of planning that would come to facilitate motorization after World War II.[8] Local and regional planning authorities were encouraged to draft proposals for highway projects with federal assistance. The records of the National Resources Planning Board show that chambers of commerce, manufacturers associations, and other business organizations encouraged individual states and local communities to build roads through making recommendations to state planning commissions. These organized groups dominated the recommendations to planning agencies. State legislation increased tax supports for municipal road building, and planners and engineers argued that these roads be built parallel to railroad rights-of-way. Under the direction of the National Resources Planning Board, development commissions within state planning commissions were oriented toward urban development and transportation planning. Automobile, oil, and rubber company representatives typically were overrepresented on these transportation planning boards (Yago, 1980).[9]

On the local level, measures were initiated to reduce the expense and inconvenience of private auto ownership. The task of regulating traffic was interpreted as the task of increasing traffic flows. Parking regulations were adapted to the needs of auto usage (Barrett, 1976: 400–401). Unlimited automobile accommodation through new taxes, improved roads, expanded parking facilities, extensive surveys, and systems of regulation became the goal of local planning policy. In the process, the neglect of public transportation development and maintenance became institutionalized. The impetus for such regulations came from the emerging profession of urban and traffic planners, automobile interests, motor clubs, and central city business interests that were worried about how regulations might harm central city shopping. Planning served as a response to situations and problems, not as a method for anticipating them. This notion of problem solving, so dominant in the urban planning tradition in the United States, was plainly exemplified by local transportation policy. Moreover, it left urban development particularly vulnerable to the corporate strategy of opposing mass transportation. Everything was done by state policy to promote the automobile, nothing to constrain it.

What developed was a largely unsystematic, almost accidental relationship between cities and transportation systems. Instead of comprehensive, long range, publicly determined goals for city and regional development (with plans for transportation systems that complement and facilitate overall urban development), we have cities that grow haphazardly and transportation facilities that provide inadequate service for many residents of the metropolitan area (Meyer et al., 1965; Ornati, 1968; Davies and Albaum, 1974). Although the structure of urban areas could be planned, for example, to minimize the need for unnecessary travel, the opposite condition came to exist. To the extent that there has been any urban planning, that planning has involved a virtual surrender to the automobile. As Flink (1975: 164) observes:

> Thus, instead of attempting to discourage the use of private passenger cars in cities, politicians and city planners adopted the expensive and ultimately unworkable policy of unlimited accommodation to the motor car. That American life would conform to the needs of automobility rather than vice versa was obvious by the early 1920's.

The industrial coalition that gave birth to bus conversions and motorization also organized the highway lobby that informally developed national transportation policy. As the Automobile Manufacturers Association (Memo of AMA Committee on Highway Economics, November 1, 1959, GM files R-89) points out:

> From the beginning of the automobile industry in the U.S., vehicle manufacturers have recognized their direct stake in highway development and financing policies. Both through industry wide programs and through leadership by industry executives, continuous activities have been carried out through the years.

On the state level the National Highway Users Conference, with 2800 lobbying groups decisively affected the creation of model state highway trust funds that were free from competition with other state budgetary items. Through lobbying, campaign contributions, control of various lobbying organizations, and the influence of corporate representatives on decision making bodies, highway building was insulated fiscally and politically from opposition.

A series of conferences in the 1950s and 1960s sponsored by the auto industry through the Automotive Safety Foundation (founded by the Automobile Manufacturers Association) and the National Committee on Urban Transportation (and later the Joint Committee on Highways) specified the issues to be considered by state and local officials, traffic engineers, and city planners in the process of transportation planning. Technically, transportation planning reinforced and expanded the patterns of auto domination that had been established by the mid-1950s (Holmes, 1973: 381–383). Through federal financing and profit planning conferences, state highway agencies were relieved of fiscal, legislative, administrative, and planning constraints in the implementation of freeway, primary and secondary route, and feeder route construction. This plethora of technical solutions provided state highway engineers with enormous power to counter any coalition of municipalities or civic groups committed to policy alternatives.

Highway planning was in essence an attempt to reorganize transportation policy at higher levels of government and, in successive stages, to remove it from the sphere of public decision making.[10] Because the 1962 and 1965 Highway Acts called for "comprehensive, cooperative, and continuous planning," (the so-called "3C" process) the Bureau of Public Roads was able, through various directives and instructional memoranda, to ensure that planning would be concentrated in and controlled by the Bureau and state highway offices. The language of participatory planning was reinterpreted to emphasize the technical factors rather than the social effects of highway construction. Public hearings were not intended as "popular referenda," but as trial balloons for testing local opposition, developing highway support, and constructing a political strategy for any proposed highway Morehouse, 1965).[11] This stands in great contrast to the tradition of participatory planning, a practice that has a long and generally successful history in many other countries. Moreover, in the United States as the 3C process of transportation planning (through a metropolitan planning organization) became institutionalized, the locus of planning control slipped from city hands.

At the state level, agency control over transportation planning was dominated largely through these provisions. Since the turn of the century, transit planning by city governments has been generally replaced by regional and state transportation planning agencies, agencies that stress intercity and suburban service. A recent study by the U.S. Department of Transportation indicates that in 24 out of 30 communities examined, the initiative for route selection, project staffing, and planning was taken by state rather than local agencies working through metropolitan planning bodies (U.S. Department of Transportation, 1976). The increased public opposition to highway construction in the 1960s resulted in several court decisions that tended to reinforce centralized planning. These decisions focused on procedural rather than substantive issues. The courts determined that construction could be halted if highway planners had made some mistake in the procedures. However, the power of the community in public hearings, the social and economic impact of highways, and other issues were left untouched by the courts.[12]

In addition to the planning biases of federal legislation, economic biases have abounded. The apportionment formulae allowing for heavy federal subsidization of highway construction make other transportation modes inconceivable. Less obvious is an antiurban bias. Until recently (1978) states have not been permitted to receive more than 12.5% of apportionment funds for other transportation modes (Mantel, 1971: 177–230). In the federal government's computation of cost and benefits of auto transportation, the valuations of land, pollution, residential dislocation, induced traffic congestion, energy waste, and other social costs were excluded.

Summary

A major determinant of national transportation policy as it has affected cities has been the corporate profit-making strategies of the auto-oil-rubber industrial complex, strategies that are designed to broaden market areas and to provide the physical infrastructure necessary to sell the commodities these and closely related industries produce. Transportation policy also has involved local and regional efforts to obtain capital to increase the development of land, to foster industrial construction and new housing so as to establish new bases to increase profits. Thus, capital at the national level involved in the most monopolized sectors of production and similar interests at local and regional levels involved in more speculative, less directly productive areas have been unified politically and economically in motorizing transportation.

In large measure, transportation policy reflects a profit-making and spatial planning interest of capital accumulation. Historically, the profit-making function of transportation had dominated national developments. Such policy has been developed within corporate circles, expanded through public policy bodies, supported by corporations, and transmitted into state policy. As rail transit became a fetter on expanded production and new industries, and on profit making in urban land and housing, pressures arose from the corporate sector to supplant rail with motorization policies. Although electrical transit had been the climax of industrial growth associated with other industries (coal, steel, electrical machinery), it became an obstacle to the emergence of an ascendent industrial group associated with the automobile, oil, and rubber industries. This new group took steps to constrain transportation policy by its own investment decisions, by its influence on the emerging economic structure, and by engaging in political struggles against older corporate interests associated with rail transit. Having created structural influences, corporate control over transportation policy was greatly strengthened through the participation of corporate leaders and allies in high levels of government dealing with transportation.

CONSEQUENCES OF PRESENT TRANSIT POLICY

Kapp (1963) vividly demonstrates how many serious social costs are generated by private production processes. He defines social costs as "all direct and indirect losses sustained by third persons or the general public as a result of unrestrained and unregulated economic activities." Such costs may take the form of immediate monetary losses, damages to human health, deterioration of property values, the premature depletion of natural resources, and the impairment of less tangible human values (such as aesthetic losses). There are several ways that we can examine the applicability of the theory of social costs to the political economy of urban transportation.

Every federal administration over the past 40 years has celebrated the objective of safe, cheap, and efficient transportation as the goal of transportation policy. Let us examine the federal government's policy criteria for urban transportation. During the last two decades consumers, as taxpayers, have begun to cast a jaundiced eye upon highway-dependent transportation, questioning why the goals of cheap, safe, and efficient transportation have not been met, in spite of steadily rising costs. Without effective mass transit, the proportion of personal transportation consumption expenditures ha[s] more than tripled (from 4.5% to 17.0%) in the last 70 years. The energy crisis ensures that these trends will continue. Transportation increasingly has become a private consumption item absorbed through rising auto purchase and operation and maintenance costs. Moreover, the resulting infrastructural investment in highways is a costly and rapidly expanding burden. It is becoming evident that the commitment to highway transportation with a concomitant neglect of public transportation exacts great fiscal and social costs. Direct federal expenditures since 1956 for the national highway program total between $200 and $300 billion; highway lobbyist Peter Koltnow, former president of the Highway Users for Safety and Mobility and former head of the Transportation Research Board predicts it will take even more than that amount to repair and maintain those same roads. Federal highway expenditures have not diminished the fiscal burden of unbalanced transportation on cities and states. Since World War II state and local highway debts have risen from $3.6 billion to $24 billion.

Overemphasis on highways generates many other fiscal burdens as well—police and safety services, local road construction and maintenance, and snow removal are a few. In 1973, the Federal Highway Administration conservatively estimated that 30%, or $7 billion, of direct highway expenses were not covered by highway user revenues or tolls. This does not include indirect costs of auto accidents, energy waste, and environmental damage associated with overdependence on highway traffic and resulting urban sprawl. Nor does it cover the expense of the expansion of social support services, declining urban taxes, and the abandonment of real estate that accompany the low-density land use of the auto age.

Not only do we spend more money traveling, it often takes more time and energy to get where we are going. Although transportation policy promoted motorization to overcome the barriers of space through decreased travel time, in many ways it created land use patterns that imposed new, special limits to mobility. The average time required to travel to work— the trek constituting most urban travel— generally remains about the same despite faster cars. In those urban centers that are more dependent on the automobile than public transportation, the average travel time to work has increased (Voorhees and Bellomo, 1970: 121–135; Guest, 1975: 220–225). Moreover, average blue-collar workers and the poor, consisting largely of minority populations, take longer to travel to work than they did after World War II (Greytak, 1970). Projections show average travel time to work increasing 15% to 20% by the year 2000.

That our highway transportation system wastes natural resources and fuel also is readily demonstrable. The motor vehicle industry alone consumes a substantial amount of the total U. S. steel, aluminum, lead, iron, rubber, and zinc production. As auto production and profits are based largely on obsolescence (annual style changes and lower annual years of use), resource depletion will increase, thus escalating future transportation costs. Environmental Protection Agency projections indicate resource reserves necessary for current levels of auto production will dissipate by the year 2000. Costlier extraction processes and new technologies will boost travel costs even further.

Transportation's share of petroleum consumption has increased over 50% since World War II. Cars, trucks, and buses consume 80% of the gasoline used in transportation, resulting in a tripling of gasoline use since 1950 (Office of Technology Assessment, 1975; 17–24). In Western European countries, by contrast, only 25–30% of their petroleum consumption goes for transportation, because of better public transportation, more fuel-efficient cars, and the maintenance of high gasoline prices. Public transportation, transit-coordinated land use planning, conservation, and alternative fuel uses account for those countries' lower per capita energy requirements than in the United States.

Our present transportation system also compromises our personal safety. Since World War II deaths from traffic accidents have catapulted from insignificance to the third major cause of mortality; for young people (15–34) it has become the major cause of death. Disabilities from motor vehicle accidents have increased for all age groups. Drivers regularly ignore the speed limits imposed during the 1973 oil crisis and casualties continue. Although consumer groups (reflecting public attitudes as expressed in opinion polls) have fought for seatbelts, safer construction, and airbags, safe travel has declined along with public transportation alternatives.

The future of automobile safety looks grim. Since auto usage began in the United States, well over 2 million people have been killed in accidents. Because mortality increases with decreased auto weight and increased travel distance, the reduction of car weight and increased fuel efficiency (downsizing) will likely result in increased mortality figures. In the rush to dominate the new small car market, the developmental response to energy shortages, producers sometimes have cut corners on safety. Environmental quality diminishes with the pursuit of current transportation policy as well. Air pollution provides a continued area of controversy among consumers, federal regulators, and the auto industry.

In short, it has become clear to many observers that urban transportation has become unnecessarily expensive, wasteful, and dangerous. Transportation policy largely has ignored the needs of the poor, elderly, young, disabled, and minorities. Access to employment, recreation, and urban services are thus distributed unequally. The effects on industrial policy and industrial decline in the automobile industry have been enormous.

HIGH-TECHNOLOGY RAIL SYSTEMS: NEW CONTRADICTIONS

Our analysis of the political economy of transportation has focused largely on corporate interests and strategies at the national level. We have done this to contrast certain aspects of transit development in the United States with transit development in European countries. Transportation systems also have strong and specific locational impacts, and local corporations, real estate interests, and other groups play active roles in shaping metropolitan transportation policies and systems. As the work of Harvey (1973), Molotch (1976), and others demonstrate, the struggle to obtain locational advantages and to maximize ground rents is the essence of metropolitan politics, in transit as in many other matters. Although we have not analyzed them here, such local struggles to control transportation policies, technologies, and routes are—in addition to the events we have examined—important not only in shaping transit at the local level, but also in influencing the strategies that are pursued at the national level.

A national-level analysis based on corporate actions and an analysis of local corporations and groups who compete for locational advantage and profits are both needed for a full understanding of the political economy of transportation in the United States. For example, part of the reason for the attempted resurgence of rail transit in the near past has been a recent coalition between business at the local level (e.g., corporate headquarters operations in the central business district [CBD], banks) and others at the national or regional level (aerospace and other high-tech firms).

Another important factor is the impact the long-dominant automobile is having on central cities. The story is a familiar one. Traffic often comes to a standstill as hoards of individuated, private, mostly single-passenger vehicles fight for freeway space during rush hours. Noise and exhaust fumes fill the air. The suburbs recede

even further away as more and more land is covered with concrete to satisfy the needs of the auto. Land also is taken off tax rolls by this process. The fiscal status of central cities further declines. Affluent commuters face longer and longer journeys and increasing delays. The inner-city poor are trapped in their neighborhoods and cannot get to employment opportunities. Corporations are also affected. Traffic tie-ups hurt downtown property values and retail sales. Decentralization of population and fragmentation of governmental units, brought about in part by automobility, make corporate management in urban areas difficult. At the local level, big businesses become worried about the possible and actual decline of CBD property values and the political challenge of poor urban minorities.

More farsighted corporate planners, trying to respond to these contradictions, [came] to realize that the auto-highway system may have reached the practical extent of its possible development in urban areas, and that the situation has often begun to decline—the auto is making things worse. What was once seen as highly useful for developing corporate and urban America is now seen as much less useful and often damaging.

Various urban redevelopment schemes and governmental reorganization plans are put forth to rescue urban land values and availability, and pacification programs are initiated to cool out protest of the urban underclass. In the 1960s and 1970s ambitious high-tech rail transit systems such as the Bay Area Rapid Transit (BART) system in San Francisco and the Metro in Washington, D.C., have been built, fundamentally, we would argue, as political tools for urban redevelopment and pacification. They are particularly initiated and supported, not by grass-roots citizens' groups, but by big corporations in the center city as a way to try to halt skid rows, to make suburb-to-central-city commuting easier for corporate executives and functionaries, to reinforce centralized dominance of headquarters firms and financial institutions, and to boost CBD property values (Whitt, 1982).

These expensive new systems are designed to try to reduce labor conflict and expenses by being as fully automated as possible. The aerospace industry, long subject to political fluctuations in government demand, sees them as attractive markets for products. Banks stand to make a lot of money by buying the bonds used to construct them. The public is told that these new systems will ease air pollution, reduce traffic congestion, benefit low-income groups, and make it easier to get around in the city. The actual effects usually are minimal as, in our view, the prime raison d'être for rail transit as currently conceived is urban growth and private corporate profit, not making life better for urban residents in general.

All of this leads to important contradictions. Urban business leaders want these systems to enhance capital accumulation, central city political hegemony, and corporate legitimacy. But voters sometimes do not see the "need" for them and often balk at paying higher taxes. Conflicts sometimes divide elements of the business community too over additional auto-related development versus mass transit, over how to pay for costly transit development, and over where routes will be laid and thus which local property owners will most benefit. A particularly sore spot in the business community is whether to tap highway funds in significant ways. The "highway lobby" still has a lot of clout, although it is somewhat diminished. The biggest contradiction is financial: Voters often cannot be persuaded to pay more taxes, government has traditionally been most reluctant to subsidize transit development, and the private corporations who stand to gain have a hard time—even if willing—raising the large amounts of capital needed.

At present, the result is a stalemate: After two decades of talk about new transit systems, and the construction of several, new construction of urban transit has virtually halted. These expensive projects cannot be financed without governmental subsidies, and the Reagan administration is strongly opposed to such aid. New proposals for urban transit systems will get nowhere, at least in the foreseeable future. Meanwhile, automobile dominance is unabated and the contradictions facing urban areas and central city firms grow worse. We interpret the historical record as suggesting the following general conclusions and policy implications.

The seemingly never-ending cycle of problems and contradictions in transportation continues. Within the present organization of urban transportation, the pursuit of profit satisfies private interests, and only on a short-run basis. The very "success" of private profitability in transit undermines its own foundation. New plans, investments, and problems must always be dealt with. In this context, the "solution" of one problems leads to another. In the process, this corporate drive for profits fails to serve the needs of commuters and cities for more rational, coordinated, efficient public transportation. The example of many European cities shows that this state of affairs need not exist. Our cities too often have become costly, ugly patchworks of wasteful automobiles, decaying neighborhoods, unplanned sprawl, and expensive but ineffective high-tech tools for profit. Without a significant degree of public control and grass-roots participation, continued corporate dominance over transit policy and development will lead merely to the usual profit-seeking, contradictory policies and the maintenance of anemic, minimal systems of public transport. More avenues for public participation in transit policymaking would be appropriate, as would a greater degree of publicly sponsored planning emphasizing an integration of such considerations as urban development and growth, transportation needs, social costs, and environmental impacts. In this regard, comparative studies suggest that much may be gained by emulating examples that exist in other countries.

NOTES

[1] Kolko (1978: 2–12) has argued convincingly that rapid economic growth occurred in the United States without the existence of centralized financial and capital control as many have assumed. He maintains that decentralization and local and regional authority were far more characteristic of the U.S. economy prior to 1900.

[2] In the cases of both electrification and automobilization, the process of innovation was faster in the United States than in Germany. Public transportation was fully electrified in the United States by 1895, with full German electrification not occurring until the turn of the century (McKay, 1976: 35–84). The same process appears to have occurred in automobilization (Kramer-Bardoni et al., 1971: 19–24).

[3] It also was a convenient way to displace social conflict. Henry Ford was noted for the aphorism "We shall solve the problems of the city by leaving the city." The point is that technological changes in transportation equipment made possible more rapid capital accumulation and affected the disorganization of the working class over commonly conceived problems of production and consumption. The spatial dislocation of working populations through transportation and urban physical changes separated the arenas of production and consumption struggles, thus diminishing the possibility of class struggle over such issues (Katznelson, 1976: 28).

⁴ The expansion of the electrical transit system often was not in the interests of rational transportation development, but advanced profit making by transit operators, land speculators, and banks. Ralph S. Bauer's testimony before the Federal Electrical Railroad Commission (1920: 1622) is illustrative of this point. Bauer, President of the Lynn, Massachusetts Board of Trade, noted:

> I found that a little later on in the nineties, banking interests in the Northeast became interested in the street railway problem, and believed that by consolidating these competing companies there could be evolved from such consolidation a unit system which would pay tremendous profits. . . . I further found that the ground hogs in the different communities—the land speculators—had brought certain influences to bear on the local governments which compelled the street railway to build extensions into property for the sake of adding rental and sales values to pasture land, and the politicians in charge of the localities in those times brought sufficient influence to bear on the railways to compel them to build the kind of extensions *which would never profit producing lines.*

⁵ Contrary to some current interpretations, the movement for public ownership of transit, utilities, ice manufacturing, and so on at the turn of the century was not simply a "petit-bourgeois" movement of the Progressive Era. Yago's archival research concerning the "Traction Question" in Chicago indicates working-class community mobilization (of community groups, Socialist and People's parties, religious groups), in alliance with many small business interests in the community, against what was called "the exploitation of people's needs" such as food, transportation, and electricity (Vickers, 1934; Goodwyn, 1976). Information on popular oppositional movements regarding transit during this period is available for the following urban areas: San Francisco (Bean, 1968), New Orleans (Jackson, 1969), Baltimore (Crooks, 1968), Detroit (Holli, 1969), Cincinnati (Miller, 1960), Philadelphia (Warner, 1976), and Milwaukee (MacShane, 1975). Cheape (1980) presents additional evidence of these referenda and mass protests in Boston, New York, and Philadelphia; and how these demands were transformed into regulatory management procedures in a bureaucratic framework.

⁶ Regarding descriptions of the market saturation problems of the major accumulation growth industries of this period (auto, oil, rubber, etc.), see Weiss (1961), Flink (1975: 148–160), and Sloan (1962: 208).

⁷ The most important break in the story of the decline of public transit has been the investigation by Bradford Snell (1984). Much of the present discussion is based on Snell's thorough study. He has pointed the way to the critical questions concerning transit's decline in the United States.

Snell's hypothesis has been widely contested. The regularity with which unsubstantiated claims are made about the technological superiority of highway transportation modes is astounding; it appears in both popular and scientific works. Dunn (1981: 75) states, "But the economics of the declining transit industry would have dictated much of this switch [from streetcars to buses] in any case, since buses were cheaper to purchase and operate (in the short run) than trolleys." Concerning automobiles, Altschuler (1980: 21) argues, "In the course of achieving this overwhelming dominance, the automobile appears to have become the less expensive mode for most purposes, as well as

the more rapid, convenient, and flexible." Neither Dunn nor Altschuler provides any evidence for these claims. In fact, the evidence from Germany and the United States, detailed by Yago (1980, 1983), appears to support just the opposite. Most recently, St. Clair (1980: 600) examined aggregate data from trade sources to compare costs and profits of motor buses, electric buses, and electric streetcars. He concludes that the "motor buses were consistently the least economical transit vehicle during the period 1935–1950." This includes consideration of both capital and operating costs and is the most definitive study of comparative modal costs.

⁸ The Reconstruction Finance Corporation was quite active in supporting bus conversion programs during the 1930s (APTA Files, 900.01, 308.01, various city files). As part of modernization and public service, the use of these subsidized loans aided the corporate strategy of bus conversions. See also U. S. National Resources Committee (1940).

⁹ For example, the National Advisory Committee on a National Highway Program consisted of General Lucius D. Clay, Chairman, Continental Can; Stephen D. Bechtel, President, Bechtel Corporation; David Beck, President, International Brotherhood of Teamsters; S. Sloan Colt, President, Bankers' Trust Company; and W. A. Roberts, President, Allis Chalmers Manufacturing Company.

¹⁰ The federal government financed but did not actually construct the highways as in Germany. This "pork barrel" nature of the U.S. strategy allowed for state highway departments to dispense with federally contracted monies as a way to curry support for highway spending. This maximized support and control for highway building and ultimately for planning centralization.

¹¹ This bureaucratic control of highway planning to dedemocratize it is reflected in numerous policy memoranda (BPR Policy and Procedure Memo, 20-8, August 10, 1956; see also Morehouse, 1965). This is consistent with findings of urban political scholars who have shown the loss of administrative power by large urban populations through organizational changes and control within the state bureaucracy.

¹² In most recent court cases judges have tended to emphasize procedural rather than substantive issues of transit planning. If a community could discover where a particular impact statement had failed to be filed or some hearing procedure overlooked, there was the possibility of halting highway construction. But over the substantive matters of what impact statements should consider or what the power of the community is in hearings, the court has tended to constrain any democratization of transit planning. In highway hearings, rights of cross-examination are not required, nor does an accurate court-like record need to be maintained. The courts have upheld that federal highway officials' decisions need not be reviewed (Morningside Lennox Park Association v. State Highway Department); that federal officials have the final say in determining whether procedures and plans were sufficient and proper (D.C. Federation of Civic Association v. Volpe); and that planning need not be intermodal (Citizens for Mass Transit Against Freeways v. Brinegar).

REFERENCES

Altschuler, A. (1980) Urban Transportation Policy. Cambridge, MA: MIT Press.

Averitt, R. (1968) The Dual Economy. New York: Norton.

Barrett, P. F. (1976) "Mass transit, the automobile, and public policy in Chicago, 1900–1930." Ph.D. dissertation, University of Illinois.

Bean, W. (1968) Boss Ruef's San Francisco. Berkeley: Univ. of California Press.

Bunting, D. (1972) "Rise of large American corporations, 1896–1905." Ph.D. dissertation, University of Oregon.

Chandler, A. D., Jr. (1968) Strategy and Structure. Garden City, NY: Doubleday.

———— and H. Daems (1974) "The rise of managerial capitalism and its impact on investment strategy in the Western world and Japan," pp. 1–34 in H. Daems and H. Van der Wee (eds.) The Rise of Managerial Capitalism. The Hague: Martinus Nijhoff.

Cheape, C. (1980) Moving the Masses. Cambridge, MA: Harvard Univ. Press.

Crooks, J. B. (1968) Politics and Progress: The Rise of Urban Progressivism in Baltimore, 1895–1911. Baton Rouge: Louisiana State Univ. Press.

Davies, C. S. and M. Albaum (1976) "The mobility problem of the poor in Indianapolis." Antipode 1: 67–86.

Dewees, D. (1970) "The decline of the American street railways." Traffic Q. 24 (September): 563–582.

Duncan, B. and S. Lieberson (1970) Metropolis and Region in Transition. Beverly Hills, CA: Sage.

Dunn, J. A. (1981) Miles to Go. Cambridge, MA: MIT Press.

Edel, M. (1973) Economies and the Environment. Englewood Cliffs, NJ: Prentice-Hall.

Edwards, C. D. (1966) Dynamics of the U.S. Automobile Industry. Columbia: Univ. of South Carolina Press.

Federal Electric Railways Commission [FERRC] (1920) Commission Proceedings. Washington, DC: Government Printing Office.

Flink, J. J. (1975) The Car Culture. Cambridge, MA: MIT Press.

———— (1970) America Adopts the Automobile, 1895–1910. Cambridge, MA: MIT Press.

Forbes, H. C. (1905) Public Safety and the Interurban Road vs. the Railroad Monopoly in Massachusetts. Cambridge: Cambridge Univ. Press.

Goodwyn, L. (1976) Democratic Promise: The Populist Movement in America. New York: Oxford Univ. Press.

Greytak, D. (1970) Residential Segregation, Metropolitan Decentralization, and the Journey to Work. Springfield, VA: National Technical Information Center.

Guest, A. M. (1973) "Urban growth and population densities." Demography 10, 1: 53–69.

Harvey, D. (1973) Social Justice and the City. Baltimore: Johns Hopkins Univ. Press.

Hilton, G. N. and J. E. Due (1960) The Electric Interurban Railways in America. Stanford, CA: Stanford Univ. Press.

Holli, M. (1969) Reform in Detroit: Hazen Pingress and Urban Progress. New York: Oxford Univ. Press.

Holmes, E. H. (1973) "The state of the art in urban transportation planning." Transportation 4: 379–402.

Jackson, J. J. (1969) New Orleans in the Guilded Age: Politics and Urban Progressivism, 1880–1896. Baton Rouge: Louisiana State Univ. Press.

Jenses, G. (1956) "The national civic federation: American business in an age of social change and reform, 1900–1910." Ph.D. dissertation, Princeton University.

Kapp, K. W. (1963) The Social Costs of Business Enterprise. Bombay: Asia Publishing.

Katznelson, I. (1976) "The patterning of class in the U.S." Presented at the annual meeting of the American Political Science Association, Chicago.

Kennedy, E. D. (1941) The Automobile Industry. New York: Reynal & Hitchcock.

Kolko, G. (1978) Main Current in Modern American History. New York: Harper & Row.

Kraemer-Badoni, T. (1971) Zur sozio-oekonomischen Bedutung des Automobils. Frankfurt/Main: Suhrkamp.

Kuhn, A. (1952) Arbitration in Transit. Philadelphia: Univ. of Pennsylvania Press.

MacShane, C. (1975) "American cities and the coming of the automobile in the 19th century." Ph.D. dissertation, University of Wisconsin-Madison.

Mantel, E. H. (1971) "Economic biases in urban transportation planning and implementation." Traffic Q. 25: 177–230.

McKay, J. (1976) Tramways and Trolleys: The Rise of Urban Mass Transit. Princeton, NJ: Princeton Univ. Press.

Meyer, J. R. and J. A. Gomez-Ibanez (1981) Autos, Transit, and Cities. Cambridge, MA: Harvard Univ. Press.

Meyer, J. R., J. F. Kain, and M. Wohl (1972) The Urban Transportation Problem. Cambridge, MA: Harvard Univ. Press.

Miller, J. A. (1960) Fares Please! New York: Dover Press.

Molotch, H. (1976) "The city as a growth machine: toward a political economy of place." Amer. J. of Sociology 82 (September): 309–332.

Morehouse, T. A. (1965) "The determinants of federal policy for urban transportation planning under the federal highway act of 1962." Ph.D. dissertation, University of Minnesota.

Office of Technology Assessment (1975) Energy, The Economy, and Mass Transit. Washington, DC: Government Printing Office.

Ornati, O. (1968) Transportation and the Poor. New York: Praeger.

Passer, H. (1953) The Electrical Manufacturing Industry. Cambridge, MA: Harvard Univ. Press.

Schmidt, E. P. (1935) "The development of the street railway." Ph.D. dissertation, University of Wisconsin-Madison.

Seltzer, L. H. (1928) A Financial History of the American Automobile Industry. Boston: Houghton-Mifflin.

Sloan, A. P., Jr. (1962) My Years with General Motors. Garden City, NY: Doubleday.

Smerk, G. (1975) Urban Transportation Policy. Bloomington: Indiana Univ. Press.

Snell, B. C. (1974) American Ground Transport. Washington, DC: Subcommittee on Antitrust and Monopoly of Judiciary Committee, U.S. Senate.

St. Clair, D. J. (1980) "The motorization and decline of urban transit, 1935–50." J. of Econ. History 41 (September): 579–600.

Tarr, J. (1973) "From city to suburb: the 'moral' influence of transportation technology," pp. 202–212 in A. B. Callow, Jr. (ed.) American Urban History. New York: Oxford Univ. Press.

U. S. Department of Transportation (1976) Urban System Study. Washington, DC: Government Printing Office.

U. S. National Resources Committee (1940) Urban Government. Vol. 1: Supplementary Report of the Urbanism Committee. Washington, DC: Government Printing Office.

Vickers, L. (1934) "Fare structures in the transit industry." Ph.D. dissertation, Columbia University.

Voorhees, A. M. and S. Bellamo (1970) "Urban travel and city structure." Highway Research Record 322: 121–135.

Ward, D. (1971) Cities and Immigrants: A Geography of Change in Nineteenth Century America, New York: Oxford Univ. Press.

Warner, S. M., Jr. (1976) Streetcar Suburbs. New York: Atheneum.

Weiss, L. (1961) Economics and American Industry. New York: John Wiley.

Whitt, J. A. (1982) Urban Elites and Mass Transportation: The Dialectics of Power. Princeton, NJ: Princeton Univ. Press.

Wilcox, D. F. (1921) Analysis of the Electrical Railway Problem. New York: author.

———— (1919) "Solving the traction problem from the public point of view." Presented at the 10th anniversary of the New York State Conference of Mayors and City Officials, Schenectady, NY, June 12.

Yago, G. (1983) The Decline of Transit. New York: Cambridge Univ. Press.

———— (1980) "Corporate power and urban transportation," pp. 296–323 in M. Zeitlin (ed.) Classes, Class Conflict, and the State. Cambridge, MA: Winthrop.

Problems in the Educational System

A Third of the Nation Cannot Read These Words

JONATHAN KOZOL

You have to be careful not to get into situations where it would leak out. . . . If somebody gives you something to read, you make believe you read it. . . .

He is meticulous and well-defended.

He gets up in the morning, showers, shaves, and dresses in a dark gray business suit, then goes downstairs and buys a New York *Times* from the small newsstand on the corner of his street. Folding it neatly, he goes into the subway and arrives at work at 9 A.M.

He places the folded New York *Times* next to the briefcase on his desk and sets to work on graphic illustrations for the advertising copy that is handed to him by the editor who is his boss.

"Run over this with me. Just make sure I get the gist of what you really want."

The editor, unsuspecting, takes this as a reasonable request. In the process of expanding on his copy, he recites the language of the text: a language that is instantly imprinted on the illustrator's mind.

At lunch he grabs the folded copy of the New York *Times,* carries it with him to a coffee shop, places it beside his plate, eats a sandwich, drinks a beer, and soon heads back to work.

At 5 P.M., he takes his briefcase and his New York *Times,* waits for the elevator, walks two blocks to catch an uptown bus, stops at a corner store to buy some groceries, then goes upstairs. He carefully unfolds his New York *Times.* He places it with mechanical precision on a pile of several other recent copies of the New York *Times.* There they will remain until, when two or three more copies have been added, he will take all but the one most recent and consign them to the trash that goes into a plastic bag that will be left for pickup by the truck that comes around during the night and, with a groaning roar, collects and crushes and compresses all the garbage of the occupants of this and other residential buildings of New York.

Then he returns upstairs. He opens the refrigerator, snaps the top from a cold can of Miller's beer, and turns on the TV.

Next day, trimly dressed and cleanly shaven, he will buy another New York *Times,* fold it neatly, and proceed to work. He is a rather solitary man. People in his office view him with respect as someone who is self-contained and does not choose to join in casual conversation. If somebody should mention something that is in the news, he will give a dry, sardonic answer based upon the information he has garnered from TV.

He is protected against the outside world. Someday he will probably be trapped. It has happened before; so he can guess that it will happen again. Defended for now against humiliation, he is not defended against fear. He tells me that he has recurrent dreams.

"Somebody says: WHAT DOES THIS MEAN? I stare at the page. A thousand copies of the New York *Times* run past me on a giant screen. Even before I am awake, I start to scream."

If it is of any comfort to this man, he should know that he is not alone. Twenty-five million American adults cannot read the poison warnings on a can of pesticide, a letter from their child's teacher, or the front page of a daily paper. An additional 35 million read only at a level which is less than equal to the full survival needs of our society.

Together, these 60 million people represent more than one third of the entire adult population.

Chapters 1 and 2 from *Illiterate America* by Jonathan Kozol, copyright © 1985 by Jonathan Kozol. Used by permission of Doubleday, a division of Bantam, Doubleday, Dell Publishing Group, Inc.

The largest numbers of illiterate adults are white, native-born Americans. In proportion to population, however, the figures are higher for blacks and Hispanics than for whites. Sixteen percent of white adults, 44 percent of blacks, and 56 percent of Hispanic citizens are functional or marginal illiterates. Figures for the younger generation of black adults are increasing. Forty-seven percent of all black seventeen-year-olds are functionally illiterate. That figure is expected to climb to 50 percent by 1990.

Fifteen percent of recent graduates of urban high schools read at less than sixth grade level. One million teenage children between twelve and seventeen cannot read above the third grade level. Eighty-five percent of juveniles who come before the courts are functionally illiterate. Half the heads of households classified below the poverty line by federal standards cannot read an eighth grade book. Over one third of mothers who receive support from welfare are functionally illiterate. Of 8 million unemployed adults, 4 to 6 million lack the skills to be retrained for hi-tech jobs.

The United States ranks forty-ninth among 158 member nations of the U.N. in its literacy levels.

In Prince George's County, Maryland, 30,000 adults cannot read above a fourth grade level. The largest literacy program in this county reaches one hundred people yearly.

In Boston, Massachusetts, 40 percent of the adult population is illiterate. The largest organization that provides funds to the literacy programs of the city reaches 700 to 1,000 people.

In San Antonio, Texas, 152,000 adults have been documented as illiterate. In a single municipal district of San Antonio, over half the adult population is illiterate in English. Sixty percent of the same population sample is illiterate in Spanish. Three percent of adults in this district are at present being served.

In the State of Utah, which ranks number one in the United States in the percent of total budget allocated to the education sector, 200,000 adults lack the basic skills for employment. Less than 5 percent of Utah's population is black or Hispanic.

Together, all federal, state, municipal, and private literacy programs in the nation reach a maximum of 4 percent of the illiterate population. The federal government spends $100 million yearly to address the needs of 60 million people. The President has asked that this sum be reduced to $50 million. Even at the present level, direct federal allocations represent about $1.65 per year for each illiterate.

In 1982 the Executive Director of the National Advisory Council on Adult Education estimated that the government would need to spend about $5 billion to eradicate or seriously reduce the problem. The commission he served was subsequently dismissed by presidential order.

Fourteen years ago, in his inaugural address as governor of Georgia, a future President of the United States proclaimed his dedication to the crisis of Illiterate America. "Our people are our most precious possession. . . . Every adult illiterate . . . is an indictment of us all. . . . If Switzerland and Israel and other people can end illiteracy, then so can we. The responsibility is our own and our government's. I will not shirk this responsibility."

Today the number of identified nonreaders is three times greater than the number Jimmy Carter had in mind when he described this challenge and defined it as an obligation that he would not shirk.

On April 26, 1983, pointing to the literacy crisis and to a collapse in standards at the secondary and the college levels, the National Commission on Excellence in Education warned: "Our Nation is at risk." . . .

> Donny wanted me to read to him. I told Donny: "I can't read." He said: "Mommy, you sit down. I'll read it to you." I tried it one day, reading from the pictures. Donny looked at me. He said, "Mommy, that's not right." He's only five. He knew I couldn't read. . . . Oh, it matters. You *believe* it matters!

One of the classic methods of equivocation, in literacy as in every other area where social justice is at stake, is to adhere to endless, self-repeating statements that "we don't yet know enough," "we need more research," "we are just not sure." A certain degree of caution is essential in an area of human misery that, by its very nature, challenges detection and fends off enumeration. A false humility, on the other hand—what certain activists have aptly called "Fake Humblehood"—can also be self-serving. Politicians can exploit a laborious sequence of reiterated doubts to postpone action even in those areas of which they are quite certain. Intellectuals can underwrite their income while purporting to be doing "the essential groundwork" that has already been done ten years before.

Dozens of studies of this subject have been conducted since the early 1970s. Many of them advance the ritual of recondite complexification to the point at which the reader's main reaction is exhaustion in the face of numbers and capitulation in the face of doubts as to "the proper definition" of the very words we use and "the criteria" by which we speak of an illiterate man or woman "in the context of American society." Fifteen years later, the same debates take place; and some of those who were contributors to the debates of 1970 are telling us once more that we may not yet have at hand "sufficient information" to be sure of "where we go from here . . ."

Taking action even in the context of a limited confusion ought to be one obligation of a conscientious scholar; but the confusion in this instance is compounded by the contradictory information that emerges from a multitude of government reports.

The U.S. Department of Education tells us (1983) that 23 million American adults are totally or functionally illiterate. An additional 23 million function at a level which is marginal at best.

In a separate statement, the Office of Vocational and Adult Education states that "74 million Americans . . . function at a marginal level or less."

A third release, distributed by the White House on September 7, 1983, states that "26 million Americans are functionally illiterate. . . . An additional 46 million Americans may be considered marginally functional, for a total of 72 million Americans who function at a marginal level or below."

In another statement, the Director of the National Institute of Education tells us (January 1984) that an estimated 23 million adults are functionally illiterate while, six months later,

Newsweek reports that 26 million are functionally illiterate. *Newsweek* adds that this is one fifth of the adult population, a calculation which diminishes the adult population of the nation by 40 million people.

The Bureau of the Census meanwhile states that "virtually 100 percent" of "the general population" are literate but that the figure is "about 96 percent" for "members of minority groups." The Bureau drew most of its figures from a written answer to a printed form.

A natural reaction to this arithmetic saga might be the unfortunate humility that paralyzes action on the pretext that "nobody knows." In actual fact, we do know now a great deal more than when the numbers game began. Some of the most compelling evidence has been assembled in a Ford Foundation study carried out by David Harman and Carman St. John Hunter and published in 1979. More recent data gathered in the six years since provides us with a realistic picture of the crisis we confront.

In 1973, the Adult Performance Level (APL), a study carried out at the University of Texas under the direction of Dr. Norvell Northcutt, employed a list of sixty-five "objectives"—areas of competence which were associated with Northcutt's definition of "adult success"—in order to identify how many adults were unable to cope with the responsibilities of everyday life. Previous efforts had done little more than to establish "simple literacy" and did so purely on the basis of the years of school a person had completed. Literacy, by this standard indicated little more than the capacity to sign one's name and perhaps to understand a handful of three-letter words. The Texas study therefore represented an important breakthrough in the effort to describe American realities in 1973.

The U.S. Office of Education, applying the standards of the APL, calculated that, during the early 1970s, 57 million Americans did not have the skills required to perform most basic tasks. Of that number, almost 23 million lacked the competencies necessary to function. The remaining 34 million were able to function, "but not proficiently."

Looking at a different body of criteria, Hunter and Harman reported that a maximum of

64 million persons sixteen and over had not completed high school (and were not presently in school) in 1979. While rejecting grade-completion levels as reliable determinants of literacy levels, Hunter and Harman drew attention to the fact that numbers drawn from two entirely different sources (grade completion and the APL) appeared to be so close. Hunter believes that a figure in excess of 60 million is a realistic estimate for 1984.

Calculations from other groups and other scholars indicate that even this is a conservative projection. Harvard professor Jeanne Chall, while understandably impatient with the numbers game, states that total estimates of 75 to 78 million seem to have some merit.

Most important in untangling these numbers, the authors of the APL have made their own updated calculations. They have done so in a manner that can render the statistics less abstract:

Given a paycheck and the stub that lists the usual deductions, 26 percent of adult Americans cannot determine if their paycheck is correct. Thirty-six percent, given a W-4 form, cannot enter the right number of exemptions in the proper places on the form. Forty-four percent, when given a series of "help-wanted" ads, cannot match their qualifications to the job requirements. Twenty-two percent cannot address a letter well enough to guarantee that it will reach its destination. Twenty-four percent cannot add their own correct return address to the same envelope. Twenty percent cannot understand an "equal opportunity" announcement. Over 60 percent, given a series of "for sale" advertisements for products new and used, cannot calculate the difference between prices for a new and used appliance. Over 20 percent cannot write a check that will be processed by their bank—or will be processed in the right amount. Over 40 percent are unable to determine the correct amount of change they should receive, given a cash register receipt and the denomination of the bill used for payment.

From these and other forms of evidence, the APL concludes that 30 million men and women are now "functionally incompetent." Another 54 million "just get by." This total of 84 million far exceeds all other estimates that we have seen.

Rather than throwing up our hands once more, we should recognize some explanations for these latest areas of disagreement. Some of the figures refer to 1973 compilations. Others represent an effort to update these figures, but all methods of updating cannot be identical. No one can be certain which of several methods is the best. Other differences depend on where we draw the line between the categories "functional" and "marginal." Again, this is a somewhat random matter and it simply isn't possible, or worth our time, to try to legislate an arbitrary line. The points that matter, in my own opinion, are the following: Nobody's updated figure for the "functional" and "marginal" together is less than 60 million. The total present adult population (1984) is 174 million. By even the most conservative calculations, then, we are speaking here of well above one third of all American adults.

In recent discussions with Hunter and with the directors of the Texas APL, I have proposed the following minimal estimates for 1984: 25 million reading either not at all or at less than fifth grade level; 35 million additional persons reading at less than ninth grade level. Note that, in both cases, I am speaking of performance, not of years of school attendance.

It requires ninth grade competence to understand the antidote instructions on a bottle of corrosive kitchen lye, tenth grade competence to understand instructions on a federal income tax return, twelfth grade competence to read a life insurance form. Employment qualifications for all but a handful of domestic jobs begin at ninth grade level. I have argued, therefore, that all of these 60 million people should be called "illiterate in terms of U.S. print communication at the present time." Both Hunter and the APL agree that these are cautious figures. These, then, are the figures I have used. . .

In this discussion I have been obliged to use grade levels as the benchmarks of desirable but unattained proficiency. The need to do this is a function of the need to offer standards that may have some meaning for those citizens whose only reference points are those which are familiar from their years in public school.

Nonetheless, a certain caveat is called for. Grade equivalents have little meaning in an era in which grade completion has, at best, occasional connection with the levels of proficiency that numbers of this sort suggest. Wherever grade levels do appear, it will be helpful to remember that I do not have in mind the level of a person who has "sat it out" in school for three or five or seven or twelve years. I am speaking of a person who can do what those who master the objectives of specific grades in excellent and successful schools can do: not what they are "certified to have attempted."

[Here] I have also been obliged to make use of the category "functionally illiterate" in order to refer to studies that have been conducted in the past. I do not like this term. Its connotations are all wrong. . . Wherever possible, I will attempt to use instead two terms of my own choice: "illiterate" in order to refer to those who scarcely read at all; "semiliterate" in order to refer to those whose reading levels are unequal to societal demands. At some moments, for the sake of unencumbered prose, I will combine both categories in the single phrase "Illiterate America." This does not indicate a loss of recognition of the spectrum that extends from marginal ability to none at all. What it does imply is that all 60 million are substantially excluded from the democratic process and the ordinary commerce of a print society. The distinctions are important for the organization of a plan of action; it is the totality, however, which defines a crisis we have yet to meet head-on.

One troublesome objection rears its head whenever we address this situation. Literacy, certain people say, is "an elitist concept," a residue of our excessive education, a "hang-up" from our years at Harvard or Ann Arbor. The ordinary person, whether literate or not, "can do a lot of things that are beyond our own hypertrophied imaginations," possesses simple virtues that elude us, demonstrates an ingenuity and basic hardihood that render us incompetent by contrast, and may only be endangered by our overeager plans. "People like that do very well without us. Why should we encumber them with cultural constraints they do not need? Why burden them with middle class ambitions which they may do very well without? Is literacy going to make someone *happy?*"

The simplest answer is provided by Jeanne Chall: "Does literacy make men happy? Only highly literate people seem to ask [this] question. And only the well-educated seem to say that it does not. They are like the rich who doubt that money makes one happy. Significantly, such doubts come only after they have accumulated enough money and do not have to worry. . . And so with the highly literate. They doubt that literacy will contribute to the happiness of those who are not yet literate only because they themselves use it so well and easily in living, working, playing, and in making choices. . ." So well, indeed, that they are unaware of the advantages and options it affords.

The idealization of "the simple and unlettered human being," unencumbered by our burden of self-serving and at times destructive words, might have some meaning for a people who were not surrounded and conditioned by the print reality from which they are excluded but whose skilled practitioners control the chief determinants of their existence. No community in the United States today, not even one that dwells apart in the most isolated village, is exempt from these determinants.

This, then, is an issue we should put to rest. No matter how decent and how earnest in their views, those who raise such arguments in printed prose deserve at most a swift riposte. Soon enough, they will return to their typewriters.

This much we know, and this much we should have the confidence to state in clean and unencumbered words: Whatever the "right number" and whatever the "right definition," we are speaking of at least one third of all adults who live in the United States in 1984. The cost to our economy, as we shall see, is very great. The cost to our presumptions and our credibility as a democracy is greater still. The cost in needless human pain may be the greatest price of all.

"At this point," wrote Michael Harrington, "I would beg the reader to forget the numbers game. Whatever the precise calibrations, it is obvious that these statistics represent an enormous, an unconscionable amount of human suffering. . . They should be read with a sense of outrage."

Harrington wrote these words in 1962. We have been entangled in the numbers game too long. It is unlikely that we shall escape these rituals with any greater ease today than when those words were written. The only hope, in my belief, lies in that "sense of outrage" which, with few exceptions, has been absent from the academic discourse on this subject for ten years. . . .

Teacher Expectations for the Disadvantaged

ROBERT ROSENTHAL

LENORE F. JACOBSON

One of the central problems of American society lies in the fact that certain children suffer a handicap in their education which then persists throughout life. The "disadvantaged" child is a Negro American, a Mexican American, a Puerto Rican or any other child who lives in conditions of poverty. He is a lower-class child who performs poorly in an educational system that is staffed almost entirely by middle-class teachers.

The reason usually given for the poor performance of the disadvantaged child is simply that the child is a member of a disadvantaged group. There may well be another reason. It is that the child does poorly in school because that is what is expected of him. In other words, his shortcomings may originate not in his different ethnic, cultural, and economic background but in his teachers' response to that background.

If there is any substance to this hypothesis, educators are confronted with some major questions. Have these children, who account for most of the academic failures in the U.S., shaped the expectations that their teachers have for them? Have the schools failed the children by anticipating their poor performance and thus in effect teaching them to fail? Are the massive public programs of educational assistance to such children reinforcing the assumption that they are likely to fail? Would the children do appreciably better if their teachers could be induced to expect more of them?

We have explored the effect of teacher expectations with experiments in which teachers were led to believe at the beginning of a school year that certain of their pupils could be expected to show considerable academic improvement during the year. The teachers thought the predictions were based on tests that had been administered to the student body toward the end of the preceding school year. In actuality the children designated as potential "spurters" had been chosen at random and not on the basis of testing. Nonetheless, intelligence tests given after the experiment had been in progress for several months indicated that on the whole the randomly chosen children had improved more than the rest.

The central concept behind our investigation was that of the "self-fulfilling prophecy." The essence of this concept is that one person's prediction of another person's behavior somehow comes to be realized. The prediction may, of course, be realized only in the perception of the predictor. It is also possible, however, that the predictor's expectation is communicated to the other person, perhaps in quite subtle and unintended ways, and so has an influence on his actual behavior.

An experimenter cannot be sure that he is dealing with a self-fulfilling prophecy until he has taken steps to make certain that a prediction is not based on behavior that has already been observed. If schoolchildren who perform poorly are those expected by their teachers to perform poorly, one cannot say in the normal school situation whether the teacher's expectation was the cause of the performance or whether she simply made an accurate prognosis based on her knowledge of past performance by the particular children involved. To test for the existence of self-fulfilling prophecy the experimenter must establish conditions in which an expectation is uncontaminated by the past behavior of the subject whose performance is being predicted.

From *Scientific American*, April 1968. Reprinted with permission. Copyright © 1968 by *Scientific American*, Inc. All rights reserved.

It is easy to establish such conditions in the psychological laboratory by presenting an experimenter with a group of laboratory animals and telling him what kind of behavior he can expect from them. One of us (Rosenthal) has carried out a number of experiments along this line using rats that were said to be either bright or dull. In one experiment 12 students in psychology were each given five laboratory rats of the same strain. Six of the students were told that their rats had been bred for brightness in running a maze; the other six students were told that their rats could be expected for genetic reasons to be poor at running a maze. The assignment given the students was to teach the rats to run the maze.

From the outset the rats believed to have the higher potential proved to be the better performers. The rats thought to be dull made poor progress and sometimes would not even budge from the starting position in the maze. A questionnaire given after the experiment showed that the students with the allegedly brighter rats ranked their subjects as brighter, more pleasant and more likable than did the students who had the allegedly duller rats. Asked about their methods of dealing with the rats, the students with the "bright" group turned out to have been friendlier, more enthusiastic and less talkative with the animals than the students with the "dull" group had been. The students with the "bright" rats also said they handled their animals more, as well as more gently, than the students expecting poor performances did.

Our task was to establish similar conditions in a classroom situation. We wanted to create expectations that were based only on what teachers had been told, so that we could preclude the possibility of judgments based on previous observations of the children involved. It was with this objective that we set up our experiment in what we shall call Oak School, an elementary school in the South San Francisco Unified School District. To avoid the dangers of letting it be thought that some children could be expected to perform poorly we established only the expectation that certain pupils might show superior performance. Our experiments had the financial support of the National Science Foundation and the cooperation of Paul Nielsen, the superintendent of the school district.

Oak School is in an established and somewhat run-down section of a middle-sized city. The school draws some students from middle-class families but more from lower-class families. Included in the latter category are children from families receiving welfare payments, from low-income families and from Mexican-American families. The school has six grades, each organized into three classes—one for children performing at above-average levels of scholastic achievement, one for average children and one for those who are below average. There is also a kindergarten.

At the beginning of the experiment in 1964 we told the teachers that further validation was needed for a new kind of test designed to predict academic blooming or intellectual gain in children. In actuality we used the Flanagan Tests of General Ability, a standard intelligence test that was fairly new and therefore unfamiliar to the teachers. It consists of two relatively independent subtests, one focusing more on verbal ability and the other more on reasoning ability. An example of a verbal item in the version of the test designed for children in kindergarten and first grade presents drawings of an article of clothing, a flower, an envelope, an apple and a glass of water; the children are asked to mark with a crayon "the thing that you can eat." In the reasoning subtest a typical item consists of drawings of five abstractions, such as four squares and a circle; the pupils are asked to cross out the one that differs from the others.

We had special covers printed for the test; they bore the high-sounding title "Test of Inflected Acquisition." The teachers were told that the testing was part of an undertaking being carried out by investigators from Harvard University and that the test would be given several times in the future. The tests were to be sent to Harvard for scoring and for addition to the data being compiled for validation. In May, 1964, the teachers administered the test to all the children then in kindergarten and grades one through five. The children in sixth grade were not tested because they would be in junior high school the next year.

Before Oak School opened the following September about 20 percent of the children were designated as potential academic spurters. There were about five such children in each classroom.

The manner of conveying their names to the teachers was deliberately made rather casual: the subject was brought up at the end of the first staff meeting with the remark, "By the way, in case you're interested in who did what in those tests we're doing for Harvard. . . ."

The names of the "spurters" had been chosen by means of a table of random numbers. The experimental treatment of the children involved nothing more than giving their names to their new teachers as children who could be expected to show unusual intellectual gains in the year ahead. The difference, then, between these children and the undesignated children who constituted a control group was entirely in the minds of the teachers.

All the children were given the same test again four months after school had started, at the end of that school year and finally in May of the following year. As the children progressed through the grades they were given tests of the appropriate level. The tests were designed for three grade levels: kindergarten and first grade, second and third grades and fourth through sixth grades.

The results indicated strongly that children from whom teachers expected greater intellectual gains showed such gains [*see illustration below*]. The gains, however, were not uniform across the grades. The tests given at the end of the first year showed the largest gains among children in the first and second grades. In the second year the greatest gains were among the children who had been in the fifth grade when the "spurters" were designated and who by the time of the final test were completing sixth grade.

At the end of the academic year 1964–1965 the teachers were asked to describe the classroom behavior of their pupils. The children from whom intellectual growth was expected were described as having a better chance of being successful in later life and as being happier, more curious and more interesting than the other children. There was also a tendency for the designated children to be seen as more appealing, better adjusted and more affectionate, and as less in need of social approval. In short, the children for whom intellectual growth was expected became more alive and autonomous

intellectually, or at least were so perceived by their teachers. These findings were particularly striking among the children in the first grade.

An interesting contrast became apparent when teachers were asked to rate the undesignated children. Many of these children had also gained in I.Q. during the year. The more they gained, the less favorably they were rated.

From these results it seems evident that when children who are expected to gain intellectually do gain, they may be benefited in other ways. As "personalities" they go up in the estimation of their teachers. The opposite is true of children who gain intellectually when improvement is not expected of them. They are looked on as showing undesirable behavior. It would seem that there are hazards in unpredicted intellectual growth.

A closer examination revealed that the most unfavorable ratings were given to the children in low-ability classrooms who gained the most intellectually. When these "slow track" children were in the control group, where little intellectual gain was expected of them, they were rated more unfavorably by their teachers if they did show gains in I.Q. The more they gained, the more unfavorably they were rated. Even when the slow-track children were in the experimental group, where greater intellectual gains were

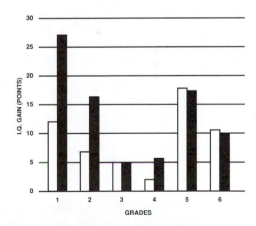

Gains in intelligence were shown by children by the end of the academic year in which the experiment was conducted in an elementary school in the San Francisco area. Children in the experimental group (dark bars) *are* the ones the teachers had been told could be expected to show intellectual gains. In fact their names were chosen randomly. Control-group children (light bars), *of whom nothing special was said, also showed gains.*

expected of them, they were not rated as favorably with respect to their control-group peers as were the children of the high track and the medium track. Evidently it is likely to be difficult for a slow-track child, even if his I.Q. is rising, to be seen by his teacher as well adjusted and as a potentially successful student.

How is one to account for the fact that the children who were expected to gain did gain? The first answer that comes to mind is that the teachers must have spent more time with them than with the children of whom nothing was said. This hypothesis seems to be wrong, judging not only from some questions we asked the teachers about the time they spent with their pupils but also from the fact that in a given classroom the more the "spurters" gained in I.Q., the more the other children gained.

Another bit of evidence that the hypothesis is wrong appears in the pattern of the test results. If teachers had talked to the designated children more, which would be the most likely way of investing more time in work with them, one might expect to see the largest gains in verbal intelligence. In actuality the largest gains were in reasoning intelligence.

It would seem that the explanation we are seeking lies in a subtler feature of the interaction of the teacher and her pupils. Her tone of voice, facial expression, touch and posture may be the means by which—probably quite unwittingly—she communicates her expectations to the pupils. Such communication might help the child by changing his conception of himself, his anticipation of his own behavior, his motivation or his cognitive skills. This is an area in which further research is clearly needed.

Why was the effect of teacher expectations most pronounced in the lower grades? It is difficult to be sure, but several hypotheses can be advanced. Younger children may be easier to change than older ones are. They are likely to have less well-established reputations in the school. It may be that they are more sensitive to the processes by which teachers communicate their expectations to pupils.

It is also difficult to be certain why the older children showed the best performance in the follow-up year. Perhaps the younger children, who by then had different teachers, needed

continued contact with the teachers who had influenced them in order to maintain their improved performance. The older children, who were harder to influence at first, may have been better able to maintain an improved performance autonomously once they had achieved it.

In considering our results, particularly the substantial gains shown by the children in the control group, one must take into account the possibility that what is called the Hawthorne effect might have been involved. The name comes from the Western Electric Company's Hawthorne Works in Chicago. In the 1920's the plant was the scene of an intensive series of experiments designed to determine what effect various changes in working conditions would have on the performance of female workers. Some of the experiments, for example, involved changes in lighting. It soon became evident that the significant thing was not whether the worker had more or less light but merely that she was the subject of attention. Any changes that involved her, and even actions that she only thought were changes, were likely to improve her performance.

In the Oak School experiment the fact that university researchers, supported by Federal funds, were interested in the school may have

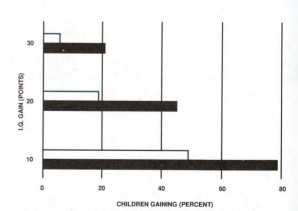

Children in lower grades showed the most dramatic gains. The chart shows the percent of children in the first and second grades by amount of their gains in I.Q. points. Again dark bars represent experimental-group children, light bars control-group children. Two lower sets of bars include children from higher groups, so that lowest set sums results.

led to a general improvement of morale and effort on the part of the teachers. In any case, the possibility of a Hawthorne effect cannot be ruled out either in this experiment or in other studies of educational practices. Whenever a new educational practice is undertaken in a school, it cannot be demonstrated to have an intrinsic effect unless it shows some excess of gain over what Hawthorne effects alone would yield. In our case a Hawthorne effect might account for the gains shown by the children in the control group, but it would not account for the greater gains made by the children in the experimental group.

Our results suggest that yet another base line must be introduced when the intrinsic value of an educational innovation is being assessed. The question will be whether the venture is more effective (and cheaper) than the simple expedient of trying to change the expectations of the teacher. Most educational innovations will be found to cost more in both time and money than inducing teachers to expect more of "disadvantaged" children.

For almost three years the nation's schools have had access to substantial Federal funds under the Elementary and Secondary Education Act, which President Johnson signed in April, 1965. Title I of the act is particularly directed at disadvantaged children. Most of the programs devised for using Title I funds focus on overcoming educational handicaps by acting on the child—through remedial instruction, cultural enrichment and the like. The premise seems to be that the deficiencies are all in the child and in the environment from which he comes.

Our experiment rested on the premise that at least some of the deficiencies—and therefore at least some of the remedies—might be in the schools, and particularly in the attitudes of teachers toward disadvantaged children. In our experiment nothing was done directly for the child. There was no crash program to improve his reading ability, no extra time for tutoring, no program of trips to museums and art galleries. The only people affected directly were the teachers; the effect on the children was indirect.

It is interesting to note that one "total push" program of the kind devised under Title I led in three years to a 10-point gain in I.Q. by 38 percent of the children and a 20-point gain by 12 percent. The gains were dramatic, but they did not even match the ones achieved by the control-group children in the first and second grades of Oak School. They were far smaller than the gains made by the children in our experimental group.

Perhaps, then, more attention in educational research should be focused on the teacher. If it could be learned how she is able to bring about dramatic improvement in the performance of her pupils without formal changes in her methods of teaching, other teachers could be taught to do the same. If further research showed that it is possible to find teachers whose untrained educational style does for their pupils what our teachers did for the special children, the prospect would arise that a combination of sophisticated selection of teachers and suitable training of teachers would give all children a boost toward getting as much as they possibly can out of their schooling.

CHAPTER
11

Ageism

"Second Childhood": Old Age in Popular Culture

ARNOLD ARLUKE

JACK LEVIN

There is an extreme and unremitting bias against older adults in America, a bias so prevalent that it has been given the name "ageism" (Butler, 1968). Psychologically, ageism can be regarded as an attitude—a negative evaluation that serves to orient individuals toward old people as a group. In particular, it frequently predisposes individuals to discriminate; that is, to avoid contact, victimize, or otherwise do injury to old people based on their age status alone. Ageism is also a tendency to stereotype old people—which is, of course, another form of injury. We picture them as rigid, meddlesome, sexless, conservative, unhealthy, inactive, lonely, forgetful, and not very bright (Levin and Levin, 1980).

Many stereotypes portray old age as a time of second childhood. This dim view of the elderly suggests that they are losing, or have lost, the very things a growing child gains. It implies a backward movement to earlier developmental stages, with no recognition of the lifetime of experience that unquestionably separates the elderly from children (Gresham, 1973).

The image of old people as childlike has been with us for a long time. Tuckman and Lorge (1953) asked graduate students in psychology to indicate their agreement or disagreement with a number of statements about old people. Despite the fact that their subjects were well acquainted with psychology and enrolled in a course involving the aging process, there was a high level of agreement that old people like to collect many useless things, are poorly coordinated, cannot taste differences in foods, have to go to bed early, need a nap every day, are in the "happiest" period of their lives, cannot manage their own affairs, and are in their second childhood.

More recent research indicates that stereotyping continues to be an integral part of public images of the aged, and that a major thrust of this stereotyping still perpetuates the second childhood image. McTavish (1971) found considerable acceptance of an image of old people that is distinctly reminiscent of the toddler image known as "the terrible twos." Many of his subjects felt that old people are likely to be annoying, complaining, and inconsiderate. In 1975, the National Council on the Aging reported the results of a survey of 4254 adult Americans (Harris, 1975). Old people were generally thought of as useless and inactive by participants in the survey. Subjects agreed that the elderly spend most of their time watching television or "doing nothing" in the true spirit of directionless adolescence.

Our society has not always mistreated or stereotyped its old people. In colonial America it was youth who encountered ageism. According to Fischer (1977), aged Americans living 200 years ago commanded inordinate respect, power, and privilege. Under Puritanism, old age was regarded as a sign of election and a special gift from God. In their dress and hairstyles, early Americans frequently tried to make themselves out to be older than they really were. Men would hide their natural hair beneath a wig, or they would powder their own hair to give it a white color associated with advanced age. Until the nineteenth century, the census taker frequently found that citizens represented themselves as older than they were. Today's census taker finds misrepresentations of age too, but in the opposite direction.

During the nineteenth century the privileged status of old age began to deteriorate as America modernized. First, as levels of literacy and education increased, there was less reliance on the older generation as a source of knowledge. Since the young became better educated, they began to hold a competitive edge with respect to jobs, status, and power. This led, second, to a retirement that reduced the standard of living and social status of the aged. Third, the nuclear family became more prevalent, so that older members of society were expected to live apart in independent households or to seek care. And finally, in the shift from agriculture to industry, older members of society lost control over land and were forced instead to compete with younger persons for nonagricultural positions.

By the twentieth century, ageism had become a cultural phenomenon—part of the normative order of our society. As such it was passed from generation to generation through the process of socialization much like other cultural phenomena—love of country and church, motherhood, the success ethic, and so forth. The result is that there is now widespread acceptance of ageism crosscutting differences in age, region, social class, and occupation. Studies have recorded agreement with age stereotypes not only among groups of physicians, nurses, ministers, and middle-aged children of aged parents, but also among institutionalized older persons and gerontologists.

Since ageism is so prevalent in society at large, it is hardly surprising to find ageism in popular culture which expresses, and in turn transmits, age prejudice. Television, in particular, has consistently assigned negatively stereotyped roles to the aged when it has not ignored the aged altogether. As revealed in his study of characters appearing in prime-time network TV drama, Aronoff (1974) reports that the aged comprised less than 5 percent of all characters, about half of the proportion that they actually occupied in the population of the United States at the time of his study. When they did appear, the aged tended to be depicted as evil, unsuccessful, and unhappy. TV commercials have similarly ignored or stereotyped the aged. One study found that only two out of 100 television commercials contained older characters (Francher, 1973). The focus of attention was on the "Pepsi Generation"—young and attractive characters who promise youthful appearance or behavior.

Newspapers are little better than television in their treatment of the elderly. According to MacDonald's (1973) analysis of 265 articles on the subject of aging, all appearing in a large Midwestern newspaper, old people who are still active in their communities are ignored. The newspaper focus is largely on the problems of old age or the mere "human interest" side, which features retirees graduating from college at seventy-five or reminiscing about the "good old days."

Age stereotypes characterize the portrayal of old people in prescription drug advertisements as well. Smith (1976) found aged models in drug ads frequently described solely on the basis of old age as disruptive, apathetic, temperamental, and out of control.

Even birthday cards perpetuate age stereotypes. A study by Demos and Jache (1981) found contemporary birthday cards often depicting old age as a time of physical, sexual, and intellectual decline.

INFANTILIZING ELDERS

Most pernicious, perhaps, of all age stereotypes is that of "second childhood." It is certainly the most widely represented in popular culture. There are at least six ways in which second childhood is portrayed:

Old people and children are paired with each other. A TV commercial for "Country-Time Lemonade" shows an elderly man with children gathered round him as he claims that this tastes as good to him as lemonade did when he was young. A DuPont commercial shows an old man and young boy floating along in a small boat enjoying their idle time. A magazine ad for Yashica cameras has an old man snapping pictures of a small girl holding a stuffed dog, while an ad for the prescription drug Isuprel features an old man blowing bubbles as a young girl sits on his lap and watches him intently.

One seemingly favorable interpretation of these juxtapositions of age and youth is that children and the elderly share a special bond and that such pairing need not suggest that old people are childlike. Yet the equally plausible interpretation—and the tone of the ads heavily leans this way—is that they both have a lot of personality characteristics in common.

Some pairings of children and elders are not subtle. They clearly suggest the second childhood image of old age. Note the 1979 movie *Just You and Me, Kid* costarring teenager Brooke Shields and elder George Burns. Newspaper ads showed the two stars playing stickup and described the film as "the story of two juvenile delinquents." In an article called "The Fun Life for Young and Old," the *Boston Globe* provided "a guide to August activities for senior citizens and children." Pictures were shown of a puppet show and a magic act. Even the "Kiddies' Menu" of a popular Massachusetts ice cream parlor portrays an older man walking hand-in-hand with a young boy. As clearly stated on the face of the menu, "for all kids under 10 and over 65," the bill of fare consists of a "hot doggie," "kiddie burger," and "peanut butter and jelly sandwich."

Old people are given the personality and moods of children. It is common in prescription drug ads to describe the symptoms of senility in terms normally associated with the personality and behavior of children. A Mellaril ad "for the agitated geriatric" shows an elderly man angrily waving his fist. "Tantrums" is printed large across the page. Other drug ads for senility use terms such as "nuisance," "torment," "disruptive," "obstreperous," and "disorderly behavior" to describe elderly behavior. The recent children's book *How Does It Feel to Be Old?* also implies a delinquent side of the aged personality. At one point, the elderly woman who is explaining to a young girl what it is like to be old compares herself to a "demon" who is "cranky." TV shows and movies characterize the personality of older people as childlike, whether it is "Mother Jefferson's" cantankerousness, the silliness of Johnny Carson's "Aunt Blabby," or the impulsiveness and recklessness of Ruth Gordon in *Harold and Maude*.

Old people are given the dress and appearance of children. On the cover of one birthday card is a blackboard with "You're only young once!" chalked on it along with various doodles. Inside, an overweight, unshaven elderly man smoking a cigar is wearing a summer camp tee shirt, shorts, sneakers, and cap and is playing with a yo-yo and baseball bat. Above his grinning face the card says "Happy Birthday, Playboy." Clearly, the card suggests that you can be young twice—so young that "playboy" literally refers to the old man playing in his

summer camp outfit. Equally childlike is an ad in *Esquire* showing an elderly woman dressed in a football helmet and varsity sweater playing an electronic football game.

Old people are given the physical problems of children. One ad for catheters, which appears in a geriatric nursing journal, shows the forearms and hands of a baby as its model instead of an elder. The caption below notes that at "Delmed, we don't want to hurt anyone's feelings." A prescription drug ad for the stool softener Doxidan features a smiling bifocaled older woman. The text reads: "Minnie moved her bowels today. The day started right for Minnie. That young doctor feller gave her Doxidan to take last night. And it worked! Minnie figures she's got the smartest doctor in town." It is not too farfetched to imagine that Minnie's smile not only expresses her physical relief but also her pride at being told she moved her bowels. Then again, on the cover of one birthday card is a large bottle of milk of magnesia wrapped in a bright red bow. Above the bottle the card says "Aging." On opening the card, the message reads: ". . . age is nature's way of telling us to wear looser underwear. May your birthday be anything but regular." One image suggested by this card is that of an elder in diapers.

Old people are given the activities and playthings of children. Parties for old people are characterized as children's parties. In a suburban small-town newspaper, a recent article reported that the patients at a local nursing home "held their very own Christmas party." The article went on to indicate that patients "planned the party, made the invitations, decorated the cookies made by the chef, and took part in the entertainment, which included group singing of Christmas Carols." The article thanked a local drugstore for supplying "Santa's gifts." The intentions were admirable, but the message rang loud and clear: Old people are like big children. Posters in a popular chain of fast-food restaurants urge customers to "have a senior birthday party at McDonald's." For the "birthday kid" who is "young at heart," McDonald's offers to provide the cake, hats, and party favors. Also consider Bell Telephone's ad for its custom phones which can be given as gifts to "celebrate any occasion." One such occasion is "Gertrude's" retirement party, complete with colorful ribbons and balloons. In honor of her retirement, Gertrude is shown receiving her own Snoopy phone from her coworkers. A similar Bell Telephone ad shows an elder receiving a Mickey Mouse phone at a party.

Even the "play" of elders is depicted to imply that they are children. A department store ad in *TV Guide* shows an elderly man riding a child's three-wheeler. The caption reads: "Wish they had Hot Cycles when I was a kid. . . . Yep, kids sure are lucky today. Hey, maybe when no one's around. . . ." Haldol, a prescription drug used to treat symptoms associated with organic brain syndrome, claims in an ad that it "usually leaves the disturbed elderly patient in the nursing home more alert, more responsive." The photograph of an elderly woman shows her smiling limply and holding a large red-and-white-checked cloth flower. Above her is the caption: "I made a flower today." A similar arts-and-crafts portrayal of the aged appears in a Roniacol ad, a drug used to improve circulation. Three elders who are "deficient in peripheral circulation" but "proficient in the 'home'" are shown hard at work making clay pots.

The role of old people is reversed. Popular culture frequently portrays old people as the children of middle-aged parents. The *Boston Globe* recently ran an article on "Foster Care for the Elderly" which included a photograph of a "foster elder" standing in his room. What particularly stresses the role reversal is the caption under the photograph. It notes that "Joe Dionne lives with a family in Charlton. He helps with their chores and joins their trips." On one TV program, a comedian told the following story: "A small boy was sitting at a curb crying. An old man passed by and kindly asked, 'Why are you crying, Sonny?' 'Because I can't do what the big boys do.' So the old man sat down and cried too." On TV's popular series "The Rockford Files," star James Garner frequently gets his aging father Rocky out of trouble.

We can also observe role reversal in prescription drug ads. In an ad for Hydergine, an older woman is shown suffering "gray area" symptoms such as confusion, lack of self-care, dizziness, moodiness, and unsociability. Large print superimposed over her face reads: "I got lost—lost in my own neighborhood. . . .

Yesterday I was going to the grocery store . . . and suddenly didn't know the way. I was all mixed up . . . I thought it was the old neighborhood. It frightened me—and it's not the first time. My children say it's my second childhood. It's not fair, I took care of them as kids. Please, doctor . . . what's happening to me?" Similarly, an ad for Pneumovax, an antipneumonia vaccine, shows an elderly man at his birthday party. Noticeably taller are a middle-aged man and woman who are throwing the party for their aged father just as they would for their children who are also in the picture. Like the baby held by the elderly man, the caption reads "Grandpa's a year older."

IMPLICATIONS

Casting old people as children has detrimental effects on old and young alike. The "second-childhood" stereotype tends to make young people feel distant from their elders. Having just graduated from childhood, what adolescent wants to endure it again by associating with the old? The stereotype may well also encourage gerontophobia, the neurotic fear of old age. How many adults want to be thought of one day as a 6-year-old who has nothing to do but play with yo-yos, or as a cranky 2-year-old who is not toilet trained?

For old people, the second-childhood stereotype creates a self-fulfilling prophecy: After being socialized from an early age, many elderly people come to accept the second-childhood stereotype and play the infantilized role with enthusiasm. But is that because they fail to see any alternative? Our society has traditionally offered certain rewards to those elderly citizens who are willing to "stay in their place." Riding on a special bus for senior citizens, or dancing with other seniors to the tune of "Yankee Doodle" may isolate elderly people. But it may be preferable to watching reruns of "Marcus Welby."

Acting like children has three negative consequences for old people. First, such behavior lowers their social status because their individual responsibility has been diminished, while their dependency has increased. Second, the perception of infantile behavior in the elderly may allow certain things to be done to them that would otherwise not be considered: the prescription of psychoactive medications, institutionalization, and declaration of legal incompetency. Third, infantilization robs the "gray power" movement of adults who might otherwise work for political change and social betterment.

But not all old people buy the second-childhood stereotype. A large number of elderly Americans are thoroughly offended by infantilization and seek to avoid the consequences of the stereotype. For many, this means making efforts to "pass" for middle-age by dying hair, lying about their age, and using youth-oriented cosmetics. A positive form of avoidance is reengagement, whereby old people seek to become either reemployed or remarried after the loss of a job or spouse. On the damaging side, an unknown number of cases of apparent senility (organic brain dysfunction) may actually represent a refusal to accept the second-childhood syndrome. Rather than comply, some elders may retreat into a more comfortable, more secure psychological state which ironically has the appearance of infantile behavior. For example, we might see lack of sexual interest, giddiness, forgetfulness, inability to maintain a stable relationship, and lack of control over bodily functions.

In contrast to mere avoidance, a growing number of elderly people have become aggressive in their response to attempts to infantilize them. This aggressive reaction seeks not to deny the second-childhood stereotype but to eliminate it. When the readers of *Retirement Living* magazine were asked to choose from a list of twelve words those that most accurately describe the way Americans over sixty are portrayed on television, their top three choices were "ridiculous," "decrepit," and "childish" (Hemming and Ellis, 1976). The Gray Panthers' Media Watch Task Force is an important example of an organized effort to improve media images of the elderly in general and to eliminate the second-childhood stereotype in particular.

Clearly, efforts ought to be made to end the media's infantilization of the aged. Yet it must be remembered that the problem does not lie with the media. Take for example the Kellogg's Rice Krispies ad which shows an elderly man and woman posed in a romantic embrace. The caption reads: "It's a perfect night for sparkin' on the front swing. For love that's still young." Aside from the ageist reference to young love, the Rice Krispies ad seems to go thoughtfully out of its way to avoid depicting older people as stereotypes. Indeed, they are portrayed in an activity—lovemaking—which although commonly associated with young adults is nonetheless not to be denied their elders as well.

Yet frustratingly, the problem is not thereby solved. The media in this case, via the Rice Krispies ad, has treated the aged with dignity. But readers' responses to the ad—"Aren't they cute! Aren't they sweet!"—are exactly those with which those same readers would greet the inappropriate behavior of children attempting to act like adults. Ageism is so deeply ingrained in our culture that an audience may interpret even the noblest ad to conform to its ageist predispositions.

REFERENCES

Aronoff, C. "Old Age in Prime-Time." *Journal of Communications* 24 (1974): 86–87.

Butler, R. "Age-ism: Another Form of Bigotry." *Gerontologist* 9 (1969): 243–46.

Demos, V., and Jache, A. "When You Care Enough: An Analysis of Attitudes toward Aging in Humorous Birthday Cards." *Gerontologist* 21 (1981): 209–15.

Francher, J. S. "It's the Pepsi Generation: Accelerated Aging and the Television Commercial." *International Journal of Aging and Human Development* 4 (1973): 245–55.

Gresham, M. "The Infantilization of the Elderly." *Nursing Forum* 15 (1976): 196–209.

Harris, L., and Associates. *The Myth and Reality of Aging in America.* New York: National Council on Aging, 1975.

Hemming, R., and Ellis, K. "How Fair Is T.V.'s Image of Older Americans?" *Retirement Living* (April 1976): 21–24.

Levin, J., and Levin, W. *Ageism: Prejudice and Discrimination against the Elderly.* Belmont, Calif: Wadsworth, 1980.

MacDonald, R. "Content Analysis of Perceptions of Aging as Represented by the News Media." Presented at the 26th Annual Meeting of the Gerontological Society, 1973.

McTavish, D. G. "Perceptions of Old People: A Review of Research, Methodologies, and Findings." *Gerontologist* 11 (1971): 90–101.

Smith, M. C. "Portrayal of the Elderly in Prescription Drug Advertising." *Gerontologist* 16 (1976): 329–34.

Tuckman, J., and Lorge, I. "Attitudes toward Old People." *Journal of Social Psychology* 37 (1953): 249–60.

Communal Life-Styles for the Old

ARLIE RUSSELL HOCHSCHILD

The 43 residents of Merrill Court (a small apartment building near the shore of San Francisco Bay), 37 of them women, mainly conservative, fundamentalist widows from the Midwest and Southwest, don't seem likely candidates for "communal living" and "alternatives to the nuclear family." Nonetheless, their community has numerous communal aspects. Without their "old-agers commune" these 60-, 70- and 80-year-olds would more than likely be experiencing the disengagement from life that most students of aging have considered biologically based and therefore inevitable.

The aged individual often has fewer and fewer ties to the outside world, and those which he or she does retain are characterized by less emotional investment than in younger years. This case study, however, presents evidence that disengagement may be situational—that how an individual ages depends largely on his social milieu, and that socially isolated older people may disengage but that older people supported by a community of appropriate peers do not.

RURAL WAYS IN URBAN SETTINGS

Merrill Court is a strange mixture of old and new, of a vanishing Oakie culture and a new blue-collar life-style, of rural ways in urban settings, of small-town communities in mass society, of people oriented toward the young in an age-separated subculture. These internal immigrants to the working-class neighborhoods of West Coast cities and suburbs perceive their new environment through rural and small-town eyes. One woman who had gone shopping at a department store observed "all those lovely dresses, all stacked like cordwood." A favorite saying when one was about to retire was, "Guess I'll go to bed with the chickens tonight." They would give directions to the new hamburger joint or hobby shop by describing its relationship to a small stream or big tree. What remained of the old custom of a funeral wake took place at a new funeral parlor with neon signs and printed notices.

The communal life which developed in Merrill Court may have had nothing to do with rural ways in an urban setting. Had the widows stayed on the farms and in the small towns they came from, they might have been active in community life there. Those who had been involved in community life before remained active and, with the exception of a few, those who previously had not, became active.

For whatever reason, the widows built themselves an order out of ambiguity, a set of obligations to the outside and to one another where few had existed before. It is possible to relax in old age, to consider one's social debts paid, and to feel that constraints that do not weigh on the far side of the grave should not weigh on the near side either. But in Merrill Court, the watchfulness of social life, the Protestant stress on industry, thrift and activity added up to an ethos of keeping one's "boots on," not simply as individuals but as a community.

FORMING THE COMMUNITY

"There wasn't nothin' before we got the coffee machine. I mean we didn't share nothin' before Mrs. Bitford's daughter brought over the machine and we sort of had our first occasion, you might say."

From *Society,* July/August 1973. Published by permission of Transaction Publishers, from *Society,* Vol. 10, No. 5. Copyright © 1973 by Transaction Publishers.

There were about six people at the first gathering around the coffee machine in the recreation room. As people came downstairs from their apartments to fetch their mail, they looked into the recreation room, found a cluster of people sitting down drinking coffee, and some joined in. A few weeks later the recreation director "joined in" for the morning coffee and, as she tells it, the community had its start at this point.

Half a year later Merrill Court was a beehive of activity: meetings of a service club; bowling; morning workshop; Bible study classes twice a week; other classes with frequently changing subjects; monthly birthday parties; holiday parties; and visits to four nearby nursing homes. Members donated cakes, pies and soft drinks to bring to the nursing home, and a five-piece band, including a washtub bass, played for the "old folks" there. The band also entertained at a nearby recreation center for a group of Vietnam veterans. During afternoon band practice, the women sewed and embroidered pillow cases, aprons and yarn dolls. They made wastebaskets out of discarded paper towel rolls, wove rugs from strips of old Wonder Bread wrappers, and Easter hats out of old Clorox bottles, all to be sold at the annual bazaar. They made placemats to be used at the nursing home, tote-bags to be donated to "our boys in Vietnam," Christmas cards to be cut out for the Hillcrest Junior Women's Club, rag dolls to be sent to the orphanage, place cards to be written out for the bowling league banquet, recipes to be written out for the recipe book that was to go on sale next month, and thank you and condolence cards.

SOCIAL PATTERNS

The social arrangements that took root early in the history of Merrill Court later assumed a life of their own. They were designed, as if on purpose, to assure an "on-going" community. If we were to visually diagram the community, it would look like a social circle on which there are centripedal and centrifugal pressures. The formal role system, centered in the circle, pulled people toward it by giving them work and rewards, and this process went on mainly "downstairs," in the recreation room. At the same time, informal loyalty networks fluctuated toward and away from the circle. They became clear mainly "upstairs," where the apartments were located. Relatives and outsiders pulled the individual away from the circle downstairs and network upstairs although they were occasionally pulled inside both.

DOWNSTAIRS

Both work and play were somebody's responsibility to organize. The Merrill Court Service Club, to which most of the residents and a half-dozen nonresidents belonged, set up committees and chairmanships that split the jobs many ways. There was a group of permanent elected officials: the president, vice-president, treasurer, secretary and birthday chairman, in addition to the recreation director. Each activity also had a chairman, and each chairman was in charge of a group of volunteers. Some officers were rotated during the year. Only four club members did not chair some activity between 1965 and 1968; and at any time about a third were in charge of something.

FRIENDSHIP NETWORKS

Shadowing the formal circle was an informal network of friendships that formed over a cup of coffee in the upstairs apartments. The physical appearance of the apartments told something about the network. Inside, each apartment had a living room, kitchen, bedroom and porch. The apartments were unfurnished when the women moved in and as one remarked, "We fixed 'em up just the way we wanted. I got this new lamp over to Sears, and my daughter and I bought these new scatter rugs. Felt just like a new bride."

For the most part, the apartments were furnished in a remarkably similar way. Many had American flag stickers outside their doors. Inside, each had a large couch with a floral design, which sometimes doubled as a hide-a-bed where a grandchild might sleep for a weekend. Often a chair, a clock or picture came from the old home and provided a material link to the past. Most had large stuffed chairs, bowls of homemade artificial flowers, a Bible and porcelain knick-knacks neatly arranged on a table. (When the group was invited to my own apartment for tea, one woman suggested sympathetically that we "had not quite moved in yet" because the apartment seemed bare by comparison.) By the window were potted plants, often grown from a neighbor's slip. A plant might be identified as "Abbie's ivy" or "Ernestine's African violet."

Photographs, usually out of date, of pink-cheeked children and grandchildren decorated the walls. Less frequently there was a photo of a deceased husband and less frequently still, a photo of a parent. On the living room table or nearby there was usually a photograph album containing pictures of relatives and pictures of the woman herself on a recent visit "back East." Many of the photographs in the album were arranged in the same way. Pictures of children came first and, of those, children with the most children appeared first, and childless children at the end.

The refrigerator almost always told a social story. One contained homemade butter made by the cousin of a woman on the second floor; berry jam made by the woman three doors down; corn bought downstairs in the recreation room, brought in by someone's son who worked in a corn-canning factory; homemade Swedish rolls to be given to a daughter when she came to visit; two dozen eggs to be used in cooking, most of which would be given away; as well as bread and fruit, more than enough for one person. Most of the women had once cooked for large families, and Emma, who raised eight children back in Oklahoma, habitually baked about eight times as much corn bread as she could eat. She made the rounds of apartments on her floor distributing the extra bread. The others who also cooked in quantities reciprocated, also gratuitously, with other kinds of food. It was an informal division of labor although no one thought of it that way.

Most neighbors were also friends, and friendships as well as information about them, were mainly confined to each floor. All but four had their *best* friends on the same floor and only a few had a next-best friend on another floor. The more one had friends outside the building, the more one had friends on other floors within the building. The wider one's social radius outside the building, the wider it was inside the building as well.

NEIGHBORING

Apart from the gratification of friendship, neighboring did a number of things for the community. It was a way of relaying information or misinformation about others. Often the information relayed upstairs influenced social arrangements downstairs. For example, according to one widow,

> The Bitfords had a tiff with Irma upstairs here, and a lot of tales went around. They weren't true, not a one, about Irma, but then people didn't come downstairs as much. Mattie used to come down, and Marie and Mr. Ball and they don't so much now, only once and again, because of Irma being there. All on account of that tiff.

Often people seated themselves downstairs as they were situated upstairs, neighbor and friend next to neighbor and friend, and a disagreement upstairs filtered downstairs. For example, when opinion was divided and feelings ran high on the issue of whether to store the club's $900 in a cigar box under the treasurer's bed or in the bank, the gossip, formerly confined to upstairs, invaded the public arena downstairs.

Relaying information this way meant that without directly asking, people knew a lot about one another. It was safe to assume that what you did was known about by at least one network of neighbors and their friends. Even the one social isolate on the third floor, Velma, was known about, and her comings and goings were talked about and judged. Talk about other people was a means of social control and it operated, as it does elsewhere, through parables; what was told of another was a message to one's self.

Not all social control was verbal. Since all apartment living rooms faced out on a common walkway that led to a central elevator, each tenant could be seen coming and going; and by how he or she was dressed, one could accurately guess his or her activities. Since each resident knew the visiting habits of her neighbors, anything unusual was immediately spotted. One day when I was knocking on the door of a resident, her neighbor came out:

> I don't know where she is, it couldn't be the doctor's, she goes to the doctor's on Tuesdays; it couldn't be shopping, she shopped yesterday with her daughter. I don't think she's downstairs, she says she's worked enough today. Maybe she's visiting Abbie. They neighbor a lot. Try the second floor.

Neighboring is also a way to detect sickness or death. As Ernestine related, "This morning I look to see if Judson's curtains were open. That's how we do on this floor, when we get up we open our curtains just a bit, so others walking by outside know that everything's all right. And if the curtains aren't drawn by midmorning, we knock to see." Mattie perpetually refused to open her curtains in the morning and kept them close to the wall by placing potted plants against them so that "a man won't get in." This excluded her from the checking-up system and disconcerted the other residents.

The widows in good health took it upon themselves to care for one or two in poor health. Delia saw after Grandma Goodman who was not well enough to go down and get her mail and shop, and Ernestine helped Little Floyd and Mrs. Blackwell who could not see well enough to cook their own meals. Irma took care of Mr. Cooper and she called his son when Mr. Cooper "took sick." Even those who had not adopted someone to help often looked after a neighbor's potted plants while they were visiting kin, lent kitchen utensils and took phone messages. One woman wrote letters for those who "wrote a poor hand."

Some of the caretaking was reciprocal, but most was not. Three people helped take care of Little Floyd, but since he was blind he could do little in return. Delia fixed his meals, Ernestine laundered his clothes, and Irma shopped for his food. When Little Floyd died fairly suddenly, he was missed perhaps more than others who died during those three years, especially by his caretakers. Ernestine remarked sadly, "I liked helping out the poor old fella. He would appreciate the tiniest thing. And never a complaint."

Sometimes people paid one another for favors. For example, Freda took in sewing for a small sum. When she was paid for lining a coat, she normally mentioned the purpose for which the money would be spent (for example, bus fare for a visit to relatives in Montana), perhaps to reduce the commercial aspect of the exchange. Delia was paid by the Housing Authority for cleaning and cooking for Grandma Goodman, a disabled woman on her floor; and as she repeatedly mentioned to Grandma Goodman, she spent the money on high school class rings for her three grandchildren. In one case, the Housing Authority paid a granddaughter for helping her grandmother with housework. In another case, a disabled woman paid for domestic help from her Social Security checks.

THE "POOR DEAR" HIERARCHY

Within the formal social circle there was a status hierarchy based on the distribution of honor, particularly through holding offices in the service club. Additionally, there was a parallel informal status hierarchy based on the distribution of luck. "Luck" as the residents defined it is not entirely luck. Health and life expectancy, for example, are often considered "luck," but an upper-class person can expect to live ten years longer than a lower-class person. The widows of Merrill Court, however, were drawn from the same social class and they saw the differences among themselves as matters of luck.

She who had good health won honor. She who lost the fewest loved ones through death won honor, and she who was close to her children won honor. Those who fell short of any of these criteria were often referred to as "poor dears."

The "poor dear" system operated like a set of valves through which a sense of superiority ran in only one direction. Someone who was a "poor dear" in the eyes of another seldom called that other person a "poor dear" in return. Rather, the "poor dear" would turn to someone less fortunate, perhaps to buttress a sense of her own achieved or ascribed superiority. Thus, the hierarchy honored residents at the top and pitied "poor dears" at the bottom, creating a number of informally recognized status distinctions among those who, in the eyes of the outside society, were social equals.

The distinctions made by residents of Merrill Court are only part of a larger old age status hierarchy based on things other than luck. At the monthly meetings of the countywide Senior Citizens Forum, to which Merrill Court sent two representatives, the term "poor dear" often arose with reference to old people. It was "we senior citizens who are politically involved versus those 'poor dears' who are active in recreation." Those active in recreation, however, did not accept a subordinate position relative to the politically active. On the other hand, they did not refer to the political activists as "poor dears." Within the politically active group there were those who espoused general causes, such as getting out an anti-pollution bill, and those who espoused causes related only to old age, such as raising Social Security benefits or improving medical benefits. Those in politics and recreation referred to the passive card players and newspaper readers as "poor dears." Uninvolved old people in good health referred to those in poor health as "poor dears," and those in poor health but living in independent housing referred to those in nursing homes as "poor dears." Within the nursing home there was a distinction between those who were ambulatory and those who were not. Among those who were not ambulatory there was a distinction between those who could enjoy food and those who could not. Almost everyone, it seemed, had a "poor dear."

At Merrill Court, the main distinction was between people like themselves and people in nursing homes. Returning from one of the monthly trips to a nearby nursing home, one resident commented:

> There was an old woman in a wheel chair there with a dolly in her arms. I leaned over to look at the dolly. I didn't touch it, well, maybe I just brushed it. She snatched it away, and said "Don't take my dolly." They're pathetic, some of them, the poor dears.

Even within the building, those who were in poor health, were alienated from their children, or were aging rapidly were considered "poor dears." It was lucky to be young and

unlucky to be old. There was more than a 20-year age span between the youngest and oldest in the community. When one of the younger women, Delia, age 69, was drinking coffee with Grandma Goodman, age 79, they compared ages. Grandma Goodman dwelt on the subject and finished the conversation by citing the case of Mrs. Blackwell, who was 89 and still in reasonably good health. Another remarked about her 70th birthday:

> I just couldn't imagine myself being 70. Seventy is old! That's what Daisy said too. She's 80 you know. It was her 70th that got her. No one likes to be put aside, you know. Laid away. Put on the shelf you might say. No sir.

She had an ailment that prevented her from bowling or lifting her flower pots, but she compared her health to that of Daisy, and found her own health a source of luck.

Old people compare themselves not to the young but to other old people. Often the residents referred to the aged back in Oklahoma Texas and Arkansas with pity in their voices:

> Back in Oklahoma, why they toss the old people away like old shoes. My old friends was all livin together in one part of town and they hardly budged the whole day. Just sat out on their porch and chewed the fat. Sometimes they didn't even do that. Mostly they didn't have no nice housing, and nothin' social was goin' on. People here don't know what luck they've fallen into.

They also compared their lot to that of other older people in the area. As one resident said:

> Some of my friends live in La Casa [another housing project]. I suppose because they have to, you know. And I tried to get them to come bowling with me, but they wouldn't have a thing to do with it. "Those senior citizens, that's old folks stuff." Wouldn't have a thing to do with it. I tried to tell them we was pretty spry, but they wouldn't listen. They just go their own way. They don't think we have fun.

On the whole, the widows disassociated themselves from the status of "old person," and accepted its "minority" characteristics. The "poor dears" in the nursing home were often referred to as childlike: "They are easily hurt, you know. They get upset at the slightest thing and they like things to be the way they've alway been. Just like kids." Occasionally, a widow would talk about Merrill Court itself in this vein, presumably excluding herself: "We're just like a bunch of kids here sometimes. All the sparring that goes on, even with church folk. And people get so hurt, so touchy. You'd think we were babies sometimes."

If the widows accepted the stereotypes of old age, they did not add the "poor dear" when referring to themselves. But younger outsiders did. To the junior employees in the Recreation and Parks Department, the young doctors who treated them at the county hospital, the middle-aged welfare workers and the young bank tellers, the residents of Merrill Court, and old people like them, were "poor dears."

Perhaps in old age there is a premium on finishing life off with the feeling of being a "have." But during old age, one also occupies a low social position. The way the old look for luck differences among themselves reflects the pattern found at the bottom of other social, racial and gender hierarchies. To find oneself lucky within an ill-fated category is to gain the semblance of high status when society withholds it from others in the category. The way old people feel above and condescend to other old people may be linked to the fact that the young feel above and condescend to them. The luck hierarchy does not stop with the old.

THE SIBLING BOND

There were rivalries and differences in Merrill Court, but neither alienation nor isolation. A club member who stayed up in her apartment during club meetings more often did it out of spite than indifference. More obvious were the many small, quiet favors, keeping an eye out for a friend and sharing a good laugh.

There was something special about this community, not so much because it was an old age subculture, but because the subculture was founded on a particular kind of relationship—the sibling bond. Most residents of Merrill Court are social siblings. The customs of exchanging cups of coffee, lunches, potted plants and curtain checking suggest reciprocity. Upstairs, one widow usually visited as much as she was visited. In deciding who visits whom, they often

remarked, "Well, I came over last time. You come over this time." They traded, in even measure, slips from house plants, kitchen utensils and food of all sorts. They watched one another's apartments when someone was away on a visit and they called and took calls for one another.

There are hints of the parent-child bond in this system, but protectors picked their dependents voluntarily and resented taking care of people they did not volunteer to help. For example, one protector of "Little Floyd" complained about a crippled club member, a nonresident:

> It wasn't considerate of Rose to expect us to take care of her. She can't climb in and out of the bus very well and she walks so slow. The rest of us wanted to see the museum. It's not nice to say, but I didn't want to miss the museum waiting for her to walk with us. Why doesn't her son take her on trips?

The widows were not only equals among themselves, they also were remarkably similar. They all wanted more or less the same things and could give more or less the same things. They all wanted to *receive* Mother's Day cards. No one in the building *sent* Mother's Day cards. And what they did was to compare Mother's Day cards. Although there was some division of labor, there was little difference in labor performed. All knew how to bake bread and can peaches, but no one knew how to fix faucets. They all knew about "the old days" but few among them could explain what was going on with youth these days. They all had ailments but no one there could cure them. They all needed rides to the shopping center, but no one among them needed riders.

Their similar functions meant that when they did exchange services, it was usually the same kinds of services they themselves could perform. For example, two neighbors might exchange corn bread for jam, but both knew how to make both corn bread and jam. If one neighbor made corn bread for five people in one day, one of the recipients would also make corn bread for the same people two weeks later. Each specialized within a specialization, and over the long run the widows made and exchanged the same goods.

Hence the "side by sideness," the "in the same boat" quality of their relations. They noticed the same things about the world and their eyes caught the same items in a department store. They noticed the same features in the urban landscape—the pastor's home, the Baptist church, the nursing homes, the funeral parlors, the places that used to be. They did not notice, as an adolescent might, the gas stations and hamburger joints.

As a result, they were good listeners for each other. It was common for someone to walk into the recreation room and launch into the details of the latest episode of a midafternoon television drama ("It seems that the baby is not by artificial insemination but really Frank's child, and the doctor is trying to convince her to tell. . ."). The speaker could safely assume that her listeners also knew the details. Since they shared many experiences, a physical ailment, a death, a description of the past, an "old age joke" could be explained, understood and enjoyed. They talked together about their children much as their children, together, talked about them. Each shared with social siblings one side of the prototypical parent-child bond.

This similarity opened up the possibility of comparison and rivalry, as the "poor dear" hierarchy suggests. Whether the widows cooperated in collecting money for flowers, or competed for prestigious offices in the service club, bowling trophies or front seats in the bus, their functions were similar, their status roughly equal, and their relations in the best and worst sense, "profane."

Not all groups of old people form this sibling bond. Although we might expect subcultures to arise in nursing homes, certain hospital wards or convalescent hospitals, the likes of Merrill Court is rare. It is not enough to put fairly healthy, socially similar old people together. There is clearly something different between institutions and public housing apartments. Perhaps what counts is the kind of relationships that institutions foster. The resident of an institution is "a patient." Like a child, he has his meals served to him, his water glass filled, his bed made, his blinds adjusted by the "mother-nurse." He cannot return the service. Although he often shares a room or a floor with "brother" patients, both siblings have a nonreciprocal relationship to attendants or nurses. Even the research on the institutionalized focuses on the relation between

patient and attendant, not between patient and patient. If there is a strong parent-child bond, it may overwhelm any potential sibling solidarity. If the old in institutions meet as equals, it is not as independent equals. The patient's relation to other patients is like the relation between *real, young siblings*, which may exaggerate rather than forestall narcissistic withdrawal.

The widows of Merrill Court took care of themselves, fixed their own meals, paid their own rent, shopped for their own food; and made their own beds; and they did these things for others. Their sisterhood rests on adult autonomy. This is what people at Merrill Court have and people in institutions do not.

THE SIBLING BOND AND AGE-STRATIFICATION

The sibling bond is delicate and emerges only when conditions are ripe. Rapid currents of social change lead to age-stratification, which, in turn, ripens conditions for the sibling bond. Tied to his fellows by sibling bonds, an individual is cemented side by side into an age stratum with which he shares the same rewards, wants, abilities and failings.

French sociologist Emile Durkheim, in his book *The Division of Labor,* describes two forms of social solidarity. In organic solidarity there is a division of labor, complementary dependence and differences among people. In mechanical solidarity there is no division of labor, self-sufficiency and similarity among people. Modern American society as a whole is based on organic solidarity, not only in the economic but in the social, emotional and intellectual spheres.

Different age strata within the general society, however, are more bound by mechanical solidarity. This is important both for the individual and the society. Although division of labor, complementary dependence and differences among people describe society's network of relations as a whole, they do not adequately describe relations among particular individuals. An individual's complementary dependence may be with people he does not know or meet—such as the person who grows and cans the food he eats, or lays the bricks for his house. And in his most intimate relations, an individual may also have complementary relations (either equal or unequal) with his spouse and children. But in between the most and least intimate bonds is a range in which there are many sibling relationships which form the basis of mechanical solidarity.

In fact, many everyday relations are with people similar and equal to oneself. Relations between colleague and colleague, student and student, friend and friend, relations within a wives' group or "the guys at the bar," the teen-age gang or army buddies are often forms of the sibling bond. These ties are often back-up relations, social insurance policies for the times when the complementary bonds of parent and child, husband and wife, student and teacher, boy friend and girl friend fail, falter or normally change.

From an individual's viewpoint, some periods of life, such as adolescence and old age, are better for forming sibling bonds than are other periods. Both just before starting a family and after raising one, before entering the economy and after leaving it, an individual is open to, and needs, these back-up relationships. It is these stages that are problematic, and it is these stages that, with longer education and earlier retirement, now last longer.

From society's point of view, the sibling bond allows more flexibility in relations between generations by forging solidarity within generations and divisions between them. This divides society into age layers that are relatively independent of one another, so that changes in one age layer need not be retarded by conditions in another. The institution that has bound the generations together—the family—is in this respect on the decline. As it declines, the sibling bond emerges, filling in and enhancing social flexibility, especially in those social strata where social change is most pronounced. The resulting social flexibility does not guarantee "good" changes and continuity is partly sacrificed to fads and a cult of newness. But whether desirable or not, this flexibility is partly due to and partly causes the growing importance of the sibling bond.

The times are ripe for the sibling bond, and or old-age communities such as Merrill Court. In the social life of old people the problem is not the sibling bond versus the parent-child bond. Rather, the question is how the one bond complements the other. The sisterhood at Merrill Court is no substitute for love of children and contact with them; but it offers a full, meaningful life independent of them.

THE MINORITY GROUP ALMOST EVERYONE JOINS

Isolation is not randomly distributed across the class hierarchy; there is more of it at the bottom. It is commonly said that old age is a leveler, that it affects the rich in the same way it affects the poor. It doesn't. The rich fare better in old age even as they fared better in youth. The poorer you are, the shorter your life expectancy, the poorer your health and health care, the lower your morale generally, the more likely you are to "feel" old regardless of your actual age, the less likely you are to join clubs or associations, the less active you are and the more isolated, even from children. Irving Rosow's study of 1200 people over 62 living in Cleveland found that roughly 40 percent of the working class but only 16 percent of the middle class had fewer than four good friends. Another study of 6000 white working-class men and women showed that of those over 65 with incomes under $3000, a full third did not visit with or speak to a friend or neighbor during the preceding week. The rock-bottom poor are isolated, but they are not the only ones.

The isolation of old people is linked to other problems. The old are poor and poverty itself is a problem. The old are unemployed and unemployment, in this society, is itself a problem. The old lack community and the lack of community is itself a problem. There is some connection between these three elements. Removed from the economy, the old have been cast out of the social networks that revolve around work. Lacking work, they are pushed down the social ladder. Being poor, they have fewer social ties. Poverty reinforces isolation. To eliminate enforced isolation, we have to eliminate poverty, for the two go together. The social life of Merrill Court residents, who had modest but not desperately low incomes, is an exception to the general link between social class and isolation.

Even if every old person were in a Merrill Court, the problem of old age would not be solved. But allowing every old person the possibility of such an arrangement could be part of the solution. The basic problem far exceeds the limits of tinkering with housing arrangements. It is not enough to try to foster friendships among the old. Even to do that, it is not enough to set up bingo tables in the lobbies of decrepit hotels or to hand out name cards to the sitters on park benches. This would simply put a better face on poverty, a cheerful face on old age as it now is, at not much social cost.

Merrill Court is not set in any island of ideal social conditions; it is essentially an adjustment to bad social conditions. For the lives of old people to change fundamentally, those *conditions* must change. In the meantime, Merrill Court is a start. It is a good example of what can be done to reduce isolation. I do not know if similar communities would have emerged in larger apartment houses or housing tracts rather than in a small apartment house, with the married rather than the widowed, with rich rather than poor residents, with people having a little in common rather than a lot, with the very old person rather than the younger old person. Only trying will tell.

Merrill Court may be a forecast of what is to come. A survey of 105 University of California students in 1968 suggested that few parents of these students and few of the students themselves expect to be living with their families when they are old. Nearly seven out of ten (69 percent) reported that "under no circumstances" would they want their aged parents to live with them, and only 3 percent expected to be living with their own children when they are old. A full 28 percent expected to be living with *other* old people, and an additional 12 percent expected to be "living alone or with other old people."

Future communities of old people may be more middle class and more oriented toward leisure. Less than 10 percent of the students expected to be working when they passed 65. A great many expected to be "enjoying life," by which they meant studying, meditating, practicing hobbies, playing at sports and traveling.

But some things about future communities may be the same. As I have suggested throughout . . . communal solidarity can renew the social contact the old have with life. For old roles that are gone, new ones are available. If the world watches them less for being old, they watch one another more. Lacking responsibilities to the young, the old take on responsibilities toward one another. Moreover, in a society that raises an eyebrow at those who do not "act their age," the subculture encourages the old to dance, to sing, to flirt and to joke. They talk frankly about death in a way less common between the old and young. They show one another how to be, and trade solutions to problems they have not faced before.

Old age is the minority group almost everyone joins. But it is a forgotten minority group from which many old people dissociate themselves. A community such as Merrill Court counters this disaffiliation. In the wake of the declining family, it fosters a "we" feeling, and a nascent "old age consciousness." In the long run, this may be the most important contribution an old age community makes.

Sexism

Unemployed Women: When "Social Support" Is Not Supportive

KATHRYN STROTHER RATCLIFF
The University of Connecticut

JANET BOGDAN
Syracuse University

Despite major changes in the social and occupational position of women in the last two decades, resistance to women's employment endures. This paper reports on 89 unemployed women who were personally interviewed and asked about their job orientations, the nature of support they received from others while unemployed and their perceptions of the unemployment period. While the women reported close and extensive social support networks, the content of the messages from those networks about work was often not supportive. The nature and extent of this non-support is documented and the effect of a non-supportive social "support" network is analyzed. Our findings suggest that while some unemployed women suffer from a lack of close friends, a more common pattern may be for a woman to be surrounded by "caring others" who may undermine her by denying the legitimacy of an activity she regards as important.

Unemployed women in this society can experience distinctive tensions because those around them often view their employment in contradictory ways. At the center of these tensions are two crosscutting realities. First, employment is important to women both as a source of income to support themselves and their families and as a defining factor in their self conceptions. Second, attitudes and social patterns persist that deny the legitimacy of women's labor and that ignore the importance these jobs have come to occupy in the lives of many working women. We believe many women feel this conflict and that it likely shapes their experience of unemployment. Our research examines two questions. First, do unemployed women, and especially those who value their prior jobs, often face friends who question the worth or legitimacy of their being employed? Second, do such clashes between personal values and others' expressed sentiments make the experience of unemployment particularly difficult for some women?

PAST RESEARCH ON UNEMPLOYMENT AND SOCIAL SUPPORT

The extensive social science literature on unemployment gives an important place to the stresses associated with job loss. Such research ranges from work done in the 1930s focusing on the psychological effects of unemployment (e.g., Eisenberg and Lazarsfeld, 1938; Komarovsky, 1940) to recent research showing that unemployment is linked to a number of negative psychological, physical and mental health

This research was supported by a Biomedical Support Grant through the Department of Psychiatry at Upstate Medical Center, Syracuse, NY and a Research Foundation Fellowship at the University of Connecticut. Thanks to Myra Marx Ferree, Richard E. Ratcliff, Jay Stewart, and members of the Women and Work Study Group. A preliminary version of this paper was presented at the Families in Crisis Conference held at Lehman College. Correspondence to: Ratcliff, Department of Sociology, University of Connecticut Box U-68, Storrs, CT 06268.

From the article originally published in *Social Problems,* Vol. 35, No. 1 (February 1988): 54–63. © 1988 by the Society for the Study of Social Problems. Used with permission.

effects (e.g., Kasl, Gore and Cobb, 1975; Liem and Rayman, 1980; Linn, Sandifor and Stein, 1985). An important finding in the more recent studies has been that the negative psychological and emotional consequences of unemployment are likely to be substantially mitigated if the unemployed person is surrounded by a supportive network of family, relatives and friends (Gore, 1978; Pearlin et al., 1981).

Few of these empirical studies of unemployment include women, and even fewer examine the possibly different ways men and women experience unemployment. Recent research, however, has begun to correct this imbalance. Now that men's and women's experiences can be compared, some important differences have emerged. For example, unemployed women report that their plight is regarded less seriously than that of men. Nowak and Snyder (1984) note that while nearly all of the women expressed displeasure with the unemployed status of their husbands, only one-third of the men were unhappy with the unemployed status of their wives. Such gender-related differences in reactions to job loss appear in part to result from a gender-segregated occupational structure that provides different financial and intrinsic benefits for men and women workers. The differences are also a function of socially defined patterns, namely, perceptions of the "proper roles" of men and women.

A common assumption of most social support research, especially of the "life event-social support-personal outcome" model, is that the messages received from one's social network, especially from one's intimates, are favorable and that they contribute to one's mental well-being. Given this, researchers have focused attention on the density of social support networks, on their intimacy and their usefulness. They have measured social support (Turner, 1983; Turner et al., 1983) by the amount of contact with a close friend (Dean and Ensel, 1982); the size, density and connectedness of a person's social network (Mitchell and Trickett, 1980); the existence of a confiding relationship (Brown and Harris, 1978); the receipt of information that one is cared for, esteemed, valued or belongs to a network of mutual obligation (Cobb, 1976); and the provision of instrumental aid (Dean, Lin and Ensel, 1981). Although there

has been some conceptual concern for the inclusion of negative aspects of social networks (Wellman, 1981; House, 1981), Rook's work (1984) on widows stands nearly alone as a piece of empirical work which examines the potentially negative impact of social involvement.

The unexamined assumption that the content of social support is consistently positive precludes research that seriously examines this content. This is a weakness of most past research. It is an especially questionable assumption to make for unemployed women. Precisely because there are sharply divided views in the society regarding the legitimacy and appropriateness of women's employment (Huber and Spitze, 1981), we would expect unemployed women to receive mixed messages about their working from those in their close social network. In particular, we expect that a job loss will be most stressful for those women caught in the contradiction between the new employment realities for women and attitudes supporting more traditional roles for women. These are the women who want to work but who are in social networks that do not support paid employment.

SAMPLE AND DATA

We drew our 89 respondents from women who visited a state unemployment office in upstate New York between December, 1983 and September, 1984. Researchers approached individual women at different times of the day and week as they came to the office, briefly explained the study and asked the women to participate. Those agreeing were contacted by an interviewer. The interview schedule was a mixture of structured, closed- and open-ended questions and we encouraged extended responses throughout the interview. The interviews, lasting about an hour, were conducted in the privacy of the women's homes. Each woman was paid fifteen dollars to participate. The interviews were tape recorded and then transcribed.

The sample is diverse both in terms of the women's prior jobs and their demographic characteristics. Past positions ranged from minimum wage jobs to specialized careers with excellent salaries and included factory and unskilled service employment as well as positions of considerable responsibility such as managers, hospital social workers and teachers. The median yearly income for the women was $11,040, with one-third making over $12,500. This median compares to $12,368 for full-time women workers in the SMSA where the unemployment office was located (U.S. Bureau of the Census, 1986:34–294). The median time on the last job was three and a half years. The length of unemployment for these women varied from one to 16 months, with a median of 4.5 months. The women ranged from 19 to 76 years of age, with two-thirds (67%) between 25 and 44. One in ten had less than a high school education, half (55%) had a high school diploma and one-third (31%) had gone beyond high school. The women lived in an assortment of social arrangements. About two-thirds of the women (63%) lived with a husband or partner (56% married and 7% not married). Among the married women, half (49%) had children under the age of 18.

THE CONTENT OF SOCIAL "SUPPORT"

First we consider the kinds of messages married women received from their husbands. Then we consider messages from other relatives and friends.

Husbands' Views on Unemployment

The husbands of our respondents were reported to have expressed a diverse range of reactions to the women's unemployment. One theme in these reactions was at least some lack of enthusiasm for the women's being employed and some satisfaction with their now being out of a job. For instance, a number of women indicated that their husbands welcomed their unemployment. Respondents said: "He loves it, he thinks it is fantastic" (ID 52); "I think he's thrilled to bits" (ID 109); and "He's glad I'm not working; if it'd been up to him, I'd quit long ago" (ID 104).

Even women with husbands who expressed sympathy for their situation sometimes said their husbands had strong preferences for a wife who stays at home. In these reports two themes stand out. The first emphasizes a cultural value preference: the wife's place is in the home while the responsibility of the husband is to provide. As one woman said, "He's very old-fashioned. He wants to start a family and do the things his Italian lineage does. He'd love to make enough money where I have to stay home. The wife is supposed to stay home and bake goodies and that's it and raise children" (ID 26). Another woman attributed her husband's idea that she should not work to his being "from the old country" (ID 105). Similar statements included "[My husband] feels it is best [for me] to be home with the kids" (ID 41) and "[My husband] thinks I should be home" (ID 51).

The second theme in wives' perceptions of their husbands' comments and actions is the practical benefits of having a wife at home. Wives said their husbands seemed to feel that their unemployment made them better homemakers. One woman reported, "He likes [my being unemployed]. I'm here when he gets home. His food is hot and his clothes are ironed" (ID 106). Another said, "He likes it—he's getting better meals" (ID 102), and yet another reported that her husband liked her unemployment because it meant she had "more time to do things around the house" (ID 45).

Wives said that despite thinking a woman's place is in the home and wanting to have housework well done, husbands also often recognized the financial importance of their wives' jobs. These husbands did not want their wives to work, yet they appreciated the additional money. It is not surprising that our respondents' families reflected conflicts about women's employment that exist in the larger society. As one woman reported: "I think my husband has mixed feelings about my unemployment. I think that for one thing he likes the idea of having a wife that's home and cooking dinner and taking care of stuff like that at home. But I think he misses the money that I was bringing in. . . ." (ID 124). Similarly, another woman said her husband thinks she "should be home, but realizes there isn't enough money—[and it] makes him feel bad that he can't support [the family]" (ID 51).

Recognizing the monetary importance of a wife's employment is not just a financial consideration. For some husbands it appeared to force a realization that their monopoly on the "provider role" had been broken. One woman's experiences illustrate this conflict:

> [My husband is] schizophrenic about [my working]. He has two opposing views and it depends on the day. One side of him thinks it is great [for me to be at home]. He loves his woman in the house. Here all day long doing the work, taking care of the kids. He really would like to see me relaxed and enjoying . . . sitting at the loom, creating, gardening, having women friends over for coffee. That's what he wants in a wife and that's not for me. . . . On the other hand, no. He doesn't like it because of his total financial responsibility and that's a big responsibility these days with a mortgage to pay and three young children to raise. . . . He can't accept the fact that he is not the provider, because he is from a family in which a male provides. His father did it, his grandfather did it. The male provides. In one sense it is a slap at his ego that he can't be the provider (ID 854).

Other respondents described husbands as basically indifferent to their unemployment and seeing no particular value in their wives' working. For instance, speaking of her former job, one woman said, "We never discussed it. . . . He never cared whether I worked or not" (ID 35). Another said, "I don't think he cares one way or another [if I'm employed or unemployed]. With the money aspect like I say he's annoyed with that part of it. But that's the only thing" (ID 130).

As these comments indicate, many of the women lived either with husbands who were hostile to their employment and who actually welcomed their unemployment or with husbands who were indifferent and gave them little to no support for working. To find which views were most common, we reviewed the transcripts to judge whether the woman's husband was basically opposed to the idea of his wife being employed. There was a fairly even split among the married women. In 40 percent of the cases, the husband was, at least at the time of the interview, opposed in principle to his wife's employment. In a similar number of instances (37%) the husband seemed, on balance, supportive of her working. In the other cases, the husband's attitude was either split or there was insufficient information to make a judgment.

In addition to these attitudes of husbands about their wives' working, we asked four questions about the practical and emotional support husbands offered while the women were unemployed: whether the husbands were helpful in listening to wives' concerns about being unemployed, whether they were helpful in job searches, whether they were concerned that their wives had lost jobs the women regarded as meaningful and whether they were concerned about the women's loss of income.

To create a general measure of husbands' opposition/support toward their wives' employment, we combined the women's responses to these four questions with our own assessment, from the transcripts, of the husbands' work attitudes. A husband was considered to have "anti-employment" attitudes if he was opposed to his wife's work in principle (40%) or if he gave limited support-support on two or fewer of the four questions (50%). Using this measure, we concluded that two out of three of the married women (66%) were in family settings where the husbands were substantially unsupportive of their wives' working outside the home.

The Views of Other Relatives and Friends

Women's relationships with friends, relatives and others can also influence how they experience unemployment. These networks can also convey important messages about the women's working. Most of the women in our sample had large and active networks of friends, relatives and acquaintances beyond their immediate families. Nearly all (89%) had at least one friend they had contact with about once a week. Three-fifths (61%) reported three or more close friends. Only a few women (7%) reported no friends. Women who said they had active support networks described the relationships as, in general, positive and caring. They said they had friends and family they spoke to regularly and in whom they confided during times of stress.

Many of the women did report receiving some form of support from others for needs related to their unemployment. Most typical was emotional assistance in the form of listening to concerns and helping the woman keep up her spirits. Others also gave instrumental help by providing information about possible jobs or giving help with childcare so the woman could look for a job.

But along with such assistance, respondents often also described messages that were indifferent or even opposed to their working. Nearly half (46%) of the women said that "most" of their friends, neighbors and relatives were not concerned that they had lost their jobs. As we might expect, this lack of concern was more common for the married women (56%) than for the unmarried (33%). Many indicated that the typical view among friends was that "it is better for the family that I am at home." Forty percent of the married and 20 percent of the unmarried women reported this.

Many of our respondents, and especially married women, received strong messages that questioned the value of women's paid work. For example, one woman described her friends as from "the church and they believe in 'mama being home and being mama'" (ID 302). Another woman reported: "Most of my friends say I should be home as a homemaker" (ID 854). A third woman whose children were all over age 15 indicated that although her friends did show concern about her job loss, the typical view was that she should stay home (ID 102).

In contrast to these "stay home" attitudes, a few of the women experienced strong support from their friends for working. One woman described this kind of assistance:

> They've allowed me to put things in perspective. To realize that it is a temporary situation. They've been helpful in terms of giving me concrete ideas about how to manage financially through this time. My girlfriend is living here with me now to help me until things get better. . . . She's encouraged me to go back to school to use this time productively instead of feeling frozen and panicky. She's helped me to think of options (ID 133).

But another woman described how her disagreements with friends over the issue of whether women should work caused tension even in the midst of a supportive relationship: "I have some very avid homemaker friends who feel that 'a woman's place is at home' and they are very happy being homemakers. I've tried to convince them that not all women get enough fulfillment doing housework" (ID 50).

In order to summarize the views of these women's friends and relatives, we considered them to be anti-employment if they contained at least two of the three negative themes described (little direct help, absence of concern about job loss, affirming the idea that a woman should stay at home). On this basis, just under half (44%) of the married women were in anti-work environments outside their immediate families. Among the unmarried, only one in four (26%) [was] in similar environments.

In Table 1 we look at the occurrence of anti-employment messages in relation to income and generation. Married women were likely (74%) to receive anti-employment messages from at least one source. Unmarried women, who can receive such messages only from relatives and friends, were much less likely (26%) to hear them. Even among these women, who have no working husbands available to provide support, one in four women said they received anti-employment sentiments from others. These anti-work messages do not seem strongly associated with the women's income levels, though those with lower incomes and whose husbands had lower incomes were slightly more likely to hear such messages. Generational patterns were somewhat more clear, but only for the married women. Older married women were more likely to hear anti-employment messages both from their husbands and from other relatives and friends.

JOB COMMITMENT

To understand how women interpret the anti- and pro-employment messages they receive, we must ask whether they place a strong value on paid work. Recent research shows that women often receive major satisfaction and an increased sense of self-control and empowerment from paid work, even when they are in lower status "women's jobs" (Ferree, 1976; Rubin, 1981). Our transcripts revealed considerable variation in our respondents' job commitment. Some said things like, "I have absolutely no sense of identity [now that I'm unemployed]" (ID 854). Others reported they felt their ". . . place is here with the kids" (ID 51). Commitment was not simply a function of

TABLE 1

Percent Women Receiving Anti-Work Messages, by Marital Status, Demographic Variables, and Source of Message

	Marital Status							
	Married				Single		All Women	
	Source							
Demographic Variables	Husbands	Others	Total		Others		Husbands & Others	
Total	66%	44%	74%	(50)	26%	(39)	53%	(89)
Age								
19–35	54	35	62	(26)	26	(23)	45	(49)
Over 35	79	54	88	(24)	25	(16)	63	(40)
Annual Income								
$11,000 or less	64	52	80	(25)	26	(19)	57	(44)
Over $11,000	68	36	68	(25)	25	(20)	49	(45)
Husband's Income								
Less than $20,000	68	36	77	(22)				
$20,000 or More	62	50	68	(26)				
Children Under 7								
No	69	47	75	(36)	24	(33)	51	(69)
Yes	57	36	71	(14)	33	(6)	60	(20)

job status. Some women in lower status jobs placed a high value on working. One woman who earned the minimum wage as a heat seal machine operator spoke of the "sense of usefulness," the enjoyment of learning and even of liking the machine she used (ID 36). Similarly, another woman, a sales consultant at a weight loss clinic, said that the job gave her "a lot of new responsibility" and that it was "rewarding to help people lose weight" (ID 39).

We wanted to assess a woman's overall job commitment. In the interviews, we asked questions about the most recent job: whether she liked the job "very much" (63 percent said they did); whether the job was "meaningful" to her (85 percent said it was) and whether the job provided her with an opportunity to learn (71 percent reported it did). We also asked questions about the general appeal of working, including whether the "satisfaction" of doing the work and the associated intellectual stimulation were "very important" reasons for working (27 and 19 percent respectively said yes). Finally, we asked if she would continue to work even if she did not need the money (76 percent said they would continue). To obtain the overall assessment of job commitment, we combined responses to these six questions. On this basis, just over half of the women (55%) had what we consider a high level of job commitment.

THE CONTENT OF SOCIAL SUPPORT, JOB COMMITMENT AND DISSATISFACTION WITH UNEMPLOYMENT

When women who want to work, who like their work and find it fulfilling in a number of ways, hear the kinds of discouraging messages that we have described, how do they react to being unemployed? To try to answer this, we asked questions that would measure the women's dissatisfaction with being unemployed. We asked them what they liked and disliked about this situation. Responses to the first question included having free time to do pleasurable things. There seemed to be a temporary adjustment to being unemployed that parallels Rosen's (1981) finding of a kind of similarly temporary respite from work. In response to the second question, women said that they disliked spending so much time at home, that there was nothing to like about being unemployed and that they missed the motivation and reason to get out of the house that work provided.

We coded these responses into simple numeric categories (from 1 to 4 for each), depending on how many things the women liked or disliked and the intensity of their expression. The more the women liked being employed, the lower the score. Thirty-nine percent of the women expressed what we consider a substantial level of dissatisfaction with being unemployed.

In Table 2 we examine the relationship between level of dissatisfaction with being unemployed by the content of work messages from one's social network and level of job commitment. Dissatisfaction with unemployment was concentrated among those receiving anti-employment messages (51%) and, looked at alternatively, among those with high job commitment (51%). The highest level of dissatisfaction with unemployment (70%) was found among those women who were in the contradictory situations we identified at the outset,

that is, women who themselves expressed a strong commitment to working but who saw their networks as unsupportive of this commitment. Those close around them sent messages that devalued their prior role as employed women.

A somewhat unexpected finding also emerged from this analysis. The other group of women who evidenced a relatively high level of personal dissatisfaction with their unemployed situation were those in an opposite form of contradictory situation. Nearly half (45%) of the women who personally had a low job commitment but received fairly consistent pro-employment messages from those around them indicated high levels of dissatisfaction. Lower levels of dissatisfaction were found among those women in consistent positions. These included those with low job commitment who heard anti-employment messages from their social networks (only 25 percent were dissatisfied) and those whose own high level of job commitment was supported by pro-employment messages from those around them (27% dissatisfied).

TABLE 2

Percent Women Dissatisfied with Unemployment Experience, by Content of Employment Messages from Others and Level of Job Commitment[a]

Job Commitment	Content of Messages from Others		
	Anti-Employment	Pro-Employment	
Low	25% (20)	45% (20)	35% (40)
High	70% (27)	27% (22)	51% (49)
	51% (47)	36% (42)	

[a] Demographic and structural characteristics, namely, financial problems, age, marital status, the size of the social support network and the woman's previous income, could have an important impact on dissatisfaction. We used a regression model including these variables and both the simple additive effects of messages and job orientation and a term for the interaction between the content of the messages and one's job commitment. This analysis shows an effect for the content of messages from one's social support network, an effect for the interaction between the messages and one's job commitment, and an effect for financial problems. Age, marital status, number of friends, and the woman's income had no significant effects.

DISCUSSION

Our research indicates that, despite the growth of the number of women in the labor force, we should be cautious in our conclusions about the support women receive for this work. Over half of the unmarried women we spoke to, and an even larger share of those who are married, received clear messages expressing disapproval to hostility to women's employment. Most others received mixed or only slight support. Only a minority reported receiving strong and consistent support for their working.

These anti-employment attitudes and the problems and challenges they present appear to be unique to women. The extensive literature on unemployed men does not discuss the legitimacy of men's employment as an issue. For a large majority of the women we interviewed, the very legitimacy of their employment appears to be a central theme in their relations with husbands or other close associates. Moreover, the conflict between their own employment values and the anti-employment messages they receive from others represents a substantial burden for many women.

These findings suggest that in social networks where value disagreements are likely, we should give careful attention to the content of messages the person receives. To ignore the content and merely assess the breadth and depth of social support is to ignore major forces that shape individual well-being. Unemployment for women is an area where the content of messages is problematic. Women who seek employment and who place a high value on that role are likely, even in an age of supposed women's freedom, to have husbands, relatives and close friends who express their disapproval. One might expect that a whole range of issues relevant to women, from abortion to women's roles in family decision making, would pose similar problems. Evaluating how women cope with stressful events is not just a matter of whether the social network is present, is "dense," provides confiding relationships or care; rather, the substantive support on a particular issue is crucial. Our findings indicate that while some women suffer from a lack of close friends and relations, a more common pattern for a woman who seeks out new roles may be for her to be surrounded by "caring others" who actually undermine her by denying the legitimacy of an activity she regards as important. In analyzing "social support" relationships, we must examine just how supportive such relationships are to those in them.

REFERENCES

Brown, George W. and T. Harris Social Origins of Depression: A Study of Psychiatric Disorder among Women. New York: Free Press. (1978).

Cobb, Sidney "Social support as a moderator of life stress." Psychosomatic Medicine 38:300–14. (1976).

Dean, Alfred, Nan Lin and William Ensel "The epidemiological significance of social support systems in depression." Research in Community and Mental Health 2:77–109. (1981).

Eisenberg, Philip and Paul F. Lazarsfeld "The psychological effects of unemployment." Psychological Bulletin 35:358–91. (1938).

Ferree, Myra M. "Working-class jobs: housework and paid work as sources of satisfaction." Social Problems 23:431–41. (1976).

Gore, Susan "The effect of social support in moderating the health consequences of unemployment." Journal of Health and Social Behavior 19:157–65. (1978).

House, James S. Work Stress and Social Support. Reading, MA: Addison Wesley. (1981).

Huber, Joan and Glenna Spitze "Wives' employment, household behaviors, and sex-role attitudes." Social Forces 60:150–69. (1981)

Kasl, Stanislav V., Susan Gore and Sidney Cobb "The experience of losing a job: reported changes in health, symptoms and illness behavior." Psychosomatic Medicine 37:106–22. (1975).

Komarovsky, Mirra The Unemployed Man and His Family. New York: Dryden Press. (1940).

Liem, Ramsay and Paula Rayman "Health and social costs of unemployment." American Psychologist 37:1116–23. (1982).

Linn, Margaret, Richard Sandifor and Shayna Stein "Effects of unemployment on mental and physical health." American Journal of Public Health 75:502–06. (1985).

Mitchell, Roger E. and Edison J. Trickett "Task force report: social networks as mediators of social support: an analysis of the effects and determinants of social networks." Community Mental Health Journal 16:27–44. (1980).

Nowak, Thomas C. and Kay A. Snyder "Job loss, marital happiness and household tension: do women fare better than men?" Presentation at the Society for the Study of Social Problems meetings, San Antonio, TX. (1984).

Pearlin, Leonard I., Elizabeth G. Menaghan, Morton A. Lieberman and Joseph T. Mullan "The stress process." Journal of Health and Social Behavior 22:337–56. (1981).

Rook, Karen "The negative side of social interaction: impact on psychological well being." Journal of Personality and Social Psychology 46:1097–1108. (1984).

Rosen, Ellen "Between a rock and a hard place: employment and unemployment among blue collar workers." Paper presented at American Sociological Association annual meetings, Toronto, Ont. (1981).

Rubin, Lillian Breslow Why Should Women Work? Working paper. Center for Research and Education for Women. University of California, Berkeley. (1981).

Turner, R. Jay "Direct, indirect, and moderating effects of social support on psychological distress and associated conditions." Pp. 105–56 in H.B. Kaplan (ed.), Psychological Stress: Trends in Theory and Research. New York: Academic Press. (1983).

Turner, R. Jay, B. Gail Frankel, Deborah Levin and Samuel Noh "Measures of social support: some instruments and their properties." Mimeo, Health Care Research Unit, the University of Western Ontario. (1983).

U.S. Bureau of the Census Current Population Reports, General Social and Economic Characteristics of the Population. Volume 1: Part 34, New York. Washington, DC: United States Government Printing Office. (1986).

Wellman, Barry "Applying network analysis to the study of support." Pp. 171–200 in B.H. Gottlieb (ed.), Social Networks and Social Support. Beverly Hills: Sage. (1981).

Incestuous Fathers and Their Families

JUDITH LEWIS HERMAN

with LISA HIRSCHMAN

These fathers . . . tend toward abuses of authority of every conceivable kind, and they not infrequently endeavor to secure their dominant position in the family by socially isolating the members of the family from the world outside. Swedish, American, and French surveys have pointed time and again to the patriarchal position of such fathers, who set up a "primitive family order."—Herbert Maisch, Incest, 1972

Forty women who had had incestuous relationships with their fathers shared their stories with us. Most were young women in their twenties or early thirties. At the time we met them, most had already married and some had already divorced; half had children. They worked at common women's jobs; they were mothers and houseworkers, typists and secretaries, waitresses and factory workers, teachers and nurses. About half came from working-class and half from middle-class families.[1] Their ethnic and religious backgrounds reflected the predominant Catholicism of the state of Massachusetts, where most of them lived (see Tables 5.1 and 5.2). To all appearances, they were an ordinary group of women.

All of the informants were white. We made the decision to restrict the interviewing to white women in order to avoid even the possibility that the information gathered might be used to fuel idle speculation about racial differences. White people have indulged for too long in discussion about the sexual capacities, behaviors, and misbehaviors of black people. There is no question, however, that incest is a problem in black families, as it is in white families. Many of the first, most daring, and most honest contributions to the public discussion of incest were made by black women, and much of our work has been inspired by theirs.[2]

All of the informants were outpatients in psychotherapy. Some allowed their therapists to discuss their histories with us; others agreed to be interviewed in person as well; and a few, having heard of our study, carried on a correspondence with us. We chose to restrict the study to women who had therapists because we believed that our work could not be carried out without causing pain. Every interview we conducted was stressful, both for the informants and for ourselves. As one woman commented, "Every time I tell about it, I hurt in a new place." By limiting the study to patients in therapy, we made certain that the informants had at least one safe place in which to deal with their renewed memories.

Informants were located primarily through an informal network of therapists in private practice in the Boston area. Cases were initially discussed with the therapists, who exercised some preliminary judgment about which patients should be approached. Patients who were in severe distress or who had not established a good therapeutic alliance were generally screened out of the study. The therapists then informed their patients about our research and invited them to participate. It is our impression that those who accepted, and especially those who agreed to be interviewed in person, had already dealt with the incest trauma to a certain extent in their therapy.

Information was gathered according to a semistructured interview protocol which covered the patient's present work and personal life, a detailed description of the patient's family

Chapter 5, "Incestuous Fathers and Their Families," from *Father–Daughter Incest*, by Judith Lewis Herman with Lisa Hirschman (Cambridge, Mass.: Harvard University Press, 1981), pp. 67–95, 267–269.

TABLE 5.1

Demographic Characteristics of Incest Victims and Comparison Group[a]

Demographic Characteristic	Incest Victims No. = 40	%	Comparison Group No. = 20	%
Age				
18–25	23	57.5	11	55
26–30	7	17.5	6	30
31–35	5	12.5	2	10
36+	5	12.5	1	5
Mean	27.7		26.8	
Marital status				
Single	15	37.5	11	55
Married	14	35	4	20
Separated or divorced	11	27.5	5	25
Children				
Yes	20	50	5	25
No	20	50	15	75
Religious background				
Catholic	17	42.5	8	40
Protestant	14	35	9	45
Jewish	5	12.5	3	15
n.a.	2	5		
Educational level				
Advanced degree	3	7.5	6	30
B.A.	12	30	7	35
Some college	11	27.5	7	35
High school graduate	10	25	0	0
< twelfth grade	4	10	0	0

[a] Comparison group for tables 5.1–5.3 and 5.5 are daughters of seductive fathers.

TABLE 5.2

Family Background of Incest Victims and Comparison Group

Family Background	Incest Victims No. = 40	%	Comparison Group No. = 20	%
Father's occupation				
Working class	19	47.5	11	55
Middle layers or self-employed	21	52.5	9	45
Mother employed outside home				
Yes	9	22.5	6	30
No	31	77.5	14	70
Parents separated or divorced				
Yes	9	22.5	5	25
No	31	77.5	15	75
Victim's place in family				
Only daughter	15	37.5	11	55
Oldest daughter	17	42.5	4	20
Other	8	20	5	25

of origin, a history of the incestuous relationship, and an assessment of the long-term effects of the incest. Interviews generally lasted two to three hours. Case discussions with therapists were recorded in the form of extensive notes; interviews with patients were recorded verbatim. The forty interviews were collected over a period of four years, beginning in 1975.

Though all the informants were patients in psychotherapy, they were not in any obvious manner a disturbed group of people. Most functioned quite well in their daily lives, and some had achieved remarkable success, particularly in their work. They were special, perhaps, only in that they had admitted to themselves that they had problems in their personal lives and were trying to do something about it. Our method of locating the informants tended to select for a relatively healthy group of patients.

Our definition of incest reflected a predominantly psychological rather than a biological or social concept of the taboo. Incest was defined to mean any sexual relationship between a child and an adult in a position of paternal authority. From the psychological point of view, it does not matter if the father and child are blood relatives. What matters is the relationship that exists by virtue of the adult's parental power and the child's dependency. In fact, most of the informants (thirty-one, or 78 percent) had been molested by their biologic fathers. Five had been molested by stepfathers, and four by adoptive fathers.

We further defined a sexual relationship to mean any physical contact that had to be kept a secret. From a biological or social point of view, only contact which might lead to defloration or pregnancy, that is vaginal intercourse, is dignified with the name of incest. This narrow definition is reflected both in the criminal codes of most states and in the popular thinking on the subject. From the point of view of the adult male, sexual activity that stops short of penile penetration is often described as "unconsummated," as though somehow it does not "count." But from a psychological point of view, especially from the child's point of view, the sexual motivation of the contact, and the fact that it must be kept secret, are far more significant than the exact nature of the act itself. From the moment that the father initiates the child into activities which serve the father's sexual needs, and which must be hidden from others, the bond between parent and child is corrupted.

The composite portrait of the incestuous family which emerged from the testimony of the informants is only one version of a complex reality. It is, first of all, a retrospective portrait, with all the simplification and distortion that inevitably degrades an adult's memory of childhood. Second, it is a portrait drawn from the perspective of the victim alone. Nevertheless, as the investigation progressed, we gained increasing confidence in the accuracy of the informants' accounts. Each individual's testimony had the vividness and integrity of well-preserved memory, and the accounts of many informants were so similar that they tended to validate each other. Finally, the general picture which emerged from the collective testimony of the informants has been corroborated in many respects by other researchers who have directly observed incestuous fathers, mothers, or entire families.

The families in which the informants grew up were conventional to a fault. Most were churchgoing and financially stable; they maintained a facade of respectability. They were for the most part unknown to mental health services, social agencies, or the police. Because they conformed to traditional family norms, their private disturbances were easily overlooked:

> *Marion:* Yes, we were what you call an intact family. My mother lived at Church and Church functions. My father sang in the choir, and he molested me while my mother was at Sunday School class parties. There was no drinking or smoking or anything the world could see. Only God knows.

The informants described their fathers as perfect patriarchs. They were, without question, the heads of their households. Their authority within the family was absolute, often asserted by force. They were also the arbiters of the family's social life and frequently succeeded in virtually secluding the women in the family. But while they were often feared within their families, they impressed outsiders as sympathetic, even admirable men.

The daughters themselves were often impressed, for their fathers did have many strengths. Most took their responsibility to provide for the family very seriously. Their daughters knew them to be hard-working, competent, and often very successful:

> *Yvonne:* My father was a jack of all trades. Throughout his life he did many interesting things. He was manager of a state agency, foreman of a construction company, and even a politician; he ran for the State Senate. He was likable and could talk anyone into helping him out when he was in a jam. I remember him as a big man, about six feet tall, and very good-looking.

> *Christine:* My sisters and I used to feel really proud to see our father dressed up in his uniform. Or when he was called away on flight duty we'd be very excited to hear him talk about bombs and how he was going to protect our country.

Thirty-one of the forty fathers were the sole support of their families. Two policemen, three military officers, two physicians, and two college professors were included in their number, as well as an assortment of businessmen, storekeepers, and skilled tradesmen. Many worked long hours and held more than one job. Their role as family breadwinner was honored with almost ritual solemnity:

> *Lily:* No matter what had gone on that week, every Friday my father would bring home his paycheck. He'd take my mother's hand and put the check in it and close her hand over it without saying a word.

The competence in work and social life of incestuous fathers has also been documented in many previous studies. I. B. Weiner, in a clinical study of five fathers referred for outpatient treatment, observed that the fathers all had "successful work histories" and their families were not in "economic distress."[3] Herbert Maisch, in his study of 72 cases reported to the German courts, characterized the offenders as working-class men with average or above-average levels of skill.[4] Several investigators remarked as well on the fathers' above-average intelligence.[5] Noel Lustig, in his study of six military men who committed incest, described the fathers as "strongly motivated to maintain a facade of role competence as the family patriarch in the eyes of society." The men were well thought of outside their families.[6]

In addition, the families of our informants adhered rigidly to the traditional sexual division of labor. Most of the mothers were full-time houseworkers who depended entirely upon their husbands for their livelihood. Six mothers did some part-time work outside the home. Only three mothers had full-time jobs. None of the mothers had the working skills or experience which would have made independent survival a realistic option.

The mothers were considered inferior to the fathers, not only in their work achievements, but also simply in their status as women. These were families in which sex roles were rigidly defined, and male superiority was unquestioned:

Christine: My father just thought women were stupid. He had a very, very low opinion of women, and he never made my mother feel like she was worth anything. Nothing she could do was any good.

The preference for males was expressed in countless ways. Boys in the family were given more freedom and privileges than girls, or were excused from household chores. Some families paid for the education of their sons but not their daughters. One daughter recalled that with each of her mother's numerous pregnancies, her father proudly informed the relatives that his wife was expecting a boy.

In many families, it was considered a male prerogative to supervise and restrict the activities of the females. Fathers exercised minute control over the lives of their wives and daughters, often virtually confining them to the house. The boys in the family were sometimes enlisted as deputies in this policing role. Many daughters reported that their fathers discouraged their mothers from driving a car, visiting friends, or participating in activities outside the home:

Yvonne: My mother was a secretary when she met my father, and she became his secretary. After they were married, my parents moved away from my mother's birthplace, to Vermont. My father told my mother she should not work or

drive there because it was too cold and too dangerous in the snow. She never drove or worked again.

Daughters were also deterred from establishing any independent social contacts. The fathers consolidated their power within the family by isolating their wives and children from the outside world:

Sheila: We had no visitors. My father was very exclusive, and my mother was afraid to let people in when he had been drinking. People just didn't come to our house. I remember my best friend who lived across the street from me: people would float in and out of her house like it was Grand Central Station. I used to think, wouldn't it be nice to be able to do that.

One of the most significant distinguishing characteristics of the incestuous fathers was their tendency to dominate their families by the use of force. Half of the informants reported that their fathers were habitually violent and that they themselves had seen their mothers beaten (see Table 5.3). Other children in the family were often beaten as well. The fathers were selective in their choice of targets: one child was often singled out as a scapegoat, while a more favored child was spared. This lesson was not lost on the daughters, who quickly recognized the advantages of being in their fathers' good graces:

Esther: My father is an extremely macho and egotistical person, an educated elitist who always felt that he married beneath him. In fact, he is extremely intelligent and artistically creative. I have always admired his superior intellect and his talent. But he is also a very willful and childishly demanding person who has always had his own way. He is and always was subject to fits of irrational violence, and the whole family is scared to death of him. Except for me, that is.

This violence, though terrifying to the mothers and children, did not exceed certain clear limits. No family member was injured seriously enough to require hospitalization, though there were some close calls, and no outside intervention was provoked. Although the fathers often appeared completely out of control in the privacy of their homes, they never made the mistake of attacking outsiders. They

TABLE 5.3

Distinguishing Characteristics of Incestuous Families and Comparison Group

Family Characteristic	Incest Families		Comparison Group	
	No. = 40	%	No. = 20	%
Father violent[a]				
Yes	20	50	4	20
No	20	50	16	80
Father alcoholic				
Yes	15	37.5	7	35
No	25	62.5	13	65
Mother ill[b]				
Yes	22	55	3	15
No	18	45	17	85
Mother-child separation[b]				
Yes	15	37.5	0	0
No	25	62.5	20	100
Daughter's family role[b]				
Maternal	18	45	1	5
Mediator	6	15	3	15
Nonmaternal	16	40	16	80
Children in family				
1	6	15	4	20
2	9	22.5	6	30
3	8	20	4	20
4	10	25	3	15
5	2	5	2	10
6	0	0	0	0
7	0	0	1	5
8	3	7.5	0	0
9	1	2.5	0	0
10–13	0	0	0	0
14	1	2.5	0	0
Mean	3.6[c]		2.85	

[a] Differences between the two groups were significant at the $p < .05$ level.
[b] Differences between the two groups were significant at the $p < .01$ level.
[c] Difference between this mean and the national mean of 2.2 was significant at the $p < .01$ level.

Many previous studies have recognized the dictatorial role of fathers in incestuous families. One explained the father's "dominant position" as resulting from his "intimidation and control of the family."[7] Another described the father as "the authoritarian head of the house."[8] Still another observer indicated that "in an overwhelming majority of all cases, the family structure was formed by . . . the dominating influence of the husband and father."[9]

Other observers, however, have described the same fathers as "ineffectual and dependent," "inadequate," or "weak, insecure and vulnerable."[10] Far from appearing as tyrants, these fathers emerge as rather pitiful men, sometimes even as victims of a "domineering or managing wife."[11] The solution to this apparent contradiction lies in the fathers' ability to assess their relative power in any situation and to vary their behavior accordingly. In the presence of men much more powerful than themselves, such as police, prosecutors, therapists, and researchers, the fathers knew how to present themselves as pathetic, helpless, and confused. Only in the privacy of their homes, where they knew they would encounter no effective opposition, did they indulge their appetites for domination. Face to face with men of equal or superior authority, they became engaging and submissive.

Male professionals who are not themselves intimidated often find it hard to imagine how women and children might be. As one expert on child abuse admits: "Many sexually abusive fathers are described as tyrants in the home. . . . Professionals who have worked with sexual abuse frequently encounter a father who has been described in these terms. When he enters the office for an interview, the professional is astonished to find this 'violent and unpredictable' man to be 5'7", 150 pounds and neatly dressed. He is of a calm disposition and appears to be a rather anxious, harassed and overburdened man, puzzled by recent events."[12] A 5'7", 150-pound man out in public and on good behavior may not seem at all frightening to a larger man in a position of authority. But the same man may be quite large enough to terrorize his wife and children behind closed doors.

Alcoholism was another common characteristic of the incestuous fathers of our informants,

were not known as bullies or troublemakers; in the presence of superior authority, they were generally ingratiating, deferential, even meek. In this, as in many other aspects of family life, they seemed exquisitely sensitive to the bounds of the male prerogative, and did not exceed the socially condoned limits of violence.

though not a distinguishing one. Over a third of the informants considered their fathers to be problem drinkers. Like the violence, however, the fathers' drinking was effectively concealed from outsiders. Family relationships were often severely disrupted by the father's excessive drinking, and in a few cases the father's health was seriously affected, but most fathers retained their ability to work and to conform to normal standards of public behavior. If the father's drinking problem was recognized at all, it usually fell into the category of "a good man's failing." Very few fathers received any medical or psychiatric treatment for alcoholism or, for that matter, for any other problem.

Alcoholism has frequently been associated with incestuous behavior. In one study of imprisoned sex offenders, for example, 46 percent of the incestuous fathers were diagnosed as alcoholic, a figure that approximates our own. But as that study points out, although sex offenders who are alcoholic often commit their crimes while drunk, it is naive to attribute the offense to demon alcohol. The sexual assault, more often than not, is planned in advance. On careful questioning, offenders often admit that they drink in order to gather courage for the approach.[13]

While the fathers of our informants preserved a facade of competent social functioning, the mothers were often unable to fulfill their traditional roles. Over half of the informants (55 percent) remembered that their mothers had had periods of disabling illness which resulted in frequent hospitalizations or in the mother's living as an invalid at home. Over a third (38 percent) of the daughters had been separated from their mothers for some period of time during childhood. The separations occurred because their mothers either were hospitalized or felt unable to cope with their child care duties and temporarily placed their daughters in the care of relatives. Three mothers died before their daughters were grown, one by suicide. Another mother committed suicide after her daughter left home.

Depression, alcoholism, and psychosis were among the most common causes of the mothers' disability. Many daughters remembered their mothers as suffering from mysterious ailments

which made them seem withdrawn, peculiar, and unavailable. One daughter reported that when she was ten, her mother developed the delusion that she was dying of cancer and took to bed for a year. Many other daughters commented on their mothers' strange maladies which seemed to elude definition:

> *Janet:* She was almost like a recluse. She was very alone. It was obvious to me by the time I reached high school that my mother was really strange. My sisters and I used to joke about it.

As in the case of the fathers, the mothers' psychiatric and medical problems usually went undiagnosed and untreated.

If the cause of the mother's ailment sometimes seemed obscure, in other cases it was only too obvious: repeated enforced pregnancies. The average number of children for this group of mothers was 3.6, well above the national mean of 2.2. Seventeen mothers had four children or more, and five had eight or more children (see Table 5.3). Although some daughters reported that their mothers loved babies and had always wanted large families, in many cases the pregnancies were more or less imposed on women who felt helpless to prevent them:

> *Rita:* I blame my father for her death, to a certain degree. After the seventh child, they found out she had cancer, and they told her not to get pregnant again. But she couldn't control it, my father being the man he is. He felt, if you're going to have sex, you have to have the child. And he was the type of man who would say, if I can't get it from my wife, I'll go elsewhere. He's also the type of man where, if she didn't want to open her legs, he'd pinch her thighs.

Whether or not they wanted to have many children, the mothers of large families often suffered physically from their multiple pregnancies and became overwhelmed with the burden of caring for many small children:

> *Christine:* Now I know she was only 98 pounds at the age of twenty-five. She was yellow, jaundiced; she had some kind of kidney infection; and she was sick with every one of her pregnancies. We were barely a year apart, and I think having kids in such rapid succession, my mother was really tired out.

Four of the mothers also had severely handicapped children, whose care absorbed virtually all their energies.

Numerous researchers have commented on the surprisingly large number of children found in incestuous families. In Maisch's German study, the average number of children was 3.48, compared to a national average of 1.8.[14] Studies of other populations have found even higher averages. For example, a study of an American inner-city population found an average of 4.7 children of incest families, compared to a mean of 3.9 in a comparison group.[15] A study of imprisoned incestuous fathers reported that they had an average of 5.1 children.[16] And a study of a rural Irish population reported an average of seven children in incestuous families, as compared to a county average of 4.5.[17] Only one researcher, however, apparently understood the connection between the large size of the family and the relative powerlessness of the mother: "The finding relating to more children in the home of incest families . . . suggests an overburdened mother, possibly tired because of early and prolonged childbearing. . . . Perhaps it gives us some insight into the mother's general forbearance and passive acceptance of the incest offender's peculiar behavior in the home."[18]

Economically dependent, socially isolated, in poor health, and encumbered with the care of many small children, these mothers were in no position to challenge their husbands' domination or to resist their abuses. No matter how badly they were treated, most simply saw no option other than submission to their husbands. They conveyed to their daughters the belief that a woman is defenseless against a man, that marriage must be preserved at all costs, and that a wife's duty is to serve and endure.

Most of our informants remembered their mothers as weak and powerless, finding their only dignity in martyrdom. The few who described their mothers as strong meant by this that there was apparently no limit to their capacity for suffering:

Rita: She held on because that's all she had. Everything she did was self-sacrifice. She made sure there was food on everyone's plate—whatever we left behind, that's what she ate. She went around in the same housedress and a pair of loafers day after day—never any new clothing. She never wore makeup, never colored her hair, never spent money on herself. Her kids came first.

Anne-Marie: She always said, give with one hand and you'll get with the other, but she gave with two hands and always went down. She was nothing but a floor mat. She sold out herself and her self-respect. She was a love slave to my father.

None of the fathers adapted to their wives' disabilities by assuming a maternal role in the family. Rather, they reacted to their wives' illnesses as if they themselves were being deprived of mothering. As the family providers, they felt they had the right to be nurtured and served at home, if not by their wives, then by their daughters.

Thirty-two (80 percent) of the informants were the oldest or the only daughters in their families.[19] Before the age of ten, almost half (45 percent) had been pressed into service as "little mothers" within the family. They cared for their younger sisters and brothers and took on responsibility for major household tasks. Many became astonishingly competent in this role. Pride in their accomplishments as little adults became their compensation for loss of childhood:

Christine: I could see that my mother needed help, but she wouldn't ask for it; she'd nag and bitch, and that would turn my sisters off. My sisters were very unproductive. So I'd pitch in without being asked. I'd vacuum, I'd do the laundry, I'd wash the dishes, I'd do this, I'd do that. This was from the time I was, oh, nine. I still think I can do a lot of things better than my mother.

Whether or not they were obliged to take on household responsibilities, most of the daughters were assigned a special duty to "keep Daddy happy." They mediated parental quarrels and placated their fathers when their mothers dared not approach them. They became their fathers' confidantes and often shared their grievances and secrets.

In their special roles as little mother or as father's consort, the daughters believed that they bore the responsibility for holding the family together. None of the informants thought that her parents were happily married;

many were well aware that their parents were miserable together. Though a few daughters wished devoutly that their parents would divorce, most dreaded this possibility, and did whatever they could to avert it. They lived in terror that their fathers would desert the family and that their mothers would fall apart completely.

Since it was their duty to provide a sympathetic audience for their fathers, many daughters heard about their parents' marital troubles in great detail. The fathers' complaints were monotonously simple. They considered themselves deprived of the care to which they felt entitled. In their estimation, their wives were not giving enough: they were cold; they were frigid; they refused sex; they withheld love.

These complaints seemed plausible enough to the daughters, who themselves often felt deprived of maternal affection. Some daughters were additionally aware that their mothers had highly negative sexual attitudes:

Janet: My mother is a terrible prude. I don't remember any of her sayings, but I remember the feeling behind them. It was so ugly, it made sex sound like the dirtiest thing around.

In retrospect, however, most daughters felt that their fathers' complaints wore a little thin and that their parents' problems must have been more complicated than their fathers' accounts had led them to believe. As adults, they puzzled over what went wrong and who was most at fault:

Marion: In my case I put most of the blame on my mother. She is a cold person—cannot show love to anyone except babies. She started a large family and ignored my father from the day she got pregnant. I have seen her many times shove Daddy away from her. I feel she drove my Dad to this thing. He was starved for affection. Still, he may have had a deeper problem; I'll never know. He couldn't seem to keep his hands to himself. I never brought a girlfriend home. He would squeeze all the neighbors' wives in the wrong places. He didn't seem to care if we saw him or not. He made me sick at my stomach.

Janet: He would just talk in very personal terms about how deprived he was. But then my mother says she always did have sex with him, so I don't know who was telling the truth.

At the time, most of the daughters took their fathers' side. It was easy enough to sympathize with the fathers' feeling of deprivation, for most of the daughters themselves felt slighted or neglected by their mothers. Though many could see that their mothers were ill or overwhelmed with their own problems, few, as children, could afford the luxury of compassion. They knew only that they bore the burden of their mothers' shortcomings and were obliged to nurture others while their own longings for nurture went unsatisfied. In these circumstances, the daughters could not escape feeling profoundly disappointed in their mothers.

At best, the daughters viewed their mothers ambivalently, excusing their weaknesses as best they could. The one daughter out of the forty who cherished a positive image of her mother did so on the basis of a fantasy which she created after her mother's death. Though her mother had endured savage beatings herself and had been helpless to prevent the abuse of her children, this daughter clung to the belief that her mother would have taken protective action, had she lived.

At worst, the relations between mother and daughter were marked by active hostility. Many of the daughters remembered their mothers only with bitterness and contempt. They described the women who had borne them as selfish, uncaring, and cruel. In their moments of despair, these daughters felt the absence of the most primary bonds of caring and trust. They believed they had been unwanted from the moment of their birth, and they cursed their mothers for bringing them into the world:

Esther: My mother was extraordinarily rejecting. I was born ten months after my brother, and I was clearly an "accident," greatly regretted.

Paula: She's an asshole. I really don't like my mom. I guess I am bitter. She's very selfish. She was seventeen when she had me, and her mother put her in a home. She blames me for ruining her life because she got pregnant with me. But I'm not the one who spread my legs.

Sandra: Why do people bother having kids? Why did my mother have me? I'm sure in those days people knew how to get rid of them. She seemed to know how. I wish she was dead so I could forget about her—or that I was dead so that she'd suffer. Why does God allow people like her to live?

Other authors have also remarked on the alienation between mothers and daughters which seems to prevail in incestuous families. Maisch found that 61 percent of the mothers and daughters in his study had a distant or hostile relationship which preceded the onset of overt incest.[20]

By contrast, most of our informants had some fond memories of their fathers. Although they feared their fathers, they also admired their competence and power. Many described their fathers as gifted, likable, and intelligent, terms that they rarely applied to their mothers. Some remembered that, as children, they had frankly adored their fathers:

Sheila: It was nice having a father who did things with you. He loved to take us on trips and show us around. He was fun to be with.

Lenore: We had long intellectual conversations. My father lectured me about history. I was a captive audience. I was so impressed. He was my idol.

Feelings of pity for the fathers were also common. With few exceptions, the daughters seemed more tolerant of their fathers' shortcomings and more forgiving of their failures than they were toward their mothers, or themselves:

Esther: I find that most of my anger is toward my mother rather than my father. I know that is not quite rational, but I can't help feeling that the bond between mother and child ought to be such that a child is assured protection. I somehow do not expect that fathers are as responsible for the welfare of offspring as mothers are.

All of the daughters received favored treatment from their fathers, in the form of gifts, privileges, or exemption from punishments. Many spent long hours in the exclusive company of their fathers, often on adventures which were kept secret from the rest of the family:

Christine: He used to call me his mama-san, and I used to massage his feet. He used to take me to stag bars. I thought that was great. I used to really like him. I was definitely Daddy's girl.

In the special alliance with their fathers, many daughters found the sense of being cared for which they craved, and which they obtained from no other source. The attentions of their fathers offered some compensation for what was lacking in their relations with their mothers.

Mothers were often suspicious and resentful of this special relationship. They perceived, correctly, that what bound father and daughter together was in part a shared hostility toward themselves. The mothers' resentment made the daughters feel guilty, but could not entirely extinguish the pleasure they derived from their favored status. Some even exulted in their mothers' mortification:

Paula: Face it, she was just jealous. The man she loved preferred me!

These daughters, in short, were alienated from their mothers, whom they saw as weak, helpless, and unable to nurture or protect them. They were elevated by their fathers to a special position in the family, in which many of the mothers' duties and privileges were assigned to them. They felt obligated to fulfill this role in order to keep their families together. Moreover, their special relationship with their fathers was often perceived as their only source of affection. Under these circumstances, when their fathers chose to demand sexual services, the daughters felt they had absolutely no option but to comply.

Most of the daughters (80 percent) were under thirteen years of age when their fathers first approached them sexually. The average age was nine (see Table 5.4). The sexual contact was limited at first to fondling and gradually proceeded to masturbation and oral-genital contact. Most fathers did not attempt vaginal intercourse, at least until their daughters had reached puberty. Force was rarely used. It was not necessary:

Yvonne: The first time I remember any sexual advances, I was about four or five. I hadn't started school yet. My parents were having a party—that is, my mother was entertaining some women. My father took my brother and me to bed to be out of the way. My brother lay on one side of him, me on the other. I remember him curling up beside me, pressing me to him

TABLE 5.4

Incest Histories

History	Number	Percentage
Child's age at onset		
<5	4	10
5–6	5	12.5
7–8	8	20
9–10	9	22.5
11–12	4	10
13+	8	20
Unknown (<13)	2	5
Mean	9.4	
Duration		
Single incident	7	17.5
0–2 years	13	32.5
3–5 years	8	20
>5 years	9	22.5
Unknown	3	7.5
Mean	3.3	
Repetition with sisters		
Yes	11	27.5
Unknown	10	25
No	6	15
No available sisters	13	32.5
Secrecy broken with child at home		
Yes	17	42.5
No	23	57.5
Mean duration before secrecy broken		3.8 years
Agency intervention		
Yes	3	7.5
No	37	92.5
Court intervention		
Yes	3	7.5
No	37	92.5

from behind and touching my vagina. I also remember him playing with my ass. I only remember lying there and him telling me that was what Adam and Eve did, so it was okay.

Those authors who restrict their definition of incest to intercourse find that the daughters are somewhat older, on the average, at the onset of the relationship. In Maisch's study, the average age of the daughter was 12¼ at the time intercourse began.[21] Other researchers who define incest, as we do, to mean any sexual contact find, as we do, that most relationships begin when the children are grade-schoolers. The

girls in one study were five to fourteen years old; those in another were between the ages of six and fourteen.[22]

The father's explanations to our informants, if any were offered, always sounded silly in retrospect. Younger girls were told, "This is how we learn about the birds and the bees," "This is our special game," or "Don't you want to make Daddy feel good?" Older girls were told, "I'm getting you ready for your husband," "You should feel comfortable about sex," or "You need me to teach you the facts of life." Many of the fathers seemed to consider it their parental prerogative to introduce their daughters to sex.

Sometimes the sexual encounter took on the aspect of an initiation rite. By introducing their daughters into secret and forbidden knowledge, the fathers compelled their daughters to leave girlhood behind and taught them something about their place in the world as women:

Jackie: That was the year I grew up. I got my period, and I gave up my dolls and stopped being a tomboy.

Sara: As a child I thought, why would someone that I love and who loves me do anything wrong to me. There seemed to be no other answer but . . . this is natural, and this is the way it is. I thought maybe, just maybe, this was my personal indoctrination into womanhood.[23]

Seven of the daughters could remember only a single incident in which they were molested by their fathers. But the majority recalled that once begun, the sexual contact was repeated whenever the father could find an opportunity. On the average, the incestuous relationship went on for three years. Other studies agree that the majority of incestuous relationships are of long duration.[24]

Although many of our informants were too young to have a clear idea of the significance of the father's behavior, the father's furtive attitude usually indicated to the daughters that there was something wrong with what they were doing:

Lenore: When I was around seven, that's when the first sexual incident happened with my father. They used to have us kids in bed with them sometimes, and he continued this after mother was in the hospital. I got more favored attention. One time he called me in. He had a hard on and he had a rubber on. He told me to jerk him off. He told me to squeeze it and he came. I was a pretty innocent kid, pretty isolated. I didn't know what it was. I can't remember whether he told me not to tell, but it was intense and hurried and he was ashamed. He sent me away right after he came. I knew he would deny it, but I have a vivid memory of it.

Few of the daughters had anything positive to say about the sexual contact itself. Though many enjoyed other aspects of their special relationship with their fathers, most dreaded the sexual encounters and invented whatever pitiful strategies they could to avoid them:

> *Rita:* I hated it all the time; it was like a nightmare. There was nothing I could do. I went along with the program. I don't know why he went along with it, because I never responded. Every time I'd say, "Daddy, I gotta go pee." You know, anything to get out of it.

Fear, disgust, and shame were the feelings most commonly remembered. Most of the daughters coped with the sexual episodes by mentally dissociating themselves from them. They "froze up" or pretended that "it wasn't really happening":

> *Sheila:* My head just died then. It was an impossible thing for me to handle, so I just didn't handle it. It's like it never happened. Every time I try to talk about it, my mind goes blank. It's like everything explodes in my head.

A few informants remembered that they had experienced some pleasure in the sexual encounters, or that they had sometimes initiated the contact once the routine of the sexual relationship had become established. These memories only exacerbated their feelings of confusion and shame:

> *Paula:* With my father, I was the aggressor. He'd come in my bed and cuddle me and eat me; then he'd threaten me not to tell. He loved me very much. He just had a sickness. He was a good man in every other way. He went to church and worked six days a week. Maybe I did go up to my father and cuddle him, but I was a child; you don't make anything of it.

In these few instances, the fathers might have been able to convince themselves that their daughters desired and enjoyed their sexual attentions. But in most cases, the fathers persisted in their sexual demands even in the face of their daughters' obvious reluctance. Why they chose to do so is a matter of speculation. Presumably, they experienced their own needs as so compelling that they chose to ignore their daughters' unhappiness.

Some researchers who have studied incestuous fathers directly emphasize the father's unfulfilled dependent wishes and fear of abandonment. In the father's fantasy life, the daughter becomes the source of all the father's infantile longings for nurturance and care. He thinks of her first as the idealized childhood bride or sweetheart, and finally as the all-good, all-giving mother. The reality, that she is the child and he the adult, becomes quite immaterial to him. In the compulsive sexual act he seeks repeated reassurance that she will never refuse or frustrate him.[25]

In addition, the father must experience the sexual act itself as powerfully rewarding. He can structure the sexual encounter exactly to his liking, with no fear that his performance will be judged or ridiculed. His excitement is heightened by the need for secrecy and the sense of indulging in the forbidden. The sexual contact becomes like an addiction, one which, unlike alcohol or other drugs, leaves no morning hangover other than possibly a guilty conscience. The incestuous father can indulge his habit repeatedly and suffer no bodily consequences; if there are any, it is the daughter who suffers them.

Finally, in some cases the daughter's unhappiness actually contributes to the father's enjoyment. Many researchers have noted that incest, like other sex crimes, fulfills the offender's hostile and aggressive wishes. Power and dominance, rather than sexual pleasure, may be the primary motivation. One researcher, who administered psychological tests to convicted incest offenders, concluded that the incest was an expression of hostility to all women, and that the daughter was selected as the victim because she was perceived as the woman least capable of retaliation.[26]

Most of our informants were warned not to tell anyone about the sexual episodes. They were threatened with the most dreadful consequences if they told: their mothers would have a nervous breakdown, their parents would divorce, their fathers would be put in jail, or they themselves would be punished and sent away from home. One way or another, the girls were given to understand that breaking secrecy would lead to separation from one or both of their parents. Those who remembered no warnings simply intuited that guarding the incest secret was part of their obligation to keep the family together:

Janet: I just knew there would be dire consequences if I told. My mother would fall apart, or they would separate. I didn't even want to imagine what would happen.

In some cases, the fathers threatened severe bodily harm:

Maggie: He told me if I told anyone he would have me shot. I believed him because he was a cop. I'm thirty years old and I'm still afraid of him.

The majority of the daughters (58 percent) never explicitly told their mothers, or anyone else, of the incest as long as they remained at home. Nevertheless, they longed for their mothers to come to their rescue. Often they tried, indirectly, to indicate to their mothers that something was wrong. Many had vague symptoms of distress: they complained of abdominal pains or pain while urinating; they became fearful or withdrawn; they had nightmares. Such "nonspecific" symptoms are typical of incestuously abused children, in the observations of many clinicians.[27] A few of our informants as children developed compulsive, ritualized sexual behaviors that would have alerted any knowledgeable observer to the fact that something was wrong. For instance, one girl, at the age of five, began approaching male acquaintances and unzipping their pants. Others "experimented" sexually with younger children, subjecting them to the same assaults to which they themselves had been subjected. These and numerous other indirect cries for help were ignored or misunderstood by the mothers. Many daughters believed that their mothers knew, or should have known, about the incest, and they bitterly resented the fact that their mothers did not intervene:

Sheila: One day she was at work, and she was so worried that something really bad was happening at home that she actually left work and came home. When she got home, I was locked in the bathroom crying, and I remember her saying to my father, "What's the matter with her?" I guess I have a hard time reconciling the fact that that happened and she still didn't realize I was in trouble. How come she never asked *me* what was happening to me? How come she never tried to find out how *I* felt?

Christine: My mother's philosophy is to ignore things and hope they'll go away. She's always a victim; even in little things she always finds stupid reasons why she can't do anything about the situation. She knew about the incest; there's no way she couldn't have known. But she's never acknowledged it. She just says men are that way and there's nothing she could do about it.

Those daughters who did confide in their mothers were uniformly disappointed in their mothers' responses. Most of the mothers, even when made aware of the situation, were unwilling or unable to defend their daughters. They were too frightened or too dependent upon their husbands to risk a confrontation. Either they refused to believe their daughters, or they believed them but took no action. They made it clear to their daughters that their fathers came first and that, if necessary, the daughters would have to be sacrificed:

Yvonne: The last time my father made these advances I was about eight or nine. My mom caught us again and my dad promised he wouldn't do it again. Then he got very drunk, went outside, and lay under a tree at night. My mom woke me up and told me my dad was drunk under the tree and wouldn't come in. She wanted me to ask him to come in before he got pneumonia. I got up, went out on the porch—it was damp and cool out—and did as my mother asked. I asked my dad to come in. He did. I decided after that that they were both pretty nuts.

Only three mothers, on learning about the incest, responded by separating from their husbands, and even in these few cases the separations were brief. The mothers found life without their husbands too hard to bear, and they took them back within a matter of months. Three other mothers, on discovering the incest secret, sent their daughters away from home:

Paula: She was afraid I'd become a lesbian or a whore. So she put me in a mental hospital. It was a good excuse to get rid of me.

In general, those daughters who told their mothers had reason to regret it. Sensing correctly that no protection would be forthcoming if they told, most of the daughters bore the incestuous relationship in silence, biding their time until they were old enough to leave home.

Some of the daughters developed close relationships with adult women outside the family, which partially compensated for their disappointment with their mothers. Though few dared to confide their secrets to these outsiders, the relationships helped the daughters to endure the misery of their family life:

Marion: My mother's sister was the only person in my childhood that I remember relating to at all. She lived on a farm with her three children, and I used to go there in the summer. I love the outdoors and that is where I would play most of the time. I never stayed at home if I could help it. I didn't tell her about my Dad, but we talked about Mom and how funny she acted sometimes. She said if I knew how they had been brought up, I would understand. She never explained it. I remember wishing she was my mother.

Sandra: My best friend's mother used to take me in when my mother threw me out. If it weren't for her, I'd be sleeping in hallways. Anyone with half a brain and half a heart would open their doors, but not too many really do it. I was well off there; I lived with them till I had my first labor pains. Marriage was a change for the worse. I wish I'd stayed with them.

The girls who found surrogate mothers were among the most fortunate. All of the women longed for a mother who could be strong, competent, and affectionate. Many desperately envied their friends and classmates who appeared to have normal mothers:

Lenore: When I hear other women complaining about their mothers, I feel like screaming,

"You stupid idiot, don't you realize how lucky you are?"

Some of the daughters expressed their disappointment in both parents by elaborating the fantasy that they were adopted and that their true parents would one day find and rescue them. Others simply resigned themselves to the fact that, from an emotional point of view, they were orphans:

Janet: I remember very clearly at age nine I decided that if they did get divorced, I didn't want to live with either one of them.

As the daughters reached adolescence, they often became more assertive and rebellious. The fathers responded with intense jealousy, bordering on paranoia. They did whatever they could to seclude and isolate their daughters and to prevent them from developing normal relationships with peers. They saw the outside world as filled with sexual dangers and opportunities, and they often regarded their daughters as untrustworthy little bitches who needed to be closely guarded. Many daughters reported that their fathers would tear up their clothes, forbid lipstick or makeup, and refuse to allow parties or dates:

Sheila: He would raise the roof because of the clothing that I wore or how I looked. I think I was the last kid in my whole group to start wearing lipstick. I didn't really understand what it was all about. All I knew was my father was telling me I was very bad for some reason and it all involved *that.*

Other fathers eventually accepted the inevitable and permitted their daughters to have some social life, but insisted on interrogating their daughters about their sexual activities:

Lenore: He would tell me not to throw myself away on some boy and sacrifice my intellect. I got the message loud and clear that you can't be sexual and have your intellect too. Later I realized that he wanted to keep me for himself. I was Daddy's little girl. When I hit high school, around age fifteen, I started screwing around a lot. I had been so isolated I never made friends. This seemed like an easy way to make contact with people. As soon as my father found out, he would find an excuse to beat the crap out of me. It happened whenever I had a new boyfriend. Supposedly his attitude was very libertarian. He wanted to hear about what I was doing. He was kind of lecherous about it.

As the fathers' jealousy and sexual demands became more and more intolerable, the daughters began to try to escape from the family. Thirteen girls ran away from home at least once (see Table 5.5). Most of the attempts were short-lived, for the girls quickly realized that they were not equipped to survive in the street,

TABLE 5.5

Distress Symptoms in Incest Victims and Comparison Group

Distress Symptom	Incest Victims No. = 40	%	Comparison Group No. = 20	%
Adolescent pregnancy[a]				
Yes	18	45	3	15
No	22	55	17	85
Runaway attempt				
Yes	13	32.5	1	5
No	27	67.5	19	95
Major depressive symptoms				
Yes	24	60	11	55
No	16	40	9	45
Suicide attempt				
Yes	15	37.5	1	5
No	25	62.5	19	95
Drug or alcohol abuse				
Yes	8	35	1	5
No	32	65	19	95
Sexual problems				
Yes	21	55	10	50
No	19	45	10	50
Promiscuity				
Yes	14	35	3	15
No	26	65	17	85
Victimization				
Yes (rape)	6	15	3	15
(beatings[a])	11	27.5	0	0
No	24	60	17	85
Self-image[b]				
Predominantly +	3	7.5	2	10
Dual or confused ±	13	32.5	16	80
Predominantly −	24	60	2	10

[a]Differences between the two groups were significant at the p < .05 level.
[b]Differences between the two groups were significant at the p < .02 level.

and they reluctantly returned home. Only two girls managed to make good their escape. From mid-adolescence, they supported themselves as strippers or prostitutes:

Paula: I ran away to New York. I was on my own at age sixteen. I never had a pimp; I wasn't that crazy. I knew a lot of women in the business and I did a lot of speed and downs. If I hadn't met up with my boyfriend, I'd be dead today.

Three girls who ran away were pursued, caught, and committed to hospitals on "stubborn child" complaints. Their incest history did not come to light during these hospitalizations. Three others tried to get away from home by requesting foster placements or admission to residential schools. They, too, were unsuccessful:

Esther: The way I was able to get away from my father was by running away with an older man. Before that I had tried to get professional help with the aim of being placed in a girls' residence. I had several sessions with a social worker to whom I was unable to reveal the reason for my intense desire to leave home. She met with my father, and she was favorably impressed with his great love and concern for me. She refused to help me gain admittance at that girls' residence.

Just as the girls' childhood distress symptoms had been ignored, their adolescent escape attempts were misunderstood. None of the professionals with whom these girls came into contact undertook to find out why they were so desperate to get away from their families.

Sooner or later, most of the daughters realized that the only way to escape from their fathers was to find another powerful male protector. A great many became pregnant or married prematurely. Eighteen of the forty women (45 percent) became pregnant during adolescence. In most cases, they had no particular desire for children, and the pregnancies were unintended. Planned or not, however, the pregnancies usually did put an end to the incest.[28]

For many of the daughters, marriage appeared to be the passport to freedom. Some confessed the incest secret for the first time to their husbands or fiancés. A number of the men responded in a very caring and appropriate manner: they were angry at the fathers and concerned about the harm that had been done to the daughters. Women who were lucky enough to find men who responded in this way usually felt extremely grateful.

As the fathers felt their daughters slipping out of their control, they began to cast about for substitutes. If there were younger sisters in the family, the fathers often transferred their sexual attentions to them. In eleven families (28 percent), incest was repeated with younger sisters. In another ten families (25 percent), the daughters suspected that their sisters had been molested but could not be positive about it. In one third of the families, there was no repetition of the incest because there were no available sisters. The phenomenon of the father's "moving on" to a younger daughter has been observed by many authors, some of whom report even higher proportions of families in which this occurs.[29]

Brothers were not molested, according to our informants. However, a number of brothers were physically abused, and several developed assaultive and abusive behavior in identification with their fathers. One of the daughters was molested by her brother as well as her father; she felt that her father, in breaching the incest taboo, had given her brother tacit permission to do the same. Others suspected that their brothers were carrying on the family tradition in the next generation:

Marion: In all your research do you think it's inherited? I hate to say this, but I think my brother has the problem. I remember we had a cottage at the ocean when his little girl was three or four. I caught them in bed one time when we were all supposed to be gone. I saw him fondling her and it made me sick. After that I saw very little of him until recently. He has two granddaughters now. I feel he's abnormally proud of the one; I can't explain it, but it's there. This I have never told anyone.

In several families, the fathers deserted once the daughters had left home. This outcome confirmed the daughters' belief that they had been responsible for keeping the family together, and that the parents' marriage depended upon the incestuous relationship for its survival.

In no case was the incestuous relationship ended by the father. The daughters put a stop to the sexual contact as soon as they could, by whatever means they could. But most felt that in their fathers' minds, the incestuous affair never ended, and that their fathers would gladly resume the sexual relationship if they were ever given an opportunity. Though all the daughters eventually succeeded in escaping from their families, they felt, even at the time of the interview, that they would never be safe with their fathers, and that they would have to defend themselves as long as their fathers lived.

NOTES

1. Class backgrounds were determined in accordance with criteria in Harry Braverman, *Labor and Monopoly Capital* (New York: Monthly Review Press, 1974). "Middle class" is shorthand for the combined categories of "middle layers of employment" and "self-employed."
2. Maya Angelou, *I Know Why the Caged Bird Sings* (New York: Random House, 1970); Anne Moody, *Coming of Age in Mississippi* (New York: Dial Press, 1968); Toni Morrison, *The Bluest Eye* (New York: Holt, Rinehart and Winston, 1970); Gayl Jones, *Corregidora* (New York: Random House, 1975).
3. I. B. Weiner, "Father-Daughter Incest: A Clinical Report," *Psychiatric Quarterly* 36 (1962): 607–632.
4. Herbert Maisch, *Incest* (New York: Stein & Day, 1972).
5. Weiner, "Father-Daughter Incest"; Hector Cavallin, "Incestuous Fathers: A Clinical Report," *American Journal of Psychiatry* 122 (1966): 1132–1138.
6. Noel Lustig, John Dresser, Seth Spellman and Thomas Murray, "Incest: A Family Group Survival Pattern," *Archives of General Psychiatry* 14 (1966): 31–40.
7. S. Kirson Weinberg, *Incest Behavior* (New York: Citadel, 1955), p. 63.
8. Bruno Cormier, Miriam Kennedy, and Jadwiga Sangowicz, "Psychodynamics of Father-Daughter Incest," *Canadian Psychiatric Association Journal* 7 (1962): 206.
9. Maisch, *Incest*, p. 139.
10. David Raphling, Bob Carpenter, and Allan Davis, "Incest: A Genealogical Study," *Archives of General Psychiatry* 16 (1967): 505–511; Narcyz Lukianowicz, "Incest," *British Journal of Psychiatry* 120 (1972) p. 304; Werner Tuteur, "Further Observations on Incestuous Fathers," *Psychiatric Annals* 2 (1972): 77.
11. Joseph Peters, "Children Who Are Victims of Sexual Assault and the Psychology of Offenders," *American Journal of Psychotherapy* 30 (1976): 411.
12. David Walters, *Physical and Sexual Abuse of Children* (Bloomington: Indiana University Press, 1975), p. 122.
13. Richard Rada, Robert Kellner, D. R. Laws, and Walter Winslow, "Drinking, Alcoholism, and the Mentally Disordered Sex Offender," *Bulletin of the American Academy of Psychiatry and Law* 6 (1978): 296–300.
14. Maisch, *Incest*.
15. Yvonne Tormes, *Child Victims of Incest* (Denver: American Humane Association, 1968).
16. Cavallin, "Incestuous Fathers."
17. Lukianowicz, "Incest," pp. 301–313.
18. Tormes, *Child Victims of Incest*, p. 26.
19. Several other authors have commented on the oldest daughter's particular vulnerability to incestuous abuse. See, e.g., Tormes, *Child Victims of Incest;* Browning and Boatman, "Children at Risk"; Weinberg, *Incest Behavior;* Karin Meiselman, *Incest* (San Francisco: Jossey-Bass, 1978).
20. Maisch, *Incest*.

21. Maisch, *Incest*.

22. Lukianowicz, "Incest"; Irving Kaufman, Alice Peck, and Consuelo Tagiuri, "The Family Constellation and Overt Incestuous Relations Between Father and Daughter," *American Journal of Orthopsychiatry* 24 (1954): 266–277.

23. Anonymous letter, May 1979, in *Reaching Out,* newsletter of RESPOND, an organization working with women and domestic violence in Somerville, Mass.

24. Weinberg, *Incest Behavior;* Maisch, *Incest;* Kaufman et al., "Family Constellation"; Lukianowicz, "Incest"; Tormes, *Child Victims of Incest*.

25. Cormier et al., "Psychodynamics"; Lustig et al., "Family Group Survival Pattern."

26. Cavallin, "Incestuous Fathers."

27. Christine Adams-Tucker, "Sex-Abused Children: Pathology and Clinical Traits," paper presented at Annual Meeting of the American Psychiatric Association, May 1980; Vincent De Francis, *Protecting the Child Victim of Sex Crimes Committed by Adults* (Denver: American Humane Association, 1969), pp. 152–180.

28. Virginia Abernethy and her colleagues describe a family constellation which they associate with a high risk for unwanted pregnancy in young women. Though overt incest is not mentioned, the family dynamics that these authors describe are similar to those observed in incestuous families. They note the presence of a powerful father, a devalued mother, an exclusive relationship between father and daughter, and the reassignment of some maternal functions to the daughter. They interpret the pregnancy as a flight from the "threateningly incestuous" situation. Virginia Abernethy, Donna Robbins, George Abernethy, Henry Grunebaum, and Justin Weiss, "Identification of Women at Risk for Unwanted Pregnancy," *American Journal of Psychiatry* 132 (1975): 1027–1031.

29. Cavallin, "Incestuous Fathers"; Lukianowicz, "Incest"; Paul Sloane and Eva Karpinski, "Effects of Incest on the Participants," *American Journal of Orthopsychiatry* 12 (1942): 666–673; A. M. Gligor, "Incest and Sexual Delinquency: A Comparative Analysis of Two Forms of Sexual Behavior in Minor Females" (Ph.D. diss., Case Western Reserve University, 1966).

Racism

Inner-City Dislocations

WILLIAM JULIUS WILSON

The social problems of urban life in advanced industrial America are, in large measure, viewed as problems of race. Joblessness, urban crime, addiction, out-of-wedlock births, female-headed families, and welfare dependency have risen dramatically in the past several decades. Moreover . . . the rates reflect an amazingly uneven distribution by race. These problems are heavily concentrated in urban areas, but it would be a mistake to assume that they afflict all segments of the urban minority community. Rather . . . these problems disproportionately plague the urban underclass—a heterogeneous grouping of families and individuals in the inner city that are outside the mainstream of the American occupational system and that consequently represent the very bottom of the economic hierarchy. It is my view that the increasing rates of social dislocation in the inner city cannot be explained simply in terms of racial discrimination or in terms of a "culture of poverty," but should be viewed as having complex and interrelated sociological antecedents, ranging from demographic changes to the problems of societal organization.

Racial discrimination is the most frequently invoked explanation of racial variation in certain forms of urban social dislocation. Proponents of the discrimination thesis, however, often fail to make a distinction between the effects of historical discrimination and the effects of contemporary discrimination.

There is no doubt that contemporary discrimination has contributed to or aggravated the social and economic problems of the black poor. But is discrimination greater today than it was in 1948, when black unemployment (5.9%) was less than half the rate in 1980 (12.3%), and when the black/white unemployment ratio (1.7) was almost a quarter less than the ratio in 1980 (2.1)? There are obviously many reasons for the higher levels of black joblessness since the mid-1950s, but to suggest contemporary discrimination as the main factor is, as I shall soon show, to obscure the impact of major demographic and economic changes and to leave unanswered the question of why black unemployment was lower not after, but prior to, the mid-1950s.

It should also be pointed out that, contrary to prevailing opinion, the black family showed signs of deterioration not before, but after, the mid-twentieth century. Until the publication of Herbert Gutman's impressive historical study of the black family, it had been widely assumed that the contemporary problems of the black family could be traced back to slavery. Gutman, however, produced data demonstrating that the black family was not particularly disorganized either during slavery or during the early years of their first migration to the urban North, thereby suggesting that the present problems of black family disorganization are a product of more recent forces. But are these problems mainly a consequence of contemporary discrimination, or are they related to other factors that ostensibly have little to do with race? If contemporary discrimination is the main culprit, why have its nefarious effects produced the most severe problems of inner-city social dislocation—including joblessness—during the *1970s,* a decade that followed an unprecedented period of antidiscrimination legislation and that ushered in the proliferation of affirmative-action programs.

To repeat, the problem is to unravel the effects of contemporary discrimination, on the one hand, and historical discrimination, on

William Julius Wilson is the Lucy Flower Professor of Urban Sociology at the University of Chicago. He is the author, most recently, of The Declining Significance of Race: Blacks and Changing American Institutions. *His book* The Hidden Agenda: Race, Social Dislocations and Public Policy *is forthcoming from the University of Chicago Press.*

From *Society,* November/December 1983. Published by permission of Transaction Publishers, from *Society,* Vol. 21, No. 1.
Copyright © 1983 by Transaction Publishers.

the other. Even if all contemporary discrimination were eliminated, the problems of social dislocation in the inner city would persist for many years, until the effects of historical discrimination disappeared. However, a full appreciation of the legacy of historical discrimination is impossible without taking into account other historical and contemporary forces that have helped shape the experiences and behavior of impoverished urban minorities.

One of the major consequences of historical discrimination is the presence of a large black underclass in our central cities, plagued by problems of joblessness and other forms of social dislocation. Whereas blacks made up 23 percent of the population of central cities in 1977, they constituted 46 percent of the poor in those cities. In accounting for the historical developments that contributed to this concentration of urban black poverty, I will draw briefly upon Stanley Lieberson's recent and original study *A Piece of the Pie: Black and White Immigrants since 1880*. On the basis of a systematic analysis of early U.S. censuses and various other data sources, Lieberson showed that in many areas of life, including the labor market, blacks in the early twentieth century were discriminated against far more severely than the new immigrants from Southern, Central, and Eastern Europe. However, he cautions against attributing this solely to racial bias. The disadvantage of skin color—the fact that the dominant white population preferred whites over nonwhites—is one that blacks have certainly shared with the Chinese, Japanese, American Indians, and other nonwhite groups. Nonetheless, even though blacks have experienced greater discrimination, the contrast with the Asians does reveal that skin color per se was "not an insurmountable obstacle." Indeed, Lieberson argues that the greater success enjoyed by Asians may well be explained largely by the different context of their contact with whites. Because changes in immigration policy cut off Asian migration to America in the late-nineteenth and earlier-twentieth century, the Japanese and Chinese populations—in sharp contrast to blacks—did not reach large numbers and therefore did not pose as great a threat to the white population. Lieberson concedes that the "response of whites to Chinese and

Japanese was of the same violent and savage character in areas where they were concentrated," but he also notes that "the threat was quickly stopped through changes in immigration policy."

Furthermore, the discontinuation of large-scale immigration from Japan and China enabled these groups to solidify networks of ethnic contact and to occupy particular occupational niches. The 1970 census records 22,580,000 blacks and only 435,000 Chinese and 591,000 Japanese. "Imagine," Lieberson exclaims, "22 million Japanese Americans trying to carve out initial niches through truck farming!"

THE IMPORTANCE OF MIGRANT FLOWS

If different population sizes accounted for a good deal of the difference in the economic success of blacks versus Asians, they also helped determine the dissimilar rates of progress of urban blacks and the new Europeans. The dynamic factor behind these differences, and perhaps the most important single contributor to the varying rates of urban ethnic progress in the twentieth century, is the flow of migrants. Changes in U.S. policy first halted Asian immigration to America and then curtailed the new European immigration. However, black migration to the urban North continued in substantial numbers several decades after the new European immigration had ceased. Accordingly, the percentage of northern blacks who are recent migrants substantially exceeds the dwindling percentage of Europeans who are recent migrants.

In this connection, Lieberson theorizes that the changes in race relations that accompany shifts in racial composition are not caused by any radical alteration in white dispositions but rather, that shifts in composition activate dispositions that were present all along. "In other words," writes Lieberson, "there is a latent structure to the race relations pattern in a given setting, with only certain parts of this structure observed at a given time." The sizable and continuous migration of blacks from the South to the North, coupled with the cessation of immigration from Eastern, Central, and Southern

Europe, created a situation in which other whites muffled their negative disposition toward the new Europeans and focused antagonism toward blacks. In the words of Lieberson, "the presence of blacks made it harder to discriminate against the new Europeans because the alternative was viewed less favorably."

The flow of migrants made it much more difficult for blacks to follow the path of the Asians and new Europeans, who had overcome the negative effects of discrimination by finding special occupational niches. Only a small percentage of a group's total work force can be absorbed in such specialties when the group's population increases rapidly or is a sizable proportion of the total population. Furthermore, the flow of migrants had a harmful effect on the earlier-arriving or longer-standing black residents of the North. Lieberson insightfully points out that

> sizable numbers of newcomers raise the level of ethnic and/or racial consciousness on the part of others in the city; moreover, if these newcomers are less able to compete for more desirable positions than are the longer-standing residents, they will tend to undercut the position of other members of the group. This is because the older residents and those of higher socioeconomic status cannot totally avoid the newcomers, although they work at it through subgroup residential isolation. Hence, there is some deterioration in the quality of residential areas, schools, and the like for those earlier residents who might otherwise enjoy more fully the rewards of their mobility. Beyond this, from the point of view of the dominant outsiders, the newcomers may reinforce stereotypes and negative dispositions that affect all members of the group.

In sum, because substantial black migration to the North continued several decades after the new European and Asian migration ceased, urban blacks, having their ranks constantly replenished with poor migrants, found it much more difficult to follow the path of the new Europeans and the Asian immigrants in overcoming the effects of discrimination. The net result is that as the nation entered the last quarter century, its large urban areas continued to have a disproportionate concentration of poor blacks who, as I shall show, have been especially vulnerable to recent structural changes in the economy.

It should also be emphasized, however, that black migration to urban areas has been minimal in recent years. Indeed, between 1970 and 1977, blacks actually experienced a net outmigration of 653,000 from the central cities. In most large cities, the number of blacks increased only moderately; in some, in fact, the number declined. As the demographer Philip Hauser pointed out, increases in the urban black population during the 1970s were "mainly due to births." This would indicate that, for the first time in the twentieth century, the ranks of blacks in our central cities are no longer being replenished by poor migrants. This strongly suggests, other things being equal, that urban blacks will experience a steady decrease in joblessness, crime, out-of-wedlock births, single-parent homes, and welfare dependency. In other words, just as the Asian and new European immigrants benefited from a cessation of migration, there is now reason to expect that the cessation of black migration will help to upgrade urban black communities. In making this observation, however, I am in no way overlooking other factors that affect the differential rate of ethnic progress at different periods of time, such as structural changes in the economy, population size, and discrimination. Nonetheless, one of the major obstacles to urban black advancement—the constant flow of migrants—has been removed.

Hispanics, on the other hand, appear to be migrating to urban centers in increasing numbers. The status of Hispanics vis-à-vis other ethnic groups is not entirely clear because there are no useful figures for 1970 on their type of residence. But data collected since 1974 indicate that their numbers are increasing rapidly in central cities, as a consequence of immigration as well as births. Indeed, in several large cities (including New York, Los Angeles, San Francisco, San Diego, Phoenix, and Denver) Hispanics apparently outnumber black Americans. Accordingly, the rapid growth of the Hispanic population in urban areas, accompanied by the opposite trend for black Americans, could contribute significantly to different outcomes for these two groups in the last two decades of the twentieth century. Specifically, whereas blacks could very well experience a decrease in their rates of joblessness, crime, out-of-wedlock births, single-parent homes, and welfare dependency, Hispanics could show a steady increase in each of these problems. Moreover, whereas blacks could experience a decrease in the ethnic hostility directed toward them, Hispanics, with their increasing visibility, could become victims of increasing ethnic antagonism.

The flow of migrants also has implications for the average age of an ethnic group. The higher the median age of a group, the greater its representation in the higher-income and professional categories where older individuals are more heavily represented. It is not mere coincidence, then, that younger ethnic groups, such as blacks and Hispanics, who are highly concentrated in age groups where unemployment and violent crime are prevalent, also tend to have high unemployment and crime rates, even if other factors are considered. In 1980, ethnic groups differed significantly in median age, ranging from 23.2 years for blacks and Hispanics to 31.3 years for whites. Only 21.3 percent of all American whites were under age 15, compared with 28.7 percent for blacks and 32 percent for Hispanics.

In the nation's central cities in 1977, the median age was 30.3 years for whites, 23.9 for blacks, and 21.8 for Hispanics. One cannot overemphasize the importance of the sudden increase of young minorities in the central cities. The number of central-city black teenagers (16–19 years old) increased by almost 75 percent from 1960 to 1969, compared with an increase of only 14 percent for whites in the same age group. Furthermore, young black adults (ages 20 to 24) in the central city increased in number by two-thirds during the same period—three times the increase for comparable whites. From 1970 to 1977, the increase in the number of young blacks slackened off somewhat but was still substantial. For example, the number of young blacks (ages 14 to 24) in the central cities of our large metropolitan areas (populations above 1 million) increased by 22 percent from 1970 to 1977; young Hispanics, by 26 percent. The number of young whites in these central cities, however, decreased by 7 percent.

On the basis of these demographic changes alone, one would expect blacks and Hispanics to account disproportionately for the increasing social problems of the central city. Indeed, in 1980, 55 percent of all those arrested for violent and property crimes in American cities were younger than 21.

Age is also related to out-of-wedlock births, female-headed homes, and welfare dependency. Teenagers accounted for almost half of out-of-wedlock births in 1978. Moreover, 80 percent of all out-of-wedlock black births in 1978 were to teenage and young-adult (ages 20 to 24) women. Further, the median age of female householders has decreased significantly in recent years because of the sharp rise in teenage and young-adult female householders. (In 1970, young black-female householders, ages 14 to 24, having children under 18 years old constituted 30.9 percent of all black female householders with children under age 18; by 1979, their proportion had increased to 37.2 percent, compared with increases from 22.4 to 27.9 percent for comparable white families and from 29.9 to 38.3 percent for comparable Hispanic families.) Finally, the explosion of teenage births has contributed significantly to an increase in the number of children on AFDC (aid to families with dependent children) from 35 per 1000 children under age 18 in 1960 to 113 per 1000 in 1979.

In short, recent increases in crime, out-of-wedlock births, female-headed homes, and welfare dependency are related to the explosion in numbers of young people, especially among minorities. However, as James Q. Wilson pointed out in his analysis of the proliferation of social problems in the 1960s, a decade of general economic prosperity, "changes in the age structure of the population cannot alone account for the social dislocations" in those years. Wilson argues, for instance, that from 1960 to 1970 the rate of serious crime in the District of Columbia increased by more than 400 percent, heroin addiction by more than 1000 percent, welfare rates by 100 percent, and unemployment rates by 100 percent; yet the number of young persons between 16 and 21 years of age increased by only 32 percent. Also, the number of murders in Detroit increased from 100 in 1960 to 500 in 1971, "yet the number of young persons did not quintuple."

Wilson, drawing from published research notes that the "increase in the murder rate during the 1960s was more than ten times greater than what one would have expected from the changing age structure of the population alone," and that "only 13.4 percent of the increase in arrests for robbery between 1950 and 1965 could be accounted for by the increase in the numbers of persons between the ages of ten and twenty-four." Speculating on this problem, Wilson advances the hypothesis that the abrupt increase in the number of young persons had an "exponential effect on the rate of certain social problems." In other words, there may be a "critical mass" of young persons such that when that mass is reached or is increased suddenly and substantially, "a self-sustaining chain reaction is set off that creates an explosive increase in the amount of crime, addiction, and welfare dependency."

This hypothesis seems to be especially relevant to densely populated inner-city neighborhoods, especially those with large public housing projects. The 1937 United States Housing Act provided federal money for the construction of housing for the poor. But, as Roncek and colleagues pointed out in a recent article in *Social Problems,* opposition from organized community groups trying to prevent public housing construction in their neighborhoods "led to massive, segregated housing projects, which become ghettos for minorities and the economically disadvantaged." As large poor families were placed in high-density housing projects in the inner city, both family and neighborhood life suffered. Family deterioration, high crime rates, and vandalism flourished in these projects. In St. Louis, for example, the Pruitt-Igoe project, which housed about 10,000 children and adults, developed serious problems only five years after it opened and became so unlivable that it was closed in 1976, less than a quarter-century after it was built.

If James Q. Wilson's critical-mass theory has any validity, it would seem to be readily demonstrated in densely populated inner-city neighborhoods having a heavy concentration of teenagers and young adults. As Oscar Newman showed in *Defensible Space,* the population concentration in these projects, the types of housing, and the surrounding population concentration have interactive effects on the occurrence and types of crimes. In other words, the crime problem, generally high in inner-city neighborhoods, is exacerbated by conditions in the housing projects. But as Lee Rainwater has suggested, in his book

Behind Ghetto Walls, the character of family life in the federal housing projects "shares much with the family life of lower-class Negroes" elsewhere. The population explosion of young minorities in already densely settled inner-city neighborhoods over the past two decades has created a situation whereby life in inner-city neighborhoods closely approximates life in the projects. In both cases, residents have greater difficulty recognizing their neighbors and, therefore, are less likely to be concerned for them or to engage in reciprocal guardian behavior. The more densely a neighborhood or block is populated, the less contact and interaction among neighbors and the less likely the potential offenders can be detected or distinguished. Events in one part of the neighborhood or block tend to be of little concern to those residing in other parts. And it hardly needs emphasizing that what observers call "the central city crisis" derives in part from the unprecedented increase in these neighborhoods of younger blacks, many of whom are not enrolled in school, are jobless, and are a source of delinquency, crime, and ghetto unrest.

It should be pointed out, however, that the cessation of black migration to the central cities and the steady black outmigration to the suburbs will help relieve the population pressures in the inner city. Perhaps even more significant is the fact that in 1977 there were overall 6 percent fewer blacks in the age group 13 and under than there were in 1970. In metropolitan areas there were likewise 6 percent fewer blacks in that age group; and in the central cities, there were 13 percent fewer black children age 13 or younger. Similarly, between 1970 and 1977, white children in this age group decreased by 14 percent overall, by 17 percent in metropolitan areas, and by 24 percent in the central cities. By contrast, Hispanic children age 13 or younger *increased* during this period—18 percent overall, 16 percent in metropolitan areas, and 12 percent in the central cities. Thus, just as the change in migration flow could contribute to differential rates of ethnic involvement in certain types of social problems, so too could changes in the age structure. In short, whereas whites and blacks—all other things being equal—are likely to experience a decrease in such problems as joblessness, crime, out-of-wedlock births, family dissolution, and welfare dependency in the near future, the growing Hispanic population is more likely to show increasing rates of social dislocation.

ECONOMIC CHANGES AND ETHNIC CULTURE

Problems of social dislocation in the inner city have also been profoundly exacerbated by recent structural changes in the economy. Indeed, the population explosion among young minorities in recent years occurred at a time when changes in the economy are posing serious problems for unskilled workers, both in and out of the labor force.

Urban minorities are particularly vulnerable to structural economic changes: the shift from goods-producing to service-producing industries, the increasing segmentation of the labor market, the growing use of industrial technology, and the relocation of manufacturing industries out of the central cities. Such economic changes serve to remind us, as John Kasarda notes in [Chapter 29], that for several decades America's urban areas have been undergoing what appears to be an irreversible structural transformation—from centers of production and distribution of material goods to centers of administration, information exchange, finance, trade, and government services. This process has effectively eliminated millions of manufacturing, wholesale, and retail jobs since 1948, a process that has accelerated since 1967. At the same time, there has been an increase in "postindustrial society" occupational positions that usually require levels of training and education beyond the reach of disadvantaged inner-city residents. These changing employment patterns have accompanied shifts in the demographic composition of our central cities—from predominantly European white to predominantly black, Hispanic, and other minorities—leading to a decrease both in the total population size of the central cities and in aggregate personal-income levels.

The cumulative effect of these technological-employment and population changes, as Kasarda points out, has been a growing mismatch between the level of skill or training of city residents and the formal prerequisites for urban jobs. Thus we have deeper "ghettoization," solidification of high levels of urban poverty, increased institutional problems in the inner city (e.g., the declining quality of public schools, poorer municipal services), and a rise in such social dislocations as joblessness, crime, single-parent homes, and welfare dependency.

The changes brought about by the cessation of migration to the central cities and by the sharp drop in the number of black children under age 13 seem to make it more likely that the economic situation of urban blacks as a group will noticeably improve in the near future. However, the present problems of black joblessness are so overwhelming (less than 30 percent of all black-male teenagers and only 62 percent of all black young-adult males [ages 20 to 24] were employed in 1978) that perhaps only an extraordinary program of economic reform can possibly prevent a significant segment of the urban underclass from being permanently locked out of the mainstream of the American occupational system.

In focusing on different explanations of the social dislocation in the inner city, I have yet to say anything about the role of ethnic culture. Even after considering racial discrimination, migrant flows, changes in ethnic demography, and structural changes in the economy, a number of readers will still maintain that ethnic cultural differences account in large measure for the disproportionate and rising rates of social dislocation in the inner city. But any cultural explanation of group behavioral differences must deal with, among other things, the often considerable variation within groups on several aspects of behavior. For example, whereas only 7 percent of urban black families having incomes of $25,000 or more in 1978 were headed by women, 85 percent of those having incomes below $4000 were headed by women. The higher the economic position of black families, the greater the percentage of two-parent households. Moreover, the proportion of black children born out of wedlock . . . is partly a function of the sharp decrease in fertility among married blacks (i.e., two-parent families) who have a higher economic status in the black community. By treating blacks and other ethnics as monolithic groups, we lose sight of the fact that *high-income* blacks, Hispanics, and Indians have *even fewer* children than their counterparts in the general population.

Nonetheless, in the face of some puzzling facts concerning rates of welfare and crime in the 1960s, the cultural explanation seems to hold validity for some observers. From the Great Depression to 1960, for example, unemployment accounted in large measure for welfare dependency. During this period, the correlation between the nonwhite-male unemployment and the rate of new AFDC cases was very nearly perfect. As the nonwhite-male unemployment rate increased, the rate of new AFDC cases increased; as the former decreased, the latter correspondingly decreased. Commenting on this relationship in his book *The Politics of a Guaranteed Income,* Daniel P. Moynihan stated that "the correlation was among the strongest known to social science. It could not be established that the men who lost their jobs were the ones who left their families, but the mathematical relationship of the two statistical series—unemployment rates and new AFDC cases—was astonishingly close." However, the relationship suddenly began to weaken at the beginning of the 1960s, had vanished by 1963, and had completely reversed itself by the end of the decade—a steady decline in the rate of nonwhite-male unemployment and a steady increase in the number of new AFDC cases.

Some observers quickly seized on these figures. Welfare dependency, they argued, had become a cultural trait; even during an economic upswing, welfare rates among minorities were increasing. Upon closer inspection, though, one sees that even though nonwhite-male unemployment did drop during the 1960s, the percentage of nonwhite males who dropped out of the labor force increased steadily throughout the decade, thereby maintaining the association between economic dislocation and welfare dependency. The importance of labor-force participation in explaining certain types of social problems was also demonstrated in a recent empirical study relating labor-market opportunities to the increasing rate of crime among youths, reported in the *Journal of Political Economy:*

The labor force/not-in-the-labor-force formulation has greater explanatory power than the non-working formulation, demonstrating the importance of participation rates relative to unemployment rates in explaining crime rates. This point is reinforced when one observes that during the middle and latter sixties, crime rates rose while unemployment rates declined. It is the decline in the participation rate which provides an explanation of the rise in crime during this period.

A well-founded sociological assumption is that different ethnic behaviors and different ethnic outcomes largely reflect different opportunities for, and external obstacles against, advancement—experiences that are in turn determined by different historical and material circumstances and by different times of arrival and patterns of settlement. In addition, even if one can show that different values are related to differences in ethnic group behavior, mobility, and success, this hardly constitutes a full explanation. By revealing cultural differences, we reach only the first step in a proper sociological investigation; analysis of the social and historical basis of those differences remains to be done. In the words of Stephen Steinberg, "only by adopting a theoretical approach that explores the interaction between cultural and material factors is it possible to assess the role of values in ethnic mobility without mystifying culture and imputing a cultural superiority to groups that have enjoyed disproportionate success."

In short, cultural values do not *determine* behavior or success. Rather, cultural values grow out of specific circumstances and life chances and reflect one's position in the class structure. Thus, if lower-class blacks have low aspirations or do not plan for the future, this is not ultimately because of different cultural norms but because the group is responding to restricted opportunities, a bleak future, and feelings of resignation originating from bitter personal experience. Accordingly, as Steinberg persuasively argues, behavior described as social-pathological and associated with lower-class ethnics should not be analyzed as a cultural aberration but as a symptom of class inequality. If impoverished conditions produced exceedingly high rates of crime among first-generation Irish, Italians, and Jews, what would have been the outcome of these groups had they been mired in poverty for five to ten generations like so many black families in the United States?

Adaptive responses to recurrent situations take the form of behavior patterns, norms, and aspirations. As economic and social opportunities change, new behavioral solutions originate, form patterns, and are later upheld and complemented by norms. If new conditions emerge, both the behavior patterns and the norms eventually undergo change. As Herbert Gans has put it: "some behavioral norms are more persistent than others, but over the long run, all of the norms and aspirations by which people live are nonpersistent: they rise and fall with changes in situations."

ALLIES NEEDED

To suggest that changes in social and economic situations will bring about changes in behavior patterns and norms raises the issue of public policy: how to deal effectively with the social dislocations that have plagued the urban underclass over the past several decades. Space does not permit a detailed discussion of public policy and social dislocations in the inner city, but it must be emphasized that any significant reduction of inner-city joblessness, and of the related problems of crime, out-of-wedlock births, single-parent homes, and welfare dependency, will call for a program of socioeconomic reform far more comprehensive than what Americans have usually regarded as appropriate or desirable.

A shift away from the convenient focus on "racism" would probably result in a greater appreciation and understanding of the complex factors that account for recent increases in the social dislocations of the inner city. Although discrimination undoubtedly still contributes to these problems, in the past twenty years they have been more profoundly affected by shifts in the American economy that have both produced massive joblessness among low-income urban minorities and exacerbated conditions stemming from historical discrimination, the continuous flow of migrants to the large metropolises,

changes in the urban-minority age structure, and population changes in the central city. For all these reasons, the urban underclass has not significantly benefited from race-specific policy programs (e.g., affirmative action) that are designed only to combat discrimination. Indeed, the economic and social plight of the underclass calls for public policies that benefit all the poor, not just poor minorities. I have in mind policies that address the broader, and more difficult to confront, problems of societal organization, including the problems of generating full employment, achieving effective welfare reform, and developing a comprehensive economic policy to promote sustained and balanced urban economic growth. Unless these problems are seriously addressed, we have little hope that public policy can significantly reduce social dislocation in the inner city.

I am reminded, in this connection, of Bayard Rustin's plea in the early 1960s—that blacks ought to recognize the importance of *fundamental* economic reform and the need for an effective and broad-based interracial coalition to achieve it. It is evident—more now than at any time in the last half of the twentieth century—that blacks and other minorities will need allies to effect a program of reform that can improve the conditions of the underclass. And since an effective political coalition will partly depend upon how the issues are defined, the political message must underscore the need for socioeconomic reform that benefits *all* groups in society. Civil rights organizations, as one important example, will have to change or expand their definition of racial problems in America and broaden the scope of their policy recommendations. They would, of course, continue to stress the immediate goal of eliminating racial discrimination; but they will have to recognize that low-income minorities are also profoundly affected by problems in social organization that go beyond race (such as structural changes in the economy) and that the dislocations which follow often include increased joblessness, rising crime, family deterioration, and welfare dependency.

READINGS SUGGESTED BY THE AUTHOR

Gans, Herbert. "Culture and Class in the Study of Poverty." In Daniel P. Moynihan, ed., *On Understanding Poverty:*

Perspectives for the Social Sciences. New York: Basic Books, 1968.

Lieberson, Stanley. *A Piece of the Pie: Black and White Immigrants since 1880.* Berkeley: University of California Press, 1981.

Rainwater, Lee. *Behind Ghetto Walls: Black Family Life in a Federal Slum.* Chicago: Aldine, 1970.

Steinberg, Stephen. *The Ethnic Myth: Race, Ethnicity, and Class in America.* New York: Atheneum, 1981.

Wilson, James Q. *Thinking about Crime.* New York: Basic Books, 1971.

The Effect of Residential Segregation on Black Social and Economic Well-Being

DOUGLAS S. MASSEY
University of Pennsylvania

GRETCHEN A. CONDRAN
University of Pennsylvania

NANCY A. DENTON
University of Pennsylvania

This paper investigates some of the consequences of black residential segregation using specially compiled data for Philadelphia in 1980. Blacks, like whites, attempt to improve their neighborhood characteristics with rising social status, but unlike whites, they face strong barriers to residential mobility. As a result, high status blacks must live in neighborhoods with fewer resources and amenities than whites of similar background. Specifically, they live in poorer, more dilapidated areas characterized by higher rates of poverty, dependency, crime, and mortality, and they must send their children to public schools populated by low income students who score badly on standardized tests. These findings suggest that racial segregation remains an important basis for stratification in U.S. society.

In December of 1985, four hundred whites stood in the streets of southwest Philadelphia shouting racial epithets and protesting the movement of a black family into the working class neighborhood. The newspaper headlines provided the city and the nation with a shocking reminder of the constraints that blacks still face in choosing where to live (Cass 1986). However, at the same time, blacks and whites across town lived together peacefully in many other areas, including some of the city's wealthiest neighborhoods, where the regular entry and exit of black families elicited no comment at all. This paper explores this apparent paradox and explains why some blacks are allowed to assimilate spatially, while others are not. Using specially prepared data from Philadelphia, we document the detrimental consequences of racial segregation for blacks in American society.

A large theoretical literature postulates a connection between spatial mobility and social mobility (Kobrin & Goldscheider 1978; Lieberson 1963, 1980; Massey & Mullan 1984; Nelli 1970; Park 1926; Thernstrom 1973; Ward 1971). This basic tenet of human ecology is usually examined from the determinants side, with social distance determining the extent of spatial separation. That is, patterns of segregation are typically explained as a function of ethnicity, race, culture, socioeconomic status, and other indicators of social distance. However, there is another side to the issue. Not only does social distance

This paper was prepared with funding from NIH Grant HD-18594, whose support is gratefully acknowledged.

produce physical separation, but physical separation, in turn, perpetuates social distance.

City neighborhoods vary on a wide range of characteristics that affect the life chances of residents (Logan 1978). Where one lives not only reflects one's past social and economic achievements (Laumann, Siegel & Hodge 1970), it also affects one's prospects for advancement, and especially those of one's children. Recently a growing research literature has suggested that racial residential segregation might undermine the relative position of blacks compared to other groups, restricting their access to jobs (Kain 1968; Kain & Persky 1969; Lewin-Epstein 1985; Madden & Hughes 1985; Parcel 1979), exposing them to greater health risks (Kitagawa & Hauser 1973), giving them poorer public services and higher taxes (Schneider & Logan 1982, 1985), increasing their cost of housing (Berry 1976; Kain & Quigley 1975; Villemez 1980), segregating them in inferior schools (Coleman, Kelly & Moore 1975; Farley 1978; Farley & Taeuber 1974), and contributing to their high risk of single parenthood (Furstenberg, Morgan & Moore 1985; Hogan & Kitagawa 1985). Residential segregation, by relegating disadvantaged minorities to areas with fewer opportunities and amenities, exacerbates the existing social distance between them and the majority (Logan 1978).

In this paper we describe the contrasting environments experienced by residents of Philadelphia in different kinds of neighborhoods. Using census tract indicators of school quality, crime, health, socioeconomic status, and physical condition, we examine the characteristics of white tracts, established black tracts, transition areas, and tracts of recent black in-movement. Our leading hypothesis is that blacks, like other groups, attempt to maximize their spatial position in society by choosing neighborhoods with greater amenities and more resources, but that unlike other groups, they are hampered by persistent barriers to residential integration. Upwardly mobile blacks are therefore less able than whites of comparable income and education to translate their hard-won status attainments into desirable spatial outcomes, giving them markedly less access to higher quality housing, better schools, safer streets, healthier neighborhoods, and regular contact with other high status people. Thus, ecological factors exert a strong effect on the process of stratification in the U.S., one not generally recognized in the status attainment literature, nor in the debate over "the declining significance of race" (Wilson 1978).

DATA

A comprehensive analysis of the consequences of segregation requires data from diverse sources, and integrating them all into a single geographically keyed file involves considerable effort. The resources available to this study did not permit carrying out these operations for a large set of cities, nor even for an entire metropolitan area, so the present analysis focuses exclusively on the City of Philadelphia in 1980, using its 359 census tracts as units of analysis. Unlike many central cities, Philadelphia contains a broad socioeconomic cross-section of both blacks and whites, ranging from the wealthiest to the poorest, providing a range of variation sufficient to sustain this study. However, Philadelphia is probably more representative of blacks than of whites, since it contains 72 percent of the SMSAs black population, but only 27 percent of its white population. The excluded whites are disproportionately middle to upper class, so confining attention to the city alone understates the socioeconomic contrast between the two groups, a bias that is conservative with respect to the direction of differentials we hypothesize.

Tract data on the characteristics of housing and population were compiled from Summary Tape File 4A of the 1980 U.S. Census. This file provides detailed tabulations on the physical and social environment of each census tract. In order to identify patterns of neighborhood change, these 1980 data were combined with tract-level counts of blacks, whites, and total population taken from the 1970 Fourth Count Summary Tapes. These census data were, in turn, supplemented by three other data sets specially compiled for the project.

Information on the quality and characteristics of schools was obtained from the Research Division of the Philadelphia Department of Education. School characteristics include economic composition, racial composition, test scores, attendance rates, and dropout rates for each public school in the city. School characteristics for each tract are described as a weighted average of characteristics of schools attended by children resident in the tract. Obviously, these data do not paint a complete picture of the educational environment facing black and white children in Philadelphia, since they exclude private schools in the city. To the extent that private schools are of higher quality than public schools, and to the degree that white students are more likely to attend them, our use of public school data alone understates the contrast between black and white educational environments, a bias that is conservative with respect to the direction of our hypothesis.

Crime data were obtained from the Philadelphia Criminal Justice Coordinating Office. Unfortunately, crime statistics are reported by 22 Police Districts instead of for 359 tracts. For our purposes, a tract was given the crime rates for the Police District in which it was located. In the few cases where a tract straddled a Police District boundary, rates were estimated as a weighted average of rates for the districts involved, where weights were the proportion of the tract's population in each district. Thus, crime rates for each tract are actually rates for a much larger area. This unfortunate attribution of district rates to individual tracts attenuates spatial variation in crime rates, and probably reduces the contrast between tracts inhabited by blacks and whites, an unavoidable bias that is conservative with respect to the hypothesized direction of effects.

The health environment of each tract was measured using information on registered births and deaths obtained from the Pennsylvania Department of Vital Statistics and the Philadelphia Department of Health. The basic data consist of individual birth and death records for the years 1979, 1980, and 1981, including all information listed on the vital certificates except names and addresses. Tract of residence was entered on the data file by the Philadelphia Health Department, so mortality rates and birth characteristics could be calculated for individual census tracts. To insure more reliable estimates, birth and death data for 1979–81 were averaged.

METHODS

Our basic hypothesis is that upwardly mobile blacks attempt to move into higher quality neighborhoods, but are inhibited from doing so by racial prejudice on the part of whites, with significant deleterious consequences. This idea will be examined using two methodological approaches developed in earlier research. First, tracts will be classified by the type of residential change they experienced between 1970 and 1980, and characteristics of neighborhoods and residents will be examined by type of change. Second, structural equations of spatial assimilation will be estimated to measure the relative extent to which black and white Philadelphians are able to translate their socioeconomic achievements into desirable spatial outcomes.

Past research generally indicates that once blacks enter neighborhoods in significant numbers, the areas cease to be attractive to potential white settlers, and in the course of residential turnover, they go from predominantly white to mostly black (Aldrich 1975; Duncan & Duncan 1957; Massey & Mullan 1984; Taeuber & Taeuber 1965). Although over the 1970s this transition process was arrested in certain instances by "gentrification," it still represents the dominant pattern of neighborhood racial change in American cities (Lee 1985; Lee, Spain & Umberson 1985).

In order to identify the characteristics of tracts at different stages of transition, and to study the socioeconomic background of blacks and whites at each stage, we adapted the classification scheme previously developed by Massey and Mullan (1984). In this scheme, tracts that contain at least 250 black residents in 1980 are classified according to the kind of change they experienced over the prior decade. "Established black tracts" were at least 60 percent black in both 1970 and 1980. "Entry tracts" had fewer than 250 blacks in 1970 but more than this number in 1980. "Transition tracts" gained black residents but lost white residents over the decade, and "decline tracts" lost both groups between the two dates. "White growth tracts" gained whites over the decade. Collectively, tracts with

250 or more black residents are referred to as "black tracts," while the remaining areas are called "white tracts." . . . tracts having more than 250 Hispanics or Asians were deleted . . .

The first four of these categories correspond roughly to classic stages in the process of residential succession (see Duncan & Duncan 1957): blacks first penetrate white areas in very small numbers (white tracts), then cross some threshold to "invade" a traditionally white area (black entry tracts); whites begin to move out (black transition tracts), initiating a process of succession that culminates ultimately in a predominantly black area (black established tracts). Black declining tracts generally do not follow as a fifth step in this logical progression. They are not predominantly black tracts that have begun to decline, but are a residual category of predominantly white tracts that are losing both racial groups. Conceptually, they are probably closest to transition tracts, since in most cases the loss of whites is greater than the loss of blacks, moving the tract closer to black dominance.

The second method used in this paper estimates structural equation models to compare the relative abilities of blacks and whites to convert status achievements into spatial outcomes. The conceptual basis for these models was developed in a series of prior papers (Massey & Bitterman 1985; Massey & Denton 1985; Massey & Mullan 1984). Ecological theory postulates that spatial mobility is a natural concomitant of social mobility. With rising social status—as measured by education, income, and occupational status—groups attempt to improve their spatial position in urban society by selecting neighborhoods with richer resources and more amenities, areas more consistent with their enhanced status. In economic terms, a move to a new neighborhood by an upwardly mobile family may be considered to be an investment in real capital (a house), in human capital (children's education), in productivity (improved health and safety), or in psychic satisfaction (neighborhood status). Families expect to reap future returns from these investments in terms of capital gains, intergenerational mobility, higher earnings, or greater prestige. . . .

. . . Our hypothesis is that coefficients linking attainment variables to outcome characteristics will be positive for both blacks and whites (assuming desirable outcomes), but that they will be smaller in magnitude for the former than the latter. . . .

. . . The article should be viewed as a preliminary exploratory analysis of segregation's socioeconomic effects rather than a definitive case study.

ANALYSIS

Resident Characteristics by Kind of Area

A basic premise of this analysis is that high status blacks seek the amenities and services that are more abundant in white residential areas, and attempt to use their education and income to attain them. This premise is supported by the data in Table 1, which shows socioeconomic characteristics of whites and blacks living in tracts that experienced different kinds of racial change between 1970 and 1980. The 308 tracts included in this table contain 844,683 whites and 568,389 blacks, roughly a 60–40 split. However, two-thirds of the city's white population live in tracts with fewer than 250 black people, while virtually all blacks (99.1%) live in tracts with more than 250 blacks.

Consistent with our underlying premise, tract groups can be ranked fairly consistently across most indicators of black SES. In general, blacks of highest status reside either in white tracts or in black entry tracts, and the lowest status blacks are found either in black established tracts or in declining areas. The variation is often quite dramatic. For example, only 10 percent of black families in white tracts are below the poverty line, compared to 20 percent in black entry areas, 22 percent in black transition areas, 29 percent in established black areas, and 47 percent in declining areas. A similar pattern is observed for the other indicators of black social status.

Interestingly, the pattern of SES across tract groups is somewhat different for whites. Educational attainment does not differ much by kind of racial change, but on other indicators, the highest status whites are almost always found in

TABLE 1

*Socioeconomic Characteristics of Whites and Blacks Living in
Different Kinds of Philadelphia Neighborhoods: 1980*

Socioeconomic Characteristics	White Tracts	Black Tracts				
		Entry	Transition	Established	Decline	Total*
Whites						
Median education	12.3	12.5	12.4	12.3	12.3	12.5
Median household income**	16.1	17.2	13.3	8.9	14.5	14.6
Families:						
% below poverty line	6.6	5.5	10.3	12.8	10.3	8.7
% on public assistance	2.1	1.3	4.0	6.2	4.2	3.3
% female headed w/child < 18	5.5	5.2	7.4	8.0	7.9	6.8
Labor force:						
% 20–64 unemployed	7.4	6.8	7.8	8.5	7.6	7.2
Median weeks unemployed	13.8	11.9	12.5	13.7	13.8	12.4
% prof/tech/manager	23.5	30.3	33.3	34.2	31.7	34.4
% of all whites in area	67.5	10.6	9.6	2.6	7.6	32.4
Blacks						
Median education	12.7	12.8	12.3	11.9	11.6	12.1
Median household income**	15.0	14.6	13.5	9.7	6.7	10.5
Families:						
% below poverty line	10.4	20.0	21.9	29.4	47.2	28.1
% on public assistance	2.5	12.6	12.5	18.0	36.3	17.3
% female headed w/child < 18	24.1	26.4	26.8	27.7	44.6	28.1
Labor force:						
% 20–64 unemployed	7.5	7.7	12.5	17.0	18.9	15.6
Median weeks unemployed	14.4	12.4	16.1	17.8	17.2	17.3
% prof/tech/manager	37.6	34.7	19.9	14.7	19.7	16.9
% of all blacks in area	0.9	1.4	23.7	69.2	4.1	99.1
Number of tracts	144	17	44	75	20	164

*Includes 8 tracts of white growth not shown in table.
**Income in thousands of dollars.
Source: U.S. Bureau of the Census, Summary Tape File 4A.

black entry areas. Indeed, they are of higher status than those in white areas generally, which may reflect resistance to black entry in blue collar ethnic neighborhoods, a possibility that is developed further later in the article. Whites of lowest SES live in black established tracts.

In short, the major premise of our leading hypothesis is amply verified. Not only do high status blacks live within predominantly white neighborhoods, but the areas where they achieve entry are those of highest white status. The problem, from the black viewpoint, is that very few are able to achieve entry into such neighborhoods. Although 16 percent of blacks aged 25 or more report some college education, only 5 percent of them live in white tracts or entry areas, and while 23 percent of black households earn at least $20,000, only 4 percent of them live

in such neighborhoods. In all, well over 90 percent of blacks live in transition or established black areas.

Neighborhood Characteristics by Kind of Area

So far, we have simply replicated a long line of research showing that high status blacks attempt spatial integration with whites (Duncan & Duncan 1957; Massey & Mullan 1984; Taeuber and Taeuber 1965). In Table 2, however, we consider other aspects of the socioeconomic and physical environment in each of the five kinds of areas. As is readily apparent, residents of white tracts and black entry tracts face a markedly better environment than people who live in other areas. White tracts and black entry tracts consist-

TABLE 2

*Indicators of the Socioeconomic and Physical Environment in
Different Kinds of Philadelphia Neighborhoods: 1980*

Socioeconomic or Physical Characteristic	White Tracts	Black Tracts				
		Entry	Transi-tion	Estab-lished	Decline	Total*
Socioeconomic						
% families below poverty line	6.7	6.7	17.5	28.7	20.0	21.9
% families on assistance	7.1	5.9	18.0	31.9	18.0	22.7
% female headed family child < 18	5.7	6.9	19.5	26.7	17.6	21.1
% unemployed	8.2	7.5	11.7	17.8	10.3	13.6
% 16+ in labor force	55.9	60.9	57.1	49.7	53.4	53.6
% 14–18 enrolled in school	86.6	85.2	86.5	84.2	81.8	84.8
% households w/out income	26.6	23.8	25.7	35.9	30.2	30.6
% births to unwed mothers	13.1	14.4	34.9	53.3	37.3	41.1
% white	99.1	92.0	37.5	5.2	73.6	32.8
% black	0.9	8.0	62.5	94.8	26.4	67.2
Physical						
% houses boarded up	0.4	0.4	2.1	6.0	3.9	4.0
% w/out complete plumbing	0.9	1.6	2.2	5.4	2.3	3.7
% w/out complete heating	4.6	4.0	13.7	20.7	9.9	15.2
Median age of housing	38.0	21.0	45.0	52.0	52.0	48.0
Median housing value**	31.6	34.0	21.6	14.1	20.9	18.0
Median rental value	244.4	294.3	220.7	171.0	206.4	204.8
% of all whites in area	67.5	10.6	9.6	2.6	7.6	32.4
% of all blacks in area	0.9	1.4	23.7	69.2	4.1	99.1
Number of tracts	144	17	44	75	20	164

*Includes 8 tracts of white growth not shown in table.
**Housing value in thousands of dollars.
Source: U.S. Bureau of the Census, Summary Tape File 4A.

ently display the best socioeconomic and physical environments, while established black tracts uniformly display the poorest. Decline and transition tracts are similar to one another and generally lie midway between the best and worst areas on most indicators. [See Table 2.]

White tracts and black entry areas have the lowest percentages of families in poverty, the smallest shares on public assistance, the lowest proportions of female-headed families with dependent children, the smallest percentages of births out of wedlock, the lowest unemployment rates, and the smallest fractions of households without income. These tracts similarly contain the lowest percentage of homes boarded up, the smallest shares without complete heating or plumbing, and the newest housing with the highest rental or resale value. In short, upper class blacks reside in predominantly white neighborhoods that contain high status people

and the newest, most marketable, and least dilapidated housing.

Table 3 paints a similar picture of the health environment faced by residents of the five tract groups. The most striking result from these data is the far better survival chances of both blacks and whites in tracts of black entry. Black death rates in these areas are lower even than those in white areas, the tract group with the next lowest mortality rates, and much lower than the rates in other black tracts. Whites have extraordinarily high death rates from cancer and cardiovascular diseases in established black areas, much higher than rates for blacks in the same places. However, the white population in established black tracts is very old (30% of whites are above age 65 compared to 10% of blacks), and age standardization by ten year age groups may not have corrected adequately for the large differences

TABLE 3

Health Environment Experienced by Whites and Blacks in Different Kinds of Philadelphia Neighborhoods: 1980

Health Indicator	White Tracts	Black Tracts				
		Entry	Transi-tion	Estab-lished	Decline	Total*
Whites						
Total deaths						
Crude rate**	13.0	10.6	17.4	30.7	13.8	14.8
Age standardized rate**	11.2	9.4	11.9	15.9	12.6	11.6
Cancer deaths 50+						
Crude rate***	597.0	408.7	688.9	1,397.0	481.5	548.6
Age standardized rate***	583.1	394.8	672.5	1,349.0	482.9	539.7
Cardiovascular deaths 50+						
Crude rate***	1,242.6	878.2	1,594.9	3,632.2	1,076.8	1,299.6
Age standardized rate***	1,181.6	783.7	1,523.1	3,381.5	1,070.8	1,198.8
Infant mortality rate**	13.3	13.3	9.9	20.1	10.2	11.7
Births						
% late or no prenatal care	22.9	19.5	22.9	33.5	24.1	22.8
% low birthweight	6.2	6.4	6.4	8.4	6.6	6.7
% of all whites in area	67.5	10.6	9.6	2.6	7.6	32.4
Blacks						
Total deaths						
Crude rate**	7.9	3.3	6.6	12.0	11.0	10.5
Age standardized rate**	11.4	7.7	13.2	14.1	15.7	13.9
Cancer deaths 50+						
Crude rate***	692.4	539.1	766.5	826.4	827.5	817.1
Age standardized rate***	747.5	594.7	971.1	918.0	904.7	923.9
Cardiovascular deaths 50+						
Crude rate***	1,218.7	628.9	1,109.8	1,176.5	1,427.6	1,171.2
Age standardized rate***	1,428.1	776.7	1,715.2	1,571.9	1,737.6	1,587.6
Infant mortality rate**	21.7	17.6	20.0	22.7	23.1	22.0
Births						
% late or no prenatal care	30.0	29.6	35.7	42.3	46.0	40.6
% low birthweight	10.5	12.2	10.8	12.9	11.7	12.3
% of all blacks in area	0.9	1.4	23.7	69.2	4.1	99.1
Number of tracts	144	17	44	75	20	164

*Includes 8 tracts of white growth not shown in table.
**Rate per 1,000 population.
***Rate per 100,000 population.
Sources: U.S. Bureau of the Census, Summary Tape File 4A; Pennsylvania Vital Statistics.

in age composition. Nonetheless, white infant mortality rates are also highest in established black tracts, suggesting that higher white mortality rates in these areas are more than statistical artifacts.

Thus, differences across areas in mortality, unarguably an important indicator of well-being, are surprisingly large. Our data cannot explain why these large differences occur. Social class differences obviously play an important role, but unequal access to medical care, especially to emergency medical care in the case of cardiovascular deaths, probably also contributes to the differential. This interpretation receives some support from figures on the proportion of black mothers receiving no or late (after the second trimester) prenatal care, which increases from 30 percent in white and entry areas to 42 percent in black established areas, and 46 percent in declining areas. In any event, the basic message of Table 3 is clear: there are large ecological variations in probabilities of dying across different kinds of residential areas. Blacks have a severe disadvantage compared to whites regardless of where they live, but that disadvantage is increased by living in predominantly black areas, and not surprisingly, high status blacks tend to reside in areas where the probabilities of dying are lowest.

Two features of neighborhoods that are very salient to prospective residents are schools and crime, which are the subjects of Tables 4 and 5. While few movers would seek out information on the cardiovascular death rates in particular areas, virtually everyone asks about the crime rates of the neighborhoods into which they might move, and parents are keenly interested in the quality of neighborhood schools. Therefore we consider them to be key tests of our leading hypothesis.

As indicated earlier, the data on crime are not ideal for the task at hand because they refer to police districts rather than census tracts, thereby attenuating the variation across different kinds of residential areas. However, to the police crime data in Table 4, we add death rates from violence or accidents, which should provide a more sensitive indicator of exposure to crime since they are tract-based calculations derived from vital registration data.

In spite of the unavoidable spatial averaging, crime rates, like the previous indicators of well-being, also vary strongly across tract groups. For every category of crime, rates are lowest in white or black entry tracts, and highest in black declining or black established tracts. The contrast is especially marked for violent crime rates. Thus, the murder, rape, and assault rates roughly triple as one moves from entry to established areas, while the robbery rate nearly doubles. These figures are paralleled by trends in the death rate for violence/accidents, which doubles for whites, and nearly doubles for blacks, moving from entry to established areas.

TABLE 4

Indicators of Exposure to Violence and Crime in Different Kinds of Philadelphia Neighborhoods: 1980

		Black Tracts				
Indicator	White Tracts	Entry	Transi- tion	Estab- lished	Decline	Total*
Violent/accidental deaths 15+						
Age adjusted white rate	60.1	61.8	75.9	127.1	92.0	79.7
Age adjusted black rate	99.3	79.7	101.6	123.9	111.1	115.6
Violent crime rates						
Murder	1.1	1.3	2.1	3.6	2.8	2.9
Rape	2.3	3.3	5.2	7.7	5.2	6.3
Assault	16.0	18.4	23.6	41.0	35.7	33.6
Robbery	25.9	39.9	47.1	73.1	56.5	62.1
Property crime rates						
Burglary	105.3	113.5	121.9	132.9	130.0	129.6
Larceny	173.8	206.6	146.6	194.4	243.0	202.2
Auto theft	67.7	86.4	83.3	87.2	95.0	88.9
Major crime rate**	392.6	470.1	431.1	540.4	568.3	526.3
Minor crime rate***	836.6	933.4	1,007.5	1,324.0	1,519.4	1,250.6
% of all whites in area	67.5	10.6	9.6	2.6	7.6	32.4
% of all blacks in area	0.9	1.4	23.7	69.2	4.1	99.1
Number of tracts	144	17	44	75	20	164

*Includes 8 tracts of white growth not shown in table.
**Major crimes include murder, rape, aggravated assault, robbery, burglary, larceny, and auto theft.
***Minor crimes include assault, arson, forgery, fraud, embezzlement, stolen property, vandalism, weapons, prostitution, sex offenses, drugs, gambling, driving under influence, liquor law, drunkenness, disorderly conduct, vagrancy, suspicion, and curfew violations.
Sources: U.S. Bureau of the Census, Summary Tape File 4A; Pennsylvania Vital Statistics; Philadelphia Police Department Crime Reports.

TABLE 5

Characteristics of Public High Schools Attended by Students from Different Kinds of Philadelphia Neighborhoods

Characteristic*	White Tracts	Black Tracts				
		Entry	Transi-tion	Estab-lished	Decline	Total**
% students low income	23.1	23.0	39.3	51.3	41.5	44.6
% testing above 85 percentile	11.8	16.9	6.2	3.7	6.0	5.8
% testing below 15 percentile	20.7	19.3	31.9	39.4	33.5	35.0
% black students	28.0	28.6	72.2	86.1	56.3	74.4
Grade retention rate	18.2	18.5	26.7	29.0	27.3	27.2
Dropout rate	9.4	7.1	10.3	12.3	11.2	11.2
Mean daily attendance	79.8	81.1	73.3	72.7	74.0	73.6
Staff absence rate	7.3	7.2	8.2	9.4	7.9	8.7
Number of tracts	144	17	44	75	20	164

*Characteristics of public schools are a weighted average of the characteristics of schools attended by public school pupils resident in the tract. Percentile test scores refer to the percentage of students above or below the national percentile on the California Achievement Test.

**Includes 8 tracts of white growth not shown in table.

Sources: U.S. Bureau of the Census, Summary Tape File 4A; Philadelphia Public Schools.

Schools in Philadelphia are very segregated. Even averaging across tracts to compute the figures for tract groups, which tends to understate the degree of school segregation, it is apparent from Table 5 that most black students go to schools that are largely black, and probably to no one's surprise, separate is not equal. Although similar results are obtained for elementary and middle schools, Table 5 focuses on high schools, where the contrasts are sharpest. On all indicators, the quality and relative integration of schools attended by residents deteriorate as one moves from white or entry areas to established black areas. For example, the percentage of black students increases from 19 to 86 between entry and established areas, and the percentage scoring above the 85th percentile on the California Achievement Test drops from 17 to 4. Similarly, the grade retention rate increases from 19 to 29 percent, the dropout rate grows from 7 to 12 percent, the percentage of low income students from 23 to 51, while average daily attendance falls steadily from 81 to 73 percent. Moreover, unpublished data show that disparities in school quality increase as children go through the school system, being least in elementary schools and greatest in high schools.

In summary, the data presented so far suggest two things. First, they unambiguously indicate that high status blacks reside in integrated residential areas of superior quality. Areas in which few blacks live, or those where they have just begun to enter, contain residents of highest SES, have the greatest number of intact families, display the least physical dilapidation, and have the highest housing values. They also tend to be neighborhoods with the most favorable mortality conditions, the lowest crime rates, and the best public schools.

In seeking to maximize their spatial position, high status blacks behave like other groups. However, a second finding is the apparent difficulty they have in achieving these desirable spatial outcomes. High quality white areas and black entry tracts remain out of reach to all but a few of Philadelphia's black citizens, but they house 68 percent of the city's whites. On the other hand, poor quality established black neighborhoods house 69 percent of blacks, but a tiny minority of whites. In other words, patterns of residential segregation have separated blacks and whites into two vastly different environments: one that is poor, crime-ridden, unhealthy, unsafe, and educationally inferior, and another that is markedly richer, safer, healthier, and educationally superior.

The key question is why so few upper class blacks are able to achieve spatial assimilation within high-quality integrated neighborhoods. Philadelphia is well known for its large black middle class, yet the small percentage of blacks in white and entry neighborhoods suggests that middle class blacks have a difficult time achieving a spatial outcome commensurate with their SES. As mentioned earlier, while 23 percent of black families earn more than $20,000, only 4 percent live in white tracts or entry areas. The obvious explanation for this anomaly is that racial prejudice does not allow high status blacks to achieve the spatial outcomes they seek. As a result, middle class blacks are much more likely than whites to live in poor quality neighborhoods inhabited by people of low social and economic status.

Direct evidence for this view comes from Table 6, which presents probabilities of residential contact between high status white and black people, on the one hand, and low status people on the other: blue collar workers, high school dropouts, unemployed workers, families on public assistance, and families headed by women. The cell entries in this table are values of *P**, which give probabilities that a random person from categories in the stub of the table will have residential contact with a person or family described in the column headings (see Lieberson 1980, 1981). For example, the contact probability of .341 in the first cell means that the average white white collar worker lives in a tract where 34 percent of the workers are blue collar.

This table shows that high status blacks are considerably more likely than high status whites to encounter poor, dependent people in their neighborhoods. For example, while a college-educated white has a 29 percent chance of encountering a high school dropout in his or her tract, the probabilities of a college-educated black doing so is 39 percent. Similarly, a high income white has only an 8 percent probability of contact with a family on welfare, but the probability for a black at the same income level is nearly three times higher, 22 percent. Patterns are the same for other black and white contact probabilities. In short, these data strongly suggest that upwardly mobile blacks are markedly less able to convert their achievements into spatial separation from poor social environments and into contact with people of comparable class backgrounds, a supposition that is confirmed in the following section.

TABLE 6

Probability of Residential Contact (P*) between Persons with Selected Characteristics: Whites and Blacks in Philadelphia, 1980

Group	Blue Collar Worker	High School Dropout	Family on Welfare	Female Headed Family	Unemployed Worker
Whites					
White collar	0.341	0.336	0.081	0.074	0.095
College educated	0.308	0.289	0.080	0.080	0.092
Income < $25,000	0.344	0.336	0.076	0.069	0.095
All whites	0.373	0.382	0.093	0.079	0.105
Blacks					
White collar	0.376	0.406	0.227	0.214	0.154
College educated	0.372	0.393	0.221	0.210	0.153
Income < $25,000	0.382	0.398	0.216	0.206	0.150
All blacks	0.348	0.466	0.284	0.250	0.184

Source: U.S. Bureau of the Census, Summary Tape File 4A.

Structural Equation Analysis of Spatial Outcomes

. . . The general pattern of results, however, is easily described. Consistent with our hypothesis, the coefficients for income's effect on spatial outcomes are generally significant and always in the expected direction for both blacks and whites. When the outcome is undesirable (e.g., the percentage of families on welfare, the probability of murder) the coefficients are negative: the higher the income, the less likely blacks and whites are to experience the characteristic; and when the outcome is desirable (median housing value, the percentage of students testing above the 85th percentile) the coefficients are positive: the higher the income, the more likely both groups are to experience the outcome. [See Table (7).]

Moreover, as we expected, the income coefficient for whites is almost always stronger than the coefficient for blacks. In 27 of the 33 comparisons, the absolute value of the white coefficient exceeds that of the black coefficient, usually by a considerable margin. For example, blacks are only able to convert household income into spatial separation from families on assistance at 58 percent of the white rate, and are able to translate income into housing value at a mere 13 percent of the rate of whites. Other particularly strong contrasts include the percentages of unwed mothers, of school dropouts, and of dilapidated housing; the probabilities of infant mortality, of murder, of rape, of robbery, and of burglary; and the percentages of low income, low achievement students in public schools. For all of these variables, whites are able to make much more effective use of their incomes to achieve the desired outcome.

. . . Compared to blacks with low education and low income, whites with the same characteristics live in much more desirable areas, with a lower percentage of families in poverty, a higher median housing value, a lower likelihood of crime, and a higher probability of sending their children to a school with other high achievers. In most cases, the black intercept is several times less favorable than the white intercept. Thus, the neighborhoods from which blacks launch their spatial attainment

efforts are generally worse off than the areas from which whites launch theirs.

Turning to the effect of education, the picture is quite different. Coefficients for both groups are less consistently significant, and less often in the expected direction. Thus, while coefficients linking education to indicators of the social, physical, health, and school environments are generally in the expected direction, coefficients associated with crime outcomes are in the opposite direction, with education being positively related to the likelihood of criminal victimization. . . .

. . . As we anticipated, both blacks and whites endeavor to convert their socioeconomic achievements into beneficial spatial outcomes. But consistent with our belief that blacks face greater barriers to spatial assimilation than other groups, they are less able than whites to translate their income gains into desired spatial results, and, in addition, they enter the assimilation process at a much more disadvantaged position. However, contrary to our expectations, blacks consistently and strongly out-perform whites in converting education into spatial achievements. . . .

Table [8] illustrates the interplay between education and income with respect to four outcome measures: two socioeconomic and two educational. Predicted outcomes were actually generated for all 33 indicators, then inspected, and these four were selected as representative. The outcomes were predicted by assuming values of education ranging from 10 to 16 years, and values of income from $8000 to $32,000, and substituting these into the relevant black and white equations from Table [7]. These limits lie within the range of tract averages actually observed for blacks and whites across census tracts in Philadelphia.

The outcomes shown in Table [8] suggest that education captures a class dimension of segregation that is independent of income. Working class or middle class blacks—those with a high school education or less but a relatively high income, such as a plumber or electrician might have—are considerably less able to achieve desirable neighborhood characteristics than working or middle class whites. Thus, with 10 years of education and a $16,000 income, a black citizen is expected to live in a

TABLE [7]

Regression Equations Linking Education and Income to Selected Spatial Outcomes: Philadelphia, 1980

	Predictor Variables			
	Median Education		Household Income	
Spatial Outcomes	Whites	Blacks	Whites	Blacks
Social Environment				
% families below poverty line	−0.108*	−0.348*	−0.147*	−0.092*
% families on assistance	−0.143*	−0.435*	−0.128*	−0.074*
% families w/child < 18	−0.056	−0.239*	−0.107*	−0.066*
% workers unemployed	−0.114*	−0.235*	−0.073*	−0.042*
% households w/out income	−0.092*	−0.200*	−0.048*	−0.051*
% births to unwed mothers	−0.067	−0.390*	−0.149*	−0.046*
% 16+ in labor force	0.075*	0.139*	0.024*	0.031*
% 14–18 in school	0.276*	0.524*	0.062*	0.003
Physical Environment				
% houses boarded up	−0.099	−0.622*	−0.163*	−0.102*
% w/out complete plumbing	0.104*	−0.277*	−0.152*	−0.074*
% w/out complete heating	−0.074*	−0.395*	−0.098*	−0.037*
Median age of housing	−0.331	−3.648*	−1.060*	−0.641*
Median housing value**	8.860*	14.415*	1.552*	0.200
Median rental value	8.933*	25.962*	5.476*	4.129*
Health Environment				
Death probability	−0.027	−0.077*	−0.018*	−0.019*
Infant death probability	−0.172*	−0.161*	−0.039*	−0.019
Cancer death probability	−0.012	−0.030	−0.011*	−0.015*
CV death probability	−0.026*	−0.020	−0.010*	−0.005
Crime Environment				
Violent death probability	−0.036	−0.160*	−0.018*	−0.020*
Murder probability	0.126*	−0.063	−0.095*	−0.044*
Rape probability	0.185*	0.074	−0.083*	−0.028*
Assault probability	0.080*	−0.055	−0.068*	−0.040*
Robbery probability	0.202*	0.083	−0.092*	−0.036*
Burglary probability	0.068*	0.047	−0.020*	−0.010
Larceny probability	0.113*	0.113*	−0.025*	−0.025*
Auto theft probability	0.097*	0.126*	−0.025*	−0.012*
Major crime probability	0.122*	0.090*	−0.034*	−0.022*
High School Environment				
% students low income	0.028	−0.180*	−0.085*	−0.043*
% students testing > 85%	0.155*	0.388*	0.084*	0.045*
% students testing < 15%	−0.084*	−0.195*	−0.099*	−0.035*
% black students	0.235*	−0.020	−0.146*	−0.048*
Grade retention probability	−0.019*	−0.039*	−0.016*	−0.011*
Dropout probability	−0.076*	−0.126*	−0.037*	−0.021*

*p < .05
**In thousands of dollars.
[NOTE: Table is abridged from original.]

tract where 26 percent of the population is below the poverty line, but a white with the same characteristics is predicted to reside in an area where only 13 percent live in poverty. Similarly, a black with a high school diploma and a $20,000 income is predicted to live in an area where 26 percent of the births are to unwed mothers, compared to a figure of 10 percent for a white with the same characteristics.

Given a high school education or lower, these differences persist at all levels of income. Indeed, because blacks convert income into spatial achievements at a much lower rate than whites, the differences widen as income rises.

Racism

TABLE [8]

***Predicted Characteristics of Tracts Inhabited by Whites and Blacks with
Different Levels of Education and Family Income: Philadelphia, 1980***

Predicted Outcome, Race, and Level of Education	Household Income						
	$8,000	$12,000	$16,000	$20,000	$24,000	$28,000	$32,000
% Families on Assistance							
Whites							
10 years	0.287	0.195	0.127	0.080	0.050	0.030	0.018
12 years	0.233	0.154	0.098	0.061	0.038	0.023	0.014
14 years	0.185	0.120	0.076	0.047	0.029	0.017	0.010
16 years	0.146	0.093	0.058	0.036	0.022	0.013	0.008
Blacks							
10 years	0.400	0.331	0.269	0.215	0.169	0.132	0.101
12 years	0.218	0.172	0.134	0.103	0.079	0.060	0.045
14 years	0.105	0.080	0.061	0.046	0.035	0.026	0.019
16 years	0.047	0.035	0.026	0.020	0.015	0.011	0.008
% Births to Unwed Mothers							
Whites							
10 years	0.440	0.302	0.193	0.116	0.068	0.038	0.022
12 years	0.407	0.275	0.173	0.103	0.060	0.034	0.019
14 years	0.375	0.249	0.154	0.091	0.053	0.030	0.017
16 years	0.344	0.224	0.138	0.081	0.046	0.026	0.015
Blacks							
10 years	0.568	0.523	0.477	0.431	0.387	0.344	0.304
12 years	0.376	0.334	0.295	0.258	0.224	0.194	0.167
14 years	0.217	0.187	0.161	0.137	0.117	0.099	0.084
16 years	0.112	0.095	0.081	0.068	0.057	0.048	0.040
% Low Income Students							
Whites							
10 years	0.442	0.360	0.286	0.222	0.169	0.126	0.093
12 years	0.455	0.373	0.298	0.232	0.177	0.133	0.098
14 years	0.469	0.386	0.309	0.242	0.185	0.139	0.103
16 years	0.483	0.400	0.322	0.252	0.194	0.146	0.108
Blacks							
10 years	0.540	0.497	0.454	0.412	0.371	0.332	0.295
12 years	0.450	0.408	0.368	0.329	0.292	0.258	0.226
14 years	0.364	0.325	0.288	0.255	0.223	0.195	0.169
16 years	0.285	0.251	0.221	0.192	0.167	0.144	0.124
% Students Scoring < 15%							
Whites							
10 years	0.433	0.340	0.257	0.189	0.136	0.095	0.066
12 years	0.393	0.303	0.226	0.165	0.117	0.082	0.057
14 years	0.353	0.269	0.198	0.143	0.101	0.700	0.048
16 years	0.316	0.237	0.173	0.123	0.087	0.060	0.041
Blacks							
10 years	0.448	0.414	0.381	0.348	0.317	0.288	0.260
12 years	0.355	0.324	0.294	0.266	0.239	0.215	0.192
14 years	0.272	0.245	0.220	0.197	0.176	0.156	0.139
16 years	0.202	0.180	0.160	0.142	0.126	0.111	0.098

Thus, while a black with 10 years of schooling and living in a household making $8,000 is 39 percent more likely than a similar white to experience contact with a family on assistance, a black with 10 years of schooling and a $32,000 income is nearly six times more likely to do so.

In short, a black plumber or electrician earning a steady, relatively high income, but only having a high school education, cannot come close to achieving the same quality neighborhood as a skilled white with a high school diploma.

The story, however, is quite different for

college-educated blacks. Although the combination of high education and low income is quite unlikely, a black college graduate earning a household income of $8,000 would actually experience a *better* tract environment than a white with the same characteristics. Because of the strong effect of black education on spatial outcomes, they live in areas with a lower share of families on assistance and a lower percentage of births to unwed mothers; and at high levels of both education and household income, whites and blacks experience comparable, high quality neighborhoods.

Both these combinations of characteristics—high education and low income, and high education and high income—are relatively uncommon. Most blacks have high school educations and moderate incomes, and in this status range the white advantage in attaining desirable spatial outcomes is decisive. In practical terms, black spatial assimilation is a viable option only for members of the upper middle class, people who have achieved high levels of education *and* income. Thus, for upwardly mobile blacks, spatial assimilation requires a quantum leap in social status. The first tentative steps away from the ghetto are likely to be exceedingly difficult.

The school outcomes depicted in the table show the kind of handicap this places on working class black parents with solid incomes who have high aspirations for their children. A black child from a family whose parents have high school educations and a household income of $32,000 attends a markedly inferior school compared to a white child from the same kind of home. The black child is predicted to attend a high school where 19 percent of students score below the 15th percentile on the California Achievement Test and where 23 percent are from low income families. In contrast, a white child with the same family background would be in a school where only 6 percent score below the 15th percentile and where only 10 percent are from low income families. Thus, given the same objective socioeconomic characteristics, black children are much more likely than white children to go to a school attended by poor children who score badly on standardized tests, providing them with a less-advantaged educational environment.

SUMMARY AND DISCUSSION

This paper has taken a detailed look at the process by which blacks attempt to improve their spatial position in urban society, and some of the consequences they face for not achieving it. High status blacks, like whites, seek to convert past socioeconomic attainments into improved residential circumstances. Specifically, high status blacks seek spatial assimilation within integrated areas that are of markedly higher quality than average, inhabited by high status residents living in newer, more valuable housing, with better schools and considerably lower mortality and crime rates.

However, very few blacks are successful in achieving these locational outcomes. The vast majority live in segregated neighborhoods where blacks long have been, or are rapidly becoming, the majority, areas characterized by high crime, poor schools, economic dependency, unstable families, dilapidated housing, and poor health. All evidence indicates that blacks are no different than whites in trying to escape such an environment, when they are able. They are just less able. For any desirable spatial outcome, blacks begin the process of spatial assimilation at a much more disadvantaged position than whites, and achieve less benefit per unit of income attained. Only through education are black people able to make up for these two strikes against them.

As a result of the interplay between education and income in the process of spatial assimilation, lower and middle class blacks who have not attended college face a distinctly disadvantaged residential environment, similar in quality to areas that only the poorest of whites must face. The simplest and most plausible explanation for these patterns is the continuing importance of racial prejudice among middle and working class whites, as in the vignette at the beginning of this paper. While there are many neighborhoods in Philadelphia where a black doctor, lawyer, or business executive might settle peacably with other professionals, be they white or black, there are few working class or middle class white neighborhoods where blacks are allowed to enter. If there is a ladder out of the ghetto for ambitious black people, the bottom rungs seem to have been chopped off by racial prejudice.

This explanation does not necessarily imply that the upper classes are paragons of racial tolerance while the lower classes are bastions of prejudice. Although survey data generally show that prejudice decreases with SES, and especially with education, an alternative explanation is that upper class whites are not threatened because they know that few blacks possess the economic resources to enter their neighborhoods. In contrast, lower class whites know very well that many blacks have both the means and the desire to settle among them. Thus, given the same level of racial intolerance, wealthy whites would not have to act on their prejudices to limit contact with blacks, while poor whites would. Another possibility is that whites of all classes are equally prejudiced against lower class blacks, but harbor no prejudice toward upper class blacks. In other words, blacks must accumulate a great deal of human capital, such as education or occupational status, before they are not threatening to whites and are allowed to settle among them.

Whatever its origin, at this point it seems fairly clear that the undeniable persistence of racial segregation in American cities is far from neutral in its effect on black social and economic well-being. At least partly because of racial segregation, and possibly largely because of it, middle class blacks are subjected to higher rates of crime, less healthy environments, and more dilapidated surroundings than their white counterparts. More important, they must live with people of considerably lower social class, and send their children to inferior schools with students from much less advantaged families than their own.

Admittedly, the data employed here are less than ideal for comparing processes of black and white spatial achievement. The crime data are so aggregated that they blur spatial distinctions, while the school data include only the public sector schools. Moreover, while basing the study on the City of Philadelphia facilitates the compilation of data, it eliminates many wealthy suburban areas which house more whites than blacks. We nonetheless believe that each of these

defects biases our results in a conservative direction, mitigating the apparent contrast between whites and blacks.

The consequences of continuing racial segregation are directly relevant to several contentious theoretical, social, and practical debates within sociology. First is the declining significance of race. Banfield (1970), Wilson (1978), and others argue that the problem of black poverty is becoming more and more a matter of class. Although class has undoubtedly become more important in recent years, this article has shown race to have a strong impact on black social and economic well-being through its impact on residential patterns. Race, operating through the discriminatory allocation of families to residences, continues to be an important variable for understanding the position of blacks in contemporary American society.

A related issue is the emergence of a black underclass. Several observers have argued that since the late 1960s the black population has bifurcated increasingly into two classes of people, an underclass of poor welfare-dependent people living in unstable single-parent households located in declining central city areas, and a middle class of stable families with one, or more often two, working adults located in suburban or wealthy urban areas (Auletta 1982; Cottingham 1982). To the extent that such a bifurcation is occurring, it seems likely that processes of residential segregation have played a role. We have demonstrated the critical role of college education in allowing higher income blacks to escape the confines of a ghetto environment. Ecological processes of segregation may, in fact, be core mechanisms by which a black underclass is created and perpetuated in American society.

Another issue is the persistently poor performance of blacks in schools and on standardized tests such as the SAT. Even controlling for income, blacks lag far behind whites in SAT scores. In 1984, for example, blacks in the highest income category ($50,000 and over) achieved average SAT scores (404 verbal, 428 math) *below* white scores (412 and 446, respectively) in the *lowest* income category (under $6,000) (Biemiller 1985). But in light of our findings, why would one expect otherwise? Controlling for income in no way equalizes the access of blacks and whites to educational resources. Because of residential segregation, middle class blacks must send their children to public schools with children far below their own class standing, children with more limited cognitive, linguistic, and social skills. Given the strong effect of peer influences and environment on aspirations, motivation, and achievement, it is hardly surprising that so many young black people, even those from stable middle class families, fail to achieve high test scores or educational distinction.

In sum, we argue that the process of stratification in the U.S. is in many ways ecologically based, operating through mechanisms that can only be understood in spatial terms. Residential segregation not only reflects social distance, it perpetuates it as well. As long as segregation is imposed on black Americans because of the color of their skin rather than the nature of their achievements, race must be considered to be a salient dimension of stratification in U.S. society.

REFERENCES

Aldrich, Howard. 1975. "Ecological Succession in Racially Changing Neighborhoods: A Review of the Literature." *Urban Affairs Quarterly* 10:327–48.

Auletta, Ken. 1982. *The Underclass.* Random House.

Banfield, Edward C. 1970. *The Unheavenly City.* Little, Brown.

Berry, Brian J. L. 1976. "Ghetto Expansion and Single-Family Housing Prices: Chicago, 1968–1972." *Journal of Urban Economics* 3:397–423.

Biemiller, Lawrence. 1985. "Black Students' Average Aptitude-Test Scores Up 7 Points in a Year." *The Chronicle of Higher Education* (January 16).

Cass, Julia. 1986. "The Elmwood Incident." *The Philadelphia Inquirer Magazine* (May 4).

Cliff, A. D., and J. K. Ord. 1973. *Spatial Autocorrelation.* Pion.

Coleman, James S., Sara D. Kelly, and John A. Moore. 1975. *Trends in School Segregation 1968–1973.* The Urban Institute.

Cottingham, Clement. 1982. "Conclusion: The Political Economy of Urban Poverty." Pp. *nnn–nn* in *Race, Poverty, and the Urban Underclass,* edited by Clement Cottingham. Heath.

Doreian, Patrick. 1980. "Linear Models with Spatially Distributed Data: Spatial Disturbances or Spatial Effects?" *Sociological Methods and Research* 9:29–60.

Duncan, Otis D., and Beverly Duncan. 1957. *The Negro Population of Chicago.* University of Chicago Press.

Farley, Reynolds. 1978. "School Integration in the United States." Pp. 15–50 in *The Demography of Racial and Ethnic Groups,* edited by Frank D. Bean and W. Parker Frisbie. Academic Press.

Farley, Reynolds, and Alma F. Taeuber. 1974. "Racial Segregation in the Public Schools." *American Journal of Sociology* 79:888–905.

Furstenberg, Frank F., Jr., S. Philip Morgan, and Kristin A. Moore. 1985. "Exploring Race Differences in the Timing of Intercourse." Working Paper, Population Studies Center, University of Pennsylvania.

Hanushek, Eric A., and John E. Jackson. 1977. *Statistical Methods for Social Scientists.* Academic Press.

Hogan, Denis P., and Evelyn M. Kitagawa. 1985. "The Impact of Social Status, Family Structure, and Neighborhood on the Fertility of Black Adolescents." *American Journal of Sociology* 90:825–55.

Kain, John F. 1968. "Housing Segregation, Negro Employment, and Metropolitan Decentralization." *Quarterly Journal of Economics* 82:175–97.

Kain, John F., and J. J. Persky. 1969. "Alternatives to the 'Guilded Ghetto.'" *The Public Interest* 14:275–97.

Kain, John F., and J. M. Quigley. 1975. *Housing Markets and Racial Discrimination: A Microeconomic Analysis.* National Bureau of Economic Analysis.

Kitagawa, Evelyn M., and Philip M. Hauser. 1973. *Differential Mortality in the United States.* Harvard University Press.

Kobrin, Frances E., and Calvin Goldscheider. 1978. *The Ethnic Factor in Family Structure and Mobility.* Ballinger.

Laumann, Edward O., Paul M. Siegel, and Robert W. Hodge. 1970. *The Logic of Social Hierarchies.* Markham.

Lee, Barrett A. 1985. "Racially Mixed Neighborhoods During the 1970s: Change or Stability?" *Social Science Quarterly* 66:346–64.

Lee, Barrett A., Daphne Spain, and Debra J. Umberson. 1985. "Neighborhood Revitalization and Racial Change: The Case of Washington, D.C." *Demography* 22:581–602.

Lewin-Epstein, Noah. 1985. "Neighborhoods, Local Labor Markets, and Opportunities for White and Nonwhite Youth." *Social Science Quarterly* 66:163–71.

Lieberson, Stanley. 1963. *Ethnic Patterns in American Cities.* Free Press.

———. 1980. *A Piece of the Pie: Black and White Immigrants Since 1880.* University of California Press.

———. 1981. "An Asymmetrical Approach to Segregation." Pp. 61–82 in *Ethnic Segregation in Cities,* edited by Ceri Peach, Vaughn Robinson, and Susan Smith. Croom Helm.

Loftin, Colin, and Sally K. Ward. 1983. "A Spatial Autocorrelation Model of the Effects of Population Density on Fertility." *American Sociological Review* 48:121–28.

Logan, John R. 1978. "Growth, Politics, and the Stratification of Places." *American Journal of Sociology* 84:404–16.

Madden, Janice, and Mark Hughes. 1985. "Residential Ghettos, Job Discrimination, and the Economic Status of Black Workers: New Evidence for an Old Debate." Unpublished Paper, Department of Regional Science, University of Pennsylvania.

Massey, Douglas S., and Brooks Bitterman. 1985. "Explaining the Paradox of Puerto Rican Segregation." *Social Forces* 64:306–31.

Massey, Douglas S., and Nancy A. Denton. 1985. "Spatial Assimilation as a Socioeconomic Outcome." *American Sociological Review* 50:94–105.

Massey, Douglas S., and Brendan P. Mullan. 1984. "Processes of Hispanic and Black Spatial Assimilation." *American Journal of Sociology* 89:836–73.

Nelli, Humbert S. 1970. *Italians in Chicago 1880–1930: A Study in Ethnic Mobility.* Oxford University Press.

Parcel, Toby. 1979. "Race, Regional Labor Markets, and Earnings." *American Sociological Review* 44:262–79.

Park, Robert E. 1926. "The Urban Community as a Spatial Pattern and a Moral Order." Pp. 3–18 in *The Urban Community,* edited by Ernest W. Burgess. University of Chicago Press.

Schneider, Mark, and John R. Logan. 1982. "Suburban Racial Segregation and Black Access to Local Public Resources." *Social Science Quarterly* 63:762–70.

———. 1985. "Suburban Municipalities: The Changing System of Intergovernmental Relations in the Mid-1970s." *Urban Affairs Quarterly* 21:87–105.

Taeuber, Karl E., and Alma F. Taeuber. 1965. *Negroes in Cities.* Aldine.

Thernstrom, Stephan. 1973. *The Other Bostonians: Poverty and Progress in the American Metropolis 1880–1970.* Harvard University Press.

Villemez, Wayne J. 1980. "Race, Class, and Neighborhood: Differences in Residential Return on Individual Resources." *Social Forces* 59:414–30.

Ward, David. 1971. *Cities and Immigrants: A Geography of Change in Nineteenth Century America.* Oxford University Press.

Wilson, William J. 1978. *The Declining Significance of Race.* University of Chicago Press.

Part THREE

The World
at Large

CHAPTER
14

Overpopulation

Family Planning and World Health

JODI L. JACOBSON

Thirty-three-year-old Socorro Cisneros de Rosales, a Central American mother of thirteen, is neither a demographer nor an economist. In describing her own plight and that of her country as "an overproduction of children and a lack of food and work," Mrs. Cisneros nevertheless speaks authoritatively on the conflict between high birthrates and declining economies that faces many in the Third World. Over the past two decades, steadily declining birthrates have contributed to significant improvements in the health and well-being of millions of people and to the growth of national economies. To date, however, only a handful of countries have reduced fertility rates sufficiently to make these gains universal or to ensure that their populations will stabilize in the foreseeable future. Countries that remain on a high fertility path will find that meeting basic subsistence needs will be increasingly difficult in the years to come.

Despite lower fertility levels for the world as a whole, population increased by 86 million people in 1987, surpassing a total of 5 billion. Although birthrates continue to fall in many developing countries, the pace has slowed markedly. Declining death rates have balanced out the modest reductions in fertility of the past few years. Slower economic growth in developing countries plagued by debt, dwindling exports, and environmental degradation mean that governments can no longer rely on socioeconomic gains to help reduce births. This uncertain economic outlook raises important questions. Can governments successfully encourage fertility reductions in the face of extensive poverty? What mix of policies is likely to promote smaller families, thereby reducing fertility and raising living standards?

Encouraging small families requires a two-pronged strategy of family planning and social change. Few countries have put family planning and reproductive health care at the top of their agendas. In most industrial nations, widely available contraceptive technologies enable couples to choose the number and spacing of their children. For the majority of women in many developing countries, contraceptive methods remain unavailable, inaccessible, or inappropriate. Surveys confirm that half the 463 million married women in developing countries outside of China do not want more children. Millions more would like to delay their next pregnancy. Meanwhile, the number of women who are in their childbearing years is increasing rapidly. With few exceptions, governments have not changed policies or invested in programs sufficiently to weaken the social conditions underlying high fertility rates. These conditions include, most significantly, the low status of women and the high illiteracy rates, low wages, and ill health that customarily accompany it. Until societal attitudes change, national fertility rates are unlikely to decline significantly.

International support for family planning has been considerably weakened in recent years by changes in United States policy. By the time the world's population surpassed 5 billion in 1987, the United States had abdicated its role as a leading supporter of reproductive rights worldwide. Political and societal disputes have converged with fiscal constraints to cut funding for contraceptive research and for both domestic and international family planning. This

Jodi L. Jacobson is a senior researcher at the Worldwatch Institute in Washington, D.C. She is coauthor of the 1987 and 1988 editions of State of the World; *and author or coauthor of several Worldwatch papers, including: "Our Demographically Divided World" and "The Future of Urbanization."*

From *Society,* July/August 1988. Published by permission of Transaction Publishers, from *Society,* Vol. 25, No. 5. Copyright © 1988 by Transaction Publishers.

329

policy change has set back by several years the worldwide efforts to reduce fertility, dimming hopes of achieving population stabilization by the end of the next century.

Reducing birthrates to speed the development process is a goal that deserves the immediate attention of the world community. Promoting smaller families throughout the Third World will benefit every segment of society. For women, bearing fewer children means better health for themselves and their offspring. For countries, reducing the average family size increases per capita investments and alleviates pressures on the natural resources underpinning national economies. For the world, slower population growth enhances the prospects for widespread security and prosperity.

Family planning is among the most basic of preventive health care strategies, although it is rarely recognized as such. Encouraging fewer and safer births among women in developing countries will reduce unacceptably high rates of maternal mortality from complications of childbirth and abortion. Moreover, by distributing condoms and increasing the public's understanding of reproductive health issues, family planning programs can help control the spread of acquired immunodeficiency syndrome (AIDS), a major threat to Third World health and economic survival.

Each year, at least a half-million women worldwide die from pregnancy-related causes. Fully 99 percent of these deaths occur in the Third World, where complications arising from pregnancy and illegal abortions are the leading killers of women in their twenties and thirties. World Health Organization (WHO) officials caution that maternal deaths—those resulting directly or indirectly from pregnancy within forty-two days of childbirth, induced abortion, or miscarriage—may actually be twice the estimated figures. What is more, for every woman who dies, many more suffer serious, often long-term, health problems. That bearing life should bring death to so many women is a distressing irony. It is even more distressing given that family planning and preventive medicine could substantially reduce these losses.

In the Third World, maternal mortality accounts for some 25 percent of deaths of women aged fifteen to forty-nine. More than 3000 maternal deaths occur per 100,000 live births annually in parts of Ethiopia and Bangladesh. By contrast, the figures in the United States and Norway are only 10 and 2, respectively. Each year, more than 20,000 women die from pregnancy or related complications in Bangladesh, compared with about 500 women in the United States, a country with more than twice as many people.

Illegal abortion is one of the major direct causes of maternal death. Rough estimates indicate that only half the estimated 54 million abortions performed annually around the world are legal. Most illegal abortions are carried out under unsanitary conditions by unskilled attendants, leaving women vulnerable to serious complications and infection. By contrast, modern abortion procedures, carried out under proper medical supervision in countries where they are legal, cause fewer maternal deaths than pregnancy or oral contraceptives do.

Forty-four percent of women in the developing world, outside of China, live in countries where abortion is allowed only to save the mother's life. Another 10 percent live in countries where abortion is totally prohibited. Millions of women unable to obtain a legal abortion on the basis of life-threatening circumstances have subsequently died from the complications of an illegal abortion. Those who advocate restrictive abortion policies rarely acknowledge this toll on women's lives. Estimates of the annual number of deaths due to abortion complications range from 155,000 to 204,000 women worldwide. Abortion-related deaths are especially common among poor and illiterate women living in countries with strict abortion laws. In Latin America, where legal abortion is generally restricted to cases of rape or endangerment of the woman's life, up to half of maternal deaths appear to be due to illegal abortions.

Pregnancy itself takes a greater toll on a woman's body in regions where malnutrition and poor health are the norm. In the Third World, pregnancy is associated with a higher incidence of health-threatening infection, vitamin and mineral deficiencies, and anemia. Due to reduced immunity, common diseases such as pneumonia and influenza cause 50 to 100 percent more deaths in pregnant than in nonpregnant women. Three groups of women face the highest risk of pregnancy-related deaths: those at either end of their reproductive cycle, those who bear children in rapid succession, and those who have more than four children. Because of biological factors, women under nineteen or over thirty-five are more susceptible to complications of pregnancy. Women giving birth to children spaced less than a year apart are twice as likely to die from pregnancy-related causes than those who have children two or more years apart. In Matlab Thana, Bangladesh, health workers recorded three times as many deaths among women giving birth to their eighth child as among those giving birth to their third.

At least half of all maternal deaths can be averted through a combined strategy of family planning, legal abortion, and primary health care. According to researchers Beverly Winikoff and Maureen Sullivan of the Population Council, in *Studies in Family Planning* in 1987, a fertility rate reduction of 25 to 35 percent resulting from more widely available family planning would also lower maternal mortality by one-fourth. Making abortions legal and safe could reduce the toll an additional 20 to 25 percent. Making all pregnancies safer through increased investments in prenatal health care and reducing the number of high-risk pregnancies would prevent another 20 to 25 percent of deaths. Winikoff and Sullivan point out that while, theoretically, this three-pronged strategy could reduce maternal mortality by three-fourths, a 50 percent decrease is more a realistic expectation, given prevailing social and political conditions, such as large desired family size and the opposition to legalizing abortion.

Establishing integrated family planning and health strategies will be well worth the investment. Village-based paramedics and midwives can teach women the benefits of birth spacing, breast-feeding, prenatal care, and contraceptive use. Small-scale maternity centers—on the order of one for every 4000 people—could promote simple solutions to some of the most pervasive maternal health problems, by providing, for instance, iron supplements to treat anemia. Linked with regional facilities run by doctors, such clinics would constitute a pivotal link between rural populations and the often urban-based medical community. Assuming that

maternal deaths run as high as 1 million per year, family planning and health care would save at least 500,000 women's lives annually and improve the health of millions more.

Ironically, new reproductive health threats may push family planning services to the top of national agendas. By October 1987, the total number of reported cases of AIDS worldwide (persons already showing signs of illness) had exceeded 60,000, more than one-sixth of which were in developing countries. Although the United States leads the world, with nearly 42,000 documented cases as of September 1987, the potential devastation from AIDS appears to be a far greater threat in developing countries. WHO estimates that between 5 million and 10 million people around the world may now be infected with the virus that can lead to AIDS, and that at least 2 million of them are in Africa. Approximately 4000 cases have been found in Latin America and the Caribbean thus far. Current health care problems may only foreshadow far more serious public health burdens.

Transmission of this new virus through sexual contact is the single greatest route of infection; therefore, AIDS prevention and education can best be carried out by family planning and related health programs. Next to total abstinence, condoms offer the best protection against the spread of sexually transmitted diseases. Yet, primarily for cultural reasons, condoms are rarely used in most of the Third World. Excluding China, fewer than one-third of the world's 45 million condom users live in developing countries.

Increasing the availability of condoms and linking their use with better health may slow the spread of AIDS. Instructing heath care workers on the dangers of reusing needles and of performing routine procedures with unsanitary implements, and securing adequate supplies of medical equipment, will ensure that the health care community itself is not responsible for spreading the virus.

Scientists currently believe that between 25 and 50 percent of those infected with the virus that can lead to AIDS will die in the next ten years. In developing countries, this disease will primarily afflict individuals aged twenty to forty-nine. Both pregnancy- and AIDS-related deaths thus strike at people in their prime, taking a tremendous toll on human life and productive capacity. The need for public education about reproductive health is stronger than ever.

CHANGING CONTRACEPTIVE TECHNOLOGIES

Nearly thirty years after the introduction of oral contraceptives, millions of couples in the developing world remain without the means to plan their families. Poor supply and distribution networks are part of the problem, but the prevalence of contraceptive use remains low in the Third World, in part because few of the methods currently available fit the life-styles or the pocketbooks of potential users. Today's technologies are not versatile enough, nor are they changing quickly enough, to meet the needs of a highly diverse and growing world population.

About 372 million of the 860 million married couples of reproductive age worldwide use modern contraceptives, a prevalence rate of 43 percent. Among couples in developing countries outside of China, the use of modern methods is much lower than the world average. Although more than half indicate a desire to practice family planning, only 27 percent actually do.

At least nine reversible contraceptives are on the market, including hormonal methods and less effective barrier devices. Their distribution is highly skewed to particular regions or countries. Eighty-three million women have intrauterine devices (IUDs), the most prevalent reversible method; nearly three-fourths of them are in China. By contrast, the 64 million users of oral contraceptives are more evenly divided between the Third World and industrialized countries. Nearly 60 million people, about two-thirds of whom live in the industrial world, rely primarily on condoms, diaphragms, and sponges.

Contraceptives vary significantly in their effectiveness, depending on the skill and consistency with which a given method is used. As a group, hormonal methods, including implants and injectables, have the lowest failure rates. Birth control pills—the most established hormonal method—have the widest failure range in that group. The effectiveness of these oral contraceptives, which must be taken every day, depends on a high level of individual motivation and an understanding of self-administered drugs. Injectable contraceptives have been on the market for about a decade and are among the most effective hormonal methods. Approximately 6.5 million around the world use injectables, one-sixth of whom are Chinese. The injectable Depo-Provera, approved in ninety countries, prevents conception for three months. Injectables effective for one month are used primarily in China and Latin America.

At the other end of the scale of effectiveness, natural family planning—also known as the rhythm method or periodic abstinence—has consistently high failure rates. Worldwide, between 10 million and 15 million people use rhythm, most of whom live in industrial countries. This technique requires a woman to time her ovulatory cycle by charting bodily functions, such as basal temperature, on a daily basis. Because a significant proportion of women everywhere experience highly variable menstrual cycles, fertile periods may be hard to calculate, and reliance on this method can often lead to unwanted pregnancy. Apart from other drawbacks, periodic abstinence requires a degree of cooperation between husband and wife that is unusual in many cultures.

No one contraceptive can fit the needs of every couple any more than one eyeglass prescription can correct all vision problems. In many cultures, for example, the diaphragm is considered undesirable because women are uncomfortable with the intimate contact with their own bodies that this method requires. It may also be impractical where water for washing is in short supply. Although the pill is relatively inexpensive, it may be a highly ineffective method where primary health care is poor and contraceptive supplies uncertain. Unexpected or unpleasant side effects can cause considerable anxiety among women in countries where medical advice is hard to come by.

First-year discontinuation rates between 20 and 40 percent among new pill and IUD users in the Third World indicate that these methods will not be effective in meeting the needs of most women in these countries. Advances in contraceptive technology that address concerns about safety and side effects will help speed the transition from high to low fertility around the world. Long-acting, inexpensive methods of birth control are more likely to serve the needs of low-income consumers in developing countries. In this category, recently developed hormonal implants show considerable promise. One such product, NORPLANT, is the most effective reversible contraceptive yet developed, offering protection against pregnancy for five years. Small permeable rods filled with timed-release hormones are implanted under the skin of the upper arm in a simple surgical procedure. The rods can be removed at any time. NORPLANT has already been approved in ten countries, including China, Colombia, Finland, Indonesia, Sweden, and Thailand, and is still undergoing evaluation in twenty-six others. A two-year implant, NORPLANT-2, is under study in several countries. The price tag for NORPLANT runs about $2.80 per year of protection, a cost that can be significantly reduced as production increases.

It can take fifteen years or more under good conditions for a new contraceptive to move from laboratory to market availability. Contraceptives evolve from a lengthy process of basic and applied research, product development, testing, marketing, and safety evaluation. In order to be registered in the United States and most other countries, experimental methods must pass muster through a series of animal and human clinical studies that usually take more than a decade to complete. Relatively few of the many leads scientists follow result in a marketable product. Not surprisingly, contraceptive development is an expensive and uncertain undertaking.

Several new hormonal methods aimed at Third World consumers are in varying stages of development. WHO is investigating two new monthly injectables, Cycloprovera and HRP102, both of which will be tested in clinical trials beginning in 1988. Biodegradable injectables and implants, which break down over time and do not require surgical removal, are in the early stages of testing. All of these are more effective and have fewer side effects than their currently available counterparts. Market introduction of more revolutionary methods, like a two-year pregnancy vaccine, a reversible contraceptive for men that reduces sperm count, and chemicals for nonsurgical female sterilization, is still far off. How quickly these methods become available hinges on the amount of money and scientific effort invested in contraceptive research and development.

Each new contraceptive technology results in an increase in the total number of users worldwide, which in turn translates into lower fertility rates. Unfortunately, the prospects for developing and disseminating new methods are not bright. Measured in constant dollars, global funding for overall reproductive research—including basic nondirected research, contraceptive research and development, and safety evaluation—peaked in 1973. Since 1973, European contributions to the field have declined in both constant and current dollars. The United States expenditure, averaging roughly 75 percent of the total since 1965, has declined by 23 percent in real terms since 1978. India alone among Third World countries has spent more than $1 million annually in these areas. Cutbacks in public support for contraceptive research funding come at a time when the private sector is moving away from developing new methods, placing the burden of contraceptive evolution on often cash-poor, nonprofit research institutions.

Reduced funding and an inhospitable political climate are delaying the development and introduction of contraceptive technology just as the demand for new methods is multiplying. About $100 million is needed annually through the year 2000 to take new products out of the laboratory and put them onto the market. Creating an international consortium of public and private groups to promote cooperation on contraceptive research and recommend uniform regulatory standards among countries would speed that development process.

INGREDIENTS OF SUCCESS

Without fertility declines, many governments cannot hope to make the investments necessary to improve human welfare and encourage economic development. A number of political and social obstacles remain for countries wishing to reduce fertility, improve health, and raise living standards. Attainment of these goals will depend on fundamental changes in several areas, including the way governments shape population policies, the degree to which they make contraceptive supplies and information accessible, and the steps they take to improve the status of women and increase their access to education.

Governments can use a mix of policies to hasten the transition to lower fertility. Population-related policies, such as laws governing minimum age at marriage, delivery of family planning services, and the importation or manufacture of contraceptive methods, directly affect the determinants of fertility. Official sanction of family planning efforts in the form of revised policies and legal codes is likely to increase acceptance of these services and help dispel widespread myths and misconceptions about contraception. Public policies concerning development indirectly affect fertility by influencing economic opportunities, social services, literacy, mortality, and the status of women.

A transformation in the laws, attitudes, and beliefs that directly and indirectly encourage high fertility will be essential to achieving population stabilization. Over the past decade, there have been promising changes in the attitudes of African officials toward population policy and family planning. Thirteen of the forty-two sub-Saharan countries have issued explicit population policies, and eleven of them have incorporated in their development plans policies specifically aimed at population problems. In discussing demographic trends, leaders have cited environmental degradation, unemployment, and the difficulty of raising living standards among their growing concerns. In the words of one Kenyan official, "If more and more people keep pouring into a country that can only deliver so much, you can expect political unrest, serious shortage of food and everything else that people need to live, and in general, chaos."

Realistic goals are an essential aspect of any national population policy. Programs that attempt to enforce norms—such as a two-child family—upon society before they have some cultural acceptance usually do not succeed. Sociologist Ronald Freedman notes, in *Studies in Family Planning* in 1987, that "setting a goal of a two child family as soon as possible may be a necessary and rational [long-term] policy goal. [But] to press for only two, when the real

potential for decreasing fertility [in the short run] is to encourage reducing desired family size from six children to four, makes the effort appear alien and ridiculous."

Countries that do not start now to reduce fertility may face stark choices later. The conflicts between individual desires and societal goals that result from excessive population growth are evident in China's one-child family program, perhaps the best known and most controversial of all fertility reduction campaigns. In 1953, the first census taken in China revealed a rapidly growing population of about 582 million. Mao Zedong, Communist party chairman at that time, did not see China's expanding millions as a problem. Fewer than thirty years later the Chinese numbered 1 billion, more than 20 percent of the world's population living on 7 percent of the world's arable land. By the late seventies, years of famine, poverty, and political upheaval had convinced the leaders in Beijing of the need for a rigorous family planning campaign.

Today's one-child family program evolved out of a series of strategies that began in the early seventies with the Wan Xi Shao (later, longer, fewer) program. This strategy encouraged delayed marriage, longer birth intervals, and smaller families. Even so, China's population continued to grow rapidly. As a result, policymakers enacted the one-child family policy in the hope of holding the population to about 1.2 billion just after the turn of the century. The policy, intended to last through the year 2000, offers a series of incentives and disincentives. Substantial pay increases, better housing, longer maternity leaves, and priority access to education are among the benefits offered to one-child families, while heavy fines and social criticism await couples who bear more than one. China's original policy, often seen as monolithic in its application, actually allows certain segments of the population to have more than one child. Urban couples are generally expected to adhere to the policy. Ethnic minorities and rural couples—80 percent of the nation's population—are allowed two or more.

Several other countries have turned to incentives in their attempts to influence fertility trends. Most of these programs have targeted individuals or couples, such as the programs in

India and Bangladesh offering financial incentives for sterilization. Several have experienced uneven success and in some cases have incited charges of coercion. On the other hand, experimental incentive programs aimed at overall community participation and development have shown some promise. A pilot program in northeastern Thailand tested the effects of community-level incentives on contraceptive prevalence. Loan funds of $2000 each were set up in several villages in conjunction with a family planning and health program. Initially, loans to individuals were based on character, creditworthiness, and the project to be carried out. After the program became established, preference was given to applicants who were practicing family planning. Members of the loan fund received shares and dividends on the basis of the contraceptive method used; more effective methods had higher values. As the prevalence of contraceptive use increased within a village, so did the total amount of the loan fund.

The Thai program was designed to prevent coercion. Money was not subtracted from a loan fund if the prevalence of contraceptive use fell; shares in the loan fund and the right to borrow were not taken away from those who chose not to continue using contraceptives. At the end of two years, loans totaling $72,000 had been granted for small-scale income-generating projects, such as pig and silk farming and cassava cultivation. During that period, the prevalence of contraceptive use in the experimental villages rose from 46 to 75 percent; in control villages, it went from 51 to 57 percent. By mixing small-family incentives with programs to increase community self-sufficiency, this experiment demonstrated the link between lower fertility and higher standards of living.

Women hold a paradoxical place in many societies. As mothers and wives, they often bear sole responsibility for child-rearing and domestic duties. In many cultures, they are bound by custom and necessity to contribute to household income; in some, they are the only breadwinners. Despite these roles as the linchpins of society, women in some societies have few rights under the law regarding land tenure, marital relations, income, or social security.

Attitudes toward familial relationships dim the prospects of reducing fertility rates in some African societies until the status of women improves. For example, payments made by a groom's family in expectation of high fertility may increase the wealth of a bride's family. Odile Frank and Geoffrey McNicoll, in a Population Council study on population policy in Kenya, note that because men bear little financial or domestic responsibility for basic subsistence, the costs of large numbers of children are invisible to them. As a result, they write, "even an emerging land shortage is not necessarily felt by men as a reason to limit fertility." Policies aimed at capping and regulating bridewealth payments as well as those recognizing and enforcing a woman's right to lay claim to land may serve to at least partially counteract the social forces that underlie high fertility in this case.

Improving the status of women, or, more specifically, reducing their economic dependence on men, is a crucial aspect of development. Until female education is widespread—until women in all societies gain at least partial control over the resources that shape their economic lives—high fertility, poverty, and environmental degradation will persist in many regions.

FILLING THE GAP

Policymakers concerned with population dynamics are faced with two objectives: reducing the unmet need for family planning in medium fertility countries and, in high fertility countries, providing an environment in which small families can become the norm. Helping couples achieve that norm will require a major commitment to family planning from both the international community and the Third World. Uncertain economic prospects, competing investment needs, and international politics have subverted the growing support for family planning in developing countries. Without the resources needed to back that commitment, the trend of declining fertility in developing countries may be reversed.

Over the past two decades, about $10 billion has been spent on family planning programs in developing countries, with $4 billion coming from donor countries and the rest from developing countries themselves. The current budget from public and private sources for family planning and population activities in developing countries is about $2.5 billion per year. The Chinese government alone spends about $1 billion, while the Indian government spends roughly $530 million.

The international community, particularly the United States, has traditionally played a significant role in international family planning, giving political as well as financial support to reducing fertility and charting demographic trends. Donor countries have been spending about $500 million per year in this area. Recently, the United States—the largest contributor in terms of absolute dollars—has scaled back its commitment to international population assistance. United States funding fell 20 percent between 1985 and 1987, from $288 million to $230 million. More significantly, the United States no longer contributes to the United Nations Fund for Population Activities (UNFPA) or to the International Planned Parenthood Federation. At the International Conference on Population in Mexico City, the Reagan administration set in motion a policy denying funds to any international organization that alerted women that abortion might be one of their options. The UNFPA funds were withdrawn as a result of United States opposition to grants made to China. More than 340 million couples in sixty-five countries are affected by this short-sighted policy.

Instead of cutting back on international family planning assistance, the United States and other industrial countries need to increase their contributions. Dr. Joseph Speidel of the Population Crisis Committee of Washington, D.C., estimates that in order to achieve population stabilization by the end of the next century, global expenditures must rise to $7 billion annually over the next decade. Industrial countries could contribute at least $2 billion of this total.

An increase in international donor assistance can be used to strengthen family planning in several key areas. First, improving the gathering of statistics and the analytical capabilities of Third World governments is essential to charting and responding to trends more accurately. Second, priority should be given to the poorest, most rapidly growing countries, such as those in sub-Saharan Africa and parts of Asia, where services are scant but sorely needed. Third,

donors can augment funding for programs in countries where current efforts are inadequate. New approaches to family planning and social change in these countries deserve more support. India and Mexico, for example, are both using the popular media to spread information and promote the concept of smaller families.

Developing countries themselves need to make a greater commitment to family planning. At the moment, the Third World spends more than four times as much on weaponry and upkeep of military forces as it does on health care—$150 billion in 1986, compared with $38 billion. Increased government funding of family planning and primary health care programs is essential as part of the effort to speed fertility rate declines. Contraceptive supplies, educational materials, prenatal health care, and information on family health are desperately needed in rural areas throughout the developing world. New approaches to contraceptive marketing and distribution, such as those that rely on local residents and shopkeepers to disseminate information and supplies, are now being tried in a number of countries, and they should be considered in others.

The primary goals of a family planning program are to reduce unmet need for fertility control, to improve maternal and child health through birth spacing, and eliminate the need for illegal abortion. But an integrated development strategy that combines family planning with income generation for women, reforestation efforts, small-scale agricultural projects, and improvements in water supply and sanitation will simultaneously reduce births and improve the quality of life.

Although national leadership is needed, encouraging the development of regional, district, and village programs that are responsive to local needs is essential too. Programs patterned after the Thai loan experiment, relying on village leaders to help develop and introduce new ideas, may be the most successful. The private sector should also be involved. Initiatives in Africa and elsewhere have shown that it is cost-effective for employers to offer primary health care and family planning services, which result in better overall health and higher productivity. In Kenya, a group of fifty companies and plantations is the second largest provider of family planning. Likewise, in Nigeria, Gulf Oil and Lever Brothers Co. are planning to introduce such programs.

Three decades of experience in international family planning hold important lessons for designing effective programs and for creating a social environment receptive to smaller families. Countries such as China, India, Mexico, and Thailand can serve as models for different approaches. Sub-Saharan African countries may find that regionwide cooperation on family planning, in the form of training and outreach programs through perhaps a new consortium on population growth, will strengthen the efforts of individual countries.

Teenage Pregnancy in Developed Countries: Determinants and Policy Implications

ELISE F. JONES

JACQUELINE DARROCH FORREST

NOREEN GOLDMAN

STANLEY K. HENSHAW

RICHARD LINCOLN

JEANNIE I. ROSOFF

CHARLES F. WESTOFF

DEIRDRE WULF

INTRODUCTION

This article summarizes the results of a comparative study of adolescent pregnancy and childbearing in developed countries, undertaken by The Alan Guttmacher Institute (AGI). The study's main purpose was to gain some insight into the determinants of teenage reproductive behavior, especially factors that might be subject to policy changes.

A 1983 article by Charles F. Westoff, Gérard Calot and Andrew D. Foster reported that although adolescent fertility rates have been declining in the United States, as they have in virtually all the countries of Western and northern Europe, teenage fertility is still considerably higher in the United States than in the great majority of other developed countries.[1] There is a large differential within the United States between the rates of white and black teenagers. However, even if only whites are considered, the rates in the United States are still much higher than those in most of the other countries. The gap between the United States and the other countries is greater among younger adolescents (for whom the great majority of births are out of wedlock and, presumably, unintended) than it is among older teenagers. Abortion rates are also higher among U.S. teenagers than among adolescents in the dozen or so countries for which there are data.[2]

Elise F. Jones directed the study upon which this article is based while she was a Senior Research Associate at The Alan Guttmacher Institute (AGI). Jacqueline Darroch Forrest is Research Director, Stanley K. Henshaw is Deputy Research Director, Richard Lincoln is Senior Vice President, Jeannie I. Rosoff is President and Deirdre Wulf is Deputy Director of Publications, of the AGI. Noreen Goldman is Research Demographer and Charles F. Westoff is Director, Office of Population Research, Princeton University. The contributions of Lynne Brenner, Karen Fuller, Ellen E. Kisker and Carolyn Makinson are gratefully acknowledged. The study was supported by the Ford Foundation.

Source: Elise F. Jones et al., "Teenage Pregnancy in Developed Countries: Determinants and Policy Implications," *Family Planning Perspectives*, Vol. 17, No. 2 (March/April 1985): pp. 53–63. © 1983 The Alan Guttmacher Institute.

Two major questions were suggested by these comparisons: Why are teenage fertility and abortion rates so much higher in the United States than in other developed countries? And, since most teenage pregnancies in the United States are unintended,[3] and their consequences often adverse,[4] what can be learned from the experience of countries with lower adolescent pregnancy rates that might be useful for reducing the number of teenage conceptions in the United States? . . .

COUNTRY CASE STUDIES

The five countries selected for the case studies in addition to the United States—

Canada, England and Wales, France, the Netherlands and Sweden—were chosen on the basis of three considerations: Their rates of adolescent pregnancy are considerably lower than that of the United States, and it was believed that sexual activity among young people is not very different; the countries are similar to the United States in general cultural background and stage of economic development. . . .

Figures 1, 2 and 3 present, for the United States and each of the five countries, 1981 birthrates, abortion rates and pregnancy rates by single year of age. The exceptional position of the United States is immediately apparent. The U.S. teenage birthrates, as Figure 1 shows, are much higher than those of each of the five countries at every age, by a considerable margin. The contrast is particularly striking for younger teenagers. In fact, the maximum relative difference in the birthrate between the United States and other countries occurs at ages under 15. With

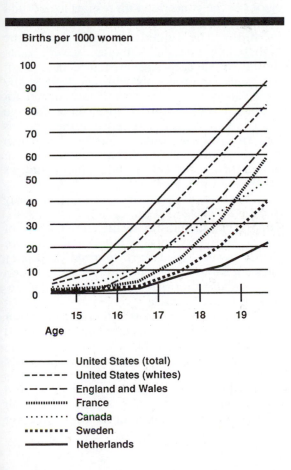

Births per 1000 women

Legend:
—— United States (total)
- - - United States (whites)
- – - England and Wales
········· France
· · · · · Canada
■■■■■ Sweden
—— Netherlands

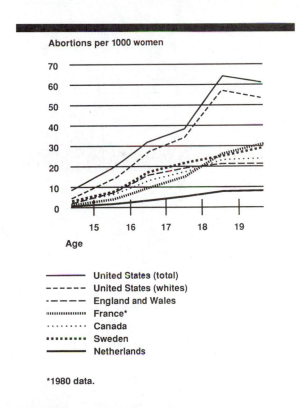

Abortions per 1000 women

Legend:
—— United States (total)
- - - United States (whites)
- – - England and Wales
········· France*
· · · · · Canada
■■■■■ Sweden
—— Netherlands

*1980 data.

FIGURE 1. Births per 1000 women under age 20, by woman's age, case-study countries, 1981.

FIGURE 2. Abortions per 1000 women, by woman's age, 1981.

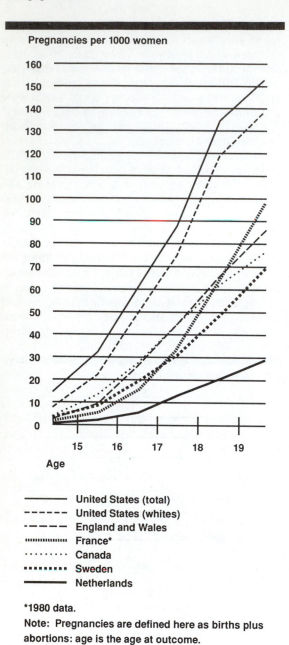

Pregnancies per 1000 women

Legend:
- —————— United States (total)
- – – – – United States (whites)
- – — – — England and Wales
- ⁙⁙⁙⁙⁙⁙ France*
- ·········· Canada
- ▪▪▪▪▪▪▪ Sweden
- —————— Netherlands

*1980 data.

Note: Pregnancies are defined here as births plus abortions: age is the age at outcome.

FIGURE 3. Pregnancy rates per 1000 women by woman's age, 1981.

more than five births per 1000 girls aged 14, the U.S. rate is around four times that of Canada, the only other country with as much as one birth per 1000 girls of comparable age.

Teenagers from the Netherlands clearly have the lowest birthrate at every age. In 1981, Dutch women aged 19 were about as likely to bear a child as were American women aged 15–16. The birthrates are also very low in Sweden, especially among the youngest teenagers. Canada, England and Wales, and France compose an intermediate group. Birthrates are relatively high for Canadian girls aged 14–16, and rise gradually with age. The French rates are low among women up to age 18, but increase very sharply among older teenagers.

In 1981, as Figure 2 shows, the relative positions of the countries with respect to abortion are surprisingly close to the pattern observed for births. The United States has by far the highest rate, and the Netherlands, very much the lowest, at each age. French teenage abortion rates climb steeply with age,* while the Canadian curve is somewhat flatter. The rate for England and Wales rises relatively little after age 17. The chief difference between the patterns for births and abortions involves Sweden, which has age-specific abortion rates as high as, or higher than, those of any of the other countries except the United States.

The teenage pregnancy rates[†] necessarily follow the same pattern, as Figure 3 reveals. The U.S. rates are distinctly higher than those of the other five countries; the Dutch rates are clearly lower. The French teenage pregnancy rates appear to be low among teenagers 16 and younger, and after that age, to be high. The reverse is true of Canada.

Thus, the six countries represent a rather varied experience. At one extreme is the United States, which has the highest rates of teenage birth, abortion and pregnancy. At the other stands the Netherlands, with very low levels on all three measures. Canada, France, and England and Wales are quite similar to one another. Sweden is notable for its low adolescent

---

*The relatively low rates among younger teenagers may be due to underreporting at those ages in France.
[†]Calculated as the sum of births and abortions experienced by women of a given age divided by the midyear estimate of the female population of that age.

birthrates, although its teenage abortion rates are generally higher than those reported for any country except the United States. It is noteworthy that the United States is the only country where the incidence of teenage pregnancy has been increasing in recent years. The increase reflects a rise in the abortion rate that has not been completely offset by a decline in the birthrate. For both younger and older teenagers, the disparity between the U.S. pregnancy rates and those for other countries increased somewhat between 1976 and 1981.

In the United States, the pregnancy rates among black teenagers are sufficiently higher than those among whites to influence the rates for the total adolescent population, even though in 1980, black teenagers represented only 14 percent of all 15–19-year-olds. Restriction of the international comparisons to pregnancy rates among white U.S. teenagers reduces the difference between the United States and other countries by about one-fifth. However, the pregnancy rate for white U.S. adolescents remains much higher than the rates for the teenage populations in the other countries, as shown in the table below. What is more, some of the other countries studied also have minority populations that appear to have higher-than-average teenage reproductive rates (e.g., Caribbean and Asian women in England), so that it would not be appropriate to compare white U.S. rates with rates for the total adolescent population in those countries.

A common approach was established for the study of the six countries selected for close examination. Detailed information on teenage births and abortions was collected, and a systematic effort was made to assemble quantitative data on the proximate determinants of preg-nancy—specifically, the proportion of teenagers cohabiting, rates of sexual activity among those not living together and levels of contraceptive practice. In addition, the investigators sought descriptive material on a number of related topics: policies and practices regarding teenage access to contraceptive and abortion services, the delivery of those services, and the formal and informal provision of sex education. Several aspects of teenage life were explored to try to enhance understanding of certain social and economic considerations that might influence the desire to bear children and contraceptive practice. These include the proportions of young people in school, employment and unemployment patterns, the move away from the family home, and government assistance programs for young people and, particularly, for young unmarried mothers.

Teams of two investigators each visited Canada, England, France, the Netherlands and Sweden for one week and conducted interviews with government officials, statisticians, demographers and other researchers, and family planning, abortion and adolescent health service providers. These interviews provided the opportunity to discuss attitudes and other less tangible factors that might not otherwise have been possible to document, and helped the investigators to identify other sources of data.

The five countries that were visited and the United States have much in common. All are highly developed nations, sharing the benefits and problems of industrialized modern societies. All belong essentially to the cultural tradition of northwestern Europe. All have reached an advanced stage in the process of demographic transition. Life expectancy is over 70 years for men and women of all the countries. Finally, all have fertility levels below that required for replacement. Yet, as Figure 3 demonstrates, teenage pregnancy rates in the six countries are quite diverse. However, the consistency of the six countries' positions in Figures 1 and 2 points to an immediate and important conclusion: The reason that adolescent birthrates are lower in the five other countries than they are in the United States is not more frequent resort to abortion in those countries. Where the birthrate is lower, the abortion rate also tends to be lower. Thus, the

Pregnancy Rate	15–19	15–17	18–19
U.S. total	96	62	144
U.S. white	83	51	129
England & Wales	45	27	75
France	43	19	79
Canada	44	28	68
Sweden	35	20	59
Netherlands	14	7	25

explanation of intercountry differences can focus on the determinants of pregnancy as the antecedent of both births and abortions.

The desire for pregnancy. Are the differences in adolescent birthrates due to the fact that in some countries, higher proportions of young women choose to become pregnant? The number of marital births per 1000 teenagers is higher in the United States than in any other of the countries studied, and the proportion of teenagers who are married is at least twice as high in the United States as in the other countries (not shown). Data on teenagers' pregnancy intentions are available only for the United States. In 1980, 76 percent of marital teenage pregnancies and only nine percent of nonmarital teenage pregnancies were intended. On the assumption that all pregnancies ending in abortions are unintended, and that a large majority of nonmarital births are the result of unintended pregnancies (except in Sweden, where nonmarital childbearing has traditionally been free of social stigma), the distribution of pregnancy outcomes illustrated in Figure 4 sheds some light on the contribution of unintended pregnancy to the differences among the six countries. The combined fraction of all pregnancies accounted for by abortions and nonmarital births is approximately three-quarters in the United States and Canada, close to two-thirds in England and Wales and France, and only about one-half in the Netherlands. Thus, in England and Wales, France and the Netherlands, unintended pregnancy appears to constitute a smaller part of adolescent pregnancy than it does in the United States. Even more striking is the fact that the abortion rate alone in the United States is about as high as, or higher than, the overall teenage pregnancy rate in any of the other countries.

Exposure to the risk of pregnancy. Figure 5 illustrates some recent findings on levels of sexual activity (defined here as the proportion who have ever had intercourse) among teenagers in the six countries. The data should be interpreted cautiously, however, as there are numerous problems of comparability and quality. (Two potentially important aspects of sexual activity among adolescents—the number of sexual partners and frequency of intercourse—could not be examined because data on them

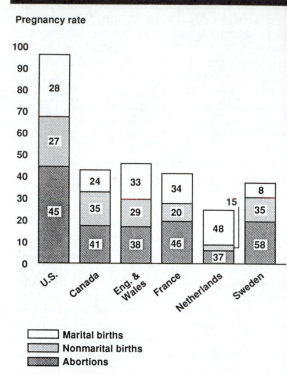

Pregnancy rate

▢ **Marital births**
▨ **Nonmarital births**
▧ **Abortions**

*The rates can be estimated by measuring the height of the bars against the vertical axis. The numbers inside the bars represent the percentage distributions.

FIGURE 4. Percentage distribution of pregnancies, and pregnancy rates, by outcome,* for women aged 15–19, 1980/1981.

were not available for most countries.) The most striking observation from the figure is that the differences in sexual activity among teenagers in the six countries do not appear to be nearly as great as the differences in pregnancy rates. Sexual activity is initiated considerably earlier in Sweden than elsewhere. By age 16, around one-third of all Swedish girls have had intercourse, and by age 18, four-fifths have done so. In Canada, by comparison, women may have had their first sexual experience later than the average for all six countries. At ages 16–17, only one out of five girls are sexually active. Smaller proportions of women are reported as having initiated sexual intercourse

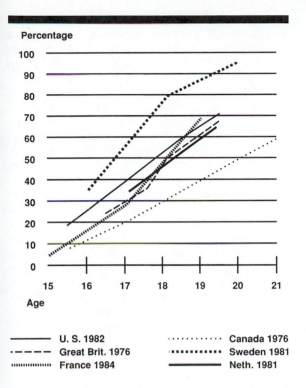

Percentage

Age

— U. S. 1982
– – – Great Brit. 1976
...... France 1984
.... Canada 1976
■■■■■ Sweden 1981
— Neth. 1981

FIGURE 5. Percentage of women ever having had intercourse, by age.

before the age of 18 in both Great Britain (England, Wales and Scotland) and France than in the United States. However, a rapid catch-up seems to take place, and in France the proportion of young women who have had intercourse by the time they are 19 appears to be higher than that found in the United States. The median age at first intercourse is very similar for the United States, France, Great Britain and the Netherlands—something under age 18—and is about a year younger in Sweden, and may be about a year higher in Canada.

These data indicate that the variation in adolescent pregnancy rates shown in Figure 3 cannot, by and large, be explained by differences in levels of sexual experience. The examples of the Netherlands and Sweden make it clear that the postponement of first intercourse is not a prerequisite for the avoidance of early pregnancy. It does seem possible that reduced sexual

exposure among younger Canadian teenagers is partly responsible for keeping their pregnancy rates relatively low. The difference in pregnancy rates between the Netherlands and Sweden may also be partly attributable to the older age at sexual initiation in the Netherlands.

Contraceptive use. The data on contraceptive practice . . . were, likewise, derived from surveys that differed widely in their design and approach to the issue.[5] Nevertheless, it is possible to make some estimates of proportions using any contraceptive method, and proportions using the pill, at various ages. Contraceptive use among French teenagers is probably underestimated because condom use was not included in the published results of the survey. It is likely, therefore, that the United States has the lowest level of contraceptive practice among teenagers of all six countries.

In particular, pill use appears to be less widespread among U.S. teenagers than among those in the other countries. This difference suggests that American adolescents use less effective contraceptives to avoid accidental pregnancy, even if they are using a birth control method.

Access to contraceptive and abortion services. Contraceptive services appear to be most accessible to teenagers in England and Wales, the Netherlands and Sweden. In England and Wales and the Netherlands, those seeking care may choose to go either to a general practitioner (limited to their own family doctor in the Netherlands) or to one of a reasonably dense network of clinics. The Dutch clinic system is less extensive than the British one, but it is directed largely toward meeting the special needs of youth, whereas in England and Wales, there are relatively few clinics specially designed for young people. In Sweden, there are two parallel clinic systems, one consisting of the primary health care centers that serve every community, and the other consisting of a less complete network providing contraceptive care and related services to the school-age population.

Canada, France and the United States also have clinic systems, but these appear to be less accessible than those found in the other countries. (In France, however, the clinic system has expanded considerably since 1981.) The Canadian clinic system is uneven, with fairly complete coverage for adolescents in Ontario and Quebec, and scattered services elsewhere. The U.S. clinic network is reasonably accessible in a strictly geographic sense. Moreover, all family planning clinics receiving federal funds are required to serve adolescents. A basic drawback of the U.S. clinic system, however, is that it was developed as a service for the poor, and is often avoided by teenagers who consider clinics places where only welfare clients go.[6]

Condoms are widely available in England and Wales, the Netherlands and Sweden. They not only are available from family planning clinics and pharmacies, but also are sold in supermarkets and other shops and in vending machines. In France and in many parts of Canada and the United States, condoms are less freely available.

Confidentiality was found to be an important issue in every country. Even where attitudes about sex are very open, as in the Netherlands and Sweden, the research teams were told that young people wish to keep their personal sex lives private. The need for confidential services is probably best met in Sweden, where doctors are specifically forbidden to inform parents about an adolescent's request for contraceptive services. Dutch doctors also are required to keep the visit confidential if the teenager requests it; and the services in Dutch clinics are entirely confidential. French official policy stipulates that clinic services for women under age 18 be absolutely confidential. Although the prescription of contraceptives to girls younger than 16 without a requirement that the parents be informed is now being legally contested in Britain, the practice was followed through the period covered by this study, and the British government is seeking to preserve confidentiality for young teenagers. In Canada and the United States, many individual doctors insist on parental consent before they will provide contraceptives to minors. However, most family planning clinics in Canada and the United States provide services to young women without any such restriction.

Like all medical care, contraceptive services, including supplies, are provided free of charge to young people in England and Wales and Sweden. Free services and supplies are available from clinics to French women under age 18; and for older teenagers, most of these expenses are reimbursable under social security. Contraceptive services provided by Dutch family doctors are covered under the national health insurance scheme, but the clinics charge a small fee. Until very recently, no charge was made to have a prescription filled at a pharmacy. In Canada, doctors' services are likewise covered by national medical insurance, and clinic services are free; but all patients except those on welfare have to pay for supplies obtained from pharmacies. The potential expense of obtaining contraceptive services in the United States varies considerably. Indigent teenagers from eligible families are able to get free care through Medicaid, and others do not have to pay anything because of individual clinic policy; otherwise, clinic fees are likely to be modest. On the other hand, consulting a private doctor usually entails appreciable expense, as does purchase of supplies at pharmacies.

An additional observation concerns the central role of the pill everywhere outside the United States. In each country, the research teams were told that the medical profession accepts the pill as a highly appropriate, usually *the most* appropriate, method for adolescents. Moreover, a pelvic examination is not necessarily required before the pill can be prescribed in some of these countries. The emphasis on pill use emerged more clearly from the interviews than from the incomplete statistics on contraceptive use. . . . By contrast, in the United States, there seems to be a good deal of ambivalence about pill use, both on the part of the medical profession and among potential young users. In the United States, medical protocol requires that a pelvic examination be performed before the pill can be prescribed, a procedure some young people find daunting.[7] Whether justified or not, this requirement undoubtedly influences method selection among young women.

Postcoital contraceptive pills have been available at many family planning clinics in the United Kingdom for a number of years. Postcoital IUD insertion and oral contraceptives are available in the clinics run by both the Dutch and the French family planning associations. However, it is unlikely that these methods are sufficiently widely utilized to influence the birthrate appreciably. In Sweden, the morning-after pill is not yet permitted for general use. The federal Food and Drug Administration has not approved postcoital use of pills in the United States, and no plan exists to market them, but they are available in some college health clinics and rape treatment centers.

Geographically, abortion services are most easily accessible in the Netherlands and Sweden. Although services are theoretically in place throughout England and Wales and France, wide differences in the abortion rates by area are believed to be attributable to variation in the availability of abortion facilities. In all three countries, as in Canada and the United States, services are likely to be found in cities. In Canada, England and Wales, and France, abortions typically involve at least an overnight hospital stay.

In Sweden, there is no charge for abortion; Canadian women usually pay only a small portion of the cost; and abortions obtained under the national health service in Britain are also free. However, because of bureaucratic delays in the national health service, almost half of British women choose to pay for an abortion in the private sector. In the Netherlands, the cost of an abortion is borne by the patient but is not high. The same was true in France up until 1982, when the service became free. Most U.S. women must pay for the abortion procedure themselves. For a second-trimester abortion, in particular, the cost may be substantial.

Sex education. Sweden has the distinction of being the first country in the world to have established an official sex education curriculum in its schools. The curriculum, which is compulsory and extends to all grade levels, gives special attention to contraception and the discussion of human and sexual relationships. Perhaps most important, there is a close, carefully established link in Sweden between the schools and contraceptive clinic services for adolescents. None of the other countries comes close to the Swedish model. Sweden established this link in 1975, following liberalization

of the abortion law, because of concern that liberalized abortion access might otherwise result in a sharp rise in teenage abortion rates. In fact, adolescent abortion rates have declined dramatically since 1975, whereas the rates for adults have not changed much. (In the other countries studied, teenage abortion rates have *not* fallen during this period.) The Swedish authorities credit the combination of sex education with the adolescent clinic program for the decline.

In Canada, England and Wales, and the United States, school sex education is a community option, and it is essentially up to the local authorities, school principals or individual teachers to determine how much is taught and at what age. In England and Wales, however, there is a national policy favoring the inclusion of topics related to sex and family life in the curriculum, whereas there is no such national policy in Canada and the United States. French policy now mandates broad coverage of sexuality for all adolescents, although in practice, interpretation of this provision similarly devolves on local decision-makers.

The Netherlands is a case apart. Coverage of sex in the school curriculum is limited on the whole to the facts of reproduction in natural science classes. The Dutch government, nevertheless, encourages the teaching of contraception indirectly by subsidizing mobile educational teams that operate under the auspices of the private family planning association. At the same time, in recent years there has been an explosion of materials on contraception and other sex-related topics in the media, much of which is of a responsible and informative nature. Youth surveys show that knowledge of how to avoid pregnancy appears to be virtually universal.

In Sweden, sex education is completely accepted by the vast majority of parents, most of whom themselves had sex education while they were in school. Objections are confined to the immigrant community, for some of whom sex education represents a direct challenge to their own traditions. British law requires schools offering sex education to notify the parents. In the United States, many of the school districts that provide sex education give parents the option of excusing their children from such courses.

THE WIDER CONTEXT

Consideration was given to a number of other social, economic and political factors that appear to be related to the phenomenon of adolescent pregnancy. The investigators who visited the four European countries were struck by the fact that in those countries, the government, as the main provider of preventive and basic health services, perceives its responsibility in the area of adolescent pregnancy to be the provision of contraceptive services to sexually active teenagers. This commitment to action and the enunciation of an unambiguous social policy appear to be associated with a positive public climate surrounding the issue. Teenage childbearing is viewed, in general, to be undesirable, and broad agreement exists that teenagers require help in avoiding pregnancies and births.

Another aspect of government involvement in and commitment to contraceptive services for teenagers has to do with the rationale for such programs. In France, the Netherlands and Sweden, the decision to develop such services was strongly linked to the desire to minimize abortions among young people. In France and the Netherlands, for example, conservative medical groups had shown some reluctance to endorse the provision of contraceptives to young, unmarried women. Apparently, the alternative of rising abortion rates among teenagers helped to persuade them that such services were justified. In Sweden, the connection was made explicit by the government, and the 1975 law that liberalized abortion also laid the groundwork for the development of contraceptive services for young people, with the specific understanding that prevention of the need for abortion could best be achieved by putting safe, effective, confidential services within the reach of all teenagers. In the United States, in contrast, some powerful public figures reflect the view that the availability of contraceptive services acts as an incitement to premarital sexual activity and claim, therefore, that such services actually cause an increase in abortions.

The use of contraceptive services is obviously made simpler in the European countries, as in Canada, by the fact that medical services of all kinds are easily accessible through national health programs, and teenagers, in particular, grow up accustomed to using public health facilities or to visiting their local general practitioner as a matter of course. This combination of ease of accessibility and familiarity with the health care system probably serves to remove many of the social, psychological and financial barriers to contraceptive services experienced by young people in the United States.

There seems to be more tolerance of teenage sexual activity in the European countries visited than there is in most of the United States and in parts of Canada. Such acceptance of adolescent sexuality is unremarkable in a country like Sweden, with its long history of support for sexual freedom, and the absence there of taboos against premarital sex. However, such acceptance represents a considerable break with traditional standards in the Netherlands, France and, in Canada, Quebec. One reason for the more successful experience of the European countries may be that public attention was generally not directly focused on the morality of early sexual activity but, rather, was directed at a search for solutions to prevent increased teenage pregnancy and childbearing.

In the United States, sex tends to be treated as a special topic, and there is much ambivalence: Sex is romantic but also sinful and dirty; it is flaunted but also something to be hidden. This is less true in several European countries, where matter-of-fact attitudes seem to be more prevalent. Again, Sweden is the outstanding example, but the contrast with the United States was evident in most of the countries visited. Survey results tend to bear out this impression, although the questions asked are not directly comparable from country to country. For instance, in 1981, 76 percent of Dutch adults agreed with the statement that "sex is natural—even outside marriage," whereas in 1978, only 39 percent of Americans thought premarital sex was "not wrong at all."[8] . . .

While the association between sexual conservatism and religiosity is not automatic, in the case of the United States the relationship appears to be relatively close. The proportion of the population who attend religious services and feel that God is important in their lives is higher in the United States than in the other case-study countries.[9] Although England and Wales and Sweden have an established church, both countries are more secular in outlook than the United States. Moreover, in the Netherlands, France and Quebec Province, increasing secularization is believed to be an important aspect of recent broad social changes. Fundamentalist groups in America are prominent and highly vocal. Such groups often hold extremely conservative views on sexual behavior, of a sort rarely encountered in most of Western Europe. Both the nature and the intensity of religious feeling in the United States serve to inject an emotional quality into public debate dealing with adolescent sexual behavior that seems to be generally lacking in the other countries. . . .

Although all six countries included in the survey are parliamentary democracies, the nature of each country's political institutions differs, and there is considerable variation in the way in which public issues are developed and public policies formulated. The U.S. political system appears to foster divisiveness and confrontation at many levels of society, while these elements seem less salient a part of political life in the other countries. In addition, the United States is distinguished by the widespread use of private funds to mount political campaigns and create myriad pressure groups. While the American confrontational style may have its political uses, it makes the resolution of certain emotionally charged issues hard to achieve. Positions tend to become polarized, and the possibilities for creative compromise are narrowed. The most interesting country to contrast with the United States, in terms of political style, is probably the Netherlands. It has strong and diverse religious and political groups, but a complex range of formal and informal conventions exists to defuse and resolve ideological conflicts before these emerge into the open. As a result, through accommodation and negotiation, the Dutch administrations of all political tendencies have, in the past 15 years or so, been able to make birth control services available to teenagers without exacerbating divisions in the society.

Directly related to this issue is the fact that with the exception of Canada, the United States is a much larger country than any of the others, in terms of both its geographic and its population size. In smaller, more compact countries, where lines of communication are more direct, it is easier than in the United States to engage in a national debate that includes all the appropriate parties to the discussion. For example, in the early 1960s, debate within the Dutch medical community over the advisability of prescribing the pill to teenagers quickly resulted in a broad consensus. A similar process would be much harder to implement in the United States. As a result, informing concerned professionals about the terms of a debate may be as hard as keeping the general population up to date on any issue.

Another closely related facet of national life is the extent to which political and administrative power is concentrated in the national government. France is often cited as the epitome of a centralized state, and even the existence of two "nations" within England and Wales is a simple arrangement compared with the federal systems of Canada and the United States. Both countries have two-tiered government structures, with some powers delegated to the central government and some reserved to the provinces or states. This structure has two main consequences: First, major differences can develop within the country in policy-making. Second, the task of giving shape to social change, in terms of public policies and programs, becomes enormously complicated because of the many bureaucracies that must be dealt with and the sometimes indeterminate boundaries of their separate jurisdictions.

Many observers from different backgrounds have suggested that early teenage childbearing in the United States is a response to social anomie and to a sense of hopelessness about the future on the part of large numbers of young people growing up in poverty. In the course of the country visits, the investigators collected information on teenage education and employment patterns, in order to explore further the possible association between career and life opportunities for young people and their attitudes toward reproductive planning. The finding was that educational opportunities in the United States appear to be as great as, or greater than, those in other countries, except, possibly, Sweden. In Sweden, about 85 percent of young people aged 18–19 are pursuing academic or vocational schooling. In Canada and France, most young people leave school at around 18, as they do in the United States, although a higher proportion of U.S. students go on to college. However, in the Netherlands, only about half of girls are still in school at age 18, while in England and Wales, the majority of young people end their full-time schooling at age 16.

The employment situation is difficult to compare or assess, since definitions of labor-force participation and unemployment differ from country to country. The most that can be concluded is that unemployment among the young is considered a very serious problem everywhere, and young people themselves are universally uneasy on this score. The chances of getting and keeping a satisfying or well-paying job do not appear to be worse in the United States than in other countries. To a greater extent than in the United States, however, all the other countries offer assistance to ease the problem, in the form of youth training, unemployment benefits and other kinds of support.

It is often suggested that in the United States, the availability of public assistance for unmarried mothers creates a financial incentive for poor women, especially the young, to bear children outside of marriage. Yet, all the countries studied provide extensive benefits to poor mothers that usually include medical care, food supplements, housing and family allowances. In most cases, the overall level of support appears to be more generous than that provided under the Aid to Families with Dependent Children program in the United States. Benefits in the other countries tend to be available regardless of women's marital or reproductive status, although in England and Wales and in France, at least, special supplementary benefit programs for poor single mothers also exist. In those countries, however, the existence of considerable financial support for out-of-wedlock childbearing does not appear to stimulate adolescent birthrates or explain the differences between their rates and the U.S. rates.

The final difference between the United States and the other countries that may be relevant to teenage pregnancy concerns the overall extent and nature of poverty. Poverty to the degree that exists in the United States is essentially unknown in Europe. Regardless of which way the political winds are blowing, Western European governments are committed to the philosophy of the welfare state. The Dutch and the Swedes have been especially successful in achieving reasonably egalitarian societies, but even in England and Wales and France, the contrast between those who are better off and those who are less well off is not so great as it is in the United States. In every country, when respondents were pressed to describe the kind of young woman who would be most likely to bear a child, the answer was the same: adolescents who have been deprived, emotionally as well as economically, and who unrealistically seek gratification and fulfillment in a child of their own. Such explanations are also given in the United States, but they tend to apply to a much larger proportion of people growing up in a culture of poverty. No data are available that would have made it possible to examine adolescent pregnancy in terms of teenagers' family income. . . .

POLICY IMPLICATIONS

. . . [T]he individual country studies provide convincing evidence that many widely held beliefs about teenage pregnancy cannot explain the large differences in adolescent pregnancy rates found between the United States and other developed countries: Teenagers in these other countries apparently are *not* too immature to use contraceptives consistently and effectively; the level and availability of welfare services does *not* seem correlated with higher adolescent fertility; teenage pregnancy rates are *lower* in countries where there is *greater* availability of contraceptive services and of sex education; levels of adolescent sexual activity in the United States are not very different from those in countries with much *lower* teenage pregnancy rates; although the teenage pregnancy rate of American blacks is much higher than that of whites, this difference does not explain the gap between the pregnancy rates in the United States and the other countries; teenage unemployment appears to be at least as serious a problem in all the countries studied as it is in the United States; and American teenagers have more, or at least as much, schooling as those in most of the countries studied. The other case-study countries have more extensive public health and welfare benefit systems, and they do not have so extensive and economically deprived an underclass as does the United States.

Clearly, then, it *is* possible to achieve lower teenage pregnancy rates even in the presence of high rates of sexual activity, and a number of countries have done so. Although no single factor has been found to be responsible for the differences in adolescent pregnancy rates between the United States and the other five countries, is there anything to be learned from these countries' experience that can be applied to improve the situation in the United States?

A number of factors that have been discussed here, of course, are not easily transferable, or are not exportable at all, to the United States: Each of the other five case-study countries is considerably smaller, and all but Canada are more compact than the United States—making rapid dissemination of innovations easier; their populations are less heterogeneous ethnically (though not so homogenous as is commonly assumed—most have substantial minority nonwhite populations, usually with higher-than-average fertility); religion, and the influence of conservative religious bodies, is less pervasive in the other countries than it is in the United States; their governments tend to be more centralized; the provision of wideranging social and welfare benefits is firmly established, whether the country is led by parties labeled conservative or liberal; income distribution is less unequal than it is in the United States; and constituencies that oppose contraception, sex education and legal abortion are not so powerful or well funded as they are in the United States.

Some factors associated with low pregnancy rates that *are,* at least theoretically, transferable receive varying levels of emphasis in each country. For example, school sex education appears to be a much more important factor in Sweden than it is in the other countries; a high level of

exposure to contraceptive information and sex-related topics through the media is prominent in the Netherlands; condoms are more widely available in England, the Netherlands and Sweden. Access to the pill by teenagers is probably easiest in the Netherlands.

On the other hand, although initiation of sexual activity may begin slightly earlier in the United States than in the other countries (except for Sweden), none of the others have developed official programs designed to discourage teenagers from having sexual relations—a program intervention that is now advocated and subsidized by the U.S. government. The other countries have tended to leave such matters to parents and churches or to teenagers' informed judgments.

By and large, of all the countries studied, Sweden has been the most active in developing programs and policies to reduce teenage pregnancy. These efforts include universal education in sexuality and contraception; development of special clinics—closely associated with the schools—where young people receive contraceptive services and counseling; free, widely available and confidential contraceptive and abortion services; widespread advertising of contraceptives in all media; frank treatment of sex; and availability of condoms from a variety of sources. It is notable that Sweden has *lower* teenage pregnancy rates than have all of the countries examined, except for the Netherlands, although teenagers begin intercourse at earlier ages in Sweden. It is also noteworthy that Sweden is the only one of the countries observed to have shown a rapid decline in teenage abortion rates in recent years, even after its abortion law was liberalized.

The study findings point to several approaches observed in countries other than Sweden that also might help reduce teenage pregnancy rates in the United States. These include upgrading the family planning clinic system to provide free or low-cost contraceptive services to *all* teenagers who want them, and publicizing the fact that these services are not limited to the poor; establishment of special adolescent clinics, including clinics associated with schools, to provide confidential contraceptive services as part of general health care;

encouraging local school districts to provide comprehensive sex education programs, where possible, closely integrated with family planning clinic services; relaxation of restrictions on distribution and advertising of nonprescription contraceptives, especially the condom; dissemination of more realistic information about the health benefits, as well as the health risks, of the pill; and approval of the use of postcoital methods.

In sum, increasing the legitimacy and availability of contraception and sex education (in its broadest sense) is likely to result in declining teenage pregnancy rates. That has been the experience of many countries of Western Europe, and there is no reason to think that such an approach would not also be successful in the United States.

Admittedly, application of any of the program and policy measures that appear to have been effective in other countries is more difficult in the United States nationally, where government authority is far more diffused. But their application may, in fact, be as easy or easier in some states and communities. Efforts need to be directed not just to the federal executive branch of government, but to Congress, the courts, state legislatures, local authorities and school superintendents and principals—as well as to families and such private-sector and charitable enterprises as insurance companies, broadcast and publishing executives, church groups and youth-serving agencies.

Among the most striking of the observations common to the four European countries included in the six-country study is the degree to which the governments of those countries, whatever their political persuasion, have demonstrated the clear-cut will to reduce levels of teenage pregnancy. Pregnancy, rather than adolescent sexual activity itself, is identified as the major problem. Through a number of routes, with varying emphasis on types of effort, the governments of those countries have made a concerted, public effort to help sexually active young people to avoid unintended pregnancy and childbearing. In the United States, in contrast, there has been no well-defined expression of political will. Political and religious leaders, particularly, appear divided

over what their primary mission should be: the eradication or discouragement of sexual activity among young unmarried people, or the reduction of teenage pregnancy through promotion of contraceptive use.

American teenagers seem to have inherited the worst of all possible worlds regarding their exposure to messages about sex: Movies, music, radio and TV tell them that sex is romantic, exciting, titillating; premarital sex and cohabitation are visible ways of life among the adults they see and hear about; their own parents or their parents' friends are likely to be divorced or separated but involved in sexual relationships. Yet, at the same time, young people get the message good girls should say no. Almost nothing that they see or hear about sex informs them about contraception or the importance of avoiding pregnancy. For example, they are more likely to hear about abortions than about contraception on the daily TV soap opera. Such messages lead to an ambivalence about sex that stifles communication and exposes young people to increased risk of pregnancy, out-of-wedlock births and abortions. . . .

REFERENCES

1. C. F. Westoff, G. Calot and A. D. Foster, "Teenage Fertility in Developed Nations," *Family Planning Perspectives,* 15:105, 1983.
2. C. Tietze, *Induced Abortion: A World Review, 1983,* fifth ed., The Population Council, New York, 1983, Tables 5 and 7.
3. M. Zelnik and J. F. Kantner, "Sexual Activity, Contraceptive Use and Pregnancy Among Metropolitan-Area Teenagers," *Family Planning Perspectives,* 12:230, 1980, Table 6.
4. See, for example: F. F. Furstenberg, Jr., R. Lincoln and J. Menken, eds., *Teenage Sexuality, Pregnancy and Childbearing,* University of Pennsylvania Press, Philadelphia, 1981, pp. 163–300.
5. R. F. Badgley, D. F. Caron and M. G. Powell, *Report of the Committee on the Operation of the Abortion Law,* Minister of Supply and Services, Ottawa, 1977, K. Dunnell, *Family Formation, 1976,* Office of Population Censuses and Surveys, Social Survey Division, Her Majesty's Stationery Office, London, 1979, "Amour: La Première fois. . . ." (Sondage SOFRES), *Le Nouvel Observateur,* Mar. 23–29, 1984, pp. 46–53. *Sex in Nederland,* Het Spectrum, Utrecht/Antwerp, 1983; M. Zelnik and J. F. Kantner, "Sexual and Contraceptive Experience of Young Unmarried Women in the United States, 1976 and 1971," *Family Planning Perspectives,* 9:55, 1977; M. Zelnik and J. F. Kantner, 1980, op. cit. (see reference 3); B. Lewin, "The Adolescent Boy and Girl: First and Other Early Experiences with Intercourse from a Representative Sample of Swedish School Adolescents," *Archives of Sexual Behavior,* Vol. 11. No. 5, 1985; and B. Andersch and I. Milsom, "Contraception and Pregnancy Among Young Women in an Urban Swedish Population," *Contraception,* 26:211, 1982.

6. E. E. Kisker, "Teenagers Talk About Sex, Pregnancy and Contraception," *Family Planning Perspectives,* 17:83, 1985.

7. L. S. Zabin and S. D. Clark, Jr., "Why They Delay: A Study of Teenage Family Planning Clinic Patients," *Family Planning Perspectives,* 13:205, 1981, Table 10.

8. *Sex in Nederland,* 1983, op. cit. (see reference 5), Table 4.8, and B. K. Singh, "Trends in Attitudes Towards Premarital Sexual Relations," *Journal of Marriage and the Family,* 42:2, 1980.

9. Center for Applied Research in the Apostolate, "Value Systems' Study Group of the Americas," Washington, D.C., July 1982, Table 8.

CHAPTER

15

The Ecological Crisis

Still Hungry after All These Years

JOSEPH COLLINS

FRANCES MOORE LAPPÉ

It takes a lot of vegetables to fill a DC-10 jumbo jet. Yet three times a week, from early December until May, a chartered cargo DC-10 takes off from Senegal's dusty Dakar airport loaded with eggplants, green beans, tomatoes, melons and paprika. Its destination? Amsterdam, Paris or Stockholm. These airlifts of food *from* the African Sahel began in 1972, the fourth year of the region's publicized drought. They increased dramatically as famine spread.

In 1971, Fritz Marschall, an executive of the Brussels affiliates of Bud Antle, Inc., visited Senegal. Perhaps you have heard of Bud Antle, the California-based corporation that trades worldwide. The world's largest iceberg lettuce grower, Bud Antle is the company that managed in 1970 to get Cesar Chavez jailed for picketing.

Marschall, formerly a sales manager for Mercedes trucks, was struck by the similarity between Senegal's sun-rich climate and that of southern California. Only two generations ago federally funded irrigation projects and ill-paid Mexican labor had helped make California an agribusiness wonderland. But as farmworkers in California began organizing, Bud Antle, like other companies, began looking for cheaper labor elsewhere. Maybe Senegal could replace California as the company's source of vegetables for the high-priced European winter market.

By 1972, the German-born Marschall—known in European vegetable circles as "the pusher"—had set up Bud Senegal as an affiliate of Bud Antle's Brussels affiliate, the House of Bud. Promoting the entire venture as "development," Marschall got the Senegalese government, the German foreign aid agency and McNamara's World Bank to put up most of the capital. The Senegalese government helpfully supplied police to clear away villagers who had always presumed the land was theirs for growing millet for themselves and the local market. The Peace Corps contributed four volunteers.

Today, more than 60 armed security officers not only guard the fields but each day search the poorly paid fieldhands, mostly women, to be sure they don't sneak vegetables home to their families. When we visited the Bud Senegal fields last winter, the American technical overseer told us that the most embarrassing incident in his life was searching a suspected field worker who was a nursing mother—and getting squirted in the face with her milk. He recently resigned.

TO THE GLOBAL SUPERMARKET

Under the banner of "food interdependence," multinational agribusiness companies like Bud Senegal are now busily creating a Global Farm to supply a Global Supermarket. Big food wholesalers, processors and retail chains have been delighted to find that land and labor costs in the Third World are often as low as 10 per cent of those in the U.S. Countries most Americans think of as agricultural basket cases—because we've seen so many photos of their starving babies—multinational agribusiness sees as potential breadbaskets, future Californias.

With the emergence of one Global Supermarket, the world's hungry are being thrown into ever more direct competition with the well-fed and the overfed. The fact that a food is grown in abundance right where they live, that their own country subsidizes its production,

"Still Hungry after All These Years," by Joseph Collins and Frances Moore Lappé is reprinted from *Mother Jones,* August 1977, pp. 27–33. Copyright 1977, Food First. Reprinted by permission.

and even that they themselves sow and harvest it, means little.

Like the women seasonal laborers on Bud Senegal's vegetable plantations, they may never eat one bit of it. Rather, the food will be destined for some branch of the Global Supermarket where everyone in the world, poor or rich, must reach for it on the same shelf. Every item has a price and, true to the market system, that price is determined by what the Global Supermarket's better-off customers are willing to pay. None without money will be able to move through the checkout line. The sad reality is that even most Fidos and Felixes in a country like the United States can outbid all of the world's hungry.

Del Monte is another example of how agribusiness creates a Global Farm to service a Global Supermarket. Though originally based entirely in the U.S., Del Monte today operates farms, fisheries and processing plants in more than two dozen countries. Board Chairperson Alfred Eames, Jr., wrote glowingly in a recent annual report: "Our business isn't just canning; it's feeding people." But which people? Del Monte has been accused of bullying self-provisioning Filipino farmers off their land to set up plantations to grow bananas for Japan; Del Monte is contracting rich, fertile land in northwestern Mexico that previously had grown a dozen local food crops in order to feed asparagus-cravers in France, Germany, Denmark and Switzerland; and Del Monte has opened a new plantation in Kenya so that no Britisher need go without his or her jet-fresh pineapple. Del Monte finds that a pineapple that would bring only eight cents in the Philippines can bring $1.50 in the Tokyo division of the Global Supermarket.

Seeing all the world as a Global Farm, agribusiness today is building on solid colonial tradition. Since the earliest outside interventions, agriculture in the colonized world has been a mine from which to extract wealth rather than the basis of livelihood and nutrition for the local people. But today, to the traditional "export crops," like coffee, sugar and cocoa, multinational agribusiness is adding items previously grown at home in the U.S. or Europe: vegetables, strawberries, mushrooms, meat and even flowers.

Jet cargo planes and swift refrigerator ships have helped make all this possible. In Africa's Upper Volta, we even saw a blimp floating above the fields, being used by a German firm experimenting with a quicker way to get fresh vegetables to the airport for jet flights to Frankfurt. And so it no longer matters that strawberries are highly perishable or that pineapples are grown more than 10,000 miles away. And while multinational agribusiness claims that the Global Farm brings unprecedented variety, the reality is that the Global Supermarket substitutes the monotony of Everything Always for the experience of the rhythm of eating local, seasonally available foods. Moreover, there is no hiding that the tomato bred for world travel doesn't taste like a tomato.

The Global Farm is spreading fast. Today in Central America and the Caribbean, for example, more than half the agricultural land—its best half—has been put into production for export. This export push goes on despite the fact that up to 70 per cent of the children under five in many of these countries are undernourished. Costa Rica's beef exports to the United States—much of it destined to become Big Macs or Whoppers—have risen to more than 60 million pounds, while Costa Ricans themselves eat much less beef than before. Many eat none at all. (There are always a few shelves for the poor countries, however: a small number of well-off Costa Ricans can afford to eat some Costa Rican beef just like Americans—at one of the three McDonald's in San José, Costa Rica's capital.)

Who helps pay for the transformation of countries like Costa Rica into farms and feedlots for the likes of Del Monte? We do—in the name of "foreign aid." The Latin American Agribusiness Development Corporation, owned by some of the largest agribusiness corporations in America, has in the past four years helped start up more than 60 projects in Central America geared to the U.S. division of the Global Supermarket. LAAD has obtained two-thirds of its capital in loans from American taxpayers, via the Agency for International Development.

During the winter and early spring, well over one-half of many vegetables in your supermarket come from Mexico. They are grown on land that could, and in many areas did, produce beans. With beans displaced and their prices rising in Mexico, many rural people find it hard to secure this basic nutritious staple. Similarly, the Brazilian military government has brought in Cargill and other giant U.S. grain-marketing firms in an all-out drive to boost soybean exports to the Japanese cattlefeed market. This soybean export drive has been at the expense of ordinary Brazilians, some of whom last year rioted, because exported soybeans had crowded out their basic food—black beans. And in Chile the junta vigorously pushes food exports, while it has been estimated by a Canadian economist that 85 per cent of the Chilean people are malnourished.

The Global Farm does more than divert land away from growing the varied, nutritious crops that used to be grown and eaten in the poorer countries. Crops for the Global Supermarket monopolize the funds and services of government agriculture programs and neglect local food crops. Finally, the Global Supermarket is the best incentive yet for the local elite to fight redistribution of agricultural resources. Unwittingly, Global Supermarket consumers in countries like the United States are becoming a suction force, absorbing land and labor that could otherwise be producing food for those who need it most.

THE GREEN REVOLUTION

Ironically, many Americans see agribusiness as the solution to hunger. Having been told that scarcity is the cause of hunger, they inevitably believe that production must be the answer. Only agribusiness, they reason, has the technical and managerial know-how to produce more food.

On the surface, this sounds logical enough. In fact, it's nonsense. Simply increasing production will never solve the problem of hunger. The real questions are *what* is grown and *who* eats it—and the answers to these questions are determined by who controls the food-producing resources. The problem is not technical. It is political.

The diagnosis of scarcity and its prescription of more production have been the central thrust of the "War on Hunger" for at least 30 years. More than enough evidence is now in to know where the philosophy has taken us. As newspaper headlines each month attest, the gap between rich and poor nations is growing, and the so-called Green Revolution is part of the cause.

Presented as an all-out effort to boost food production, governments, international agencies like the U.N., the World Bank and multinational corporations have promoted agricultural "modernization" of all sorts. This means large-scale irrigation, chemical fertilizers, pesticides, tractors and combines and new high-response seeds. The result has been that Third World agriculture, once the basis of livelihood for millions of self-provisioning farmers, has become the latest way for a small elite to get rich. As sheer control over the "right" piece of land begins to virtually ensure financial success, a catastrophic chain of events has been set into motion.

Competition for land by a new class of "farmers"—moneylenders, military officers, bureaucrats, city-based speculators and foreign corporations—has sent land values soaring. Land values have jumped three to five times in the "Green Revolution" areas of India. For people who owned the land they worked, that's fine; but most do not. Higher rents force tenants and sharecroppers into the ranks of the landless, who now make up the majority of the rural population in many countries. With their profits, the powerful new class buys out the small landholders who have gone bankrupt.

Thus, fewer people are gaining control over more land. In Sonora, Mexico, before the "Green Revolution," the average farm size was 400 acres. After 20 years of publicly funded modernization, the average around the "Green Revolution" hub city of Hermosillo has now climbed to 2000 acres. Some holdings run as large as 25,000 acres. In contrast, more than three-quarters of Sonora's rural labor force have no land at all. (A similar process moves ahead right here in the United States. Where government funds have subsidized costly irrigation schemes, the legal holding for one person is

160 acres. Yet today, the average irrigated farm operation in California is 2047 acres.)

Moreover, with vast acreages planted uniformly in the most profitable crop, commercial operators from Brazil to Indonesia mechanize to avoid "labor-management problems." By conservative estimate, two and a half million laborers have already been displaced by tractors and harvesters in Latin America alone. Fewer than a third of these will find other rural jobs. They have no choice but to join the ranks of the urban unemployed. Thus come about the rapidly swelling slums of cities like Calcutta or Mexico City.

We have found this process happening in every country where farmland is allowed to be the source of individual wealth. And *to be cut out of production is to be cut out of consumption.* No one expressed it better than an agricultural laborer in Bihar, India, who earns 36¢ a day: "If you don't own any land, you may never get enough to eat, even if the land is producing well."

Once Green Revolutionist landholders are established, they start growing crops not in the local diet. We found landowners in Mexico's Sinaloa and Sonora provinces switching to grapes for brandy; we found entrepreneurs in Colombia switching from growing wheat to growing carnations. Thus, for laborers forced off the land, the price of the food crops that remain is still higher.

The end result is tragic, ironic and predictable: more food *is* being produced, yet more people are hungry. This point is hardly speculative. International Labor Organization studies document that in the very Asian countries—Pakistan, India, Bangladesh, Sri Lanka, Malaysia, the Philippines and Indonesia— where the Green Revolution has been pushed, and where, indeed, food production per person has risen, the rural poor are worse off than before. The study concludes that "the *increase* in poverty has been associated not with a fall but with a *rise* in cereal production per head, the main component of the diet of the poor" (our emphasis). These seven countries account for well over half of the rural population of the nonsocialist Third World. Other studies by the United Nations Research Institute for Social Development confirm the pattern: in the Third World, on the whole, there is more food and less to eat.

DESTROYING THE LAND

Bud Senegal is using giant Caterpillar earthmovers to uproot scores of centuries-old baobab trees, some as much as 25 feet in diameter. One Senegalese guard proudly informed us that it often takes two "Cats" just to pull over a single tree. The trees, according to the technical overseer, have to go to make way for Bud's tractors. What is being lost here is more than beauty. The baobab's roots are essential to hold the soil in place against strong winds.

In its lust to harvest new riches, agribusiness is treating the soil carelessly all over the world. It can afford to, because profits are high and there is always new land to move on to when the old develops problems. In Mexico's Zamora Valley, the strawberry export industry treats cheaply the land that it has acquired cheaply. Too much irrigation and pesticide spraying result in infested and exhausted soil. But the few strawberry millionaires merely count on taking over new sites where the process can be started all over again. In supplying the Global Supermarket, Mexico's strawberry growers are competing with the greater expertise of U.S. producers. To compete, according to a major study of the Mexican strawberry industry, "they plunder resources to the fullest, i.e., getting the maximum out of them without investing more than strictly necessary. . . ."

In Brazil, one of the last remaining great natural preserves, the Amazon river basin, is rapidly being stripped of its forests. Giant multinational firms like Anderson Clayton, Goodyear, Volkswagen, Nestlé, Liquigas, Borden, Mitsubishi and Universe Tank Ship (owned by multibillionaire D. K. Ludwig) are bulldozing hundreds of millions of acres to raise cattle for export. Liquigas plans call for floating barges of cattle downstream to Belém at the mouth of the Amazon. There, workers will slaughter and cut up the meat; more workers will quickly plastic-wrap it in packages complete with weight and prices in lire. The meat will be flown to Milan for immediate distribution to Italian supermarkets. The company figures it will save on refrigeration, since the meat will be chilled "naturally" at 30,000 feet.

But the environmental consequences of clearing land for cattle are likely to be disastrous. Tampering with a tropical forest, it turns out, is not the same as same as cutting down trees in the temperate zone. Once the multi-canopied vegetation of the forest is stripped away, the torrential tropical rains, which sometimes dump six to eight inches in a single day, wash away unshielded topsoil, and the equatorial sun bakes what remains into a bricklike wasteland. Ecologists warn that by altering the Amazonian forest so vastly, drainage and water evaporation rates might well set off chain reactions that would significantly alter climate throughout the world.

ONE COUNTRY, ONE CROP

Most Americans learned about single-crop agriculture in high school geography classes: everyone can remember the brightly colored maps of the world with a banana superimposed on Ecuador, a coffee tree on Brazil, and so on. Indeed, there seems something so logical about all this, the "natural advantage" idea. Why shouldn't every country grow what it can grow best and then trade for what it can't? Why not grow pineapples in the Philippines or Kenya, get strawberries from Mexico or fly carnations in from Colombia, if these countries can grow them more cheaply?

But our learning now must begin with unlearning: there is nothing "natural" and no "advantage" about just growing luxury agricultural exports. Applied to most underdeveloped countries today, the idea of natural advantage is inherently deceptive. It hides what really happens, namely that those who benefit from the foreign exchange earned by the agricultural exports are not the people whose labor produces the exported crops.

Even when a Third World country uses part of its foreign earnings to import food, the imports generally are not staples but Western-style or semi-luxury food for the better-off, urban classes. In Senegal, peasants are forced by taxation to dedicate their better land to growing peanuts for export to Europe. The government uses a good portion of the foreign exchange this earns to import wheat for foreign-owned mills that turn out flour for French-style white bread for city dwellers. On a recent research trip to Niger, we discovered that foreign exchange even goes to import ice cream straight from a shop on the Champs-Elysées!

The whole process debunks a myth much in the news these days: that higher prices for the Third World's agricultural exports will help the hungry. The very success of export agriculture often pushes the rural population further into poverty. This happens because of the land speculation we talked about earlier: when commodity prices go up, land farmed by tenants and self-provisioning farmers gets taken over by big landholders who can now make a larger profit. In addition, plantation workers' wages can actually decline. For instance, when the world price of sugar more than doubled in 1974, the real wage of a cane cutter in the Dominican Republic actually fell to less than it was ten years earlier. A nominal increase in cane cutters' wages did not compensate for the inflation set off by the sugar boom.

Moreover, governments pushing agricultural exports are governments that relentlessly suppress land reform. Minimum wage laws for farmworkers are killed because they might make the country's exports "uncompetitive." Land growing food for export gets exempted from land reform: and growers shift faster from local foods to export crops to avoid having to sell their land. Thus, in the Philippines in 1974–75, 232,000 more acres were planted in sugar (and therefore exempted from land reform) than just three years earlier.

Finally, large-scale Global Farming demands chemical fertilizers and pesticides, to maximize yields as well as to meet the foreign market's "beauty standard" and processing specifications (the Unbruisable Tomato Syndrome). Basing an agricultural system on imported technologies helps ensure that whatever is produced will be exported to pay the import bill—a vicious circle of dependency.

One fast-expanding crop on the Global

Farm is what the Department of Agriculture calls ornamental crops—cut flowers and foliage. Certain worldwide firms, such as Sears, Green Giant, Ralston Purina ("Green Thumb Division"), Pillsbury and United Brands are getting into this business, along with the big grocery chains. All of them have their eyes on the profits to be made by mass-producing flowers in underdeveloped countries at low costs, then air-freighting them to the Global Supermarket's divisions in North America and Europe (where, on the average, consumers spend 3 per cent of their food budget on fresh flowers).

The agribusiness corporations will thus begin gaining control of the flower business from seed to customer. Historically, the flower business in countries like the United States has consisted of large numbers of independent enterprises: small nurseries, growers, larger grower-shippers and tens of thousands of retail shops. But now a few corporations hope to change all that. They plan to brand-name flowers, as United Brands did with bananas in the 1960s ("Chiquita"), and market them through the supermarket chains and franchised outlets. Flowers from the Global Farm might well mean neighborhood florist shops will go the way of tens of thousands of other mom-and-pop stores—out of business.

BRINGING IT ALL BACK HOME

It's temptingly easy to believe our food problems are different from those of the poor countries—that their problem is scarcity and ours is oversupply. In reality, however, we and the world's hungry face a common threat: the tightening of control over the most basic human need—food—both within our own country and on a global scale. The same increasing concentration of control over land and marketing that directly causes hunger in underdeveloped countries is going on right here at home:

- Only 5.5 per cent of all agricultural corporations in the United States now operate over one-half of all land in farms. The result is landlessness, joblessness and sometimes even hunger in rural America.

- Almost 90 per cent of vegetable production in the United States is controlled, through contracts or directly, by major processing corporations. Many farmers already have no choice but to sign with Del Monte, or whoever, or go out of business.

- Fewer than 0.2 per cent of all U.S. food manufacturers control about 50 per cent of all the industry's assets. The top four firms in any given line control, on average, more than half of the market. In 1972, the Federal Trade Commission staff calculated that such oligopolies in 13 food lines were responsible for $2.1 billion in overcharges. For the one of ten Americans who must spend an average of 69 per cent of all income on food, such inflated prices mean malnutrition.

It is many of these same oligopolistic corporations, helped by governments and international agencies, that are now penetrating the Third World. Farmers, farmworkers, meat packers and cannery workers lose their jobs as agribusiness roams abroad. The United States already is importing roughly $14 billion worth of food annually—more than half of which competes directly with what U.S. farms grow.

The Global Farm and Global Supermarket do *not* bring American consumers cheaper food. Do Ralston Purina's and Green Giant's mushrooms grown in Korea and Taiwan sell to Americans for less than those produced in the United States? Not one cent, according to a U.S. government study. Del Monte's and Dole's Philippine pineapples actually cost American consumers more than those produced by a small company in Hawaii. On top of it all, flying food from Global Farm to Global Supermarket makes little sense in a fuel-scarce world.

Glorifying it as "food interdependence," multinational agribusiness corporations right now are creating a single world agricultural system in which they will control all stages of food production, from the soil in Afghanistan to the grocery shelf in Des Moines. Eventually, they will be able to effectively manipulate supply and prices for the first time on a worldwide basis. The process is well under way; we are already seeing the effects in the rising food prices we face today.

The opposite of such fake interdependence is not isolationism, just as the opposite of the narrow production focus is not stagnation. We have to redefine the world hunger problem as a *social* one, not a technical one. People freed from exploitation by landlords, elitist governments and corporate power—people who know that together they are working for themselves—have shown that not only will they make the land produce, but they can make it ever more productive. After decades of heavy dependence on food imports, Cuba is now producing rice, beef, dairy products and an increasingly wide variety of fruits and vegetables. The Chinese people, through equalizing and localizing control over food-producing resources, have freed themselves from hunger. And, in countries such as Jamaica, where half the protein intake has been coming from foreign sources, even minor moves toward land reform can lead to some diversification and less hunger.

Once people use their own land to feed themselves first, trade can become an organic outgrowth of development—no longer the fragile hinge on which basic survival hangs. No country can hope to "win" in international trade as long as its very survival depends on selling only one or two products every year. A country simply cannot hold out for just prices for its exports if it is desperate for foreign exchange with which to import food. Once the basic needs are met, however, trade can become a healthy extension of *domestic need* rather than being determined strictly by foreign demand. Cuba and China have shown that food trade does not have to be at the cost of a decently fed population.

In contrast, the Global Farm and the Global Supermarket are the type of interdependence no one needs. They are a smokescreen for the usurpation of land and labor by a few for a few.

The Dirty Seas

ANASTASIA TOUFEXIS
Reported by
Andrea Dorfman/New York,
Eugene Linden/Boston and
Edwin M. Reingold/Seattle

The very survival of the human species depends upon the maintenance of an ocean clean and alive, spreading all around the world. The ocean is our planet's life belt. —Marine Explorer Jacques-Yves Cousteau (1980)

After sweltering through a succession of torrid, hazy and humid days, thousands of New Yorkers sought relief early last month by heading for the area's public beaches. What many found, to their horror and dismay, was an assault on the eyes, the nose and the stomach. From northern New Jersey to Long Island, incoming tides washed up a nauseating array of waste, including plastic tampon applicators and balls of sewage 2 in. thick. Even more alarming was the drug paraphernalia and medical debris that began to litter the beaches: crack vials, needles and syringes, prescription bottles, stained bandages and containers of surgical sutures. There were also dozens of vials of blood, three of which tested positive for hepatitis-B virus and at least six positive for antibodies to the AIDS virus.

To bathers driven from the surf by the floating filth, it was as if something precious—*their* beach, *their* ocean—had been wantonly destroyed, like a mindless graffito defacing a Da Vinci painting. Susan Guglielmo, a New York City housewife who had taken her two toddlers to Robert Moses State Park, was practically in shock: "I was in the water when this stuff was floating around. I'm worried for my children. It's really a disgrace." Said Gabriel Liegey, a veteran lifeguard at the park: "It was scary. In the 19 years I've been a lifeguard, I've never seen stuff like this."

Since the crisis began, more than 50 miles of New York City and Long Island beaches have been declared temporarily off limits to the swimming public because of tidal pollution. Some of the beaches were reopened, but had to be closed again as more sickening debris washed in. And the threat is far from over: last week medical waste was washing up on the beaches of Rhode Island and Massachusetts. "The planet is sending us a message," says Dr. Stephen Joseph, New York City's health commissioner. "We cannot continue to pollute the oceans with impunity."

As federal and state officials tried to locate the source of the beach-defiling materials, an even more mysterious—and perhaps more insidious—process was under way miles off the Northeast coast. Since March 1986, about 10 million tons of wet sludge processed by New York and New Jersey municipal sewage-treatment plants has been moved in huge barges out beyond the continental shelf. There, in an area 106 nautical miles from the entrance to New York harbor, the sewage has been released underwater in great, dark clouds.

The dumping, approved by the Environmental Protection Agency, has stirred noisy protests from commercial and sport fishermen from South Carolina to Maine. Dave Krusa, a Montauk, N.Y., fisherman, regularly hauls up hake and tilefish with ugly red lesions on their bellies and fins that are rotting away. Krusa is among those who believe that contaminants from Dump Site 106 may be borne back toward shore by unpredictable ocean currents. "In the past year, we've seen a big increase of fish in this kind of shape," he says. Who will eat them? New Yorkers, says a Montauk dockmaster. "They're

 From *Time*, August 1, 1988, pp. 44–50. Copyright 1988 Time Inc. Reprinted by permission.

going to get their garbage right back in the fish they're eating."

This summer's pollution of Northeastern beaches and coastal waters is only the latest signal that the planet's life belt, as Cousteau calls the ocean, is rapidly unbuckling. True, there are some farsighted projects here and there to repair the damage, and there was ample evidence in Atlanta last week that the Democrats hope to raise the national consciousness about environmental problems. The heightened interest comes not a moment too soon, since marine biologists and environmentalists are convinced that oceanic pollution is reaching epidemic proportions.

The blight is global, from the murky red tides that periodically afflict Japan's Inland Sea to the untreated sewage that befouls the fabled Mediterranean. Pollution threatens the rich, teeming life of the ocean and renders the waters of once famed beaches about as safe to bathe in as an unflushed toilet. By far the greatest, or at least the most visible, damage has been done near land, which means that the savaging of the seas vitally affects human and marine life. Polluted waters and littered beaches can take jobs from fisherfolk as well as food from consumers, recreation from vacationers and business from resorts. In dollars, pollution costs billions; the cost in the quality of life is incalculable.

In broadest terms, the problem for the U.S. stems from rampant development along the Atlantic and Pacific coasts and the Gulf of Mexico. Between 1940 and 1980, the number of Americans who live within 50 miles of a seashore increased from 42 million to 89 million—and the total is still mounting. Coastal waters are getting perilously close to reaching their capacity to absorb civilization's wastes.

Today scientists have begun to shift the focus of research away from localized sources of pollution, like oil spills, which they now believe are manageable, short-term problems. Instead, they are concentrating on the less understood dynamics of chronic land-based pollution: the discharge of sewage and industrial waste and—possibly an even greater menace—the runoff from agricultural and urban areas.

Conveyed to the oceans through rivers, drainage ditches and the water table, such pollutants include fertilizers and herbicides washed from farms and lawns, motor oil from highways and parking lots, animal droppings from city streets and other untreated garbage that backs up in sewer systems and spills into the seas. Says Biologist Albert Manville of Defenders of Wildlife, a Washington-based environmental group: "We're running out of time. We cannot continue to use the oceans as a giant garbage dump."

The oceans are broadcasting an increasingly urgent SOS. Since June 1987 at least 750 dolphins have died mysteriously along the Atlantic Coast. In many that washed ashore, the snouts, flippers and tails were pocked with blisters and craters; in others, huge patches of skin had sloughed off. In the Gulf of Maine, harbor seals currently have the highest pesticide level of any U.S. mammals, on land or in water. From Portland to Morehead City, N.C., fishermen have been hauling up lobsters and crabs with gaping holes in their shells and fish with rotted fins and ulcerous lesions. Last year's oyster haul in Chesapeake Bay was the worst ever; the crop was decimated by dermo, a fungal disease, and the baffling syndrome MSX (multinucleate sphere X).

Suffocating and sometimes poisonous blooms of algae—the so-called red and brown tides—regularly blot the nation's coastal bays and gulfs, leaving behind a trail of dying fish and contaminated mollusks and crustaceans. Patches of water that have been almost totally depleted of oxygen, known as dead zones, are proliferating. As many as 1 million fluke and flounder were killed earlier this summer when they became trapped in anoxic water in New Jersey's Raritan Bay. Another huge dead zone, 300 miles long and ten miles wide, is adrift in the Gulf of Mexico.

Shellfish beds in Texas have been closed eleven times in the past 18 months because of pollution. Crab fisheries in Lavaca Bay, south of Galveston, were forced to shut down when dredging work stirred up mercury that had settled in the sediment. In neighboring Louisiana 35% of the state's oyster beds are closed because of sewage contamination. Says Oliver Houck, a professor of environmental law at Tulane: "These waters are nothing more than cocktails of highly toxic substances."

The Pacific coastal waters are generally cleaner than most, but they also contain pockets of dead—and deadly—water. Seattle's Elliott Bay is contaminated with a mix of copper, lead, arsenic, zinc, cadmium and polychlorinated biphenyls (PCBs), chemicals once widely used by the electrical-equipment industry. "The bottom of this bay is a chart of industrial history," says Thomas Hubbard, a water-quality planner for Seattle. "If you took a core sample, you could date the Depression, World War II. You could see when PCBs were first used and when they were banned and when lead was eliminated from gasoline." Commencement Bay, Tacoma's main harbor, is the nation's largest underwater area designated by the Environmental Protection Agency as a Superfund site, meaning that pollution in the bay is so hazardous that the Federal Government will supervise its cleanup.

Washington State fisheries report finding tumors in the livers of English sole, which dwell on sediment. Posted signs warn, BOTTOMFISH, CRAB AND SHELLFISH MAY BE UNSAFE TO EAT DUE TO POLLUTION. Lest anyone fail to get the message, the caution is printed in seven languages: English, Spanish, Vietnamese, Cambodian, Laotian, Chinese and Korean.

San Francisco Bay is also contaminated with copper, nickel, cadmium, mercury and other heavy metals from industrial discharges. Last year toxic discharges increased 23%. In Los Angeles urban runoff and sewage deposits have had a devastating impact on coastal ecosystems, notably in Santa Monica Bay, which gets occasional floods of partly processed wastes from a nearby sewage-treatment plant during heavy rainstorms. Off San Diego's Point Loma, a popular haunt of skin divers, the waters are so contaminated with sewage that undersea explorers run the risk of bacterial infection.

U.S. shores are also being inundated by waves of plastic debris. On the sands of the Texas Gulf Coast one day last September, volunteers collected 307 tons of litter, two-thirds of which was plastic, including 31,733 bags, 30,295 bottles and 15,631 six-pack yokes. Plastic trash is being found far out to sea. On a four-day trip from Maryland to Florida that ranged 100 miles offshore, John Hardy, an Oregon State University marine biologist, spotted "Styrofoam and other plastic on the surface, most of the whole cruise."

Nonbiodegradable plastic, merely a nuisance to sailors, can kill or maim marine life. As many as 2 million seabirds and 100,000 marine mammals die every year after eating or becoming entangled in the debris. Sea turtles choke on plastic bags they mistake for jellyfish, and sea lions are ensnared when they playfully poke their noses into plastic nets and rings. Unable to open their jaws, some sea lions simply starve to death. Brown pelicans become so enmeshed in fishing line that they can hang themselves. Says Kathy O'Hara of the Center for Environmental Education in Washington: "We have seen them dangling from tree branches in Florida."

Some foreign shores are no better off. Remote beaches on Mexico's Yucatán Peninsula are littered with plastics and tires. Fish and birds are being choked out of Guanabara Bay, the entryway to Rio de Janeiro, by sewage and industrial fallout. Japan's Inland Sea is plagued by 200 red tides annually; one last year killed more than 1 million yellowtail with a potential market value of $15 million. In the North Sea chemical pollutants are believed to have been a factor in the deaths of 1,500 harbor seals this year. Last spring the Scandinavian fish industry was hard hit when millions of salmon and sea trout were suffocated by an algae bloom that clung to their gills and formed a slimy film. Farmers towed their floating fishponds from fjord to fjord in a desperate effort to evade the deadly tide.

For five years, at 200 locations around the U.S., the National Oceanic and Atmospheric Administration has been studying mussels, oysters and bottom-dwelling fish, like flounder, that feed on the pollutant-rich sediment. These creatures, like canaries placed in a coal mine to detect toxic gases, serve as reliable indicators of the presence of some 50 contaminants. The news is not good. Coastal areas with dense populations and a long history of industrial discharge show the highest levels of pollution. Among the worst, according to Charles Ehler of NOAA: Boston Harbor, the Hudson River–Raritan estuary on the New Jersey coast, San Diego harbor and Washington's Puget Sound.

Last week the EPA added six major estuaries to the half a dozen already on the list of ecologically sensitive coastal areas targeted for long-term study. Estuaries, where rivers meet the sea, are the spawning grounds and nurseries for at least two-thirds of the nation's commercial fisheries, as well as what the EPA calls sources of "irreplaceable recreation and aesthetic enjoyment."

Although the poisoning of coastal waters strongly affects vacationers, homeowners and resort operators, its first (and often most vocal) victims are fishermen. Commercial fishing in the U.S. is a $3.1 billion industry, and it is increasingly threatened. Fisherman Richard Hambley of Swansboro, N.C., recalls that only a few years ago, tons of sturgeon and mullet were pulled out of the White Oak River. "Now that is nonexistent," he says. "There are no trout schools anymore. Crabs used to be like fleas. I'm lucky to get a few bushels." Ken Seigler, who works Swansboro's Queens Creek, has seen his income from clams and oysters drop 50% in seven years; this year he was forced to apply for food stamps. New Jersey Fisherman Ed Maliszewski has used his small boat for only two weeks this year. He is trying to bail out, and so are others.

In the diet-and-wellness '80s, fish has been widely touted as a healthful food. Not only do smaller catches mean ever higher prices, but also the incidence of illnesses from eating contaminated fish—including gastroenteritis, hepatitis A and cholera—is rising around the U.S. Pesticide residues and other chemicals so taint New York marine waters that state officials have warned women of childbearing age and children under 15 against consuming more than half a pound of bluefish a week; they should never eat striped bass caught off Long Island. Says Mike Deland, New England regional administrator for the EPA: "Anyone who eats the liver from a lobster taken from an urban area is living dangerously."

Fish and shellfish that have absorbed toxins can indirectly pass contaminants to humans. Birds migrating between Central America and the Arctic Circle, for example, make a stopover in San Francisco's wetlands, where they feast on clams and mussels that contain high concentrations of cadmium, mercury and lead. Says

Biologist Gregory Karras of Citizens for a Better Environment: "The birds become so polluted, there is a risk from eating ducks shot in the South Bay."

Despite the overwhelming evidence of coastal pollution, cleaning up the damage, except in a few scattered communities, has a fairly low political priority. One reason: most people assume that the vast oceans, which cover more than 70% of the world's surface, have an inexhaustible capacity to neutralize contaminants, by either absorbing them or letting them settle harmlessly to the sediment miles below the surface. "People think 'Out of sight, out of mind,'" says Richard Curry, an oceanographer at Florida's Biscayne National Park. The popular assumption that oceans will in effect heal themselves may carry some truth, but scientists warn that this is simply not known. Says Marine Scientist Herbert Windom of Georgia's Skidaway Institute of Oceanography: "We see things that we don't really understand. And we don't really have the ability yet to identify natural and unnatural phenomena." Notes Sharron Stewart of the Texas Environmental Coalition: "We know more about space than the deep ocean."

Marine scientists are only now beginning to understand the process by which coastal waters are affected by pollution. The problem, they say, may begin hundreds of miles from the ocean, where nutrients, such as nitrogen and phosphorus, as well as contaminants, enter rivers from a variety of sources. Eventually, these pollutants find their way into tidal waters. For the oceans, the first critical line of defense is that point in estuaries, wetlands and marshes where freshwater meets salt water. Marine biologists call this the zone of maximum turbidity—literally, where the water becomes cloudy from mixing.

There, nutrients and contaminants that have dissolved in freshwater encounter the ionized salts of seawater. The resulting chemical reactions create particles that incorporate the pollutants, which then settle to the bottom. As natural sinks for contaminants, these turbidity zones protect the heart of the estuary and the ocean waters beyond.

But the fragile estuarine systems can be overtaxed in any number of ways. Dredging can stir up the bottom, throwing pollutants back into circulation. The U.S. Navy plans to build a port in Puget Sound for the aircraft carrier U.S.S. *Nimitz* and twelve other ships; the project will require displacement of more than 1 million cu. yds. of sediment, with unknown ecological consequences. Similarly, natural events such as hurricanes can bestir pollutants from the sediment. The estuarine environment also changes when the balance of freshwater and salt water is disturbed. Upstream dams, for example, diminish the flow of freshwater into estuaries; so do droughts. On the other hand, rainstorms can cause an excess of freshwater runoff from the land.

Whatever the precise cause, trouble begins when the level of pollutants in the water overwhelms the capacity of estuaries to assimilate them. The overtaxed system, unable to absorb any more nutrients or contaminants, simply passes them along toward bays and open coastal areas. "When the system is working," says Maurice Lynch, a biological oceanographer at the Virginia Institute of Marine Science, "it can take a lot of assault. But when it gets out of whack, it declines rapidly."

It is then that the natural growth of sea grass may be ended, as has happened in Chesapeake Bay, or sudden blooms of algae can occur, particularly in stagnant waters. The exact reasons for these spurts of algal growth are unknown. They can be triggered, for example, by extended periods of sunny weather following heavy rains. Scientists believe algal growth is speeded up by the runoff of agricultural fertilizers. The burgeoning algae form a dense layer of vegetation that displaces other plants. As the algae die and decay, they sap enormous amounts of oxygen from the water, asphyxiating fish and other organisms.

Some kinds of algae contain toxic chemicals that are deadly to marine life. When carcasses of more than a dozen whales washed up on Cape Cod last fall, their deaths were attributed to paralytic shellfish poisoning that probably passed up the food chain through tainted mackerel consumed by the whales. Carpets of algae can turn square miles of water red, brown or yellow. Some scientists speculate that the account in Exodus 7:20 of the Nile's indefinitely turning red may refer to a red tide.

When such blights occur in coastal areas, the result can be devastating. Last November a red tide off the coast of the Carolinas killed several thousand mullet and all but wiped out the scallop population. Reason: the responsible species, *Ptychodiscus brevis,* contains a poison that causes fish to bleed to death. Brown tides, unknown to Long Island waters before 1985, have occurred every summer since; they pose a constant threat to valuable shellfish beds.

A study of satellite photographs has led scientists to believe that algae can be conveyed around the world on ocean currents. The Carolinas algae, which had previously been confined to the Gulf of Mexico, apparently drifted to Atlantic shores by way of the Gulf Stream. One species that is native to Southern California is thought to have been carried to Spain in the ballast water of freighters.

The effects of man-made pollution on coastal zones can often be easily seen; far less clear is the ultimate impact on open seas. The ocean has essentially two ways of coping with pollutants: it can dilute them or metabolize them. Pollutants can be dispersed over hundreds of square miles of ocean by tides, currents, wave action, huge underwater columns of swirling water called rings, or deep ocean storms caused by earthquakes and volcanoes.

Buried toxins can also be moved around by shrimp and other creatures that dig into the bottom and spread the substances through digestion and excretion. Though ocean sediment generally accumulates at a rate of about one-half inch per thousand years, Biogeochemist John Farrington of the University of Massachusetts at Boston cites discoveries of plutonium from thermonuclear test blasts in the 1950s and 1960s located 12 in. to 20 in. deep in ocean sediment. Thus contaminants can conceivably lie undisturbed in the oceans indefinitely—or resurface at any time.

There is little question that the oceans have an enormous ability to absorb pollutants and even regenerate once damaged waters. For example, some experts feared that the vast 1979 oil spill in the Gulf of Mexico would wipe out the area's shrimp industry. That disaster did not occur, apparently because the ocean has a greater capacity to break down hydrocarbons than scientists thought. But there may be a limit to how much damage a sector of ocean can take. Under assault by heavy concentrations of sludge, for example, the self-cleaning system can be overwhelmed. Just like decaying algae, decomposing sludge robs the water of oxygen, suffocating many forms of marine life. What effect chronic contamination from sludge and other wastes will have on the oceans' restorative powers is still unknown.

Rebuckling the planet's life belt may prove formidable. The federal Clean Water Act of 1972 overlooked runoff pollution in setting standards for water quality. Meanwhile, the nation's coasts are subject to the jurisdiction of a bewildering (and often conflicting) array of governmental bodies. One prime example of this confusion, reports *Time* Houston Bureau Chief Richard Woodbury, is found in North Carolina's Albemarle-Pamlico region. There both the federal Food and Drug Administration and a state agency regulate the harvesting of shellfish. A third agency, the state's health department, surveys and samples the water and shellfish. And another state body sets the guidelines for opening or closing shellfish beds. Complains Douglas Rader of the Environmental Defense Fund: "The crazy mix of agencies hurts the prospects for good management."

Lax enforcement of existing clean-water policies is another obstacle. According to Clean Ocean Action, a New Jersey–based watchdog group, 90% of the 1,500 pipelines in the state that are allowed to discharge effluent into the sea do so in violation of regulatory codes. Municipalities flout the rules as well. Even if Massachusetts keeps to a very tight schedule on its plans to upgrade sewage treatment, Boston will not be brought into compliance with the Clean Water Act until 1999—22 years after the law's deadline. Meanwhile, the half a billion gallons of sewage that pour into Boston Harbor every day receive treatment that is rudimentary at best.

Some communities are leading the way in trying to preserve their shores and coastal waters. In March the legislature of Suffolk County on Long Island passed a law forbidding retail food establishments to use plastic grocery bags, food containers and wrappers beginning next year. Sixteen states have laws requiring that the plastic yokes used to hold six-packs of soda or beer together be photo- or biodegradable. Last December the U.S. became the 29th nation to ratify an amendment to the Marpol (for marine pollution) treaty, which prohibits ships and boats from disposing of plastics—from fishing nets to garbage bags—anywhere in the oceans. The pact goes into effect at the end of this year.

Compliance will not be easy. Merchant fleets dump at least 450,000 plastic containers overboard every day. The U.S. Navy, which accounts for four tons of plastic daily, has canceled a contract for 11 million plastic shopping bags, and is testing a shipboard trash compactor. It is also developing a waste processor that can melt plastics and turn them into bricks. The Navy's projected cost of meeting the treaty provision: at least $1 million a ship. Supporters of the Marpol treaty readily acknowledge that it will not totally eliminate plastic pollution. "If a guy goes out on deck late at night and throws a bag of trash overboard," says James Coe of NOAA's National Marine Fisheries Service in Seattle, "there's no way that anyone will catch him."

Stiff fines and even prison sentences may get the attention of landbound polluters. Under Administrator Mike Deland, the EPA's New England office has acquired a reputation for tough pursuit of violators. In November 1986 the agency filed criminal charges against a Providence boatbuilder for dumping PCBs into Narragansett Bay. The company was fined $600,000 and its owner $75,000; he was put on probation for five years.

Washington is one of the few states with a comprehensive cleanup program. Three years ago, the Puget Sound water-quality authority developed a master plan for cleaning up the heavily polluted, 3,200-sq.-mi. body of water. The state legislature has levied an 8¢-a-pack surtax on cigarettes to help pay the bill; this year the tax will contribute an estimated $25 million to the cleanup. The Puget Sound authority and other state agencies closely monitor discharge of industrial waste and are working with companies on ways to reduce effluent.

An aggressive effort is being made to limit runoff as well. Two counties have passed ordinances that regulate the clearing of land and the installation and inspection of septic tanks. Farmers are now required to fence cattle away from streams. Zoning has become more stringent for construction in a critical watershed area: a single-family house requires at least two acres of land. The number of livestock and poultry per acre is also controlled.

The Puget Sound group has an educational program that teaches area residents everything from the history of the sound to what not to put down the kitchen sink. Controlling pollution is promoted as everyone's task. High school students take water samples, and island dwellers have been trained in what to do if they spot an oil spill. Says Seattle Water-Quality Planner Hubbard: "Bridgetenders are great at calling in with violations. They are up high, and when they see a black scum or a little slick, they let us know about it."

Officials hope the cleanup program will have the same result as a decade-long effort mounted by the Federal Government and four states in the Delaware River estuary, an area ringed by heavy industry and home to almost 6 million people. The Delaware's pollution problem began in Benjamin Franklin's day. By World War II, the river had become so foul that air-plane pilots could smell it at 5,000 ft. President Franklin Roosevelt even considered it a threat to national security. In 1941 he ordered an investigation to determine whether gases from the water were causing corrosion at a secret radar installation on the estuary.

Although the Delaware will never regain its precolonial purity, the estuary has been vastly improved. Shad, which disappeared 60 years ago, are back, along with 33 other species of fish that had virtually vanished. Estuary Expert Richard Albert calls the Delaware "one of the premier pollution-control success stories in the U.S."

Such triumphs are still rare, and there is all too little in the way of concerted multinational activity to heal the oceans. That means pollution is bound to get worse. Warns Clifton Curtis, president of the Oceanic Society, a Washington-based environmental organization: "We can expect to see an increase in the chronic contamination of coastal waters, an increase in health advisories and an increase in the closing of shellfish beds and fisheries. Those are grim tidings indeed, for both the world's oceans and the people who live by them."

Problems in International Relations

Will the Stealth Bomber Work?

MALCOLM W. BROWNE

Some time around election day this November, America's putative wonder weapon for the 21st century—the Northrop Corporation's B–2 "Stealth bomber"—will lumber into the air for the first time. As the boomerang-shaped machine climbs away from its birthplace at Palmdale, Calif., for a 25-mile flight to Edwards Air Force Base, a cluster of generals, industrial leaders and politicians will be on hand, their fingers tightly crossed.

Will the B–2 perform as advertised? Will it provide the United States with a strategic bomber that is nearly invisible to radar and able to fly undetected into the heart of the Soviet Union after an exchange of nuclear missiles in order to drop its thermonuclear bombs on the remaining Soviet weapons? Or is the Stealth a high-priced boondoggle that is devouring an unconscionably large fraction of America's limited defense budget?

As the time nears for the first completed B–2 to prove its mettle in the air, the sometimes heated debate between supporters and critics of the project has cooled.

"Even some Congressmen who have backed the program to the hilt up to now are leery of being made to look like fools once the plane actually flies," a Congressional aide privately acknowledges. "The secrecy gag imposed on Congressional insiders is actually a very handy thing."

The runways at Edwards are within view of the perimeter fence, and outsiders without security clearances are likely to be watching the B–2's maiden flight: curious passers-by, inquisitive journalists, concerned taxpayers, probably even a few Soviet spies. The Air Force seems content to let them glimpse the super-secret B–2, if only to demonstrate to the world that the plane finally exists in some form more concrete than scale models and rhetoric.

Stung by mounting criticism of the secrecy that has shrouded Stealth technology for the past decade, the Reagan Administration took a dramatic step this April by allowing the Air Force to release the first official picture of the B–2. It was only an artist's rendering and Air Force officials acknowledged that some details had been "masked"; nevertheless, they assured questioners, the overall shape was accurately portrayed.

Defenders of the Stealth program were delighted by the partial relaxation of secrecy. But many aviation experts, including some outspoken supporters of Pentagon programs, were none too satisfied. A pungent editorial in the influential trade magazine *Aviation Week and Space Technology* offered a friendly warning to sponsors of the B–2:

"As Northrop and the Air Force prepare for the B–2's first flight this fall, they should consider the high expectations pervasive on Capitol Hill. Lowering those expectations to a sensible level and sharing data is the smart way to maintain Congressional support, which will take a beating when the B–2's shake-down problems become public—in an austere fiscal climate."

Some Congressional leaders have already expressed doubt as to whether the B–2's virtues will justify its immense cost. The House Armed Services Committee Chairman, Les Aspin, Democrat of Wisconsin, recently asked "How can we know whether or not the B–2 will be cost effective? At this point we don't even know how much it's going to cost."

There is no doubt that the B–2 will be one of the costliest flying machines ever built

Malcolm W. Browne is a science writer for The New York Times.

From *The New York Times Magazine,* July 17, 1988. Copyright © 1988 by The New York Times Company. Reprinted by permission.

Last January, the Air Force broke its long public silence on the cost of the bomber with a cryptic announcement that Northrop had been awarded a $2 billion contract to build the first B–2. Although plans call for construction of 132 of the big airplanes at a total cost of $36.6 billion in 1981 dollars, overruns have already made that estimate obsolete. The latest Air Force guess is that the B–2 fleet will cost more like $59 billion (in 1988 dollars). This would bring the cost for each bomber to almost one-half of a billion dollars, and even that figure could rise significantly before the last bomber is delivered in the late 1990's. Already, the General Accounting Office, the Congressional investigative agency, estimates the program will cost almost $69 billion, or $520 million for each plane.

Indeed, many supporters of the B–2 now acknowledge that the airplane's pre-eminent mission is economic: to compel the Soviet Union to spend an equivalent fortune on countermeasures. Senator Sam Nunn, Democrat of Georgia, the Chairman of the Senate Armed Services Committee, claims that the B–2 "will render obsolete billions of dollars of Soviet investment in their current air defense."

But many American critics would like to see the B–2 scrapped altogether. Since its inception during the Carter Administration, the Air Force's "black" (secret) Advanced Technology Bomber project—as the Stealth is officially called—has been plagued by management problems, cost overruns, technical snags and production delays. If the B–2 finally leaves the ground in November, its maiden flight will be more than one year behind schedule. The Rev. Jesse Jackson is only the most prominent of those who contend that since the Air Force has just taken delivery of a new fleet of 100 Rockwell B–1B strategic bombers (at a cost of $28 billion), the nation could easily get along without another strategic bomber.

Some experts, meanwhile, question the survivability of *any* manned bomber, stealthy or otherwise, during a nuclear war. The editors of Jane's *All the World's Aircraft* pointed out in the 1987–88 edition of their authoritative aviation compendium that since airfields would be prime targets at the outset of a nuclear war, the only airplanes likely to survive the first wave of missiles (aside from those airborne when the missiles hit) would be those that do not use airfields—like the British-designed Harrier fighter, which can take off vertically from any small patch of ground.

This being the case, the Jane's editors wondered whether "America is prepared to pay too high a price for the advantages that can be derived from low observability," and urged the Pentagon to spend its money on vertical-takeoff aircraft rather than Stealth bombers.

But backers of Stealth aircraft have never flagged in their enthusiasm since former Defense Secretary Harold Brown's disclosure of the Stealth program during a press conference in 1980. As recently as last March, Dr. Lawrence W. Woodruff, the Deputy Undersecretary of Defense for Strategic and Theater Nuclear Forces, told Congress that the B–2 is virtually indispensable to national security. Noting that Stealth's major role is to attack Soviet mobile missiles after an initial exchange of nuclear missiles, Dr. Woodruff testified that the B–2 "will be ever more important as the Soviets continue to augment and modernize their air defense capabilities and to deploy more and more of their strategic war-fighting assets in mobile or highly dispersed modes for survivability."

Stealth's job will be to slip through Soviet defenses and destroy important targets that have not been leveled during the initial phase of a nuclear war—a job that may become more important as mobile missiles make up a larger portion of Soviet land-based missiles. By the same token, if mobile missiles are banned—an American proposal currently on the table at Geneva—the Stealth's role, and its importance, becomes even more debatable.

During the early years of the B–2 program, skeptics were deprived of debating points by the extreme secrecy imposed by the Government. But outside experts eventually began drawing on information from unclassified technical journals and other sources about the potential strengths and limits of the B–2.

Moreover, some holes inevitably opened in the veil of official secrecy. At Northrop alone, some 14,000 men and women have worked on or near the Stealth bomber. Large numbers of workers are also involved in production of Lockheed's equally secret Stealth fighter (reportedly designated the F–19). Many scientists and technicians at air bases, military test facilities, subcontracting manufacturers and universities have also played roles in the Stealth program.

The result has been the gradual creation of what experts believe to be a fairly comprehensive portrait of the Stealth bomber.

The B–2 is a "flying wing" with neither a fuselage nor a tail. (The design is a descendent of Northrop's experimental flying-wing bombers of the 1940s, including the YB–49. . . . The wing is about 175 feet across. (By comparison, the wing span of the Boeing 747 jumbo jet is 196 feet, that of the Rockwell B–1B bomber 137 feet.) The B–2 weighs about 180 tons, around the same as the B–1B, but it is believed that it can carry only about 40,000 pounds of bombs, compared with the B–1B's 75,000. Depending on its weapons load, the B–2 reportedly could carry enough fuel to fly 7,500 miles.

Viewed from above, the B–2 as depicted in the Air Force sketch has a peculiar saw-toothed appearance with awkwardly squared wing tips. Aeronautical engineers say the plane must be so unstable in flight that it would be virtually impossible to fly without the continuous control of a so-called "fly-by-wire" system, in which a computer automatically and continuously adjusts flight controls to maintain stability. In this system, the pilot exercises his own control only indirectly, sending his instructions through the computer to the machinery that changes the aircraft's altitude.

The airplane's four jet engines are concealed inside the wing structure; air flows through ducts to them from inlets on top of the wing, and the exhaust is fed through heat-dispersing baffles to the rear. Carbon-fiber, glass-fiber and other composite plastics have replaced radar-reflective metals in some of the bomber's structure. Radar-deflecting shields inside the aircraft are said to prevent incoming radar beams from striking the compressor blades of the jet engines and bouncing back as detectable echoes. A transparent layer of gold that coats the glass cockpit canopy is said to deflect enemy emissions that could create radar echoes from objects in the cockpit.

Although aerospace scientists and engineers with direct knowledge of the B–2 program will not discuss details or speak on the record, in interviews many of them express reservations about the probable performance of the airplane. In all cases, the Pentagon has refused to answer these charges, noting the highly classified nature of the program.

Many aviation and defense specialists argue, for example, that designers of the B–2 have had to make large—some say fatal—sacrifices in order to make it "stealthy." Because its jet engines have been muffled to reduce the heat and noise of their exhausts, for example, the bomber has almost certainly been deprived of afterburners—devices that spray fuel directly into the exhausts of jet engines to give an airplane extra thrust. Since the Korean War, pilots have considered brute engine thrust and afterburners essential to air combat, especially when bursts of speed are needed for escape or pursuit.

These modifications were necessary to make a stealthy aircraft, since all warm objects, including exhaust gases, emit infrared radiation, and enemy night-vision devices and missile homing systems can detect hot spots in the sky as if they were beacons. But the B–2's exhaust cooling system probably makes supersonic speeds unattainable.

"The B–2 crews will fly with all their eggs in the Stealth basket," one engineer says. "Once the bad guys spot them, they won't stand a chance of outrunning the enemy fighters."

Another set of problems imposed by Stealth technology arises from the need to keep the contours of the aircraft absolutely "clean"—free of such radar-reflecting protuberances as antennas, gun muzzles, external bomb and rocket launching pylons, external fuel tanks, even the booms and probes used to fuel warplanes in flight from aerial tankers.

Since it will lack external "drop tanks," the B–2 will have to carry all its fuel in huge internal tanks that can neither be jettisoned in emergencies nor exchanged for larger payloads. And midair refueling in the vicinity of enemy radar is ruled out, since it would immediately reveal the plane's position (unless the Air Force plans to call for the development of Stealth tankers to supply its Stealth fighters and bombers).

The internal weapon bays of the B–2, moreover, are likely to be much less adaptable to specific missions than underwing pylons are. In conventional warplanes, a wide variety of bombs, missiles and guns can be slung from pylons at the discretion of a mission commander, without the need to modify the aircraft. None of this will be possible with the B–2.

Indeed, the B–2's relative slowness (the new B–1, for example, can travel at supersonic speed) and its lack of defensive weapons mean that it will be something of a sitting duck if detected. Some insiders say that in most cases the plane will in fact be performing a "suicide mission," its object to reach the target undetected and drop its bombs, after which it is unlikely to survive— or, if it does, to find a landing field that has not been destroyed by bombs.

But despite the sacrifices in performance that appear to have been made to insure the B–2's stealthiness, major questions remain about just how invisible the bomber will be. The radar visibility of an object, its "Radar Cross Section" (R.C.S.), is measured in terms of the surface area of a reflective sphere that would produce an equivalent radar echo. An eight-engine, Vietnam-era B–52 bomber has a head-on R.C.S. of about 1,100 square feet, a B–1A bomber one of about 100 square feet, and a B–1B, much more stealthy than its predecessor, an R.C.S. of only about 10 feet. The B–2, by comparison, is said to have an R.C.S. of only about one-half of one square foot—making it, according to project supporters, no more detectable than a bird.

An object's size is only one factor in determining the magnitude of its radar echo. For example, the radar cross section of a pickup truck is twice that of a wide-body airliner, even though the truck could fit inside the airplane with lots of room to spare. The reason has to do with the respective shapes of the two vehicles. A radar beam projected at an oncoming truck is almost certain to bounce from one surface to another and back in the direction of the radar beam, producing a strong echo. Radar aimed at the nose of a slim, smoothly contoured airplane, on the other hand, may reflect back only very slightly.

The B–2 has been designed to eliminate all sharp angles likely to reflect a radar signal. Viewed from ahead or from one side, a flying wing presents very few features from which a radar beam can bounce back toward the radar transmitter.

In general, materials that readily conduct electricity—metals in particular—are good radar reflectors, and therefore undesirable in stealthy aircraft. Radar tends to pass right through such nonconductors as glass-fiber-reinforced plastics, and the carbon-fiber composite plastics that make up large portions of many modern aircraft (including the B–2) absorb rather than reflect radar.

But apart from certain problems that composites and plastics present in aircraft— vulnerability to lightning strikes, for example, which can wreck structural members and electronic equipment—they do not offer perfect immunity to radar. Even the high-technology B–2 requires a great deal of metal in its structure, not only in its engines but in its spars and some of its covering as well; and the seams where plastic is joined to metal form discontinuities likely to produce radar reflections. Designers smooth over these blip-producing seams by joining dissimilar materials in a saw-tooth pattern and then coating their surfaces with a special paint, which is intermediate in conductivity between metal and plastic and thus helps blend discontinuities in an airplane's structure.

Assuming that the B–2's shape and materials have reduced its radar cross section to the barest minimum, could an enemy still detect it? The answer appears to be yes, although the bomber would be much harder to identify and track than ordinary aircraft. Sources in the military say that the assessment of Stealth aircraft made in 1980 by Dr. William J. Perry, then the Undersecretary of Defense for Research and Engineering, still stands: "The term 'invisible' is strictly a figure of speech," he said. "It is not an invisible airplane. . . . You can see it. And it is also not invisible to radar. It can be seen by radars if you get the airplane close enough to radars."

One way the Russians might better "see" the B–2 would be to direct radar at it from above or below. Although the B–2's radar cross section is expected to be minuscule, this measures only how the plane will appear to radar hitting it head on—that is, directed at the plane's nose. But radar beamed from above or below the flying wing would impinge on a much larger surface, which would be likely to reflect a much larger echo.

"It's a bit like holding a sheet of paper between yourself and a light," according to Dr. Leon Peters, a radar specialist at Ohio State University. "Viewed edgewise, the paper hardly impedes the light at all. But held perpendicular to your line of vision, the paper blocks the light, scattering it back toward the light source. In many respects, radar behaves the same way as light."

The powerful ground-based radar installations used by the Soviet Union and the United States to detect attacking aircraft look outward, shining their beams at the noses of approaching aircraft. This works to the advantage of aircraft like the B–2. But both nations not only possess aircraft—the Soviet Sukhoi–27 and MIG–29 fighters, for example—with radar that can look downward and track planes beneath them; they are both experimenting with satellite-borne radar systems, which some experts forecast will eventually be capable of detecting and tracking aircraft in flight.

How successful the B–2 may be at evading overhead radar remains an open and troubling question.

"Bistatic" radar—in which the site of the radar receiver is separate from the transmitter site—could also pose problems for the B–2. Such a system, radar experts say, could pick up glancing radar reflections that would otherwise be lost, and thereby detect a Stealth aircraft.

Finally, and paradoxically, the Stealth bomber may be markedly conspicuous to the naked eye. Many late-vintage American attack aircraft, including the F–111 fighter-bomber, rely for surprise upon their ability to fly at high speed only a few feet above the ground in what is called a "nap-of-the-earth profile." The airplane's finely tuned radar altimeters constantly inform an on-board computer of the bomber's exact altitude, and the computer directs the lightning-fast maneuvers needed to leap over or skirt obstacles.

But even the modest emissions of radar altimeters can sometimes be detected by enemy sensors. For this and other reasons, William Gunston, a British aviation analyst, believes the Stealth bomber will fly at moderate rather than ground-hugging altitudes—which means it is likely to be visible from some distance. Thus,

even with its cooled engine exhausts, the B–2 risks streaking the sky with white condensation trails certain to attract the notice of enemy fighters and missile batteries.

A major reason for misgivings about the B–2 is that no one can predict how truly stealthy it will be until it actually flies. Industry officials say a small-scale version of the airplane has been flying for several years, and has provided useful radar data. Designers have also gained experience from the F–19 Stealth fighter, at least two of which seem to have been destroyed in crashes. (But the F–19, with a reported wingspan of only 24 feet 1 1/2 inches, presents a much smaller radar target than the B–2.) Mathematical models and scale models tested in radar-absorbing chambers have also helped engineers make predictions about the B–2's performance.

Yet experts agree that only a rough prediction of the radar response of a full-scale airplane is possible. "You would not want to make big-bucks decisions on the basis either of scale modeling or computer calculations," a radar-testing specialist says. "When you get to making hard decisions, you'd better have some full-scale or very nearly full-scale data."

In the defense budget passed this spring, Congress belatedly approved $25 million for Stealth testing ranges (called Dynamic Coherent Measurement Systems, or Dycoms), probably to be situated in Nevada and other Western states, that will allow Air Force engineers to test the radar characteristics of an aircraft in flight. A real airplane, unlike a model, bends and warps under load, opens and closes doors to dispense weapons or antimissile decoys, moves the control surfaces that maneuver the plane and presents many other potential radar reflectors to an enemy beam. The Dycoms ranges are supposed to provide a realistic evaluation of the effects of all these things on the radar reflectance of the B–2—but it will not be completed until the 1990's.

Meanwhile, the Air Force itself has avoided direct confrontation with experts who doubt the virtues of the B–2. "Look," says a spokesman, "a lot of the technical questions these people are raising are good questions, although we're obviously not going to breach security to respond to them. This much we acknowledge: the B–2 will not be invisible to radar. All we're saying is that the B–2 will be so hard to detect from a distance that the Soviets will not have much warning before it arrives. Sure, they can develop systems to cope with the B–2, but they don't have them now. An airplane like this is going to force them to spend huge amounts of money and resources against a relatively small force—only 100 or so B–2 bombers."

Whether Moscow will respond to the economic challenge remains to be seen. To date, the Russians do not appear to have made changes in their defenses to confront the B–2, nor has the Soviet Air Force demonstrated any particular interest in developing Stealth aircraft of its own. American critics speculate that this is because, quite simply, the Russians don't regard Stealth bombers as sufficiently effective to be worth working on. Of course, there's no way to know for sure.

For some military men, the quest for invisibility has an appeal that seems to transcend mere tactics. The dream of Stealth is at least as old as the Tarnhelm—the magic helmet of Germanic myth that conferred invisibility upon the warrior who wore it. The perfect cloak of invisibility has always eluded military inventors, however, and the B–2 seems unlikely to break the pattern. Nevertheless, some experts say, the B–2 has been a fruitful exercise.

"The work that went into the B–2 will certainly be good experience for designers, who will have to incorporate a certain degree of stealth in all future combat planes," an aerospace engineer says. "It's a natural trend in military aviation, just as it was inevitable that British soldiers should eventually trade their red coats for less conspicuous garb.

"But as for the B–2 itself," he adds, "if it doesn't work out, it won't be the first expensive freak to end up gathering dust in some air museum. It's too bad the failures cost so much, though."

Nuclear War and Climatic Catastrophe: Some Policy Implications

CARL SAGAN

It is not even impossible to imagine that the effects of an atomic war fought with greatly perfected weapons and pushed by the utmost determination will endanger the survival of man. —Edward Teller, *Bulletin of the Atomic Scientists,* February 1947

The extreme danger to mankind inherent in the proposal by [Edward Teller and others to develop thermonuclear weapons] wholly outweighs any military advantage. —J. Robert Oppenheimer, et al., *Report of the General Advisory Committee, AEC,* October 1949

The fact that no limits exist to the destructiveness of this weapon makes its very existence and the knowledge of its construction a danger to humanity. . . . It is . . . an evil thing. —Enrico Fermi and I. I. Rabi, Addendum, *ibid.*

A very large nuclear war would be a calamity of indescribable proportions and absolutely unpredictable consequences, with the uncertainties tending toward the worse. . . . All-out nuclear war would mean the destruction of contemporary civilization, throw man back centuries, cause the deaths of hundreds of millions or billions of people, and, with a certain degree of probability, would cause man to be destroyed as a biological species. . . . —Andrei Sakharov, *Foreign Affairs,* Summer 1983

Apocalyptic predictions require, to be taken seriously, higher standards of evidence than do assertions on other matters where the stakes are not as great. Since the immediate effects of even a single thermonuclear weapon explosion are so devastating, it is natural to assume—even without considering detailed mechanisms—that the more or less simultaneous explosion of ten thousand such weapons all over the Northern Hemisphere might have unpredictable and catastrophic consequences.

And yet, while it is widely accepted that a full nuclear war might mean the end of civilization at least in the Northern Hemisphere, claims that nuclear war might imply a reversion of the human population to prehistoric levels, or even the extinction of the human species, have, among some policymakers at least, been dismissed as alarmist or, worse, irrelevant. Popular works that stress this theme, such as Nevil Shute's *On the Beach,* and Jonathan Schell's *The Fate of the Earth,* have been labeled disreputable. The apocalyptic claims are rejected as unproved and unlikely, and it is judged unwise to frighten the public with doomsday talk when nuclear weapons are needed, we are told, to preserve the peace. But, as the above quotations illustrate, comparably dire warnings have been made by respectable scientists with

Carl Sagan is David Duncan Professor of Astronomy and Space Sciences and Director of the Laboratory for Planetary Studies at Cornell University. He has played a leading role in the Mariner, Viking and Voyager expeditions to the planets, for which he has received the NASA medals for Exceptional Scientific Achievement and (twice) for Distinguished Public Service. Study of the Martian atmosphere led to the research by Dr. Sagan and his colleagues described here. He has served as Chairman of the Division for Planetary Sciences of the American Astronomical Society; as President of the Planetology Section of the American Geophysical Union; and, for 12 years, as Editor of Icarus, *the leading professional journal in planetary science. Dr. Sagan is also a recipient of the Peabody Award and the Pulitzer Prize.*

Copyright © 1983 by Carl Sagan. All rights reserved. First published in *Foreign Affairs*. Reprinted by permission of the author.

diverse political inclinations, including many of the American and Soviet physicists who conceived, devised and constructed the world nuclear arsenals.

Part of the resistance to serious consideration of such apocalyptic pronouncements is their necessarily theoretical basis. Understanding the long-term consequences of nuclear war is not a problem amenable to experimental verification—at least not more than once. Another part of the resistance is psychological. Most people—recognizing nuclear war as a grave and terrifying prospect, and nuclear policy as immersed in technical complexities, official secrecy and bureaucratic inertia—tend to practice what psychiatrists call denial: putting the agonizing problem out of our heads, since there seems nothing we can do about it. Even policymakers must feel this temptation from time to time. But for policymakers there is another concern: if it turns out that nuclear war could end our civilization or our species, such a finding might be considered a retroactive rebuke to those responsible, actively or passively, in the past or in the present, for the global nuclear arms race.

The stakes are too high for us to permit any such factors to influence our assessment of the consequences of nuclear war. If nuclear war now seems significantly more catastrophic than has generally been believed in the military and policy communities, then serious consideration of the resulting implications is urgently called for.

It is in that spirit that this article seeks, first, to present a short summary, in lay terms, of the climatic and biological consequences of nuclear war that emerge from extensive scientific studies conducted over the past two years, the essential conclusions of which have now been endorsed by a large number of scientists. These findings were presented in detail at a special conference in Cambridge, Mass., involving almost 100 scientists on April 22–26, 1983, and were publicly announced at a conference in Washington, D.C., on October 31 and November 1, 1983. They have been reported in summary form in the press, and a detailed statement of the findings and their bases will be published in *Science*.[1] The present summary is designed particularly for the lay reader.

Following this summary, I explore the possible strategic and policy implications of the new findings.[*] They point to one apparently inescapable conclusion: the necessity of moving as rapidly as possible to reduce the global nuclear arsenals below levels that could conceivably cause the kind of climatic catastrophe and cascading biological devastation predicted by the new studies. Such a reduction would have to be to a small percentage of the present global strategic arsenals.

II

The central point of the new findings is that the long-term consequences of a nuclear war could constitute a global climatic catastrophe.

The immediate consequences of a single thermonuclear weapon explosion are well known and well documented—fireball radiation, prompt neutrons and gamma rays, blast,

[1]R. P. Turco, O. B. Toon, T. P. Ackerman, J. B. Pollack and Carl Sagan [TTAPS], "Global Atmospheric Consequences of Nuclear War," *Science,* in press; P. R. Ehrlich, M. A. Harwell, Peter H. Raven, Carl Sagan, G. M. Woodwell, *et al.,* "The Long-Term Biological Consequences of Nuclear War," *Science,* in press.

[*]For stimulating discussions, and/or careful reviews of an earlier version of this article, I am grateful to Hans Bethe, McGeorge Bundy, Joan Chittester, Freeman Dyson, Paul Ehrlich, Alton Frye, Richard Garwin, Noel Gayler, Jerome Grossman, Averell Harriman, Mark Harwell, John P. Holden, Eric Jones, George F. Kennan, Robert S. McNamara, Carson Mark, Philip Morrison, Jay Orear, William Perry, David Pimentel, Theodore Postel, George Rathjens, Joseph Rotblat, Herbert Scoville, Brent Scowcroft, John Steinbruner, Jeremy Stone, Edward Teller, Brian Toon, Richard Turco, Paul Warnke, Victor Weisskopf, Robert R. Wilson, and Albert Wohlstetter. They are however in no way to be held responsible for the opinions stated or the conclusions drawn. I deeply appreciate the encouragement, suggestions and critical assessments provided by Lester Grinspoon, Steven Soter and, especially, Ann Druyan, and the dedicated transcriptions, through many drafts, by Mary Roth.

This article would not have been possible without the high scientific competence and dedication of my co-authors on the TTAPS study, Richard P. Turco, Owen B. Toon, Thomas P. Ackerman, and James B. Pollack, and my 19 coauthors of the accompanying scientific paper on the long-term biological consequences of nuclear war. Finally, I wish to thank my Soviet colleagues, V. V. Alexandrov, E. I. Chazov, G. S. Golitsyn, and E. P. Velikhov among others, for organizing independent confirmations of the probable existence of a post-nuclear-war climatic catastrophe, and for helping to generate a different kind of climate—one of mutual concern and cooperation that is essential if we are to emerge safely from the trap that our two nations have jointly set for ourselves, our civilization, and our species.

and fires.[2] The Hiroshima bomb that killed between 100,000 and 200,000 people was a fission device of about 12 kilotons yield (the explosive equivalent of 12,000 tons of TNT). A modern thermonuclear warhead uses a device something like the Hiroshima bomb as the trigger—the "match" to light the fusion reaction. A typical thermonuclear weapon now has a yield of about 500 kilotons (or 0.5 megatons, a megaton being the explosive equivalent of a million tons of TNT). There are many weapons in the 9 to 20 megaton range in the strategic arsenals of the United States and the Soviet Union today. The highest-yield weapon ever exploded is 58 megatons.

Strategic nuclear weapons are those designed for delivery by ground-based or submarine-launched missiles, or by bombers, to targets in the adversary's homeland. Many weapons with yields roughly equal to that of the Hiroshima bomb are today assigned to "tactical" or "theater" military missions, or are designated "munitions" and relegated to ground-to-air and air-to-air missiles, torpedoes, depth charges and artillery. While strategic weapons often have higher yields than tactical weapons, this is not always the case.[3] Modern tactical or theater missiles (e.g., Pershing II, SS–20) and air support weapons (e.g., those carried by F–15 or MiG–23 aircraft) have sufficient range to make the distinction between "strategic" and "tactical" or "theater" weapons increasingly artificial. Both categories of weapons can be delivered by land-based missiles, sea-based missiles, and aircraft; and by intermediate-range as well as intercontinental delivery systems. Nevertheless, by the usual accounting, there are around 18,000 strategic

thermonuclear weapons (warheads) and the equivalent number of fission triggers in the American and Soviet strategic arsenals, with an aggregate yield of about 10,000 megatons.

The total number of nuclear weapons (strategic plus theater and tactical) in the arsenals of the two nations is close to 50,000, with an aggregate yield near 15,000 megatons. For convenience, we here collapse the distinction between strategic and theater weapons, and adopt, under the rubric "strategic," an aggregate yield of 13,000 megatons. The nuclear weapons of the rest of the world—mainly Britain, France and China—amount to many hundred warheads and a few hundred megatons of additional aggregate yield.

No one knows, of course, how many warheads with what aggregate yield would be detonated in a nuclear war. Because of attacks on strategic aircraft and missiles, and because of technological failures, it is clear that less than the entire world arsenal would be detonated. On the other hand, it is generally accepted, even among most military planners, that a "small" nuclear war would be almost impossible to contain before it escalated to include much of the world arsenals.[4] (Precipitating factors include command and control malfunctions, communications failures, the necessity for instantaneous decisions on the fates of millions, fear, panic and other aspects of real nuclear war fought by real people.) For this reason alone, any serious attempt to examine the possible consequences of nuclear war must place major emphasis on large-scale exchanges in the five-to-seven-thousand-megaton range, and many studies have done so.[5] Many of the effects described below, however, can be triggered by much smaller wars.

---

[2]Samuel Glasstone and Philip J. Dolan, *The Effects of Nuclear War,* 3rd ed., Washington: Department of Defense, 1977.

[3]The "tactical" Pershing I, for example, is listed as carrying warheads with yields as high as 400 kilotons, while the "strategic" Poseidon C–3 is listed with a yield of only 40 kilotons. *World Armaments and Disarmament, SIPRI Yearbook 1982,* Stockholm International Peace Research Institute, London: Taylor and Francis, 1982; J. Record, *U.S. Nuclear Weapons in Europe,* Washington: Brookings Institution, 1974.

[4]See, e.g., D. Ball, Adelphi Paper 169, London: International Institute for Strategic Studies, 1981; P. Bracken and M. Shubik, in *Technology in Society,* Vol. 4, 1982, p. 155.

[5]National Academy of Sciences/National Research Council, *Long-term Worldwide Effects of Multiple Nuclear Weapons Detonations,* Washington: National Academy of Sciences, 1975; Office of Technology Assessment, *The Effects of Nuclear War,* Washington, 1979; J. Peterson (Ed.), *Nuclear War: The Aftermath,* special issue *Ambio,* Vol. 11, Nos. 2–3, Royal Swedish Academy of Sciences, 1982; R. P. Turco, *et al., loc. cit.* footnote 1; S. Bergstrom, *et al., Effects of Nuclear War on Health and Health Services,* Rome: World Health Organization, Publication No. A36.12, 1983; National Academy of Sciences, new 1983 study in press.

The adversary's strategic airfields, missile silos, naval bases, submarines at sea, weapons manufacturing and storage locales, civilian and military command and control centers, attack assessment and early warning facilities, and the like are probable targets ("counterforce attack"). While it is often stated that cities are not targeted "per se," many of the above targets are very near or colocated with cities, especially in Europe. In addition, there is an industrial targeting category ("countervalue attack"). Modern nuclear doctrines require that "war-supporting" facilities be attacked. Many of these facilities are necessarily industrial in nature and engage a work force of considerable size. They are almost always situated near major transportation centers, so that raw materials and finished products can be efficiently transported to other industrial sectors, or to forces in the field. Thus, such facilities are, almost by definition, cities, or near or within cities. Other "war-supporting" targets may include the transportation systems themselves (roads, canals, rivers, railways, civilian airfields, etc.), petroleum refineries, storage sites and pipelines, hydroelectric plants, radio and television transmitters and the like. A major countervalue attack therefore might involve almost all large cities in the United States and the Soviet Union, and possibly most of the large cities in the Northern Hemisphere.[6] There are fewer than 2,500 cities in the world with populations over 100,000 inhabitants, so the devastation of all such cities is well within the means of the world nuclear arsenals.

Recent estimates of the immediate deaths from blast, prompt radiation, and fires in a major exchange in which cities were targeted range from several hundred million to 1.1 billion people—the latter estimate is in a World Health Organization study in which targets were assumed not to be restricted entirely to NATO and Warsaw Pact countries.[7] Serious injuries requiring immediate medical attention (which would be largely unavailable) would be suffered by a comparably large number of people, perhaps an additional 1.1 billion.[8] Thus it is possible that something approaching half the human population on the planet would be killed or seriously injured by the direct effects of the nuclear war. Social disruption; the unavailability of electricity, fuel, transportation, food deliveries, communications and other civil services; the absence of medical care; the decline in sanitation measures; rampant disease and severe psychiatric disorders would doubtless collectively claim a significant number of further victims. But a range of additional effects—some unexpected, some inadequately treated in earlier studies, some uncovered only recently—now make the picture much more somber still.

Because of current limitations on missile accuracy, the destruction of missile silos, command and control facilities, and other hardened sites requires nuclear weapons of fairly high yield exploded as groundbursts or as low airbursts. High-yield groundbursts will vaporize, melt and pulverize the surface at the target area and propel large quantities of condensates and fine dust into the upper troposphere and stratosphere. The particles are chiefly entrained in the rising fireball; some ride up the stem of the mushroom cloud. Most military targets, however, are not very hard. The destruction of cities can be accomplished, as demonstrated at Hiroshima and Nagasaki, by lower-yield explosions less than a kilometer above the surface. Low-yield airbursts over cities or near forests will tend to produce massive fires, some of them over areas of 100,000 square kilometers or more. City fires generate enormous quantities of black oily smoke which rise at least into the upper part of the lower atmosphere, or troposphere. If firestorms occur, the smoke column rises vigorously, like the draft in a fireplace, and may carry some of the soot into the lower part of the upper atmosphere, or stratosphere. The smoke from forest and grassland fires would initially be restricted to the lower troposphere.

The fission of the (generally plutonium) trigger in every thermonuclear weapon and the reactions in the (generally uranium–238) casing added as a fission yield "booster" produce a witch's brew of radioactive products, which are

---

[6]See, e.g., J. Peterson, *op. cit.* footnote 5.

[7]S. Bergstrom, *op. cit.* footnote 5.

[8]*Ibid.*

also entrained in the cloud. Each such product, or radioisotope, has a characteristic "half-life" (defined as the time to decay to half its original level of radioactivity). Most of the radioisotopes have very short half-lives and decay in hours to days. Particles injected into the stratosphere, mainly by high-yield explosions, fall out very slowly—characteristically in about a year, by which time most of the fission products, even when concentrated, will have decayed to much safer levels. Particles injected into the troposphere by low-yield explosions and fires fall out more rapidly—by gravitational settling, rainout, convection, and other processes—before the radioactivity has decayed to moderately safe levels. Thus rapid fallout of tropospheric radioactive debris tends to produce larger doses of ionizing radiation than does the slower fallout of radioactive particles from the stratosphere.

Nuclear explosions of more than one-megaton yield generate a radiant fireball that rises through the troposphere into the stratosphere. The fireballs from weapons with yields between 100 kilotons and one megaton will partially extend into the stratosphere. The high temperatures in the fireball chemically ignite some of the nitrogen in the air, producing oxides of nitrogen, which in turn chemically attack and destroy the gas ozone in the middle stratosphere. But ozone absorbs the biologically dangerous ultraviolet radiation from the Sun. Thus the partial depletion of the stratospheric ozone layer, or "ozonosphere," by high-yield nuclear explosions will increase the flux of solar ultraviolet radiation at the surface of the Earth (after the soot and dust have settled out). After a nuclear war in which thousands of high-yield weapons are detonated, the increase in biologically dangerous ultraviolet light might be several hundred percent. In the more dangerous shorter wavelengths, larger increases would occur. Nucleic acids and proteins, the fundamental molecules for life on Earth, are especially sensitive to ultraviolet radiation. Thus, an increase of the solar ultraviolet flux at the surface of the Earth is potentially dangerous for life.

These four effects—obscuring smoke in the troposphere, obscuring dust in the stratosphere, the fallout of radioactive debris, and the partial destruction of the ozone layer—constitute the four known principal adverse environmental consequences that occur after a nuclear war is "over." There may be others about which we are still ignorant. The dust and, especially, the dark soot absorb ordinary visible light from the Sun, heating the atmosphere and cooling the Earth's surface.

All four of these effects have been treated in our recent scientific investigation.[9] The study, known from the initials of its authors as TTAPS, for the first time demonstrates that severe and prolonged low temperatures would follow a nuclear war. (The study also explains the fact that no such climatic effects were detected after the detonation of hundreds of megatons during the period of U.S.–Soviet atmospheric testing of nuclear weapons, ended by treaty in 1963: the explosions were sequential over many years, not virtually simultaneous; and, occurring over scrub desert, coral atolls, tundra and wasteland, they set no fires.) The new results have been subjected to detailed scrutiny, and half a dozen confirmatory calculations have now been made. A special panel appointed by the National Academy of Sciences to examine this problem has come to similar conclusions.[10]

Unlike many previous studies, the effects do not seem to be restricted to northern mid-latitudes, where the nuclear exchange would mainly take place. There is now substantial evidence that the heating by sunlight of atmospheric dust and soot over northern mid-latitude targets would profoundly change the global circulation. Fine particles would be transported across the equator in weeks, bringing the cold and the dark to the Southern Hemisphere. (In addition, some studies suggest that over 100 megatons would be dedicated to equatorial and Southern Hemisphere targets, thus generating fine particles locally.)[11] While it would be less cold and less dark at the ground in the Southern Hemisphere than in the Northern, massive

---

[9]R. P. Turco, *et al., loc. cit.* footnote 1.

[10]National Academy of Sciences, 1983, *loc. cit.* footnote 5.

[11]J. Peterson, *op. cit.* footnote 6.

climatic and environmental disruptions may be triggered there as well.

In our studies, several dozen different scenarios were chosen, covering a wide range of possible wars, and the range of uncertainty in each key parameter was considered (e.g., to describe how many fine particles are injected into the atmosphere). Five representative cases are shown in Table 1, below, ranging from a small low-yield attack exclusively on cities, utilizing, in yield, only 0.8 percent of the world strategic arsenals, to a massive exchange involving 75 percent of the world arsenals. "Nominal" cases assume the most probable parameter choices; "severe" cases assume more adverse parameter choices, but still in the plausible range.

Predicted continental temperatures in the Northern Hemisphere vary after the nuclear war according to the curves shown in Figure 1 on the following page. The high heat-retention capacity of water guarantees that oceanic temperatures will fall at most by a few degrees. Because temperatures are moderated by the adjacent oceans, temperature effects in coastal regions will be less extreme than in continental interiors. The temperatures shown in Figure 1 are average values for Northern Hemisphere land areas.

Even much smaller temperature declines are known to have serious consequences. The explosion of the Tambora volcano in Indonesia in 1815 led to an average global temperature decline of only 1°C, due to the obscuration of sunlight by the fine dust propelled into the stratosphere; yet the hard freezes the following year were so severe that 1816 has been known in Europe and America as "the year without a summer." A 1°C cooling would nearly eliminate wheat growing in Canada.[12] In the last thousand years, the maximum global or Northern Hemisphere temperature deviations have been around 1°C. In an Ice Age, a typical long-term temperature decline from preexisting conditions is about 10°C. Even the most modest of the cases illustrated in Figure 1 give temporary temperature declines of this order. The Baseline Case is much more adverse. Unlike the situation in an Ice Age, however, the global temperatures after nuclear war plunge rapidly and take only months to a few years to recover, rather than thousands of years. No new Ice Age is likely to be induced by a Nuclear Winter.

Because of the obscuration of the Sun, the daytime light levels can fall to a twilit gloom or worse. For more than a week in the northern mid-latitude target zone, it might be much too dark to see, even at midday. In Cases 1 and 14 (Table 1), hemispherically averaged light levels

TABLE 1

Nuclear Exchange Scenarios

Case	Total Yield (MT)	% Yield Surface Bursts	% Yield Urban or Industrial Targets	Warhead Yield Range (MT)	Total Number of Explosions
1. Baseline Case, countervalue and counterforce[a]	5,000	57	20	0.1–10	10,400
11. 3,000 MT nominal, counterforce only[b]	3,000	50	0	1 –10	2,250
14. 100 MT nominal, countervalue only[c]	100	0	100	0.1	1,000
16. 5,000 MT "severe," counterforce only [b, d]	5,000	100	0	5 –10	700
17. 10,000 MT "severe," countervalue and counterforce[c, d]	10,000	63	15	0.1–10	16,160

[a]In the Baseline Case, 12,000 square kilometers of inner cities are burned; on every square centimeter an average of 10 grams of combustibles are burned, and 1.1% of the burned material rises as smoke. Also, 230,000 square kilometers of suburban areas burn, with 1.5 grams consumed at each square centimeter and 3.6% rising as smoke.
[b]In this highly conservative case, it is assumed that no smoke emission occurs, that not a blade of grass is burned. Only 25,000 tons of the fine dust is raised into the upper atmosphere for every megaton exploded.
[c]In contrast to the Baseline Case, only inner cities burn, but with 10 grams per square centimeter consumed and 3.3% rising as smoke into the high atmosphere.
[d]Here, the fine (submicron) dust raised into the upper atmosphere is 150,000 tons per megaton exploded.

[12]National Academy of Sciences, 1975, *op. cit.* footnote 5.

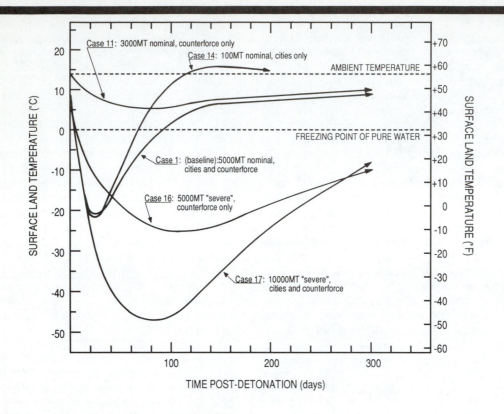

FIGURE 1. Temperature effects of nuclear war cases.

NOTE: In this Figure, the average temperature of Northern Hemisphere land areas (away from coastlines) is shown varying with time after the five Cases of nuclear war defined in Table 1. The "ambient" temperature is the average in the Northern Hemisphere over all latitudes and seasons: thus, normal winter temperatures at north temperate latitudes are lower than is shown, and normal tropical temperatures are higher than shown. Cases described as "nominal" assume the most likely values of parameters (such as dust particle size or the frequency of firestorms) that are imperfectly known. Cases marked "severe" represent adverse but not implausible values of these parameters. In Case 14 the curve ends when the temperatures come within a degree of the ambient values. For the four other Cases the curves are shown ending after 300 days, but this is simply because the calculations were not extended further. In these four Cases the curves will continue to the directions they are headed.

fall to a few percent of normal values, comparable to those at the bottom of a dense overcast. At this illumination, many plants are close to what is called the compensation point, the light level at which photosynthesis can barely keep pace with plant metabolism. In Case 17, illumination, averaged over the entire Northern Hemisphere, falls in daytime to about 0.1 percent of normal, a light level at which plants will not photosynthesize at all. For Cases 1 and especially 17, full recovery to ordinary daylight takes a year or more (Figure 1).

As the fine particles fall out of the atmosphere, carrying radioactivity to the ground, the light levels increase and the surface warms. The depleted ozone layer now permits ultraviolet light to reach the Earth's surface in increased proportions. The relative timing of the multitude of adverse consequences of a nuclear war is shown in Table 2, on the following page.

Perhaps the most striking and unexpected consequence of our study is that even a comparatively small nuclear war can have devastating climatic consequences, provided cities are

TABLE 2

Effects of the Baseline Nuclear War

Effect	Time After Nuclear War										U.S./S.U. Population at risk	N.H. Population at risk	S.H. Population at risk	Casualty rate for those at risk	Potential global deaths
	1 hr	1 day	1 wk	1 mo	3 mo	6 mo	1 yr	2 yr	5 yr	10 yr					
Blast											H	M	L	H	M-H
Thermal Radiation											H	M	L	M	M-H
Prompt Ionizing Radiation											L	L	L	H	L-M
Fires											M	M	L	M	M
Toxic Gases											M	M	L	L	L
Dark											H	H	M	L	L
Cold											H	H	H	H	M-H
Frozen Water Supplies											H	H	M	M	M
Fallout Ionizing Radiation											H	H	L-M	M	M-H
Food Shortages											H	H	H	H	H
Medical System Collapse											H	H	M	M	M
Contagious Diseases											M	M	L	H	M
Epidemics and Pandemics											H	H	M	M	M
Psychiatric Disorders											H	H	L	L	L-M
Increased Surface Ultraviolet Light											H	H	M	L	L
Synergisms						?					?	?	?	?	?

NOTE: This is a schematic representation of the time scale for the effects, which are most severe when the thickness of the horizontal bar is greatest. The columns at the right indicate the degree of risk of the populations of the United States and the Soviet Union, the Northern Hemisphere, and the Southern Hemisphere—with H, M, and L standing for High, Medium, and Low respectively.

targeted (see Case 14 in Figure 1; here, the centers of 100 major NATO and Warsaw Pact cities are burning). There is an indication of a very rough threshold at which severe climatic consequences are triggered—around a few hundred nuclear explosions over cities, for smoke generation, or around 2,000 to 3,000 high-yield surface bursts at, e.g., missile silos, for dust generation and ancillary fires. Fine particles can be injected into the atmosphere at increasing rates with only minor effects until these thresholds are crossed. Thereafter, the effects rapidly increase in severity.[13]

As in all calculations of this complexity, there are uncertainties. Some factors tend to work towards more severe or more prolonged effects; others tend to ameliorate the effects.[14] The detailed TTAPS calculations described here are one-dimensional; that is, they assume the fine particles to move vertically by all the appropriate laws of physics, but neglect the spreading in latitude and longitude. When soot or dust is moved away from the reference locale, things get better there and worse elsewhere. In addition, fine particles can be transported by weather systems to other locales, where they are carried more rapidly down to the surface. That would ameliorate obscuration not just locally but globally. It is just this transport away from the northern mid-latitudes that involves the equatorial zone and the Southern Hemisphere in the effects of the nuclear war. It would be helpful to perform an accurate three-dimensional calculation on the general atmospheric circulation following a nuclear war. Preliminary estimates suggest that circulation might moderate the low temperatures in the Northern Hemisphere predicted in our calculations by some 30 percent, lessening somewhat the severity of the effects, but still leaving them at catastrophic levels (e.g., a 30°C rather than a 40°C temperature drop). To provide a small margin of safety, we neglect this correction in our subsequent discussion.

There are also effects that tend to make the results much worse: for example, in our calculations we assumed that rainout of fine particles occurred through the entire troposphere. But under realistic circumstances, at least the upper troposphere may be very dry, and any dust or soot carried there initially may take much longer to fall out. There is also a very significant effect deriving from the drastically altered structure of the atmosphere, brought about by the heating of the clouds and the cooling of the surface. This produces a region in which the temperature is approximately constant with altitude in the lower atmosphere and topped by a massive temperature inversion. Particles throughout the atmosphere would then be transported vertically very slowly—as in the present stratosphere. This is a second reason why the lifetime of the clouds of soot and dust may be much longer than we have calculated. If so, the worst of the cold and the dark might be prolonged for considerable periods of time, conceivably for more than a year. We also neglect this effect in subsequent discussion.

Nuclear war scenarios are possible that are much worse than the ones we have presented. For example, if command and control capabilities are lost early in the war—by, say, "decapitation" (an early surprise attack on civilian and military headquarters and communications facilities)—then the war conceivably could be extended for weeks as local commanders make separate and uncoordinated decisions. At least some of the delayed missile launches could be retaliatory strikes against any remaining adversary cities. Generation of an additional smoke pall over a period of weeks or longer following the initiation of the war would extend the magnitude, but especially the duration of the climatic consequences. Or it is possible that more cities and forests would be ignited than we have assumed, or that smoke emissions would be larger, or that a greater fraction of the world arsenals would be committed. Less severe cases are of course possible as well.

These calculations therefore are not, and cannot be, assured prognostications of the full consequences of a nuclear war. Many refinements in them are possible and are being pursued. But there is general agreement on the overall conclusions: in the wake of a nuclear war there is likely to be a period, lasting at least for months, of extreme cold in a radioactive gloom, followed—after the soot and dust fall out—by an extended period of increased ultraviolet light reaching the surface.[15]

---

[13]The climatic threshold for smoke in the troposphere is about 100 million metric tons, injected essentially all at once; for sub-micron fine dust in the stratosphere, about the same.

[14]The slow warming of the Earth due to a CO_2 greenhouse effect attendant to the burning of fossil fuels should not be thought of as tempering the nuclear winter: the greenhouse temperature increments are too small and too slow.

[15]These results are dependent on important work by a large number of scientists who have previously examined aspects of this subject; many of these workers are acknowledged in the articles cited in footnote 1.

We now explore the biological impact of such an assault on the global environment.

III

The immediate human consequences of nuclear explosions range from vaporization of populations near the hypocenter, to blast-generated trauma (from flying glass, falling beams, collapsing skyscrapers and the like), to burns, radiation sickness, shock and severe psychiatric disorders. But our concern here is with longer-term effects.

It is now a commonplace that in the burning of modern tall buildings, more people succumb to toxic gases than to fire. Ignition of many varieties of building materials, insulation and fabrics generates large amounts of such pyrotoxins, including carbon monoxide, cyanides, vinyl chlorides, oxides of nitrogen, ozone, dioxins, and furans. Because of differing practices in the use of such synthetics, the burning of cities in North America and Western Europe will probably generate more pyrotoxins than cities in the Soviet Union, and cities with substantial recent construction more than older, unreconstructed cities. In nuclear war scenarios in which a great many cities are burning, a significant pyrotoxin smog might persist for months. The magnitude of this danger is unknown.

The pyrotoxins, low light levels, radioactive fallout, subsequent ultraviolet light, and especially the cold are together likely to destroy almost all of Northern Hemisphere agriculture, even for the more modest Cases 11 and 14. A 12° to 15°C temperature reduction by itself would eliminate wheat and corn production in the United States, even if all civil systems and agricultural technology were intact.[16] With unavoidable societal disruption, and with the other environmental stresses just mentioned, even a 3,000-megaton "pure" counterforce attack (Case 11) might suffice. Realistically, many fires would be set even in such an attack (see below), and a 3,000-megaton war is likely to wipe out U.S. grain production. This would represent by itself an unprecedented global catastrophe: North American grain is the principal reliable source of export food on the planet, as well as an essential component of U.S. prosperity. Wars just before harvesting of grain and other staples would be incrementally worse than wars after harvesting. For many scenarios, the effects will extend . . . into two or more growing seasons. Widespread fires and subsequent runoff of topsoil are among the many additional deleterious consequences extending for years after the war.

Something like three-quarters of the U.S. population lives in or near cities. In the cities themselves there is, on average, only about one week's supply of food. After a nuclear war it is conceivable that enough of present grain storage might survive to maintain, on some level, the present population for more than a year. But with the breakdown of civil order and transportation systems in the cold, the dark and the fallout, these stores would become largely inaccessible. Vast numbers of survivors would soon starve to death.

In addition, the sub-freezing temperatures imply, in many cases, the unavailability of fresh water. The ground will tend to be frozen to a depth of about a meter—incidentally making it unlikely that the hundreds of millions of dead bodies would be buried, even if the civil organization to do so existed. Fuel stores to melt snow and ice would be in short supply, and ice surfaces and freshly fallen snow would tend to be contaminated by radioactivity and pyrotoxins.

In the presence of excellent medical care, the average value of the acute lethal dose of ionizing radiation for healthy adults is about 450 rads. (As with many other effects, children, the infirm and the elderly tend to be more vulnerable.) Combined with the other assaults on survivors in the postwar environment, and in the probable absence of any significant medical care, the mean lethal acute dose is likely to decline to 350 rads or even lower. For many outdoor scenarios, doses within the fallout plumes that drift hundreds of kilometers downwind of targets are greater than the mean lethal dose. (For a 10,000-megaton war, this is true for more than 30 percent of northern mid-latitude land areas.) Far from targets, intermediate-timescale chronic doses from delayed radioactive fallout

[16]David Pimentel and Mark Sorrells, private communication, 1983.

Problems in International Relations

may be in excess of 100 rads for the baseline case. These calculations assume no detonations on nuclear reactors or fuel-reprocessing plants, which would increase the dose.

Thus, the combination of acute doses from prompt radioactive fallout, chronic doses from the delayed intermediate-timescale fallout, and internal doses from food and drink are together likely to kill many more by radiation sickness. Because of acute damage to bone marrow, survivors would have significantly increased vulnerability to infectious diseases. Most infants exposed to 100 rads as fetuses in the first two trimesters of pregnancy would suffer mental retardation and/or other serious birth defects. Radiation and some pyrotoxins would later produce neoplastic diseases and genetic damage. Livestock and domesticated animals, with fewer resources, vanishing food supplies and in many cases with greater sensitivity to the stresses of nuclear war than human beings, would also perish in large numbers.

These devastating consequences for humans and for agriculture would not be restricted to the locales in which the war would principally be "fought," but would extend throughout northern mid-latitudes and, with reduced but still significant severity, probably to the tropics and the Southern Hemisphere. The bulk of the world's grain exports originate in northern mid-latitudes. Many nations in the developing as well as the developed world depend on the import of food. Japan, for example, imports 75 percent of its food (and 99 percent of its fuel). Thus, even if there were no climatic and radiation stresses on tropical and Southern Hemisphere societies—many of them already at subsistence levels of nutrition—large numbers of people there would die of starvation.

As agriculture breaks down worldwide (possible initial exceptions might include Argentina, Australia and South Africa if the climatic impact on the Southern Hemisphere proved to be minimal), there will be increasing reliance on natural ecosystems—fruits, tubers, roots, nuts, etc. But wild foodstuffs will also have suffered from the effects of the war. At just the moment that surviving humans turn to the natural environment for the basis of life,

that environment would be experiencing a devastation unprecedented in recent geological history.

Two-thirds of all species of plants, animals, and microorganisms on the Earth live within 25° of the equator. Because temperatures tend to vary with the seasons only minimally at tropical latitudes, species there are especially vulnerable to rapid temperature declines. In past major extinction events in the paleontological record, there has been a marked tendency for tropical organisms to show greater vulnerability than organisms living at more temperate latitudes.

The darkness alone may cause a collapse in the aquatic food chain in which sunlight is harvested by phytoplankton, phytoplankton by zooplankton, zooplankton by small fish, small fish by large fish, and, occasionally, large fish by humans. In many nuclear war scenarios, this food chain is likely to collapse at its base for at least a year and is significantly more imperiled in tropical waters. The increase in ultraviolet light available at the surface of the earth approximately a year after the war provides an additional major environmental stress that by itself has been described as having "profound consequences" for aquatic, terrestrial and other ecosystems.[17]

The global ecosystem can be considered an intricately woven fabric composed of threads contributed by the millions of separate species that inhabit the planet and interact with the air, the water and the soil. The system has developed considerable resiliency, so that pulling a single thread is unlikely to unravel the entire fabric. Thus, most ordinary assaults on the biosphere are unlikely to have catastrophic consequences. For example, because of natural small changes in stratospheric ozone abundance, organisms have probably experienced, in the fairly recent geologic past, ten percent fluctuations in the solar near-ultraviolet flux (but not fluctuations by factors of two or more). Similarly, major continental temperature changes of the magnitude and extent addressed here may not have been experienced for tens of thousands and possibly not for millions of years. We have no experimental information, even for aquaria or terraria, on the simultaneous effects of cold,

[17]C. H. Kruger, R. B. Setlow, *et al., Causes and Effects of Stratospheric Ozone Reduction: An Update,* Wash.: Nat. Acad. of Sciences, 1982.

dark, pyrotoxins, ionizing radiation, and ultraviolet light as predicted in the TTAPS study.

Each of these factors, taken separately, may carry serious consequences for the global ecosystem: their interactions may be much more dire still. Extremely worrisome is the possibility of poorly understood or as yet entirely uncontemplated synergisms (where the net consequences of two or more assaults on the environment are much more than the sum of the component parts). For example, more than 100 rads (and possibly more than 200 rads) of external and ingested ionizing radiation is likely to be delivered in a very large nuclear war to all plants, animals and unprotected humans in densely populated regions of northern mid-latitudes. After the soot and dust clear, there can, for such wars, be a 200 to 400 percent increment in the solar ultraviolet flux that reaches the ground, with an increase of many orders of magnitude in the more dangerous shorter-wavelength radiation. Together, these radiation assaults are likely to suppress the immune systems of humans and other species, making them more vulnerable to disease. At the same time, the high ambient-radiation fluxes are likely to produce, through mutation, new varieties of microorganisms, some of which might become pathogenic. The preferential radiation sensitivity of birds and other insect predators would enhance the proliferation of herbivorous and pathogen-carrying insects. Carried by vectors with high radiation tolerance, it seems possible that epidemics and global pandemics would propagate with no hope of effective mitigation by medical care, even with reduced population sizes and greatly restricted human mobility. Plants, weakened by low temperatures and low light levels, and other animals would likewise be vulnerable to preexisting and newly arisen pathogens.

There are many other conceivable synergisms, all of them still poorly understood because of the complexity of the global ecosystem. Every synergism represents an additional assault, of unknown magnitude, on the global ecosystem and its support functions for humans. What the world would look like after a nuclear war depends in part upon the unknown synergistic interaction of these various adverse effects.

We do not and cannot know that the worst would happen after a nuclear war. Perhaps there is some as yet undiscovered compensating effect or saving grace—although in the past, the overlooked effects in studies of nuclear war have almost always tended toward the worst. But in an uncertain matter of such gravity, it is wise to contemplate the worst, especially when its probability is not extremely small. The summary of the findings of the group of 40 distinguished biologists who met in April 1983 to assess the TTAPS conclusions is worthy of careful consideration:[18]

> Species extinction could be expected for most tropical plants and animals, and for most terrestrial vertebrates of north temperate regions, a large number of plants, and numerous freshwater and some marine organisms. . . . Whether any people would be able to persist for long in the face of highly modified biological communities; novel climates; high levels of radiation; shattered agricultural, social, and economic systems; extraordinary psychological stresses; and a host of other difficulties is open to question. It is clear that the ecosystem effects *alone* resulting from a large-scale thermonuclear war could be enough to destroy the current civilization in at least the Northern Hemisphere. Coupled with the direct casualties of perhaps two billion people, the combined intermediate and long-term effects of nuclear war suggest that eventually there might be no human survivors in the Northern Hemisphere.
>
> Furthermore, the scenario described here is by no means the most severe that could be imagined with present world nuclear arsenals and those contemplated for the near future. In almost any realistic case involving nuclear exchanges between the superpowers, global environmental changes sufficient to cause an extinction event equal to or more severe than that at the close of the Cretaceous when the dinosaurs and many other species died out are likely. In that event, the possibility of the extinction of *Homo sapiens* cannot be excluded.

. . . .

---

[18]P. Ehrlich, *et al., loc. cit.* footnote 1.

VI

We have, by slow and imperceptible steps, been constructing a Doomsday Machine. Until recently—and then, only by accident—no one even noticed. And we have distributed its triggers all over the Northern Hemisphere. Every American and Soviet leader since 1945 has made critical decisions regarding nuclear war in total ignorance of the climatic catastrophe. Perhaps this knowledge would have moderated the subsequent course of world events and, especially, the nuclear arms race. Today, at least, we have no excuse for failing to factor the catastrophe into long-term decisions on strategic policy.

Since it is the soot produced by urban fires that is the most sensitive trigger of the climatic catastrophe, and since such fires can be ignited even by low-yield strategic weapons, it appears that the most critical ready index of the world nuclear arsenals, in terms of climatic change, may be the total *number* of strategic warheads. (There is some dependence on yield, to be sure, and future very low-yield, high-accuracy burrowing warheads could destroy strategic targets without triggering the nuclear winter . . .) For other purposes there are other indices—numbers of submarine-launched warheads, throw-weight (net payload deliverable to target), total megatonnage, etc. From different choices of such indices, different conclusions about strategic parity can be drawn. In the total number of strategic warheads, however, the United States is "ahead" of the Soviet Union and always has been.

Very roughly, the level of the world strategic arsenals necessary to induce the climatic catastrophe seems to be somewhere around 500 to 2,000 warheads—an estimate that may be somewhat high for airbursts over cities, and somewhat low for high-yield groundbursts. The intrinsic uncertainty in this number is itself of strategic importance, and prudent policy would assume a value below the low end of the plausible range.

National or global inventories above this rough threshold move the world arsenals into a region that might be called the "Doomsday Zone." If the world arsenals were well below this rough threshold, no concatenation of computer malfunction, carelessness, unauthorized acts, communications failure, miscalculation and madness in high office could unleash the nuclear winter. When global arsenals are above the threshold, such a catastrophe is at least possible. The further above threshold we are, the more likely it is that a major exchange would trigger the climatic catastrophe.

Traditional belief and childhood experience teach that more weapons buy more security. But since the advent of nuclear weapons and the acquisition of a capacity for "overkill," the possibility has arisen that, past a certain point, more nuclear weapons do not increase national security. I wish here to suggest that, beyond the climatic threshold, an increase in the number of strategic weapons leads to a pronounced *decline* in national (and global) security. National security is not a zero-sum game. Strategic insecurity of one adversary almost always means strategic insecurity for the other. Conventional pre-1945 wisdom, no matter how deeply felt, is not an adequate guide in an age of apocalyptic weapons.

If we are content with world inventories above the threshold, we are saying that it is safe to trust the fate of our global civilization and perhaps our species to all leaders, civilian and military, of all present and future major nuclear powers; and to the command and control efficiency and technical reliability in those nations now and in the indefinite future. For myself, I would far rather have a world in which the climatic catastrophe cannot happen, independent of the vicissitudes of leaders, institutions and machines. This seems to me elementary planetary hygiene, as well as elementary patriotism.

Something like a thousand warheads (or a few hundred megatons) is of the same order as the arsenals that were publicly announced in the 1950s and 1960s as an unmistakable strategic deterrent, and as sufficient to destroy either the United States or the Soviet Union "irrecoverably." Considerably smaller arsenals would, with present improvements in accuracy and reliability, probably suffice. Thus it is possible to contemplate a world in which the global strategic arsenals are below threshold, where mutual deterrence is in effect to discourage the use of those surviving warheads, and where, in the unhappy event that some warheads are detonated, there is little like-lihood of the climatic catastrophe.[19]

To achieve so dramatic a decline in the global arsenals will require not only heroic measures by both the United States and the Soviet Union—it will also require consistent action by Britain, France and China, especially when the U.S. and Soviet arsenals are significantly reduced. Currently proposed increments in the arsenals at least of France would bring that nation's warhead inventory near or above threshold. I have already remarked on the strategic instability, in the context of the climatic catastrophe only, of the warhead inventories of these nations. But if major cuts in the U.S. and Soviet arsenals were under way, it is not too much to hope that the other major powers would, after negotiations, follow suit. These considerations also underscore the danger of nuclear weapons proliferation to other nations, especially when the major inventories are in steep decline. . . .

It is widely agreed—although different people have different justifications for this conclusion—that world arsenals must be reduced significantly. There is also general agreement, with a few demurrers, that at least the early and middle stages of a significant decline can be verified by national technical means and other procedures. The first stage of major arms reduction will have to overcome a new source of reluctance, when almost all silos could be reliably destroyed in a sub-threshold first strike. To overcome this reluctance, both sides will have prudently maintained an invulnerable retaliatory force, which itself would later move to sub-threshold levels. (It would even be advantageous to each nation to provide certain assistance in the development of such a force by the other.)

As arsenals are reduced still further, the fine tuning of the continuing decline may have to be worked out very carefully and with additional safeguards to guarantee continuing rough strategic parity. As threshold inventories are approached, some verifiable upper limits on yields as well as numbers would have to be worked out, to minimize the burning of cities if a nuclear conflict erupted. On the other hand, the deceleration of the arms race would have an inertia of its own, as the acceleration does; and successful first steps would create a climate conducive to subsequent steps. . . .

No one contends it will be easy to reverse the nuclear arms race. It is required at least for the same reasons that were used to justify the arms race in the first place—the national security of the United States and the Soviet Union. It is necessarily an enterprise of great magnitude. John Stuart Mill said: "Against a great evil, a small remedy does not produce a small result. It produces no result at all." . . .

In the deployment of more stabilizing weapons systems, in the possible development—especially in later stages of arms reductions—of novel means of treaty verification, and (perhaps) in the augmentation of conventional armaments, it will, of course, be expensive.

But, given the stakes, a prudent nuclear power should be willing to spend more every year to defuse the arms race and prevent nuclear war than it does on all military preparedness. For comparison, in the United States the annual budget of the Department of Defense is about 10,000 times that of the Arms Control and Disarmament Agency, quite apart from any questions about the dedication and effectiveness of the ACDA. The equivalent disparity is even greater in many other nations. I believe that the technical side of guaranteeing a major multilateral and strategically secure global arms reduction can be devised and deployed for considerably less—perhaps even a factor of 100 less—than the planet's direct military expenditures of $540 billion per year.[20]

Such figures give some feeling for the chasm that separates a prudent policy in face of our present knowledge of nuclear war from the actual present policies of the nuclear powers. Likewise, nations far removed from the conflict, even nations with little or no investment in the quarrels among the nuclear powers, stand to be

---

[19]Since higher-yield tactical warheads can also be used to burn cities, and might do so inadvertently, especially in Europe, provision for their elimination should also eventually be made. But initial attention should be directed to strategic warheads and their delivery systems.

[20]Ruth Leger Sivard, *World Military and Social Expenditures,* Leesburg (Va.): World Priorities, 1983.

destroyed in a nuclear war, rather than benefiting from the mutual annihilation of the superpowers. They too, one might think, would be wise to devote considerable resources to help ensure that nuclear war does not break out.

VII

In summary, cold, dark, radioactivity, pyrotoxins and ultraviolet light following a nuclear war—including some scenarios involving only a small fraction of the world strategic arsenals—would imperil every survivor on the planet. There is a real danger of the extinction of humanity. A threshold exists at which the climatic catastrophe could be triggered, very roughly around 500–2,000 strategic warheads. A major first strike may be an act of national suicide, even if no retaliation occurs. Given the magnitude of the potential loss, no policy declarations and no mechanical safeguards can adequately guarantee the safety of the human species. No national rivalry or ideological confrontation justifies putting the species at risk. Accordingly, there is a critical need for safe and verifiable reductions of the world strategic inventories to below threshold. At such levels, still adequate for deterrence, at least the worst could not happen should a nuclear war break out.

National security policies that seem prudent or even successful during a term of office or a tour of duty may work to endanger national—and global—security over longer periods of time. In many respects it is just such short-term thinking that is responsible for the present world crisis. The looming prospect of the climatic catastrophe makes short-term thinking even more dangerous. The past has been the enemy of the present, and the present the enemy of the future.

The problem cries out for an ecumenical perspective that rises above cant, doctrine and mutual recrimination, however apparently justified, and that at least partly transcends parochial fealties in time and space. What is urgently required is a coherent, mutually agreed upon, long-term policy for dramatic reductions in nuclear armaments, and a deep commitment, embracing decades, to carry it out.

Our talent, while imperfect, to foresee the future consequences of our present actions and to change our course appropriately is a hallmark of the human species, and one of the chief reasons for our success over the past million years. Our future depends entirely on how quickly and how broadly we can refine this talent. We should plan for and cherish our fragile world as we do our children and our grandchildren: there will be no other place for them to live. It is nowhere ordained that we must remain in bondage to nuclear weapons.

Name Index

Abel, G.G., 217
Abelson, H.I., 214
Ackerman, T.P., 375n
Adler, A., 166
Adler, P.A., 107–119
Adler, Peter, 107–119
Agnew, S.T., 170
Agopian, M., 11
Albaum, M., 240
Albert, R., 366
Aldrich, H., 312
Alexandrov, V.V., 375n
Allen, D., 202, 211
Allen, P., 48
Alstrom, J., 125
Aponte, R., 129–138
Arluke, A., 261–265
Aronoff, C., 262
Aspin, L., 368
Atkinson, T.-G., 166
Atkyns, R.L., 107
Auletta, K., 60, 324
Avedon, R., 214
Averitt, R., 234
Aviram, U., 49, 50, 51

Ball, D., 376n
Ballantine, C., 197
Bane, M.J., 136
Banfield, E.C., 324
Banzhaf, J., 87
Barbaree, H.E., 217
Barlow, D.H., 217
Baron, R.A., 214, 215, 216
Barrett, P.F., 236, 240
Barry, K., 211
Bassuk, E., 123
Becker, H., 202
Bell, P.A., 215, 216
Bellomo, S., 243
Bellows, K., 99
Belmont, A., 236
Belvin, R.J., 77
Bergstrom, S., 376n, 377n
Berkman, L.F., 38
Berry, B.J.L., 223n, 311
Best, J., 11–16, 117, 202
Bethe, H., 375n
Biemiller, L., 324
Biernacki, P., 109
Biggar, J.M., 80

Bingham, R., 126
Birenbaum, A., 7
Birnbaum, H.J., 217n
Bitterman, B., 313
Blanchard, E.B., 217
Blauner, R., 139–156
Bleda, P.R., 91
Blum, F.H., 150
Blum, R.H., 107, 109, 113n
Blumer, H., 3, 4, 5
Bogdan, J., 276–283
Boggs, V., 55–61
Borland, B.L., 91
Bosco, J.J., 3n
Bovard, E.W., 41
Bowles, S., 135
Boyer, D.K., 202, 210
Bracken, P., 376n
Bradford, G.L., 85n
Brady, J., 73
Brandt, A., 29, 32
Braucht, G.N., 213, 217n
Brenner, L., 338n
Brody, A., 83
Brody, B., 83
Brody, J.E., 87, 89n, 91
Brown, G.W., 277
Brown, H., 369
Brown, N.O., 166
Brown, M.W., 368–373
Brownmiller, S., 213, 219
Bruce-Briggs, B., 74
Bryan, J., 211
Buchanan, P.J., 29
Buchsbaum, H.K., 197
Bullough, B., 214n
Bullough, V., 214n
Bundy, M., 375n
Bunting, D., 234
Burns, G., 263
Bykofsky, S., 121, 128

Cain, G., 130
Califano, J.A., Jr., 84, 86, 92
Calot, G., 338
Carey, J.T., 107n, 108, 109, 113n
Carnegie, D., 166
Carson, J., 263
Carter, J., 84n, 250, 369
Cass, J., 310
Cassel, J., 37, 41, 43

Centers, R., 140n
Chaiken, J., 63
Chaiken, M., 63
Chall, J., 252, 253
Chandler, A.D., J., 234, 237, 238
Chase, J., 49, 50
Chavez, C., 353
Chazov, E.I., 375n
Cherry, N., 91
Chilton, R., 82n
Chinoy, E., 145
Chittester, J., 375n
Chodorow, N., 219n
Chu, F., 50, 51
Cisneros de Rosales, S., 329
Clements, P.F., 124–125
Cloninger, C.R., 101
Cobb, S., 37, 43, 277
Coe, J., 365
Cogan, J., 135
Cole, R.J., 87
Coleman, J.S., 311
Collins, J., 353–359
Condon, J.C., 87–88
Condran, G.A., 310–326
Connery, R.H., 49
Conrad, P., 27–34, 82n
Conway, T., 238
Cook, P., 69
Coombs, N.R., 202
Cottingham, C., 324
Cousteau, J.-Y., 360, 361
Craft, M., 202
Cronkite, W., 86
Cubbernuss, D., 82n
Cullen, F., 211
Currie, E., 57
Curry, R., 363
Curtis, C., 366

Dallek, G., 19–26
Daly, K., 121n
Danziger, S., 130
Darwin, C., 36
Davies, C.S., 240
Davies, D.L., 105
Davis, F.J., 7
Davis, K., 213, 217n
Davis, N., 202, 210
Dean, A., 277
Decker, J., 210

Deisher, R., 202
Deland, M., 363, 365
DeMan, H., 143, 144, 150
Demos, V., 262
Dentler, R.A., 3
Denton, N.A., 310–326
DeVries, W., 23
Dewees, D., 236, 237
Diamond, I., 214
Dienstbier, R.A., 219
Dobson, J., 170
Dolan, P.J., 376n
Donnerstein, E., 214, 215, 216
Dorfman, A., 360–366
Dorsey, P.A., 3n
Douglas, J.D., 109
Doyle, R., 33
Drucker, P., 151
Druyan, A., 375n
Due, J.E., 237
Duncan, B., 237, 312, 313, 314
Duncan, O.D., 312, 313, 314
Dunham, E., 49
Durant, B., 237
Durkheim, E., 36, 42, 272
Dworkin, A., 213
Dyson, F., 375n

Eames, A., Jr., 354
Ebert, R., 217
Edel, M., 239
Edwards, C.D., 234
Edwards, G., 104
Ehler, C., 362
Ehrlich, P.R., 375n, 385n
Eisenberg, P., 276
Ellis, K., 265
Emerson, R.M., 202n
English, D., 218, 219
Ensel, W., 277
Epstein, S., 87n
Ermann, D., 20
Espenshade, T., 190
Eysenck, H.J., 91

Farley, R., 311
Farrington, J., 364
Fattah, Sr. F., 59
Faunce, W.A., 147
Faust, B., 219
Fermi, E., 374
Ferree, M.M., 276n, 280
Fingarette, H., 95–106
Firestine, R.E., 133n
Fischer, A.K., 91
Fischer, C., 261

Fisher, J.M., 91
Fleder, J.R., 76
Fleming, E.L., 45n
Fletcher, E., 90
Flink, J.J., 237, 238, 240
Forbes, H.C., 235
Ford, H., 237–238
Forrest, J.D., 338–351
Foster, A.D., 338
Francher, J.S., 262
Frank, O., 335
Freedman, R., 334
Freud, S., 166
Freyhan, F., 202
Friedan, B., 186
Friedman-Kein, A., 31
Fromm, E., 166
Frye, A., 375n
Fuller, K., 338n
Furstenberg, F.F., Jr., 311

Gabel, J., 20
Gallup, G.H., 88
Gandy, P., 202
Gans, H., 308
Gardner, R.A., 91
Garner, J., 264
Garwin, R., 375n
Gayler, N., 375n
Gernreich, R., 167
Gerzon, M., 170
Gesell, A., 170
Ginsburg, K.N., 202
Gintis, H., 135
Glasstone, S., 376n
Goertzel, V., 48
Goffman, E., 30, 46
Goldman, N., 338–351
Goldscheider, C., 310
Goldstein, M.J., 216–217
Golitsyn, G.S., 375n
Gomez-Ibanez, J.A., 232
Goodchilds, J.D., 219
Goode, E., 108, 109
Gordon, R., 263
Goodwin, D., 100–101
Gore, S., 277
Gottschalk, P., 130
Gouldner, A.W., 146
Gray, D., 202, 210, 211
Gray, 213–221
Green, R.E., 126
Greenley, J., 51
Greenstein, R., 130
Greenwood, P.W., 63
Gresham, M., 261

Greytak, D., 243
Grinspoon, L., 375n
Gros, E., 76, 77
Grossman, J., 375n
Groth, A.N., 217n
Guerrette, M., 79
Guest, A.M., 243
Guglielmo, S., 360
Guild, D., 217
Gunderson, J., 48
Gunston, W., 372
Gusfield, J.R., 82–83
Gutman, H., 301

Hallam, J., 216
Hambley, R., 363
Hamilton, R., 121n
Hammer, A.R., 90
Hanley, J.A., 91
Hanneman, G.J., 107
Hardy, J., 362
Harman, D., 251–252
Harriman, A., 375n
Harrington, M., 253–254
Harris, L., 261
Harris, M., 202
Harris, T., 277
Hartog, J.B., 76
Harvey, D., 244
Harwell, M.A., 375n
Hauser, P.M., 303, 311
Hawkins, P., 15
Hemming, R., 265
Henshaw, S.K., 338–351
Herman, J.L., 284–299
Heron, A., 151
Heyl, B., 211
Hill, G., 84
Hill, J.J., 62
Hillabush, P.E., 79
Hilton, G.N., 237
Hinckley, J., 73
Hirschman, L., 284–299
Hochschild, A.R., 266–274
Hodge, R.W., 311
Hodges, W.F., 197
Hofferth, S., 195
Hoffman, M., 205
Hoffman, S., 187
Hogan, D.P., 311
Holden, J.P., 375n
Holmes, E.H., 241
Holmes, J., 187
Hoppock, R., 140, 147, 153
Horton, P.B., 7
Hoskins, J., 86

Houck, O., 361
House, J.S., 36–44, 277
Howard, J.L., 216
Howell, J., 15
Hoyvald, N.L., 75–80
Hubbard, T., 362, 366
Huber, J., 277
Hudson, R., 33–34
Hughes, M., 311
Hunter, C.S.J., 251–252

Infanger, C.L., 85n
Irini, S., 202, 210, 211

Jache, A., 262
Jackson, J., 369
Jacobs, M.A., 91
Jacobson, J.L., 329–337
Jacobson, L.F., 255–259
Jaffe, J.H., 91
Jaffe, Y., 216n
James, J., 202, 210
Jellinek, E.M., 97–98
Jensen, G., 236
Jensen, M.C., 85, 86
Johnsey, B., 77
Johnson, B.D., 109
Johnson, L.B., 213, 259
Johnson, P., 219
Jones, D.L., 124
Jones, Elise F., 338–351
Jones, Eric, 375n
Joseph, S., 360
Jost, K.L., 77
Julian, J., 7

Kagan, J., 172
Kain, J.F., 311
Kaminer, W., 213
Kant, H.S., 216–217
Kaplan, A., 5
Kaplan, G.A., 38
Kaplansky, Z., 76, 77, 80
Kapp, K.W., 242
Karras, G., 363
Kasarda, J.D., 134, 135, 223–231, 306
Kasl, S.V., 277
Katz, H., 20, 21
Keely, C.B., 3n
Keller, M., 103
Kellert, S.R., 49
Kellogg, S.M., 164–178
Kelly, J., 186, 196
Kelly, S.D., 311
Kennan, G.F., 375n
Kennedy, E.D., 234, 237

Kennedy, E.M., 84, 85
Kennedy, L., 23
Kercher, G.A., 217
Kierman, K., 91
Kimelman, S., 77
King, W., 90
Kirk, S.A., 45–53
Kisker, E.E., 338n
Kitagawa, E.M., 311
Kitsuse, J.I., 82n
Knickbocker, I., 76, 77
Kobrin, F.E., 310
Koch, E., 127
Koltnow, P., 242
Komarovsky, M., 276
Kornblum, W., 55–61
Kornhauser, A., 140n
Kozol, J., 249–254
Kramer, R., 82n
Krim, M., 31
Kruger, C.H., 384n
Krusa, D., 360
Kuhn, A., 235
Kuhn, T.S., 3
Kutchinsky, B., 216n
Kuttner, B., 49

Lafon, G.R., 22
Lamb, H.R., 48
Landis, K.R., 36–44
Langer, J., 108
Lappé, F.M., 353–359
Laumann, E.O., 311
Lavery, J.F., 75–80
Lazarsfeld, P.F., 276
Lazure, L., 46
Lederer, L., 213
Lee, B.A., 312
Lemert, E., 114n
Leslie, G.R., 7
Levin, J., 261–265
Levin, W., 261
Levine, H.G., 82n
Lewin-Epstein, N., 311
LiCari, J.J., 76–77, 78, 80
Lieb, J., 108, 109, 113
Lieberson, S., 237, 302–303, 310, 319
Liegey, G., 360
Liem, R., 277
Lin, N., 277
Lincoln, R., 338–351
Lindecker, C.L., 203
Linden, E., 360–366
Linder, H., 215
Linn, M., 277
Lipset, S.M., 139n

Lipsky, M., 157–162
Lloyd, R., 203
Lofland, J., 203, 206
Logan, J.R., 311
Lorge, I., 261
Luce, C.B., 165
Luckenbill, D.F., 117, 202–212
Ludwig, D.K., 356
Lustig, N., 287
Lynch, M., 364

MacDonald, R., 262
MacNamara, D., 202
Madden, J., 311
Maisch, H., 284, 286, 290, 292, 293
Makinson, C., 338n
Malamuth, N.N., 214
Maliszewski, E., 363
Mancuso, J., 49
Manis, J.G., 3–10
Mann, C.K., 85n, 86
Mann, J., 216
Mantel, E.H., 241
Manville, A., 361
Mao Zedong, 334
Marcuse, H., 166
Mark, C., 375n
Markle, G.E., 82–94
Marlatt, A., 102
Marlowe, K., 202
Marschall, F., 353
Martinson, R., 58, 64
Marx, K., 139, 153
Maslow, A., 166
Massey, D.S., 310–326
Massey, J., 19
Mavissakian, M., 217
Mayo, E., 149
McGee, R., 4
McKay, J., 235
McNamara, R.S., 375n
McNicoll, G., 335
McShane, C., 235
McTavish, D.G., 261
Meltzer, B.N., 3n
Meredith, E.E., 13, 15
Merton, R.K., 3, 5, 8
Methvin, E.H., 62–64
Meyer, J.R., 232, 240
Meyer, T., 214, 215
Mill, J.S., 387
Miller, G., 111
Mills, C.W., 150
Mintz, S., 164–178
Mitchell, R.E., 277
Molotch, H., 244

Mondale, W., 171
Monkkonen, E.H., 125
Moore, J.A., 311
Moore, K.A., 311
Morehouse, T.A., 241
Morgan, S.P., 311
Morrison, P., 375n
Morse, N.C., 140n
Mouledoux, J., 108
Moynihan, D.P., 136, 307
Mullan, B.P., 310, 312, 313, 314
Murphy, P., 91
Murray, C., 129–130, 136
Myers, D.J., 45n

Nash, C.W., 237
Nawy, H., 214
Neckerman, K., 129–138
Nelli, H.S., 310
Nemeth, R., 82n
Nerem, R.M., 41
Newman, O., 305
Nicholas, F.C., 76, 77
Nichols, R., 91
Nielsen, P., 256
Nixon, R.M., 171–172
Northcutt, N., 251
Nowak, T.C., 277
Nuehring, E., 83, 87, 88, 89n, 92
Nunn, S., 369

O'Hara, K., 362
Olson, S., 108, 109, 113
Oppenheimer, J.R., 374
Orear, J., 375n
Ornati, O., 240
Orth-Gomer, K., 38

Palmer, G.L., 140n
Palmquist, A., 203
Panzetta, A., 49
Parcel, T., 311
Park, R.E., 310
Passer, H., 235
Pattison, R., 20, 21
Patz, E., 11
Pearlin, L.I., 277
Perrucci, R., 6
Perry, W.J., 371, 375n
Persky, J.J., 311
Peters, L., 372
Petersen, J., 82n, 376n, 377n, 378n
Pfohl, S.J., 82n
Phillips, D., 49
Pilisuk, M., 6
Pimentel, D., 375n, 383n

Planck, M., 3
Platt, T.C., 75
Pollack, J.B., 375n
Postel, T., 375n
Preston, S.H., 195
Prus, R., 202, 210, 211

Quigley, J.M., 311
Quinn, T.M., 79

Rabi, I.I., 374
Rader, D., 365
Rae, G., 91
Rainwater, L., 305
Ratcliff, K.S., 276–283
Ratcliff, R.E., 276n
Rathjens, G., 375n
Raven, P.H., 375n
Rayman, P., 277
Reagan, R., 59, 73, 128, 245, 336,
    368
Regnery, A., 64
Reingold, E.M., 360–366
Reinhardt, U., 25
Reiss, A.J., 202, 205
Reynolds, C., 91
Reynolds, L.G., 140n
Riemer, J.W., 109
Riesman, D., 146
Ritzer, R., 111
Robertson, M., 126–127
Robin, S.S., 3n, 82n
Robinson, J.C., 91
Roche, T.H., 75, 77
Rogers, C., 166
Roncek, D.W., 305
Rood, W.B., 86
Rook, K., 277
Roosevelt, F.D., 239
Roper, E., 142n
Rose, V.N., 82n
Rosen, E., 281
Rosenthal, R., 255–259
Rosenzweig, A., 78–79
Rosoff, J.I., 338–351
Rosow, I., 273
Ross, H.L., 133
Rossi, P.H., 66, 121n, 122, 127
Rosten, L., 142n
Rotblat, J., 375n
Roth, M., 375n
Rothschild-Whitt, J., 232n
Rubin, L.B., 280
Rudolph, J.P., 91
Rush, B., 97
Russell, D.H., 202

Rustin, B., 308
Rutter, M., 172

Safire, W., 91
Sagan, C., 374–388
Sagarin, E., 7
Sager, A., 22
St.Clair, D.J., 237, 238
Sakharov, A., 374
Salk, L., 170
Salpukas, A., 91n
Sandifor, R., 277
Sandman, P.H., 91
Sapolsky, B.S., 215
Sarbin, T., 49
Sawhill, I., 133
Saxe, L., 104
Scheff, T., 49
Schell, J., 374
Schmidt, E.P., 235
Schneider, J.W., 82n
Schneider, M., 311
Schoenbach, V.J., 38
Schuckit, M., 99
Schutz, A., 5
Scoville, H., 375n
Scowcroft, B., 375n
Segal, S.P., 49, 50, 51
Seigler, K., 363
Seltzer, L.H., 234, 237
Setlow, R.B., 384n
Shields, B., 263
Shister, J., 140n
Shonholtz, R., 60
Shubik, M., 376n
Shuffett, D.M., 86
Shute, N., 374
Siegel, P.M., 311
Silberman, C., 58, 59
Silkworth, W., 97
Simon, P., 11
Sivard, R.L., 387n
Sloan, A., 237, 238
Smerk, G., 235
Smith, D.D., 214
Smith, G.M., 91
Smith, H.E., 202n
Smith, M.C., 262
Smith, R.H., 97
Snell, B.C., 233, 238
Snyder, K.A., 277
Sobell, L., 105
Sobell, M., 105
Sontag, S., 27
Sorrells, M., 383n
Soter, S., 375n

Sowell, T., 56
Spain, D., 312
Spector, M., 82*n*
Speidel, J., 336
Spilkin, A.Z., 91
Spinner, B., 214
Spitze, G., 277
Spock, B., 170
Srole, L., 91
Stein, S., 277
Steinberg, S., 307
Steinbruner, J., 375*n*
Stewart, J., 276*n*
Stewart, S., 363
Stoller, R.J., 218, 219
Stone, J., 375*n*
Stuart, R., 46
Sullivan, B.V., Jr., 75
Sullivan, M., 331
Syme, S.L., 38

Taeuber, A.F., 311, 312, 314
Taeuber, K.E., 312, 314
Tallman, I., 4
Tarr, J., 235
Tauke, T., 13
Teller, E., 374, 375*n*
Thayer, L., 64
Thernstrom, S., 310
Therrien, M.E., 45–53
Theuer, R.C., 75, 80
Tibblin, G., 38
Tierney, C.W., 197
Toon, O.B., 375*n*

Toufexis, A., 360–366
Traub, J., 75–80
Trickett, E.J., 277
Trotter, S., 49, 50, 51
Troyer, R.J., 82–94
Tuckman, J., 261
Turco, R.P., 375*n*, 376*n*, 378*n*
Turner, R.J., 277

Umberson, D.J., 36–44, 312

Vaillant, G., 99, 105
Velikhov, E.P., 375*n*
Villemez, W.J., 311
Voorhees, A.M., 243

Waldorf, D., 108, 109, 113*n*, 114*n*
Walker, C.E., 217
Walker, C.R., 148, 151
Wallerstein, J., 186, 196
Walsh, A., 11
Walsh, J., 11, 13, 14
Ward, D., 234, 310
Warner, K.E., 90*n*
Warner, S.M., Jr., 235
Warnke, P., 375*n*
Weber, D., 121*n*
Weber, M., 144
Wechsler, R.C., 197
Wedow, S., 114*n*
Weiner, I.B., 286
Weiner, S., 47, 51
Weinstein, B.L., 133*n*
Weiss, L., 237

Weiss, R.S., 140*n*, 186, 190
Weisskopf, V., 375*n*
Weitzman, L.J., 179–200
Welin, L., 38
Wellman, B., 277
Wells, J.W., 202
Wells, R.H., 80
Westoff, C.F., 338–351
White, S.B., 126
Whitt, J.A., 232–247
Wilcox, D.F., 233, 235
Wilson, J.Q., 56, 304–305
Wilson, R.R., 375*n*
Wilson, W., 97
Wilson, W.C., 214
Wilson, W.J., 129–138, 301–309,
    311, 324
Windom, H., 363
Winikoff, B., 331
Wohlstetter, A., 375*n*
Wolfgang, M., 62–63
Woodbury, R., 365
Woodruff, L.W., 369
Woodwell, G.M., 375*n*
Worthy, J., 151
Wright, J.D., 65–74, 121–128
Wulf, D., 338–351

Yago, G., 232–247

Zillman, D., 215
Zusman, J., 46

Subject Index

Abortion:
illegal, 330
rates in selected industrial countries, 339, 340–341
rates, U.S. teenagers, 338–341
and Reagan administration, 336
teenage access to, 343–345
Acquired immunodeficiency syndrome (AIDS), 330, 331–332
deadliness of, 30
effects of, 30–33
normalizing, 33–34
public reaction to, 27–28
resistance to information about, 32–33
risk groups, 28–29
role of contagion, 29–30
sexual transmission of, 29
social meaning of, 27–34
Action on Smoking and Health (ASH), 87
Activism, and identification of problems, 12
Adolescence:
problems of, 169–170
and sibling bonds, 273
and teenage pregnancy, 338–351
Adult Performance Level (APL), 251–252
Adventurous deviant act, 206
Advertising industry, and smoking, 86
Age:
median, of ethnic group, 304
and start in crime, 63
Ageism, 260–274
and communal life-styles, 266–274
second childhood bias, 261–265
Age-stratification, and sibling bond, 272–273
Aggression:
against infantilization, 265
and hard-core pornography, 214–216
Agribusiness:
and competition with the hungry, 353–355
and forests, 356–357
and land destruction, 356–357

Agriculture, single-crop, 357–358
Aid to Families with Dependent Children (AFDC), 123, 125, 129–130, 168, 196, 304, 348
AIDS-Related Complex (ARC), 27, 30
Alan Guttmacher Institute (AGI), 338
Alcohol, and incestuous fathers, 288–289
Alcoholics Anonymous, 97–98
Alcoholism:
biological causes of, 99–100
causes of, 101–102
and control, 102–103
conventional wisdom concerning, 96
disease concept of, 95–106
and genes, 100–101
identification of, and treatment, 103–105
new approaches to, 105–106
origins of disease myth of, 96–98
phases of, 98–99
"Alcoholism movement," 98
Alienation, of welfare workers, 159, 160–161
Analysis, units of, 7–8
Anderson Clayton, 356
Anger:
and pornography, 213–221
as social problem, 217–218
Assembly line work, 145–146
ways to humanize, 151–152
Asylums (Goffman), 46
Automobile:
private, promotion of, 240–241
reliance on, 232–233
Automobile industry, 152
and assembly line work, 145–146
and cities, 237–239
and state policy, 239–241

Baby boom, and homelessness, 126
Bay Area Rapid Transit (BART), 244
Beech-Nut Nutrition Corporation, 75–80
Bias:
cultural, in research, 152
second childhood, 261–265, 270–271

Biological markers, and alcoholism, 99–100
Birth control:
hormonal implants, 333
pills, 332, 344–345
See also Contraception; Family planning
Birthrate, 164
reducing, 330
Bistatic radar, 372
Black Americans:
family disintegration, and welfare, 129–138
and residential segregation, 310–326
and social integration, 40
teenage pregnancy among, 341
versus Asians, 302
Western, 132–133
Boarding homes, 50–51, 52
Books, child-rearing manuals, 170
Borden Inc., 356
Bud Antle, Inc., 353
Bud Senegal, 353, 356
Burnout, in drug dealing, 113
Bustout, in drug dealing, 116

Catchment area, 45, 48–49
Causality:
and alcoholism, 99
and primacy of social problems, 6–7
Central problem (see Primary social problem)
Centro de Orientación y Servicios (Ponce, Puerto Rico), 59, 60
Change:
and the city, 223–231
economic, and black male jobless, 133–136
economic, effect on the family of, 130–133
economic, and ethnicity, 306–308
in family, since 1960, 164–178
Child Find, 11
Child(ren):
day care, 171–173
disadvantaged, and teacher expectations, 255–259
and divorce, 168–169, 173–174
homeless, 123

Child(ren) (continued)
    number of, and incest, 289–290
    old people portrayed as, 262–264
    and postdivorce income,
        179–181, 195–197
    missing, statistics on, 11–16
    redefining abduction of, 13–14
Child-rearing:
    manuals for, 170
    since 1960, 168–174
    and television, 170–171
"Chronics" (mental hospital
        patients), 47–48
Cigarette smoking:
    antismoking forces, 86–88
    attitudes and patterns, 88–90
    coercive control, 88, 89
    as deviance, 82–94
    emerging confrontations over,
        90–92
    prosmoking forces, 84–86
    recent history of, 83–84
City:
    central, crisis in, 305
    and change, 223–231
    Chicago, 226, 227, 229–230
    demographic change, 228
    Detroit, 226, 227, 228
    employment change in, 226,
        226–228
    future of, 230–231
    high-technology rail systems,
        244–245
    mismatch of jobs and skills,
        226–228, 228–230
    New York, 226, 227, 229, 230
    of 1920s, and the automobile, 237
    and nuclear war, 377
    Philadelphia, 226, 227–228, 230
    population decline, 227–228
    present transit policy, 242–244
    problems of, 223–247
    and public housing projects, 305
    and racism, 301–309
    rural ways in, 266–274
    as socioeconomic springboard,
        224–226
    transit, and corporate strategy,
        232–247
    unemployment in, 229–230
Clean Water Act (1972), 365
Cocaine, 108–109
    See also Drugs
Commission on Obscenity and
        Pornography (1970), 213
Community:

concept of, 48–49
    and crime prevention, 58
    of drug dealers, 109
    empowerment, in anticrime
        model, 60
    forming of, 266–267
    information transfer in, 268–269
    occupational, 149–150
    and old age, 266–274
    and the sibling bond, 271–273
Community Boards Program (San
        Francisco), 60
Competence, and divorce, 191–193
Compulsive smoking syndrome, 91
Contagion, response to, 29–30
Contraception:
    changing technologies, 332–333
    condoms, 331, 344
    postcoital pill, 344–345
    and teenagers, 343–345
    unequal access to, 329
    See also Birth control; Family
        planning
Control:
    and incestuous fathers, 286–288
    and occupation, 144–147
Courtesy stigma, 30
Crime, 54–80
    and aging of population, 55
    and community empowerment,
        60–61
    data on, 312
    and decriminalization, 57
    and employment intervention,
        58–60
    get-tough strategies, 56–57
    and guns, 67–69
    individual rate of, 62–63
    key to control of, 62–64
    and neighborhood, 317
    new alternatives for fighting,
        55–61
    of passion, and gun control,
        69–70
    pragmatic trends in fighting,
        57–58
    rates of (1970–1980), 55
    severity of, 8
    superfelons, 62
    white-collar, 75–80
Critical-mass theory (Wilson), 305
Cultural bias, in research, 152

Day care, 171–173
Death:
    accidental, and guns, 68

and drug dealing, 116
    and guns, 67–68
    and the homeless, 125–126
    rates of, 315–317
Defensible Space (Newman), 305
Defensive deviant act, 203
Definitions, importance of, 14
Dehumanization, in welfare system,
        159
Del Monte Corporation, 354
Deprivation, postdivorce, 179–181
Deserving poor, 121
Deviance:
    assimilative model of, 82–83
    careers in, drug dealing, 107–119
    cigarette smoking as, 82–94
    coercive model of, 83
    incest, 284–299
    male prostitution, 202–212
    public conception of, 4
    sexual, 201–221
Diagnosis-related group (DRG)
        payment system, 19, 21, 25
Disadvantaged, and teacher
        expectations, 255–259
Discrimination, 301–302
Disease:
    compared to illness, 27
    concept of, 95–96
Divorce:
    attitudes toward, 165
    and children, 168–169, 173–174
    and competence and self-esteem,
        191–193
    economic effects of, 174,
        179–200
    feminist attitude toward, 166–167
    and impoverishment of women
        and children, 187–189
    and loss of social networks,
        185–186
    and mental and physical health,
        193–194
    and per capita income, 181–186
    rate of, since 1960, 164
    social consequences of, 190–194
    societal consequences of,
        194–197
    and standards of living, 188,
        189–190
    and the two-tier society, 197–198
Dole Corporation, 358
Drug dealing, 107–119
    aging in the career, 113–114
    alternative occupations, 115
    bustout, 116

Drug dealing *(continued)*
  career shifts and oscillations, 113–118
  leaving, 118
  low and upper level, 108–109
  low-level entry, 109–110
  middle, straight, and wholesale, 108
  middle-level entry, 110–111
  phasing-out, 114–116
  re-entry into, 116–117
  research setting and method, 108–109
  routes into, 109–112
  smuggling, 111–112
Drugs:
  alcohol, 95–106, 288–289
  cigarette smoking, 82–94
  dealing (*see* Drug dealing)
  decriminalization of, 57
  "soft," 107*n*
  use of, by superfelons, 63
  use of, by teenage homeless, 124
  See also Cocaine; Marihuana
Dynamic Coherent Measurement Systems (Dycoms), 372

Earned Income Tax Credit (1975), 130
Ecology, 352–366
  water pollution, 360–366
Economics:
  change in, and ethnic culture, 306–308
  of divorce, 174, 179–200
  of national transportation policy, 234–242
Education, 248–259
  compromise in, 160
  cross-cultural comparison, 347–348
  data on city schools, 311–312
  illiteracy, 249–254
  and segregation, 320–323
  sex, 345, 349
  standardized test performance, 324–325
  teacher expectations, 255–259
  See also Schools
Employment:
  and crime, 58–60
  growth by region, 133
  supported work programs, 59–60
Entry:
  into drug dealing, 109–112

into male prostitution, 202–203, 203–208
Environmental Protection Agency, 360
Ethnic community, 49
  and economic change, 306–308

Family(ies):
  changes since 1960, 164–178
  disintegration of, and welfare, 129–138
  homeless, 122–124
  and incestuous fathers, 284–299
  and joblessness, 130–133
  and new morality, 165–168
  problems of, 163–200
  redefinition of, 165
  and sibling bond, 273
Family Assistance Plan, 161
Family planning, 329–337
  China, 334
  and confidentiality, 344
  financing of, 335–337
  ingredients of success, 333–335
  Thailand, 335
  and U.S. policy, 329–330, 336
  See also Birth control; Contraception
Federal Bureau of Investigation (FBI), 12–13
Federal government:
  and day care, 172
  and tobacco controversy, 85–87
Flanagan Tests of General Ability, 256
Food Complex, 78
Food stamp program, 160
Functional illiteracy, 252, 253

Gay Related Immune Deficiency Syndrome (GRID), 29
General Motors Corporation, 239
Genetic research, and alcoholism, 100–101
Global Supermarket and Global Farm, 353–355
Goal displacement, in welfare system, 158
Goodyear Corporation, 356
Gray Panthers, 265
Great Society programs, 129
Green Giant Corporation, 358
Green Revolution, 355–356
Group Against Smokers Pollution (GASP), 87
Gun control, 65–74

and crime, 67–69
and crimes of passion, 69–70
demand and supply, 69
effects of laws, 67
international comparisons, 70–71
meaning of, 66–67
and public opinion, 71
reactions to research on, 73–74
and Saturday Night Special, 71–73

HTLV-III, 27
Hawthorne effect, 258–259
Head Start program, 171, 172
Health:
  data on, 312
  and divorce, 193–194
  and social relationships, 36–44
  world, and family planning, 329–337
Heterosexuality, and male prostitution, 205–206
Hispanics, migration of, 303–304
Homeless:
  age and sex differences in, 124
  families, 122–124
  lone adult men, 125–126
  lone disabled men, 127
  lone veterans, 126–127
  lone women and children, 123, 124–125
  shelter and street, 122
  worthy and unworthy, 121–128
Homicide, and guns, 68
Homophobia, 29, 31
Homosexuality:
  and AIDS, 29, 31
  and male prostitution, 202–212
Hospital Corporation of America (HCA), 19, 22–23
Hospitals:
  costs of care, 20–21
  and the poor, 22–23
  for profit, 19–26
  profit versus nonprofit, 23–24
  unneeded, 21
House of Umoja (Philadelphia), 59
Housing:
  classification of, 312–313
  data on, 311
  public projects, 305
  racial segregation in, 310–326
Human potential movement, and the family, 166
Humana, Incorporated, 19, 21, 22, 23
Hunger, world, 353–359

Illiteracy, 249–254
  contradictory information on, 251
  functional and marginal, 252
  rates of, by age, race, and ethnicity, 250
Illiterate America, 253
Illness:
  compared to disease, 27
  metaphorical aspects of, 27
  stigmatized, 28–29
Immigration:
  and the city, 225
  and racism, 302–306
Incest, 284–299
  characteristics of victims, 285
  definition, 285–286, 293
  distress symptoms in victims, 297
  as initiation rite, 293
  mother's response to, 295–296
Income, and segregation, 320–323
Income Maintenance Experiments, 130
Information transfer, and community, 268–269
International relations, 367–388
Intrauterine device (IUD), 332
Isolation:
  and old age, 273–274
  of postdivorce women, 191

Job commitment, of women, 280–282
Job Corps, 59
Job satisfaction:
  and control, 144–147
  factors in, 143–150
  and industrial trends, 139–156
  and integrated work groups, 147–149
  and occupational communities, 149–150
  occupational differences in, 141–142
  and occupational prestige, 143–144
  research on, 140–141, 152–153
  and supervision, 147
Joblessness:
  black, 301
  of black males, 133–136
  in cities, 229–230
  versus welfare effects, 129–138
  of women, 276–283
  See also Unemployment

Kaposi's sarcoma, 30
Kevin Collins Foundation for Missing Children, 14
Kidnapping, of children, 11–16
Kinder-Care, 172

Latin American Agribusiness Development Corporation (LAAD), 354
Law enforcement, compromise in, 160
Losing Ground (Murray), 129

Magnitude, of social problems, 7–8
Male marriageable pool index (MMPI), 130–133, 135, 136–137
Male prostitution, 202–212
  adventurous involvement, 206–208
  and contextual conditions, 210
  defensive involvement, 203–206
  entry into, 202–203, 203–208
  regular involvement, 208–210
  research sample and method, 203
Manual labor, attitude toward, 143–144
Marginal illiteracy, 252
Marihuana:
  dealing in, 108–109
  as social problem, 4
  See also Drugs
Marriage:
  lasting 11–17 years, and postdivorce income, 182–183
  long, and postdivorce income, 183–186
  remarriage, 174
  shorter, and postdivorce income, 180–181
Mechanical solidarity, 272–273
Medical care:
  and AIDS stigma, 31–32
  managed system approach, 21
  and political ideology, 24–26
  for profit, 19–26
  and recruitment of doctors, 23
Medicare:
  diagnosis-related group (DRG) payment, 19
  policy of, 25
Men:
  incestuous fathers, 284–299
  views on wives' unemployment, 278–279

Mental health, 35–53
  community programs, 45–53
  and divorce, 193–194
  former hospitalized patients, 45–53
  and the homeless, 127
  patient placement, 47
Merrill Court community, 266–274
Metro (Washington, D.C.), 244
Mining, job satisfaction in, 146, 149–150
Missing children, 11–16
  magnitude of problem, 11–12
  policy suggestions, 15
"Mr. Rogers' Neighborhood," 171
Mitsubishi Corporation, 356
Monetary savings, myth of, 49–51
Morality:
  changes in, 165–168
  and economic affluence, 165–166
Mortality:
  among the homeless, 125–126
  prospective studies of, 37–40
  and social integration, 36, 39, 40–41
Myth:
  of alcoholism as disease, 95–106
  of community mental health programs, 45–53
  of continuity of care, 51–52
  of monetary savings, 49–51
  of rehabilitation, 46–48
  of reintegration of mental health patients, 48–49

National Center for Missing and Exploited Children (NCMEC), 12, 13–14, 15
National Civic Federation (NCF), 236
National Clearinghouse for Smoking and Health, 86
National Council on Alcoholism (NCA), 98
National Health Care for the Homeless Program (HCH), 122–123
National Health Law Program, 19n
National Interagency Council on Smoking (NIC), 87
National Medical Enterprises (NME), 19, 20
National Oceanic and Atmospheric Administration (NOAA), 362
National Rifle Association (NRA), 65, 66, 67, 73

Neighborhood Watch program, 62
Nestlé Food Corporation, 77–78, 79–80, 356
New Deal, and urban highways, 239
Newspapers, ageism of, 262–264
NORPLANT (contraceptive), 333
Nuclear war:
    Baseline Case, 379–381
    biological impact of, 383–385
    environmental consequences of, 378
    and Hiroshima bomb, 376
    temperature effects of, 380
Nuclear winter, 374–388
    Doomsday Zone, 386

Obscenity (*see* Pornography)
Occupational prestige, 143–144
Oceans, pollution of, 360–366
Office of Civil Rights (OCR), 22
Office of Juvenile Justice and Delinquency Prevention (OJJDP), 11, 15, 64
Old age:
    communal life-styles in, 266–274
    loss of status of, 261–262
    as minority group, 273–274
    and neighboring, 268–269
    "poor dear" hierarchy, 269–271
    as second childhood, 261–265, 270–271
    and the sibling bond, 271–273
Oral contraceptives, 332
Organic solidarity, 272
Overpopulation, 328–351
Ozone layer, and nuclear war, 378

Paranoia:
    defined, 114*n*
    of drug dealer, 114
Pedophiles, 216–217
Peripheral problem (*see* Secondary social problem; Tertiary social problem)
Phillip Morris, Incorporated, 85, 86, 90
Physical health problems, 18–34
Placement, of mental health patients, 47
Police Special, 73
"Poor dear" hierarchy, 269–271
Population, 328–351
    family planning, 329–337
    teenage pregnancy, 338–351
Pornography:
    and aggression, 213–221

defined, 213–214
    as fantasy, 218
    future research on, 219–220
    long-term effects of, 216–217
    soft-core and hard-core, 214, 215
Post-traumatic stress syndrome, 126
Poverty:
    of children, post-divorce, 195–197
    and educational expectations, 255–259
    feminization of, 168, 194–195
    and medical care, 22–23
    and post-divorce women and children, 187–190
    and teenage pregnancy, 348
    renewed visibility of, 121
Pregnancy, teenage, and homelessness, 124
Primacy, and causality, 6–7
Primary social problem, 6–7
Prisoner's dilemma, 239
Processed Apples Institute, 78–79
Proprietary hospital, 19
Prostitution:
    as acceptable activity, 204, 205–206, 208–209
    female and male, 210–211
    male, 202–212
    teenage, 124
Public Health Service, 86
Public housing projects, 305
Public opinion:
    and gun control, 71
    and social problems, 3–4
Public policy, cross-cultural comparison of, 347
Public welfare, and mental health programs, 50, 52

R.J. Reynolds Industries, Incorporated, 85, 86
Race:
    declining significance of, 324
    family and public policy, 136–137
    and social integration, 40
Racism, 300–326
    and inner city, 301–309
    and migration, 302–306
    and residential segregation, 310–326
Radar Cross Section (R.C.S.), 371
Railroad workers, 147, 150
Railways, high-technology, 244–245

Ralston Purina Company, 358
Rapists, 216–217
Reading, 249–254
    grade equivalents use, 252–253
Recidivism, criminal:
    and employment, 58–60
    and prison, 64
Reengagement, in old age, 265
Rehabilitation:
    criminal, and recidivism, 64
    myth of, 46–48
Reimbursement system, of hospital payment, 19–20, 21
Reintegration, myth of, 48–49
Relative deprivation, 179–181
Religion, and attitudes toward sex, 346–347
Remarriage, 174
Rhythm method, 332

Sado-masochism, 214
Safer Foundation, 60
Saturday Night Special, 71–73
Scholastic Aptitude Test (SAT), 324
Schools:
    segregation in, 318
    See also Education
Science:
    objectivity of, 5–6
    social responsibility of, 5
    values of, 5
Second childhood stereotype, 261–265
Secondary social problem, 6–7
Selective incapacitation, of criminals, 63
Self-esteem, and divorce, 191–193
Self-fulfilling prophecy, 255–259
    second childhood stereotype as, 264–265
Self-realization, as cultural goal, 166
Semi-literacy, 253
Sex:
    and anger, 217–218
    equalizing effect of guns, 70
Sex education, 345, 349
Sex roles:
    and incestuous fathers, 287
    and unemployment, 277
Sexism, 167, 275–299
    and incest, 284–299
    and unemployed women, 276–283
Sexual activity, of adolescents, 342–343

Sexual codes, 164
  and family, 166
  and the sexual revolution,
    167–168
  in United States, 346–347
Sexual deviance, 201–221
  male prostitution, 202–212
  pornography and anger, 213–221
"Sesame Street," 171
Shop talk, and community,
    149–150
Sibling bond, 271–272
  and age-stratification, 272–273
Sick tax, 24
Singles culture, 167
SmokEnders, 87–88
Smuggling, of drugs, 111–112
Social control, neighboring as,
    268–269
Social mobility:
  and the city, 224–226
  downward, of postdivorce
    women, 182, 185
  and spatial mobility, 310–311, 313
Social network:
  and old age, 267–268
  post-divorce, 185–186
  and unemployed women,
    279–280
Social network index, 38
Social pathology, 162
Social problems:
  assessing seriousness of, 3–10
  classification model, 7
  identification of, 4–6
  magnitude of, 7–8
  physical health as, 18–34
  primacy of, 6–7
  professional view of, 4–5
  public definition of, 3–4
  severity of, 8
  sociology of, 1–16
  subjective definition of, 3
  subjective definition versus
    objective data, 7
Social relationships:
  determinants of, 43–44
  and health, 36–44
  theory and research on, 37
Social solidarity, 272–273
Social support:
  content of, 278–280
  and unemployed women,
    276–283
  See also Social relationships

Society:
  impact of divorce on, 194–197
  two-tier, 197–198
Sociology, and social problems, 5
Spatial mobility, and social
    mobility, 310–311, 313
Specialization, in welfare system,
    159, 161
Squibb Corporation, 76
Standardized tests, black
    performance on, 324–325
Statistics, misleading, 11–16
Stealth bomber (B-2), 368–373
  radar visibility of, 371
Stereotypes:
  "bag lady," 125
  old age as second childhood,
    261–265, 270–271
Stigma, and illness, 28–29
Street homeless, 122
Stress:
  in post-divorce women, 191
  and unemployment, 276–277
Suicide:
  and guns, 68
  and social integration, 36

Teacher, and expectations for
    disadvantaged, 255–259
Teenage pregnancy, 304, 338–351
  cross-cultural research on,
    339–345
  intended, 342
  public climate of, 346–348
  and public policy, 348–350
Television:
  age prejudice in, 262–264
  and child-rearing, 170–171
  Gray Panthers' Media Watch Task
    Force, 265
Tertiary social problem, 6–7
"Third force" psychology, 166
Third World, and family planning,
    329–337
Tobacco industry, 85–86
Tobacco Institute, 85
Transportation:
  national policy, and economics,
    234–242
  present policy's effects, 242–244
  public, fall of, 236–239
  public, growth period of,
    234–236
  urban, 232–247
Truck drivers, 147

Underclass, The (Auletta), 60
Underground economy, 230–231
Unemployment:
  research on, 276–277
  of women, and husbands' views
    of, 278–279
  See also Joblessness
United Nations Fund for Population
    Activities (UNFPA), 336
Units of analysis, 7–8
Universal Juice, 76
Universe Tank Ship, 356
Urban programs, 223
Urban transit, and corporate
    strategy, 232–247

Values, scientific, 5
Venereal disease, 29
Victim Offender Reconciliation
    Program (VORP), 60–61
Victimless crime, 57
Violence:
  of incestuous fathers, 287–288
  and neighborhood, 317
Volkswagen, 356

Wan Xi Shao program, 334
Water pollution, 360–366
  algae, 361, 362, 364
  and runoff, 361
Welfare economy, 230–231
Welfare system:
  compromises in, 159–160
  versus direct income-support,
    161
  and ethnic culture, 307
  goal displacement in, 158
  inadequate resources, 157
  and marriage, 168
  as workplace, 157–162
White-collar crime, 75–80
Women:
  aggression toward, and
    pornography, 213–221
  "bag lady" homeless, 125
  disabled, and incest, 289
  displaced homemakers, 183–186
  as family heads, 131–132, 164,
    168, 304
  and homelessness, 123, 124–125
  job commitment of, 280–282
  post-divorce income, 179–181,
    187–190
  and poverty, 194–195
  status of, 335

Women (*continued*)
  Third World maternal mortality,
    330–331
  unemployed, 276–283
  unemployed, and social support,
    278–280
  working mothers, 171–173
  working wives, 164

Women Against Pornography, 213,
  214
Women's Liberation movement:
  and cigarette smoking, 90
  and family, 166–168
  and male anger, 217–218
Work ethic, 151
  and alcohol, 97

World hunger, 353–359
  and the Green Revolution,
    355–356
  and United States, 358–359

Youth Development and Research
  Center (North Carolina), 59–60
Yuppies, 126